1st Workshop on NLP for Science (NLPScience 2024)

Miami, Florida, USA
16 November 2024

ISBN: 979-8-3313-0852-0

Printed from e-media with permission by:

Curran Associates, Inc.
57 Morehouse Lane
Red Hook, NY 12571

Some format issues inherent in the e-media version may also appear in this print version.

Printed with permission by Curran Associates, Inc. (2025)

Association for Computational Linguistics
209 N. Eighth Street
Stroudsburg, Pennsylvania 18360

Phone: 1-570-476-8006
Fax: 1-570-476-0860

acl@aclweb.org

Additional copies of this publication are available from:

Curran Associates, Inc.
57 Morehouse Lane
Red Hook, NY 12571 USA
Phone: 845-758-0400
Fax: 845-758-2633
Email: curran@proceedings.com
Web: www.proceedings.com

NLP4Science 2024

The 1st Workshop on NLP for Science

Proceedings of the Workshop

November 16, 2024

Order copies of this and other ACL proceedings from:

Association for Computational Linguistics (ACL)
317 Sidney Baker St. S
Suite 400 - 134
Kerrville, TX 78028
USA
Tel: +1-855-225-1962
acl@aclweb.org

Introduction

We are excited to welcome you to the NLP4Science workshop, part of EMNLP 2024, taking place in Miami, Florida, on November 16, 2024. This on-site workshop delves into an important frontier in natural language processing (NLP): leveraging NLP to deepen our understanding of the human mind and behavior.

In recent years, NLP and large language models (LLMs) have become pivotal tools in the scientific modeling of the human mind and behavior, influencing fields such as social science, psychology, psychiatry, healthcare, neuroscience, and behavioral economics. At NLP4Science, we will explore these advances through keynote talks, an expert panel, and a poster session featuring papers accepted to the workshop. Topics will include the principles of NLP-driven scientific modeling, methods for statistically robust evaluation of NLP models, experimental designs for NLP-based scientific research, and more.

This year, we received over 40 submissions, each carefully reviewed by our program committee. We are pleased to accept 22 papers, which will be presented as posters during the workshop. We extend our gratitude to all authors for their contributions, and we look forward to seeing how this work will advance our understanding of the human mind and behavior through NLP.

In addition to the poster session, we are honored to host several invited speakers who will present their cutting-edge research, including Amit Sharma (Microsoft Research), Rita Goldstein (Mount Sinai), Roger Levy (MIT), and Hadas Raviv (Princeton University). We will also hold a panel session where experts from multiple disciplines will discuss the future of NLP in scientific discovery. The panel, moderated by Roi Reichart (Technion), will feature Elliot Ash (ETH Zurich), Lyle Ungar (University of Pennsylvania), Diyi Yang (Stanford University), and Jekaterina Novikova (AI Risk and Vulnerability Alliance).

We would like to thank the organizing committee and workshop chairs, the authors for submitting their outstanding work, the reviewers for their hard work, and, of course, the workshop participants.

We hope this workshop fosters fruitful discussions and collaborations that push the boundaries of NLP's potential as a critical tool for scientific modeling of the human mind and behavior.

Organizing Committee

Organizing Committee

Lotem Peled-Cohen, Technion- Israel Institute for Technology
Nitay Calderon, Technion - Israel Institute for Technology
Alex Chapanin, Technion - Israel Institute for Technology
Rotem Dror, Haifa University
Amir Feder, Columbia University, Google Research
Ariel Goldstein, The Hebrew University
Anna Korhonen, University of Cambridge
Shir Lissak, Technion - Israel Institute for Technology
Yaakov Ophir, University of Cambridge
Ilanit Sobol, Technion - Israel Institute for Technology
Roi Reichart, Technion - Israel Institute for Technology
Refael Tikochinski, Technion - Israel Institute for Technology
Mor Ventura, Technion - Israel Institute for Technology

Program Committee

Program Committee

Dana Atzil-Slonim, Bar Ilan University, Israel
Aron Culotta, Tulane University, USA
Dan Goldwasser, Purdue University, USA
Justin Grimmer, Stanford University, USA
Vivek Gupta, University of Pennsylvania, USA
Nora Hollenstein, University of Copenhagen, Denmark
Qiao Jin MD, National Institutes of Health, USA
David Jurgens, Michigan University, USA
Jack LaViolette, Columbia University, USA
Marina Litvak, Shamoon College of Engineering, Israel
Emaad Manzoor, Cornell University, USA
Antonio Moreno Sandoval, Madrid University, Spain
Tristan Naumann, Microsoft
Reid Pryzant, Microsoft
Paul Rayson, Lancaster University, UK
Omer Shubi, Technion- Israel Institute for Technology
Hiroya Takamura, Tokyo Institute of Technology, Japan
Inbal Yahav, Tel Aviv University, Israel
Andrew Yates, University of Amsterdam, Netherlands
Zach Wood-Doughty, Northwest University, USA
Ayah Zirikly, Johns Hopkins University, USA
Carolina Zheng, Columbia University, USA

Keynote Talk
Teaching Causal Reasoning to Transformers

Amit Sharma
Microsoft Research, India

Sat, November 16, 2024 – Time: **09:00 – 09:45** –

Abstract: Large language models (LLMs) have demonstrated remarkable accuracy in identifying cause-and-effect relationships across various scientific fields. However, their ability to reason over these relationships remains inconsistent. In this work, we introduce an axiomatic approach to enhance causal reasoning in transformer models. By training on synthetic demonstrations of causal axioms, we show that even models with fewer than 100 million parameters can achieve reasoning capabilities comparable to much larger models, such as Phi and GPT-4. This suggests that axiomatic training offers a new method for imparting causal reasoning to LLMs, without the need for active interventions. Additionally, it may help explain how models like GPT-4, which are trained solely on observational data, can exhibit seemingly sophisticated reasoning.

Keynote Talk
Natural Language Processing of Spontaneous Speech in Drug Addiction: A Brain Biomarker of Treatment Effects and a Predictor of Outcomes

Rita Z. Goldstein
Icahn School of Medicine at Mount Sinai, USA

Sat, November 16, 2024 – Time: **09:45 – 10:30** –

Abstract: Escalating morbidity and mortality with opioid and stimulant use disorders makes it imperative to identify reliable and valid behavioral markers of brain function that change with treatment and predict outcomes. A naturalistic approach targeting spontaneous speech can serve as a readily accessible behavioral marker of neural plasticity with treatment, amenable for analyses with innovative artificial intelligence (AI), including natural language processing (NLP) approaches. Language, a ubiquitous, dense and measurable yet complex brain function that engages numerous higher-order executive functions (including the prefrontal cortex, PFC), is a distinctively human medium to express emotions, thoughts, and perceptions and to communicate. Concomitant with evidence for PFC recovery with treatment and abstinence in people with heroin and cocaine use disorders, using NLP our results show the impact of 3-months of treatment also on verbal movie-recall, further tracking the brain's shared representation of this drug-themed complex stimulus, and its change with time; in contrast to common lab-based tasks, movies establish a dynamic narrative context, approximating real world processing by allowing a glimpse into the way groups of individuals with common addiction related experiences collectively attribute salience in their environment, addressing the social nature of drug use and recovery. Our results also show that NLP of speech about the consequences of drug use or abstinence outperformed numerous other models (including those incorporating drug use itself) as a predictor of 1-year outcomes, suggesting that hidden predictors of longitudinal craving, withdrawal, abstinence and drug use are embedded in peoples' verbal outputs at baseline. The machine-learning community could only unlock the power of AI by first painstakingly curating large-scale training datasets. Using rich data that can be collected at scale, here we demonstrate a naturalistic ecologically valid approach to identify prognostic bio-markers of vulnerability and resilience in drug addiction. These bio-markers could ultimately facilitate the identification and design of neuroscience-informed empirically-based individually-tailored intervention and prevention approaches, timely deployed to improve outcomes, optimize recovery and save lives in people with drug addiction.

Keynote Talk

Cognitive Science of Language in the Era of Large Language Models

Roger Levy
Department of Brain and Cognitive Sciences at MIT, USA

Sat, November 16, 2024 – Time: **13:00 – 13:45** –

Abstract: Large language models (LLMs) are the first human-created artifacts whose text processing and generation capabilities seem to approach our own. But the hardware they run on is vastly different than ours, and the software implementing them probably is too. How, then, can we use LLMs to advance the science of language in the human mind? In this talk I give examples of three key ways LLMs can contribute to the cognitive science of language: they can help us place lower bounds on the learnability of linguistic generalizations; they can help us reverse-engineer human language processing mechanisms; and they can help us develop hypotheses for the interface between language and other cognitive mechanisms.

Keynote Talk

The First 1000 Days - Harnessing Real-World Data to Model the Complexity of Language Acquisition

Hadas Raviv
Princeton Neuroscience Institute, USA

Sat, November 16, 2024 – Time: **13:45 – 14:30** –

Abstract: Human motor, cognitive, and social skills undergo extraordinary development during life's first 1000 days (1kD). Babies are born helpless, equipped with minimal cognitive-motor skills, and must rely on their caregivers to provide for their needs. However, within a few years, they walk, climb, talk, and reason about the world. Despite the large body of research devoted to studying the first 1000 days, our understanding of the developmental processes that shape children's future outcomes is limited. One of the biggest impediments to modeling human development is the lack of dense measurements of children's lives during their first few years of life. Until recently, capturing, managing, and analyzing large longitudinal datasets containing the rich sensory input with which the child is immersed has been technologically challenging.

Keynote Talk

The Role of NLP Interpretability in Advancing the Human Mind and Social Science Research

Nitay Calderon
The Faculty of Data and Decision Sciences at the Technion, Israel

Sat, November 16, 2024 – Time: **16:15 – 16:45** –

Abstract: The role of language in modern science goes far beyond its use as a tool for communicating research, sharing knowledge, or exploring new ideas. Language is fundamental to understanding human behavior, thoughts, and social development, serving as a gateway to comprehending the human mind. Given this centrality, it is no surprise that recent advances in Natural Language Processing (NLP) and the rise of Large Language Models (LLMs) have led researchers to leverage NLP for modeling scientific phenomena, decoding complex patterns, and uncovering insights about humanity. In this talk, I will explore how NLP interpretability methods are instrumental for the NLP4Science approach. Specifically, interpretability enables us to understand the underlying mechanisms and patterns the NLP model identifies, facilitating deeper comprehension and advancing scientific discoveries. I will review key interpretability paradigms, compare their strengths and limitations, and showcase their application in diverse scientific disciplines. For example, probing techniques are commonly used in neuroscience by aligning NLP representations with brain signals, and causal NLP methods such as counterfactuals are used in political science. I will then present a comprehensive analysis of over two thousand interpretability papers, highlighting trends in NLP interpretability paradigms and comparing them to those in other fields. Finally, I will discuss the broader implications of these findings and offer recommendations for promoting the adoption of NLP interpretability techniques in fields beyond NLP.

Table of Contents

Program

Saturday, November 16, 2024

08:45 - 09:00	*Gathering and Welcome*
09:00 - 09:45	*Invited Speaker 1 - Amit Sharma*
09:45 - 10:30	*Invited Speaker 2 - Rita Goldstein*
10:30 - 11:00	*Coffee Break*
11:00 - 12:00	*Panel Discussion & Q&A*
12:00 - 13:00	*Lunch Break*
13:00 - 13:45	*Invited Speaker 3 - Roger Levy*
13:45 - 14:30	*Invited Speaker 4 - Hadas Raviv*
14:30 - 16:00	*Poster Session + Coffee Break*
16:00 - 16:15	*Best Paper Announcement + Short Oral*
16:15 - 16:45	*Invited Speaker 5 - Nitay Calderon*
16:45 - 17:00	*Closing Remarks*

TokenSHAP: Interpreting Large Language Models with Monte Carlo Shapley Value Estimation

Miriam Horovicz
NI
Tel Aviv, Israel
miriam.horovicz@ni.com

Roni Goldshmidt
Nexar
Tel Aviv, Israel
roni.goldshmidt@getnexar.com

Abstract

As large language models (LLMs) become increasingly prevalent in critical applications, the need for interpretable AI has grown. We introduce TokenSHAP, a novel method for interpreting LLMs by attributing importance to individual tokens or substrings within input prompts. This approach adapts Shapley values from cooperative game theory to natural language processing, offering a rigorous framework for understanding how different parts of an input contribute to a model's response. TokenSHAP leverages Monte Carlo sampling for computational efficiency, providing interpretable, quantitative measures of token importance. We demonstrate its efficacy across diverse prompts and LLM architectures, showing consistent improvements over existing baselines in alignment with human judgments, faithfulness to model behavior, and consistency.

Key contributions include:

- A theoretical framework extending Shapley values to variable-length text LLM inputs.
- An efficient Monte Carlo sampling approach tailored for language models.
- Comprehensive evaluation across various prompts and model types.
- Capability to effortlessly visualize the insights.

Our method's ability to capture nuanced interactions between tokens provides valuable insights into LLM behavior, enhancing model transparency, improving prompt engineering, and aiding in the development of more reliable AI systems. TokenSHAP represents a significant step towards the necessary interpretability for responsible AI deployment, contributing to the broader goal of creating more transparent, accountable, and trustworthy AI systems.

1 Introduction

Large language models (LLMs) have greatly advanced natural language processing, delivering near or at human-level performance on many tasks. However, their "black box" nature poses interpretability challenges, crucial for applications in fields like healthcare and legal analysis, where understanding AI decision-making is vital.

This paper introduces TokenSHAP, a method enhancing LLM interpretability by adapting Shapley values from game theory. TokenSHAP treats input tokens as players, assessing their contribution to model outputs. This allows for a deeper understanding of how LLMs process information, crucial for improving model transparency and reliability.

We propose a Monte Carlo sampling method for practical Shapley value estimation, accommodating the variable lengths and contextual nature of language inputs. Our evaluations across different prompts and models confirm TokenSHAP's versatility and effectiveness in revealing LLM decision-making processes. This breakthrough aids the development of more accountable AI systems, ensuring their responsible use as they become more integrated into critical applications.

2 Related Work

2.1 Interpretability in Machine Learning

Interpretability in machine learning has gained significant attention as models become increasingly complex. Methods for explaining AI systems can be broadly categorized into two approaches: black box methods and white box methods (Guidotti et al., 2018).

Black box methods, such as LIME (Ribeiro et al., 2016) and SHAP (Lundberg and Lee, 2017), have emerged as popular approaches for explaining predictions across various ML models without requiring access to the model's internal architecture or parameters. LIME provides local approximations of model behavior by perturbing input data, while SHAP unifies several feature attribution methods under the Shapley value framework. These meth-

Proceedings of the 1st Workshop on NLP for Science (NLP4Science), pages 1–8
November 16, 2024 ©2024 Association for Computational Linguistics

ods are particularly valuable when working with proprietary or complex models where internal access is limited or impractical (Molnar, 2020).

White box methods, on the other hand, require knowledge of and access to the model's internal structure. These include techniques like gradient-based saliency maps (?) and layer-wise relevance propagation (LRP) (Bach et al., 2015). While these methods can provide more detailed insights into the model's decision-making process, they are limited to scenarios where the model architecture is fully accessible and understood (Gilpin et al., 2018).

Recent advancements include counterfactual explanations (Wachter et al., 2018), which explore how altering inputs changes model predictions. While these methods offer valuable insights for tabular and image data, they face challenges when applied to the sequential and contextual nature of language, highlighting the need for specialized NLP interpretability techniques (Danilevsky et al., 2020).

2.2 Interpretability in Natural Language Processing

In the NLP domain, attention visualization techniques (Vig, 2019) have gained popularity, offering insights into which parts of the input a model focuses on. However, these visualizations often lack quantitative rigor. More sophisticated methods like Integrated Gradients (Sundararajan et al., 2017) and Layer-wise Relevance Propagation (LRP) (Bach et al., 2015) provide continuous importance scores for input tokens but can struggle with gradient saturation and non-linearity in deep models.

Probing tasks (Tenney et al., 2019) have also been employed to examine the representations learned by language models, revealing the types of linguistic information encoded at different layers. However, these methods do not directly interpret how inputs lead to specific outputs in inference tasks.

2.3 Shapley Values in Machine Learning and NLP

Shapley values, originating from cooperative game theory, have emerged as a powerful tool for feature importance estimation in machine learning. Lundberg and Lee's SHAP method (Lundberg and Lee, 2017) unified several feature attribution techniques under the Shapley value framework, ensuring consistency and local accuracy. However, the computational intensity of exact Shapley value calculation has led to approximations like KernelSHAP and TreeSHAP, which are primarily designed for fixed-length feature vectors.

Applying Shapley values to NLP tasks presents unique challenges due to the combinatorial explosion of possible token subsets in variable-length text. Recent work by Sundararajan et al. (Sundararajan et al., 2017) introduced TracIn to track the influence of training data points on predictions, but it doesn't provide granular token-level insights for individual predictions.

3 Methodology

3.1 TokenSHAP Overview

TokenSHAP attributes importance to individual tokens or substrings in an input prompt by estimating their Shapley values. The Shapley value for a token represents its average marginal contribution to the model's output across all possible combinations of tokens. This approach provides a rigorous framework for understanding how each part of the input influences the final response of large language models (LLMs).

3.2 Tokenization and Sampling

Given an input prompt $x = (x_1, ..., x_n)$, where x_i represents individual tokens or substrings, we consider all possible subsets $S \subseteq N$, where $N = \{1, ..., n\}$. The exponential number of subsets (2^n) makes exact computation impractical, so we employ Monte Carlo sampling to estimate Shapley values efficiently. This sampling approach balances the need for computational feasibility with the accuracy of Shapley value estimations.

3.3 Monte Carlo Shapley Estimation

We adapt the Monte Carlo sampling approach to the context of text inputs. For each token x_i, we estimate its Shapley value ϕ_i as follows:

1. Generate a set of combinations that includes:
   (a) All combinations where x_i is the only token removed (essential combinations)
   (b) A random sample of other combinations based on a specified sampling ratio
2. For each combination:
   (a) Generate the model's response

(b) Calculate the cosine similarity between this response and the full prompt response

3. Compute the average similarity for combinations with and without x_i

4. Calculate ϕ_i as the difference between these averages

This Monte Carlo estimation approach ensures a balance between computational efficiency and estimation accuracy. The use of essential combinations alongside random samples provides a robust basis for estimating Shapley values, even with a relatively small number of samples.

3.4 Value Function

We define the value function $v(S)$ as the cosine similarity between the TF-IDF vectors of the model's response to the subset S and the response to the full prompt. Formally:

$$v(S) = \text{cosine\_similarity}(\text{TF-IDF}(r(S)), \text{TF-IDF}(r(N))) \quad (1)$$

where $r(S)$ is the model's response to the subset S, and $r(N)$ is the response to the full prompt. This formulation allows us to measure how closely the response to a subset resembles the response to the entire input, providing a quantitative basis for attributing importance to individual tokens.

3.5 Model Interaction

For each sampled subset S, we query the LLM to generate a response. The prompt for a subset is constructed by concatenating the tokens or substrings corresponding to the indices in S. This step ensures that the model's behavior is consistently evaluated across varying subsets of the input.

3.6 Shapley Value Computation

The estimated Shapley value for token x_i is computed as:

$$\begin{aligned}\phi_i =& (\text{average similarity of combinations including } x_i) \\ &- (\text{average similarity of combinations excluding } x_i)\end{aligned} \quad (2)$$

This difference in average similarities provides a measure of the token's importance to the model's output. The final Shapley values are normalized to ensure comparability across different inputs and models.

Algorithm 1 TokenSHAP

Require: Input prompt x, model name, sampling ratio r, tokenizer/splitter

Ensure: Shapley values ϕ_i for each token x_i

Tokenize or split x into n tokens $(x_1, \ldots, x_n)$
Calculate baseline response b for full prompt x
Initialize essential combinations $E \leftarrow \{\}$
for $i = 1$ to n **do**
  $E \leftarrow E \cup (x_1, \ldots, x_{i-1}, x_{i+1}, \ldots, x_n)$
end for
$N \leftarrow \min(n, \lfloor (2^n - 1) \cdot r \rfloor)$ ▷ Number of sampled combinations
if $N < n$ **then**
  $C \leftarrow E$ ▷ Use only first-order samples
else
  $S \leftarrow$ Random sample of $N - n$ combinations excluding E
  $C \leftarrow E \cup S$ ▷ All combinations to process
end if
for each combination c in C **do**
  Get model response R_c for c
  Calculate cosine similarity $\text{sim}(b, R_c)$
end for
for $i = 1$ to n **do**
  $\text{with}_i \leftarrow$ average similarity of combinations including x_i
  $\text{without}_i \leftarrow$ average similarity of combinations excluding x_i
  $\phi_i \leftarrow \text{with}_i - \text{without}_i$
end for
Normalize $\phi_1, \ldots, \phi_n$
return $\phi_1, \ldots, \phi_n$

3.7 Visualization

We present the results using a color-coded visualization of the input text. The color intensity represents the magnitude of the Shapley value for each token or substring, with a diverging color map (e.g., coolwarm) to distinguish positive and negative values. This visualization aids in intuitively understanding the model's decision-making process by highlighting the most influential parts of the input.

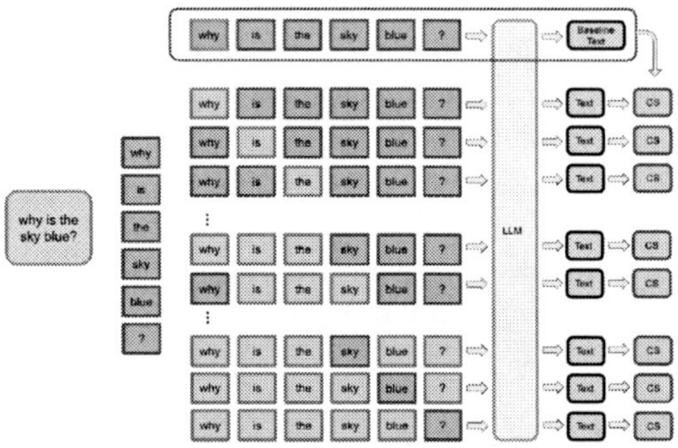

Figure 1: Flowchart of the TokenSHAP algorithm illustrating the process of Shapley value estimation for token importance in large language models by accepting parts of the text to the players and a cosine similarity measure to the base prompt as a gain.

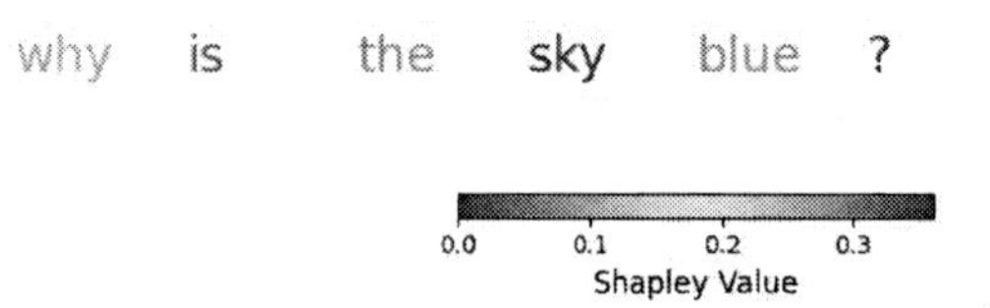

Figure 2: A graph that shows the visualization of the prompt in blue-red colors.

By providing a clear and quantitative analysis of token importance, TokenSHAP enhances the interpretability of LLMs, offering insights that are critical for improving model transparency, trustworthiness, and overall performance.

4 Experiments

4.1 Injection of Random Words and Method Comparison

This experiment evaluates the ability of different interpretability methods to accurately assign low importance to randomly injected words within prompts. The goal is to test each method's sensitivity and precision in identifying extraneous words that should not significantly impact model decisions.

4.1.1 Experimental Design

We selected random prompts from the Alpaca dataset and injected each with random words at random places. We examined the performance of the following explainability methods in assigning low importance to those random words:

1. **Random**: This method uses a random baseline, assigning random importance to each token.

2. **Prompt Engineer**: This method uses relevant prompts to derive the tokens' importance from an LLM model. Llama3 was used with few-shot in-context learning.

3. **TokenSHAP**: Utilizes Shapley values to quantify the impact of each token within a prompt on the model's output, effectively identifying tokens with low importance.

4.1.2 Results and Evaluation

This section details the performance of each interpretability method when applied to both regular and injected prompts. Effective methods are expected to demonstrate the ability to discern between 'real' and injected words by assigning significantly lower importance to the latter.

Statistical Analysis The analysis focused on comparing the average importance values and standard deviations for 'real' words against those for injected words. Effective discrimination by a method would manifest as a substantial difference in these metrics, with lower values for injected words indicating better performance.

Results Summary Table 1 presents the differences in mean importance values and standard deviations between non-injected and injected words for each evaluated method. Notably, a method performing well should show a larger mean difference and a controlled standard deviation.

Method	Δ Mean Importance	Δ Std Dev
Random	0.017	-0.017
Prompt Engineer	0.019	-0.001
TokenSHAP	**0.033**	**0.011**

Table 1: Differential importance values between non-injected and injected words across methods

4.1.3 Visual Analysis

Boxplots were generated to visually depict the distribution of importance values for each method, contrasting injected versus non-injected words. These plots underscore the quantitative findings and highlight how each method manages the variance and central tendency of importance values across conditions.

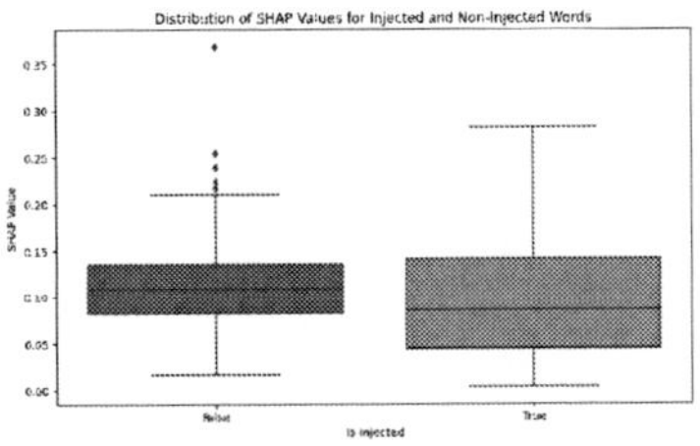

Figure 3: Box plot showing the distribution of importance values for the Random Baseline method.

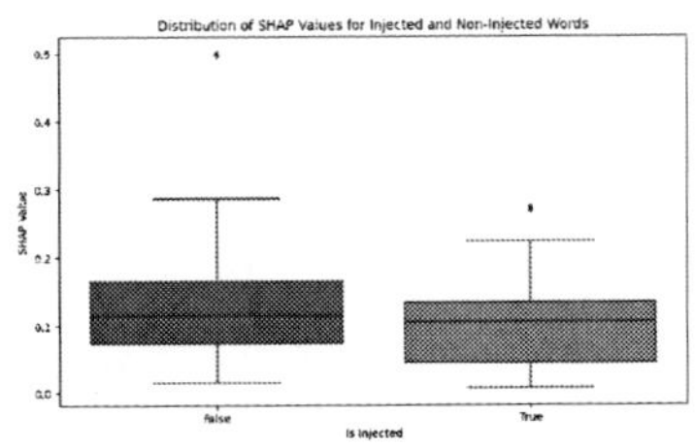

Figure 4: Box plot showing the distribution of importance values for the Prompt Engineering method.

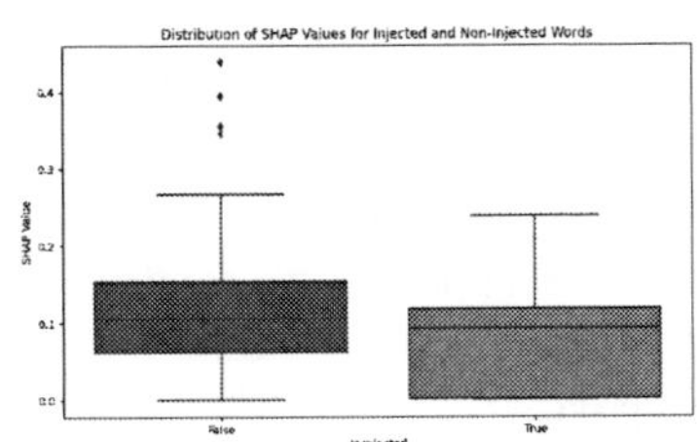

Figure 5: Box plot showing the distribution of importance values for TokenSHAP.

4.1.4 Discussion

As anticipated, the Random method performed the poorest, showing minimal differentiation between real and injected words. Prompt Engineering demonstrated slight improvement but remained limited in discriminative power. In contrast, **TokenSHAP** significantly excelled, effectively distinguishing between relevant and irrelevant tokens with its realistic and lower SHAP values for injected words, thus proving to be the most reliable method for ensuring model interpretability and transparency.

4.2 Monte Carlo Shapley Value Approximation

4.2.1 Experimental Setup

To assess the effectiveness of Monte Carlo sampling in approximating Shapley values under diverse conditions, we designed an experiment comparing different sampling ratios, both with and without the inclusion of first-order omission conditions. The first-order omission condition entails always including subgroups that omit exactly one token, offering a consistent baseline for comparison. This condition was tested alongside scenarios where it was entirely excluded, allowing us to explore the impact of this methodological choice on the approximation accuracy.

4.2.2 Methodology

The experiment involved calculating the cosine similarity between true Shapley values and those approximated by the Monte Carlo method across various sampling ratios. These ratios ranged from 1.0 (full sampling) down to 0.0. The true Shapley values were computed comprehensively, and then the similarity to these values was measured by comparing the results from the Monte Carlo approximations to the original Shapley value vector through cosine similarity. This metric provides a clear measure of how closely the approximations match the true values, highlighting the accuracy of the sampling method.

4.2.3 Results and Analysis

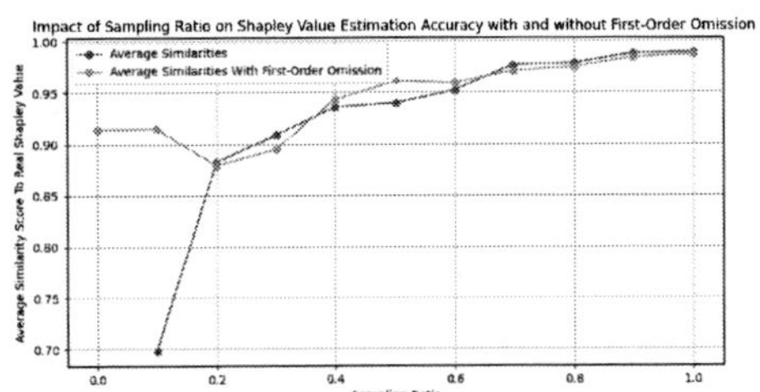

Figure 6: Change in average similarity between true Shapley values and their approximations under different sampling ratios, with and without the condition of first-order omission.

Figure 6 presents the results, demonstrating significant differences in approximation accuracy depending on the presence of the first-order omission condition. The sampling ratio plays a crucial role in determining the number of combinations considered beyond the essential first-order samples.

4.2.4 Implications

These findings underscore the importance of including first-order omissions in Monte Carlo sampling to maintain robustness and reliability in Shapley value approximations. This approach validates the Monte Carlo sampler's capability to accurately estimate Shapley values, highlighting its utility in practical applications where computational efficiency is critical.

5 Discussion

5.1 Interpretability Insights

TokenSHAP offers several advantages for interpreting LLM outputs:

1. **Quantitative Measure:** It provides a rigorous, quantitative assessment of token importance, utilizing the Shapley value framework to quantify the contribution of each token to the model's output in a consistent and objective manner.

2. **Context-awareness:** The method captures the interdependence between tokens, reflecting how the model processes the entire input. This contextual sensitivity is essential for accurately interpreting the sophisticated dynamics of LLMs.

3. **Model-agnostic:** TokenSHAP can be applied to any LLM without requiring access to its internal architecture, making it a versatile tool for users working with proprietary or black-box models. This positions TokenSHAP as a powerful black box method in the landscape of explainable AI, contrasting with white box methods that require detailed knowledge of model internals.

4. **Granularity:** The approach allows for analysis at both token and substring levels, offering significant flexibility and enabling detailed exploration of how linguistic constructs larger than single tokens influence the model's decisions.

5.2 Limitations

1. **Computational Cost:** Despite the efficiency gains from Monte Carlo sampling, TokenSHAP remains more computationally intensive than simpler interpretability methods, due to the need for repeated model evaluations.

2. **Sensitivity to Sampling:** The stochastic nature of Monte Carlo sampling introduces variability in the importance scores, which may slightly vary between runs, affecting reproducibility in sensitive applications.

3. **Assumption of Additivity:** The theoretical foundation of Shapley values assumes that contributions from individual tokens can be additively combined, which may not always be accurate in cases where complex interactions and non-linear dynamics dominate.

5.3 Future Work

1. **Exploring Alternative Value Functions:** Future research could include developing more sophisticated value functions that better capture nuanced aspects of semantic similarity and contextual alignment. Usage of LLM can also be considered for this task.

2. **Investigating Shapley Value Stability:** Further studies are needed to assess the stability of Shapley values across different LLM architectures and input sizes, to understand their robustness and generalizability.

3. **Developing Interactive Tools:** There is a substantial opportunity to create interactive, user-friendly tools that allow practitioners to dynamically explore token importance, enhancing the accessibility and practical utility of TokenSHAP.

4. **Extending to Multi-turn Conversations:** Applying TokenSHAP to multi-turn conversational contexts could provide insights into how contextual understanding evolves in dialogue systems.

5. **Bias Analysis:** Utilizing TokenSHAP for systematic identification and analysis of potential biases in LLM outputs could contribute to the development of more ethical and fair AI systems.

6 Conclusion

TokenSHAP offers a significant advancement in the interpretability of large language models (LLMs) by adapting Shapley values to natural language processing and employing Monte Carlo estimation for feasibility. This approach overcomes the challenges of variable input lengths and contextual dependencies, offering a scalable solution for complex language models.

Key achievements include:

- A novel framework that extends Shapley values to natural language, providing a rigorous, theoretically grounded method for interpreting token importance.
- An efficient Monte Carlo sampling method that enhances the computational feasibility of applying TokenSHAP to large-scale models.
- Superior performance over existing methods in terms of alignment with human judgments, model behavior faithfulness, and consistency.
- Detailed insights into LLM behavior, revealing how models process and prioritize input components.

Our method's capacity to capture detailed token interactions enhances model transparency and aids in debugging, bias mitigation, and regulatory compliance, which is essential as LLMs are increasingly deployed in critical domains.

Future research will explore sophisticated value functions, the stability of Shapley values across models, and the extension of TokenSHAP to conversational AI. Developing interactive tools based on TokenSHAP could also enhance its accessibility and practical utility for practitioners.

TokenSHAP represents a vital step towards making AI systems not only powerful but also transparent and accountable, ensuring their responsible development and deployment in transformative applications.

Limitations

While TokenSHAP provides a valuable framework for interpreting large language models, it is not without limitations. The computational cost associated with Monte Carlo sampling can be significant, especially for very large models or long input texts. Additionally, the method assumes additivity in token contributions, which may not fully capture complex non-linear interactions in some models. The stochastic nature of the sampling process may also introduce variability in the results, affecting reproducibility in certain applications.

Ethics Statement

The development of TokenSHAP is motivated by the need for transparency and accountability in AI systems, particularly large language models that are increasingly used in sensitive domains. By providing interpretable insights into model behavior, TokenSHAP aims to mitigate risks associated with black-box models, such as unintended biases or unfairness. We acknowledge that interpretability methods can also be misused, for example, to manipulate model outputs or infer proprietary information. Therefore, we advocate for responsible use of TokenSHAP, aligned with ethical guidelines and regulatory standards in AI.

Acknowledgments

We would like to thank Alon Malki for his valuable feedback and contributions to this work.

References

Sebastian Bach, Alexander Binder, Grégoire Montavon, Frederick Klauschen, Klaus-Robert Müller, and Wojciech Samek. 2015. On pixel-wise explanations for non-linear classifier decisions by layer-wise relevance propagation. *PLOS ONE*, 10(7):e0130140.

Marina Danilevsky, Ke Qian, Ranit Aharonov, Yannis Katsis, Batool Kawas, and Prithviraj Sen. 2020. A survey of the state of explainable ai for natural language processing. *arXiv preprint arXiv:2010.00711*.

Leilani H Gilpin, David Bau, Ben Z Yuan, Ayesha Bajwa, Michael Specter, and Lalana Kagal. 2018. Explaining explanations: An overview of interpretability of machine learning. In *2018 IEEE 5th International Conference on Data Science and Advanced Analytics (DSAA)*, pages 80–89. IEEE.

Riccardo Guidotti, Anna Monreale, Salvatore Ruggieri, Franco Turini, Fosca Giannotti, and Dino Pedreschi. 2018. A survey of methods for explaining black box models. *ACM Computing Surveys (CSUR)*, 51(5):1–42.

Scott M Lundberg and Su-In Lee. 2017. A unified approach to interpreting model predictions. In *Advances in Neural Information Processing Systems*, volume 30, pages 4765–4774. Curran Associates, Inc.

Christoph Molnar. 2020. *Interpretable Machine Learning*. Lulu. com.

Marco Tulio Ribeiro, Sameer Singh, and Carlos Guestrin. 2016. Why should i trust you? explaining the predictions of any classifier. In *Proceedings of the 22nd ACM SIGKDD International Conference on Knowledge Discovery and Data Mining*, pages 1135–1144. ACM.

Mukund Sundararajan, Ankur Taly, and Qiqi Yan. 2017. Axiomatic attribution for deep networks. In *Proceedings of the 34th International Conference on Machine Learning*, pages 3319–3328. PMLR.

Ian Tenney, Dipanjan Das, and Ellie Pavlick. 2019. Bert rediscovers the classical nlp pipeline. In *Proceedings of the 57th Annual Meeting of the Association for Computational Linguistics*, pages 4593–4601.

Jesse Vig. 2019. A multiscale visualization of attention in the transformer model. In *Proceedings of the 57th Annual Meeting of the Association for Computational Linguistics: System Demonstrations*, pages 37–42.

Sandra Wachter, Brent Mittelstadt, and Chris Russell. 2018. Counterfactual explanations without opening the black box: Automated decisions and the gdpr. *Harvard Journal of Law & Technology*, 31:841.

.

DeepFM-Crispr: Prediction of CRISPR On-Target Effects via Deep Learning

Condy Bao
condybao@gmail.com

Fuxiao Liu
fl3es@umd.edu

Abstract

Since the advent of CRISPR-Cas9, a groundbreaking gene-editing technology that enables precise genomic modifications via a short RNA guide sequence, there has been a marked increase in the accessibility and application of this technology across various fields. The success of CRISPR-Cas9 has spurred further investment and led to the discovery of additional CRISPR systems, including CRISPR-Cas13. Distinct from Cas9, which targets DNA, Cas13 targets RNA, offering unique advantages for gene modulation. We focus on Cas13d, a variant known for its collateral activity where it non-specifically cleaves adjacent RNA molecules upon activation, a feature critical to its function. We introduce DeepFM-Crispr, a novel deep learning model developed to predict the on-target efficiency and evaluate the off-target effects of Cas13d. This model harnesses a large language model to generate comprehensive representations rich in evolutionary and structural data, thereby enhancing predictions of RNA secondary structures and overall sgRNA efficacy. A transformer-based architecture processes these inputs to produce a predictive efficacy score. Comparative experiments show that DeepFM-Crispr not only surpasses traditional models but also outperforms recent state-of-the-art deep learning methods in terms of prediction accuracy and reliability.

1 Introduction

The discovery and development of Clustered Regularly Interspaced Short Palindromic Repeats (CRISPR) and their associated Cas proteins have revolutionized biotechnology and biomedical sciences. Initially identified within the adaptive immune systems of bacteria and archaea, these CRISPR-Cas systems have been ingeniously adapted for genome editing. They exploit their inherent ability to make precise and efficient genetic alterations (Doudna and Charpentier, 2013; Jinek et al., 2012). The CRISPR locus is characterized by repetitive base sequences interspersed with spacers derived from past viral and plasmid invaders. This locus is transcribed into a long precursor CRISPR RNA (pre-crRNA), which is then processed into mature guide RNAs (crRNAs). These crRNAs direct the Cas proteins to cleave complementary sequences in invading genetic elements, thereby providing adaptive immunity. Among the various CRISPR-Cas systems, CRISPR-Cas9 of Type II has attracted significant attention due to its simplicity and versatility in genome editing. It employs a dual-RNA structure consisting of crRNA and trans-activating crRNA (tracrRNA), guiding the Cas9 enzyme to specific DNA targets (Jinek et al., 2012; Doudna and Charpentier, 2014).

CRISPR-Cas12, a Type V system, offers unique advantages over Cas9 by utilizing a single RNA for both CRISPR array processing and target DNA recognition. This system cleaves target DNA in a staggered manner, increasing the diversity of editable sequences and enhancing the potential for multiplex editing. Another innovative addition to the CRISPR toolkit is CRISPR-Cas13, which targets RNA instead of DNA, facilitating not only gene modulation without altering the genome but also enabling novel diagnostic applications due to its collateral cleavage activity upon target recognition (Gootenberg et al., 2017). The specificity and efficacy of guide RNA design are crucial for maximizing on-target actions and minimizing off-target effects, which are particularly concerning with Cas9's potential DNA off-targets and Cas13's RNA-targeted collateral activity (Abudayyeh et al., 2017). CRISPR screens, including those for viability and FACS-sorting, have become instrumental in evaluating the effectiveness and specificity of CRISPR systems. These screens employ a multitude of guide RNAs to ascertain factors influencing knockout efficiency and to refine guide designs to balance activity and specificity (Doench et al.,

Proceedings of the 1st Workshop on NLP for Science (NLP4Science), pages 9–15
November 16, 2024 ©2024 Association for Computational Linguistics

2016). Unlike tools focused solely on CRISPR-Cas9, those designed for Cas13 must account for RNA secondary structures, significantly impacting guide RNA efficiency (Wessels et al., 2020).

To address challenges related to data scarcity and the complexity of integrating structural and evolutionary information, we introduce DeepFM-Crispr. This model leverages advanced transformer-based architectures and large language models, which have revolutionized fields ranging from natural language processing (Liu et al., 2023a, 2024, 2023b; Li et al., 2023) to bioinformatics due to their ability to handle large datasets and extract deep, contextual relationships within data. Our transformer (Vaswani et al., 2017) model processes a wide array of inputs, offering a predictive score for on-target efficiency based on enriched representations of evolutionary and structural insights. Validated against a dataset of 22,599 Cas13d sgRNAs (Cheng et al., 2023), DeepFM-Cas13d outperforms conventional machine learning methods and existing prediction tools, particularly in targeting non-coding RNAs (Shmakov et al., 2015).

2 Method

Our methodology integrates multiple deep learning architectures and data representation techniques to predict the on-target efficiency of sgRNAs based on their sequences and secondary structures. This approach harnesses the power of large language models, convolutional networks, and transformer encoders to process and analyze the complex biological data. The details of DeepFM-Crispr shown in Fig. 1.

2.1 Data Representation

sgRNA sequences were encoded using a one-hot encoding scheme, where each nucleotide (A, C, G, U) is represented by a binary vector. The vectors for adenine (A), cyto- sine (C), guanine (G), and uracil (U) are respectively [1,0,0,0], [0,1,0,0], [0,0,1,0], and [0,0,0,1]. This methodological choice ensures a uniform input structure for all sequences, facilitating the computational handling of genetic data across diverse sgRNA samples. By transforming the nucleotide sequences into binary vectors, the model can effectively learn from the positional and compositional nuances of the sgRNA without the biases and variances inherent in raw textual data.

The one-hot encoded vectors serve as the primary input for the subsequent layers of the machine learning architecture. They are fed into a series of deep learning models that are designed to extract and learn complex patterns and relationships. This initial representation forms the basis for all further transformations and feature extractions performed by the RNA large language model and other components of our predictive framework. The standardized format ensures that each sgRNA is represented in a consistent manner, allowing the deep learning algorithms to focus on learning the underlying biological mechanisms rather than adjusting to variations in data format.

2.2 RNA Large Language Model

RNA-FM (Chen et al., 2022) is designed as an end-to-end deep learning model that efficiently extracts latent features from RNA sequences and leverages an attention mechanism to capture contextual information. It features 12 layers of transformer-based bidirectional encoder blocks equipped with positional embeddings. This structure allows RNA-FM to accurately discern the positional context of ncRNA sequences. The encoder within RNA-FM utilizes self-attention and feedforward connections to generate complex representations that integrate context from every sequence position. Furthermore, the model is adept at constructing pairwise interactions between nucleotides, enhancing its ability to depict direct nucleotide-nucleotide interactions and providing a nuanced representation of the input data. These capabilities make RNA-FM particularly effective in correlating internal representations with RNA secondary structures. As a result, the model produces high-dimensional embeddings for each sgRNA (Abudayyeh et al., 2017), encapsulating both local and global contextual relationships within the sequences. These embeddings are subsequently utilized as inputs for further predictive modeling to determine sgRNA efficacy scores, and also serve as inputs for a secondary structure prediction model, enhancing our understanding and prediction of RNA structural configurations.

2.3 Secondary Structure Prediction

The secondary structure of each sgRNA was predicted using a ResNet model (Krishna et al., 2017) that processes inputs derived from the RNA-FM representations. This model outputs a probability matrix where each nucleotide position is labeled as either paired (1) or unpaired (0). These binary

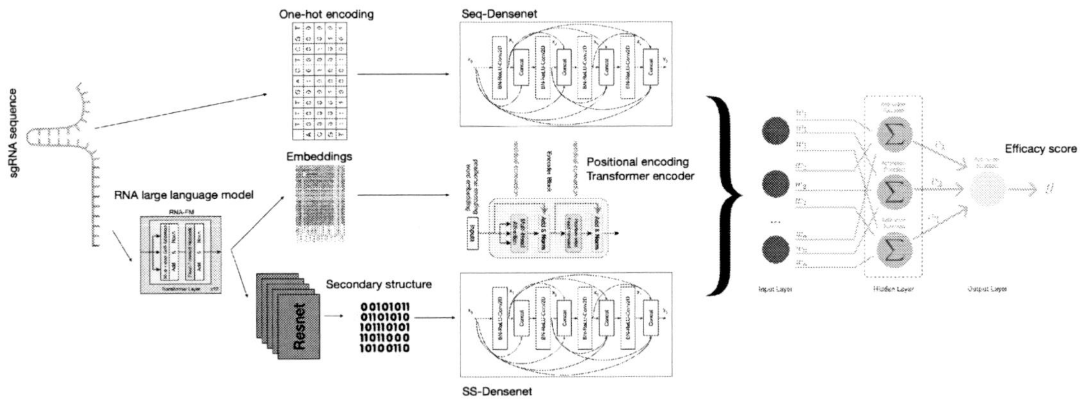

Figure 1: **The Overall Architecture of *DeepFM-Crispr*.**

sequences are then further processed using a deep convolutional network based on the ResNet architecture, which is particularly adept at capturing spatial hierarchies in structured data (He et al., 2016). This approach allows for effective integration of contextual and spatial information, enhancing the accuracy of the secondary structure predictions for the sgRNAs.

2.4 Feature Integration and Processing

The embeddings from the RNA-FM and the outputs from the secondary structure prediction ResNet are integrated and further processed to refine the feature representation.

DenseNet architecture. Seq-DenseNet (Wei et al., 2021) and SS-DenseNet (Zhao et al., 2021), was employed to process integrated features. This architecture benefits from dense connectivity patterns that improve the flow of information and gradients throughout the network, aiding in the robust learning of features from both sequence and structural data (Wei et al., 2021). **Positional Encoding Transformer Encoder.** The output embedding of RNA-FM are passed through a positional encoding transformer encoder. This module incorporates positional encodings to the input features to maintain the sequence order, which is crucial for capturing dependencies that are positionally distant in the sgRNA sequence. The transformer encoder refines these features by focusing on the most relevant parts of the sgRNA for efficacy prediction (Huang et al., 2017).

2.5 Efficacy Prediction

The final prediction of sgRNA efficacy is performed using a multi-layer perceptron (MLP) (Riedmiller and Lernen, 2014). The MLP comprises an input layer that receives the processed features, several hidden layers with non-linear activation functions to capture complex relationships in the data, and an output layer that produces a continuous efficacy score for each sgRNA.

3 Dataset

To explore the efficiency and specificity of the Cas13d system, we performed a comprehensive two-vector CRISPR/Cas13d proliferation screen on the A375 melanoma cell line, guided by protocols from a well-established benchmark study (Cheng et al., 2023). The screening library consisted of 10,830 sgRNAs targeting a total of 426 genes, including 192 protein-coding genes and 234 long non-coding RNAs (lncRNAs). This selection included 94 essential genes and 14 non-essential genes, previously identified in A375 cells via RNA interference and CRISPR-based screenings. Our library design aimed to robustly model the efficiencies of Cas13d sgRNAs, allocating approximately 30 guides per gene. This strategy was intended to overcome potential biases observed in previous tiling screens that were limited to only 2-3 genes, thereby enhancing the representativity of the sgRNA library.

Following the screening, sgRNA abundance was quantitatively assessed through high-throughput sequencing. Data analysis was conducted using the MAGeCK algorithm to evaluate sgRNA performance and gene essentiality. Quality control checks were stringent, with an average of 5.6 million reads per sample, ensuring reliable data capture. Each guide was represented by over 300 reads, with fewer than four guides missing per gene—indicative of comprehensive coverage. The

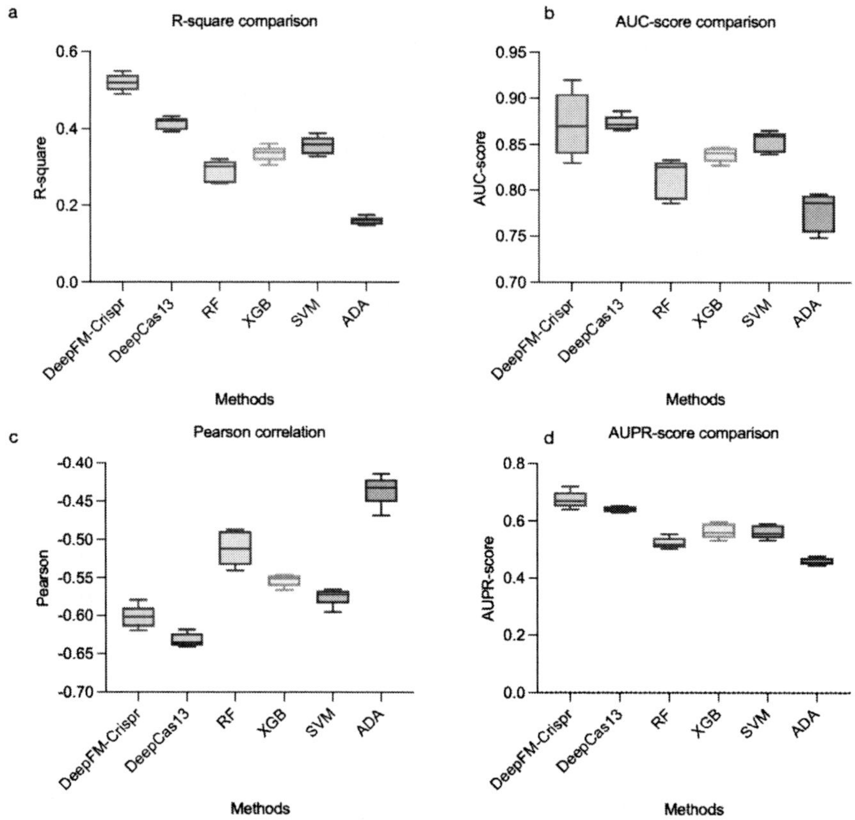

Figure 2: **Comparison Result between *DeepFM-Crispr* with baselines.**

Gini coefficient was maintained below 0.06, confirming a uniform and non-biased distribution of guide representation across the dataset. Most notably, 20 of the essential genes demonstrated significant depletion, with a false discovery rate (FDR) of less than 10%, underscoring the screening's effectiveness in identifying gene functionalities crucial for cell proliferation in melanoma.

4 Experiments

4.1 Implementation

Batch Size: The model was trained with a batch size of 128 sgRNAs to balance computational efficiency with memory constraints.

Learning Rate: We employed a learning rate of 1e-4, utilizing a learning rate scheduler to decrease the rate by 10% every two epochs to stabilize training as it progressed.

Epochs: The model was trained for up to 50 epochs, with early stopping implemented if the validation loss did not improve for 5 consecutive epochs. This approach prevented overfitting and ensured that the model generalized well to new, unseen data.

Optimizer: The Adam optimizer (Zhang, 2018) was used for its adaptive learning rate capabilities, which helped in converging faster and more effectively than traditional stochastic gradient descent. L2 regularization (Cortes et al., 2012) was applied to all trainable parameters to prevent overfitting by penalizing large weights. A dropout rate of 0.1 was used in each transformer layer to randomly omit a subset of features during training, further helping the model to generalize better. To handle the varying lengths of sgRNA sequences, attention masks were used within the transformer layers to ignore padding tokens during the self-attention calculations.

Baseline Methods: In the evaluation of guide RNA (gRNA) efficacy prediction, the DeepFM-Crispr model was compared against several established machine learning methods, including Random Forest (RF) (Rigatti, 2017), XGBoost (XGB) (Chen and Guestrin, 2016), Support Vector Machine (SVM) (Suthaharan and Suthaharan, 2016), AdaBoost (ADA) (Ying et al., 2013), and a recent deep learning method, DeepCas13 (Wessels et al., 2020).

4.2 Evaluation

Conventional machine learning algorithms were applied using 185 curated features consistent with previous studies. Each model was trained and validated on three publicly available Cas13d tiling screening datasets, encompassing a total of 5,726 sgRNAs, employing five-fold cross-validation to ensure robustness. The evaluation of our models focused on two primary metrics: (1) the prediction accuracy of sgRNA efficacy across the entire dataset, and (2) the ability to classify sgRNAs into efficient or non-efficient categories based on their performance.

4.3 Result Discussion

Prediction Accuracy. The first metric of evaluation was the coefficient of determination (R^2) and the Pearson correlation coefficient (PCC) between the predicted efficacy scores and the actual log fold changes (LFCs). DeepFM-Crispr demonstrated superior performance in this regard, achieving a higher R^2 value and a more pronounced negative Pearson correlation. These results, illustrated in Fig. 2, indicate that DeepFM-Crispr provides more accurate predictions of sgRNA efficacy, aligning closely with experimental outcomes.

Classification of sgRNA Efficiency. For the classification task, sgRNAs were categorized based on their LFC values; those with LFC smaller than -0.5 were classified as positive (efficient), and all others as negative (non-efficient). The effectiveness of each model in this binary classification was measured by the area under the Receiver Operating Characteristic (ROC) curve (AUC) and the area under the precision-recall curve (AUPR). DeepFM-Crispr not only matched the top AUC performance of DeepCas13 at an average of 0.88 across five-fold cross-validation (as shown in Fig. 2) but also significantly outperformed other methods, which exhibited AUC scores ranging from 0.78 to 0.85.

Furthermore, DeepFM-Crispr excelled in the precision-recall metric, achieving an average AUPR score of 0.69. This score was notably higher than those achieved by DeepCas13 and other traditional approaches, which varied between 0.45 and 0.58 (depicted in Fig. 2). This indicates a stronger capability of DeepFM-Crispr to differentiate between strong and weak knockdown effects. The high AUPR score is particularly significant in the context of the dataset's imbalance, where positive samples are less frequent, underscoring the model's robustness in distinguishing positives from negatives.

Implications for Gene Editing Applications. These findings underscore the enhanced predictive accuracy of DeepFM-Crispr in assessing sgRNA efficacy, affirming its utility in gene editing applications where precise guide RNA selection is crucial. The ability of DeepFM-Crispr to accurately predict and classify sgRNA efficiency supports its potential as a valuable tool in optimizing CRISPR-based gene editing. This is particularly in therapeutic contexts where the precision of genetic modification can dictate treatment efficacy.

5 Related Work

The CRISPR-Cas systems (Doudna and Charpentier, 2013; Jinek et al., 2012) have revolutionized the field of genetic engineering, offering unprecedented precision in gene editing (Jinek et al., 2012; Doudna and Charpentier, 2014; Khalil, 2020). Since its inception, the CRISPR-Cas9 system has been extensively studied and applied across various biological contexts due to its ability to make targeted DNA modifications. However, the discovery of CRISPR-Cas13 (Abudayyeh et al., 2017), which targets RNA, has opened new avenues for gene modulation without altering the DNA itself. Among the variants, Cas13d is particularly notable for its collateral activity, where it cleaves nearby non-target RNA sequences upon activation, offering potential for diagnostic as well as therapeutic applications (Barrangou et al., 2007).

Recent advancements have leveraged computational models to enhance the predictability and efficiency of CRISPR systems. For instance, models like CRISPRpred-seq (Muhammad Rafid et al., 2020) and DeepCas (Wessels et al., 2020) have utilized traditional machine learning and deep learning techniques to predict sgRNA efficacy, primarily focusing on CRISPR-Cas9. These models often rely on sequence-based features and have shown significant promise in reducing off-target effects and enhancing on-target efficiency. However, the unique mechanisms and RNA targeting properties of Cas13d (Gupta et al., 2022) present distinct challenges and opportunities that these models are not tailored to address.

DeepFM-Crispr introduces an innovative approach by integrating large language models and transformer-based architectures to specifically enhance the performance of CRISPR-Cas13d systems. This model surpasses traditional and recent computational approaches by effectively capturing and processing extensive evolutionary and structural information pertinent to RNA. The use of a large language model allows DeepFM-Crispr to understand and predict the complex dynamics of RNA interactions (Cheng et al., 2023), which are crucial for achieving high precision in RNA-targeted gene editing. Our model not only builds upon the existing body of knowledge but also sets a new benchmark for computational tools in the CRISPR field, particularly for RNA-targeting systems. By focusing on Cas13d, DeepFM-Crispr addresses a critical gap in the existing tools, offering refined predictions and insights that are vital for both research and therapeutic applications.

6 Conclusion

The DeepFM-Crispr model has proven to be exceptionally versatile and robust, demonstrating not only its efficacy with the Cas13d system but also its potential applicability to other CRISPR-Cas systems. Leveraging advanced large language model techniques, DeepFM-Crispr adeptly captures complex genetic interactions and sequence nuances essential for precise genome editing. The model's strength lies in its ability to integrate sophisticated deep learning techniques with large-scale genomic data, enabling it to surpass traditional models in both predictive accuracy and operational efficiency. This adaptability positions DeepFM-Crispr as a valuable asset across a broad spectrum of CRISPR technologies, potentially revolutionizing gene editing methodologies across diverse applications.

7 Future Work

Looking forward, our research will extend the application of DeepFM-Crispr to other widely used CRISPR systems (Barrangou and Doudna, 2016), such as Cas9 and Cas12. These systems play crucial roles in both basic research and clinical settings. By tailoring DeepFM-Crispr to these platforms, we aim to enhance the specificity and efficiency of sgRNA design, thereby minimizing off-target effects and optimizing therapeutic outcomes. Future developments will also focus on refining the model's architecture to incorporate a more comprehensive range of genomic features and environmental factors, which are expected to further enhance its predictive capabilities.

As CRISPR technology continues to evolve, the integration of sophisticated computational models like DeepFM-Crispr is poised to drive significant advancements in the field of genetic engineering. This synergy between cutting-edge biotechnology and computational innovation opens new avenues for medical research and treatment strategies, holding promise for transformative impacts on healthcare and disease management.

References

Omar O Abudayyeh, Jonathan S Gootenberg, Patrick Essletzbichler, Shuo Han, Julia Joung, Joseph J Belanto, Vanessa Verdine, David BT Cox, Max J Kellner, Aviv Regev, et al. 2017. Rna targeting with crispr–cas13. *Nature*, 550(7675):280–284.

Rodolphe Barrangou and Jennifer A Doudna. 2016. Applications of crispr technologies in research and beyond. *Nature biotechnology*, 34(9):933–941.

Rodolphe Barrangou, Christophe Fremaux, Hélène Deveau, Melissa Richards, Patrick Boyaval, Sylvain Moineau, Dennis A Romero, and Philippe Horvath. 2007. Crispr provides acquired resistance against viruses in prokaryotes. *Science*, 315(5819):1709–1712.

Jiayang Chen, Zhihang Hu, Siqi Sun, Qingxiong Tan, Yixuan Wang, Qinze Yu, Licheng Zong, Liang Hong, Jin Xiao, Tao Shen, et al. 2022. Interpretable rna foundation model from unannotated data for highly accurate rna structure and function predictions. *arXiv preprint arXiv:2204.00300*.

Tianqi Chen and Carlos Guestrin. 2016. Xgboost: A scalable tree boosting system. In *Proceedings of the 22nd acm sigkdd international conference on knowledge discovery and data mining*, pages 785–794.

Xiaolong Cheng, Zexu Li, Ruocheng Shan, Zihan Li, Shengnan Wang, Wenchang Zhao, Han Zhang, Lumen Chao, Jian Peng, Teng Fei, et al. 2023. Modeling crispr-cas13d on-target and off-target effects using machine learning approaches. *Nature communications*, 14(1):752.

Corinna Cortes, Mehryar Mohri, and Afshin Rostamizadeh. 2012. L2 regularization for learning kernels. *arXiv preprint arXiv:1205.2653*.

John G Doench, Nicolo Fusi, Meagan Sullender, Mudra Hegde, Emma W Vaimberg, Katherine F Donovan, Ian Smith, Zuzana Tothova, Craig Wilen, Robert Orchard, et al. 2016. Optimized sgrna design to maximize activity and minimize off-target effects of crispr-cas9. *Nature biotechnology*, 34(2):184–191.

J Doudna and E Charpentier. 2013. Genome editing. the new frontier of genome engineering with crispr-cas9.(2014). *Science*, 346:6213.

Jennifer A Doudna and Emmanuelle Charpentier. 2014. The new frontier of genome engineering with crispr-cas9. *Science*, 346(6213):1258096.

Jonathan S Gootenberg, Omar O Abudayyeh, Jeong Wook Lee, Patrick Essletzbichler, Aaron J Dy, Julia Joung, Vanessa Verdine, Nina Donghia, Nichole M Daringer, Catherine A Freije, et al. 2017. Nucleic acid detection with crispr-cas13a/c2c2. *Science*, 356(6336):438–442.

Rahul Gupta, Arijit Ghosh, Rudra Chakravarti, Rajveer Singh, Velayutham Ravichandiran, Snehasikta Swarnakar, and Dipanjan Ghosh. 2022. Cas13d: a new molecular scissor for transcriptome engineering. *Frontiers in Cell and Developmental Biology*, 10:866800.

Kaiming He, Xiangyu Zhang, Shaoqing Ren, and Jian Sun. 2016. Deep residual learning for image recognition. In *Proceedings of the IEEE conference on computer vision and pattern recognition*, pages 770–778.

Gao Huang, Zhuang Liu, Laurens Van Der Maaten, and Kilian Q Weinberger. 2017. Densely connected convolutional networks. In *Proceedings of the IEEE conference on computer vision and pattern recognition*, pages 4700–4708.

Martin Jinek, Krzysztof Chylinski, Ines Fonfara, Michael Hauer, Jennifer A Doudna, and Emmanuelle Charpentier. 2012. A programmable dual-rna–guided dna endonuclease in adaptive bacterial immunity. *science*, 337(6096):816–821.

Ahmad M Khalil. 2020. The genome editing revolution. *Journal of genetic engineering and biotechnology*, 18(1):68.

Ranjay Krishna, Kenji Hata, Frederic Ren, Li Fei-Fei, and Juan Carlos Niebles. 2017. Dense-captioning events in videos. In *Proceedings of the IEEE International Conference on Computer Vision*.

Zongxia Li, Paiheng Xu, Fuxiao Liu, and Hyemi Song. 2023. Towards understanding in-context learning with contrastive demonstrations and saliency maps. *arXiv preprint arXiv:2307.05052*.

Fuxiao Liu, Kevin Lin, Linjie Li, Jianfeng Wang, Yaser Yacoob, and Lijuan Wang. 2023a. Aligning large multi-modal model with robust instruction tuning. *arXiv preprint arXiv:2306.14565*.

Fuxiao Liu, Xiaoyang Wang, Wenlin Yao, Jianshu Chen, Kaiqiang Song, Sangwoo Cho, Yaser Yacoob, and Dong Yu. 2023b. Mmc: Advancing multimodal chart understanding with large-scale instruction tuning. *arXiv preprint arXiv:2311.10774*.

Xiaoyu Liu, Paiheng Xu, Junda Wu, Jiaxin Yuan, Yifan Yang, Yuhang Zhou, Fuxiao Liu, Tianrui Guan, Haoliang Wang, Tong Yu, et al. 2024. Large language models and causal inference in collaboration: A comprehensive survey. *arXiv preprint arXiv:2403.09606*.

Ali Haisam Muhammad Rafid, Md Toufikuzzaman, Mohammad Saifur Rahman, and M Sohel Rahman. 2020. Crisprpred (seq): a sequence-based method for sgrna on target activity prediction using traditional machine learning. *BMC bioinformatics*, 21:1–13.

Martin Riedmiller and A Lernen. 2014. Multi layer perceptron. *Machine Learning Lab Special Lecture, University of Freiburg*, 24.

Steven J Rigatti. 2017. Random forest. *Journal of Insurance Medicine*, 47(1):31–39.

Sergey Shmakov, Omar O Abudayyeh, Kira S Makarova, Yuri I Wolf, Jonathan S Gootenberg, Ekaterina Semenova, Leonid Minakhin, Julia Joung, Silvana Konermann, Konstantin Severinov, et al. 2015. Discovery and functional characterization of diverse class 2 crispr-cas systems. *Molecular cell*, 60(3):385–397.

Shan Suthaharan and Shan Suthaharan. 2016. Support vector machine. *Machine learning models and algorithms for big data classification: thinking with examples for effective learning*, pages 207–235.

Ashish Vaswani, Noam Shazeer, Niki Parmar, Jakob Uszkoreit, Llion Jones, Aidan N Gomez, Łukasz Kaiser, and Illia Polosukhin. 2017. Attention is all you need. *Advances in neural information processing systems*, 30.

Shunjun Wei, Qizhe Qu, Xiangfeng Zeng, Jiadian Liang, Jun Shi, and Xiaoling Zhang. 2021. Self-attention bi-lstm networks for radar signal modulation recognition. *IEEE Transactions on Microwave Theory and Techniques*, 69(11):5160–5172.

Hans-Hermann Wessels, Alejandro Méndez-Mancilla, Xinyi Guo, Mateusz Legut, Zharko Daniloski, and Neville E Sanjana. 2020. Massively parallel cas13 screens reveal principles for guide rna design. *Nature biotechnology*, 38(6):722–727.

Cao Ying, Miao Qi-Guang, Liu Jia-Chen, and Gao Lin. 2013. Advance and prospects of adaboost algorithm. *Acta Automatica Sinica*, 39(6):745–758.

Zijun Zhang. 2018. Improved adam optimizer for deep neural networks. In *2018 IEEE/ACM 26th international symposium on quality of service (IWQoS)*, pages 1–2. Ieee.

Chunhui Zhao, Boao Qin, Tong Li, Shou Feng, and Yiming Yan. 2021. Hyperspectral image classification based on dense convolution and conditional random field. In *2021 IEEE International Geoscience and Remote Sensing Symposium IGARSS*, pages 3653–3656. IEEE.

What an Elegant Bridge: Multilingual LLMs are Biased Similarly in Different Languages

Viktor Mihaylov **Aleksandar Shtedritski**

Oxford Artificial Intelligence Society, University of Oxford

Abstract

This paper investigates biases of Large Language Models (LLMs) through the lens of grammatical gender. Drawing inspiration from seminal works in psycholinguistics, particularly the study of gender's influence on language perception, we leverage multilingual LLMs to revisit and expand upon the foundational experiments of Boroditsky (2003). Employing LLMs as a novel method for examining psycholinguistic biases related to grammatical gender, we prompt a model to describe nouns with adjectives in various languages, focusing specifically on languages with grammatical gender. In particular, we look at adjective co-occurrences across gender and languages, and train a binary classifier to predict grammatical gender given adjectives an LLM uses to describe a noun. Surprisingly, we find that a simple classifier can not only predict noun gender above chance but also exhibit cross-language transferability. We find a strong social influence of language on the way multilingual LLMs reason.

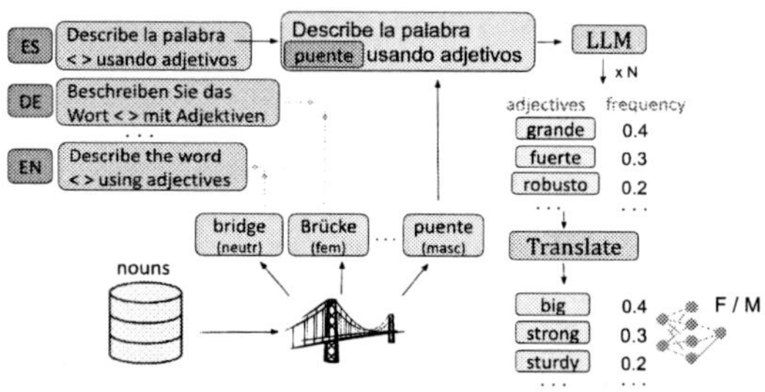

Figure 1: **Probing the bias of multilingual LLMs.** We prompt a LLM to describe gendered nouns using adjectives. This allows us to study psycholinguistic biases of LLMs. For example, if the generated adjectives are predictive of the nouns's gender, we can, by training a binary classifier, predict grammatical gender by only looking at the adjectives a LLM uses to describe a word.

1 Introduction

The way we perceive the world is not only affected by our culture (Oyserman and Lee, 2008; Masuda et al., 2008), but also the language we speak (Boroditsky et al., 2003; Boroditsky, 2001). The relationship between cognition and language has been of interest for a long time (Langacker, 1993), especially through the lens of gender (Boroditsky et al., 2003; Gygax et al., 2008). Recent advances in Large Language Models (LLMs), that match human performance on multiple tasks, provide an exciting opportunity to study the relationship between the psycholinguistic biases of humans and those of machines. While it is unclear whether the latter relationship exists, it would be a more scalable, affordable, and even ethical (Banyard and Flanagan, 2013) alternative to human studies.

In this work, we revisit the study of (Boroditsky et al., 2003) in the era of LLMs. To see how grammatical gender affects cognition, Boroditsky et al. (2003) ask speakers of languages with grammatical gender (where nouns have assigned genders) to describe various objects, finding that the language a person speaks affects the attribution of masculine or feminine characteristics to objects. For example, a Spanish speaker (where "bridge" is masculine) might describe a bridge with words like "strong" or "sturdy", while a German speaker (where "bridge" is feminine) might use terms like "elegant" or "beautiful". However, several subsequent studies fail to replicate such results (Haertlé; Mickan et al., 2014; Samuel et al., 2019), which is but a symptom of the replication crisis in psychology (Wiggins and Christopherson, 2019; Shrout and Rodgers, 2018; Maxwell et al., 2015). Similarly, studies in the field of NLP that examine the way gendered nouns are used in text corpora (Williams et al., 2021; Kann, 2019), find conflicting evidence on whether there is a relationship between grammatical gender and cognition.

The existence of gender bias has been well stud-

Proceedings of the 1st Workshop on NLP for Science (NLP4Science), pages 16–23
November 16, 2024 ©2024 Association for Computational Linguistics

ied for word embeddings (Bolukbasi et al., 2016; Basta et al., 2019; Caliskan et al., 2017), as well as a range of NLP systems, such as ones for machine translation (Stanovsky et al., 2019; Vanmassenhove et al., 2018), image and video captioning (Tatman, 2017; Hall et al., 2023), or sentiment analysis (Kiritchenko and Mohammad, 2018). More recently, the social biases of LLMs have been studied (Kirk et al., 2021). While the multilingual capabilities of LLMs have been extensively evaluated, showing they perform well on machine translation (Hendy et al., 2023; Jiao et al., 2023; Wang et al., 2023) as well as various multilingual benchmarks (Ahuja et al., 2023; Bang et al., 2023), the evaluation of biases in the multilingual setting is less mature. Contrary to recent work showing that multilingual LLMs have different biases for different languages Mukherjee et al. (2023), we find that when it comes to gendered nouns, LLMs are biased in a similar way, as the biases are predictive of each other.

In this paper, we loosely follow the protocol of Boroditsky et al. (2003) and prompt LLMs to describe nouns using adjectives in different languages. Specifically, we focus on open-sourced LLMs (Llama-2 (Touvron et al., 2023) and Mistral (Jiang et al., 2023)). We select 10 languages that have grammatical gender (e.g, German and Spanish), and use the LLMs to describe gendered nouns using adjectives. This allows us to see how adjectives co-occur across languages. Our most important findings are that (i) a simple classifier can predict the gender of a noun using the adjectives used to describe it, and (ii) such a classifier reliably transfers across languages, suggesting LLMs are biased similarly in different languages.

2 Method

In this work, we are interested in the adjectives a multilingual LLM uses to describe gendered nouns when asked in different languages. Here, we describe how we generate such adjectives, and how we examine whether they are predictive of the grammatical gender of the nouns.

2.1 Describing nouns in different languages

We show our pipeline for describing gendered nouns with adjectives in Figure 1. More formally, for a language l we have a database of K gendered nouns $\mathcal{N}^l = \{n_1^l, n_2^l, ..., n_K^l\}$, with corresponding grammatical genders $g(n_i^l) = \{\mathrm{f}, \mathrm{m}\}$ for feminine and masculine, respectively. We prompt the LLM to describe a noun n_k^l using adjectives, which we parse into a list of M adjectives $\mathcal{A}(n_k^l) = \{a_1^l, a_2^l, ..., a_M^l\}$. For every noun n, we repeat the prompting N times and compute the frequencies f with which the adjectives appear:

$$f(a_i) = \frac{\sum_{j=1}^{N} \mathbb{1}(a_i \in \mathcal{A}(n_j))}{N}. \quad (1)$$

Finally, we keep the adjectives with top-p frequencies. In practice, we use $N = 50$ and $p = 50$.

2.2 Predicting gender from descriptions

To examine to what extent the adjectives an LLM uses to describe a noun are predictive of its grammatical gender, we train a binary classifier Φ to predict grammatical gender:

$$\hat{g}(n_i^l) = \Phi\left(\sum_{i=1}^{p} f\left(a_i^l\right) e_g\left(a_i^l\right)\right),$$

where the input to the classifier are GloVe (Pennington et al., 2014) word embeddings e_g of the adjectives weighted by the adjectives frequencies f. In practice, we use a modified version of f, where $f' = -30/\log(f)$ to give us a better scaling. The classifier Φ is a 2-layer MLP and we train it with binary cross-entropy loss.

As shown in Figure 1, we first translate the generated adjectives to English. We do this for two reasons. Firstly, adjectives in some languages are also gendered and that would help the classifier learn this shortcut (e.g. *pretty* in Spanish is *bonito* and *bonita* for masculine and feminine, respectively). Adjectives in English are not gendered, so the classifier Φ has no way of inferring the gender of the noun from the grammatical form. Secondly, this allows for easy transfer of the classifier across languages – e.g. we can train Φ on words generated in Hindi, and evaluate on Italian.

3 Experiments

3.1 Implementation details

Languages We conduct experiments on the languages Bulgarian, Czech, French, German, Greek, Hindi, Italian, Latvian, Portuguese, and Spanish.

Nouns We automatically collect commonly used nouns from every language, and their corresponding grammatical gender. For details on the way we collect those nouns, and the number of nouns per language, please refer to the Appendix. We exclude neuter nouns as such nouns do not exist

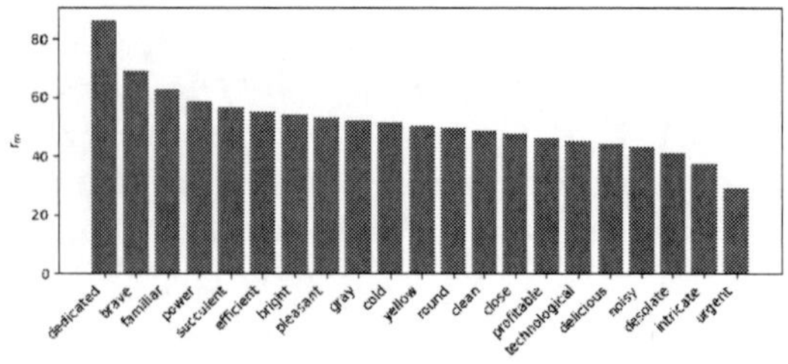

Figure 2: **Bias when describing gendered nouns.** Here we prompt an LLM in Spanish and for a random sample of adjectives, show the percentage of *masculine* nouns they were used for.

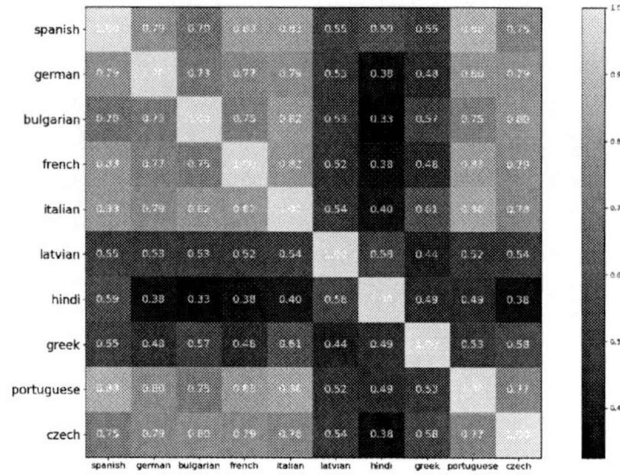

Figure 3: **Gendered adjective similarity sccores.**

in every language. We subsample the feminine or masculine nouns in each gender to ensure a uniform distribution for each language.

LLMs In our experiments we use the open-sourced Mistral-7B (Jiang et al., 2023) model, unless stated otherwise. We also repeat our experiments with Llama2-7B (Touvron et al., 2023).

Prompts We prompt the LLM to describe the given noun in the corresponding language using comma-separated adjectives. In practice, we use few-shot prompts, which we show in the Appendix.

Translation Where we translate nouns, adjectives, or prompts, we use Google Translate [1].

3.2 Bias in generated adjectives

First, we look at adjectives that commonly occur for masculine or feminine nouns.

For every adjective a_i, we look at the ratio r_m:

$$r_m(a_i) = \frac{\sum_{n \in \mathcal{N}, g(n)=\mathrm{m}} \mathbb{1}(a_i \in \mathcal{A}(n)))}{\sum_{n \in \mathcal{N}} \mathbb{1}(a_i \in \mathcal{A}(n)))}, \quad (2)$$

which shows the proportion of masculine words it was used to describe. We randomly sample adjectives and show their r_m in Figure 2. We see that adjectives like intricate and desolate are associated with feminine nouns, whereas adjectives like dedicated and brave are associated with masculine nouns. We show more examples for different languages in the Appendix.

3.3 Do languages show similar biases?

Next, we explore whether adjectives describing masculine and feminine nouns tend to co-occur in different languages. To this end, we compute a gendered-adjective similarity score S_{pq} for every language pair of languages l_p and l_q. We do that as follows. We take the set of N adjectives $a_1, a_2, ..., a_N$ that are used to describe at least 15 nouns in both l_p and l_q. Then for both languages, we construct a gendered-adjective score vector $\sigma \in \mathbb{R}^N$, where $\sigma[i] = r_m(a_i)$. Now, σ_p and σ_q contain the gender ratio for all N adjectives. Finally, we define the gendered-adjective similarity score S_{pq} as the cosine similarity between σ_p and σ_q.

In Figure 3 we show the score S for all language pairs. We see that in Romance languages (Spanish, Italian, French Portuguese), Slavic languages (Bulgarian, Czech), and Germanic languages (German), the LLM shows a high gendered-adjective similarity score, meaning that the adjectives in these languages tend to have similar value of r_m. On the other hand, Greek, Hindi and Latvian have a low score between themselves and others.

3.4 Predicting the gendered nouns

Can we predict the gender of a noun in some language given the adjectives used to describe it? Following Section 2.2, we train binary classifiers to predict the grammatical gender of a noun from the adjectives used to describe it (translated to English). We train a separate classifier for each language. As seen in Table 1, for all languages the classifier reliably does better than random – meaning that the adjectives are predictive of gender.

3.5 Transfer between languages

If we train a grammatical gender classifier, like in Section 3.4, can we predict the gender of a noun in an **unseen** language? To answer this, where we train grammatical gender classifiers on adjectives from 9 languages (translated to English), and eval-

[1]Google Translate, `https://translate.google.com/`

Language	F1	Accuracy Overall	Masc.	Fem.
Bulgarian	0.64	68.4%	72.4%	63.3%
Czech	0.52	59.0%	58.3%	60.2%
French	0.63	56.5%	55.8%	56.8%
German	0.60	60.0%	52.7%	69.4%
Greek	0.68	69.0%	62.7%	77.6%
Hindi	0.53	54.3%	57.5%	51.2%
Italian	0.46	68.2%	73.0%	54.3%
Latvian	0.64	62.6%	60.0%	65.0%
Portuguese	0.55	62.0%	62.7%	60.1 %
Spanish	0.62	63.3%	59.6%	68.0%

Table 1: **Predicting grammatical gender.** We train a classifier to predict the gender of nouns given the adjectives the LLM uses to describe them.

Language	F1	Accuracy Overall	Masc.	Fem.
Bulgarian	0.56	62.5%	64.4%	59.8%
Czech	0.45	60.6%	70.6%	43.5%
French	0.62	54.8%	50.3%	57.3%
German	0.54	58.6%	73.1%	46.0%
Greek	0.64	60.6%	47.8%	75.3%
Hindi	0.53	48.8%	37.9%	60.2%
Italian	0.40	60.1%	61.6%	55.6%
Latvian	0.41	51.7%	81.2%	29.7%
Portuguese	0.55	62.8%	63.0%	62.4%
Spanish	0.59	58.8%	56.7%	60.1%

Table 2: **Unseen Language Results.** We train on all other languages and predict the genders of nouns in the given language. We train a separate leave-one-out classifier for each language.

uate on the final language. As we see in Table 2, such classifiers can reliably predict gender across languages. Interestingly, they even work better than random for Greek, Hindi and Latvian, despite the results reported in Section 3.3. We suggest that although the LLM uses different adjectives to describe masculine and feminine nouns in different languages (hence low S_{pq}), they are semantically similar (hence high accuracy when evaluating the classifier on an unseen language).

4 Discussion

4.1 Reproducibility

Studying the phenomena relating cognition to grammatical gender in psychology has led to inconclusive results(Boroditsky, 2001; Haertlé; Mickan et al., 2014; Samuel et al., 2019). These could be explained by different experimental settings with speakers of different languages, which are difficult to control in a human study. Similarly, prior works that examine text corpora using NLP techniques show conflicting results (Williams et al., 2021; Kann, 2019). The results of these works heavily depend on the text corpora analyzed, and the methods used to identify adjective-noun pairs, which might be subpar for languages other than English. Our method presents more consistent results by ensuring consistent evaluation across languages.

LLM	Eval	F1	Accuracy Overall	Masc.	Fem.
Mistral-7B	Same	0.59	62.3%	61.5%	62.6%
Llama2-7B	Same	0.59	64.6%	67.9%	59.9%
Mistral-7B	Unseen	0.53	57.9%	60.7%	55.1%
Llama2-7B	Unseen	0.54	59.1%	62.6%	54.9%

Table 3: **Evaluating Llama-2.** We compare grammatical gender classifiers Llama-2 to Mistral when tested on the *same* language (as in Section 3.4), or an *unseen* language (as in Section 3.5). We show mean results over all 10 languages. We see that we observe a similar predictive performance on adjectives used by Llama-2 as those by Mistral.

4.2 Importance of our results

Our results are only valid for noun-adjective associations in LLMs. However, these associations have been learnt through co-occurences of these words in text corpora, which have been produced by speakers of the respective languages. Future work should study how well such biases in LLMs are predictive of biases of humans.

The results we present suggest a consistent bias that associates nouns with adjectives, depending on their grammatical gender. This could be important when LLMs are used to describe humans using objects, or vice versa (anthropomorphism, personification, metaphors, ...), where traits of these objects are transferred to the human. Furthermore, using LLMs to perform machine translation of such phrases could lead to a loss of meaning or unexpected biases.

5 Conclusion

In this work, we revisit the psycholinguistic experiments of Boroditsky et al. (2003), confirming the hypothesis of their work applies to LLMs, where different words are used to described masculine and feminine nouns. Our most surprising finding is that we can reliably zero-shot transfer a classifier that predicts grammatical gender across languages. This shows that while LLMs might think differently on different languages, they are biased similarly when it comes to grammatical gender. We hope this work inspires others to explore psycholonguistic experiments applied to LLMs, and to drive a discussion of whether such results can be useful to inform or motivate human experiments.

6 Limitations

We only conducted experiments and observed these effects for the opens-sourced Mistral-7B and Llama2-7B models. It is not clear if similar effects can be observed in larger LLMs, or commercial LLMs such as GPT-4. While we ensured to cover a wide range of languages, the ones we used are by no means exhaustive and only cover indo-european languages. Finally, we only explore the biases of general-purpose, multilingual LLMs. Looking into specialised LLMs, fine-tuned for the specific language, might be more representative of what models would be used in practice.

7 Acknowledgements

This work has been completed with the support of the Oxford AI student society, the EPSRC Centre for Doctoral Training in Autonomous Intelligent Machines Systems [EP/S024050/1] (A.S.) and compute resources from the AWS Responsible AI Grant.

References

Kabir Ahuja, Rishav Hada, Millicent Ochieng, Prachi Jain, Harshita Diddee, Samuel Maina, Tanuja Ganu, Sameer Segal, Maxamed Axmed, Kalika Bali, et al. 2023. Mega: Multilingual evaluation of generative ai. *arXiv preprint arXiv:2303.12528*.

Yejin Bang, Samuel Cahyawijaya, Nayeon Lee, Wenliang Dai, Dan Su, Bryan Wilie, Holy Lovenia, Ziwei Ji, Tiezheng Yu, Willy Chung, et al. 2023. A multitask, multilingual, multimodal evaluation of chatgpt on reasoning, hallucination, and interactivity. *arXiv preprint arXiv:2302.04023*.

Philip Banyard and Cara Flanagan. 2013. *Ethical issues in psychology*. Routledge.

Christine Basta, Marta R Costa-Jussà, and Noe Casas. 2019. Evaluating the underlying gender bias in contextualized word embeddings. *arXiv preprint arXiv:1904.08783*.

Tolga Bolukbasi, Kai-Wei Chang, James Y Zou, Venkatesh Saligrama, and Adam T Kalai. 2016. Man is to computer programmer as woman is to homemaker? debiasing word embeddings. *Advances in neural information processing systems*, 29.

Lera Boroditsky. 2001. Does language shape thought?: Mandarin and english speakers' conceptions of time. *Cognitive psychology*, 43(1):1–22.

Lera Boroditsky, Lauren A Schmidt, and Webb Phillips. 2003. Sex, syntax, and semantics. *Language in mind: Advances in the study of language and thought*, 22:61–79.

Aylin Caliskan, Joanna J Bryson, and Arvind Narayanan. 2017. Semantics derived automatically from language corpora contain human-like biases. *Science*, 356(6334):183–186.

Pascal Gygax, Ute Gabriel, Oriane Sarrasin, Jane Oakhill, and Alan Garnham. 2008. Generically intended, but specifically interpreted: When beauticians, musicians, and mechanics are all men. *Language and cognitive processes*, 23(3):464–485.

Izabella Haertlé. Does grammatical gender influence perception? a study of polish and french speakers. *Psychology of Language and Communication*, 21(1):386–407.

Siobhan Mackenzie Hall, Fernanda Gonçalves Abrantes, Hanwen Zhu, Grace Sodunke, Aleksandar Shtedritski, and Hannah Rose Kirk. 2023. Visogender: A dataset for benchmarking gender bias in image-text pronoun resolution.

Amr Hendy, Mohamed Abdelrehim, Amr Sharaf, Vikas Raunak, Mohamed Gabr, Hitokazu Matsushita, Young Jin Kim, Mohamed Afify, and Hany Hassan Awadalla. 2023. How good are gpt models at machine translation? a comprehensive evaluation. *arXiv preprint arXiv:2302.09210*.

Albert Q Jiang, Alexandre Sablayrolles, Arthur Mensch, Chris Bamford, Devendra Singh Chaplot, Diego de las Casas, Florian Bressand, Gianna Lengyel, Guillaume Lample, Lucile Saulnier, et al. 2023. Mistral 7b. *arXiv preprint arXiv:2310.06825*.

Wenxiang Jiao, Wenxuan Wang, Jen-tse Huang, Xing Wang, and Zhaopeng Tu. 2023. Is chatgpt a good translator? a preliminary study. *arXiv preprint arXiv:2301.08745*.

Katharina Kann. 2019. Grammatical gender, neo-whorfianism, and word embeddings: A data-driven approach to linguistic relativity. *arXiv preprint arXiv:1910.09729*.

Svetlana Kiritchenko and Saif M Mohammad. 2018. Examining gender and race bias in two hundred sentiment analysis systems. *arXiv preprint arXiv:1805.04508*.

Hannah Rose Kirk, Yennie Jun, Filippo Volpin, Haider Iqbal, Elias Benussi, Frederic Dreyer, Aleksandar Shtedritski, and Yuki Asano. 2021. Bias out-of-the-box: An empirical analysis of intersectional occupational biases in popular generative language models. *Advances in neural information processing systems*, 34:2611–2624.

Ronald W Langacker. 1993. Universals of construal. In *Annual Meeting of the Berkeley Linguistics Society*, volume 19, pages 447–463.

Takahiko Masuda, Mikako Akase, MH Radford, and Huaitang Wang. 2008. Effect of contextual factors on patterns of eye-movement: Comparing sensitivity to background information between japanese and westerners. *Shinrigaku Kenkyu: The Japanese Journal of Psychology*, 79(1):35–43.

Scott E Maxwell, Michael Y Lau, and George S Howard. 2015. Is psychology suffering from a replication crisis? what does "failure to replicate" really mean? *American Psychologist*, 70(6):487.

Anne Mickan, Maren Schiefke, and Anatol Stefanowitsch. 2014. Key is a llave is a schlüssel: A failure to replicate an experiment from boroditsky et al. 2003. *Yearbook of the German Cognitive Linguistics Association*, 2(1):39–50.

Anjishnu Mukherjee, Chahat Raj, Ziwei Zhu, and Antonios Anastasopoulos. 2023. Global voices, local biases: Socio-cultural prejudices across languages. *arXiv preprint arXiv:2310.17586*.

Daphna Oyserman and Spike WS Lee. 2008. Does culture influence what and how we think? effects of priming individualism and collectivism. *Psychological bulletin*, 134(2):311.

Jeffrey Pennington, Richard Socher, and Christopher Manning. 2014. GloVe: Global vectors for word representation. In *Proceedings of the 2014 Conference on Empirical Methods in Natural Language Processing (EMNLP)*, pages 1532–1543, Doha, Qatar. Association for Computational Linguistics.

Steven Samuel, Geoff Cole, and Madeline J Eacott. 2019. Grammatical gender and linguistic relativity: A systematic review. *Psychonomic bulletin & review*, 26:1767–1786.

Patrick E Shrout and Joseph L Rodgers. 2018. Psychology, science, and knowledge construction: Broadening perspectives from the replication crisis. *Annual review of psychology*, 69:487–510.

Gabriel Stanovsky, Noah A. Smith, and Luke Zettlemoyer. 2019. Evaluating gender bias in machine translation. In *Proceedings of the 57th Annual Meeting of the Association for Computational Linguistics*, pages 1679–1684, Florence, Italy. Association for Computational Linguistics.

Rachael Tatman. 2017. Gender and dialect bias in YouTube's automatic captions. In *Proceedings of the First ACL Workshop on Ethics in Natural Language Processing*, pages 53–59, Valencia, Spain. Association for Computational Linguistics.

Hugo Touvron, Louis Martin, Kevin Stone, Peter Albert, Amjad Almahairi, Yasmine Babaei, Nikolay Bashlykov, Soumya Batra, Prajjwal Bhargava, Shruti Bhosale, et al. 2023. Llama 2: Open foundation and fine-tuned chat models. *arXiv preprint arXiv:2307.09288*.

Eva Vanmassenhove, Christian Hardmeier, and Andy Way. 2018. Getting gender right in neural machine translation. In *Proceedings of the 2018 Conference on Empirical Methods in Natural Language Processing*, pages 3003–3008, Brussels, Belgium. Association for Computational Linguistics.

Longyue Wang, Chenyang Lyu, Tianbo Ji, Zhirui Zhang, Dian Yu, Shuming Shi, and Zhaopeng Tu. 2023. Document-level machine translation with large language models. *arXiv preprint arXiv:2304.02210*.

Bradford J Wiggins and Cody D Christopherson. 2019. The replication crisis in psychology: An overview for theoretical and philosophical psychology. *Journal of Theoretical and Philosophical Psychology*, 39(4):202.

Adina Williams, Ryan Cotterell, Lawrence Wolf-Sonkin, Damián Blasi, and Hanna Wallach. 2021. On the relationships between the grammatical genders of inanimate nouns and their co-occurring adjectives and verbs. *Transactions of the Association for Computational Linguistics*, 9:139–159.

Appendix

A Collecting nouns

We collect words in German [2] and Spanish [3] from a blog post that lists commonly used words in these languages, and shows their grammatical gender. For Bulgarian [4], Greek [5], Czech [6], French [7], Hindi [8], Italian [9], Latvian [10] and Portuguese [11], we take a list of words and their grammatical gender from Wikipedia. Following that, we only select words whose English translation is in the list of commonly used words in either German or Spanish.

Language	Total	Masc.	Fem.
Bulgarian	1414	839	575
Czech	2383	1501	882
French	2763	996	1767
German	2031	952	1089
Greek	1257	670	587
Hindi	830	425	405
Italian	2919	2219	700
Latvian	1223	522	701
Portuguese	1766	1119	647
Spanish	1758	896	862

Table 4: **Dataset Statistics.** We present the number of masculine and feminine words we consider for all 10 languages. The languages are sorted alphabetically.

We show the number of collected nouns per language in Table 4. We use 90% of the nouns in each language for training, and 10% for testing.

B Excluding animate nouns

Following prior works that look into grammatical gender by looking at word co-occurrence in text corpora (Williams et al., 2021), we exclude animate nouns from our datasets in all languages (e.g. "uncle", "cashier", "engineer", etc.). We repeat the experiments from Section 3.4 in Table 6, and see that the inclusion of animate nouns does not affect overall results.

[2]https://frequencylists.blogspot.com/2016/01/the-2980-most-frequently-used-german.html

[3]https://frequencylists.blogspot.com/2015/12/the-2000-most-frequently-used-spanish.html

[4]https://en.wiktionary.org/wiki/Category:Bulgarian_nouns_by_gender

[5]https://en.wiktionary.org/wiki/Category:Greek_nouns_by_gender

[6]https://en.wiktionary.org/wiki/Category:Czech_nouns_by_gender

[7]https://en.wiktionary.org/wiki/Category:French_nouns_by_gender

[8]https://en.wiktionary.org/wiki/Category:Hindi_nouns_by_gender

[9]https://en.wiktionary.org/wiki/Category:Italian_nouns_by_gender

[10]https://en.wiktionary.org/wiki/Category:Latvian_nouns_by_gender

[11]https://en.wiktionary.org/wiki/Category:Portuguese_nouns_by_gender

LLM	F1	Accuracy		
		Overall	Male	Female
Mistral-7B	0.57	55.0%	50.0%	60.0%
Llama2-7B	0.70	65.0%	50.0%	80.0%

Table 5: **Evaluating the agreement with native English.** We evaluate the agreement of our classifier trained on 10 gendered languages to the perceived grammatical gender of native English speakers, which we treat as ground truth.

Language	F1	Accuracy		
		Overall	Masc.	Fem.
Bulgarian	0.70	71.1%	73.8%	68.3%
German	0.69	63.8%	63.1%	64.2%
Spanish	0.56	55.3%	56.2%	54.4%
Italian	0.51	65.2%	64.5%	67.1%
Czech	0.55	57.2%	54.3%	61.2%
Greek	0.68	69.5%	79.6%	60.1%
Portuguese	0.60	61.1%	56.7%	67.2%
Hindi	0.59	58.1%	67.7%	51.2%
Latvian	0.70	63.2%	60.0%	64.8%
French	0.60	57.0%	58.8%	55.8%

Table 6: **Gendered Nouns Predictions.** This table is for the filtered dictionaries, i.e. without jobs/mother/father etc.

C Gendered adjectives

We show more examples of adjectives that are predominantly used for masculine (or feminine) nouns in Figure 4, similarly to Section 3.2.

D Promps

The prompt we use in English is as follows:

Question: Describe the word "bottle" using comma-separated adjectives. ***Answer***: glass, sleek, thin, brittle, elegant, transparent, clear, tall, fragile, shiny
Question: Describe the word "stone" using comma-separated adjectives. ***Answer***: round, old, strong, cold, solid, ancient, sturdy, dense, natural, durable
Question: Describe the word <> using comma-separated adjectives. ***Answer***:

For the other languages we translate the prompt, e.g. in Spanish we use:

Pregunta: Describe la palabra "botella" usando adjetivos separados por comas. ***Respuesta***: vidrio, liso, delgado, quebradizo, elegante, transparente, claro, alto, frágil, brillante

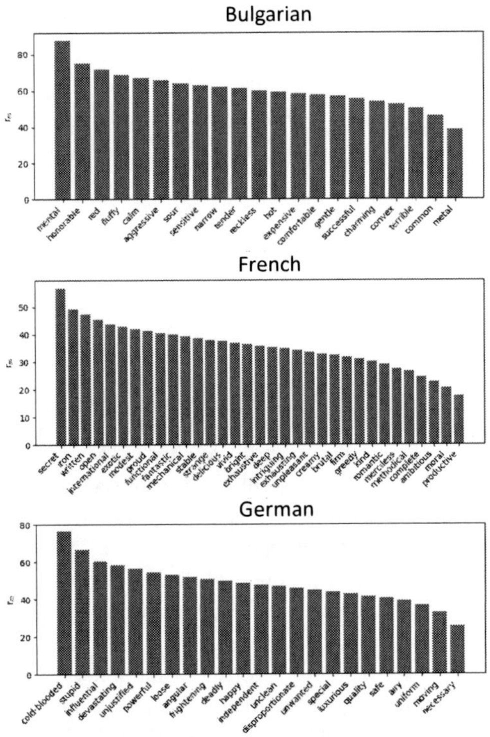

Figure 4: **Bias when describing gendered nouns**. Here we prompt an LLM in Bulgarian, French, and German and for a random sample of adjectives, show the percentage of masculine nouns they were used for.

```
***Pregunta***: Describe la palabra “piedra” usando adjetivos separados por comas. ***Respuesta***: redondo, viejo, fuerte, frío, sólido, antiguo, robusto, denso, natural, duradero
***Pregunta***: Describe la palabra <> usando adjetivos separados por comas. ***Respuesta***:
```

PsychoLex: Unveiling the Psychological Mind of Large Language Models

Mohammad Amin Abbasi[1], Farnaz Sadat Mirnezami[2], Hassan Naderi[1]
[1]Department of Computer Engineering, Iran University of Science and Technology, Tehran, Iran
[2]Department of Computer Engineering, University of Guilan, Rasht, Iran
m_abbasi1378@comp.iust.ac.ir
farnaz.mirnezami@gmail.com
naderi@iust.ac.ir

Abstract

This paper explores the intersection of psychology and artificial intelligence through the development and evaluation of specialized Large Language Models (LLMs). We introduce PsychoLex [1], a suite of resources designed to enhance LLMs' proficiency in psychological tasks in both Persian and English. Key contributions include the PsychoLexQA dataset for instructional content and the PsychoLexEval dataset for rigorous evaluation of LLMs in complex psychological scenarios. Additionally, we present the PsychoLexLLaMA model, optimized specifically for psychological applications, demonstrating superior performance compared to general-purpose models. The findings underscore the potential of tailored LLMs for advancing psychological research and applications, while also highlighting areas for further refinement. This research offers a foundational step towards integrating LLMs into specialized psychological domains, with implications for future advancements in AI-driven psychological practice.

1 Introduction

The rise of Large Language Models (LLMs) has significantly advanced artificial intelligence (AI), providing remarkable capabilities in natural language processing and understanding (Guo et al., 2023; Minaee et al., 2024; Wu et al., 2023). These models have shown proficiency in generating human-like text, translating languages, and engaging in sophisticated dialogues (Agrawal, 2023). However, as users increasingly rely on LLMs for psychological and therapeutic questions (Lai et al., 2023), the limitations of these models in specialized domains have become apparent. Notably, there is a critical absence of datasets designed to evaluate and enhance LLMs' performance in the field of psychology.

Despite considerable progress in general AI research, the integration of psychological expertise into LLMs remains underdeveloped. Existing methodologies often lack the depth required to understand and respond accurately to complex psychological inquiries. Moreover, the field is hindered by the lack of comprehensive datasets that include not only questions and answers but also instructional content tailored to psychological contexts. This gap is significant because it restricts the practical applications of LLMs in psychological research, therapy, and education, where nuanced and precise information is essential.

Our research seeks to address this gap by introducing PsychoLex, a suite of resources and models specifically designed for psychological applications in both Persian and English. The primary objectives of this study are to develop and evaluate specialized datasets, namely PsychoLexQA and PsychoLexEval, and to introduce PsychoLexLLaMA, an LLM developed for psychologyical tasks. These contributions include: (i) PsychoLexQA, which provides comprehensive instructional content and detailed questions and answers to enhance LLM training; (ii) PsychoLexEval, a multiple-choice question and answer (MCQA) dataset designed for rigorous evaluation

[1]https://huggingface.co/collections/aminabbasi/psycholex-66b64e3768da519596e49de9

Proceedings of the 1st Workshop on NLP for Science (NLP4Science), pages 24–35
November 16, 2024 ©2024 Association for Computational Linguistics

of LLMs in psychological contexts, ensuring they can handle complex psychological queries accurately and contextually;(iii) PsychoLexLLaMA, which improves the performance of LLMs in psychological tasks through continual pre-training and fine-tuning of LLaMA 3.1.(Dubey et al., 2024) Together, these contributions aim to provide robust solutions to existing challenges, enhancing the accuracy and relevance of AI-driven psychological tools and paving the way for future advancements in integrating AI with psychological practice.

The structure of this paper is organized as follows: Section 2 reviews related work in LLMs and their applications in psychology. Section 3 details the datasets developed for this study, including their creation and validation processes. Section 4 discusses the development and fine-tuning of the PsychoLexLLaMA model. Section 5 presents the evaluation methodology and results, comparing PsychoLexLLaMA with other state-of-the-art models. Section 6 provides a comprehensive discussion of the findings, and Section 7 concludes the paper with insights into future research directions and potential applications.

By exploring the intersection of AI and psychology, this paper aims to unveil the psychological capabilities of LLMs and demonstrate their potential to advance both fields significantly.

2 Related Works

In this section, we review existing research that benchmarks the capabilities of large language models (LLMs) in Persian, followed by studies that explore the integration of LLMs into psychological research and applications. This dual-focus review establishes the context for our work, emphasizing both the linguistic challenges specific to Persian and the broader implications of applying LLMs in the field of psychology.

2.1 Benchmarking Large Language Models for Persian

Recent advancements in large language models (LLMs), particularly ChatGPT, have generated significant interest in their evaluation across various languages and tasks. ChatGPT's performance on various Persian natural language processing tasks is evaluated by Abaskohi et al. (2024). they present a comprehensive evaluation of large language models (LLMs) for the Persian language, focusing on models like GPT-3.5-turbo (OpenAI, 2023a), GPT-4 (OpenAI, 2023b), and OpenChat-3.5. This study, which is the first extensive benchmarking effort for Persian, aims to address the challenges posed by Persian as a low-resource language with unique linguistic features. The evaluation covers a broad range of natural language processing (NLP) tasks, including sentiment analysis, question answering, natural language inference, and translation. the study highlights the model's superior performance in multiple-choice questions(MCQs) related to math and general knowledge from the ParsiNLU dataset (Khashabi et al., 2020). These benchmarks are particularly important for assessing the models' reasoning capabilities in Persian. While ChatGPT-4 excels across several benchmarks, its application in psychology has not been tested, underscoring a critical area for future research.

2.2 Khayyam Challenge (PersianMMLU)

Recent advancements have focused on optimizing the performance of Large Language Models (LLMs). The PersianMMLU (Ghahroodi et al., 2024) is particularly significant as it concentrates on the Persian language capabilities of these models. It evaluates their proficiency in answering multiple-choice questions across diverse fields such as mathematics, science, logic, and intelligence testing. This comprehensive evaluation involved advanced models like GPT-3.5, GPT-4(OpenAI, 2023b), Aya (Ustun et al., 2024), PersianMind(Rostami et al., 2024), mT0 (Muennighoff et al., 2023), mGPT (Shliazhko et al., 2022), and Claude3-haiku (Anthropic, 2024). The study utilized a robust dataset derived from Iran's national university entrance exams and educational assessments. While GPT-4 emerged as the superior model, its efficacy in psychological applications remains untested. This gap highlights the necessity of our current research, which aims to specifically evaluate the performance of LLMs in psychology-related scenarios.

2.3 Using large language models in psychology

Demszky et al. (2023) explores the integration of LLMs, particularly GPT-3 and GPT-4, into psychological research practices. These models' adeptness at text generation, dialogue engagement, persona simulation, and information synthesis provides innovative approaches to studying various psychological subfields. The primary aim is to evaluate the extent to which LLMs can enrich psychological research methodologies. Despite their potential, LLMs often fall short in delivering contextually accurate advice consistently. This study highlights the importance of refining LLMs through fine-tuning and reinforcement learning from human feedback to ensure their practical efficacy in real-world psychological settings. The extensive datasets used to train these models, encompassing diverse sources of human language data, are aimed at tailoring LLMs to better serve both theoretical and applied psychology.

2.4 Exploring the Frontiers of LLMs in Psychological Applications

The application of Artificial Intelligence (AI), especially large language models (LLMs), is revolutionizing psychological research. A study by Ke et al. (2024) underscores significant advances in language models and their profound impact on the field of psychology. LLMs like OpenAI's ChatGPT facilitate various research activities, including literature reviews, hypothesis formulation, experiment design, data analysis, and scholarly writing across several psychological domains such as cognitive, behavioral, clinical, educational, developmental, and social psychology. While these models offer substantial benefits, the review also delineates key technical and ethical challenges, including data privacy concerns and inherent limitations of LLMs. The authors advocate for the careful integration of these technologies in psychological research to enhance our understanding of the human mind and improve the methodologies employed in psychological studies.

In conclusion, the existing body of research on large language models (LLMs) highlights both significant advancements and notable limitations in applying these models to Persian natural language processing and psychological applications. However, challenges persist due to the low-resource nature of the Persian language and the limited evaluation of LLMs in psychological settings. While LLMs hold potential for improving psychological research, they often lack consistency and contextual accuracy. Future work is needed to refine these models for specialized fields, addressing their current limitations and improving their reliability in practical applications.

3 Dataset

This section outlines the datasets developed to investigate the application of large language models (LLMs) in psychology. We detail the creation and utilization of three pivotal datasets: the foundational pretraining data, the PsychoLexQA dataset for instructional content, and the PsychoLexEval dataset for evaluating model comprehension and performance.

3.1 Pretraining Data

For the pretraining phase, we employed "Introduction to Psychology" by Hilgard (1953), a seminal textbook noted for its comprehensive insights into psychology. This text was used in both its Persian and English versions to establish a bilingual foundation for our models. The dataset comprised approximately 1.3 million tokens, offering a rich and diverse corpus that spans a broad spectrum of psychological topics. This extensive pretraining data enabled our models to develop a deep understanding of essential psychological concepts and terminology, facilitating their application in both Persian and English contexts.

3.2 PsychoLexQA

For the instructional dataset, we adopted two distinct methodologies to generate detailed and comprehensive instructional content in both Persian and English

3.2.1 Document-Based Instructions

The first method involved extracting instructional content from "Introduction to Psychology" in both languages. This process was automated using the GPT-4o model, where paragraphs from the textbook were analyzed to grasp key concepts. For each paragraph, the model generated a series of questions and answers aimed at testing material comprehension. Each question was crafted to be clear and precise, with detailed answers provided to ensure a thorough understanding of the discussed psychological concepts. Paragraphs lacking sufficient content for question generation were identified and noted. This method resulted in a dataset containing 7,055 entries. Appendix A demonstrates an example of PsychoLexQA dataset based on psychology document.

3.2.2 Self-Instruct

The second method focuses on creating structured instructional tasks for various psychological subcategories in both Persian and English. This semi-automated approach, inspired by the Self-Instruct framework (Wang et al., 2022), utilizes a predefined list of subcategories such as Clinical and Cognitive Psychology and tasks such as Case Study Analysis and Experiment Design to generate detailed bilingual task instructions. Through iterative processes, the model generates comprehensive inputs and outputs, resulting in a dataset of 3,001 entries covering multiple psychological domains, ensuring a diverse and realistic range of scenarios. Figures 3, 4, 5, 6 in the Appendix A depicts several examples of PsychoLexQA dataset which has been created using a self-instruct method.

3.2.3 Scope of PsychoLexQA

The PsychoLexQA dataset, focuses on simulating real-world psycho-logical scenarios through a range of instructional tasks. These tasks challenge LLMs with exercises like: (1) Case Study Analysis: Identifying psychological issues and proposing interventions; (2) Experiment Design: Developing experimental methodologies, hypotheses, and variables; (3) Data Interpretation: Analyzing statistical or experimental data; (4) Scenario Response: Offering interventions for hypothetical psychological scenarios; (5) Theoretical Explanation: Explaining psycho-logical theories or concepts; (6) Diagnostic Evaluation: Simulating diagnostic processes for psychological conditions; (7) Ethical Dilemma Resolution: Proposing ethical resolutions in psychological practice; (8) Intervention Planning: Crafting treatment plans for psychological conditions; (9) Literature Review: Summarizing key findings from psychological research; (10) Comparative Analysis: Comparing psychological theories, interventions, or case outcomes.

The dataset further breaks down into subcategories that reflect distinct psychological areas, such as Clinical Psychology, Cognitive Psychology, Developmental Psychology, Social Psychology, Biological Psychology, Industrial-Organizational Psychology, Neuropsychology, Health Psychology, and Educational Psychology. Each subcategory is paired with tasks de-signed to simulate challenges and interventions relevant to that field. Together, both datasets provide a comprehensive tool for evaluating and training LLMs in diverse and realistic psycho-logical scenarios, with PsychoLexEval assessing broad understanding and PsychoLexQA focusing on task-based problem-solving.

3.3 PsychoLexEval

The PsychoLexEval dataset, a multiple-choice question and answer (MCQA) format in both Persian and English, is designed to assess the comprehension and performance of LLMs in psychology. This section will describe the data collection and review process, the methods employed to ensure quality and compliance, and the broad scope and coverage of this MCQA dataset. An example of the PsychoLexEval dataset can be found in Appendix A.

3.3.1 Data Collection

To construct this dataset, we compiled questions from multiple significant sources: (1) Graduate Entrance Exams: questions from psychology entrance exams (2014-2024) that cover advanced topics; (2) Employment Exams: questions from various job tests, including both specialized and general psychology; (3) Online Sources: Questions from trusted psychology test websites; (4) GPT-4 Generated Content: questions from Psychology books, covering a wide range of topics.

3.3.2 Filtering and Review

To ensure high quality and legal compliance, we implemented rigorous filtering and review processes for the dataset. Initially, a human review was conducted where a sample of questions was meticulously scrutinized by experts. This step was crucial to ensure that each question was relevant, complete, and clearly articulated. During this phase, we specifically retained only those questions that had exactly four answer options, ensuring consistency and clarity in the evaluation process. Additionally, to avoid any legal complications, we carefully removed any content that potentially violated copyright laws. This step was essential to maintain the integrity of the dataset and ensure that all included materials were legally compliant for use in our research and broader academic dissemination. These measures collectively reinforced the dataset's reliability and adherence to legal standards, providing a robust foundation for evaluating large language models within psychological contexts.

3.3.3 Scope of PsychoLexEval

The PsychoLexEval dataset is meticulously designed to evaluate the comprehension and performance of large language models (LLMs) in psychology, encompassing a broad spectrum of psychological fields. These include general psychology, developmental psychology, and clinical psychology, along with psychometrics, cognitive tests, and industrial-organizational psychology. The dataset also covers social and educational psychology, exceptional children's needs, and foundational concepts from Introduction to Psychology. With 3,430 rows of diverse content, it serves as an invaluable resource for researchers to assess LLMs' capabilities across various psychology domains.

4 PsychoLexLLaMA

In this section, we detail the development of PsychoLexLLaMA, a specialized large language model (LLM) designed explicitly for psychology. Our goal was to surpass the performance of general-purpose models by optimizing our model to require minimal data and hardware resources. the model benefits significantly from the integration of the PsychoLexQA dataset, which includes tasks such as case study analysis, experiment design, and diagnostic evaluation. This dataset allows PsychoLexLLaMA to handle complex psychological scenarios across a variety of domains like clinical, cognitive, and developmental psychology, making it a highly valuable tool for both practical and research-oriented applications.

The integration of PsychoLexQA significantly enhances PsychoLexLLaMA's role in applied psychology and psychological science. It assists clinical practitioners with diagnostics and interventions, supports research with experiment design and data interpretation, and enriches education by generating tailored instructional content. Overall, it provides specialized, accurate responses, making it a valuable tool across clinical, research, and educational domains in psychology.

We utilized the Transformers[2] library for model development. The process of constructing our model is illustrated in Figure 1.

[2] https://github.com/huggingface/transformers

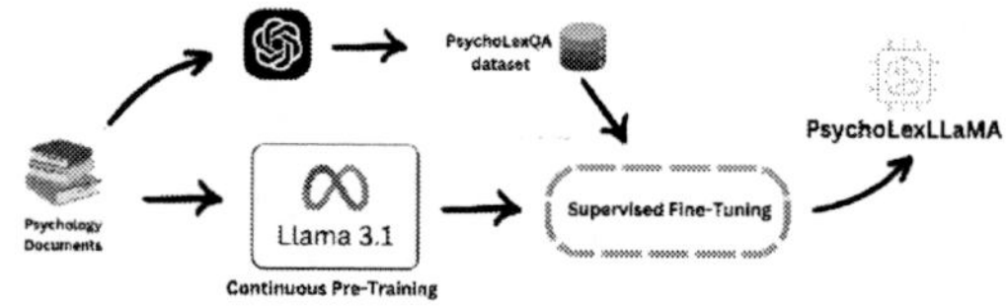

Figure 1: Process of constructing PsychoLexLLaMA model.

4.1 Continuous Pre-Training

For continuous pre-training (Zhou et al., 2024), we employed the LoRA technique (Hu et al., 2021) on the bilingual texts of "Introduction to Psychology" by Hilgard. This foundational work was processed in both Persian and English, leveraging the established pretraining data. We utilized LLaMA 3.1(Dubey et al., 2024) as our base models in two configurations: 8B and 70B. This stage was critical for aligning the base models with psychological content, thereby enhancing their understanding and application of complex psychological concepts efficiently. The pre-training for the 8B model took 8 minutes using a single A100 80GB GPU, while the 70B model required 41 minutes on two A100 80GB GPUs. Table 1 provides a detailed overview of the LoRA training configurations used during this phase.

Lr	Rank	Alpha	Dropout
1e-5	8	16	0.0

Table 1: LoRA training configurations

4.2 Supervised Fine-Tuning

The supervised fine-tuning phase was essential for tailoring our models to meet the specific demands of psychological analysis. Utilizing the PsychoLexQA dataset, which includes both instructional content and a comprehensive set of questions and answers, we applied the LoRA technique to further train the pre-trained models. This phase was pivotal in refining the models' abilities to interpret and respond accurately to intricate psychological queries and scenarios within the dataset. The supervised fine-tuning for the 8B model took 22 minutes using a single A100 GPU, while the 70B model required 32 minutes on two A100 GPUs. The LoRA training configurations used during this phase were the same as those in the continuous pre-training.

4.3 Linear Weight Combination

To bolster the final model's robustness and preserve the integrity of previous training advances, we implemented a linear weight combination strategy. This involved merging the weights of the LLaMA 3.1 Instruct model with our continuously pre-trained and finely-tuned models. Each model contributed 50% of its weight to the final composite. This method synergistically combined the foundational capabilities of LLaMA with our newly developed psychological expertise, producing a balanced and potent tool adept at handling sophisticated psychological inquiries.

Through these meticulous steps, PsychoLexLLaMA has been meticulously tailored to meet the unique needs of psychological applications. It stands as a robust resource for researchers and practitioners in both psychology and artificial intelligence, providing a reliable platform for further explorations and advancements in these fields. The next sections will evaluate PsychoLexLLaMA's performance in detail, comparing it with other models to underscore its enhanced capabilities in the realm of psychological research and practice.

5 Evaluation

In this study, we conducted a comprehensive evaluation of various language models that operate in both Persian and English, focusing on their ability to understand and accurately respond to psychological questions. The models assessed include include Qwen2 (Yang et al., 2024), Aya-23 (Aryabumi et al., 2024), Phi-3 (Abdin et al., 2024), Llama-3, Llama-3.1(Dubey et al., 2024), Gemma 1.1 (Team et al., 2024), command-r, PersianLLaMA (Abbasi et al., 2023), PersianMind (Rostami et al., 2024b), and PsychoLexLLaMA. Our focus on open-source models was intended to enhance the accessibility and reproducibility of our findings. The generation configuration for all the LLMs evaluated is consistent across the experiments and is detailed in Table 2.

Temp	Max new tokens	top p	Do sample
0.01	16	0.9	True

Table 2: Generation configurations for all evaluated LLMs.

5.1 Zero-shot Setting

In the zero-shot setting, models were tested without any prior contextual examples, relying solely on their pre-existing knowledge. This setting evaluated the models' intrinsic ability to generate accurate responses based solely on their training.

5.2 One-shot Setting

The one-shot setting involved presenting each model with a single relevant example before it answered a question. This setting was used to assess the impact of a minimal context on the accuracy of the models, providing insights into their ability to leverage new information quickly

5.3 Five-shot Setting

In the five-shot setting, models were given five related examples before responding to questions. This scenario tested the models' capacity to utilize more extensive contextual information to enhance their accuracy, offering a deeper understanding of their learning capabilities.

5.4 Evaluation Metric

The effectiveness of each model across the zero-shot, one-shot, and five-shot settings was measured using accuracy as the primary metric. Accuracy was defined as the proportion of correct answers provided by the models relative to the total number of questions posed. This rigorous evaluation approach allowed us to discern the strengths and weaknesses of each model in processing and understanding psychological content comprehensively.

Through these methodical evaluations, we aimed to illustrate the varying capabilities of each model under different contextual conditions. This analysis not only sheds light on how models adapt to incremental information but also highlights their potential applicability in psychological settings, where understanding nuanced human behavior is crucial.

6 Results

This section outlines the outcomes of our evaluation of selected large language models (LLMs) using the PsychoLexEval dataset in both Persian and

English. The primary focus was on assessing the models' proficiency in understanding and responding to psychological questions.

Tables 3 and 4 illustrate the accuracy results of the models on the PsychoLexEval dataset for Persian and English, respectively. These tables quantify how effectively each model comprehends and addresses psychology-related questions across languages.

6.1 Discussion

The results from Tables 3 and 4 provide significant insights into the performance of various LLMs, showcasing their competencies in both Persian English. Notably, these findings highlight the influence of model architecture and parameter size on handling specialized tasks, such as interpreting and responding to psychology-related questions.

		Accuracy			
Model	**# Param**	**0-shot**	**1-shot**	**5-shot**	**Avg**
Qwen2 Instruct	7B	03.55	06.18	08.63	6.12
Gemma 1.1 it	7B	43.07	40.68	27.57	37.11
PersianMind	7B	35.78	35.96	24.63	32.12
Aya-23	8B	39.64	41.42	27.02	36.03
Llama-3 Instruct	8B	33.88	10.66	34.49	26.34
Llama-3.1 Instruct	8B	45.89	41.36	35.78	41.01
PsychoLexLLaMA-pretrain-sft	8B	47.30	43.13	46.61	45.68
PsychoLexLLaMA-average	**8B**	**48.52**	**41.97**	**47.05**	**45.85**
PersianLLaMA	13B	20.13	18.52	19.89	19.51
Aya-23	35B	21.07	10.47	22.69	18.08
c4ai-command-r-v01	35B	35.96	21.75	46.20	34.64
Llama-3 Instruct	70B	19.54	09.31	0.5	9.78
Llama-3.1 Instruct	**70B**	**70.34**	**67.83**	**70.40**	**69.52**
PsychoLexLLaMA-pretrain-sft	70B	67.79	45.34	68.07	60.4
PsychoLexLLaMA-average	70B	65.84	53.06	69.66	62.85
Qwen2 Instruct	72B	31.37	05.82	50.3	29.16

Table 3 : Accuracy of LLMs on the PsychoLexEval dataset in Persian.

		Accuracy			
Model	**# Param**	**0-shot**	**1-shot**	**5-shot**	**Avg**
Qwen2 Instruct	7B	89.31	42.74	83.76	71.94
Gemma 1.1 it	7B	84.75	55.06	65.86	68.56
Aya-23	8B	73.62	33.80	77.05	61.49
Llama-3 Instruct	8B	85.77	78.57	68.22	77.52
Llama-3.1 Instruct	8B	88.97	89.25	87	88.41
PsychoLexLLaMA-pretrain-sft	8B	88.97	81.21	62.03	77.4
PsychoLexLLaMA-average	**8B**	**90.10**	**89.03**	**90.04**	**89.72**
Aya-23	35B	81.32	79.02	82	80.78
c4ai-command-r-v01	35B	87	78.06	75.08	80.05
Llama-3 Instruct	70B	90.55	88.58	76.77	85.3
Llama-3.1 Instruct	**70B**	**93.02**	**92.63**	**92.1**	**92.58**
PsychoLexLLaMA-pretrain-sft	70B	91.45	90.24	90.85	90.85
PsychoLexLLaMA-average	70B	92.13	91.85	91.87	91.95
Qwen2 Instruct	72B	91.11	73.79	92.29	85.73

Table 4 : Accuracy of LLMs on the PsychoLexEval dataset in English.

6.1.1 Performance Trends Across Models

The data reveal substantial variability in performance across models and settings. For instance, the Llama-3.1 Instruct with 70B parameters exhibits superior performance in all scenarios, suggesting a positive correlation between larger parameter sizes and enhanced comprehension and response accuracy. This trend is consistent in the English data, where models with larger parameters, such as Llama-3.1 Instruct 70B, also demonstrate robust performance, especially in zero-shot and five-shot settings.

Conversely, models with fewer parameters sometimes perform well in lower-shot settings but typically exhibit decreased performance as the complexity of tasks increases. For example, the Qwen2 Instruct with 7B parameters faces greater challenges in the Persian context than in English, potentially indicating linguistic or dataset-specific hurdles that are more effectively managed by larger models.

6.1.2 Language-Specific Observations

Our evaluation underscores distinct language-specific differences. In Persian, the increase in model accuracy from zero to five shots is more marked, indicating that Persian language models significantly benefit from added context. Conversely, English language models tend to have higher baseline performances, likely reflecting the advantages of more extensive pre-training datasets available in English.

6.1.3 Impact of Training and Fine-Tuning

The results particularly underscore the critical importance of targeted training and fine-tuning, as seen with the PsychoLexLLaMA models. Designed to surpass its predecessor, Llama 3.1, the 70B PsychoLexLLaMA occasionally does not reach its ambitious targets but consistently matches or exceeds the performance of the original Llama 3.1 model. This consistency indicates that while specific enhancements did not universally lead to improvements, they significantly bolstered the model's capabilities. The 70B version, with its vast parameter count, possesses the capacity to acquire a broader knowledge base, making it challenging to add new knowledge without forgetting previously learned information. Consequently, fine-tuning such a large model demands considerably more data to achieve better outcomes due to its complexity.

In contrast, the 8B version of PsychoLexLLaMA often outperforms larger models, suggesting that precise, domain-specific fine-tuning can yield remarkable effectiveness, even with fewer parameters. This success highlights the potential of smaller models, particularly when equipped with tailored enhancements for specific applications like psychological evaluations.

The varying impacts of scaling between the 8B and 70B versions suggest that while larger models possess a broad knowledge base enhancing their general performance, strategic fine-tuning is crucial for maximizing efficacy in specialized domains. This observation encourages further research into training strategies that optimize both large and small models for specific tasks, ensuring that they not only retain previous knowledge but also effectively integrate new information.

7 Conclusion

This study has significantly advanced our understanding of how large language models (LLMs) can be effectively tailored for applications within psychology. Through the integration of specialized psychological content, the development of the PsychoLexQA and PsychoLexEval datasets, and the creation of the PsychoLexLLaMA model, we have demonstrated the substantial benefits of targeted model training and fine-tuning.

Our findings indicate that specific pretraining and fine-tuning strategies substantially enhance the performance of LLMs in psychological settings, underscoring the critical role of thoughtful model architecture and training approaches. Notably, while larger models typically show strong performance, our results reveal that even smaller models can achieve exceptional outcomes when subjected to precise, domain-specific adjustments. This suggests a scalable potential for LLMs in psychological applications that can be adapted to different contexts and constraints.

In conclusion, this research not only sheds light on the current capabilities and challenges of using LLMs in psychology but also sets a foundation for future work. It encourages ongoing refinement of these models to improve their relevance and accuracy, thereby enhancing their utility in real-world psychological applications. Moving forward, we anticipate that continued advancements in model training methodologies and evaluation strategies will drive significant progress in the field, making

LLMs an indispensable tool in the arsenal of psychological research and practice.

Limitations

This study highlights the potential of customizing large language models (LLMs) for psychological applications, but several limitations may affect the generalizability of our findings. The PsychoLexQA and PsychoLexEval datasets, which are key to this research, contain inherent biases from the selected materials and question designs, restricting the application of results to broader psychological contexts. The reliance on freely licensed sources, particularly Hilgard's Introduction to Psychology (1953), limits the diversity and depth of psychological topics in this study. While the text provides a solid foundation in core principles, it does not reflect the significant advancements in psychology, such as developments in cognitive-behavioral therapy, neuropsychology, and cross-cultural psychology. Due to copyright restrictions, more recent, relevant texts could not be used, potentially limiting the model's engagement with modern psychological paradigms. Future iterations will aim to include up-to-date psychological literature to address this limitation and enhance the model's applicability to contemporary practice. Another major limitation is the need for high-performance hardware, such as GPUs, which can hinder replicability and limit access for researchers with fewer resources. Balancing model performance with minimal data and hardware remains challenging, often requiring trade-offs that reduce practical utility. Future research should aim to diversify training data and develop more resource-efficient methods to enhance the deployment of LLMs in psychology.

References

Amirhossein Abaskohi, Sara Baruni, Mostafa Masoudi, Nesa Abbasi, Mohammad Hadi Babalou, Ali Edalat, Sepehr Kamahi, Samin Mahdizadeh Sani, Nikoo Naghavian, Danial Namazifard, Pouya Sadeghi, & Yadollah Yaghoobzadeh. (2024). Benchmarking Large Language Models for Persian: A Preliminary Study Focusing on ChatGPT. *ArXiv, abs/2404.02403.*

Mohammad Amin Abbasi, Arash Ghafouri, Mahdi Firouzmandi, Hassan Naderi, & Behrouz Minaei-Bidgoli. (2023). PersianLLaMA: Towards Building First Persian Large Language Model. *ArXiv, abs/2312.15713.*

Marah Abdin, Sam Ade Jacobs, Ammar Ahmad Awan, Jyoti Aneja, Ahmed Awadallah, Hany Awadalla, Nguyen Bach, Amit Bahree, Arash Bakhtiari, & Harkirat Behl. (2024). Phi-3 technical report: A highly capable language model locally on your phone. *arXiv preprint arXiv:2404.14219.*

Shrivats Agrawal. (2023). Are LLMs the Master of All Trades? : Exploring Domain-Agnostic Reasoning Skills of LLMs. *ArXiv, abs/2303.12810.*

Anthropic. (2024,). The Claude 3 Model Family: Opus, Sonnet, Haiku.

Viraat Aryabumi, John Dang, Dwarak Talupuru, Saurabh Dash, David Cairuz, Hangyu Lin, Bharat Venkitesh, Madeline Smith, Kelly Marchisio, & Sebastian Ruder. (2024). Aya 23: Open weight releases to further multilingual progress. *arXiv preprint arXiv:2405.15032.*

Dorottya Demszky, Diyi Yang, David S. Yeager, Christopher J. Bryan, Margarett Clapper, Susannah Chandhok, Johannes C. Eichstaedt, Cameron A. Hecht, Jeremy P. Jamieson, Meghann Johnson, Michaela Jones, Danielle Krettek-Cobb, Leslie Lai, Nirel JonesMitchell, Desmond C. Ong, Carol S. Dweck, James J Gross, & James W. Pennebaker. (2023). Using large language models in psychology. *Nature Reviews Psychology, 2*, 688 - 701.

Abhimanyu Dubey, Abhinav Jauhri, Abhinav Pandey, Abhishek Kadian, Ahmad Al-Dahle, Aiesha Letman, Akhil Mathur, . . . Zhiwei Zhao. (2024). The Llama 3 Herd of Models.

Omid Ghahroodi, Marzia Nouri, Mohammad V. Sanian, Alireza Sahebi, Doratossadat Dastgheib, Ehsaneddin Asgari, Mahdieh Soleymani Baghshah, & Mohammad Hossein Rohban. (2024). Khayyam Challenge (PersianMMLU): Is Your LLM Truly Wise to The Persian Language? *ArXiv, abs/2404.06644.*

Zishan Guo, Renren Jin, Chuang Liu, Yufei Huang, Dan Shi, Supryadi, Linhao Yu, Yan Liu, Jiaxuan Li, Bojian Xiong, & Deyi Xiong. (2023). Evaluating Large Language Models: A Comprehensive Survey. *ArXiv, abs/2310.19736.*

J. Edward Hu, Yelong Shen, Phillip Wallis, Zeyuan Allen-Zhu, Yuanzhi Li, Shean Wang, & Weizhu Chen. (2021). LoRA: Low-Rank Adaptation of Large Language Models. *ArXiv, abs/2106.09685.*

Luoma Ke, Song Tong, Peng Cheng, & Kaiping Peng. (2024). Exploring the Frontiers of LLMs in Psychological Applications: A Comprehensive Review. *ArXiv, abs/2401.01519.*

Daniel Khashabi, Arman Cohan, Siamak Shakeri, Pedram Hosseini, Pouya Pezeshkpour, Malihe Alikhani, Moin Aminnaseri, . . . Yadollah Yaghoobzadeh. (2020). ParsiNLU: A Suite of Language Understanding Challenges for Persian. *Transactions of the Association for Computational Linguistics, 9,* 1147-1162.

Tin Lai, Yukun Shi, Zicong Du, Jiajie Wu, Ken Fu, Yichao Dou, & Ziqi Wang. (2023). Psy-LLM: Scaling up Global Mental Health Psychological Services with AI-based Large Language Models. *ArXiv, abs/2307.11991.*

Shervin Minaee, Tomáš Mikolov, Narjes Nikzad, Meysam Asgari Chenaghlu, Richard Socher, Xavier Amatriain, & Jianfeng Gao. (2024). Large Language Models: A Survey. *ArXiv, abs/2402.06196.*

Niklas Muennighoff, Thomas Wang, Lintang Sutawika, Adam Roberts, Stella Biderman, Teven Le Scao, M Saiful Bari, Sheng Shen, Zheng-Xin Yong, Hailey Schoelkopf, Xiangru Tang, Dragomir R. Radev, Alham Fikri Aji, Khalid Almubarak, Samuel Albanie, Zaid Alyafeai, Albert Webson, Edward Raff, & Colin Raffel. (2023). Crosslingual Generalization through Multitask Finetuning. Annual Meeting of the Association for Computational Linguistics,

OpenAI. (2023a). *Gpt-3.5.* https://www.openai.com/. Accessed: 2023-06-13.

OpenAI. (2023b). *Gpt-4 technical report.* https://arxiv.org/abs/2303.08774

Pedram Rostami, Ali Salemi, & Mohammad Javad Dousti. (2024). PersianMind: A Cross-Lingual Persian-English Large Language Model. *ArXiv, abs/2401.06466.*

Oleh Shliazhko, Alena Fenogenova, Maria Tikhonova, Vladislav Mikhailov, Anastasia Kozlova, & Tatiana Shavrina. (2022). mGPT: Few-Shot Learners Go Multilingual. *Transactions of the Association for Computational Linguistics, 12,* 58-79.

Gemma Team, Thomas Mesnard, Cassidy Hardin, Robert Dadashi, Surya Bhupatiraju, Shreya Pathak, Laurent Sifre, Morgane Rivière, Mihir Sanjay Kale, & Juliette Love. (2024). Gemma: Open models based on gemini research and technology. *arXiv preprint arXiv:2403.08295.*

A. Ustun, Viraat Aryabumi, Zheng-Xin Yong, Wei-Yin Ko, Daniel D'souza, Gbemileke Onilude, Neel Bhandari, Shivalika Singh, Hui-Lee Ooi, Amr Kayid, Freddie Vargus, Phil Blunsom, Shayne Longpre, Niklas Muennighoff, Marzieh Fadaee, Julia Kreutzer, & Sara Hooker. (2024). Aya Model: An Instruction Finetuned Open-Access Multilingual Language Model. *ArXiv, abs/2402.07827.*

Yizhong Wang, Yeganeh Kordi, Swaroop Mishra, Alisa Liu, Noah A. Smith, Daniel Khashabi, & Hannaneh Hajishirzi. (2022). Self-Instruct: Aligning Language Models with Self-Generated Instructions. Annual Meeting of the Association for Computational Linguistics,

Qingyun Wu, Gagan Bansal, Jieyu Zhang, Yiran Wu, Beibin Li, Erkang Zhu, Li Jiang, Xiaoyun Zhang, Shaokun Zhang, Jiale Liu, Ahmed Hassan Awadallah, Ryen W White, Doug Burger, & Chi Wang. (2023). AutoGen: Enabling Next-Gen LLM Applications via Multi-Agent Conversation.

An Yang, Baosong Yang, Binyuan Hui, Bo Zheng, Bowen Yu, Chang Zhou, Chengpeng Li, Chengyuan Li, Dayiheng Liu, & Fei Huang. (2024). Qwen2 technical report. *arXiv preprint arXiv:2407.10671.*

Da-Wei Zhou, Hai-Long Sun, Jingyi Ning, Han-Jia Ye, & De-chuan Zhan. (2024). Continual Learning with Pre-Trained Models: A Survey. *ArXiv, abs/2401.16386.*

A Dataset samples

Figures 2 shows an example of PsychoLexQA dataset based on psychology document. Figure 3, 4, 5, 6 illustrates example of PsychoLexQA dataset based on self-instruct method. Figure 7 shows an example of the PsychoLexEval dataset that includes a multiple-choice question and answer. Each example is presented in English and Persian to enhance understanding.

Question: How do researchers measure brain activity during sleep and meditation?

Answer: Researchers measure brain activity during sleep and meditation using neuroimaging techniques such as electroencephalograms (EEGs), magnetic resonance imagery (MRI), and positron emission tomography (PET). These techniques record electrical changes in the brain, brain wave patterns, and activation of specific brain areas, allowing researchers to observe and analyze different states of consciousness.

سوال: محققان چگونه فعالیت مغز را در هنگام خواب و مدیتیشن اندازه گیری می کنند؟

پاسخ: محققان با استفاده از تکنیک‌های تصویربرداری عصبی مانند الکتروانسفالوگرام (EEG)، تصویربرداری تشدید مغناطیسی (MRI) و توموگرافی گسیل پوزیترون (PET)فعالیت مغز را در طول خواب و مدیتیشن اندازه‌گیری می‌کنند. این تکنیک‌ها تغییرات الکتریکی در مغز، الگوهای امواج مغزی و فعال‌سازی نواحی خاص مغز را ثبت می‌کنند و به محققان این امکان را می‌دهند تا حالت‌های مختلف هوشیاری را مشاهده و تجزیه و تحلیل کنند.

Figure 2: Example of PsychoLexQA dataset (Document-based).

Literature Review:

Instruct: Conduct a literature review on the effects of brain plasticity on learning and memory. Summarize key findings and theoretical themes.

Output: Literature review shows that brain flexibility significantly affects learning and memory. Most of the findings indicate that engaging in new activities causes neuronal growth, while stress can decrease flexibility. Theoretical themes emphasize the need for educational strategies that foster environments that foster learning and resilience.

دستور: یک مرور ادبیات درباره تأثیر انعطاف پذیری مغز بر یادگیری و حافظه انجام دهید. یافته های کلیدی و مضامین نظری را خلاصه کنید.

خروجی: مرور ادبیات نشان میدهد که انعطافپذیری مغز به طور قابل توجهی بر یادگیری و حافظه تأثیرگذار است. عمده ی یافته ها حاکی از آن است که درگیر شدن در فعالیت های جدید باعث رشد نورونی میشود، در حالی که استرس میتواند موجب کاهش انعطاف پذیری شود. مضامین نظری بر نیاز به استراتژی های آموزشی که محیط هایی را که یادگیری و تاب آوری را تقویت میکنند، مورد تأکید قرار میدهند.

Biological Psychology

Figure 3: Example of PsychoLexQA dataset (Self-instruct).

Experiment Design :

Instruct: Design an experiment to evaluate the effect of a growth mindset intervention on students' persistence in academic tasks. Include methods for measuring sustainability and outcomes.

Output: The experiment will include two groups of students: one group that will participate in a growth mindset intervention that includes workshops on the benefits of facing challenges and learning from failure, and a control group that will receive no specific intervention. Persistence is measured by the time spent on a challenging academic task and the number of tasks completed. The hypothesis is that compared to the control group, students in the growth mindset group show more persistence and performance in academic assignments and highlight the impact of mindset on learning behaviors.

دستور: یک آزمایش طراحی کنید تا تأثیر مداخله ذهنیت رشد را بر پایداری دانش‌آموزان در وظایف تحصیلی ارزیابی کنید. شامل روش‌هایی برای اندازه‌گیری پایداری و نتایج باشد.

خروجی: این آزمایش شامل دو گروه از دانش‌آموزان خواهد بود: یک گروه که در مداخله ذهنیت رشد شرکت می‌کنند که شامل کارگاه‌هایی درباره مزایای روبه‌رو شدن با چالش‌ها و یادگیری از شکست است و گروه کنترل که هیچ مداخله خاصی دریافت نمی‌کند. پایداری از طریق زمان صرف شده بر روی یک وظیفه تحصیلی چالش‌برانگیز و تعداد وظایف کامل شده اندازه‌گیری خواهد شد. فرضیه این است که دانش‌آموزان در گروه ذهنیت رشد در مقایسه با گروه کنترل پایداری و عملکرد بیشتری در وظایف تحصیلی نشان خواهند داد و تأثیر ذهنیت بر رفتارهای یادگیری را برجسته می‌کند.

Cognitive Psychology

Figure 4: Example of PsychoLexQA dataset (Self-instruct).

Scenario Response:

Instruct: In a scenario where a student has difficulty managing time, identify specific strategies to help him improve his skills.

Output: 1. Teach the student to create a prioritized to-do list to Organize tasks by urgency and importance 2. Introduce the concept of timing, where the student sets aside specific times for studying and taking breaks 3. Use digital tools such as calendars or time management apps to set reminders for deadlines. 4. Encourage regular reviews of their schedule so they can adjust and review their time management practices. 5. Promote self-evaluation of their time and productivity to identify and improve their patterns.

دستور: در سناریویی که دانش آموز در مدیریت زمان مشکل دارد، استراتژی های خاصی را برای کمک به او در بهبود مهارت های خود شناسایی کنید.

خروجی: 1. به دانش آموز بیاموزید که فهرست کارهای اولویت بندی شده ایجاد کند تا وظایف را بر اساس فوریت و اهمیت سازماندهی کند. 2. مفهوم زمان بندی را معرفی کنید، جایی که دانش آموز زمان های خاصی را برای مطالعه و استراحت اختصاص می دهد. 3. از ابزارهای دیجیتالی مانند تقویم استفاده کنید. یا برنامه های مدیریت زمان برای تنظیم یادآوری برای مهلت ها. 4. بازبینی منظم برنامه خود را تشویق کنید تا بتوانند شیوه های مدیریت زمان خود را تنظیم و مرور کنند. 5. خود ارزیابی زمان و بهره وری خود را برای شناسایی و بهبود الگوهای آنها ارتقا دهید.

Cognitive Psychology

Figure 5: Example of PsychoLexQA dataset (Self-instruct).

Case Study Analysis:
Instruct: Analyze a 6-year-old boy who resorts to aggression in times of frustration. Explore possible causes and suggest strategies to manage his behavior.

Output: Case analysis of a 6-year-old boy who resorted to aggressive behaviors in times of frustration can reveal several potential factors. This behavior may be due to difficulty in regulating emotions, which may be related to the lack of coping strategies for frustration and anger. He may imitate aggressive behaviors he has observed in his environment, such as at home or in the media, or he may seek attention through these crises. Suggested strategies for managing his behavior could include teaching him emotion regulation techniques such as deep breathing and using 'I feel' sentences to express his feelings. Setting up a consistent behavior management plan, including clear rules and consequences, can help create structure. Finally, involving parents in reinforcing positive behavior at home and providing a loving environment can support the boy in constructively managing his frustrations.

دستور: یک پسر 6 ساله که در مواقع ناامیدی به تهاجم متوسل می‌شود را تحلیل کنید. علل احتمالی را بررسی کرده و استراتژی‌هایی برای مدیریت رفتار او پیشنهاد کنید.

خروجی: تحلیل مورد مربوط به پسر 6 ساله‌ای که در مواقع ناامیدی به رفتارهای تهاجمی متوسل می‌شود، می‌تواند چندین عامل بالقوه را نشان دهد. این رفتار ممکن است ناشی از دشواری در تنظیم احساسات باشد که ممکن است به عدم وجود استراتژی‌های مقابله‌ای برای ناامیدی و خشم مربوط باشد. او ممکن است شیوه‌های تهاجمی را که در محیط خود، مانند خانه یا رسانه‌ها مشاهده کرده است، تقلید کند یا ممکن است از طریق این بحران‌ها توجه جلب کند. استراتژی‌های پیشنهادی برای مدیریت رفتار او می‌تواند شامل آموزش تکنیک‌های تنظیم احساسات مانند تنفس عمیق و استفاده از جملات 'من احساس می‌کنم' باشد تا احساسات خود را ابراز کند. تنظیم یک برنامه مدیریت رفتار منسجم، از جمله قوانین و عواقب واضح، می‌تواند به ایجاد ساختار کمک کند. در نهایت، درگیر کردن والدین برای تقویت رفتار مثبت در خانه و فراهم کردن محیطی دوست داشتنی می‌تواند از پسر در مدیریت سازنده ناامیدی‌هایش حمایت کند.

Developmental Psychology

Figure 6: Example of PsychoLexQA dataset (Self-instruct).

Multiple-Choice QA:
Question: Which strategy is NOT considered a form of problem-focused coping?

Choices:
1) Defining the problem
2) Seeking emotional support
3) Generating alternative solutions
4) Changing personal goals

Correct Answer is 2.

سوال: کدام استراتژی به عنوان شکلی از مقابله متمرکز بر مشکل در نظر گرفته نمی شود؟

گزینه ها:
1) تعریف مسئله
2) جستجوی حمایت عاطفی
3) ایجاد راه حل های جایگزین
4) تغییر اهداف شخصی

پاسخ صحیح 2 است.

Figure 7: Example of PsychoLexEval dataset.

B Prompt template

In the below, we provide an example prompt for each task.

Generate a dataset with 40 detailed and comprehensive instructions for specific tasks in the subcategory defined below. The dataset should be structured with three components: input, and output. Each task should be available in both Persian and English. Inputs and outputs should be detailed and extensive.

Output Format:
```
[
{
"id": 1,
"Language": "English",
"Subcategory": "Subcategory",
"Task": "Task",
"Input": "A clear and concise description of the task and specific details or data needed to perform the task if needed.",
"Output": "The expected result or answer based on the input provided and should have long text."
},
{
"id": 2,
"Language": "Persian",
"Subcategory": "زیرمجموعه",
"Task": "تسک",
"Instruction": "توضیح واضح و مختصر وظیفه.",
"Input": "اختیاری: جزئیات یا داده‌های خاص مورد نیاز برای انجام وظیفه.",
"Output": "نتیجه یا پاسخ مورد انتظار بر اساس ورودی ارائه شده."
},
...
]
```
....

Each language should have 20 rows (totaling 40 rows), covering the following tasks:

Case Study Analysis
Experiment Design
Data Interpretation
Scenario Response
Theoretical Explanation
Diagnostic Evaluation
Ethical Dilemma Resolution
Intervention Planning
Literature Review
Comparative Analysis
....

Ensure that the instructions, inputs, and outputs are diverse and cover a wide range of scenarios within each task type. and ensure to generate all 20 rows and not say it is a sample or something like this.

Subcategory:
```
[
  "Clinical Psychology",
  "Cognitive Psychology",
  "Developmental Psychology",
  "Social Psychology",
  "Biological Psychology",
  "Industrial-Organizational Psychology",
  "Neuropsychology",
  "Health Psychology",
  "Educational Psychology",
]
```

Two-Stage Graph-Augmented Summarization of Scientific Documents

Rezvaneh Rezapour[1], **Yubin Ge**[2], **Kanyao Han**[2], **Ray Jeong**[2], **Jana Diesner**[2,3]
[1] Drexel University
[2] University of Illinois at Urbana-Champaign
[3] Technical University of Munich
shadi.rezapour@drexel.edu jana.diesner@tum.de
{yubinge2, kanyaoh2, yj25}@illinois.edu

Abstract

Automatic text summarization helps to digest the vast and ever-growing amount of scientific publications. While transformer-based solutions like BERT and SciBERT have advanced scientific summarization, lengthy documents pose a challenge due to the token limits of these models. To address this issue, we introduce and evaluate a two-stage model that combines an extract-then-compress framework. Our model incorporates a "graph-augmented extraction module" to select order-based salient sentences and an "abstractive compression module" to generate concise summaries. Additionally, we introduce the *BioConSumm* dataset, which focuses on biodiversity conservation, to support underrepresented domains and explore domain-specific summarization strategies. Out of the tested models, our model achieves the highest ROUGE-2 and ROUGE-L scores on our newly created dataset (*BioConSumm*) and on the *SUMPUBMED* dataset, which serves as a benchmark in the field of biomedicine.

1 Introduction

The scientific community has experienced an unprecedented surge in the number of scientific publications (Erera et al., 2019). This exponential growth has resulted in a state of information overload, presenting both opportunities and challenges for researchers. Navigating the vast amount of information, filtering out relevant studies, and extracting essential insights have become increasingly challenging (Levy, 2008). To address this issue, researchers have turned to automatic summarization methods, which leverage various NLP techniques to condense the essential findings, methodologies, and contributions of research articles into concise and informative summaries.

The use of transformer-based language models (LMs), such as BERT (Devlin et al., 2019), BART (Lewis et al., 2020), SciBERT (Beltagy et al., 2019), and T5 (Raffel et al., 2020) has significantly improved text summarization. Particularly SciBERT's performance in handling science-related documents, and BERTSUM (Zhong et al., 2020), an extension of BERT for extractive summarization, have advanced scientific summarization in terms of domain-specific performance, accuracy, and coherency (Liu, 2019; Sefid and Giles, 2022). Large language models (LLMs) have further reshaped the field of text summarization. For example, OpenAI's GPT-3 and its successors (Achiam et al., 2023) have shown remarkable capabilities in generating coherent and informative summaries (Tang et al., 2023; Jin et al., 2024). These models can perform both extractive and abstractive summarization with high accuracy and fluency. For instance, Zhang et al. (2024) highlight how LLMs can generate summaries that not only capture the main ideas of the source text but also reformulate them in novel ways, often providing additional context or explanations.

Despite recent advancements in text summarization, there are strong reasons to continue refining BERT-based models for scientific summarization: SciBERT, for instance, is trained on scientific texts, which provides with an edge in identifying academic papers' unique language and structure. They are also computationally more efficient and have smaller memory requirements than LLMs, making them faster and more accessible for processing large volumes of scientific papers (Zhu et al., 2023). Additionally, such models offer greater interpretability, allowing for insights into the summarization process, which is crucial in the context of science (White et al., 2024). Their open-source nature further aligns with scientific principles of transparency and reproducibility, reducing privacy concerns associated with proprietary models like GPT. Although BERT-based models offer numerous advantages for scientific summarization, they struggle with processing lengthy documents due

Proceedings of the 1st Workshop on NLP for Science (NLP4Science), pages 36–46
November 16, 2024

to token limits. To address this issue, two-stage summarization models have been proposed, where the first stage focuses on identifying and extracting salient sentences or passages, and the second stage on generating a concise and coherent summary based on the extracted sentences (Galanis and Androutsopoulos, 2010; Zhang et al., 2019a; Ma et al., 2021; Rezapour et al.).

In this paper, we build upon the previous work and propose a model for summarizing scientific documents that incorporates the extract-then-compress framework. Our model integrates a "graph-augmented extraction module" that first selects order-based salient sentences from the complete text of long documents in the initial step (see §4.1), and then employs an "abstractive compression module" to generate concise and relevant summaries using the extracted drafts (see §4.2). We test our model on two datasets: First, *SUMPUBMED*, a benchmark dataset for abstractive summarization of biomedical scientific articles (Gupta et al., 2021). Second, *BioConSumm*, a new dataset that we created, which was curated for the purpose of this work and is from the domain of biodiversity conservation. One limitation of existing scientific text summarization tasks is their strong reliance on datasets from well-established domains like computer science and biomedicine, neglecting other research areas. This lack of attention has resulted in a shortage of comprehensive exploration and rich datasets in these underrepresented domains. To address this disparity, we introduce the *BioConSumm* dataset, which also serves as a valuable resource for training and evaluating text summarization models across domains. With the *BioConSumm* dataset, we can investigate the unique challenges and characteristics of summarizing scientific texts in low-resourced fields, assess the effectiveness of existing summarization techniques, and develop domain-specific or domain-agnostic models.

2 Related Work

2.1 Scientific Paper Summarization

Scientific paper summarization involves the generation of a concise summary that captures the essential information and findings of a publication while preserving its core meaning (Yasunaga et al., 2019; An et al., 2021). Automatic text summarization methods can be broadly categorized into two types: extractive (Mihalcea and Tarau, 2004) and abstractive ones (Nenkova and McKeown, 2012). Extractive models focus on identifying the most important information, such as sentences or key phrases, from the original text, and constructing a summary based on these selections. Abstractive models aim to grasp the key ideas from the text and generate new, coherent summaries. Unsupervised, graph-based ranking methods (Mihalcea and Tarau, 2004; Erkan and Radev, 2004) are widely used for extractive summarization. These methods assign weights to sentences in a document using scoring systems like eigenvector centrality or cosine similarity. The sentences with the highest scores are then extracted to form the summaries. Caragea et al. (2014) proposed a key phrase extraction framework that uses a citation network. By identifying important nodes and relationships within the graph, their approach extracts key phrases from scientific papers and incorporates the citation context into the summary. Cohan and Goharian (2015) considered both content and citation contexts for summarizing scientific papers, and showed improved performance over purely content-based methods. Similarly, Abu-Jbara et al. (2013) proposed a hybrid method that uses both citation relationships and text content to summarize scientific papers more effectively. Multi-document summarization techniques have been developed, which combine extractive and abstractive techniques to generate concise summaries from multiple related scientific papers. Yasunaga et al. (2017) proposed a graph-based neural network model for summarizing scientific documents by leveraging multi-document inputs, showing that the combination of citation networks and multiple documents can create more informative summaries. Ding et al. (2014); Ge et al. (2021) incorporated domain-specific ontologies and semantic graphs to enrich the content-based summarization process and showed improved coverage and accuracy in summarizing scientific papers.

Recent improvements in deep learning and neural architectures have resulted in significant improvements in extractive models (Liu, 2019; Nallapati et al., 2017). For instance, BertSumExt (Liu and Lapata, 2019) leverages a decoder and encoder architecture as well as a classifier to select the most salient sentences from a document and generate more coherent summaries compared to the previous models. Liu (2019) introduced BERTSUM, which set new performance benchmarks across domains, including scientific text, by incorporating inter-sentence dependencies and sentence-level classification. Nallapati et al. (2016) developed a sequence-to-sequence model with attention mechanisms that generate more fluent and human-like summaries by capturing long-range dependencies within the text. Further developments, such as PEGASUS (Zhang et al., 2020) and T5 (Raffel et al., 2020), have expanded on this sequence-to-sequence architecture with large-scale pretraining on text generation tasks, enhancing abstractive summarization capabilities.

2.2 Two-stage Summarization

Hybrid, two-stage document summarization systems combine both extractive and abstractive techniques to improve summary quality (Galanis and Androutsopoulos, 2010; Zhang et al., 2019a; Ma et al., 2021; Rezapour et al.). The first stage typically involves the extraction of salient fragments from the original text as raw summaries. In the second stage, these fragments are arranged into summaries. For example, Chen and Bansal (2018) and Bae et al. (2019) followed a hybrid extract-then-rewrite architecture, with policy-based RL to bring the extraction and rewriting modules together. Lebanoff et al. (2019); Xu and Durrett (2019); Mendes et al. (2019) adopted the extract-then-compress paradigm, namely compressive summarization, which first trains an extractor to select salient sentences that are later input to a decoder to generate the summaries. Gehrmann et al. (2018) first selected key sentences through extractive methods and then rewrote them using abstractive techniques, balancing factual accuracy and fluency. Zhong et al. (2020) proposed a matching-based extractive summarization framework, which can be viewed as an extract-then-match framework. This framework employs a sentence extractor to first generate candidate summaries. It then refines these summaries to align more closely with the source document in the learned semantic space.

3 Data

3.1 Data collection

BioConSumm. Our dataset consists of a collection of academic papers in the domain of biodiversity and bio-conservation. In contrast to high-resourced fields such as biomedicine and computer science, where meticulously curated, high-quality datasets for training models are available, obtaining data for low-resourced domains like biodiversity conservation may require a multi-step approach: We first collected paper records from the Web of Science (WoS). These records include meta-information such as author details, paper titles, and digital object identifiers (DOIs), among other relevant data. Given that WoS has already organized its records according to predefined research domains, including biodiversity conservation, we used the WoS query system to specify the category as biodiversity conservation. As of October 2020, there were over 120,000 records pertaining to journal and conference papers within the field of biodiversity conservation. To narrow down the search, we additionally specified the WoS topic as biodiversity, focusing on papers where the title, abstract, or keywords contained the term "biodiversity." Finally, we downloaded more than 20,000 records as *ciw* files, imported them into Endnote X9[1], and leveraged the Endnote API to find and download full papers in the format of PDF based on the WoS records. Note that the Endnote API is limited to downloading papers from databases that permit automatic downloading and are subscribed to by the researchers' organizations. As a result, we downloaded 12,168 full papers in the format of PDF. Given that the texts in some PDF files use unknown encoding, we extracted texts from 11,579 PDF files as our final dataset. This data collection process can be extended to other domains that have limited resources or lack well-curated computational datasets but for which WoS contains records. While we are not allowed to share the full text of the papers, our data extraction pipeline is reproducible, and using the paper titles and our pipeline, researchers can extract the data.

SUMPUBMED. We used *SUMPUBMED* (Gupta et al., 2021), a dataset for abstractive summarization of biomedical scientific articles built from 33,772 scientific articles in Bio Med Central (BMS), as a point of comparison. *SUMPUBMED* processed these articles by ensuring that the text and abstract in each article have the same named entities. As Figure 1 shows, unlike the abstracts in *BioConSumm*, every sentence in each *SUMPUBMED* abstract must contain biomedical named entities such as gene identifiers (i.e., H2A.Z) that also appear in the processed main body of the same article.

Conducting experiments on these two datasets from different domains enables a more thorough evaluation of the proposed model and allows us to assess how the model's performance is influenced

[1]https://endnote.com/

Conservation

The Chinese government initiated one of the world's largest conservation programs involving agricultural ecosystems with the implementation of the 'Grain for Green' (*Tui Geng Huan Lin*) forest policy between 1999 and 2003. This is the first study to systematically quantify multiple dimensions of biodiversity, phytochemical quality and economic benefits associated with (1) the Grain for Green's tea (*Camellia sinensis*; Theaceae) initiative; (2) the state's previous forest policy involving tea populations in protected areas and; (3) the indigenous tea agro-ecosystems replaced or overlooked by this conservation program. There are several novel and unexpected findings. While forest populations contained the greatest ecological diversity, agro-forests and mixed crop plots were associated with the greatest genetic diversity, phytochemical quality and economic benefits. Indigenous management practices should be incorporated into conservation in China in order to create policies that are more aligned towards biodiversity conservation and sustainable livelihoods while allowing local communities to maintain their cultural identity through agrarian practices.

SUMPUBMED

By comparing H2A.Z binding to global gene expression in budding yeast strains engineered so that normally unstable transcripts are abundant, we show that H2A.Z is required for normal levels of antisense transcripts as well as sense ones. High levels of H2A.Z at antisense promoters are associated with decreased antisense transcript levels when H2A.Z is deleted, indicating that H2A.Z has an activating effect on antisense transcripts. Decreases in antisense transcripts affected by H2A.Z are accompanied by increased levels of paired sense transcripts. The effect of H2A.Z on protein coding gene expression is a reflection of its importance for normal levels of both sense and antisense transcripts. We now find that H2A.Z is also significantly enriched in gene coding regions and at the 3' ends of genes in budding yeast, where it co-localizes with histone marks associated with active promoters. The histone variant H2A.Z, which has been reported to have both activating and repressive effects on gene expression, is known to occupy nucleosomes at the 5' ends of protein-coding genes.

Figure 1: Example summaries in BioConSumm and SUMPUBMED datasets

by some data characteristics via quantitative metrics and human evaluation. For *BioConSumm*, we used the body of raw scientific articles as the input data, while the ground truth is the abstracts of these articles. Similarly, for *SUMPUBMED*, we use the body and the processed version of abstracts, as described above.[2]

4 Methodology

This section presents our proposed framework for long document summarization, which follows the extract-then-compress paradigm. Our model incorporates a *graph-augmented extraction module* that extracts salient sentences from the full text of long documents as drafts, and a subsequent *abstractive compression module* that generates concise and coherent summaries based on the extractive drafts.

4.1 Graph-Augmented Extraction Module

Motivated by prior studies that leveraged sentence graphs based on TF-IDF cosine similarities in summarization tasks (Erkan and Radev, 2004; Yasunaga et al., 2017), we extended this methodology by incorporating SciBERT (Beltagy et al., 2019) and Graph Convolution Network (GCN) (Kipf and Welling, 2017) to build our graph-augmented extraction module.

4.1.1 Graph-Based Encoder

Given a source document represented as a sequence of sentences $S = [s_1, s_2, ..., s_n]$, we construct an undirected sentence graph $\mathcal{G} = (\mathcal{N}, \mathcal{E})$, where $\mathcal{N}$ denotes the set of nodes comprising the sentences in the source document, and $\mathcal{E}$ indicates the significant similarity between connected sentences. We computed sentence similarity by following Erkan and Radev (2004) to first derive the TF-IDF feature for each sentence and then calculate the cosine similarity between any two sentences. We set a predefined threshold of 0.1 for cosine similarity based on the optimal performance observed in (Erkan and Radev, 2004). If the computed cosine similarity between two sentences exceeded this threshold, an edge was added to link the two sentences. We denote the adjacency matrix of the resulting graph $\mathcal{G}$ as $\mathbf{A} \in \mathbb{R}^{n \times n}$, where n is the number of sentences.

We next obtained the initial node feature matrix $\mathbf{X} \in \mathbb{R}^{n \times d}$, where d is the dimension of the feature vector, by leveraging sentence embeddings produced from SciBERT (Devlin et al., 2019). We inserted a special tag `[CLS]` at the beginning of each sentence. The final hidden state that corresponds to `[CLS]` was used as the sentence embedding.

To facilitate the identification of salient content in the source document, we applied GCN on top of the sentence graph. This technique propagates information across nodes based on the graph structure and refines the node representations. Specifically, we performed a symmetric normalization of the adjacency matrix $\mathbf{A}$ as follows:

$$\hat{\mathbf{A}} = \tilde{\mathbf{D}}^{-\frac{1}{2}} \tilde{\mathbf{A}} \tilde{\mathbf{D}}^{-\frac{1}{2}}, \tag{1}$$

where $\tilde{\mathbf{A}}$ is the adjacency matrix $\mathbf{A}$ with self-loops such as $\tilde{\mathbf{A}} = \mathbf{A} + \mathbf{I}_n$ and $\tilde{\mathbf{D}}$ is the degree matrix of $\tilde{\mathbf{A}}$ such as $\tilde{D}_{ii} = \sum_j \tilde{A}_{ij}$. To propagate information across layers, we use the following rule for each layer of GCN:

$$\mathbf{H}^{(l+1)} = \sigma(\hat{\mathbf{A}} \mathbf{H}^{(l)} \mathbf{W}^{(l)}), \tag{2}$$

where $\mathbf{H}^{(l)} \in \mathbb{R}^{n \times d^{(l)}}$ is the hidden states for each node in the l-th layer, $d^{(l)}$ is the dimension of hidden states in the l-th layer, σ is a non-linear activation function such as ReLU(.), and $\mathbf{W}^{(l)} \in \mathbf{R}^{d^{(l)} \times d^{(l+1)}}$ is the weight matrix to be learned in the l-th layer. Particularly, we initialize the hidden states in the first layer as the initial node embedding: $\mathbf{H}^{(0)} = \mathbf{X}$, and the final sentence representations are denoted as $\mathbf{H}^{(L)} \in \mathbb{R}^{n \times d^{(L)}}$.

[2]Both datasets are in English.

4.1.2 Sentence Order-Based Extraction

We treat our *graph-augmented extraction module* as an extractive summarization. The common ground-truth labels were derived from target summaries using a greedy algorithm (Nallapati et al., 2017). However, the resulting labels are typically binary, indicating only whether a sentence should be extracted or not. Consequently, the model is trained to extract sentences as unordered sets, which does not preserve the coherence of the target summaries. We believe that such binary labels can hinder the performance of the subsequent *abstractive compression module* as they fail to consider the order of sentences even if they are correctly extracted as a set.

In order to address this issue, we propose a new labeling method for our extraction module, which produces soft labels that reflect ranked source sentences following the sentence orders in a target summary. We denote the set of ground-truth sentences $G = \{g_1, g_2, ..., g_x\}$ indicating the sentences in a source document that should be extracted, and the target summary as a sequence of sentences $T = [t_1, t_2, ..., t_y]$. We looped through each $t_i \in T$ and found its most similar source sentence in G based on ROUGE-2 such as $g_{i^*} = \operatorname{argmax}_{g_j \in G} \text{ROUGE}(t_i, g_j)$. To reflect the sentence order, we recorded the ROUGE-2 score c_i between the current summary C_i after adding g_{i^*} and the target summary T:

$$C_i = C_{i-1} \cup g_{i^*} \tag{3}$$

$$c_i = \text{ROUGE}(C_i, T) \tag{4}$$

Once we finished the loop, we normalized the ordered sequence of c_i into a predefined range $[l, u]$ in decreasing order such that a source sentence corresponding to a lower-indexed target sentence receives a higher score, and after training, it is expected to be extracted earlier. Lastly, we used label smoothing (Szegedy et al., 2016) to mix the normalized score $\tilde{c}_k$ and the independent ROUGE score calculated between each source sentence and the target summary (Narayan et al., 2018) for all source sentences $s_k \in S$ as the final score:

$$r_k = \epsilon \cdot \tilde{c}_k + (1 - \epsilon) \cdot \text{ROUGE}(s_k, T), \tag{5}$$

where $\epsilon \in [0, 1]$ is an adaptation factor and we set it to a big value, such as 0.9, so that the final scores are mainly based on the normalized scores derived from sentence orders.

During the training, we added an MLP upon the final sentence representation to predict the score: $\hat{y}_k = \text{MLP}(\mathbf{H}^{(L)}_{k,})$, where $\mathbf{H}^{(L)}_{k,}$ means the k-th row of $\mathbf{H}^{(L)}$ representing the final sentence representation for s_k. We adopted cross-entropy loss to calculate the loss and set the minimization of the loss as the training objective:

$$\mathcal{L} = -\sum_{s_k \in S} r_k \cdot \log(\hat{y}_k) \tag{6}$$

4.2 Abstractive Compression Module

While our graph-augmented extraction module effectively compresses long documents into concise summaries, the resulting summaries are extractive in nature, lacking sentence coherence, which diminishes readability and could mislead readers. To address this limitation, we introduce an *abstractive compression module* that converts the extracted salient sentences into complete and coherent summaries. For this purpose, we employed a Transformer-based pre-trained model (Vaswani et al., 2017) and fine-tuned it to generate the target summary given the output from the graph-augmented extraction module as its input.

We explored two widely used models for text generation in our investigation:

- **T5** (Raffel et al., 2020), an encoder-decoder model pre-trained on a diverse set of unsupervised and supervised tasks. Each task is converted into a text-to-text format to facilitate training and inference.
- **BART** (Lewis et al., 2020), a transformer-based denoising autoencoder designed for pre-training sequence-to-sequence tasks.

By leveraging the abstractive model, we aim to transform the extractive summaries into final summaries that are both coherent and informative, enhancing the overall quality and readability of the summarization output.

5 Experiments

In this section, we first introduce implementation details, and then show experimental results from both quantitative and qualitative evaluation.

5.1 Implementation Details

All models were implemented using the PyTorch framework (Paszke et al., 2019) and Huggingface transformers (Wolf et al., 2020). For the graph-augmented extraction module, we initialized SciBERT with *allenai/scibert-scivocab-uncased*, and built a 2-layered GCN. We set the dimensions of the hidden layer and output layer for GCN as 200 and, 100 respectively. The dimension of the hidden layer of MLP was set to 32 and we used ReLU as the activation function in MLP. This module was optimized by Adafactor (Shazeer and Stern, 2018) with the learning rate of $5e-5$. As for the abstractive compression module, we initialized BART with *facebook/bart-base* and T5 with *t5-base*. During training, we optimized the model with AdamW (Loshchilov and Hutter, 2018) and set the learning rate to $5e-5$.

5.2 Quantitative Evaluation

To evaluate the performance of our proposed model, we conducted experiments on *BioConSumm*, the conservation dataset that we have curated, as well as with *SUMPUBMED*. To evaluate the quality of the generated summaries, we utilized the widely-used ROUGE scores (Lin, 2004), which were assessed against the ground truth data comprising abstracts of scientific articles. Specifically, we calculated the ROUGE-1, ROUGE-2, and ROUGE-L metrics, which offer insights into the generated summaries' quality.

For both evaluations, we compared our model, referred to as **Ordered**, against several baselines:

- **T5**: We follow a similar approach to the BART baseline by fine-tuning the T5 model on the dataset. Similarly, we truncated the input documents to comply with the maximum token limit imposed by T5.
- **BART**: We directly fine-tuned the BART model on the dataset. In this process, we truncated the input documents to fit within the maximum token limit imposed by BART.
- **Unordered**: This baseline shares the same structure as our model, but we trained the extraction module based on the ROUGE score between each sentence in an input document and the target summary as in Narayan et al. (2018).

5.2.1 Results on BioConSumm

Table 1 shows that BART consistently outperformed T5 across all evaluation scenarios in terms of ROUGE-1 and ROUGE-L. This observation aligns with the widespread success of BART for summarization (Zhang et al., 2021; Lewis et al., 2020). Also, all two-staged models outperformed abstractive models, namely T5 and BART. This could be due to the fact that crucial information that needs to be included in the summary may not always be found at the beginning of the scientific documents, unlike documents in other domains such as news articles (Grenander et al., 2019; Xing et al., 2021). By contrast, two-staged models can encode entire documents, which enables them to capture salient content regardless of its position in a document.

Model	R1	R2	RL
T5	42.97	12.16	20.13
BART	43.55	12.97	20.25
Unordered + T5	45.76	14.37	21.89
Unordered + BART	45.96	14.40	21.69
Ordered + T5	**46.18**	15.16	22.10
Ordered + BART	46.09	**15.51**	**22.86**

Table 1: Experimental results on BioConSumm.

Model	R1	R2	RL
T5	42.16	12.38	19.78
BART	44.87	13.83	20.30
Unordered + T5	46.56	15.35	21.25
Unordered + BART	**46.72**	15.85	21.57
Ordered + T5	46.43	15.72	21.42
Ordered + BART	46.55	**15.88**	**21.77**

Table 2: Experimental results on SUMPUBMED.

Among the two-staged models, those incorporating sentence order-based extraction (referred to as "Ordered") outperformed the models that do not explicitly consider sentence order (referred to as "Unordered"). This finding validates our initial hypothesis that considering sentence order in the extractive module matters, which is often disregarded in traditional extractive summarization. Our proposed method, which incorporates sentence order into the training of the extractive module, preserves sentence order and explicitly models the inherent coherence and structure within a document during the first stage of summarization. We believe that this feature contributes to the better performance of our proposed models; enabling it to better capture the essence and flow of the original content.

5.2.2 Results on SUMPUBMED

We conducted additional experiments on *SUMPUBMED* (Table 2). Consistent with our findings on *BioConSumm*, all order-based two-staged models outperformed the single abstractive models or unordered models in terms of ROUGE-2 and ROUGE-L. This reaffirms the effectiveness of order-based two-staged models for long document summarization. The improvement on *BioConSumm* data is notably larger (specifically for ROUGE-L) than for *SUMPUBMED*. We conducted a human evaluation to investigate the characteristics of summaries and the reason for this difference.

5.3 Human Evaluation

We sampled 10 articles from each of the two datasets and asked four students fluent in English to read the full papers with their abstracts removed. The abstract (ground truth) and the model-generated summaries of each paper were rated by two students with respect to four aspects: Content coverage, Coherence, Hallucination, and Overall quality (Howcroft et al., 2020). The evaluators were unaware of whether they were assessing the original abstract or a model-generated summary during the evaluation process. The four evaluation aspects are further explained below:

- **Content Coverage**: This includes five items, which aim to evaluate how well a model-generated summary or an abstract covers the main points of the corresponding full paper: 1) research background, 2) research questions or goals, 3) methods, 4) findings, and 5) conclusion or discussion.
- **Coherence**: Three coherence items aim to evaluate 1) how logical a summary or abstract is organized (e.g., background → research questions → methods → findings → contribution), 2) whether bullet points/numbering is correctly formed in a reasonable order if applicable, and 3) how fluent the summary reads.
- **Hallucination**: This aspect aims to evaluate whether a summary or abstract contains any information not mentioned in the paper.
- **Overall Quality**: We asked the evaluators to rate a summary or abstract for its overall quality.

We used a rating scale ranging from 1 to 4 (bad, fair, good, and excellent) for all metrics except numbering and hallucination, which were assessed by a yes-or-no evaluation, with 1 representing "yes" and 0 representing "no."

	BioConSumm		SumPubMed	
	A	M	A	M
Background	3.45	3.2	2.88	2.13
Question	3.05	3.28	2.56	2.67
Method	2.76	2.56	2.75	2.67
Finding	3.25	3.1	2.8	2.8
Conclusion	2.9	2.9	2.33	2.1
Organization	3.4	3.45	2.3	2
Numbering	1	1	1	1
Fluency	3.55	3.35	2.5	2.6
Hallucination	0	0.1	0	0
Overall Quality	3.15	2.8	2.3	2.1

Table 3: Human evaluation of abstracts (A) and model-generated summaries (M) for *BioConSumm* and *SUMPUBMED* data. Since Ordered + BART model is consistently the best model in terms of ROUGE-2 and ROUGE-L as well as the human evaluation scores, we only show results of these models.

Table 3 shows the average human ratings for abstracts and model-generated summaries. The abstracts from *SUMPUBMED* got lower ratings than those from *BioConSumm*, particularly for coherence; a metric that represents the logical order of abstracts in the training data and the generated summaries. This is because *SUMPUBMED* processed all indexed articles by ensuring that the named entities in both the text and abstract in each article were the same. Sentences without shared named entities between the text and abstract were removed, resulting in lower coherence. The higher coherence of the raw texts and abstracts from *BioConSumm* dataset likely provides superior information for training a more effective order-based sentence extraction model, resulting in a more substantial improvement of the final model performance represented by ROUGE scores.

6 Conclusions and Future Work

This paper presents a novel dataset for summarizing scientific articles from the domain of biodiversity conservation, which distinguishes it from existing datasets in this field. Additionally, we proposed a two-staged summarization model that employs the "extract-then-compress" approach to effectively summarize lengthy scientific documents. To evaluate the effectiveness of our model, we compared its performance using both our newly introduced dataset and a benchmark summarization dataset from the biomedical domain. The results demonstrate that our model outperforms well-established summarization methods.

7 Limitations

While our model exhibits promising performance, there are still challenges to address, particularly in modeling cross-domain datasets. Furthermore, it is important to recognize that evaluating the quality of summaries is a complex task that goes beyond the scope of a single metric. While ROUGE scores have been widely used and accepted as a standard evaluation measure in summarization research (Fabbri et al., 2021; Rezapour et al., 2022), they have inherent limitations, e.g., their focus on lexical overlap, which may not fully capture the nuances of semantic salience. Future work should focus on incorporating additional evaluation methods (e.g., Bertscore (Zhang et al., 2019b)) that consider semantic relevance and coherence and provide a more comprehensive assessment of the summaries.

Finally, expanding datasets to low-resourced domains beyond biodiversity conservation can advance summarization techniques across scientific disciplines. In addition, exploring cross-domain summarization tasks, despite limited training data, addresses the challenges of varying terminology and writing styles. Overcoming these challenges enables the wider application of summarization techniques, promoting knowledge dissemination and interdisciplinary research.

8 Ethical Statement

Our dataset consists exclusively of English-language texts, which may introduce limitations in terms of linguistic diversity and inclusivity. We are committed to promoting open and collaborative research practices. While we cannot share the full texts of our new dataset, a list of paper titles and detailed instructions for reproducing our data collection process are available for future research endeavors [3]. Furthermore, in this analysis, we deliberately chose not to employ any LLMs, whether closed- or open-weight, out of respect for the proprietary nature of our data, ensuring that our methods are fully aligned with ethical standards regarding data usage and model selection.

[3] https://github.com/khan1792/BioConSumm

9 Acknowledgement

We gratefully acknowledge the support from the John D. and Catherine T. MacArthur Foundation.

References

Amjad Abu-Jbara, Jefferson Ezra, and Dragomir Radev. 2013. Purpose and polarity of citation: Towards nlp-based bibliometrics. In *Proceedings of the 2013 conference of the North American chapter of the association for computational linguistics: Human language technologies*, pages 596–606.

Josh Achiam, Steven Adler, Sandhini Agarwal, Lama Ahmad, Ilge Akkaya, Florencia Leoni Aleman, Diogo Almeida, Janko Altenschmidt, Sam Altman, Shyamal Anadkat, et al. 2023. Gpt-4 technical report. *arXiv preprint arXiv:2303.08774*.

Chenxin An, Ming Zhong, Yiran Chen, Danqing Wang, Xipeng Qiu, and Xuanjing Huang. 2021. Enhancing scientific papers summarization with citation graph. In *Proceedings of the AAAI conference on artificial intelligence*, volume 35, pages 12498–12506.

Sanghwan Bae, Taeuk Kim, Jihoon Kim, and Sang-goo Lee. 2019. Summary level training of sentence rewriting for abstractive summarization. In *Proceedings of the 2nd Workshop on New Frontiers in Summarization*, pages 10–20.

Iz Beltagy, Kyle Lo, and Arman Cohan. 2019. Scibert: A pretrained language model for scientific text. In *Proceedings of 2019 Conference on Empirical Methods in Natural Language Processing and the 9th International Joint Conference on Natural Language Processing (EMNLP-IJCNLP)*.

Cornelia Caragea, Florin Bulgarov, Andreea Godea, and Sujatha Das Gollapalli. 2014. Citation-enhanced keyphrase extraction from research papers: A supervised approach. In *Proceedings of the 2014 conference on empirical methods in natural language processing (EMNLP)*, pages 1435–1446.

Yen-Chun Chen and Mohit Bansal. 2018. Fast abstractive summarization with reinforce-selected sentence rewriting. In *Proceedings of the 56th Annual Meeting of the Association for Computational Linguistics (Volume 1: Long Papers)*, pages 675–686.

Arman Cohan and Nazli Goharian. 2015. Scientific article summarization using citation-context and article's discourse structure. In *Proceedings of the 2015 Conference on Empirical Methods in Natural Language Processing*, pages 390–400.

Jacob Devlin, Ming-Wei Chang, Kenton Lee, and Kristina Toutanova. 2019. Bert: Pre-training of deep bidirectional transformers for language understanding. In *Proceedings of 2019 Conference of the North American Chapter of the Association for Computational Linguistics: Human Language Technologies (NAACL-HLT)*.

Ying Ding, Guo Zhang, Tamy Chambers, Min Song, Xiaolong Wang, and Chengxiang Zhai. 2014. Content-based citation analysis: The next generation of citation analysis. *Journal of the association for information science and technology*, 65(9):1820–1833.

Shai Erera, Michal Shmueli-Scheuer, Guy Feigenblat, Ora Peled Nakash, Odellia Boni, Haggai Roitman, Doron Cohen, Bar Weiner, Yosi Mass, Or Rivlin, et al. 2019. A summarization system for scientific documents. *arXiv preprint arXiv:1908.11152*.

Günes Erkan and Dragomir R Radev. 2004. Lexrank: Graph-based lexical centrality as salience in text summarization. *Journal of artificial intelligence research*, 22:457–479.

Alexander R Fabbri, Wojciech Kryściński, Bryan McCann, Caiming Xiong, Richard Socher, and Dragomir Radev. 2021. Summeval: Re-evaluating summarization evaluation. *Transactions of the Association for Computational Linguistics*, 9:391–409.

Dimitrios Galanis and Ion Androutsopoulos. 2010. An extractive supervised two-stage method for sentence compression. In *Human Language Technologies: The 2010 Annual Conference of the North American Chapter of the Association for Computational Linguistics*, pages 885–893.

Yubin Ge, Ly Dinh, Xiaofeng Liu, Jinsong Su, Ziyao Lu, Ante Wang, and Jana Diesner. 2021. Baco: A background knowledge-and content-based framework for citing sentence generation. In *Proceedings of the 59th Annual Meeting of the Association for Computational Linguistics and the 11th International Joint Conference on Natural Language Processing (Volume 1: Long Papers)*, pages 1466–1478.

Sebastian Gehrmann, Yuntian Deng, and Alexander M Rush. 2018. Bottom-up abstractive summarization. In *Proceedings of the 2018 Conference on Empirical Methods in Natural Language Processing*, pages 4098–4109.

Matt Grenander, Yue Dong, Jackie Chi Kit Cheung, and Annie Louis. 2019. Countering the effects of lead bias in news summarization via multi-stage training and auxiliary losses. In *Proceedings of the 2019 Conference on Empirical Methods in Natural Language Processing and the 9th International Joint Conference on Natural Language Processing (EMNLP-IJCNLP)*, pages 6019–6024.

Vivek Gupta, Prerna Bharti, Pegah Nokhiz, and Harish Karnick. 2021. Sumpubmed: Summarization dataset of pubmed scientific articles. In *Proceedings of the 59th Annual Meeting of the Association for Computational Linguistics and the 11th International Joint Conference on Natural Language Processing: Student Research Workshop*, pages 292–303.

David M Howcroft, Anya Belz, Miruna Clinciu, Dimitra Gkatzia, Sadid A Hasan, Saad Mahamood, Simon Mille, Emiel Van Miltenburg, Sashank Santhanam, and Verena Rieser. 2020. Twenty years of confusion in human evaluation: Nlg needs evaluation sheets and standardised definitions. In *13th International Conference on Natural Language Generation 2020*, pages 169–182. Association for Computational Linguistics.

Hanlei Jin, Yang Zhang, Dan Meng, Jun Wang, and Jinghua Tan. 2024. A comprehensive survey on process-oriented automatic text summarization with exploration of llm-based methods. *arXiv preprint arXiv:2403.02901*.

Thomas N Kipf and Max Welling. 2017. Semi-supervised classification with graph convolutional networks. In *International Conference on Learning Representations*.

Logan Lebanoff, Kaiqiang Song, Franck Dernoncourt, Doo Soon Kim, Seokhwan Kim, Walter Chang, and Fei Liu. 2019. Scoring sentence singletons and pairs for abstractive summarization. In *Proceedings of the 57th Annual Meeting of the Association for Computational Linguistics*, pages 2175–2189.

David M Levy. 2008. Information overload. *The handbook of information and computer ethics*, pages 497–515.

Mike Lewis, Yinhan Liu, Naman Goyal, Marjan Ghazvininejad, Abdelrahman Mohamed, Omer Levy, Veselin Stoyanov, and Luke Zettlemoyer. 2020. BART: Denoising sequence-to-sequence pre-training for natural language generation, translation, and comprehension. In *Proceedings of the 58th Annual Meeting of the Association for Computational Linguistics*, pages 7871–7880, Online. Association for Computational Linguistics.

Chin-Yew Lin. 2004. ROUGE: A package for automatic evaluation of summaries. In *Text Summarization Branches Out*, pages 74–81, Barcelona, Spain. Association for Computational Linguistics.

Yang Liu. 2019. Fine-tune bert for extractive summarization. *arXiv preprint arXiv:1903.10318*.

Yang Liu and Mirella Lapata. 2019. Text summarization with pretrained encoders. In *Proceedings of the 2019 Conference on Empirical Methods in Natural Language Processing and the 9th International Joint Conference on Natural Language Processing (EMNLP-IJCNLP)*, pages 3730–3740.

Ilya Loshchilov and Frank Hutter. 2018. Decoupled weight decay regularization. In *International Conference on Learning Representations (ICLR)*.

Tinghuai Ma, Qian Pan, Huan Rong, Yurong Qian, Yuan Tian, and Najla Al-Nabhan. 2021. T-bertsum: Topic-aware text summarization based on bert. *IEEE Transactions on Computational Social Systems*, 9(3):879–890.

Alfonso Mendes, Shashi Narayan, Sebastião Miranda, Zita Marinho, André FT Martins, and Shay B Cohen. 2019. Jointly extracting and compressing documents with summary state representations. In *Proceedings of the 2019 Conference of the North American Chapter of the Association for Computational Linguistics: Human Language Technologies, Volume 1 (Long and Short Papers)*, pages 3955–3966.

Rada Mihalcea and Paul Tarau. 2004. Textrank: Bringing order into text. In *Proceedings of the 2004 conference on empirical methods in natural language processing*, pages 404–411.

Ramesh Nallapati, Feifei Zhai, and Bowen Zhou. 2017. Summarunner: A recurrent neural network based sequence model for extractive summarization of documents. In *Proceedings of the AAAI conference on artificial intelligence*, volume 31.

Ramesh Nallapati, Bowen Zhou, Cicero dos Santos, Çağlar Gulçehre, and Bing Xiang. 2016. Abstractive text summarization using sequence-to-sequence rnns and beyond. In *Proceedings of the 20th SIGNLL Conference on Computational Natural Language Learning*, pages 280–290.

Shashi Narayan, Shay B. Cohen, and Mirella Lapata. 2018. Ranking sentences for extractive summarization with reinforcement learning. In *Proceedings of the 2018 Conference of the North American Chapter of the Association for Computational Linguistics: Human Language Technologies, Volume 1 (Long Papers)*, pages 1747–1759, New Orleans, Louisiana. Association for Computational Linguistics.

Ani Nenkova and Kathleen McKeown. 2012. A survey of text summarization techniques. *Mining text data*, pages 43–76.

Adam Paszke, Sam Gross, Francisco Massa, Adam Lerer, James Bradbury, Gregory Chanan, Trevor Killeen, Zeming Lin, Natalia Gimelshein, Luca Antiga, Alban Desmaison, Andreas Kopf, Edward Yang, Zachary DeVito, Martin Raison, Alykhan Tejani, Sasank Chilamkurthy, Benoit Steiner, Lu Fang, Junjie Bai, and Soumith Chintala. 2019. Pytorch: An imperative style, high-performance deep learning library. In *Advances in Neural Information Processing Systems (NeurIPS)*.

Colin Raffel, Noam Shazeer, Adam Roberts, Katherine Lee, Sharan Narang, Michael Matena, Yanqi Zhou, Wei Li, and Peter J Liu. 2020. Exploring the limits of transfer learning with a unified text-to-text transformer. *The Journal of Machine Learning Research*, 21(1):5485–5551.

Rezvaneh Rezapour, Sravana Reddy, Ann Clifton, and Rosie Jones. Spotify at trec 2020: Genre-aware abstractive podcast summarization.

Rezvaneh Rezapour, Sravana Reddy, Rosie Jones, and Ian Soboroff. 2022. What makes a good podcast summary? In *Proceedings of the 45th International ACM SIGIR Conference on Research and Development in Information Retrieval*, pages 2039–2046.

Athar Sefid and C Lee Giles. 2022. Scibertsum: Extractive summarization for scientific documents. In *Document Analysis Systems: 15th IAPR International Workshop, DAS 2022, La Rochelle, France, May 22–25, 2022, Proceedings*, pages 688–701. Springer.

Noam Shazeer and Mitchell Stern. 2018. Adafactor: Adaptive learning rates with sublinear memory cost. In *International Conference on Machine Learning*, pages 4596–4604. PMLR.

Christian Szegedy, Vincent Vanhoucke, Sergey Ioffe, Jon Shlens, and Zbigniew Wojna. 2016. Rethinking the inception architecture for computer vision. In *Proceedings of the IEEE conference on computer vision and pattern recognition*, pages 2818–2826.

Liyan Tang, Zhaoyi Sun, Betina Idnay, Jordan G Nestor, Ali Soroush, Pierre A Elias, Ziyang Xu, Ying Ding, Greg Durrett, Justin F Rousseau, et al. 2023. Evaluating large language models on medical evidence summarization. *npj Digital Medicine*, 6(1):158.

Ashish Vaswani, Noam Shazeer, Niki Parmar, Jakob Uszkoreit, Llion Jones, Aidan N Gomez, Łukasz Kaiser, and Illia Polosukhin. 2017. Attention is all you need. *Advances in neural information processing systems*, 30.

Matt White, Ibrahim Haddad, Cailean Osborne, Ahmed Abdelmonsef, Sachin Varghese, et al. 2024. The model openness framework: Promoting completeness and openness for reproducibility, transparency and usability in ai. *arXiv preprint arXiv:2403.13784*.

Thomas Wolf, Lysandre Debut, Victor Sanh, Julien Chaumond, Clement Delangue, Anthony Moi, Pierric Cistac, Tim Rault, Remi Louf, Morgan Funtowicz, Joe Davison, Sam Shleifer, Patrick von Platen, Clara Ma, Yacine Jernite, Julien Plu, Canwen Xu, Teven Le Scao, Sylvain Gugger, Mariama Drame, Quentin Lhoest, and Alexander Rush. 2020. Transformers: State-of-the-art natural language processing. In *Proceedings of the 2020 Conference on Empirical Methods in Natural Language Processing: System Demonstrations*, pages 38–45, Online. Association for Computational Linguistics.

Linzi Xing, Wen Xiao, and Giuseppe Carenini. 2021. Demoting the lead bias in news summarization via alternating adversarial learning. In *Proceedings of the 59th Annual Meeting of the Association for Computational Linguistics and the 11th International Joint Conference on Natural Language Processing (Volume 2: Short Papers)*, pages 948–954.

Jiacheng Xu and Greg Durrett. 2019. Neural extractive text summarization with syntactic compression. In *Proceedings of the 2019 Conference on Empirical Methods in Natural Language Processing and the 9th International Joint Conference on Natural Language Processing (EMNLP-IJCNLP)*, pages 3292–3303.

Michihiro Yasunaga, Jungo Kasai, Rui Zhang, Alexander R Fabbri, Irene Li, Dan Friedman, and Dragomir R Radev. 2019. Scisummnet: A large annotated corpus and content-impact models for scientific paper summarization with citation networks. In *Proceedings of the AAAI conference on artificial intelligence*, volume 33, pages 7386–7393.

Michihiro Yasunaga, Rui Zhang, Kshitijh Meelu, Ayush Pareek, Krishnan Srinivasan, and Dragomir Radev. 2017. Graph-based neural multi-document summarization. In *Proceedings of the 21st Conference on Computational Natural Language Learning (CoNLL 2017)*, pages 452–462.

Haoyu Zhang, Jingjing Cai, Jianjun Xu, and Ji Wang. 2019a. Pretraining-based natural language generation for text summarization. In *Proceedings of the 23rd Conference on Computational Natural Language Learning (CoNLL)*, pages 789–797.

Jingqing Zhang, Yao Zhao, Mohammad Saleh, and Peter Liu. 2020. Pegasus: Pre-training with extracted gap-sentences for abstractive summarization. In *International conference on machine learning*, pages 11328–11339. PMLR.

Tianyi Zhang, Varsha Kishore, Felix Wu, Kilian Q Weinberger, and Yoav Artzi. 2019b. Bertscore: Evaluating text generation with bert. *arXiv preprint arXiv:1904.09675*.

Tianyi Zhang, Faisal Ladhak, Esin Durmus, Percy Liang, Kathleen McKeown, and Tatsunori Hashimoto. 2024. Benchmarking large language models for news summarization. *Transactions of the Association for Computational Linguistics*, 12.

Yusen Zhang, Ansong Ni, Tao Yu, Rui Zhang, Chenguang Zhu, Budhaditya Deb, Asli Celikyilmaz, Ahmed Hassan Awadallah, and Dragomir Radev. 2021. An exploratory study on long dialogue summarization: What works and what's next. *arXiv preprint arXiv:2109.04609*.

Ming Zhong, Pengfei Liu, Yiran Chen, Danqing Wang, Xipeng Qiu, and Xuanjing Huang. 2020. Extractive summarization as text matching. In *Proceedings of the 58th Annual Meeting of the Association for Computational Linguistics*, pages 6197–6208, Online. Association for Computational Linguistics.

Xunyu Zhu, Jian Li, Yong Liu, Can Ma, and Weiping Wang. 2023. A survey on model compression for large language models. *arXiv preprint arXiv:2308.07633*.

GCD-TM: Graph-Driven Community Detection for Topic Modelling in Psychiatry Texts

Anusuya Krishnan
Department of Mathematics
College of Science
United Arab Emirates University, UAE
anusuyababy@uaeu.ac.ae

Isaias Mehari Ghebrehiwet
Department of Computer Science
College of IT
United Arab Emirates University, UAE
ighebrehiwet@uaeu.ac.ae

Abstract

Psychiatry texts provide critical insights into patient mental states and therapeutic interactions. These texts are essential for understanding psychiatric conditions, treatment dynamics, and patient responses. However, the complex and diverse nature of psychiatric communications poses significant challenges for traditional topic modeling methods. The intricate language, subtle psychological nuances, and varying lengths of text segments make it difficult to extract coherent and meaningful topics. Conventional approaches often struggle to capture the depth and overlap of themes present in these texts. In this study, we present a novel approach to topic modeling that addresses these limitations by reformulating the problem as a community detection task within a graph constructed from the text corpus. Our methodology includes lemmatization for data standardization, TF-IDF vectorization to create a term-document matrix, and cosine similarity computation to produce a similarity matrix. This matrix is then binarized to form a graph, on which community detection is performed using the Louvain method. The detected communities are subsequently analyzed with Latent Dirichlet Allocation (LDA) to extract topics. Our approach outperforms traditional topic modeling methods, offering more accurate and interpretable topic extraction with improved coherence and lower perplexity.

1 Introduction

Psychiatric disorders like depression, bipolar disorder, anxiety, schizophrenia, and substance abuse are major contributors to disability, significantly impacting individuals' quality of life due to their prevalence and duration (James et al., 2018; Figueroa et al., 2020; Cuijpers et al., 2012). Traditionally, psychiatrists diagnose these conditions through detailed consultations, with linguistic research highlighting key speech patterns in various disorders (Cohen et al., 2008; Patra et al., 2020). Mental health interventions, including psychosocial, behavioral, pharmacological, and telemedicine methods, are vital for improving well-being but face systemic obstacles (DeRubeis et al., 2008; Miranda et al., 2008). The absence of objective diagnostic tools, variability in treatment quality, clinician shortages, especially in rural areas, and the high costs of training reduce the effectiveness of psychological therapies, underscoring the need for improved diagnostic and treatment tools (Firth et al., 2017; Wang et al., 2007).

Recently, there has been a surge in research aimed at diagnosing psychiatric disorders through Natural Language Processing (NLP). Studies have targeted a range of disorders, including schizophrenia, depression, bipolar disorder, obsessive-compulsive disorder, autism spectrum disorders, and dementia (Malgaroli et al., 2023; Rumshisky et al., 2016). Topic modeling has emerged as a key NLP technique for extracting meaningful patterns and themes from psychiatric texts (Nikolenko et al., 2017). Topic modeling algorithms are designed to uncover latent topics within large corpora of text by analyzing word co-occurrence patterns (Tong and Zhang, 2016). This approach can reveal underlying themes in patient narratives, therapy session transcripts, and clinical notes, providing valuable insights into the content and dynamics of psychiatric disorders. By applying topic modeling to mental health data, researchers can gain a deeper understanding of prevalent issues, treatment efficacy, and patient experiences, ultimately contributing to the improvement of diagnostic and therapeutic processes (Nikolenko et al., 2017).

Latent Dirichlet Allocation (LDA) is a widely used topic modeling technique based on the premise that documents are mixtures of topics and topics are distributions over words (Blei et al., 2003). Latent Semantic Analysis (LSA) is another topic modeling technique that employs singular value decomposition to reduce dimensionality

Proceedings of the 1st Workshop on NLP for Science (NLP4Science), pages 47–57
November 16, 2024

and uncover underlying semantic structures (Dumais, 2004). Non-Negative Matrix Factorization (NMF) is also one of the topic modeling techniques, which factorizes term-document matrices into non-negative components, focusing on additive topic combinations (Lee and Seung, 2000). BERTopic enhances topic modeling by utilizing contextual embeddings from models like BERT and MPNet, combined with advanced term weighting, which improves topic identification, particularly in specialized domains such as legal documents (Grootendorst, 2022). Spectral clustering further refines topic coherence by analyzing document similarity structures, though it requires careful parameter tuning and can be sensitive to noise (Ng et al., 2001). K-means clustering is used to extract precise topics from unstructured data, such as biomedical texts, with improvements in accuracy and efficiency (Sinaga and Yang, 2020).

Existing topic modeling approaches, such as LDA and similar models, often face challenges in accurately capturing specific concepts of substantive interest within a corpus (Chemudugunta et al., 2008; Chang et al., 2009). While these models can explore the themes present in the data, they frequently produce multiple topics with overlapping content or merge distinct themes into a single topic. This can lead to difficulties in interpreting the topics and measuring key concepts accurately (Lei, 2012). Additionally, these models do not inherently incorporate information about the topics of interest, making it challenging for researchers to determine whether the generated topics align with the intended substantive concepts until after the model has been fitted (Brookes and McEnery, 2019). This limitation highlights the need for human validation to ensure the relevance and accuracy of the topics.

To address these issues, our graph-based method offers a more refined approach by constructing a network of terms, which better captures the relationships and nuances in the data, ultimately leading to clearer interpretations and more accurate measurements of the underlying thematic structures. In this study, we propose a novel approach to improve topic modeling in psychiatric text analysis by leveraging graph-driven community detection topic modelling (GCD-TM). This approach involves three key concepts:

- We build a graph based on cosine similarity computed from TF-IDF vectorized text data, where each document is represented as a node and edges denote the semantic similarity between nodes. This enables the identification of closely related groups of documents that share similar themes (Singh and Shashi, 2019).
- We apply the Louvain method for community detection on the constructed graph (Meo et al., 2011). This technique identifies densely connected subgroups within the graph, which correspond to communities of documents with closely related content. This step allows for more accurate grouping of related documents before topic modeling.
- Once communities are detected, Latent Dirichlet Allocation (LDA) is used to extract topics within each community. By focusing on these pre-grouped communities, the resulting topics are more coherent and accurately represent the underlying themes in the text, addressing the limitations of traditional topic models that often mix different themes or create overlapping topics.

The paper is structured as follows: Section 2 reviews related work, Section 3 describes the methodology, Section 4 discusses the results, section 5 gives the limitation, and Section 6 concludes with findings and future directions.

2 Related Works

This section explains topic modeling methodologies, including word-assisted, clustering-based, and sequence-based approaches.

Word-assisted topic modelling: Topic modeling is a technique used to identify themes and patterns in large text corpora by analyzing the co-occurrence of words and documents. Traditionally, fully automated models such as Latent Dirichlet Allocation (LDA) have been used to extract topics without requiring prior knowledge (Blei et al., 2003; Wood et al., 2017). However, these models often struggle with interpretability and can produce overlapping or ambiguous topics. To address these limitations, the keyATM approach has been proposed, which integrates human input by requiring researchers to specify a few keywords related to the topics of interest before fitting the model (Eshima et al., 2024; Lu et al., 2011). This enhancement has been shown to significantly improve both the interpretability and classification performance of the topics generated, providing more accurate and actionable insights from textual data. A model similar to the base keyATM assumes that each document has a single keyword topic, while other topics may lack keywords. In contrast, keyATM allows each document to belong to multiple keyword topics, providing a more flexible approach (Li et al., 2019).

Clustering based topic modelling: This study explores a hybrid topic modeling approach combining Bidirectional Encoder Representations (BERT) with Latent Dirichlet Allocation (LDA) and unsupervised clustering methods (George and Sumathy, 2023; Lim et al., 2017; Mu et al., 2022). Dimensionality reduction techniques such as PCA, t-SNE, and UMAP are employed to address computational inefficiencies in high-dimensional data. The approach, applied to the CORD19 dataset, integrates LDA's probabilistic topic assignments with BERT's sentence embeddings. Clustering is performed with k-means, and the Elbow Method identifies the optimal number of clusters (Subramani et al., 2018; Alharbi et al., 2021). The results indicate that this hybrid framework enhances topic coherence and effectiveness in topic modeling applications. STELLAR is an interactive tool for topic exploration, using BERT embeddings with UMAP and HDBSCAN to model topics. Human evaluation of the generated topics demonstrated their coherence and relevance (Eklund and Forsman, 2022).

3 Methodology

The proposed method, illustrated in Figure 1, involves several key stages: text preprocessing, text vectorization, graph construction, community detection, and topic modeling.

3.1 Text Preprocessing

Text preprocessing plays a crucial role in the quality of topic modeling results, and the pipeline for this study involved several key steps. First, text cleaning was applied to remove special characters, digits, non-informative tokens such as URLs, and excessive white spaces, while also converting all text to lowercase for consistency. Next, stopword removal was conducted using the NLTK library, eliminating common English stopwords (e.g., 'and', 'the', 'is') as well as domain-specific stopwords to prevent them from influencing topic formation. Finally, lemmatization was performed using the WordNet lemmatizer in NLTK, reducing words to their base or dictionary forms to standardize vocabulary and improve topic coherence by ensuring that variations like "running" and "ran" were treated as the same term, "run." This process helped reduce redundancy and enhance the overall clarity of the topics.

3.2 Text Vectorization

Text data is vectorized using TF-IDF with the term-document matrix X given by (Singh and Shashi, 2019):

$$X_{ij} = \text{TF-IDF}(t_i, d_j) \tag{1}$$

where $\text{TF-IDF}(t_i, d_j)$ represents the TF-IDF score of term t_i in document d_j.

3.3 Graph Creation

Cosine similarity is computed for the TF-IDF matrix X to obtain a similarity matrix S: The cosine similarity between documents i and j is computed using:

$$S_{ij} = \frac{\sum_k X_{ki} \cdot X_{kj}}{\sqrt{\sum_k X_{ki}^2} \cdot \sqrt{\sum_k X_{kj}^2}} \tag{2}$$

where S_{ij} represents the cosine similarity between the term vectors of documents i and j. Here, X_{ki} denotes the TF-IDF score of term k in document i, and X_{kj} denotes the TF-IDF score of term k in document j. The numerator $\sum_k X_{ki} \cdot X_{kj}$ calculates the dot product of the term vectors for the two documents, which measures their similarity in terms of term distributions. The denominator $\sqrt{\sum_k X_{ki}^2} \cdot \sqrt{\sum_k X_{kj}^2}$ normalizes this dot product by the magnitudes of the term vectors for both documents, ensuring the similarity score lies between 0 and 1, where 1 indicates identical term distributions.

A binary distance matrix B is then created using a threshold τ:

$$\tau = k \times (\mu + 3\sigma) \tag{3}$$

where μ is the mean and σ is the standard deviation of the similarity values in the matrix S. The parameter k is optimized through hyperparameter tuning to determine the appropriate threshold for binarization. This binarization step, which converts the similarity matrix into a binary form based on the threshold, plays a crucial role in influencing the quality of the resulting topics.

To evaluate the sensitivity of topics to binarization, different threshold levels τ were tested by adjusting the value of k. If the threshold τ is set too

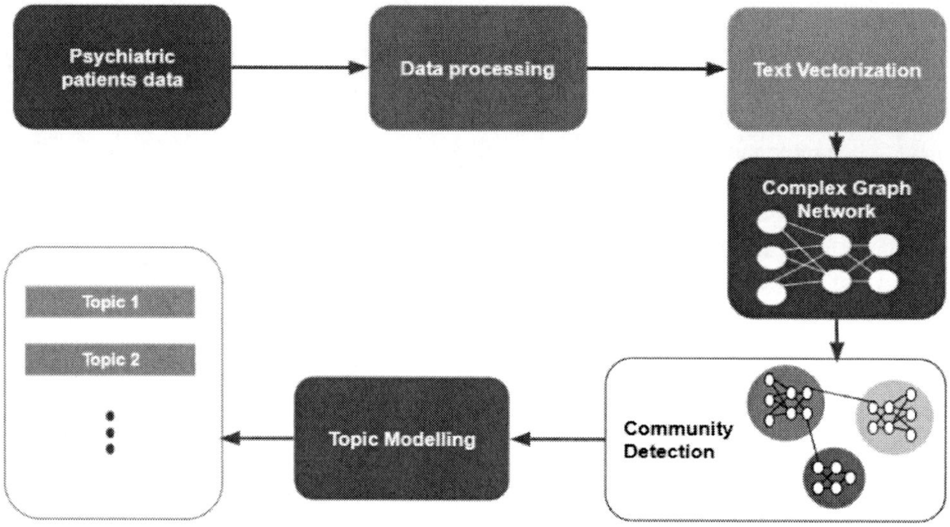

Figure 1: Proposed Architecture of Graph-Driven Community Detection for Topic Modelling.

low, many connections between documents are lost, leading to a sparse graph with fewer edges. This can result in over-fragmentation, where documents that should be grouped together are isolated, thus producing incoherent topics. Conversely, setting a higher threshold results in a densely connected graph, which diminishes the distinction between communities and blurs topic separation. Therefore, tuning k is critical to achieving the right balance between graph connectivity and effective community separation.

The binary distance matrix B is defined by:

$$B_{ij} = \begin{cases} 1, & \text{if } S_{ij} < \tau \\ 0, & \text{if } S_{ij} \geq \tau \end{cases} \tag{4}$$

In this matrix, B_{ij} represents the presence or absence of an edge between documents i and j. If the cosine similarity S_{ij} is less than the threshold τ, B_{ij} is set to 1, indicating a connection. If S_{ij} is greater than or equal to τ, B_{ij} is set to 0, indicating no connection. This binary matrix is used to construct a graph for subsequent community detection.

A graph G is constructed from the binary distance matrix B.

3.4 Community Detection

Community detection is performed using the Louvain method on G. The Louvain method is an algorithm designed to optimize the modularity of a partition of the graph into communities. Modularity is a metric that measures the density of edges within communities compared to edges between different communities.

Modularity Q for a given partition of the graph into communities is defined as:

$$Q = \frac{1}{2m} \sum_{i,j} \left[B_{ij} - \frac{k_i k_j}{2m} \right] \delta(c_i, c_j) \tag{5}$$

where B_{ij} is the adjacency matrix of G, where $B_{ij} = 1$ if there is an edge between nodes i and j, and $B_{ij} = 0$ otherwise. k_i and k_j represent the degrees of nodes i and j, respectively, and m is the total number of edges in the graph. The term $\delta(c_i, c_j)$ is the Kronecker delta, which equals 1 if nodes i and j are in the same community and 0 otherwise.

The Louvain algorithm maximizes modularity in two phases. In the Local Moving Phase, each node starts in its own community and is iteratively moved to increase modularity (Meo et al., 2011). Once no further improvement is possible, the Aggregation Phase begins, where communities are combined into single nodes, and the process repeats. These steps are iterated until no more modularity gains can be achieved. The result is a partition of the graph into non-overlapping communities with denser internal connections compared to external ones.

3.5 Topic Modelling

The Latent Dirichlet Allocation (LDA) model is employed to extract latent topics from the communities detected in the previous steps. For this, a corpus and a dictionary are first prepared using the words from each community. The corpus consists of a bag-of-words (BoW) representation of the text, where each document (community) is represented by a list of tuples. Each tuple contains a word and its corresponding frequency in that community. The dictionary maps each unique word to an integer ID. The LDA model is then trained on this corpus, with the dictionary providing the mapping between words and their IDs. The model is configured to extract a predefined number of topics, denoted as K. The training involves iterating over the corpus multiple times, controlled by the parameter 'passes', to refine the topic distribution for each document. In this study, the model is trained with $K = 5$ topics and 15 passes to ensure convergence and optimal topic extraction. The result is a set of topics, each represented by a distribution over the words in the dictionary, which characterizes the underlying themes within the communities.

4 Experimental Discussion

4.1 Experimental setup

Dataset: The datasets utilized in this study, sourced from Kaggle, include the Suicidal Mental Health Dataset, Reddit Mental Health Data, and Predicting Anxiety in Mental Health Data. Each dataset comprises three key features: patient IDs, textual statements, and corresponding mental health status labels.

The Suicidal Mental Health Dataset(SMH) encompasses a wide range of textual data related to suicide, capturing personal experiences, mental health struggles, and appeals for help. Reddit Mental Health Data (RMH) comprises posts and comments from mental health-focused subreddits, offering candid insights into everyday experiences with conditions like depression and anxiety. The Predicting Anxiety in Mental Health Data (AMH) focuses on anxiety-related content, including forum posts and social media comments, detailing symptoms, triggers, and coping mechanisms. Together, these datasets provide a rich foundation for analyzing mental health themes and language patterns in written communication. Table 1 summarizes the stastistics of the three datasets.

Dataset	Total Number of samples
SMH	5000
RMH	10000
AMH	3500

Table 1: A summary of the datasets used in this work. Dataset statistics including total number, majority samples, and minority samples.

Evaluation Measures: To evaluate the effectiveness of topic modeling, we use two key measures in this study: coherence score and perplexity. The coherence score assesses how coherent the topics are by evaluating the degree to which the top words of a topic frequently appear together in the text. A higher coherence score indicates that the topics are more semantically consistent and meaningful. On the other hand, perplexity measures the model's ability to predict a set of words within the text. It provides an indication of how well the model captures the underlying structure of the data, with lower perplexity values suggesting better predictive performance and a more accurate representation of the text (Newman et al., 2011).

Baseline Models and Implementation Details: We performed a comprehensive comparison between our proposed method and four baseline approaches: Latent Dirichlet Allocation (LDA), Spectral Clustering (SC), BERTopic, and K-means Clustering (KMC). This evaluation encompasses a range of traditional topic modeling techniques to ensure thorough benchmarking. Each topic modeling method was tested with multiple configurations, and hyperparameter tuning was employed to optimize their performance.

Our proposed method was developed using Python version 3.11. All experiments were conducted on a desktop computer equipped with a Ryzen 9 5950X processor, 128GB of RAM, and an NVIDIA GeForce RTX 3090 graphics card with 24GB of memory.

4.2 Comparative Analysis on SMH Dataset

The table 2 presents a performance comparison of different topic modeling techniques on the Suicide Mental Health (SMH) dataset. The results highlight the effectiveness of each method based on two metrics: Coherence and Perplexity.

GCD-TM outperforms all other methods with a coherence score of 0.67, indicating that it generates the most semantically meaningful and internally consistent topics. This suggests that GCD-TM is particularly effective at identifying coherent patterns within the text data. Additionally, GCD-TM has the lowest perplexity score (-8.48), demonstrating its strong ability to generalize to new data. This

Figure 2: Wordcloud for SMH Dataset.

low perplexity value means that the topics generated by GCD-TM are not only coherent but also accurate in representing the underlying structure of the dataset.

In comparison, BERTopic shows a decent performance with a coherence score of 0.45, which is better than LDA, SC, and KMC, but still falls short of GCD-TM. Its perplexity score of -7.32, while better than some methods, is also not as low as GCD-TM, indicating room for improvement in predictive accuracy. SC and KMC perform moderately, with coherence scores of 0.41 and 0.39, respectively, and perplexity scores of -7.35 and -8.01. These results suggest that while these methods can produce somewhat coherent topics, they do not perform as well in terms of generalization. Finally, LDA has the lowest coherence score (0.38) and a relatively high perplexity score (-6.15), indicating that it struggles the most with producing coherent topics and accurately modeling the dataset compared to the other techniques.

Methods	Coherence	Perplexity
LDA	0.38	-6.15
SC	0.41	-7.35
KMC	0.39	-8.01
BERTopic	0.45	-7.32
GCD-TM	0.67	-8.48

Table 2: Performance Comparison of different topic modelling techniques on Suicide Mental Health dataset (SMH).

Figure 2 shows the word cloud for the SMH dataset, highlighting prominent terms such as "life", "tired", "hate", "suicide," "kill," and "dead." Table 3 lists the top five words for each topic generated by five different topic modeling methods (LDA, SC, KMC, BERTopic, and GCD-TM). This table demonstrates how GCD-TM uniquely segments the dataset into distinct topics using the most relevant keywords, showcasing its capability to organize the text data into meaningful clusters, distinguishing itself from the other methods.

Topics	Top five words by LDA
1	Time, worry, stress, sadness, solitude
2	Event, joyful, bad, pressure, decision
3	Workplace, chat, help, colleague, hear
4	Prepare, harm, daybreak, close, shadow
5	Love, people, nurture, optimism, remain
Topics	**Top five words by SC**
1	Right, worry, nothing, sadness, isolation
2	Life, individuals, conflict, better, dead
3	Support, idea, advice, partner, attention
4	Passing, back, hope, someone, void
5	Every, bonds, empathy, always, endure
Topics	**Top five words by KMC**
1	Years, fear, anxiety, depression, alone
2	Thing, happy, worst, tension, choice
3	Office, talk, support, friend, listen
4	Ready, kill, morning, end, dark
5	Love, family, care, hope, stay
Topics	**Top five words by BERTopic**
1	Exhaustion, dread, nervous, sad, solitude
2	Living, society, struggle, urge, kill
3	Comfort, chat, courage, buddy, care
4	End, suffer, gloom, silence, empty
5	Warm, connection, kind, belief, family
Topics	**Top five words by GCD-TM**
1	Suicide, fear, anxiety, depression, alone
2	Life, people, kill, tension, hate
3	Help, talk, support, friend, listen
4	Death, pain, hopeless, end, dark
5	Love, family, care, hope, stay

Table 3: Sample topics generated by different topic modelling techniques (top 5 topics) from the Suicide Mental Health dataset (SMH).

4.3 Comparative Analysis on RMH Dataset

Table 4 compares different topic modeling techniques on the Reddit Mental Health Data (RMH) dataset using coherence and perplexity. GCD-TM is the top performer with a coherence score of 0.73

Figure 3: Wordcloud for RMH Dataset.

and a perplexity score of -6.52, indicating it produces the most coherent topics and excels in predicting new data. Spectral Clustering (SC) follows with a coherence score of 0.54 and a perplexity score of -6.08, demonstrating good topic coherence and prediction but not as effectively as GCD-TM.

K-Means Clustering (KMC) scores 0.49 in coherence and has the highest perplexity score of -4.28, showing that while it offers better coherence than some methods, it struggles with generalizing to new data. Latent Dirichlet Allocation (LDA) achieves a coherence score of 0.43 and a perplexity score of -5.51, suggesting moderate coherence and weaker predictive performance. BERTopic, with the lowest coherence score of 0.36 and a perplexity score of -5.37, exhibits the least interpretable topics and only moderate prediction capability.

Methods	Coherence	Perplexity
LDA	0.43	-5.51
SC	0.54	-6.08
KMC	0.49	-4.28
BERTopic	0.36	-5.37
GCD-TM	0.73	-6.52

Table 4: Performance Comparison of different topic modelling techniques on Reddit Mental Health Data (RMH).

Table 5 presents the topics generated by five topic modeling methods applied to the Reddit Mental Health (RMH) dataset, with each topic represented by its top five associated words. This table highlights the key themes identified, with the GCD-TM model outperforming the other methods. Figure 3 displays the word cloud for the RMH dataset.

Topics	Top five words by LDA
1	Hopes, first, better, best, calm
2	Year, stress, rooms, dawns, change
3	Love, thing, bliss, rough, worse
4	Goals, share, ties, smile, hurt
5	Family, odds, paths, trusts, days
Topics	**Top five words by SC**
1	Lives, weary, buddy, tough, right
2	Worry, pains, house, early, major
3	Weeks, close, relax, worst, anger
4	Hopes, trusts, cares, loves, happy
5	Hard, worse, plans, helps, times
Topics	**Top five words by KMC**
1	Life, better, tired, friend, hard
2	Patient, issue, home, long, first
3	Week, family, rest, best, hate
4	Wish, help, support, love, happy
5	Hard, worse, right, care, month
Topics	**Top five words by BERTopic**
1	Goals, heavy, buddy, tough, quiet
2	Tasks, worries, homes, early, shift
3	Break, folks, peace, rough, anger
4	Dreams, gives, bonds, laugh, cheer
5	Trials, risks, steps, trusts, weeks
Topics	**Top five words by GCD-TM**
1	Depression, sadness, tired, empty, life
2	People, struggle, daily, difficult, survive
3	Sleep, insomnia, restless, night, wake
4	Therapy, help, support, treatment, better
5	Pain, cry, tears, hurt, sorrow

Table 5: Sample topics generated by different topic modelling techniques (top 5 topics) from the Reddit Mental Health Data (RMH).

4.4 Comparative Analysis on AMH Dataset

Table 6 compares the performance of various topic modeling techniques on the Anxiety Mental Health Data (AMH) dataset, evaluating each method based on coherence and perplexity. GCD-TM demonstrates the highest coherence score of 0.69 and the lowest perplexity score of -7.92, indicating that it produces the most coherent topics and performs the best in terms of predictive accuracy among the methods evaluated.

In comparison, BERTopic has a coherence score of 0.46 and a perplexity score of -6.77, showing relatively strong performance but not as effective

Figure 4: Wordcloud for RMH Dataset.

as GCD-TM. K-Means Clustering (KMC) follows with a coherence score of 0.45 and a perplexity score of -6.54, indicating reasonable topic coherence but higher perplexity. Spectral Clustering (SC) and Latent Dirichlet Allocation (LDA) have coherence scores of 0.44 and 0.41, respectively, with perplexity scores of -6.08 and -6.18. Both methods show lower coherence and higher perplexity compared to GCD-TM and BERTopic, reflecting their less effective performance in generating and predicting topics.

Methods	Coherence	Perplexity
LDA	0.41	-6.18
SC	0.44	-6.08
KMC	0.45	-6.54
BERTopic	0.46	-6.77
GCD-TM	0.69	-7.92

Table 6: Performance Comparison of different topic modelling techniques on Anxiety Mental Health Data (AMH).

Table 7 presents the top five words associated with each topic generated by different topic modelling methods from the Anxiety Mental Health Data (AMH).Figure 4 illustrates the wordcloud of AMH dataset.

4.5 Performance Analysis and Insights

The superior performance of the Graph-Driven Community Detection for Topic Modeling (GCD-TM) method over traditional techniques like LDA, Spectral Clustering (SC), K-Means Clustering

Topics	**Top five words by LDA**
1	Hate, anxious, reason, little, long
2	Times, haste, able, point, fear
3	Today, crowd, worry, stress, every
4	Sleep, noise, dreams, hours, rush
5	Quiet, calm, clear, focus, panic
Topics	**Top five words by SC**
1	Stress, worse, shock, creep, today
2	Month, speed, thank, every, always
3	Long, alone, past, shame, nerves
4	Cause, awake, noise, hours, rush
5	Quiet, ease, focus, peace, clear
Topics	**Top five words by KMC**
1	Worry, tensed, month, first, strain
2	Heart, fear, able, time, days
3	Friends, good, alone, avoid, good
4	Sleep, awake, night, dream, chest
5	Calm, heart, relax, focus, hour
Topics	**Top five words by BERTopic**
1	Worry, thing, head, doubt, strain
2	Pain, back, ache, gasp, dread
3	Groups, throng, always, year, crowd
4	Snooze, uneasy, dusk, alert, life
5	Peace, every, ease, days, steer
Topics	**Top five words by GCD-TM**
1	Anxiety, nervous, panic, worry, stress
2	Heart, race, chest, breath, fear
3	Social, crowd, alone, avoid, public
4	Sleep, restless, night, awake, thoughts
5	Calm, breathing, relax, focus, control

Table 7: Sample topics generated by different topic modelling techniques (top 5 topics) from the Anxiety Mental Health Data (AMH).

(KMC), and BERTopic is primarily due to its innovative integration of graph-based community detection with topic modeling. This approach enables GCD-TM to uncover more coherent and contextually meaningful topics, resulting in higher coherence scores and lower perplexity values.

One of the key reasons GCD-TM achieves better results is its ability to capture the intricate relationships between words by constructing a graph where nodes represent terms, and edges represent the similarities between them. Unlike traditional methods that rely solely on statistical distributions, GCD-TM's use of graph theory allows it to identify clusters (or communities) of related words that are more likely to appear together in meaningful contexts. This graph-based approach is particularly effective in detecting nuanced and contextually relevant word associations, which often go unnoticed in methods like LDA, SC, or KMC, where the focus is more on word frequency and document-term distributions. The Louvain method, used for community detection within GCD-TM, further enhances the model's performance by optimizing modularity, which measures the strength of the division of a network into communities. By maximizing modularity, the Louvain method ensures that the communities (or clusters of words) identified are densely connected internally but sparsely connected with other communities. This results in well-defined groups of related words that contribute to more coherent topic extraction during the subsequent LDA phase.

Furthermore, GCD-TM's approach to binarizing the similarity matrix, based on a carefully tuned threshold, allows it to effectively filter out noise and focus on the most significant word associations. This selective process leads to the construction of a more accurate and representative graph, which is crucial for the success of community detection and, ultimately, topic modeling. By integrating these techniques, GCD-TM is able to provide a more detailed and accurate representation of the underlying thematic structure in the data. This holistic approach not only captures the global context within the text but also reveals the subtle, localized patterns that are often missed by other models. As a result, GCD-TM produces topics that are not only more coherent but also more reflective of the actual content and structure of the dataset, leading to its superior performance compared to traditional topic modeling methods.

5 Limitations

Despite its strong performance, GCD-TM has certain limitations. First, the method's reliance on graph construction and community detection makes it computationally intensive, especially with large datasets, which can lead to increased processing times. Second, the model's effectiveness is sensitive to the choice of threshold for graph binarization and the number of topics specified, requiring careful hyperparameter tuning to achieve optimal results. Additionally, while GCD-TM excels at capturing well-defined themes, it may struggle with topics that are highly interrelated or overlap significantly, potentially leading to less distinct topic separation. Finally, the complexity of the method might make it less accessible for users who are not familiar with graph-based approaches or community detection techniques, limiting its broader applicability in different research contexts.

6 Conclusion

In this study, we introduced the Graph-Driven Community Detection for Topic Modeling (GCD-TM) methodology and demonstrated its effectiveness in uncovering thematic structures within mental health datasets. By leveraging a combination of text preprocessing, TF-IDF vectorization, graph-based community detection, and topic modeling with LDA, GCD-TM offers a robust approach to identifying and analyzing latent topics. Our method outperforms traditional techniques in terms of coherence and perplexity, highlighting its capacity to deliver a more nuanced and accurate representation of underlying themes.

The comparative evaluation reveals that GCD-TM not only achieves superior results but also provides a more detailed understanding of thematic structures compared to methods like LDA, SC, KMC, and BERTopic. The combination of community detection and topic modeling enhances the model's ability to capture complex relationships within the data, leading to more meaningful and interpretable topics. To further enhance the GCD-TM methodology, it would be beneficial to explore the integration of additional data features and modalities, experiment with alternative algorithms, and assess the model's performance across more diverse datasets to improve robustness and adaptability. Additionally, investigating methods to address computational efficiency and scalability will be crucial for handling larger and more complex datasets. Finally, applying GCD-TM to other domains and comparing its performance with emerging techniques could provide valuable insights and drive innovation in topic modeling.

References

Adel R. Alharbi, Mohammad Hijji, and Amer Aljaedi. 2021. Enhancing topic clustering for arabic security news based on k-means and topic modelling. *IET Networks*, 10(6):278–294.

David M. Blei, Andrew Y. Ng, and Michael I. Jordan. 2003. Latent dirichlet allocation. *Journal of Machine Learning Research*, 3(Jan):993–1022.

Gavin Brookes and Tony McEnery. 2019. The utility

of topic modelling for discourse studies: A critical evaluation. *Discourse Studies*, 21(1):3–21.

Jonathan Chang, Sean Gerrish, Chong Wang, Jordan Boyd-Graber, and David Blei. 2009. Reading tea leaves: How humans interpret topic models. *Advances in Neural Information Processing Systems*, 22:288–296.

Chaitanya Chemudugunta, America Holloway, Padhraic Smyth, and Mark Steyvers. 2008. Modeling documents by combining semantic concepts with unsupervised statistical learning. In *Proceedings of the 7th International Conference on The Semantic Web (ISWC '08)*, pages 229–244, Berlin, Heidelberg. Springer-Verlag.

Trevor Cohen, Brett Blatter, and Vimla Patel. 2008. Simulating expert clinical comprehension: Adapting latent semantic analysis to accurately extract clinical concepts from psychiatric narrative. *Journal of Biomedical Informatics*, 41(6):1070–1087.

Pim Cuijpers, Ellen Driessen, Steven D Hollon, Patricia van Oppen, Jürgen Barth, and Gerhard Andersson. 2012. The efficacy of non-directive supportive therapy for adult depression: a meta-analysis. *Clinical Psychology Review*, 32:280–291.

Robert J DeRubeis, Greg J Siegle, and Steven D Hollon. 2008. Cognitive therapy versus medication for depression: treatment outcomes and neural mechanisms. *Nature Reviews Neuroscience*, 9:788–796.

Susan T. Dumais. 2004. Latent semantic analysis. *Annual Review of Information Science and Technology (ARIST)*, 38:189–230.

Anton Eklund and Mona Forsman. 2022. Topic modeling by clustering language model embeddings: Human validation on an industry dataset.

Shusei Eshima, Kosuke Imai, and Tomoya Sasaki. 2024. Keyword-assisted topic models. *American Journal of Political Science*, 68(2):730–750.

Jose F Figueroa, Jessica Phelan, E John Orav, Vikram Patel, and Ashish K Jha. 2020. Association of mental health disorders with health care spending in the medicare population. *JAMA Netw Open*, 3:e201210.

Joseph Firth, John Torous, Jennifer Nicholas, Rebekah Carney, Abhishek Pratap, Simon Rosenbaum, and Jerome Sarris. 2017. The efficacy of smartphone-based mental health interventions for depressive symptoms: a meta-analysis of randomized controlled trials. *World Psychiatry*, 16:287–298.

Lijimol George and P. Sumathy. 2023. An integrated clustering and bert framework for improved topic modeling. *International Journal of Information Technology*, 15(4):2187–2195.

Maarten Grootendorst. 2022. Bertopic: Neural topic modeling with a class-based tf-idf procedure. *arXiv preprint arXiv:2203.05794*.

Spencer L James, Degu Abate, Kalkidan Hassen Abate, Solomon M Abay, Cristiana Abbafati, Nooshin Abbasi, Hedayat Abbastabar, Foad Abd-Allah, Jemal Abdela, Ahmed Abdelalim, et al. 2018. Global, regional, and national incidence, prevalence, and years lived with disability for 354 diseases and injuries for 195 countries and territories, 1990–2017: a systematic analysis for the global burden of disease study 2017. *Lancet*, 392:1789–1858.

Daniel Lee and H. Sebastian Seung. 2000. Algorithms for non-negative matrix factorization. *Advances in Neural Information Processing Systems*, 13.

David M. Lei. 2012. Probabilistic topic models. *Communications of the ACM*, 55(4):77–84.

Chenliang Li, Shiqian Chen, Jian Xing, Aixin Sun, and Zongyang Ma. 2019. Seed-guided topic model for document filtering and classification. *ACM Transactions on Information Systems*, 37(1):1–37.

Kwan Hui Lim, Shanika Karunasekera, and Aaron Harwood. 2017. Clustop: A clustering-based topic modelling algorithm for twitter using word networks. In *2017 IEEE International Conference on Big Data (Big Data)*, pages 2009–2018. IEEE.

Bin Lu, Myle Ott, Claire Cardie, and Benjamin Tsou. 2011. Multi-aspect sentiment analysis with topic models. In *Proceedings of the 2011 IEEE 11th International Conference on Data Mining Workshops*, pages 81–88, Vancouver, BC, Canada. IEEE.

Matteo Malgaroli, Thomas D Hull, James M Zech, and Tim Althoff. 2023. Natural language processing for mental health interventions: A systematic review and research framework. *Translational Psychiatry*, 13(1):309.

Pasquale De Meo, Emilio Ferrara, Giacomo Fiumara, and Alessandro Provetti. 2011. Generalized louvain method for community detection in large networks. In *Proceedings of the 11th International Conference on Intelligent Systems Design and Applications*, pages 88–93. IEEE.

Jeanne Miranda, Thomas G McGuire, David R Williams, and Philip Wang. 2008. Mental health in the context of health disparities. *American Journal of Psychiatry*, 165:1102–1108.

Wenchuan Mu, Kwan Hui Lim, Junhua Liu, Shanika Karunasekera, Lucia Falzon, and Aaron Harwood. 2022. A clustering-based topic model using word networks and word embeddings. *Journal of Big Data*, 9(1):38.

David Newman, Edwin V. Bonilla, and Wray Buntine. 2011. Improving topic coherence with regularized topic models. *Advances in Neural Information Processing Systems*, 24.

Andrew Ng, Michael Jordan, and Yair Weiss. 2001. On spectral clustering: Analysis and an algorithm. *Advances in Neural Information Processing Systems*, 14.

Sergey I Nikolenko, Sergei Koltcov, and Olessia Koltsova. 2017. Topic modelling for qualitative studies. *Journal of Information Science*, 43(1):88–102.

Braja Gopal Patra, Reshma Kar, Kirk Roberts, and Hulin Wu. 2020. Mental health severity detection from psychological forum data using domain-specific unlabelled data. *AMIA Summits on Translational Science Proceedings*, 2020:487.

Anna Rumshisky, Marzyeh Ghassemi, Tristan Naumann, Peter Szolovits, VM Castro, TH McCoy, and RH Perlis. 2016. Predicting early psychiatric readmission with natural language processing of narrative discharge summaries. *Translational psychiatry*, 6(10):e921–e921.

Kristina P. Sinaga and Miin-Shen Yang. 2020. Unsupervised k-means clustering algorithm. *IEEE Access*, 8:80716–80727.

Anita Kumari Singh and Mogalla Shashi. 2019. Vectorization of text documents for identifying unifiable news articles. *International Journal of Advanced Computer Science and Applications*, 10(7).

Sandhya Subramani, Vaishnavi Sridhar, and Kaushal Shetty. 2018. A novel approach of neural topic modelling for document clustering. In *2018 IEEE Symposium Series on Computational Intelligence (SSCI)*, pages 2169–2173. IEEE.

Zhou Tong and Haiyi Zhang. 2016. A text mining research based on lda topic modelling. In *Proceedings of the International Conference on Computer Science, Engineering and Information Technology*, pages 201–210.

Philip S Wang, Sergio Aguilar-Gaxiola, Jordi Alonso, Matthias C Angermeyer, Guilherme Borges, Evelyn J Bromet, Ronny Bruffaerts, Giovanni De Girolamo, Ron De Graaf, Oye Gureje, et al. 2007. Use of mental health services for anxiety, mood, and substance disorders in 17 countries in the who world mental health surveys. *Lancet*, 370:841–850.

J. Wood, P. Tan, W. Wang, and C. Arnold. 2017. Source-lda: Enhancing probabilistic topic models using prior knowledge sources. In *Proceedings of the 2017 IEEE 33rd International Conference on Data Engineering (ICDE)*, pages 411–422, San Diego, CA, USA. IEEE.

SCITUNE: Aligning Large Language Models with Human-Curated Scientific Multimodal Instructions

Sameera Horawalavithan, Sai Munikoti, Ian Stewart, Henry Kvinge, Karl Pazdernik
Pacific Northwest National Laboratory, Richland, WA

Abstract

Instruction finetuning is a popular paradigm to align large language models (LLM) with human intent. Despite its popularity, this idea is less explored in improving LLMs to align existing foundation models with scientific disciplines, concepts and goals. In this work, we present *SciTune* as a tuning framework to improve the ability of LLMs to follow multimodal instructions generated from scientific publications. To test our methodology, we train a large multimodal model LLaMA-SciTune that connects a vision encoder and LLM for science-focused visual and language understanding. LLaMA-SciTune significantly outperforms the state-of-the-art models in the generated figure types and captions in SciCap and VisText benchmarks. In comparison to the models that are finetuned with synthetic data only, LLaMA-SciTune surpasses human performance on average and in many subcategories on the ScienceQA benchmark. Our results demonstrate that human-generated scientific multimodal instructions remain highly valuable in tuning LLMs to perform well on science tasks, despite their lower volume and relative scarcity compared to synthetic data. We publicly release the SciTune codebase[1].

1 Introduction

Instruction finetuning has gained significant traction in the NLP community as a means of enhancing the capabilities of large language models (LLMs), allowing them to accurately balance desired outcomes, context, and human preferences, leading to more relevant and coherent responses. More recently, AI assistants have been trained to comprehend and execute multimodal vision-and-language instructions, aligned with human intent, to accomplish diverse real-world tasks in complex multimodal environments. In one of the latest developments, MiniGPT-4 (Zhu et al., 2023), LLaVA (Liu et al., 2023) and LLaMA-Adapter (Gao et al., 2023) have focused on expanding language-only instruction models to incorporate multimodal capabilities, thereby granting LLMs the ability to perform visual grounded reasoning tasks.

Recent research suggests that high-quality multimodal pretraining data and instructions, such as high-resolution images and diverse multimodal data are important for effective model performance (McKinzie et al., 2024). However, one of the primary bottlenecks is the scarcity of high-quality data for multimodal pretraining and instruction tuning. To mitigate the challenges associated with data scarcity, many recent multimodal models rely on synthetically generated instructions (training data distilled from responses from other models) for fine-tuning instead of human annotations (Liu et al., 2023; Cascante-Bonilla et al., 2023; Bai et al., 2022).

However, using synthetic data to align AI models can create confusion and uncertainty, since synthetic data, being artificially generated, often fails to capture the complexities of human values (Liu et al., 2024; Zhou et al., 2024). This can cause AI models to learn from biased (Feng et al., 2023; Liu et al., 2021), ungrounded (Liu et al., 2022; Patel and Pavlick, 2022) or inaccurate data (Ji et al., 2023; Weidinger et al., 2021). Additionally, training models on recursively generated data can lead to a loss of true data distribution, resulting in less varied and misaligned outputs (Shumailov et al., 2024). Furthermore, models tuned with synthetic data often fail to meet the standards required by certain scientific subdomains, such as medicine (Li et al., 2023; Xia et al., 2024). For example, several open-source medical vision-language models such as LLaVA-Med (Li et al., 2023), Med-Flamingo (Moor et al., 2023), MedVInT (Zhang et al., 2023b), and RadFM (Wu et al., 2023) failed to satisfy the trustfulness, fairness, safety, privacy,

[1] https://github.com/pnnl/scitune

Proceedings of the 1st Workshop on NLP for Science (NLP4Science), pages 58–72

and robustness conditions in the recently introduced CARES (Xia et al., 2024) benchmark. As a result, AI systems relying on synthetic data might behave unpredictably and could potentially cause unintended or harmful outcomes (Anderljung et al., 2023; Zou et al., 2023).

We believe this is mainly due to the absence of alignment methods designed to synchronize existing foundation models with scientific disciplines, concepts, and goals and to ensure that the generated content meets the standards and expectations of the scientific community. Our hypothesis is that scientifically aligned multimodal models can learn from unique patterns and structures present in scientific language generated by human scientists, thus would be able to follow precise instructions about complex procedures, protocols, and guidelines in the scientific environments. This leads to the question: *To what extent, can LLMs align solely with human-curated scientific multimodal instructions?*

To this end, we build on top of the LLaVA (Liu et al., 2023) model architecture to perform scientific multimodal instruction tuning (*SciTune*) on top of a decoder-based pretrained LLM and vision encoder. The *SciTune* training method includes two stages for *scientific multimodal instruction tuning*, i) *scientific concept alignment* to learn across various scientific visual signals (e.g., plots, charts, equation, diagram, etc.), and textual signals (e.g., captions, optical character recognition (OCR) and paragraph mentions), ii) *scientific instruction tuning* to fine-tune on a multimodal scientific reasoning task. To validate our approach, we train our models on top of LLaMA (Touvron et al., 2023a) and the CLIP (Radford et al., 2021) vision encoder model. We show that our model surpasses human performance on the ScienceQA multimodal reasoning benchmark and performs significantly better than state-of-the-art vision-language models in a variety of scientific image understanding tasks. Our results demonstrate that human-curated scientific multimodal instructions remain highly valuable in tuning LLMs to perform well on science tasks, despite their lower volume and relative scarcity compared to synthetic data.

2 Methodology

In this section, we describe the SciTune framework in two stages of Scientific Multimodal Concept Alignment and Multimodal Task-specific Instruction Tuning and the design choices and multimodal architecture used for the experiments.

2.1 Scientific Multimodal Instructions

We use an *early-fusion* strategy (Liu et al., 2023) to jointly reason over the text, images, and other modalities with a shared multifaceted representation as presented as SciTune instructions. The SciTune instruction template $x = (s_D, s_I, s_T)$ includes a system message s_D to help the model to understand the role and context, instruction s_I randomly sampled from the visual-grounded questions, and s_T to encode the multimodal data.

Human-curated Scientific Instructions This work solely focuses on multimodal instructions curated by humans instead of machine generated content used in other visual instruction tuned models (Liu et al., 2023; Gao et al., 2023). Our goal is to align the pretrained foundation models with natural scientific concepts and the intentions of humans (scientists). To this end, we chose scientific publications (PDFs) as the medium of scientific instructions that demonstrate various stages of scientific discovery.

We use the SciCap (Hsu et al., 2021) dataset with more than 400,000 scientific figure images extracted from various arXiv papers, including their respective captions and relevant paragraphs. This dataset is composed of arXiv papers from January 2010 to October 2020. It consists eight distinct categories: Computer Science, Economics, Electrical Engineering and Systems Science, Mathematics, Physics, Quantitative Biology, Quantitative Finance, and Statistics. We use the 333,472 examples provided in the SciCap training split for pretraining and use the validation split to evaluate the performance.

We introduce scientific captions (s_c), figure types (s_t), optical character recognition (OCR)(s_o) and paragraph mentions(s_m) in the instruction template ($s_T = \{s_c, s_t, s_o, s_m\}$) to convert the SciCap dataset into a multimodal instruction-tuning dataset. Figure-captioning (s_c) data typically includes brief text that is highly specific to the associated figure. In contrast, interleaved data such as paragraph mentions (s_m) generally features longer and more varied text, which is broadly relevant to the figures it associates. Please see the Appendix (Table 6) for a SciTune instruction sample.

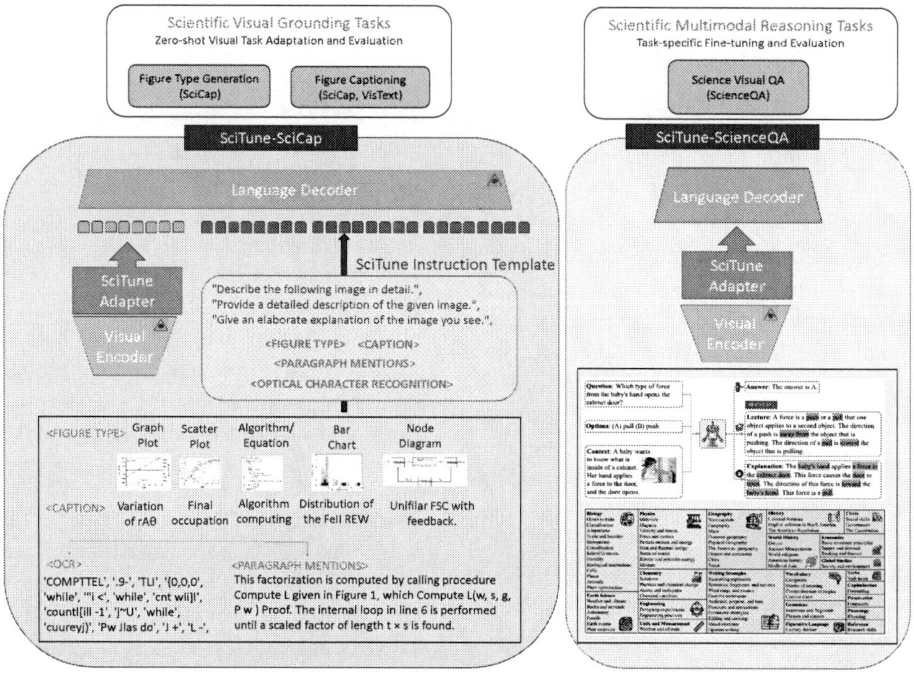

Figure 1: SciTune enables models to learn *scientific concept alignment* across various visual signals (e.g., plots, charts, equation, diagram), and textual signals (e.g., captions, OCR and paragraph mentions); shown in the left graphic in the figure. After alignment, the model can be used to perform various scientific visual grounding tasks (e.g., figure type generation, captioning) with zero demonstrations at inference time (shown in the upper-left graphic). The pretrained model can be further finetuned on a multimodal scientific reasoning task (e.g., ScienceQA; shown in the upper-right graphic).

2.2 Multimodal Architecture

Architecture We build on top of the most recent multimodal architectures (e.g., LLaVA (Liu et al., 2023), LLaMA-Adapter (Zhang et al., 2023a)) that guide LLMs to follow multimodal instructions. We noticed that adapter-based multimodal training serves as the most efficient technique for injecting multimodal knowledge to a pretrained LLM decoder model. Our goal was to improve the existing LLMs to perform better on science-focused multimodal reasoning and visual grounded tasks. To this end, we chose LLaMA-1 (Touvron et al., 2023a) as the LLM decoder, and CLIP visual encoder (Radford et al., 2021) to experiment with multimodal adapter training as shown in Figure 1.

The SciTune adapter transforms the output of the visual encoder model as inputs to the language decoder with a linear projection layer. While we keep the language decoder and the visual encoder models frozen, the multimodal adapter is updated during the pretraining stage. This modular architecture can be filled by any language decoder and a visual encoder model. We conduct the experiments with LLaMA 7B and 13B model variants for better comparison with other baseline models. It is worthwhile to note that we chose LLaMA due to its superior performance in the public benchmarks and its open-source accessibility.

We do not use any instruction-tuned LLaMA variants (e.g., Vicuna, Guanaco) in our experiments due to two main reasons. First, we mainly focus on improving the base LLM decoder models with multimodal instructions generated by humans in order to eliminate all confounding factors such as machine generated instruction tuning. Since a majority of instruction-tuned models developed on top of LLaMA are knowledge-distilled from closed-source, proprietary models like GPT-4, we want to avoid any unexpected performance advantages. Second, we want to make a fair comparison with other baseline models proposed in this area developed on top of the base LLaMA model, and test whether the multimodal instruction tuning proposed in this work could lead into better scientific concept understanding compared to those models.

Training We model the language distribution $p(x)$ from a set of SciTune instructions $(x_1, x_2, .., x_m)$ as the product of conditional multimodal token probabilities as shown in Equation 1.

$$p(x) = \prod_{j=1}^{n} p(s_{T>j} | s_V, s_I, s_{T<j}) \quad (1)$$

We model s_V with the multimodal tokens after projection from the respective plot visuals V. We sample the instruction s_I from the list of questions presented in the Appendix (Table 7). Note that we skip the token descriptors in s_T for brevity, unless the model is trained autoregressively to generate exact tokens across all textual modalities in $s_T = \{s_c, s_t, s_o, s_m\}$. More importantly, the model is able to jointly generate all modality tokens in a single-turn conversation. For example, given a scientific plot and an instruction, the model first generates the figure type (e.g., Graph Plot, Scatterplot, Node Diagram, Equation, Bar Chart), then the visual content through captioning and OCR, and finally the cited paragraph.

As presented in Figure 1, *LlaMA-SciTune-Scicap* is tuned to align the LLM towards scientific concepts. *LlaMA-SciTune-Scicap* can be further finetuned on a multimodal scientific reasoning task. In our experiments, we name the task finetuned model variant as *LlaMA-SciTune-ScienceQA*.

3 Experiments

In this section, we report the performance of *LLaMA-SciTune* models across a variety of science-focused downstream tasks. Our goal is to assess the performance of the models in visual grounded language understanding and multimodal reasoning tasks. For example, we want to show how much difference the training stages contribute to the model performance, or whether adding various scientific modalities in the instruction template improves the overall performance. Note that our objective is not to introduce a model that tops the leaderboard across various downstream tasks. Instead, we aim to demonstrate the extent to how human-curated scientific multimodal instructions can be useful in aligning vision-language models.

To this end, we trained three *LLaMA-SciTune-SciCap* models and finetuned them with scientific multimodal reasoning dataset (e.g., ScienceQA) for the corresponding *LLaMA-SciTune-ScienceQA* models. Three *LLaMA-SciTune-SciCap* models differ on the text input types (e.g., Caption, Figure Type, OCR, and Figure Mentions) and the scale of the LLM (e.g., 7B and 13B) used in the model training. For example, *LLaMA-SciTune-SciCap-13B (CTOM)* model uses the base LLaMA-1 13B checkpoint and figure **c**aption, figure **t**ype, **O**CR, and figure **m**entions in the training. Similarly, *LLaMA-SciTune-ScienceQA-13B (CTOM)* model is finetuned on the *LLaMA-SciTune-SciCap-13B (CTOM)* with the ScienceQA (Lu et al., 2022) training split. While *LLaMA-SciTune-SciCap* model tunes the LLM to better understand scientific concepts, *LLaMA-SciTune-ScienceQA* is further finetuned for scientific reasoning.

First, we report the performance of *LLaMA-SciTune-SciCap* in two science-focused visual grounded tasks to assess the scientific concept alignment training stage (Section 3.1). Finally, we use the ScienceQA benchmark to test the multimodal reasoning abilities of *LLaMA-SciTune-ScienceQA* across three scientific subject areas (Section 3.2).

3.1 Vision Grounded Tasks Performance

In this section, we report the performance of the *LLaMA-SciTune-SciCap* model for two zero-shot downstream tasks. Note that, we reference the *LLaMA-SciTune-SciCap-13B (CTOM)* model in this performance analysis. In the first task, we evaluate how well the *LLaMA-SciTune-SciCap* model is able to align the associated figure types with the actual image. In the second task, we evaluate the performance of the *LLaMA-SciTune-SciCap* model in generating the figure captions.

3.1.1 Scientific Figure Type Generation

In the scientific concept alignment stage, one of the learning tasks is to align the scientific visuals with the correct figure type. For example, the model should be able to distinguish a graph plot from a scatter plot. We compare the performance of our model of generating the figure types with a standalone vision encoder. For example, we use the CLIP model (Radford et al., 2021) to perform figure type classification in the zero-shot manner given five candidate types (e.g., Graph Plot, Scatterplot, Node Diagram, Equation, Bar Chart). We use the validation data released by the SciCap challenge to perform our experiments. This validation dataset includes plots and the associated figure types. We locate the figure types in the generated SciTune outputs, and compare it with the ground truth. As shown in Table 1, *LLaMA-*

SciTune-SciCap shows 57% performance improvement over the standalone CLIP model used in the figure type classification.

It is important to note that the *LLaMA-SciTune-SciCap* used the same CLIP model as the visual encoder, but the additional multimodal adapter was optimized towards aligning figure types with the plots during the pretraining stage. This multimodal adapter is able to project the outputs of vision encoder into the LLM to improve its understanding on the scientific plots. One could argue that a more ideal comparison would be between the *LLaMA-SciTune-SciCap* model and a version of the CLIP model that is specifically tuned with the same dataset, rather than comparing it with the vanilla (untuned) CLIP model. In this experiment, our objective was to evaluate how much the SciTune adapter (Figure 1) contributes to improving the LLM's performance in understanding scientific plots, as opposed to improvements gained merely through the use of the tuned visual encoder.

Table 1: Accuracy of Generating the Figure Types. We also report the zero-shot figure type classification performance of the CLIP model.

Figure Type	CLIP	SciTune-SciCap
Graph Plot	52.58	**93.63**
Scatterplot	52.20	**70.14**
Node Diagram	77.67	**95.40**
Equation	60.47	**89.54**
Bar Chart	32.67	**80.33**
All	55.11	**85.81**

3.1.2 Scientific Figure Captioning

In this section, we test the model performance of generating scientific figure captions given only the scientific plot. Previous works show that scientific figure captioning is an extremely challenging task due to complex image understanding required in vision-to-language modeling (Huang et al., 2023). We take the first sentence in the generated SciTune output as the generated caption. We compare *LLaMA-SciTune-SciCap* model performance with the SOTA image captioning model, BLIP (Li et al., 2022), trained with more than 14M image-text pairs. We use two text evaluation metrics, BLEU and ROUGE, to measure the quality of generated captions with respect to the ground truth captions. We evaluate the models in two scientific image captioning benchmarks, SciCap and VisText (Tang et al., 2023). We used the validation split with 47639 and 1202 images in two benchmarks, respectively.

As shown in Table 2, the *LLaMA-SciTune-SciCap* model outperforms the BLIP model in both automated text evaluation metrics. This suggests that *LLaMA-SciTune-SciCap* may have a better understanding of the scientific plot in comparison to the BLIP model finetuned towards image captions. Table 8 (see Appendix) shows a few generated captions in comparison to the baseline and ground truth image captions.

Table 2: In-distribution (SciCap) and out-of-distribution (VisText) Evaluation of Generated Figure Captions

Benchmark	Model	BLEU	ROUGE
SciCap	BLIP	0.02±0.02	0.11±0.07
	SciTune-SciCap	**0.05±0.03**	**0.13±0.08**
VisText	BLIP	0.06±0.05	0.23±0.11
	SciTune-SciCap	**0.10±0.07**	**0.23±0.12**

3.2 Scientific Multimodal Reasoning Task Performance

In this section, we evaluate the model performance on science-focused multimodal reasoning question and answering (QA). We report the *LLaMA-SciTune-ScienceQA* model performance in the ScienceQA benchmark (Lu et al., 2022) that includes 21k multimodal multiple choice questions with rich domain diversity across 3 subjects, 26 topics, 127 categories, and 379 skills. We use the ScienceQA training split (12726 examples) to tune the *LLaMA-SciTune-SciCap* model further as shown in Figure 1. Table 3 reports the performance of the models on the ScienceQA test split (4241 test questions). While lectures are shared between training and test splits, there are new questions associated with multimodal contexts, and explanations in the test split. We have three main observations from this table.

First, *LLaMA-SciTune-ScienceQA-13B (CTOM)* model outperforms the human performance on average and in four other sub-groupings. For example, this model records 90.03% accuracy in correctly answering the multimodal reasoning questions in the ScienceQA benchmark, where humans record only 88.40% accuracy. This performance benefit is consistent across social science questions, questions with text or no contexts, and higher-grade questions. More importantly, we noticed that this

Table 3: Results (accuracy %) on ScienceQA dataset. Question classes: NAT = natural science, SOC = social science, LAN = language science, TXT = text context, IMG = image context, NO = no context, G1-6 = grades 1-6, G7-12 = grades 7-12. We present two variants, *LLaMA-SciTune-ScienceQA (C)* and *LLaMA-SciTune-ScinceQA (CTOM)*. Acronyms inside the parenthesis represent the text inputs used in the SciTune instruction template. E.g., **C**aption, Figure **T**ype, **O**CR, and Figure **M**entions. We use the notation ♠ to denote the models finetuned with GPT-3.5/4 synthetic instructions, or use GPT-3.5/4 for any support during the inference time. We bold the accuracy values that are greater than what humans achieved.

Method	#Params	Avg	NAT	SOC	LAN	TXT	IMG	NO	G1-6	G7-12
Random Chance	-	39.83	40.28	46.13	29.25	47.45	40.08	33.66	39.35	40.67
Human Average	-	88.40	90.23	84.97	87.48	89.60	87.50	88.10	91.59	82.42
UnifiedQA	223M	70.12	68.16	69.18	74.91	63.78	61.38	77.84	72.98	65.00
UnifiedQA (CoT)	223M	74.11	71.00	76.04	78.91	66.42	66.53	81.81	77.06	68.82
♠ GPT-3 (Zero Shot)	175B	74.04	75.04	66.59	78.00	74.24	65.74	79.58	76.36	69.87
♠ GPT-3 (CoT) (ALE)	175B	75.17	75.44	70.87	78.09	74.68	67.43	79.93	78.23	69.68
♠ ChatGPT CoT	175B+	78.31	78.82	70.98	83.18	77.37	67.92	86.13	80.72	74.03
♠ GPT-4 CoT	1T+	83.99	85.48	72.44	**90.27**	82.65	71.49	**92.89**	86.66	79.04
Multimodal-CoT	223M	84.91	87.52	77.17	85.82	87.88	82.90	86.83	84.65	**85.37**
Multimodal-CoT	770M	**91.68**	**95.91**	82.00	**90.82**	**95.26**	**88.80**	**92.89**	**92.44**	**90.31**
♠ LLaMA-Adapter	13B	85.19	84.37	**88.30**	84.36	83.72	80.32	86.90	85.83	**84.05**
♠ LLaVa	13B	**90.92**	**90.36**	**95.95**	88.00	89.49	**88.00**	**90.66**	90.93	**90.90**
♠ LLaVa + GPT-4 (judge)	13B	**92.53**	**91.56**	**96.74**	**91.09**	**90.62**	**88.99**	**93.52**	**92.73**	**92.16**
♠ Chameleon (ChatGPT)	175B+	79.93	81.62	70.64	84.00	79.77	70.80	86.62	81.86	76.53
♠ Chameleon (GPT-4)	1T+	86.54	89.83	74.13	**89.82**	88.27	77.64	**92.13**	88.03	**83.72**
SciTune-ScienceQA (C)	7B	85.61	84.36	**92.23**	82.81	89.56	81.26	**88.29**	81.28	**86.03**
SciTune-ScienceQA (CTOM)	7B	86.11	84.50	**94.15**	82.91	88.35	83.64	**88.74**	85.05	**85.60**
SciTune-ScienceQA (CTOM)	13B	**90.03**	89.30	**95.61**	87.00	**93.08**	86.67	**91.75**	84.37	**91.30**

model reaches a comparable performance with the LLaVA model, which is trained with synthetic data and twice the size of the training data than what the former model has seen, and in some cases has additional support from GPT-4 during inference.

Second, we noticed that *LLaMA-SciTune-ScienceQA-7B (CTOM)* model performs better than *LLaMA-SciTune-ScienceQA-7B (C)* model pretrained only with captions. For example, CTOM variant (86.11) slightly outperforms C variant (85.11) on average performance and across many other sub-groupings. This suggests the importance of interleaved multimodal data in the scientific concept alignment stage which lifts the downstream task performance over the model tuned only with figure-caption data.

Finally, we noticed a significant performance advantage of the models trained with larger language decoder model (13B) compared to the relatively smaller model (7B). For example, the *LLaMA-SciTune-ScienceQA-13B (CTOM)* model has nearly 5% performance advantage over the 7B model variant. This advantage is 5x bigger than what reported by the LLaVA model when scaled from 7B to 13B (Liu et al., 2023). While this observation suggests that the larger language decoder model helps to improve the multimodal reasoning performance, we believe it could lead to huge performance benefit with even larger models (LLaMA-65B) when trained with highly-curated scientific multimodal instruction tuning datasets.

Explanation Performance Analysis In addition to generating the specific answers to the questions asked, *LLaMA-SciTune-ScienceQA* models also generate a corresponding lecture and explanation for the answers. Please see Figures 3 and 4 and in the Appendix for several examples of generated lectures and explanations. In order to better understand the behavior of generated solution, we manually investigate a few random test examples. Specifically, we picked 50 samples from both the correct and incorrect predictions. We observe that even the correct samples contain a certain amount of incorrect solutions, i.e., around 8% in C and 2% in CTOM version of the 7B models. These results indicate that solution may not always benefit the final answer, and the model is robust to some extent, i.e., it can predict the correct answer even with incorrect rationales. The incorrect solutions are further divided into two major categories, namely commonsense that requires commonsense knowledge such as factual information and counting numbers in the images, and the logical mistakes which shows contradictions in the reasoning. In our experiment, commonsense mistakes are dominant compared to logical, which aligns with previous work (Zhang et al., 2023d). Furthermore, there are cases where solutions are correct in an absolute sense but their final answers are wrong. We also noticed that solutions generated by the CTOM version of the model are more accurate compared to the C version of the model, further emphasizing the importance of multi-modal training with additional scientific modalities. There are certain task categories where our model performs extremely well compared to baselines. In our manual analysis, we found the model is very good with numerical questions, including temperatures and distances, and can answer all topological/map related questions such as "which ocean is highlighted" in the image.

While we observe high performance in aggregate, it is also important to determine whether this performance persists in cases with minimal training examples. We evaluate the performance of the model for questions whose accompanying lectures are only observed a few times in the training data. For these few-shot examples, the model will be less likely to have the exact lecture memorized and ready to use in its generation of the answer, which could lead to lower performance.

We show the model performance on questions for which the lectures were viewed in 5, 10, 25, and 50 times during training, in Table 4. The model performance drops substantially for questions with only 5 or fewer lectures in the training data but quickly recovers after the lecture is viewed at least 10 times. This suggests that the *LLaMA-SciTune-ScienceQA* model doesn't require substantial exposure to a particular type of knowledge to achieve adequate performance. Furthermore, this performance drop is worse for the 7B model as compared to the 13B model, which means that the 13B model is able to learn more quickly from fewer examples or may have more knowledge "baked in" from pretraining that can be leveraged for few-shot examples. Future extensions of the model to other datasets should test performance on completely unseen data, e.g. a more standard VQA dataset not used during training, to determine whether the model is similarly robust in other domains.

Table 4: Few-shot performance analysis. We report the number of times lectures seen during the training in frequency, and the number of test questions with the lecture.

Frequency	#Questions	Accuracy (7B)	Accuracy (13B)
5	36	75.00	83.33
10	125	81.60	85.60
25	412	80.34	85.92
50	1140	81.05	86.14

Chain of Thought Reasoning Performance Outside of the coarse-grained accuracy metric (did the model get the answer right?), we also need to determine whether the model's overall process of reasoning was correct (did the model accurately explain the reasoning that supports the answer?). We investigate the accuracy of the generated text, outside of the answer alone, assessing if the model is able to accurately recover the lecture and the solution that it was trained to generate and to help its reasoning toward the final answer. We report the BLEU and ROUGE scores over all the generated text, separated into the lecture and solution components and compared with the corresponding ground-truth data, e.g. compare the generated lecture component with the ground-truth lecture.

The aggregate results for the generation metrics are shown in Table 5. When considering all the questions, the model generates the solution text with higher accuracy than the lecture text. However, in cases where the model answers incorrectly, the trend reverses and the model has a higher accuracy in generating the lecture text as compared to the solution text. Therefore, the model may be failing to answer these questions due to a failure to reason in the "solution stage" of its generation. Furthermore, for the 13B model we see that the lecture generation performance is higher for incorrect answers than correct answers (ROUGE score of 0.924 for incorrect vs. 0.861 for correct). This could indicate overfitting, where the model "memorizes" lectures that apply to the problem but fails to apply the lectures to the actual solution.

This problem is apparent with an example question about object properties, where the model must determine the property shared by an icicle, a fish bowl, a glass, and a tea cup. The model correctly generates the lecture about object properties required to reason through the problem ("An object has different properties. A property of an object can tell you how it looks, feels, tastes, or smells."). However, in the solution stage the model incorrectly reasons that all the objects were transparent instead of fragile, based on a failure to infer the properties of the objects from the image ("You can see clearly through a transparent object. All four objects are transparent.").

Incorrect reasoning can be attributed to two factors, i.e., linguistic and visual features. In a manual analysis of 100 test samples, we found that linguistic features are a weakness for mainly two use cases, namely retrieving commonsense facts (e.g. characteristics of bird song) and semantic understanding of words in terms of figure of speech and relative position of words in the dictionary. In contrast, visual features appear to be strong in use-cases such as identifying geographic areas but it lags in counting numbers in images and retrieving properties of objects such as color, texture and states.

These observations suggest that to improve model training, we need a wide variety of human-curated instructions, especially datasets that include both text and visuals explained by humans. Such diverse explanations would help the model understand various scenarios that require different types of reasoning.

Table 5: Evaluation of generated lectures and solutions.

	7B Model		13B Model	
	BLEU	ROUGE	BLEU	ROUGE
All answers				
Lecture	0.763	0.778	0.854	0.868
Solution	0.791	0.838	0.872	0.921
Correct answers				
Lecture	0.765	0.780	0.847	0.861
Solution	0.829	0.873	0.893	0.937
Incorrect answers				
Lecture	0.751	0.767	0.909	0.924
Solution	0.565	0.631	0.694	0.778

4 Related Work

Zhang et al. (2023a) proposed LLaMA-Adapter to guide the LLaMA model to follow multimodal instructions. Specifically, they proposed a zero-init attention with gating as a Parameter-Efficient Fine-Tuning (PEFT) technique to prepend learnable multimodal adaptation prompts to the input text tokens at higher transformer layers in the LLaMA model. The same authors proposed LLaMA-Adapter-V2 (Gao et al., 2023) that distributes the learnable parameters across all layers in the LLaMA model to improve performance in multimodal reasoning. MiniGPT-4 (Zhu et al., 2023) combined the frozen LLM (Vicuna) and a vision encoder with a single projection layer and fine-tuned with a highly-curated visual conversation dataset. More recently, Liu et al. (2023) introduce *visual instruction tuning* to develop general-purpose visual assistant (LLaVA) that follows multimodal instructions. They present several data reformation techniques to construct multimodal instruction-following data from the standard image-text pairs. For example, the LLaVA model was trained with 595K image-text pairs filtered from the CC3M dataset (Sharma et al., 2018), and 158K unique language-image instruction-following data generated from ChatGPT/GPT-4 (Liu et al., 2023). This multimodal instruction set includes image-based *conversations* and *detailed descriptions* and *complex reasoning* questions. LLaVA (Liu et al., 2023) reaches the best performance in the ScienceQA benchmark with support from GPT-4 that acts as a judge to evaluate the generated answers. LLaVAR (Zhang et al., 2023c) extends the LLaVA for text-rich images by training with additional 422K image-OCR and 16K conversations generated from GPT-4.

5 Conclusion

In this work, we present scientific multimodal instruction tuning to align LLMs with scientific concepts and goals. To this end, we use human-generated multimodal instructions curated from visual signals (e.g., plots, charts, equations), and textual signals (e.g., captions, optical character recognition (OCR) and paragraph mentions) found within scientific publications. We train several models built on top of LLaMA language decoder model and CLIP vision encoder model and test the models on science-focused multimodal downstream tasks. In evaluation, we show that the resulting *LLaMA-SciTune-SciCap* models can perform better on classifying scientific visuals and generating figure captions compared with SOTA vision-to-language models. Furthermore, the *LLaMA-SciTune-ScienceQA* model surpasses the human performance in ScienceQA, the standard multimodal science-focused reasoning QA benchmark.

Our results suggest human-curated scientific multimodal data remains highly valuable despite the advancements in synthetic data generation techniques. While it is fast and easy to generate large volume of synthetic training data with closed-source models such as GPT-4, they may contain inaccuracies or biases due to lack of expert review. In contrast, although existing human-generated scientific multimodal datasets are comparatively smaller, they provide reliable ground truth for tuning LLMs, which leads to better generalization and performance in downstream science applications.

Acknowledgements

This work was supported by the NNSA Office of Defense Nuclear Nonproliferation Research and Development, U.S. Department of Energy, and Pacific Northwest National Laboratory, which is operated by Battelle Memorial Institute for the U.S. Department of Energy under Contract DE-AC05–76RLO1830. This article has been cleared by PNNL for public release as PNNL-SA-186641.

References

Markus Anderljung, Joslyn Barnhart, Anton Korinek, Jade Leung, Cullen O'Keefe, Jess Whittlestone, Shahar Avin, Miles Brundage, Justin Bullock, Duncan Cass-Beggs, et al. 2023. Frontier ai regulation: Managing emerging risks to public safety. *arXiv preprint arXiv:2307.03718*.

Yuntao Bai, Saurav Kadavath, Sandipan Kundu, Amanda Askell, Jackson Kernion, Andy Jones, Anna Chen, Anna Goldie, Azalia Mirhoseini, Cameron McKinnon, et al. 2022. Constitutional ai: Harmlessness from ai feedback. *arXiv preprint arXiv:2212.08073*.

Paola Cascante-Bonilla, Khaled Shehada, James Seale Smith, Sivan Doveh, Donghyun Kim, Rameswar Panda, Gul Varol, Aude Oliva, Vicente Ordonez, Rogerio Feris, et al. 2023. Going beyond nouns with vision & language models using synthetic data. In *Proceedings of the IEEE/CVF International Conference on Computer Vision*, pages 20155–20165.

Shangbin Feng, Chan Young Park, Yuhan Liu, and Yulia Tsvetkov. 2023. From pretraining data to language models to downstream tasks: Tracking the trails of political biases leading to unfair nlp models. *arXiv preprint arXiv:2305.08283*.

Peng Gao, Jiaming Han, Renrui Zhang, Ziyi Lin, Shijie Geng, Aojun Zhou, Wei Zhang, Pan Lu, Conghui He, Xiangyu Yue, Hongsheng Li, and Yu Qiao. 2023. Llama-adapter v2: Parameter-efficient visual instruction model. *Preprint*, arXiv:2304.15010.

Ting-Yao Hsu, C Lee Giles, and Ting-Hao'Kenneth' Huang. 2021. Scicap: Generating captions for scientific figures. *arXiv preprint arXiv:2110.11624*.

Chieh-Yang Huang, Ting-Yao Hsu, Ryan Rossi, Ani Nenkova, Sungchul Kim, Gromit Yeuk-Yin Chan, Eunyee Koh, Clyde Lee Giles, and Ting-Hao'Kenneth' Huang. 2023. Summaries as captions: Generating figure captions for scientific documents with automated text summarization. *arXiv preprint arXiv:2302.12324*.

Ziwei Ji, Nayeon Lee, Rita Frieske, Tiezheng Yu, Dan Su, Yan Xu, Etsuko Ishii, Ye Jin Bang, Andrea Madotto, and Pascale Fung. 2023. Survey of hallucination in natural language generation. *ACM Computing Surveys*, 55(12):1–38.

Chunyuan Li, Cliff Wong, Sheng Zhang, Naoto Usuyama, Haotian Liu, Jianwei Yang, Tristan Naumann, Hoifung Poon, and Jianfeng Gao. 2023. Llava-med: Training a large language-and-vision assistant for biomedicine in one day. *arXiv preprint arXiv:2306.00890*.

Junnan Li, Dongxu Li, Caiming Xiong, and Steven Hoi. 2022. Blip: Bootstrapping language-image pretraining for unified vision-language understanding and generation. In *International Conference on Machine Learning*, pages 12888–12900. PMLR.

Haotian Liu, Chunyuan Li, Qingyang Wu, and Yong Jae Lee. 2023. Visual instruction tuning. *arXiv preprint arXiv:2304.08485*.

Ruibo Liu, Chenyan Jia, Jason Wei, Guangxuan Xu, Lili Wang, and Soroush Vosoughi. 2021. Mitigating political bias in language models through reinforced calibration. In *Proceedings of the AAAI Conference on Artificial Intelligence*, volume 35, pages 14857–14866.

Ruibo Liu, Jason Wei, Shixiang Shane Gu, Te-Yen Wu, Soroush Vosoughi, Claire Cui, Denny Zhou, and Andrew M Dai. 2022. Mind's eye: Grounded language model reasoning through simulation. *arXiv preprint arXiv:2210.05359*.

Ruibo Liu, Jerry Wei, Fangyu Liu, Chenglei Si, Yanzhe Zhang, Jinmeng Rao, Steven Zheng, Daiyi Peng, Diyi Yang, Denny Zhou, et al. 2024. Best practices and lessons learned on synthetic data for language models. *arXiv preprint arXiv:2404.07503*.

Pan Lu, Swaroop Mishra, Tanglin Xia, Liang Qiu, Kai-Wei Chang, Song-Chun Zhu, Oyvind Tafjord, Peter Clark, and Ashwin Kalyan. 2022. Learn to explain: Multimodal reasoning via thought chains for science question answering. *Advances in Neural Information Processing Systems*, 35:2507–2521.

Brandon McKinzie, Zhe Gan, Jean-Philippe Fauconnier, Sam Dodge, Bowen Zhang, Philipp Dufter, Dhruti Shah, Xianzhi Du, Futang Peng, Floris Weers, et al. 2024. Mm1: Methods, analysis & insights from multimodal llm pre-training. *arXiv preprint arXiv:2403.09611*.

Michael Moor, Qian Huang, Shirley Wu, Michihiro Yasunaga, Yash Dalmia, Jure Leskovec, Cyril Zakka, Eduardo Pontes Reis, and Pranav Rajpurkar. 2023. Med-flamingo: a multimodal medical few-shot learner. In *Machine Learning for Health (ML4H)*, pages 353–367. PMLR.

Roma Patel and Ellie Pavlick. 2022. Mapping language models to grounded conceptual spaces. In *International conference on learning representations*.

Alec Radford, Jong Wook Kim, Chris Hallacy, Aditya Ramesh, Gabriel Goh, Sandhini Agarwal, Girish Sastry, Amanda Askell, Pamela Mishkin, Jack Clark, et al. 2021. Learning transferable visual models from natural language supervision. In *International conference on machine learning*, pages 8748–8763. PMLR.

Piyush Sharma, Nan Ding, Sebastian Goodman, and Radu Soricut. 2018. Conceptual captions: A cleaned, hypernymed, image alt-text dataset for automatic image captioning. In *Proceedings of the 56th Annual Meeting of the Association for Computational Linguistics (Volume 1: Long Papers)*, pages 2556–2565.

Ilia Shumailov, Zakhar Shumaylov, Yiren Zhao, Nicolas Papernot, Ross Anderson, and Yarin Gal. 2024. Ai models collapse when trained on recursively generated data. *Nature*, 631(8022):755–759.

Benny J Tang, Angie Boggust, and Arvind Satyanarayan. 2023. Vistext: A benchmark for semantically rich chart captioning. *arXiv preprint arXiv:2307.05356*.

Hugo Touvron, Thibaut Lavril, Gautier Izacard, Xavier Martinet, Marie-Anne Lachaux, Timothée Lacroix, Baptiste Rozière, Naman Goyal, Eric Hambro, Faisal Azhar, et al. 2023a. Llama: Open and efficient foundation language models. *arXiv preprint arXiv:2302.13971*.

Hugo Touvron, Louis Martin, Kevin Stone, Peter Albert, Amjad Almahairi, Yasmine Babaei, Nikolay Bashlykov, Soumya Batra, Prajjwal Bhargava, Shruti Bhosale, et al. 2023b. Llama 2: Open foundation and fine-tuned chat models. *arXiv preprint arXiv:2307.09288*.

Laura Weidinger, John Mellor, Maribeth Rauh, Conor Griffin, Jonathan Uesato, Po-Sen Huang, Myra Cheng, Mia Glaese, Borja Balle, Atoosa Kasirzadeh, et al. 2021. Ethical and social risks of harm from language models. *arXiv preprint arXiv:2112.04359*.

Chaoyi Wu, Xiaoman Zhang, Ya Zhang, Yanfeng Wang, and Weidi Xie. 2023. Towards generalist foundation model for radiology. *arXiv preprint arXiv:2308.02463*.

Peng Xia, Ze Chen, Juanxi Tian, Yangrui Gong, Ruibo Hou, Yue Xu, Zhenbang Wu, Zhiyuan Fan, Yiyang Zhou, Kangyu Zhu, et al. 2024. Cares: A comprehensive benchmark of trustworthiness in medical vision language models. *arXiv preprint arXiv:2406.06007*.

Renrui Zhang, Jiaming Han, Aojun Zhou, Xiangfei Hu, Shilin Yan, Pan Lu, Hongsheng Li, Peng Gao, and Yu Qiao. 2023a. Llama-adapter: Efficient fine-tuning of language models with zero-init attention. *arXiv preprint arXiv:2303.16199*.

Xiaoman Zhang, Chaoyi Wu, Ziheng Zhao, Weixiong Lin, Ya Zhang, Yanfeng Wang, and Weidi Xie. 2023b. Pmc-vqa: Visual instruction tuning for medical visual question answering. *arXiv preprint arXiv:2305.10415*.

Yanzhe Zhang, Ruiyi Zhang, Jiuxiang Gu, Yufan Zhou, Nedim Lipka, Diyi Yang, and Tong Sun. 2023c. Llavar: Enhanced visual instruction tuning for text-rich image understanding. *Preprint*, arXiv:2306.17107.

Zhuosheng Zhang, Aston Zhang, Mu Li, Hai Zhao, George Karypis, and Alex Smola. 2023d. Multimodal chain-of-thought reasoning in language models. *arXiv preprint arXiv:2302.00923*.

Xuhui Zhou, Zhe Su, Tiwalayo Eisape, Hyunwoo Kim, and Maarten Sap. 2024. Is this the real life? is this just fantasy? the misleading success of simulating social interactions with llms. *arXiv preprint arXiv:2403.05020*.

Deyao Zhu, Jun Chen, Xiaoqian Shen, Xiang Li, and Mohamed Elhoseiny. 2023. Minigpt-4: Enhancing vision-language understanding with advanced large language models. *arXiv preprint arXiv:2304.10592*.

Andy Zou, Zifan Wang, J Zico Kolter, and Matt Fredrikson. 2023. Universal and transferable adversarial attacks on aligned language models. *arXiv preprint arXiv:2307.15043*.

A SciTune Multimodal Instructions

Table 6 shows two SciTune instruction examples used in the scientific concept alignment training stage. Table 7 presents the LLaVA questions that used to sample the s_I instructions.

B Training Details

We use the LLaVA codebase (Liu et al., 2023) for multimodal adapter training with SciTune instructions. We train the model for 1 epoch with 128 batch size with a 0.002 learning rate and 2048 context length. LLaMA-SciTune 7B and 13B model variants took 6.5 and 11.2 hours to train, respectively with 8 x A100 GPUs. We use Pytorch Fully Sharded Data Parallel (FSDP) to recursively wrap the language models decoder layers in the task-specific instruction finetuning stage. We finetuned the models for 12 epochs with the ScienceQA training example to make a fair comparison with LLaVA.

C LLaMA-1 and LLaMA-2 Base Model Comparison

We also test our methodology with LLaMA-2 (Touvron et al., 2023b) as the base language decoder

Table 6: SciTune Multimodal Instruction Examples. We distinguish the system message s_D, natural language instruction s_I, scientific figure type s_t, caption s_c, OCR s_o and paragraph mentions s_m. The list of instructions used to sample s_I are presented at Table 7.

A chat between a curious human and an artificial intelligence assistant. The assistant gives helpful, detailed, and polite answers to the human's questions.
Human: Give an elaborate explanation of the image you see.

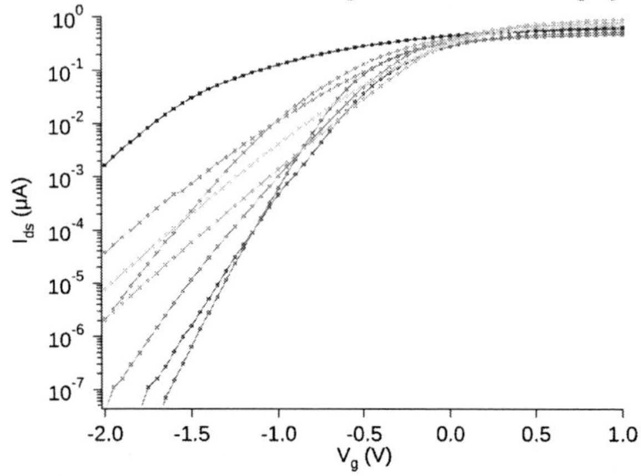

Assistant: Graph Plot Room temperature characteristics (drain-source current versus gate voltage) for a set of nominally identical samples from the same wafer. Sample to sample variations are very important, especially below the threshold voltage (-0.5 V for the best device, in red). In the most extreme case (blue curve) the many decades of excess current compared to the best device are attributed to direct transport through individual arsenic dopants which have diffused into the channel after doping and annealing steps.
The source-drain voltage is 10mV for these data.
FIG. 6: figure S1: Room temperature characteristics (drain-source current versus gate voltage) for a set of nominally identical samples from the same wafer.

A chat between a curious human and an artificial intelligence assistant. The assistant gives helpful, detailed, and polite answers to the human's questions.
Human: Describe the following image in detail.

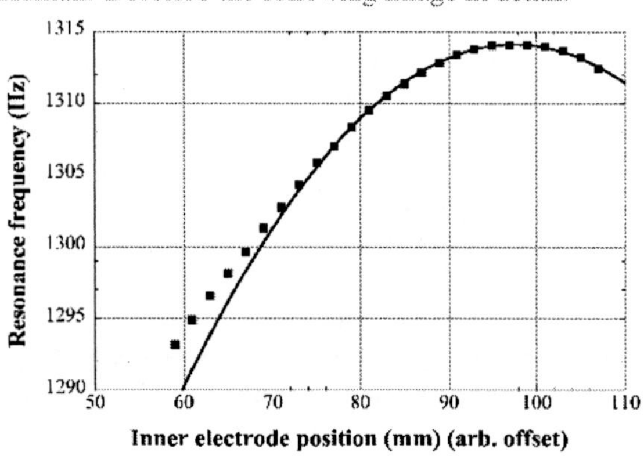

Assistant: Graph Plot Resonance frequency of the (1, 0) mode of the r1 = 4 cm cavity filled with 1 atm of N2 as a function of the vertical position of the central electrode.
Inner electrode position, (arb , offset)
In Fig. 10 we have an example of this behavior: the resonance frequency shows a maximum which corresponds to a minimum in the eccentricity of the electrode [39].

Table 7: LLaVA Instructions for detailed image descriptions

"Describe the following image in detail."
"Provide a detailed description of the given image."
"Give an elaborate explanation of the image you see."
"Share a comprehensive rundown of the presented image."
"Offer a thorough analysis of the image."
"Explain the various aspects of the image before you."
"Clarify the contents of the displayed image with great detail."
"Characterize the image using a well-detailed description."
"Break down the elements of the image in a detailed manner."
"Walk through the important details of the image."
"Portray the image with a rich, descriptive narrative."
"Narrate the contents of the image with precision."
"Analyze the image in a comprehensive and detailed manner."
"Illustrate the image through a descriptive explanation."
"Examine the image closely and share its details."
"Write an exhaustive depiction of the given image."

model. LLaMA-2 was reported to have superior performance compared to LLaMA-1 with additional pretraining corpus (2x tokens), larger context length (2x), and adopted grouped-query attention. In addition, there were additional steps taken to improve the safety of LLaMA-2 models. We do not use the LLaMA-2 model variants optimized for chat and dialogue use cases to make a fair comparison with LLaMA-1 model. In this experiment, we repeat the entire training (CTOM) pipeline (as shown in Figure 1) with the LLaMA-2 (13B) model. Figure 2 shows a comparison of ScienceQA performance with LLaMA-1 and LLaMA-2 base language models. Despite the reported performance improvements in the LLaMA-2 model over the LLaMA-1, we do not observe any performance advantage of the former model in the ScienceQA benchmark. This may be due to the effect of larger pretraining data or a different dataset mix used to pretrain LLaMA-2. For example, LLaMA-2 authors reported an increase in toxicity of the new models with more than 7B parameters (Touvron et al., 2023b). It remains as a future work to reason this performance difference with more empirical results. We use the LLaMA-1 as the base language decoder model in the rest of the experiments unless explicitly mentioned.

D Visual Grounded Task Performance

Table 8 shows a few generated captions for the SciCap images used to test the model performance on visual grounded tasks. We report the gold-standard captions as they appeared in the arXiv articles used to collect SciCap dataset, and the captions generated from the BLIP and LLaMA-SciTune (13B, CTOM) models for the comparisons.

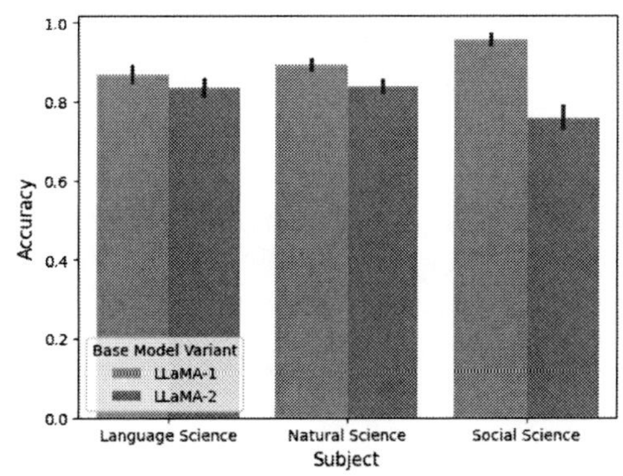

Figure 2: ScienceQA Performance of the LLaMA-SciTune models with LLaMA-1 and LLaMA-2 as the base language decoder models

E ScienceQA Chain of Thought Reasoning Examples

Figures 3 and 4 show a few answers, lectures and solutions generated by LLaMA-SciTune (13B, CTOM) for ScienceQA test instances.

Table 8: A Sample of Generated Captions. We highlight the gold standard caption in red, and generated captions from the BLIP (Li et al., 2022) model in gray. LLaMA-SciTune model first generates the figure types followed with the captions colored in blue.

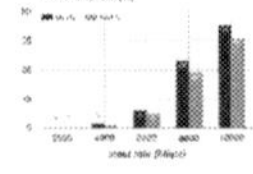

Packet drop rate
a chart of a bar chart with a number of different items
Bar Chart Packet drop rate for each method.

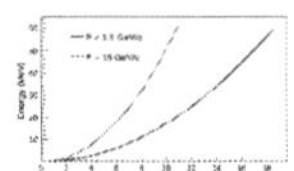

The kinetic energy of the recoil protons as a function of the recoil angle at beam momenta P=1.5 and 15 GeV/c, blue and red, respectively.
a plot of a curve with a blue line and a red line.
Graph Plot The angular distribution of the electron recoil spectrum in the 1.5 GeV/c and 15 GeV/c electron beams.

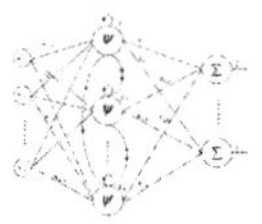

Artificial neural network structure.
a diagram of a network with several different paths.
Node Diagram The generative neural network.

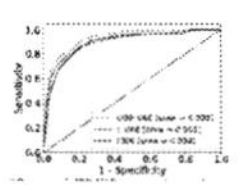

ROC curves of cIBP-VAE in comparison to alternative models on the clinical ECG data set.
a plot of the average and average time of a cell phone.
Graph Plot ROC curves of c-VAE, CNN, and c-VAE+CNN on the cerebellar atrophy dataset.

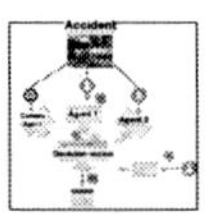

Functional architecture of the developed prototype.
a diagram of a camera and a person on a phone.
Node Diagram An overview of the system architecture of the proposed method.

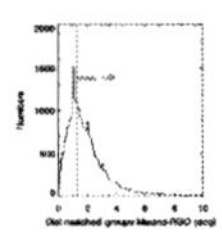

Distance between matched groups in Madrid and RGO catalogs (bins of 0.1 degrees). The red line represents the mean value.
a plot of a line of data with a red line and a white line.
Graph Plot Distance correlation between groups matched by Madrid RGO.

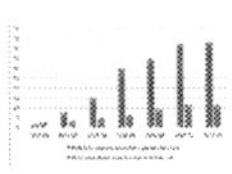

Comparison of penetration rate of mobile broadband subscribers with that of fixed broadband subscribers.
a chart of the number of people who are using the internet.
Bar Chart The average rate of mobile broadband subcribers and fixed broadband subscribers for each quarter (in thousands).

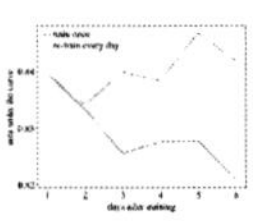

Model staleness of the one-off trained model vs. the model retrained every day.
a diagram of a graph with a line graph and a line graph.
Graph Plot Prediction accuracy of model trained once and fine-tuned every day.

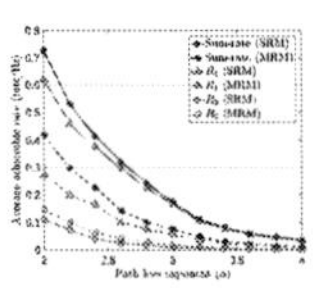

Comparison of the effect of the path loss exponent α on rates achieved by both transmitters, M = 4.
a plot of a line graph with a blue line and red line.
Graph Plot The sum-rate and sum-rate of RRM-RRM with respect to the path loss exponent γ for the two cases: $\gamma = 2$ and $\gamma = 3$.

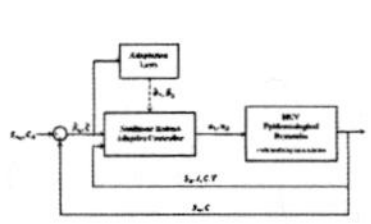

Conceptual diagram of nonlinear adaptive method developed to control the HCV epidemic in the existence of uncertainties on parameters of the model.
a diagram of a block diagram of a nuclear system.
Node Diagram Block diagram of the proposed non-linear SIR epidemic model with adaptive controllers.

Problem

Question: Which ocean is highlighted?

Context: N/A

Options: (A) the Indian Ocean (B) the Atlantic Ocean (C) the Pacific Ocean (D) the Southern Ocean

Ground-truth: (A)

Ground-truth Rationale: LECTURE: Oceans are huge bodies of salt water. The world has five oceans. All of the oceans are connected, making one world ocean. SOLUTION: This is the Indian Ocean.

Answer: (A)

Explanation: LECTURE: Oceans are huge bodies of salt water. The world has five oceans. All of the oceans are connected, making one world ocean. SOLUTION: This is the Indian Ocean

(a) An example with right answer and right explanation

Problem

Question: Which property matches this object ?

Context: Select the better answer.

Options: (A) transparent (B) bouncy

Ground-truth: (A)

Ground-truth Rationale: LECTURE/SOLUTION: An object has different properties. A property of an object can tell you how it looks, feels, tastes, or smells. Properties can also tell you how an object will behave when something happens to it.

Answer: (B)

Explanation: LECTURE: An object has different properties. A property of an object can tell you how it looks, feels, tastes, or smells. Properties can also tell you how an object will behave when something happens to it. SOLUTION: Look at the object.

(b) An example with incorrect answer and incorrect explanation

Figure 3: Two Multimodal QA examples with answer and explanation generated by LLaMA-SciTune

Problem

Question: How long is a hiking trail?

Context: Select the best

None

Options: (A) 4 meters (B) 4 millimeters (C) 4 kilometers (D) 4 centimeters

Ground-truth: (c)

Ground-truth Rationale: LECTURE: Measurements are written with both a number and a unit. The unit comes after the number. The unit shows what the number means. When you are using metric units, length can be written with units of millimeters, centimeters, meters, or kilometers. One meter contains 100 centimeters or 1,000 millimeters. So, 1 meter is larger than 1 centimeter, and 1 centimeter is larger than 1 millimeter. The tip of the pencil shown here is only 1 millimeter wide, but the pencil is about 16 centimeters long. A red fox is about 1 meter long. The Sydney Harbour Bridge in Australia is about 1,000 meters, or 1 kilometer, in length. SOLUTION: The best estimate for the length of a hiking trail is 4 kilometers. 4 millimeters, 4 centimeters, and 4 meters are all too short.

Answer: (c)

Explanation: LECTURE: Measurements are written with both a number and a unit. The unit comes after the number. The unit shows what the number means. When you are using metric units, length can be written with units of millimeters, centimeters, meters, or kilometers. One meter contains 100 centimeters or 1,000 millimeters. So, 1 meter is larger than 1 centimeter, and 1 centimeter is larger than 1 millimeter. The tip of the pencil shown here is only 1 millimeter wide, but the pencil is about 16 centimeters long. A red fox is about 1 meter long. The Sydney Harbour Bridge in Australia is about 1,000 meters, or 1 kilometer, in length. SOLUTION: The best estimate for the length of a hiking trail is 4 kilometers. 4 millimeters, 4 centimeters, and 4 meters are all too short.

(a) An example with right answer and right explanation

Problem

Question: Would you find the word bruise on a dictionary page with the following guide words? Blush-buffalo

Context: N/A

None

Options: (A) no (B) yes

Ground-truth: (B)

Ground-truth Rationale: LECTURE: Guide words appear on each page of a dictionary. They tell you the first word and last word on the page. The other words on the page come between the guide words in alphabetical order. To put words in alphabetical order, put them in order by their first letters. If the first letters are the same, look at the second letters. If the second letters are the same, look at the third letters, and so on. If one word is shorter, and there are no more letters to compare, then the shorter word comes first in alphabetical order. For example, becomes before bed. SOLUTION: Put the words in alphabetical order. Since bruise is between the guide words blush - buffalo, it would be found on that page.

Answer: (A)

Explanation: LECTURE: Guide words appear on each page of a dictionary. They tell you the first word and last word on the page. The other words on the page come between the guide words in alphabetical order. To put words in alphabetical order, put them in order by their first letters. If the first letters are the same, look at the second letters. If the second letters are the same, look at the third letters, and so on. If one word is shorter, and there are no more letters to compare, then the shorter word comes first in alphabetical order. For example, becomes before bed. SOLUTION: Put the words in alphabetical order. Since bruise is not between the guide words blush - buffalo, it would not be found on that page

(b) An example with incorrect answer and incorrect explanation

Figure 4: Two Unimodal QA examples with answer and explanation generated by LLaMA-SciTune

RACER: An LLM-powered Methodology for Scalable Analysis of Semi-structured Mental Health Interviews

Satpreet H Singh[1*]
Baylor College of Medicine
satpreetsingh@gmail.com

Kevin Jiang[1]
Baylor College of Medicine,
(Houston, TX)

Kanchan Bhasin[2]
Rice University
(Houston, TX)

Ashutosh Sabharwal[2†]
Rice University

Nidal Moukaddam[1†]
Baylor College of Medicine

Ankit B Patel[1,2†]
Baylor College of Medicine
Rice University

Abstract

Semi-structured interviews (SSIs) are a commonly employed data-collection method in healthcare research, offering in-depth qualitative insights into subject experiences. Despite their value, manual analysis of SSIs is notoriously time-consuming and labor-intensive, in part due to the difficulty of extracting and categorizing emotional responses, and challenges in scaling human evaluation for large populations. In this study, we develop RACER, a Large Language Model (LLM) based expert-guided automated pipeline that efficiently converts raw interview transcripts into insightful domain-relevant themes and sub-themes. We used RACER to analyze SSIs conducted with 93 healthcare professionals and trainees to assess the broad personal and professional mental health impacts of the COVID-19 crisis. RACER achieves moderately high agreement with two human evaluators (72%), which approaches the human inter-rater agreement (77%). Interestingly, LLMs and humans struggle with similar content involving nuanced emotional, ambivalent/dialectical, and psychological statements. Our study highlights the opportunities and challenges in using LLMs to improve research efficiency and opens new avenues for scalable analysis of SSIs in healthcare research.

1 Introduction

Semi-structured interviews (SSIs) are a widely used qualitative research method in healthcare research that provide an in-depth understanding of subjects' experiences in their own words (Adams, 2010). SSIs require interviewers to ask pre-specified 'root' questions, along with the option to ask follow-up questions to gain clarity on the interviewee's responses. This flexibility is a key characteristic of SSIs, allowing for a more dynamic and responsive data collection process, especially in areas where exploratory forays are needed. The adaptability of SSIs is particularly beneficial in exploring complex or sensitive topics such as mental health. SSIs allow rapport building between interviewer and subject and facilitate candid responses on sensitive matters. The open-ended nature of follow-up questions gives subjects the freedom to reflect on experiences and articulate thoughts without judgement. This helps reveal the nuances, contradictions, and diversity of perspectives that traditional fixed quantitative surveys may overlook. However, the traditional manual analysis of these interviews is a time-consuming and resource-intensive process. The advent of Large Language Models (LLMs), such as GPT-4 (Lee et al., 2023b,a,e), offers a novel and efficient method to extract and interpret data from such text corpora. Yet, the validity of LLMs in analyzing emotional states may be limited in circumstances where participants express multiple emotions or conflicting (dialectical) states.

As a case-study, we leveraged data from SSIs, conducted during the peak of the COVID-19 crisis in 2020, to understand the mental well-being of 93 healthcare professionals and trainees. The COVID-19 pandemic brought to the forefront profound personal and professional challenges experienced by healthcare workers. Fear of infecting family members, grief over patient deaths, moral dilemmas in resource allocation, and anxieties about professional preparedness collectively introduced a heightened level of psychological complexity and stress in the lives of healthcare professionals. The stigma surrounding the pursuit of mental health support exacerbated these challenges, leaving healthcare workers hesitant to openly discuss their difficulties or seek assistance.

In this paper, we developed **RACER**, an expert-guided automated pipeline that **R**etrieved responses to about 40 questions per SSI, **A**ggregated responses to each question across all subjects, **C**lustered these responses for each question into insightful domain-relevant **E**xpert-guided themes (Lee et al., 2023c), and finally **Re**-clustered

Proceedings of the 1st Workshop on NLP for Science (NLP4Science), pages 73–98
November 16, 2024 ©2024 Association for Computational Linguistics

responses to produce a robust result. Human evaluation on a subset of the total population revealed moderately high agreement (McHugh, 2012) between humans and RACER outputs, and similarities between inter-human disagreement and human-machine disagreement. We summarize our findings from applying RACER to our SSI-survey on the experiences of healthcare professionals and trainees during COVID-19, to reveal the power of this approach. Our results demonstrate both the capabilities and the limitations leveraging LLMs to efficiently process and extract insights from a large corpus of SSIs.

Related Work

Our research is related to a growing body of research that applies state-of-the-art and open-source LLMs to medical (Clusmann et al., 2023; Shah et al., 2023a) and psychological text corpora (Stade et al., 2024), with the most common and related applications being in mental health chatbots (Lee et al., 2023a) and medical evidence summarization and documentation (Tang et al., 2023a; Wornow et al., 2023a; Shah et al., 2023b). This literature reports broad improvements in performance over previous methods using classic Natural Language Processing (NLP) techniques in such domains (Raveau et al., 2023) Our research is most similar to very recent work assessing the use of LLMs in psychiatric mental health assessment (Kjell et al., 2024) and thematic analysis more broadly (Dai et al., 2023; Lee et al., 2023d; Stefano De Paoli, 2023), where the authors produce one-off examples of LLMs applied to specific use-cases replacing traditional research methods. In contrast, we present an expert-guided, reliable, and scalable methodology for SSI analysis, and an end-to-end case study applying our methodology to a real-world dataset, to demonstrate the efficacy of our methods for mental-health and burnout related SSIs. Furthermore, our analyses reveal intriguing similarities between inter-human disagreement and the self-consistency of LLM outputs.

2 Results

Recruitment and interview of a diverse sample of healthcare professionals and trainees

Healthcare professionals and trainees across different specialties and career stages were recruited via snowball sampling method (Goodman, 1961),

Characteristic	Percentage
Gender	
Male	54.84%
Female	45.16%
Age Group	
22-33 years	39.78%
34-45 years	32.26%
46-60 years	16.13%
61+ years	5.38%
Unclear/Excluded	6.45%
Healthcare Professional/Student Type (non-exclusive membership)	
Physicians	54.84%
Medical Students	21.51%
Nurses	8.60%
Residents	7.53%
Other Professionals	12.90%
Unclear/Excluded	1.08%
Location	
Houston, Texas	44.09%
Other Texas	21.50%
Florida	10.75%
Mid-West US	13.98%
Other US	5.38%
Unclear/Excluded	4.30%
Marital Status	
Not married	41.94%
Married	52.69%
Unclear/Excluded	5.37%
Have Kids?	
Yes	51.61%
No	45.16%
Unclear/Excluded	3.23%
Specialty Area (non-exclusive membership)	
Emergency Medicine	26.88%
Psychiatry	16.13%
Pulmonary Critical Care	16.13%
Internal Medicine	11.83%
Neurology/Neurocritical Care	5.38%
Surgery/ER	5.38%
Pediatrics	5.38%
Other Specialties	17.22%
Unclear/Excluded	2.15%
Years of Practice (Non-students)	
Under 15 Years	71.23%
15-30 Years	20.55%
Over 30 Years	5.48%
Unclear/Excluded	2.74%

Table 1: Demographic Characteristics of the Study Population. Note that some categories are non-exclusive. e.g. practicing faculty are categorized under both Physicians and Other Professionals.

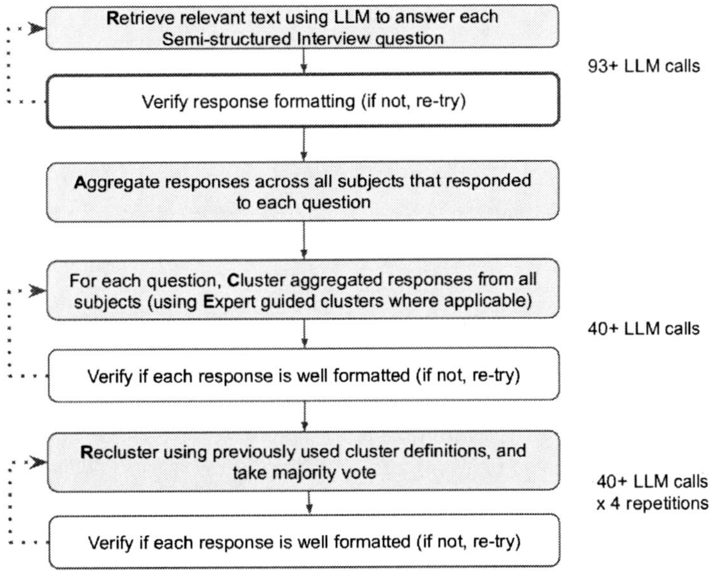

Figure 1: **Stages of the RACER (Retrieve, Aggregate, Cluster with Expert guidance, and Re-cluster) Semi-Structured Interview (SSI) processing pipeline:** First, **R**etrieve relevant responses to each SSI question. **A**ggregate responses across subjects before **C**lustering them into themes (and subthemes) defined by **E**xperts. To assess robustness, **Re**-cluster multiple times and make assignments by majority vote. The pipeline efficiently and robustly converts SSI text into meaningful themes.

described as follows. The investigators asked colleagues if they knew of anyone willing to participate in interviews about their COVID-19 experiences. Announcements were also posted online and through professional networks. Participation was voluntary with no compensation provided. Approval was obtained from the Baylor College of Medicine (Houston, TX) Institutional Review Board. The interviews were performed by a team of two research coordinators with healthcare backgrounds, and a third-year medical student, under the supervision of the investigators.

The study population of healthcare professionals and trainees consisted of 93 subjects (51 male, 42 female) with diverse demographics (Table 1). Subjects were from 22 years to over 61 years in age, and were located predominantly in Texas. Over half were married and had children. Most subjects had no care-taking responsibilities in addition to child-care. Professionally, the sample included physicians, medical students, nurses, residents and other healthcare professionals. Subjects trained at multiple institutions, with prominent representation from Baylor College of Medicine and University of Texas systems. Various specialties were represented in the cohort, with emergency medicine, psychiatry and pulmonary/critical care among the most common.

SSIs were conducted over videoconferencing using a standard template consisting of a total of 41 questions, including four questions that were only asked to students, and seven questions that were asked to only non-students. Questions were either *factual*, concerning demographics and personal and professional background, or *open ended*, where interviewees were asked to talk about their experiences during the COVID-19 pandemic, focusing on their exposure to the virus, work impacts, emotional responses, future outlooks, and coping strategies. Interviewees discussed how they had practiced in high-risk areas, their concerns for personal and family safety, and modifications made to their routines. They also reflected on the physical toll the crisis had taken. The impact on their work included changes in working hours, shifts in patient care quality, and altered management approaches. Emotional and psychological questions revealed how the crisis affected them emotionally, the level of support they received, family dynamics, and changes in burnout levels. Looking ahead, they pondered the crisis's short-term and long-term impacts on their careers and specialty choices. Finally, they shared their openness to seeking help for burnout or mental overwhelm and identified potential obstacles in obtaining this help. Students were not asked clinical-practice related questions, and were instead asked about how their training was being affected by pandemic-related changes. Interviews lasted on average 26.7 +/- 8.9 s.d. minutes. When transcribed from raw interview audio into text transcripts (using Otter.AI(Otter.ai, 2023)), were on average 4044.30 +/- 1348.34 s.d. words long.

RACER extracts relevant interviewee responses and robustly clusters them

We developed an LLM-based automated pipeline called **RACER** (Figure 1) that converts a corpus of text SSI transcripts into insightful themes per interview question. RACER, consists of four stages, **R**etrieve, **A**ggregate, **C**luster with **E**xpert guidance, and **R**ecluster:

Retrieve: We first structured interview transcripts by using an LLM (OpenAI's GPT-4(Lee et al., 2023b)) to *retrieve* relevant SSI text in response to each of the questions in the interview template. (See Appendix A for LLM prompt details) To avoid LLM 'hallucinations' (Tonmoy et al., 2024), we asked the LLM to provide 'evidence' in the form of text quoted verbatim from the transcript, to back up its response to each question. LLM outputs missing either answers or backing evidence to any question were automatically detected and re-run.

Aggregate: For each question, we then aggregated the retrieved responses across all subjects who were asked that question.

Cluster with Expert guidance: We then asked the LLM to *semantically cluster* the responses into primary and secondary clusters ('themes' and 'sub-themes'). For most questions, we provided the LLM expert-guidance in the form of primary-cluster definitions. These definitions were derived through a combination of theoretical foundations from burnout literature and practical insights from ongoing research during the COVID-19 pandemic (Moukaddam et al., 2022; Innstrand, 2022; Edú-Valsania et al., 2022). The primary clusters were selected on the basis of well-established symptom categories of burnout, such as emotional exhaustion, depersonalization/detachment, and cynicism, as well as factors exacerbated by the pandemic, like involvement with COVID-19 patients, fear of spreading the disease, and COVID-19 induced stress. This process involved expert review of early LLM experiments, where we observed that the LLM's autonomous clustering could be too variable or too fine-grained for statistical analysis. We then designed a few primary clusters per question such that clusters were mutually exclusive and collectively exhaustive.

For questions where primary clusters were not derived from expert-guidance, we allowed the LLM to autonomously discover primary clusters. In these cases, the LLM's discovered clusters were reviewed by experts to ensure they were meaningful and useful for subsequent analysis.

The LLM discovered secondary clusters (or subthemes) automatically. Expert-provided cluster definitions were always mutually exclusive and collectively exhaustive, while those discovered by the LLM were not constrained to be so. Similar to before, invalid LLM responses, e.g. those missing cluster assignments for any subjects, were automatically re-run.

This approach thus leveraged the strengths of both expert knowledge and LLM capabilities. See Supplementary Tables 2 and 3 for expert-guided and LLM-discovered primary clusters respectively.

Re-Cluster: Leveraging the probabilistic nature of LLMs, we assessed the *robustness* of the clustering process by re-running it four more times, employing the same cluster definitions and validation criteria as in the initial step. We used a majority vote over 5 runs to assign subjects to clusters, to get robust cluster assignments for all downstream processing. The number of votes (3, 4 or 5 out of total 5 LLM calls) additionally provided a synthetic measure of LLM *self-consistency* (Kompa et al., 2021; Tanneru et al., 2023) that we have quantified as a 'self-concordance score'. Only a very small fraction of subject-question pairs (12 out of 3342, 0.36%) had no 'self-concordant' cluster assignments after applying the majority voting process.

All together, we found that RACER was able to take unstructured transcriptions and extract relevant and insightful, clustered responses in a robust manner for downstream human analysis.

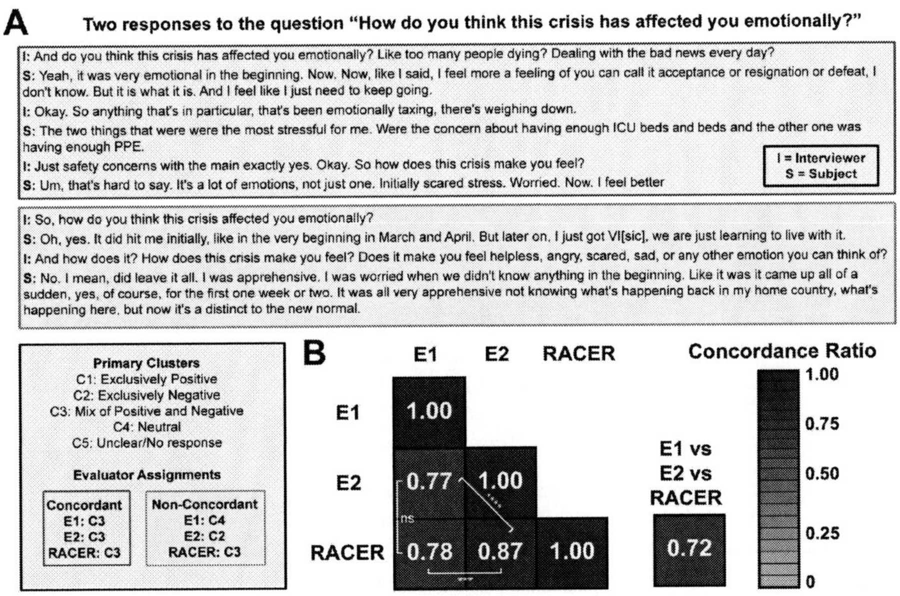

Figure 2: **Human-RACER approaches resembles human-human disagreement:** (A) Transcript segments from two different subjects being asked "How do you think this [COVID-19] crisis has affected you emotionally?". Responses were evaluated as either all concordant or all non-concordant between both evaluators and RACER, demonstrating the ambiguity that exists in parsing free responses. (B) The concordance ratio calculated between evaluator pairs, and between RACER and both evaluators simultaneously. Chi-squared test with Yates continuity correction between the three different evaluator pairings showed human evaluator concordance did not differ from evaluator one's concordance with RACER. * $p < 0.5$, ** $p < 0.01$, *** $p < 0.001$, **** $p < 0.0001$.

Human-machine disagreement approaches inter-human disagreement

To validate the output of running RACER on our SSI dataset, two human evaluators cross-checked the resulting cluster assignments for 20 randomly-selected subjects across 28 open ended questions (See Figure 2A for an example). Using the same cluster definitions as were previously used by RACER, each human evaluator (E1 and E2) independently read the raw transcript file and assigned each subject's answers to the primary clusters. Evaluator cluster assignments were then compared to RACER's robust cluster assignments. To quantify agreement, we defined a *concordance score* and a *concordance ratio* as follows: If the clusters for a given subject-question pair matched exactly (for mutually exclusive clusters), or matched partially (for mutually non-exclusive clusters) they were assigned a concordance score of 1. Conversely, mismatch was assigned a concordance score of 0. The overall concordance ratio is the proportion of matched subject-question pairs between evaluators.

We observed a concordance ratio of 78% (E1) and 87% (E2) between each of the human evaluators and RACER, and a 77% (E1-E2) inter-rater concordance ratio (Figure 2B). When the two human evaluators and RACER were compared simultaneously, there was only a small decrease in the concordance ratio (72%), indicating that across the majority of subject-question pairings, cluster assignments produced by humans and RACER were all in agreement. (See Appendix A for additional details)

Machine "confusion" resembles human confusion

We examined the self-concordance produced by RACER per subject-question pair to see how it might affect the subject-question pair's inter-rater concordance (Figure 3).

Amongst the 443 subject-question pair sample evaluated by humans, 392 (87.7%) had a self-concordance of 1 (5 of 5 repeated primary clusters), which was not different proportionally to that of the whole population: 88.2% (1852 of 2099 subject-question pairs), thus RACER's self-

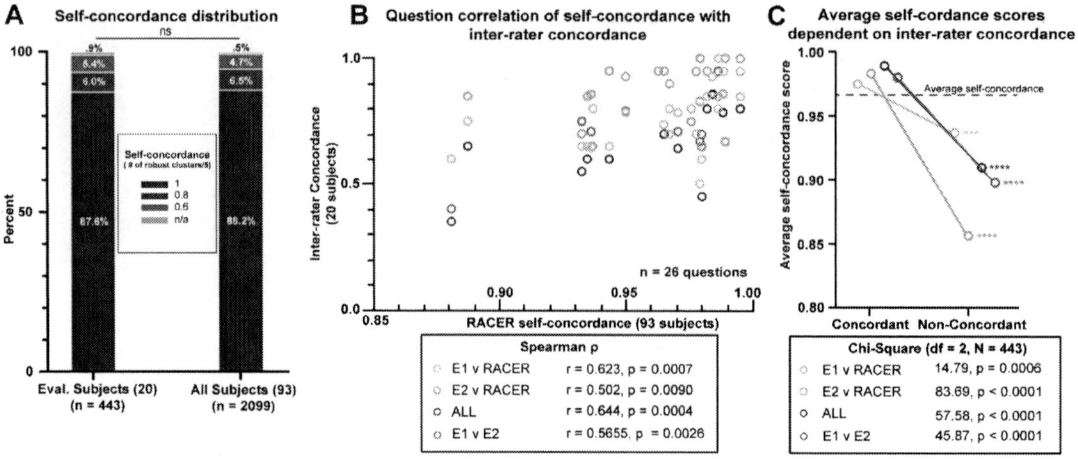

Figure 3: **RACER "self-concordance" correlates with inter-evaluator concordance and reveals areas of human disagreement:** (A) Distribution of the proportion of subject-question pair self-concordance, calculated as the fraction of identical primary cluster assignments across five runs. The self-concordance for the subject-question pairs reviewed by human evaluators (20 subjects) were not significantly different from those for all subject-question pairs (93 subjects), as determined by a Chi-squared test. (B) Average RACER self-concordance for each question (n = 93) show a significant correlation with the concordance between evaluator pairs for the same questions (n = 20), using Spearman Rank correlation. (C) Comparison of RACER self-concordance within concordant versus non-concordant subject-question pairs between human evaluators. The Chi-squared test indicates significant differences in the distribution of self-concordance between these groups. Correlation significance: * $p < 0.05$, ** $p < 0.01$, *** $p < 0.001$, **** $p < 0.0001$.

concordance across the evaluated 20 subjects was representative of its general performance in primary cluster assignment. When RACER's average self-concordance across all subjects for a given question was correlated with the question's inter-rater concordance from the 20 human evaluated subjects, there was a significant and positive correlation between self- and inter-rater concordance. Additionally, we observed that the self-concordance of subject-question pairs that had inter-rater concordance were higher than those that did not regardless of the rater pair compared: human evaluators or RACER.

Interestingly, when we juxtaposed RACER self-concordance against human-human inter-rater concordance, we observed that RACER self-concordance was lower when humans were non-concordant. This suggests that areas where RACER was less self-concordant or 'confused' were also areas where human evaluators tended to disagree. Thus the RACER self-concordance generated via repeated clustering could also serve as an indicator of ambiguity or difficulty of understanding the semi-structured interview and parsing human free-responses.

3 Insights using RACER on healthcare worker experience during COVID-19

We summarize RACER-derived insights from analyzing our 93-subject SSI corpus in Appendix B.

4 Discussion

Summary

Our study demonstrates the utility of RACER for efficiently analyzing semi-structured interviews (SSIs), particularly those exploring complex mental health topics within the healthcare domain. We introduce a novel approach by employing RACER to analyze emotions and psychological behaviors, opening new possibilities for exploration in mental health. By providing expert-guided constraints and using automated response validation steps, RACER accurately extracts and robustly clusters relevant responses from interview transcripts. Automating these laborious manual tasks significantly enhances the scalability of SSI analysis. The inter-rater agreement between LLM-assigned clusters and human expert clusters further bolsters our claims. The automated pipeline achieved moderately high concordance compared with manual evaluation by human annotators. The overall concordance ratio of

0.72 for RACER versus both human evaluators approaches the 0.77 concordance ratio between the two human evaluators.

The robust semantically clustered summary of the SSI corpus is useful to researchers in multiple ways: Clusters reveal common themes and experiences across the population, allowing identification of major issues and concerns. The quantitative breakdowns by cluster provide an overview of the distribution of different sentiments and impacts. These could potentially be used for clinical applications such as early burnout detection, and operational improvements through triage of targeted interventions and support. Since semi-structured textual data has been converted to structured data, comparisons between subgroups (e.g. by demographics or professions) can be used to identify disparities and facilitate equitable allocation of resources. RACER also enables large-scale, multi-site analyses of SSIs by providing a consistent and reproducible methodology for extracting insights from free-text responses, reducing inconsistencies arising from inherent variability between human evaluators across different sites.

Limitations

Our findings reveal both the promises and current pitfalls of LLMs for SSI analysis. We found that when RACER struggled with robust clustering, both humans and machines were more likely to be non-concordant, suggesting shared limitations in handling complex emotions or psychologically nuanced statements (Boag et al., 2021) or ambiguity of the underlying SSI. This underscores the indispensable role of human expertise in reviewing and interpreting LLM outputs, where RACER's self-concordance can guide expert scrutiny.

While RACER provided evidence in the form of quoting relevant interview text to support its response in the Retrieval step, the underlying methodology remains opaque. In contrast, human evaluators were able to describe their techniques, even if subjective. For instance, humans considered different amounts of contextual information outside the question scope, and inferred subject intentions to varying degrees, i.e. whether the subject needed to explicitly say certain phrases, or if they could be inferred from previous statements or knowledge of the subject matter. An LLM's ability to consider large amount of contextual information can be a double-edged sword; beneficial if relevant information appears elsewhere in the transcript, but misleading if the research is indeed directed towards a narrow window of text around the question.

We demonstrated that LLMs can help discover knowledge by automatically extracting themes and topics from subject responses. However, good performance requires clear, mutually exclusive category definitions. We found it highly useful to involve domain experts early to precisely define mutually exclusive thematic clusters. For certain questions, where succinct mutually exclusive categorization was not possible, we chose to use LLM-discovered clusters. However, validation of such non-exclusive categorization is challenging. Our results showed higher LLM accuracy and inter-rater agreement for questions with non-overlapping expert-defined clusters versus those allowing multiple clusters.

Additionally, human evaluators exhibited biases, such as default cluster tendencies requiring countering evidence (e.g. starting from a default of 'no' and requiring evidence to switch to a 'yes', or vice versa). Thus, expert human analysis also demonstrates cognitive variability and individual biases. Rather than definitive classifications, both human and machine outputs should be considered informed yet inherently biased perspectives on complex qualitative responses (Atari et al., 2024). Thus, in the future, clearly delineating the parameters of evaluations with humans and RACER may improve concordance.

While RACER's cluster assignments may deviate slightly from human reviewers, RACER was internally consistent and demonstrated high clustering repeatability for most questions. Furthermore, unlike humans, RACER was able to efficiently process an extensive dataset of 93 subjects and can scale to significantly larger data set sizes that would otherwise be infeasible for human evaluators to handle.

Future work

For researchers undertaking projects in this emerging domain, both optimism and caution are warranted (Badal et al., 2023; Dash et al.; Chiu et al., 2024; Tang et al., 2023b; Wornow et al., 2023b; Shah et al., 2023b). With appropriate constraints and validation, LLMs can accelerate knowledge extraction from SSIs. We implemented safeguards against hallucination risks like requiring verbatim textual evidence for an answer, which constrained the LLM to mostly avoid fabricating content. While this is already an area of active research, the possibility of a few false positives remains and needs to be accounted for in downstream use.

While evaluation of LLM outputs through comparison to multiple human raters is helpful, inter-rater agreement must also be looked at to assess inherent ambiguity. To further improve performance, we recommend specialized training for both SSI interviewers and human evaluators.

We found it useful to generate an ensemble of LLM clustering outputs from repeated runs, and used it to extract robust cluster assignments and to get a measure of model uncertainty. Future work exploring this direction could produce useful methods that help build trust in LLM-assisted analyses and inform human-in-the-loop processes for high-stakes applications (Bienefeld et al., 2023).

References

Eike Adams. 2010. The joys and challenges of semi-structured interviewing. *Community Practitioner*, 83(7):18–22.

Mohammad Atari, Mona J. Xue, Peter S. Park, Damián Blasi, and Joseph Henrich. 2024. Which Humans? Publisher: OSF.

Kimberly Badal, Carmen M. Lee, and Laura J. Esserman. 2023. Guiding principles for the responsible development of artificial intelligence tools for healthcare. *Communications Medicine*, 3(1):47.

Nadine Bienefeld, Jens Michael Boss, Rahel Lüthy, Dominique Brodbeck, Jan Azzati, Mirco Blaser, Jan Willms, and Emanuela Keller. 2023. Solving the explainable AI conundrum by bridging clinicians' needs and developers' goals. *npj Digital Medicine*, 6(1):94.

William Boag, Olga Kovaleva, Thomas H. McCoy, Anna Rumshisky, Peter Szolovits, and Roy H. Perlis. 2021. Hard for humans, hard for machines: predicting readmission after psychiatric hospitalization using narrative notes. *Translational Psychiatry*, 11(1):1–6. Number: 1 Publisher: Nature Publishing Group.

Yu Ying Chiu, Ashish Sharma, Inna Wanyin Lin, and Tim Althoff. 2024. A Computational Framework for Behavioral Assessment of LLM Therapists. *arXiv preprint*. ArXiv:2401.00820 [cs].

Jan Clusmann, Fiona R. Kolbinger, Hannah Sophie Muti, Zunamys I. Carrero, Jan-Niklas Eckardt, Narmin Ghaffari Laleh, Chiara Maria Lavinia Löffler, Sophie-Caroline Schwarzkopf, Michaela Unger, Gregory P. Veldhuizen, Sophia J. Wagner, and Jakob Nikolas Kather. 2023. The future landscape of large language models in medicine. *Communications Medicine*, 3(1):141.

Shih-Chieh Dai, Aiping Xiong, and Lun-Wei Ku. 2023. Llm-in-the-loop: Leveraging large language model for thematic analysis. In *Findings of the Association for Computational Linguistics: EMNLP 2023*, pages 9993–10001.

Debadutta Dash, Rahul Thapa, Juan M Banda, Akshay Swaminathan, Mehr Kashyap, Nikesh Kotecha, Jonathan H Chen, Saurabh Gombar, Lance Downing, Rachel Pedreira, Ethan Goh, Angel Arnaout, Garret K Morris, Matthew P Lungren, Eric Horvitz, and Nigam H Shah. Evaluation of GPT-3.5 and GPT-4 for supporting real-world information needs in healthcare delivery.

Sergio Edú-Valsania, Ana Laguía, and Juan A Moriano. 2022. Burnout: A review of theory and measurement. *International journal of environmental research and public health*, 19(3):1780.

Leo A Goodman. 1961. Snowball sampling. *The annals of mathematical statistics*, pages 148–170.

Siw Tone Innstrand. 2022. Burnout among health care professionals during covid-19. *International Journal of Environmental Research and Public Health*, 19(18):11807.

Oscar N.E. Kjell, Katarina Kjell, and H. Andrew Schwartz. 2024. Beyond rating scales: With targeted evaluation, large language models are poised for psychological assessment. *Psychiatry Research*, 333:115667.

Benjamin Kompa, Jasper Snoek, and Andrew L Beam. 2021. Second opinion needed: communicating uncertainty in medical machine learning. *NPJ Digital Medicine*, 4(1):4.

Peter Lee, Sebastien Bubeck, and Joseph Petro. 2023a. Benefits, limits, and risks of gpt-4 as an ai chatbot for medicine. *New England Journal of Medicine*, 388(13):1233–1239.

Peter Lee, Carey Goldberg, and Isaac Kohane. 2023b. *The AI revolution in medicine: GPT-4 and beyond*. Pearson.

V. Vien Lee, Stephanie C. C. van der Lubbe, Lay Hoon Goh, and Jose M. Valderas. 2023c. Harnessing ChatGPT for thematic analysis: Are we ready? *arXiv preprint*. ArXiv:2310.14545 [cs].

V. Vien Lee, Stephanie C. C. van der Lubbe, Lay Hoon Goh, and Jose M. Valderas. 2023d. Harnessing ChatGPT for thematic analysis: Are we ready? *Preprint*, arxiv:2310.14545.

V Vien Lee, Stephanie CC van der Lubbe, Lay Hoon Goh, and Jose M Valderas. 2023e. Harnessing chatgpt for thematic analysis: Are we ready? *arXiv preprint arXiv:2310.14545*.

Mary L McHugh. 2012. Interrater reliability: the kappa statistic. *Biochemia medica*, 22(3):276–282.

Nidal Moukaddam, Vishwanath Saragadam, Mahsan Abbasi, Matt Barnett, Anil Kumar Vadathya, Ashok Veeraraghavan, and Ashutosh Sabharwal. 2022. Evolution of mood symptomatology through the covid-19 pandemic: findings from the covidsense longitudinal study. *Cureus*, 14(10).

Otter.ai. 2023. Otter.ai: Voice meeting notes transcription service. Accessed: 2023-12-10.

María P. Raveau, Julián I. Goñi, José F. Rodríguez, Isidora Paiva-Mack, Fernanda Barriga, María P. Hermosilla, Claudio Fuentes-Bravo, and Susana Eyheramendy. 2023. Natural language processing analysis of the psychosocial stressors of mental health disorders during the pandemic. *npj Mental Health Research*, 2(1):17.

Nigam H. Shah, David Entwistle, and Michael A. Pfeffer. 2023a. Creation and Adoption of Large Language Models in Medicine. *JAMA*, 330(9):866.

Nigam H. Shah, David Entwistle, and Michael A. Pfeffer. 2023b. Creation and Adoption of Large Language Models in Medicine. *JAMA*, 330(9):866.

Elizabeth C Stade, Shannon Wiltsey Stirman, Lyle H Ungar, Cody L Boland, H Andrew Schwartz, David B Yaden, João Sedoc, Robert J DeRubeis, Robb Willer, and Johannes C Eichstaedt. 2024. Large language models could change the future of behavioral healthcare: a proposal for responsible development and evaluation. *npj Mental Health Research*, 3(1):12.

Stefano De Paoli. 2023. Performing an Inductive Thematic Analysis of Semi-Structured Interviews With a Large Language Model: An Exploration and Provocation on the Limits of the Approach. *Social science computer review*.

Liyan Tang, Zhaoyi Sun, Betina Idnay, Jordan G. Nestor, Ali Soroush, Pierre A. Elias, Ziyang Xu, Ying Ding, Greg Durrett, Justin F. Rousseau, Chunhua Weng, and Yifan Peng. 2023a. Evaluating large language models on medical evidence summarization. *npj Digital Medicine*, 6(1):158.

Liyan Tang, Zhaoyi Sun, Betina Idnay, Jordan G. Nestor, Ali Soroush, Pierre A. Elias, Ziyang Xu, Ying Ding, Greg Durrett, Justin F. Rousseau, Chunhua Weng, and Yifan Peng. 2023b. Evaluating large language models on medical evidence summarization. *npj Digital Medicine*, 6(1):158.

Sree Harsha Tanneru, Chirag Agarwal, and Himabindu Lakkaraju. 2023. Quantifying uncertainty in natural language explanations of large language models. *arXiv preprint arXiv:2311.03533*.

SM Tonmoy, SM Zaman, Vinija Jain, Anku Rani, Vipula Rawte, Aman Chadha, and Amitava Das. 2024. A comprehensive survey of hallucination mitigation techniques in large language models. *arXiv preprint arXiv:2401.01313*.

Michael Wornow, Yizhe Xu, Rahul Thapa, Birju Patel, Ethan Steinberg, Scott Fleming, Michael A. Pfeffer, Jason Fries, and Nigam H. Shah. 2023a. The shaky foundations of large language models and foundation models for electronic health records. *npj Digital Medicine*, 6(1):135.

Michael Wornow, Yizhe Xu, Rahul Thapa, Birju Patel, Ethan Steinberg, Scott Fleming, Michael A. Pfeffer, Jason Fries, and Nigam H. Shah. 2023b. The shaky foundations of large language models and foundation models for electronic health records. *npj Digital Medicine*, 6(1):135.

APPENDICES

A Methods

Semi-structured interviews

Study was approved by the Baylor College of Medicine (Houston, TX) Institutional Review Board [Protocol H-47690]. Consent was obtained by reading the consent text and documenting approval to participate, as the interviews were virtual. All interviewees were adults. Interviewers were provided with a standard template to guide their discussions. The subjects were all healthcare professionals or trainees, including physicians, nurses, and medical students. The interviews followed a semi-structured format, where the interviewers were instructed to cover a previously decided list of questions, and were allowed to ask exploration questions if the 'root' question was not answered. The questions covered in the SSIs are listed in Appendices 2 and 3. Raw audio and video interview files were transcribed into text format using the Otter.AI transcription service (Otter.ai, 2023). Out of 100 interviews conducted, 7 were compromised due to data-corruption/loss issues, providing a total of 93 transcriptions for further processing. Voice to text transcription was carried out using Otter.AI(Otter.ai, 2023), which attempts to perform automated speaker diarization, but does not do so perfectly. To the best of our knowledge, this shortcoming did not seem to influence the subsequent processing steps.

RACER

We used the OpenAI GPT-4 LLM for all our work, except for prompts which exceeded GPT-4's limits, where we used GPT-4-32k.

Retrieval: In this step, the model was tasked with retrieving relevant responses for each question from a predefined list of questions (listed in Appendix E) from the transcript. The prompt for the LLM consisted of instructions and a template consisting of the aforementioned list of questions and what format each question's response should be in, followed by the entire SSI transcript. The full prompt is detailed in Appendix E.

LLM Response Validation for Retrieval: By asking the LLM to respond in a structured format, we could partially automate the process of verifying the LLM's response. The LLM is called once for each subject, and then the response is parsed using the Python Pandas library. The LLM's response is marked invalid if it is ill-formatted (not parsable in tab-separated-values format) or incomplete (wrong number of rows, i.e. questions, or columns, i.e. incomplete response). The LLM is called again on invalid responses till the LLM returns a valid response. We found that at most 4-5 (5%-6%) subjects would have invalid responses in the first attempt, and in total, we were making about 10% additional calls to get valid responses for all subjects. The most common issues were that the LLM would sometimes be incomplete (skip questions, end output before final question) and sometimes use the specified tab-delimiter incorrectly.

Cluster with Expert guidance: In this step, we employed a semantic clustering approach which grouped responses based on the underlying themes or sentiments ("semantic clusters") they conveyed.

Expert Guidance: In preliminary explorations, we found that the LLM is able to automatically generate interesting semantic clusters from a list of the subjects' responses without additional human guidance. We observed that these clusters could change between subsequent LLM calls, could be mutually non-exclusive (subjects could belong to multiple clusters), and could be too fine-grained for statistical analysis. However, in many cases (29 out of ≈40 questions, see Appendix C), we felt like it was important to exercise more control over the LLM's response to improve response robustness, to facilitate statistical analysis and for easier human evaluation. So, we provided expert guidance in the form of a list of primary clusters or "themes" (defined on a per-question basis), which were included in the prompt using a template (detailed in Appendix F). Secondary clusters or "sub-themes" were discovered automatically by the LLM. Each subject's response was mapped exclusively to one primary cluster and could furthermore be associated with one or more secondary clusters.

LLM Response Validation for Clustering: The LLM returned two lists in its response: one of the cluster labels and their definitions, and the other of the cluster-labels (single or two-level clustering) assigned to each subject. The LLM was called once for each of 40 questions, and these responses were parsed using the Python Pandas library. A LLM response is marked invalid if it was ill-formatted (not in tab-separated-values format) or incomplete. The LLM was called again on invalid responses till the LLM returned a valid response. We found that almost 20 questions would have invalid responses in the first attempt, and in total, we were making almost 80% additional calls to get valid responses for all questions. We suspect that the rate of invalid responses in this step is higher than in the previous step due to the added complexity of the task i.e. the response needs to first produce a valid clustering-schema, and then additionally assign each of 93 subjects to the clusters according to the clustering schema.

Recluster: We repeated the above clustering step four additional times using a prompt similar to the previous clustering prompt (detailed in Appendix G). In this reclustering step, we used the same cluster definitions as were used in the previous steps, that is, a mix of expert-defined and LLM-generated (but expert-reviewed) cluster definitions. As in the original clustering, any invalid LLM responses were automatically detected and re-processed until a valid response was obtained. For the final cluster assignments used in downstream analysis, we applied a majority vote rule based on the 5 clustering repetitions. That is, each subject was assigned to the cluster they most commonly belonged to across the trials. This approach helps make the cluster assignments robust to the occasional variability in the LLM outputs. In a few cases ($< 1\%$ of all subject-question pairs), this process failed to find any cluster assignments that passed the majority-vote.

Human evaluation of LLM responses

Our study employed human evaluation to verify the alignment between RACER-generated clusters and human interpretation, utilizing two independent evaluators who analyzed the responses of 20 randomly selected subjects from a pool of 93. Each evaluator individually reviewed the raw interview transcript files for the selected 20 subjects and used the same cluster definitions as RACER to assign subjects to clusters. Human evaluators spent approximately 30 minutes per subject on average for a comprehensive review and categorization of the responses. This time investment reflects the thoroughness and attention to detail applied by the evaluators in their analysis, and also highlights the limits of this process to scale to large study populations. To validate the semantic clustering results produced by the LLM, each human evaluator compared their assigned scores with those generated by the LLM. An inter-rater comparison was also conducted, involving a detailed examination of the scores and evaluations independently made by both human evaluators (E1 and E2) for the same set of subjects. Concordance scores of 1 were assigned to clusters that precisely matched or were sub- or super-sets of each other, while discrepancies received a concordance score of 0. The overall concordance ratio represented the proportion of clusters aligning between the evaluators.

Additionally, the evaluators' findings were juxtaposed with RACER's cluster assignments to gauge both inter-evaluator consistency and the degree of correspondence with the LLM's outcomes. We also compared the use of Cohen's kappa coefficient with our concordance score and found them to be similar. Due to the nature of the comparison across questions which varied in the number of possible clusters as well as probability of different cluster assignment across questions, the concordance scores were used as they better described the intended comparisons. Instances where RACER did not produce any robust cluster assignments were categorized as 'mismatch' during the evaluation process.

B Insights using RACER on healthcare worker experience during COVID-19

Here we summarize the insights gleaned from analyzing SSIs with 93 subjects using RACER.

COVID-19 exposure, response, work impact and work changes:

The vast majority of practicing healthcare professionals reported having professional contact with COVID-19 patients in the past two months. Most subjects expressed safety concerns for themselves and loved ones, especially regarding viral exposure risks. Common protective measures adopted included heightened hygiene practices, using personal protective equipment, limiting travel and social interactions, and modifying routines at work and home to minimize transmission risks. Over half of the subjects reported physical tolls from the crisis, frequently citing exhaustion, disturbed sleep, and dietary changes (Figure 4).

Most subjects felt personally prepared to handle the pandemic, attributing this largely to their medical knowledge, experience, and ability to adapt. Assessment of institutional preparedness was more varied, with around 60% expressing their hospital/unit was prepared, but around 25% felt improvements were still needed.

Working hours markedly increased for most subjects during the pandemic, with over 80% reporting working more than 40 hours per week compared to pre-COVID times. For many, this resulted from escalations in patient load and administrative duties. Approaches to patient management also evolved, with the vast majority of practicing healthcare professionals stating their methods differed from usual practices. This included increased reliance on technology, more precautions with patients, and adjustments to treatments due to COVID-19. Most still felt capable of handling the situation professionally, though some desired more protections and support systems.

Among students and trainees, the majority believed they adhered closely to the Hippocratic oath during the pandemic. Their views on their educational institution's policies regarding medical students' roles during that time were divided, with half in agreement and others expressing mixed or negative sentiments, reflecting a spectrum of perspectives on the adequacy and effectiveness of institutional responses to the crisis.

Emotional and psychological impact, and support and coping strategies

The COVID-19 crisis negatively affected the emotional state of most subjects, with many reporting feelings of anxiety, stress, sadness, or anger. However, around 25% indicated a mix of both positive emotions like gratitude as well as negative feelings. Despite those challenges, the overwhelming majority felt supported by peers and family, suggesting strong social networks within and outside the workplace. Family dynamics had been affected for some, with around a quarter reporting increased family problems during the pandemic. This data underscored the profound emotional and psychological effects of the crisis on healthcare professionals, juxtaposed with the resilience and support systems that helped them navigate these challenges.

In regards to burnout, over 60% of subjects assessed their pre-pandemic burnout as low or mild. When asked about current burnout, around 40% still reported mild or no burnout, but the percentage reporting severe burnout rose from around 15% pre-pandemic to 20% during the crisis. If feeling burned out, nearly 90% stated they would seek help, with most mentioning professional resources like counseling. Over 60% also reported they would seek professional help if feeling mentally overwhelmed, with therapists and workplace programs being commonly cited options. However, around 45% still anticipated obstacles in getting help, including logistical barriers and stigma concerns (Figure 5).

Future considerations and professional outlook

When asked about near-term impacts, over 50% expressed concerns about anticipated difficulties, health risks, economic instability, and significant lifestyle changes. However, around 15% hoped for new opportunities and growth resulting from the crisis. Looking 5 years ahead, around 20% expected advancements in healthcare practices and systems due to learned lessons. Though nearly 10% feared lingering personal and professional impact. Among non-students considering job changes, around 15% expressed an immediate willingness to switch fields while around 18% would change contingent on worsening conditions.

Regarding effects on career plans, 35% of students reported the crisis has impacted their spe-

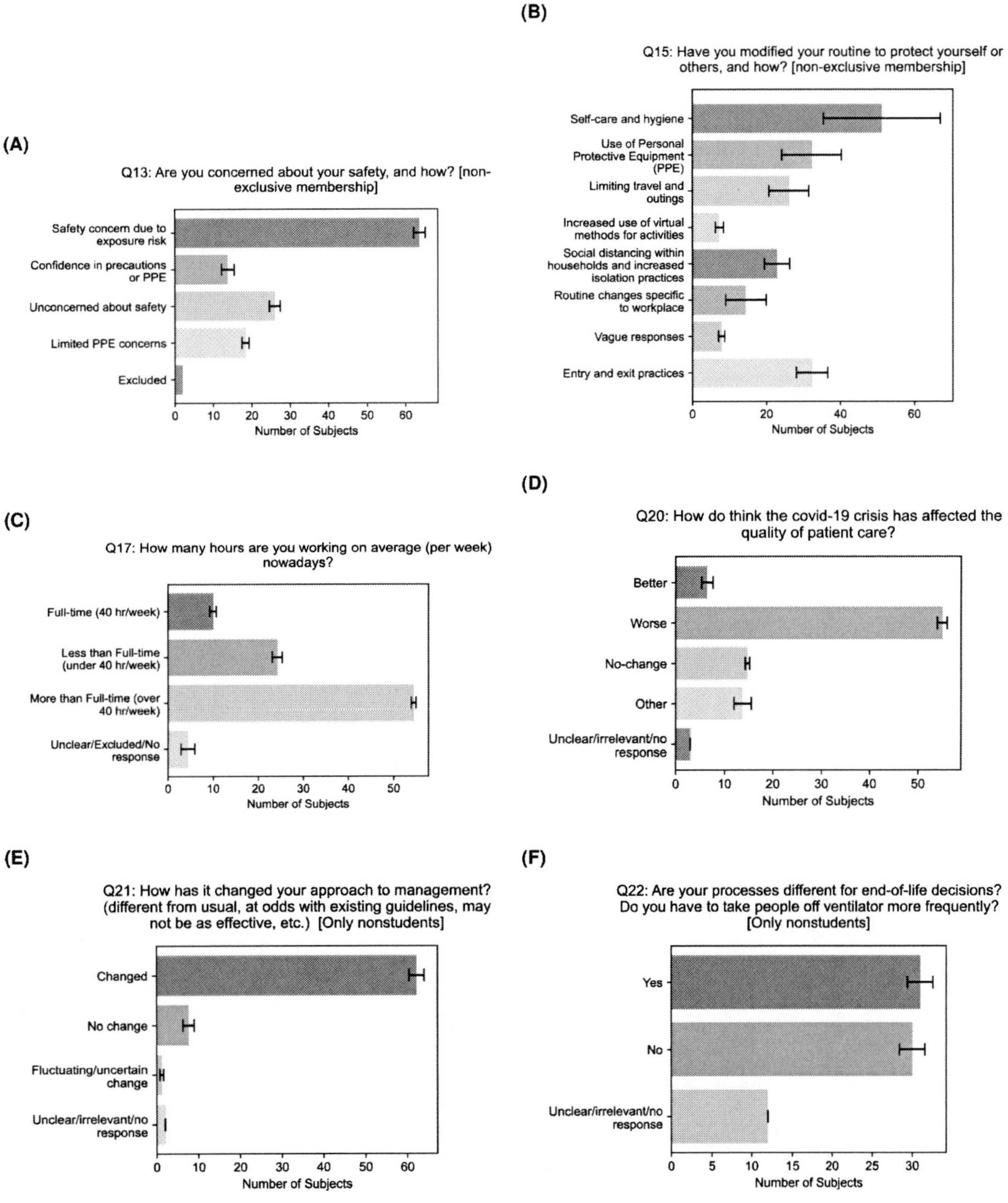

Figure 4: **Aggregated interview responses to selected questions about safety concerns arising from COVID-19 exposure, work impact, and medical management decisions.** Error bars reflect cluster-assignment variability arising from re-clustering step in RACER. Bar plot labels are primary clusters.

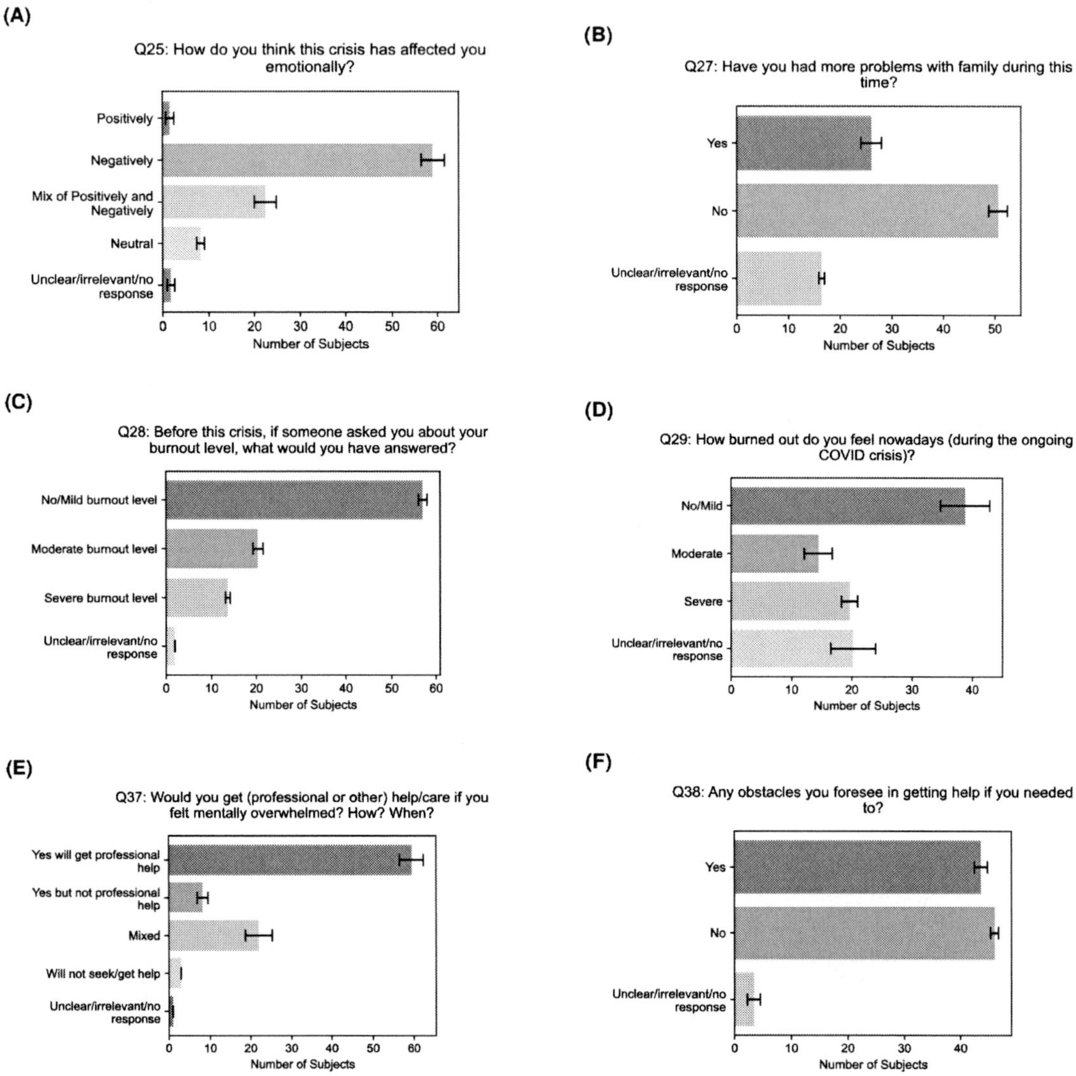

Figure 5: **Aggregated interview responses to selected questions about emotional and psychological impact, and support and coping strategies.** Error bars reflect cluster-assignment variability arising from re-clustering step in RACER. Bar plot labels are primary clusters.

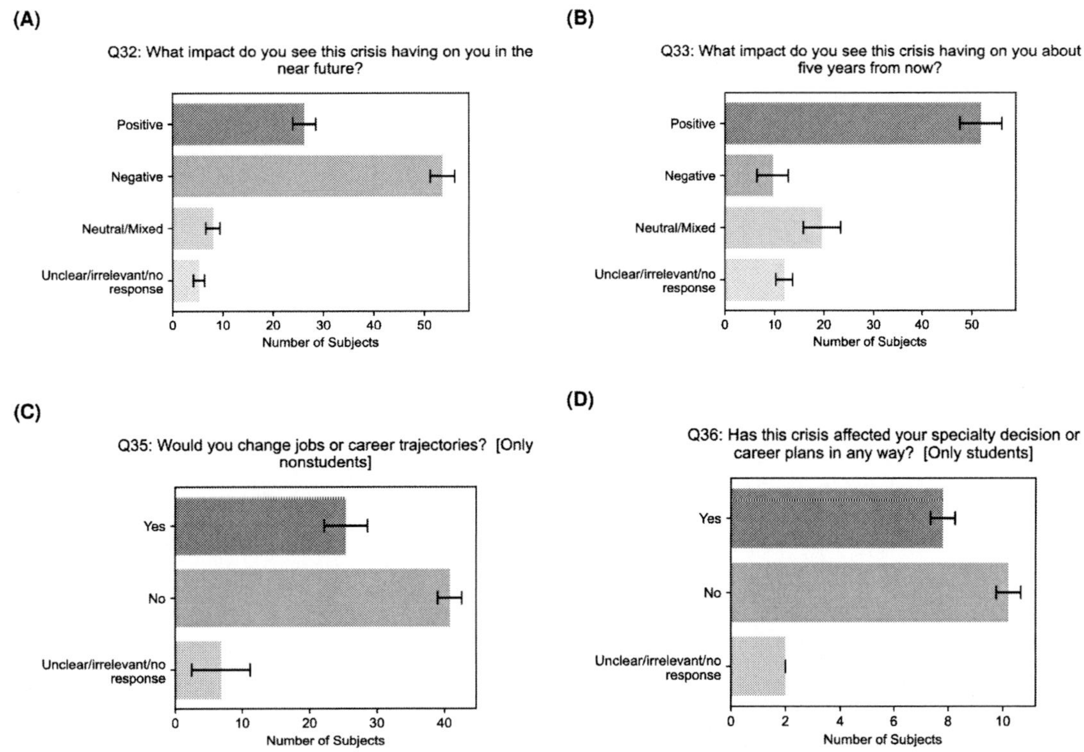

Figure 6: **Aggregated interview responses to selected questions about future considerations and professional outlook, as it relates to working in healthcare during or after the pandemic.** Error bars reflect cluster-assignment variability arising from re-clustering step in RACER. Bar plot labels are primary clusters.

cialty choices or work preferences. Specifically, around 20% described reconsidering their specialty choice due to the pandemic. Another 15% mentioned shifting their preferences regarding research involvement, practice locations, and other factors. However, 50% of students stated the crisis has not affected their professional plans or specialty decisions. Over 50% of students explicitly stated adherence to their Hippocratic oath obligations, while 10% conveyed adherence through descriptions of their clinical actions and interventions. Of students agreeing with their school's pandemic policies, 40% expressed unqualified agreement and 10% provided positive justifications. However, around 15% agreed tentatively due to concerns over student safety and curriculum changes (Figure 6).

C Interview questions and associated expert-guided primary clusters

Table 2: Expert provided primary clusters for questions.
Q1-Q13 and Q18 are *factual*, remaining are *subjective*. Q14-41 underwent human evaluation.

Q#	Question	Top-Level Cluster Guidance
1	How old are you?	(1) Young Adults (22 to 33), (2) Middle-aged Adults (34 to 45), (3) Older Adults (46 to 60), (4) Seniors (61 and above), and (5) Unclear/irrelevant/no response
2	Where do you live?	(1) Houston, TX, (2) San Antonio, TX, (3) TX (Other), (4) Florida, (5) Mid-West US, (6) US (Other) and (7) Unclear/Excluded/No response
3	What is your marital status?	(1) Not currently married, (2) Married currently, and (3) Unclear/Excluded/No response
15	Are you concerned about safety of loved ones, and how?	(1) Yes, (2) No, and (3) Unclear/irrelevant/no response
17	Has this crisis taken a toll on you physically in any way?	(1) Yes, (2) No, and (3) Unclear/irrelevant/no response
18	How many hours are you working on average (per week) nowadays?	(1) Full-time, (2) Less than Full-time, (3) More than Full-time, and (4) Unclear/Excluded/No response
19	How has your working schedule and logistics changed?	(1) Increased hours, (2) Decreased hours, (3) No change, (4) Other, and (5) Unclear/irrelevant/no response
20	How do your working hours compare to pre-covid-19 crisis?	(1) Increased hours, (2) Decreased hours, (3) No change, (4) Other, and (5) Unclear/irrelevant/no response
21	How do think the covid-19 crisis has affected the quality of patient care?	(1) Better, (2) Worse, (3) No-change, (4) Other and (5) Unclear/irrelevant/no response
22	How has it changed your approach to management?	(1) Changed, (2) No change, (3) Fluctuating/uncertain change, and (4) Unclear/irrelevant/no response
23	Are your processes different for end-of-life decisions? Do you have to take people off ventilator more frequently?	(1) Yes, (2) No, and (3) Unclear/irrelevant/no response
24	How prepared do you feel for the COVID-19 pandemic on a personal level?	(1) Prepared, (2) Unprepared, and (3) Unclear/irrelevant/no response
25	How prepared do you feel the unit/hospital is for the COVID-19 pandemic?	(1) Prepared, (2) Unprepared, and (3) Unclear/irrelevant/no response
26	How do you think this crisis has affected you emotionally?	(1) Positively (e.g. excitement), (2) Negatively, (3) Mix of Positively and Negatively, (4) Neutral, and (5) Unclear/irrelevant/no response
27	Do you feel supported by peers and/or family during this time?	(1) Yes, (2) No, (3) Mixed, (4) Fluctuating over time and (5) Unclear/irrelevant/no response
28	Have you had more problems with family during this time?	(1) Yes, (2) No, and (3) Unclear/irrelevant/no response
29	Before this crisis, if someone asked you about your burnout level, what would you have answered?	(1) No/Mild (e.g. 1, 2 or 3 out of 10), (2) Moderate (e.g. 4, 5 or 6 out of 10), (3) Severe (e.g. 7, 8, 9 or 10 out of 10), and (4) Unclear/irrelevant/no response

Continued on next page

Table 2 continued from previous page

Q#	Question	Top-Level Cluster Guidance
30	How burned out do you feel nowadays (during the ongoing COVID crisis)?	(1) No/Mild (e.g. 1, 2 or 3 out of 10), (2) Moderate (e.g. 4, 5 or 6 out of 10), (3) Severe (e.g. 7, 8, 9 or 10 out of 10), and (4) Unclear/irrelevant/no response
31	How do you feel about working from home OR at the frontlines?	(1) Positively (e.g. excitement), (2) Negatively, (3) Neutral/Mixed and (4) Unclear/irrelevant/no response
32	Do you feel you should be able to handle this as a healthcare professional?	(1) Yes, (2) No, (3) Mixed, and (4) Unclear/irrelevant/no response
33	What impact do you see this crisis having on you in the near future?	(1) Positive, (2) Negative, (3) Neutral/Mixed and (4) Unclear/irrelevant/no response
34	What impact do you see this crisis having on you about five years from now?	(1) Positive, (2) Negative, (3) Neutral/Mixed and (4) Unclear/irrelevant/no response
35	Would you seek help if you felt burned out? How?	(1) Yes, (2) No, and (3) Unclear/irrelevant/no response
36	Would you change jobs or career trajectories?	(1) Yes, (2) No, and (3) Unclear/irrelevant/no response
37	Has this crisis affected your specialty decision or career plans in any way?	(1) Yes, (2) No, and (3) Unclear/irrelevant/no response
38	Would you get (professional or other) help/care if you felt mentally overwhelmed? How? When?	(1) Yes will get professional help, (2) Yes but not professional help, (3) Mixed, (4) Will not seek/get help and (5) Unclear/irrelevant/no response
39	Any obstacles you foresee in getting help if you needed to?	(1) Yes, (2) No, and (3) Unclear/irrelevant/no response
40	If student or trainee, how closely do you feel that you are adhering to the Hippocratic oath during this time?	(1) Adhering Closely, (2) Not adhering closely OR Adhering conditionally, and (3) Unclear/irrelevant/no response
41	If student or trainee, do you agree with your school's policies regarding medical students' roles at this time?	(1) Yes, (2) No, (3) Mixed/Conditionally, and (4) Unclear/irrelevant/no response

D Interview questions with LLM-discovered primary clusters

Table 3: LLM-discovered (but expert-reviewed) Primary Clusters for remaining questions. Q1-Q13 and Q18 are *factual*, remaining are *subjective*. Q14-41 underwent human evaluation.

Q#	Question	LLM-discovered Primary Clusters
4	Do you have kids?	(1) Parents, (2) Non-parents, (3) Excluded
5	If you do have kids, provide details	[Non-exclusive membership] (1) No Information, (2) Single Child, (3) Two Children, (4) Three Children, (5) Four or more Children, (6) Child Age Provided, (7) Child Age Not Provided, (8) Children Living at Home, (9) Children No Longer Living at Home
6	Are you a caretaker otherwise? (if not own kids, e.g., elderly parents, adopted family member, etc.)	(1) Caretakers of Family Members, (2) Caretakers of Animals, (3) Partial Caretakers, (4) Financially Supportive, (5) No Caretaking Responsibilities, (6) Excluded

Continued on next page

Table 3 continued from previous page

Q#	Question	LLM-discovered Primary Clusters
7	What type of healthcare professional or student/trainee are you?	[Non-exclusive membership] (1) Physicians, (2) Medical Students, (3) Nurses, (4) Healthcare Professionals, (5) Residents, (6) Excluded
8	If student or trainee, what year are you in?	(1) First Year, (2) Second Year, (3) Third Year, (4) Fourth Year, (5) Unclear Training Year, (6) Excluded
9	What institution did you complete your (or are currently) training at?	[Non-exclusive membership] (1) Baylor College of Medicine, (2) University of Texas, (3) Texas Institutions, (4) Multiple Institutions, (5) Out of US Training, (6) Unspecified or Missing Information
10	If you are a physician, did you train in the US at any point?	(1) Trained in US, (2) Did not train in US, (3) No clear response
11	What is your specialty (if student, what specialty are you thinking of)?	[Non-exclusive membership] (1) Cardiology/Respiratory, (2) Neurology/Neurocritical Care, (3) Pediatrics, (4) Head and neck surgery/Related Surgery, (5) Fertility, (6) Psychiatry, (7) Emergency Medicine, (8) Pulmonary Critical Care, (9) Oncology, (10) OBGYN, (11) Infectious Diseases, (12) Anesthesiology and Critical Care, (13) Surgery/ER, (14) Internal Medicine, (15) Pathology, (16) Excluded
12	How long have you been practicing?	(1) Years under 15, (2) Years 15-30, (3) Years over 30, (4) Excluded
13	Over the past two months, have you practiced clinically in areas where you could be in touch with patients who have COVID-19?	(1) COVID-19 Patient Contact, (2) No COVID-19 Patient Contact
14	Are you concerned about your safety, and how?	[Non-exclusive membership] (1) Safety concern due to exposure risk, (2) Confidence in precautions or PPE, (3) Unconcerned about safety, (4) Limited PPE concerns
16	Have you modified your routine to protect yourself or others, and how?	[Non-exclusive membership] (1) Self-care and hygiene, (2) Use of Personal Protective Equipment (PPE), (3) Limiting travel and outings, (4) Increased use of virtual methods for activities, (5) Social distancing within households and increased isolation practices, (6) Routine changes specific to workplace, (7) Vague responses, (8) Entry and exit practices

E Prompt 1: Retrieving relevant responses from interview transcripts

```
Here is a template (tab-separated-values) of an interview (conducted
    ↪ in 2020) between an interviewer and a healthcare professional
    ↪ or medical student.
Populate the 'answer' column of the template below using the
    ↪ interview transcript appended after the template.
Be sure to note any positive, negative or neutral emotions expressed
    ↪ by the interviewee in the answer.
If a template question was not asked in the appended transcript (or
    ↪ is not applicable), the answer should be "NA".
For the last 'evidence' column, provide evidence, by quoting verbatim
    ↪  (except for newlines) the parts of the transcript that were
    ↪ most relevant to answering the question.

question_number question        answer  evidence
1       How old are you?        [numeric]
2       Where do you live?      [city, state, country]
3       What is your marital status?    [single/married/divorced/
    ↪ widowed/etc]
4       Do you have kids?       [yes/no]
5       If you do have kids, provide details    [details]
6       Are you a caretaker otherwise? (if not own kids, eg elderly
    ↪ parents, adopted family member, etc)       [yes/no; details]
7       What type of healthcare professional or student/trainee are
    ↪ you?        [details]
8       If student or trainee, what year are you in?    [year of
    ↪ program]
9       What institution did you complete your (or are currently)
    ↪ training at?  [name and location of institution]
10      If you are a physician, did you train in the US at any point?
    ↪    [yes/no]
11      What is your specialty (if student, what specialty are you
    ↪ thinking of)?        [details]
12      How long have you been practicing?      [in years, or NA for
    ↪ student]
13      Over the past two months, have you practiced clinically in
    ↪ areas where you could be in touch with patients who have covid
    ↪ -19?   [yes/no]
14      Are you concerned about your safety, and how?   [yes/no;
    ↪ details]
15      Are you concerned about safety of loved ones, and how?  [yes/
    ↪ no; details]
16      Have you modified your routine to protect yourself or others,
    ↪  and how?  [yes/no; details]
17      Has this crisis taken a toll on you physically in any way?
    ↪        [yes/no; details]
18      How many hours are you working on average (per week) nowadays
    ↪ ?  [numeric]
19      How has your working schedule and logistics changed?    [
    ↪ details]
20      How do your working hours compare to pre-covid-19 crisis?
```

```
    [details]
  How do think the covid-19 crisis has affected the quality of patient care?     [details]
  How has it changed your approach to management? (different from usual, at odds with existing guidelines, may not be as effective, etc.) [details]
  Are your processes different for end-of-life decisions? Do you have to take people off ventilator more frequently?     [ details]
  How prepared do you feel for the COVID-19 pandemic on a personal level? [details]
  How prepared do you feel the unit/hospital is for the COVID -19 pandemic?        [details]
  How do you think this crisis has affected you emotionally?     [note emotions recognized from interviewee;details]
  Do you feel supported by peers and/or family during this time ?  [details]
  Have you had more problems with family during this time?     [details]
  Before this crisis, if someone asked you about your burnout level, what would you have answered?       [score (e.g. 6 out of 10) and/or details]
  How burned out do you feel nowadays (during the ongoing COVID  crisis)?  [score (e.g. 6 out of 10) and/or details]
  How do you feel about working from home OR at the frontlines?   [Home/Frontlines/Other; details]
  Do you feel you should be able to handle this as a healthcare  professional?     [yes/no; details]
  What impact do you see this crisis having on you in the near future?    [details]
  What impact do you see this crisis having on you about five years from now?     [details]
  Would you seek help if you felt burned out? How?        [yes/ no; details]
  Would you change jobs or career trajectories?   [yes/no; details]
  Has this crisis affected your specialty decision or career plans in any way?    [yes/no; details]
  Would you get (professional or other) help/care if you felt mentally overwhelmed? How? When?    [yes/no; details]
  Any obstacles you foresee in getting help if you needed to?    [yes/no; details]
  If student or trainee, how closely do you feel that you are adhering to the Hippocratic oath during this time?  [closely/ not-closely; details]
  If student or trainee, do you agree with your school's policies regarding medical students' roles at this time? [yes/ no; details]
```

TRANSCRIPT:

[Interview Transcript Appended]

F Prompt 2: Template for semantic Clustering of responses aggregated across all subjects

Out of 41 questions in our template in E, 29 questions had expert-provided templates that defined the primary clusters but left secondary-cluster definitions to the LLM. Two questions (Q14, Q16) used LLM-discovered (but expert-reviewed) single-level clustering with non-exclusive membership. The following Python code shows the template used for generating the prompt associated with each question (note the use of zero-indexing):

```
TEMPLATE = """Cluster the responses in the table below at two levels.
Top level clusters must be {clusters}.
Top level clusters have mutually-exclusive cluster membership.
For the next level, cluster the responses from subjects belonging to
    ↪ each top-level cluster highlighting the common theme per
    ↪ cluster.
Subjects can belong to multiple clusters at this level.

Your response should be in tab-separated-values format, with the
    ↪ following columns:
subject_id  top_level_cluster_id     secondary_cluster_ids

Example output line:
C-002    C1   "C1.1,C1.2,C1.4"

Start your response by defining each top and secondary cluster in tab
    ↪ -separated-values format, with columns:
cluster_id  cluster_name    cluster_description

Note that some subject_ids may not be present in the prompt, and so
    ↪ should also not be present in your response.
Provide both the (tab-separated) cluster-definitions table and the (
    ↪ tab-separated) cluster-assignments table in your response.
\n"""

prompts = {
    "default": """Cluster the responses in the table below
        ↪ highlighting the common theme per cluster.
Group subjects that provide unclear, irrelevant, or no responses into
    ↪  a separate "excluded" cluster.
Subjects can belong to multiple clusters. Your response should be in
    ↪ tab-separated-values format,
with the following columns: subject_id, cluster_ids

Example output line:
subject_id  cluster_ids
C-002    "C2,C3"

Start your response by defining each cluster in tab-separated-values
    ↪ format, with columns:
cluster_id, cluster_name, cluster_description

Note that some subject_ids may not be present in the prompt, and so
    ↪ should also not be present in your response.
```

```
Provide both the (tab-separated) cluster-definitions table and the (
    ↪ tab-separated) cluster-assignments table in your response.
\n""",
    0: TEMPLATE.format(
        clusters="(1) Young Adults (22 to 33), (2) Middle-aged Adults
            ↪  (34 to 45), (3) Older Adults (46 to 60), (4) Seniors
            ↪ (61 and above), and (5) Unclear/irrelevant/no response"
    ),
    1: TEMPLATE.format(
        clusters="(1) Houston, Texas, (2) San Antonio, Texas, (3)
            ↪ Texas (Other), (4) Florida, (5) Mid-West US, (6) US (
            ↪ Other) and (7) Unclear/Excluded/No response"
    ),
    2: TEMPLATE.format(
        clusters="(1) Not currently married, (2) Married currently,
            ↪ and (3) Unclear/Excluded/No response"
    ),
    14: TEMPLATE.format(
        clusters="(1) Yes, (2) No, and (3) Unclear/irrelevant/no
            ↪ response"
    ),
    16: TEMPLATE.format(
        clusters="(1) Yes, (2) No, and (3) Unclear/irrelevant/no
            ↪ response"
    ),
    # 17: Numeric: How many hours are you working on average (per
        ↪ week)?
    17: TEMPLATE.format(
        clusters="(1) Full-time, (2) Less than Full-time, (3) More
            ↪ than Full-time, and (4) Unclear/Excluded/No response"
    ),
    18: TEMPLATE.format(
        clusters="(1) Increased hours, (2) Decreased hours, (3) No
            ↪ change, (4) Other, and (5) Unclear/irrelevant/no
            ↪ response"
    ),
    # 19: How does this compare to pre-covid-19 crisis?
    19: TEMPLATE.format(
        clusters="(1) Increased hours, (2) Decreased hours, (3) No
            ↪ change, (4) Other, and (5) Unclear/irrelevant/no
            ↪ response"
    ),
    20: TEMPLATE.format(
        clusters="(1) Better, (2) Worse, (3) No-change, (4) Other and
            ↪  (5) Unclear/irrelevant/no response"
    ),
    21: TEMPLATE.format(
        clusters="(1) Changed, (2) No change, (3) Fluctuating/
            ↪ uncertain change, and (4) Unclear/irrelevant/no
            ↪ response"
    ),
    22: TEMPLATE.format(
```

```
    clusters="(1) Yes, (2) No, and (3) Unclear/irrelevant/no
        ↪ response"
),
23: TEMPLATE.format(
    clusters="(1) Prepared, (2) Unprepared, and (3) Unclear/
        ↪ irrelevant/no response"
),
24: TEMPLATE.format(
    clusters="(1) Prepared, (2) Unprepared, and (3) Unclear/
        ↪ irrelevant/no response"
),
25: TEMPLATE.format(
    clusters="(1) Positively (e.g. excitement), (2) Negatively,
        ↪ (3) Mix of Positively and Negatively, (4) Neutral, and
        ↪ (5) Unclear/irrelevant/no response"
),
26: TEMPLATE.format(
    clusters="(1) Yes, (2) No, (3) Mixed, (4) Fluctuating over
        ↪ time and (5) Unclear/irrelevant/no response"
),
27: TEMPLATE.format(
    clusters="(1) Yes, (2) No, and (3) Unclear/irrelevant/no
        ↪ response"
),
28: TEMPLATE.format(
    clusters="(1) No/Mild (e.g. 1, 2 or 3 out of 10), (2)
        ↪ Moderate (e.g. 4, 5 or 6 out of 10), (3) Severe (e.g.
        ↪ 7, 8, 9 or 10 out of 10), and (4) Unclear/irrelevant/no
        ↪  response"
),
29: TEMPLATE.format(
    clusters="(1) No/Mild (e.g. 1, 2 or 3 out of 10), (2)
        ↪ Moderate (e.g. 4, 5 or 6 out of 10), (3) Severe (e.g.
        ↪ 7, 8, 9 or 10 out of 10), and (4) Unclear/irrelevant/no
        ↪  response"
),
30: TEMPLATE.format(
    clusters="(1) Positively (e.g. excitement), (2) Negatively,
        ↪ (3) Neutral/Mixed and (4) Unclear/irrelevant/no
        ↪ response"
),
31: TEMPLATE.format(
    clusters="(1) Yes, (2) No, (3) Mixed, and (4) Unclear/
        ↪ irrelevant/no response"
),
32: TEMPLATE.format(
    clusters="(1) Positive, (2) Negative, (3) Neutral/Mixed and
        ↪ (4) Unclear/irrelevant/no response"
),
33: TEMPLATE.format(
    clusters="(1) Positive, (2) Negative, (3) Neutral/Mixed and
        ↪ (4) Unclear/irrelevant/no response"
```

```
    ),
    34: TEMPLATE.format(
        clusters="(1) Yes, (2) No, and (3) Unclear/irrelevant/no
            ↪ response"
    ),
    35: TEMPLATE.format(
        clusters="(1) Yes, (2) No, and (3) Unclear/irrelevant/no
            ↪ response"
    ),
    36: TEMPLATE.format(
        clusters="(1) Yes, (2) No, and (3) Unclear/irrelevant/no
            ↪ response"
    ),
    37: TEMPLATE.format(
        clusters="(1) Yes will get professional help, (1) Yes but not
            ↪  professional help, (3) Mixed, (4) Will not seek/get
            ↪ help and (5) Unclear/irrelevant/no response"
    ),
    38: TEMPLATE.format(
        clusters="(1) Yes, (2) No, and (3) Unclear/irrelevant/no
            ↪ response"
    ),
    39: TEMPLATE.format(
        clusters="(1) Adhering Closely, (2) Not adhering closely OR
            ↪ Adhering conditionally, and (3) Unclear/irrelevant/no
            ↪ response"
    ),
    40: TEMPLATE.format(
        clusters="(1) Yes, (2) No, (3) Mixed/Conditionally, and (3)
            ↪ Unclear/irrelevant/no response"
    ),
}
```

G Prompt 3: Re-Clustering using previously defined clusters

```
Cluster the responses in the table below highlighting the common
   ↪ theme per cluster.
Group subjects that provide unclear, irrelevant, or no responses into
   ↪  a separate "excluded" cluster.
Subjects can belong to multiple clusters. Your response should be in
   ↪ tab-separated-values format,
with the following columns: subject_id, cluster_ids

Example output line:
subject_id  cluster_ids
C-002   "C2,C3"

Note that some subject_ids may not be present in the prompt, and so
   ↪ should also not be present in your response.
Provide both the (tab-separated) cluster-definitions table and the (
   ↪ tab-separated) cluster-assignments table in your response.

subject_id      Are you a caretaker otherwise? (if not own kids, eg
   ↪ elderly parents, adopted family member, etc)
C001    No
C002    No
C003    No
C004    No
C005    No

...

C086    Yes, looks after his mother-in-law's finances
C087    No
C090    Yes; Partial caretaker for parents
C099    No
C100    No
C101    No
C102    No

Use the following cluster definitions (Do not repeat this in output):
cluster_id      cluster_name    cluster_description
C1      Caretakers of Family Members    Subjects who responded that
   ↪ they take care of relatives (elderly parents, children,
   ↪ siblings or others).
C2      Caretakers of Animals   Subjects who take care of animals.
C3      Partial Caretakers      Subjects who participate in
   ↪ caretaking but not as primary caretakers.
C4      Financially Supportive  Subjects who provide financial
   ↪ support instead of physical caretaking.
C5      No Caretaking Responsibilities  Subjects who stated that they
   ↪  do not take care of anyone.
C6      Excluded        Responses that are unclear, irrelevant, or
   ↪ did not provide a response to the question.
```

Soft Measures for Extracting Causal Collective Intelligence

Maryam Berijanian[1], Spencer Dork [1,3], Kuldeep Singh[2], Michael Riley Millikan[1], Ashlin Riggs[1], Aadarsh Swaminathan[1], Sarah L. Gibbs[4], Scott E. Friedman [5], Nathan Brugnone[1,3]

[1]Department of Computational Mathematics, Science, & Engineering, Michigan State University
[2]Department of Computer Science, Michigan State University
[3]Complex & Social Systems Lab, Two Six Technologies, [4]University of South Alabama, [5]SIFT
{berijani, dork, singhku2, millika6, riggsash, swamina9, brugnone}@msu.edu
slg2221@jagmail.southalabama.edu, friedman@sift.net

Abstract

Understanding and modeling collective intelligence is essential for addressing complex social systems. Directed graphs called fuzzy cognitive maps (FCMs) offer a powerful tool for encoding causal mental models, but extracting high-integrity FCMs from text is challenging. This study presents an approach using large language models (LLMs) to automate FCM extraction. We introduce novel graph-based similarity measures and evaluate them by correlating their outputs with human judgments through the Elo rating system. Results show positive correlations with human evaluations, but even the best-performing measure exhibits limitations in capturing FCM nuances. Fine-tuning LLMs improves performance, but existing measures still fall short. This study highlights the need for soft similarity measures tailored to FCM extraction, advancing collective intelligence modeling with NLP.

1 Introduction

Social science has long sought to understand and model the collective intelligence underlying humanity's most pressing problems such as climate change, sustainable food supply, and violent conflict driven by inequitable resource distribution. These are *social-ecological systems* (SES) problems characterized by complex, interwoven feedback loops involving human and natural systems (Ostrom, 2009; Partelow, 2018). To model collective intelligence about SES, we can leverage mental models of causal system structure.

Researchers in the social sciences have formally encoded SES mental models using *fuzzy cognitive maps* (FCMs) that represent causal systems as signed, weighted digraphs, where edges represent causal relationships among natural language concepts (Kosko, 1986) like that depicted in Figure 1. FCMs are inspired by human *causal mental models* that people use to explain causal mechanisms and generate predictions (Craik, 1967).

FCMs have been widely used to facilitate cross-disciplinary communication within research teams (Gray et al., 2013), make qualitative and numerical predictions, and assess collective intelligence (Gray et al., 2020; Aminpour et al., 2020; Voinov et al., 2018). However, little work has explored extracting high-integrity FCMs from textual corpora. The development of a robust text-to-FCM method would enable more rapid synthesis of science- and stakeholder-informed perspectives to provide access to latent collective intelligence about SES.

This work presents a *natural language processing* (NLP) approach to (1) extracting FCMs from text with *large language models* (LLMs) and (2) measuring extracted FCM quality with novel *soft* F1 measures that permit approximate semantic matches rather than requiring exact node and edge matches. This helps capture and accumulate diverse causal collective intelligence of SES domains. We provide code and datasets for reproducibility.[1]

2 Background and Objectives

Extracting FCM edges is a specialization of extracting semantic relations or causal graphs: each node is a textual span describing causal factors, and each edge is a directed causal *increase* or *decrease* rela-

[1]The source codes and dataset are available at https://github.com/kuldeep7688/soft-measures-causal-intelligence.

Proceedings of the 1st Workshop on NLP for Science (NLP4Science), pages 99–116
November 16, 2024

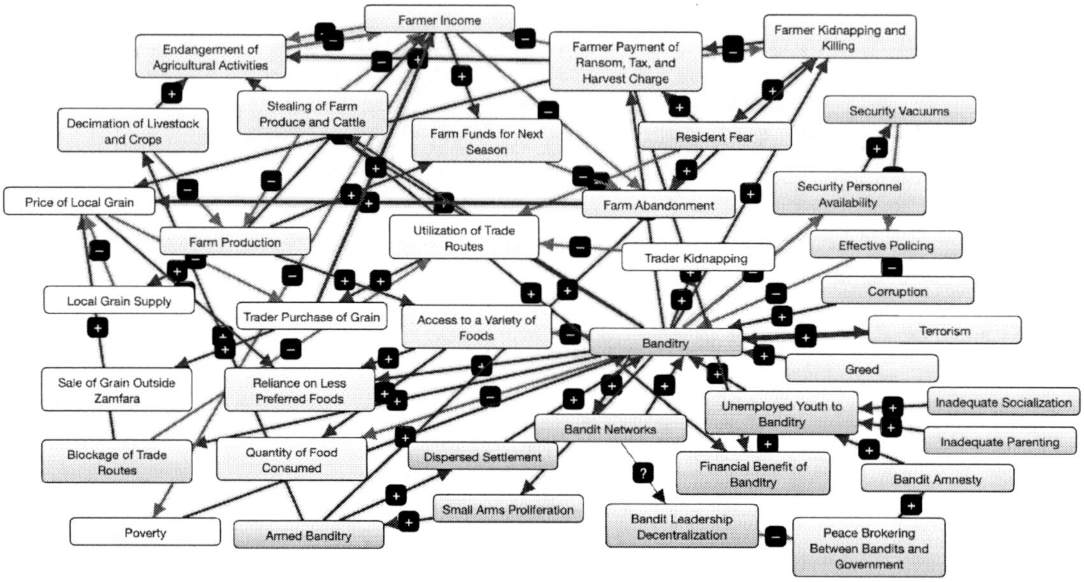

Figure 1: FCM describing the Mmahi and James (2023) mental model of conflict and food system dynamics in Zamfara State, Nigeria; blue (resp. red) edges indicate causally increasing (resp. decreasing) relations; visualized with Mental Modeler.

tionship where the source of the edge quantitatively increases or decreases the target. Two issues distinguish FCM extraction from previous graph-based extraction tasks: (1) high expressiveness and (2) partial correctness. We describe these two issues briefly to motivate our approach.

High expressiveness. Causal variables (i.e., FCM nodes) and relations may be expressed multiple ways, so human annotators may disagree and a machine prediction may actually outperform a pre-determined human-generated *gold standard* according to human judges. Many graph extraction approaches are validated by their proximity to a singular gold standard generated by human experts, where small deviations from the standard greatly affect the measure. This includes neural network loss functions. Some relaxed matching strategies help account for textual containment or overlap (Chen et al., 2019; Toba et al., 2010), but these have not been adequately extended to graph extraction.

Partial correctness. A sub-optimal node or edge that captures a valid causal relationship is often useful to report as a component of an FCM—especially in data-poor contexts, as even limited information can improve the understanding of a given system—so an NLP model's capability to produce partially correct edges is important to capture (Table 1).

Consequently, binary judgments of correctness—

Source	Target	Direction	Issue
turbine structures	blue mussels	increase	NA (gold standard)
numbers of blue mussels	turbine structures	increase	source & target swapped; extra source text
turbines	mussel populations	decrease	simplified source; extra target text; incorrect direction
turbine structures	blue mussels	decrease	incorrect direction

Table 1: Examples of partially correct causal relationships. Original text: "Some fishermen described the establishment of large numbers of blue mussels on the turbine structures" (ten Brink et al., 2021, p. 245).

such as precision, recall, and F1 scores—are sub-optimal measures for our task. Decades of research has produced numerical measures to score the similarity (or distance) between spans of text to avoid the need for absolute correctness (Mihalcea et al., 2006; Bär et al., 2012; Lavie and Denkowski, 2009), but development of textual similarity measures for graphs, and FCMs in particular, has been limited (Pilehvar and Navigli, 2015).

This paper (1) assesses fine-tuned LLM-based methods to extract FCMs from text and (2) introduces and evaluates edge-based similarity measures for validating FCM quality, addressing the limitations of previous measures. Additionally, it (3) initiates an approach for validating graph-based NLP predictions by (a) ranking predictions through pairwise comparative human judgments using Elo and (b) comparing the rankings produced by humans and similarity measures. This proof-of-concept study suggests a methodology by which to improve the qualitative evaluation of NLP-generated FCMs en masse and, thereby, takes a step towards improved collective intelligence models.

3 Methods and Data

3.1 Dataset

We curated a dataset of 318 short text passages extracted from a diverse set of research articles on SES. These articles cover a wide range of SES topics including offshore wind farm development, the impact of banditry on the food system in northern Nigeria, the distribution of food and medical aid in conflict regions, and maternal and child health in countries with low Human Development Index scores. We annotated each text passage with (`source, target, direction`) tuples.

3.2 Annotation Ranking

To rank annotations for each text passage, we (1) generated multiple annotations for each of a subset of passages, (2) presented pairs of annotations to raters, and (3) applied the Elo rating system.

3.2.1 Annotation Generation

Each of a subset of 20 passages were manually annotated with (`source, target, direction`) tuples by all authors. This subset was further augmented with LLM annotations. This was achieved through two distinct methods: few-shot learning and instruction tuning with LoRA (Wei et al., 2021; Hu et al., 2021). We employed the Llama-2-7B-chat-hf (Touvron et al., 2023a,b), Llama-3-8B-Instruct (Meta AI, 2024), and Mistral-7B-Instruct-v0.2 (Jiang et al., 2023) models from Hugging Face (Hugging Face, 2024). Fine-tuning was accomplished using splits of the 318 data points. A detailed presentation of these methods appears in Appendices F, C, and E.

3.2.2 The Elo Rating System

The Elo rating system, introduced by Arpad Elo (Elo, 1967, 1978), is a widely used method for quantifying the relative skill levels of players in two-player competitive games. It has been demonstrated to effectively rank models based on human judgment (Boubdir et al., 2023), benchmark LLMs (Zheng et al., 2023), and rank preferences, such as humor in Twitter posts (Zheng et al., 2023) through pairwise comparisons. Inspired by previous research (Berijanian et al., 2024; SEE-Insight, 2024), we used the Elo system to rank annotations and then compared these rankings with those generated by the candidate similarity measures.

3.2.3 Elo Tournaments

Each author was presented with a series of comparisons between annotations via a web interface (Appendix G). Raters were instructed to select the better annotation as 'winner' or to choose 'tie' following a set of guidelines (see Appendix I). Elo scores were computed *per passage*, so each passage acted as an individual 'tournament'. Raters did not rate their own annotations to avoid potential bias. Inter- and intra-rater reliability were captured through overlaps (Appendix H.1).

3.3 Similarity Measures

We devised five candidate FCM similarity measures based on the established textual similarity measures in Table 2. The similarity between an FCM and a gold standard is computed as a *softly thresholded F1 score* between edge sets. Given a textual similarity measure $S(\cdot,\cdot)$, a threshold T, and edge sets E and E_{gold}, as well as any textual edge attributes A (we use $\mathsf{A} = \{\texttt{source}, \texttt{target}\}$) and non-textual edge attributes N (we use $\mathsf{N} = \{\texttt{direction}\}$):

TP: For each $e \in E$, our method counts a *true positive* if there exists an $e_{\text{gold}} \in E_{\text{gold}}$ such that $S\left(e.\mathsf{a}, e_{\text{gold}}.\mathsf{a}\right) \geq T$ for every $\mathsf{a} \in \mathsf{A}$ and $e.\mathsf{n} = e_{\text{gold}}.\mathsf{n}$ for every $\mathsf{n} \in \mathsf{N}$;

PP: For each $e \in E$, our method counts a *partial positive* if there exists an $e_{\text{gold}} \in E_{\text{gold}}$ such that $S\left(e.\mathsf{a}, e_{\text{gold}}.\mathsf{a}\right) \geq T$ for every $\mathsf{a} \in \mathsf{A}$ and there exists an $\mathsf{n} \in \mathsf{N}$ such that $e.\mathsf{n} \neq e_{\text{gold}}.\mathsf{n}$;

FP: For each $e \in E$, our method counts a *false positive* if for every $e_{\text{gold}} \in E_{\text{gold}}$, we have $S\left(e.\mathsf{a}, e_{\text{gold}}.\mathsf{a}\right) < T$ for any $\mathsf{a} \in \mathsf{A}$;

FN: For each $e_{\text{gold}} \in E_{\text{gold}}$, our method counts a *false negative* if for every $e \in E$, we have $S\left(e.\mathsf{a}, e_{\text{gold}}.\mathsf{a}\right) < T$ for any $\mathsf{a} \in \mathsf{A}$.

For any S, once the TP, PP, FP, and FN have been counted, the corresponding edge-based measure can be calculated using the F1-like formula:

$$\frac{2 \cdot \text{TP} + \text{PP}}{2 \cdot \text{TP} + \text{PP} + \text{FP} + \text{FN}}. \quad (1)$$

Measure	Strengths	Weaknesses
Exact match	Simple and direct measurement.	Sensitive to minor textual differences.
BLEU (Papineni et al., 2002)	Considers n-gram precision and brevity.	Does not account for synonyms or grammatical meaning.
ROUGE (Lin, 2004)	Flexible in measure type and n-gram method.	Does not account for synonyms or grammatical meaning.
METEOR (Banerjee and Lavie, 2005)	Accounts for synonyms, stems, and word order.	Does not account for context or grammatical meaning.
BLEURT (Sellam et al., 2020)	Captures abstract meanings using neural networks.	Potential biases and limited user control.

Table 2: Text similarity/matching strategies.

For each S, a threshold T is chosen by grid search (Appendix D.3). Note that by disallowing for partial positives, when $S(\cdot, e.\mathsf{a}) = \mathbf{1}_{e.\mathsf{a}}(\cdot)$—an exact match criterion—and $T = 1$, this reduces to the classical F1 score between edge sets.

For BLEU, ROUGE, METEOR, and BLEURT, we refer to our novel edge-based measures as BLEU-E, ROUGE-E, METEOR-E, and BLEURT-E, respectively.

3.4 Correlation Analysis

The winning annotation of each tournament was deemed the gold standard. We then produced a ranking of annotations *per passage* using each candidate similarity measure applied to each (`gold standard, annotation`) FCM pair. The Spearman correlations (Spearman, 1904) between human- and similarity measure-generated rankings were computed. We then applied the measure with highest correlation to evaluate LLM-generated FCMs and compared with an LLM-only tournament.

4 Results

4.1 Spearman Correlation

The Spearman correlation coefficients for each measure, averaged across all passages, are summarized in Table 3. Higher values indicate greater mean correlation with human rankings. Novel measure-produced rankings have positive mean correlations with human-generated rankings, and each improves upon vanilla F1 in this regard (Table 4).

Measure	Mean	90% CI	95% CI
F1	0.016	(-0.057, 0.089)	(-0.072, 0.104)
BLEU-E*	0.109	(-0.018, 0.237)	(-0.045, 0.263)
METEOR-E*	**0.126**	**(0.001, 0.252)**	(-0.025, 0.278)
ROUGE-E*	**0.124**	**(0.007, 0.241)**	(-0.018, 0.266)
BLEURT-E*	**0.152**	**(0.038, 0.265)**	**(0.014, 0.289)**
BLEU-E	**0.415**	**(0.257, 0.574)**	**(0.223, 0.607)**
METEOR-E	**0.333**	**(0.146, 0.520)**	**(0.106, 0.559)**
ROUGE-E	**0.387**	**(0.205, 0.570)**	**(0.166, 0.608)**
BLEURT-E	**0.338**	**(0.178, 0.498)**	**(0.144, 0.532)**

Table 3: Mean correlations of similarity measures with human judgment and their confidence intervals. E* scores are computed without partial positives.

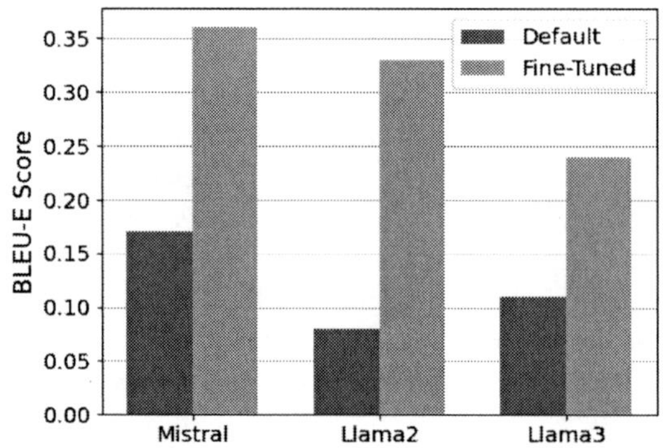

Figure 2: Mean BLEU-E across model variants.

4.2 LLM Inferences

Figure 2 presents the average BLEU-E scores for FCM inferences on the test set by each LLM before and after fine-tuning. As expected, fine-tuned models outperform their default counterparts, with Mistral scoring highest, followed by Llama-2 and then Llama-3.is consistent with the human-generated ranking.

5 Discussion and Conclusions

This paper presents an evaluation of fine-tuned LLM-based methods for extracting FCMs from text, while also introducing and assessing novel edge-based similarity measures to validate the quality of these FCMs. The study highlights the limitations of traditional measures, which often fail to capture the nuances and partial correctness in FCMs, especially in the context of SES research. For instance, there were cases where LLMs outperformed human annotators, yet these instances might have been overlooked if we relied solely on traditional measures like the F1 score or validation set loss. The novel edge-based measures allowing for partial positives show markedly greater correlation with human judgments.

In addition to examining similarity measures, this work initiates a new approach for validating graph-based NLP predictions by employing pairwise comparative human judgments, using the Elo rating system, to rank predictions. This method was used to compare human-derived rankings with those generated by similarity measures, providing a proof of concept for enhancing the qualitative evaluation of NLP-generated FCMs.

Fine-tuning LLMs proved beneficial, resulting in higher BLEU-E scores and improved model performance. Whereas the validation set losses for all fine-tuned LLMs appear similar (Figure 3 in Appendix C), their qualitative performances differed significantly. Although BLEU-E offers a more accurate assessment than validation set loss, these improvements do not fully resolve the underlying issues with the current similarity measures.

The study's findings emphasize the necessity of developing more specialized measures that are better aligned with human judgment and capable of capturing the complexities of FCM extraction. This study represents an initial step towards that goal, highlighting the limitations of current approaches and setting the stage for future research.

Future work will focus on developing and validating new similarity measures that can better capture the complexities and partial correctness in FCM extraction. For instance, greater correlation with human judgment should be achievable by parameterizing TP and PP with scalars and employing optimization. Additionally, integrating human-in-the-loop approaches may help refine LLM outputs, leading to more accurate FCMs. We also imagine a range of applications and extensions. For instance, the proposed measures can be straightforwardly extended to knowledge hypergraphs. Furthermore, by symmetrizing any one of our typically asymmetric measures we may interpret it as a kernel (Kriege et al., 2020; Scholkopf and Smola, 2018). Explicitly, let $f =$ BLEURT-E and G_1 and G_2 be FCMs, and define a kernel K as,

$$K(G_1, G_2) = \frac{f(G_1, G_2) + f(G_2, G_1)}{2}.$$

This interpretation brings to bear the entire suite of kernel methods for the study of FCMs to facilitate visualization, classification, and general pattern recognition.

In conclusion, this study has provided insights into the evaluation of LLM-generated FCMs and also underscores the need for continued research. Our framework provides a structured approach for these evaluations. This paper marks just the beginning of a journey towards improving the overall evaluation framework for FCMs and enhancing the role of LLMs in collective intelligence research, particularly in SES contexts with small quantities of low quality textual data.

Acknowledgments

We thank Krithi Sachithanand, Anna Jeffries, and Stephen Lee for input during the exploratory phase of this project. We express deep gratitude to MSU professors Dirk Colbry, Paul Speaker, and Steven A. Gray as well as Dr. Holden Harris and Willem Kajbor of NOAA for enabling this research collaboration. SD was supported by NSF grant RC112900, Collaborative Research: Integrating Perspective-taking and Systems Thinking for Complex Problem-Solving. NB and SLG were supported by the National Oceanic and Atmospheric Administration's RESTORE Science Program under award NA22NOS4510203 to the National Center for Ecological Analysis and Synthesis at the University of California, Santa Barbara as part of the Offshore Wind & Fisheries Gulf Ecosystem Initiative. NB, SLG, and SEF were supported by the Army Contracting Command, DARPA, and ARO under contract no. W911NF-21-C-0007. The views, opinions and/or findings expressed are those of the authors and should not be interpreted as representing the official views or policies of the Department of Defense or the U.S. Government.

References

Payam Aminpour, Steven A Gray, Antonie J Jetter, Joshua E Introne, Alison Singer, and Robert Arlinghaus. 2020. Wisdom of stakeholder crowds in complex social–ecological systems. *Nature Sustainability*, 3(3):191–199.

Satanjeev Banerjee and Alon Lavie. 2005. METEOR: An automatic metric for MT evaluation with improved correlation with human judgments. In *Proceedings of the ACL Workshop on Intrinsic and Extrinsic Evaluation Measures for Machine Translation and/or Summarization*, pages 65–72, Ann Arbor, Michigan. Association for Computational Linguistics.

Maryam Berijanian, Katrina Gensterblum, Doruk Alp Mutlu, Katelyn Reagan, Andrew Hart, and Dirk Colbry. 2024. A labeled array distance metric for measuring image segmentation quality. *arXiv preprint arXiv:2406.07851*.

Meriem Boubdir, Edward Kim, Beyza Ermis, Sara Hooker, and Marzieh Fadaee. 2023. Elo uncovered: Robustness and best practices in language model evaluation. *Proceedings of the Third Workshop on Natural Language Generation, Evaluation, and Metrics (GEM)*, page 339–352.

Daniel Bär, Chris Biemann, Iryna Gurevych, and Torsten Zesch. 2012. UKP: Computing semantic textual similarity by combining multiple content similarity measures. In *First Joint Conference on Lexical and Computational Semantics (*SEM)*, pages 435–440.

Liang Chen, Liting Song, Yue Shao, Dewei Li, and Keyue Ding. 2019. Using natural language processing to extracct clinically useful information from Chinese electronic medical records. *International Journal of Medical Informatics*, 124:6–12.

Kenneth James Williams Craik. 1967. *The nature of explanation*, volume 445. CUP Archive.

Arpad E. Elo. 1967. The proposed USCF rating system, its development, theory, and applications. *Chess Life*, XXII(8):242–247.

Arpad E. Elo. 1978. *The Rating Of Chess Players, Past and Present*. Arco Pub., New York.

Steven A Gray, Payam Aminpour, Caitie Reza, Steven Scyphers, Jonathan Grabowski, Robert Murphy Jr, Alison Singer, David Baltaxe, Rebecca Jordan, Antonie Jetter, et al. 2020. Harnessing the collective intelligence of stakeholders for conservation. *Frontiers in Ecology and the Environment*, 18(8):465–472.

Steven A Gray, Erin Zanre, and Stefan RJ Gray. 2013. Fuzzy cognitive maps as representations of mental models and group beliefs. In *Fuzzy cognitive maps for applied sciences and engineering: From fundamentals to extensions and learning algorithms*, pages 29–48. Springer.

Edward J Hu, Yelong Shen, Phillip Wallis, Zeyuan Allen-Zhu, Yuanzhi Li, Shean Wang, Lu Wang, and Weizhu Chen. 2021. LoRA: Low-rank adaptation of large language models. *International Conference on Learning Representations*.

Hugging Face. 2024. `https://huggingface.co`. Accessed: 6/14/2024.

Albert Q. Jiang, Alexandre Sablayrolles, Arthur Mensch, Chris Bamford, Devendra Singh Chaplot, Diego de las Casas, Florian Bressand, Gianna Lengyel, Guillaume Lample, Lucile Saulnier, Lélio Renard Lavaud, Marie-Anne Lachaux, Pierre Stock, Teven Le Scao, Thibaut Lavril, Thomas Wang, Timothée Lacroix, and William El Sayed. 2023. Mistral 7B. *arXiv preprint arXiv:2310.06825*.

Bart Kosko. 1986. Fuzzy cognitive maps. *International journal of man-machine studies*, 24(1):65–75.

Nils M Kriege, Fredrik D Johansson, and Christopher Morris. 2020. A survey on graph kernels. *Applied Network Science*, 5:1–42.

Alon Lavie and Michael J. Denkowski. 2009. The METEOR metric for automatic evaluation of Machine Translation. *Machine Translation*, 23:105–115.

Chin-Yew Lin. 2004. ROUGE: A package for automatic evaluation of summaries. In *Text Summarization Branches Out*, pages 74–81, Barcelona, Spain. Association for Computational Linguistics.

Meta AI. 2024. Build the future of AI with Meta Llama 3. `https://llama.meta.com/llama3/`. Accessed: 6/12/2024.

Rada Mihalcea, Courtney Coley, and Carlo Strapparava. 2006. Corpus-based and knowledge-based measures of text semantic similarity. *American Association of Artificial Intelligence*, 6:775–780.

Okoro Paul Mmahi and Fadeyi Taofiq James. 2023. Brigandage and criminal victimization in Nahuche community, Zamfara state: impact on food security. *Environment, Development and Sustainability*, pages 1–18.

Elinor Ostrom. 2009. A general framework for analyzing sustainability of social-ecological systems. *Science*, 325(5939):419–422.

Kishore Papineni, Salim Roukos, Todd Ward, and Wei-Jing Zhu. 2002. BLEU: a method for automatic evaluation of machine translation. In *Proceedings of the 40th Annual Meeting of the Association for Computational Linguistics*, pages 311–318, Philadelphia, Pennsylvania, USA. Association for Computational Linguistics.

Stefan Partelow. 2018. A review of the social-ecological systems framework. *Ecology and Society*, 23(4).

Mohammad Taher Pilehvar and Roberto Navigli. 2015. From senses to texts: An all-in-one graph-based approach for measuring semantic similarity. *Artificial Intelligence*, 228:95–128.

Plotly. 2024. Dash Python User Guide. `https://dash.plotly.com`. Accessed: 6/14/2024.

Bernhard Scholkopf and Alexander J Smola. 2018. *Learning with kernels: support vector machines, regularization, optimization, and beyond*. MIT press.

SEE-Insight. 2024. Which is better. `https://github.com/see-insight/SEE-Which-is-Better`. Accessed: 5/23/2024.

Thibault Sellam, Dipanjan Das, and Ankur P Parikh. 2020. BLEURT: Learning robust metrics for text generation. In *Proceedings of ACL*.

Charles Spearman. 1904. The proof and measurement of association between two things. *The American Journal of Psychology*, 15(1):72–101.

Talya ten Brink, Tracey Dalton, and Julia Livermore. 2021. Integrating social and ecological research on the impacts of offshore wind farms in North America. *Researching People and the Sea: Methodologies and Traditions*, pages 239–258.

Hapnes Toba, Syandra Sari, Mirna Adriani, and Ruli Manurung. 2010. Contextual approach for paragraph selection in question answering task. In *Cross Language Evaluation Forum (CLEF)*.

Hugo Touvron, Thibaut Lavril, Gautier Izacard, Xavier Martinet, Marie-Anne Lachaux, Timothée Lacroix, Baptiste Rozière, Naman Goyal, Eric Hambro, Faisal Azhar, Aurelien Rodriguez, Armand Joulin, Edouard Grave, and Guillaume Lample. 2023a. LLaMA: Open and efficient foundation language models. *arXiv preprint arXiv:2302.13971*.

Hugo Touvron, Louis Martin, Kevin Stone, Peter Albert, Amjad Almahairi, Yasmine Babaei, Nikolay Bashlykov, Soumya Batra, Prajjwal Bhargava, Shruti Bhosale, ..., and Thomas Scialom. 2023b. Llama 2: Open foundation and fine-tuned chat models. *arXiv preprint arXiv:2307.09288*.

Alexey Voinov, Karen Jenni, Steven Gray, Nagesh Kolagani, Pierre D. Glynn, Pierre Bommel, Christina Prell, Moira Zellner, Michael Paolisso, Rebecca Jordan, Eleanor Sterling, Laura Schmitt Olabisi, Philippi J. Giabbanelli, Zhanli Sun, Christophe Le Page, Sondoss Elsawah, Todd K. BenDor, Klaus Hubacek, Bethany K. Laursen, Antonie Jetter, Laura Basco-Carrera, Alison Singer, Laura Young, Jessica Brunacini, and Alex Smajgl. 2018. Tools and methods in participatory modeling: Selecting the right tool for the job. *Environmental Modelling & Software*, 109:232–255.

Jason Wei, Maarten Bosma, Vincent Y. Zhao, Kelvin Guu, Adams Wei Yu, Brian Lester, Nan Du, Andrew M. Dai, and Quoc V. Le. 2021. Finetuned language models are zero-shot learners. *International Conference on Learning Representations*.

Weights & Biases. 2024. Track and evaluate LLM applications. `https://wandb.ai/site/`. Accessed: 6/15/2024.

Lianmin Zheng, Ying Sheng, Wei-Lin Chiang, Hao Zhang, Joseph E. Gonzalez, and Ion Stoica. 2023. Chatbot Arena: Benchmarking LLMs in the wild with Elo ratings. `https://lmsys.org/blog/2023-05-03-arena/`. Accessed: 5/23/2024.

A Limitations

While our approach is robust, it is important to acknowledge potential limitations that could impact the generalizability and effectiveness of our findings.

Firstly, the passages we selected for our study are specific to a particular context and may not be representative of different domains, which could limit the generalizability of our findings across other contexts. Future research should explore cross-domain evaluations to validate the effectiveness of our approach in various settings.

Secondly, our methodology relies on initial human annotations, then selecting between human and LLM annotations as the gold standard, which introduces the possibility of bias due to the diversity of cultural and disciplinary backgrounds of the annotators. The initial annotations may not encompass all possible interpretations or nuances present in the text. Future work will focus on expanding the dataset to include a wider variety of texts and annotations, which will help in creating a more comprehensive and representative gold standard.

Furthermore, while we aimed to fine-tune LLMs for improved performance, we did not tune all hyperparameters. Specifically, we only optimized the rank parameter r for LoRA. The primary reason for not extensively tuning all hyperparameters, such as the learning rate, was that the focus of this paper was on measure alignment instead of optimizing hyperparameter settings. Future studies should aim to explore a broader range of hyperparameter tuning to fully explore the capabilities of the LLMs.

Additionally, our experiment was conducted with a limited number of annotation samples for LLM training and Elo ranking. Although the sample selection aimed to cover a broad spectrum of text complexities, the small sample size may not fully capture the variability in real-world data. Furthermore, the samples were selected to provide difficult examples, which may not represent typical data. Moreover, the limited sample size may limit the capabilities of LLMs due to a lack of surplus of data available for fine tuning. Elo rankings may have marginally deviated due to a limited sample size. Expanding the number of samples in future experiments will enhance the reliability and applicability of our results.

Moreover, our current approach does not leverage human-in-the-loop (HITL) strategies to iteratively improve LLM inferences based on human feedback. Integrating HITL mechanisms with the Elo rating system could significantly enhance the quality and accuracy of LLM-generated annotations. By continuously integrating human judgment, this iterative process would allow for ongoing refinement and improvement of LLM outputs. Future work should explore implementing HITL strategies to capture real-time human feedback and use it to fine-tune and validate LLM performance.

To summarize, our approach demonstrates promise. However, addressing these limitations in future work will be crucial for further validating and enhancing the robustness, reliability, and applicability of our findings.

B Ethical Considerations

This study involves the extraction and validation of fuzzy cognitive maps (FCMs) from text using large language models (LLMs). Several ethical considerations are relevant to this work, particularly regarding data use, annotation processes, biases, and the environmental impact of our research.

Data Use and Privacy: The data used in this study were created and annotated by the authors. This ensures that we have complete control over the data's provenance and the conditions under which it was generated. Since the data were produced specifically for this research, issues related to intellectual property and participant privacy are minimized.

Annotation Process: All annotations were carried out by the authors, ensuring a consistent understanding of the task and eliminating the need for external annotators. This method addresses concerns about fair compensation and working conditions for annotators, as the work was part of the authors' research activities.

Bias and Fairness: Inherent biases in language models can affect the outcomes. Researchers should explore methods to identify and mitigate such biases to enhance the fairness and reliability of FCM extractions.

Environmental Impact: The environmental impact of training and fine-tuning LLMs is a significant concern in NLP research. In our study, each training session lasted approximately 40 minutes, which is relatively short. This brevity was due to our primary focus on developing and validating measures for extracting and evaluating FCMs from text, rather than optimizing LLM performance. Consequently, we did not extensively tune the LLM hyperparameters, such as the learning rate, as our focus was on measure alignment rather than finding the ideal hyperparameter settings. This approach not only aligns with our research goals but also minimizes the environmental footprint of our computational experiments.

Potential Misuse: NLP technologies can be misused in various ways, such as generating misleading information or reinforcing harmful stereotypes. Researchers and practitioners should be aware of these risks and take steps to mitigate them when deploying such technologies.

Researchers should incorporate comprehensive strategies to address these ethical challenges, ensuring that the development and application of NLP technologies are aligned with broader societal values and ethical standards.

C Fine-Tuning Parameters and Hyperparameters

For fine-tuning the models with instruction tuning, we focused on adjusting the rank r in LoRA, while maintaining other training parameters at constant values. The cost function for training and validation was cross-entropy loss. The Huggingface library (Hugging Face, 2024) was utilized to run the training jobs with 4-bit quantization.

The common hyperparameters and their corresponding values used for fine-tuning the three models are listed below. Note that while the maximum number of training epochs was set to 15, early stopping was employed, so not all experiments reached the full 15 epochs. The early stopping mechanism halted training when the validation loss did not improve for 3 consecutive epochs.

- `Maximum number of training epochs: 15 (subject to early stopping)`
- `Batch size: 4`
- `Optimizer: Paged AdamW 32-bit`
- `Learning rate: 2e-4`
- `Learning rate scheduler: Cosine decay`
- `Gradient accumulation steps: 1`
- `Gradient clipping: 0.3`
- `Gradient checkpointing : True (to save memory)`
- `Weight decay: 0.001`
- `Warmup ratio: 0.1`
- `Use of 4-bit precision: Enabled (to reduce memory and computational cost)`
- `Data type for 4-bit computations: bfloat16`
- `Quantization type for 4-bit precision: nf4`
- `Nested quantization: Disabled`
- `LoRA dropout rate: 0.1`

The following hyperparameters were optimized during the fine-tuning process:

- `LoRA rank (r): 2, 4, 8, 16, 32, 64, 128, 256`

- LoRA $\alpha : 2 * r$

We used one Nvidia V100 GPU to execute the training jobs. On average, each experiment took approximately 40 minutes to complete.

C.1 Optimal Rank (r) Values for LoRA Fine-Tuning

To determine the optimal rank r for each model, we experimented with various r values and monitored the validation loss.

The best r values, based on the minimum validation set loss for Llama-2-7B-chat-hf, Llama-3-8B-Instruct, and Mistral-7B-Instruct-v0.2 after testing different r values, are as follows:

- `Llama-2-7B-chat-hf: 128`
- `Llama-3-8B-Instruct: 64`
- `Mistral-7B-Instruct-v0.2: 128`

As shown in Figure 3, all three models achieved similar validation losses with their respective optimal r values.

D Other Formulas and Hyperparameters

D.1 Elo Rating System

The Elo rating system (Elo, 1967, 1978), is a method for quantifying the relative skill levels of players in two-player competitive games such as chess. It assigns a numerical rating to each player, representing their skill level.

The Elo rating system updates players' ratings after each game based on the outcome. The formula to update the rating involves several steps. First, the expected score for player A against player B is calculated using the formula:

$$E_A = \frac{1}{1 + 10^{(R_B - R_A)/400}},$$

where R_A and R_B are the current ratings of players A and B, respectively. Similarly, the expected score for player B is:

$$E_B = \frac{1}{1 + 10^{(R_A - R_B)/400}}.$$

Note that $E_A + E_B = 1$. The actual score S_A is 1 if player A wins, 0 if player A loses, and 0.5 in the case of a draw. Similarly, S_B is 1 if player B wins, 0 if player B loses, and 0.5 for a draw. The new ratings for players A and B are updated using the formulas:

$$R'_A = R_A + K(S_A - E_A)$$
$$R'_B = R_B + K(S_B - E_B)$$

Here, K is a constant known as the $K-$factor, which determines the sensitivity of the rating system. A higher $K-$factor means ratings change more significantly after each game, making the system more responsive to recent results. Conversely, a lower K-factor results in smaller changes, making the ratings more stable and less sensitive to new results. The $K-$factor can vary; in chess, it is often set to 32 for new players and 16 for established players, but these values can be adjusted depending on the specific application and the desired stability of the ratings.

It can be shown that while the values of K and the initial Elo ratings R_A and R_B affect the numerical scores obtained after calculation, the *relative ranking* of players remains unchanged. Additionally, the order of "games" does not affect the final ranking, ensuring the consistency of the system regardless of the sequence in which games are played.

D.2 Hyperparameters for Elo Rating Calculation

In the process of calculating Elo ratings for annotation evaluations, we utilized the following hyperparameters:

- `K-factor: 32`
- `Initial Elo rating: 1000`

D.3 Hyperparameters for Similarity Measures

The English-trained checkpoint bleurt-base-128 and ROUGE-1 were used in this study. We considered a range of thresholds, T, for each measure through exploratory data analysis and adaptive grid search. The T chosen for each measure coordinates to the highest achieved Spearman correlation to the human-generated rankings. The T selected for each measure is:

- `BLEURT-E: -0.1532`
- `BLEU-E: 0.352`
- `METEOR-E: 0.01`
- `ROUGE-E: 0.45.`

E Prompts Format for Instruction Tuning

This section details the prompts format used for instruction tuning. This format ensures that the model clearly understands the task and generates the appropriate response based on the given instruction.

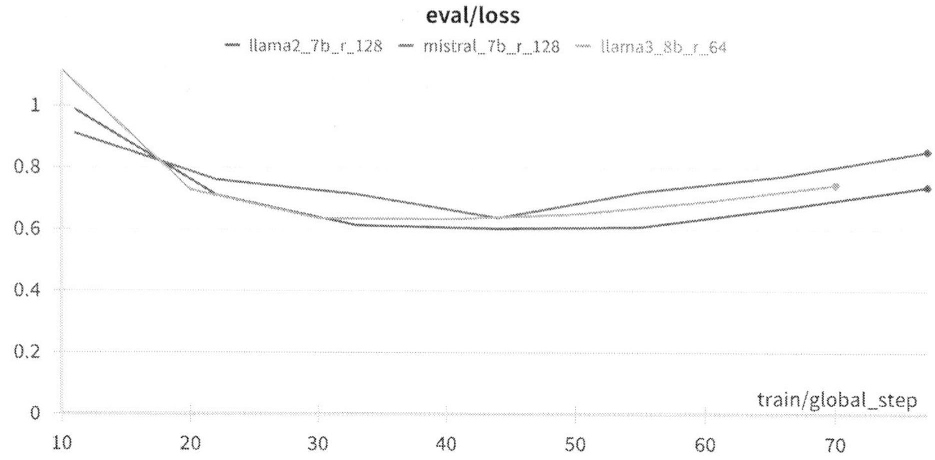

Figure 3: Validation losses for Mistral-7B-Instruct-v0.2, Llama-2-7B-chat-hf, and Llama-3-8B-Instruct during training with their respective optimal ranks r in LoRA. Plot generated using WandB (Weights & Biases, 2024).

E.1 Llama-2-7B and Mistral-7B

Both Llama-2-7B-chat-hf and Mistral-7B-Instruct-v0.2 use the same prompt format for instruction tuning. We provide the instructions for the model within the [INST] and [/INST] tags, and the model generates everything following the [/INST] tag. The entire prompt is enclosed within <s> and </s> tags.

The prompt format used is mentioned below:

```
<s>[INST] Given the input sentence, identify
    all the triplets of entities and the
    corresponding causal relationships between
    them. The entities should be phrases from
    the input sentence, and the relationships
    should either be 'Positive' or 'Negative'.
    Each new extracted triplet should start
    with the <triplet> token, followed by the
    subject phrase, the object phrase, and the
    relationship, separated by <subj> and <obj>
    tokens.

Input Sentence: <Sentence> [/INST]

Causal Relation Triplets : <triplet> Subject_1
    <subj> Target_1 <obj> Relationship_1
<triplet> Subject_2 <subj> Target_2 <obj>
    Relationship_2 </s>
```

A complete example, including the prompt, a sample sentence, and its causal relation triplets used for instruction tuning, is provided below:

```
<s>[INST] Given the input sentence, identify
    all the triplets of entities and the
    corresponding causal relationships between
    them. The entities should be phrases from
    the input sentence, and the relationships
    should either be 'Positive' or 'Negative'.
    Each new extracted triplet should start
    with the <triplet> token, followed by the
    subject phrase, the object phrase, and the
    relationship, separated by <subj> and <obj>
    tokens.

Input Sentence: Islamist violence in Mali has
    also hit cattle herding areas, forcing
    farmers to abandon their trade. Climate
    change too has led to competition for
    grazing lands and water, leading to
    intercommunal conflicts. The result,
    increased costs for breeders. [/INST]

Causal Relation Triplets : <triplet> islamist
    violence <subj> cattle herding <obj>
    negative
<triplet> climate change <subj> competition for
    grazing lands and water <obj> positive
<triplet> competition for grazing lands and
    water <subj> intercommunal conflicts <obj>
    positive
<triplet> intercommunal conflicts <subj>
    increased costs for breeders <obj> positive
    </s>
```

E.2 Llama-3-8B

Llama-3-8B-Instruct follows a different prompt format compared to Llama-2 or Mistral. An example of the prompt format for Llama-3-8B-Instruct is provided below:

```
<|begin_of_text|><|start_header_id|>
    system<|end_header_id|>

Given the input sentence, identify all the
    triplets of entities and the corresponding
    causal relationships between them. The
    entities should be phrases from the input
    sentence, and the relationships should
    either be 'Positive' or 'Negative'. Each
    new extracted triplet should start with the
```

```
    <triplet> token, followed by the subject
    phrase, the object phrase, and the
    relationship, separated by <subj> and <obj>
    tokens. <|eot_id|><|start_header_id|>
    user<|end_header_id|>

Input Sentence : A direct negative effect that
    for example a wind farm can have on the
    trawl fishery (reduced fishing activity),
    <|eot_id|><|start_header_id|>
    assistant<|end_header_id|>

Casual Relation Triplets : <triplet> wind farm
    <subj> trawl fishery <obj> negative
    <|eot_id|>
```

F Prompts Format For Zero- and Three-Shot Learning

F.1 Zero-Shot Learning

To achieve structured output in zero-shot and three-shot in-context learning, we optimized the prompts. Examples of the prompts used in zero-shot in-context learning for all the models are as follows:

F.1.1 Llama-2-7B-chat-hf

```
<s>[INST] <<SYS>> Given the input sentence,
    identify all the triplets (subject,
    object and causal relation) . The
    subject and object should be phrases
    from the input sentence.
The causal relation between subject and
    object should strictly be either
    "Positive" or "Negative" and nothing
    else.
Each new extracted triplet i.e. subject,
    object and relation should start with a
    newline should be within <triple> and
    </triplet>. The subject should be
    within <subj> and </subj> tokens. The
    object should be within <obj> and
    </obj> tokens. The causal relation
    should be within <relation> and
    </relation> tokens. The format of
    output of each triplet should be
    strictly like below:

<triplet>
    <subj> </subj>
    <obj> </obj>
    <relation> </relation>
</triplet>
<</SYS>>
Input Sentence : pastoralists in the arid
    and semi-arid regions of Mali continue
    to face increasing risk due to low
    levels of rainfall [/INST]
Causal Relation Triplet :

<triplet>
    <subj> pastoralists</subj>
    <obj> low levels of rainfall</obj>
    <relation> Negative</relation>
</triplet>
<triplet>
    <subj> Mali</subj>
    <obj> increasing risk</obj>
    <relation> Positive</relation>
</triplet>

Note: The subject and object phrases are
    enclosed within <subj> and <obj>
    tokens, respectively, and the causal
    relation is enclosed within <relation>
    and </relation> tokens.
```

F.1.2 Llama-3-8B-Instruct

```
<|begin_of_text|> <|start_header_id|> system
    <|end_header_id|>Given the input
    sentence, identify all the triplets
    (subject, object and causal relation).
    The subject and object should be
    phrases from the input sentence.
The causal relation between subject and
    object should strictly be either
    "Positive" or "Negative" and nothing
    else.
Each new extracted triplet i.e. subject,
    object and relation should start with a
    newline should be within <triple> and
    </triplet>. The subject should be
    within <subj> and </subj> tokens. The
    object should be within <obj> and
    </obj> tokens. The causal relation
    should be within <relation> and
    </relation> tokens.
The format of output of each triplet should
    be strictly like below:
<triplet>
    <subj> </subj>
    <obj> </obj>
    <relation> </relation>
</triplet> <|eot_id|><|start_header_id|>
    user <|end_header_id|>
Input Sentence : Women identified forced sex
    and men highlighted lack of awareness
    about contraception and fear of side
    effects as important causes of kunika.
    <|eot_id|><|start_header_id|> assistant
    <|end_header_id|>
<triplet>
    <subj>Women</subj>
    <obj>forced sex</obj>
    <relation>Positive</relation>
</triplet>

<triplet>
    <subj>men</subj>
    <obj>lack of awareness about
        contraception and fear of side
        effects</obj>
    <relation>Positive</relation>
</triplet>

<triplet>
    <subj>men</subj>
    <obj>kunika</obj>
    <relation>Negative</relation>
</triplet>
```

F.1.3 Mistral-7B-Instruct-v0.2

```
<s>[INST] Given the input sentence, identify
    all the triplets (subject, object and
    causal relation) . The subject and
    object should be phrases from the input
    sentence.
The causal relation between subject and
    object should strictly be either
    "Positive" or "Negative" and nothing
    else.
Each new extracted triplet i.e. subject,
    object and relation should start with a
    newline should be within <triple> and
    </triplet>. The subject should be
    within <subj> and </subj> tokens. The
    object should be within <obj> and
    </obj> tokens. The causal relation
    should be within <relation> and
    </relation> tokens. The format of
    output of each triplet should be
    strictly like below:
<triplet>
    <subj> </subj>
    <obj> </obj>
    <relation> </relation>
</triplet>

Input Sentence : pastoralists in the arid
    and semi-arid regions of Mali continue
    to face increasing risk due to low
    levels of rainfall [/INST]
Causal Relation Triplet :
 <triplet>
    <subj> pastoralists in the arid and
        semi-arid regions of Mali </subj>
    <obj> face increasing risk </obj>
    <relation> Positive </relation>
</triplet>
<triplet>
    <subj> Low levels of rainfall </subj>
    <obj> cause pastoralists in the arid and
        semi-arid regions of Mali to face
        increasing risk </obj>
    <relation> Negative </relation>
</triplet>
```

F.2 Three-Shot Learning

To achieve structured output in three-shot in-context learning, we optimized the prompts. Below are examples of the prompts used in three-shot in-context learning for all the models:

F.2.1 Llama-2-7B-chat-hf

```
<s>[INST] <<SYS>> Given the input sentence,
    identify all the triplets of entities
    and the corresponding causal
    relationships between them. The
    entities should be phrases from the
    input sentence, and the relationships
    should either be 'Positive' or
    'Negative'. Each new extracted triplet
    should start with the <triplet> token,
    followed by the subject phrase, the
    object phrase, and the relationship,
    separated by <subj> and <obj> tokens.
Don't add extra sentences.
<</SYS>>
Input Sentence : the current price of local
    rice (sold loose) at the local market
    is 1850 ngn/1kg. the price is expected
    to rise to 2100 ngn/1kg in 6 weeks, due
    to the high cost of oil. [/INST]
Causal Relation Triplets : <triplet> high
    cost of oil <subj> price of local rice
    <obj> positive
</s>
[INST]
Input Sentence : Participants also believed
    that illiteracy and low levels of
    education among some of the women were
    barriers to seeking skilled pregnancy
    health care. [/INST]
Causal Relation Triplets : <triplet>
    illiteracy among women <subj> access to
    skilled pregnancy health care <obj>
    negative
<triplet> low education among women are
    understaffed <subj> access to skilled
    pregnancy health care <obj> negative
</s>
[INST]
Input Sentence : Other health sources of
    protein are lean meats, low-fat milk,
    nuts, and beans such as kidney beans.
    [/INST]
Causal Relation Triplets : <triplet> nuts
    <subj> health sources of protein <obj>
    positive
<triplet> meats <subj> health sources of
    protein <obj> positive </s>
<triplet> milk <subj> health sources of
    protein <obj> positive </s>
<triplet> beans <subj> health sources of
    protein <obj> positive </s>
</s>
[INST]
Input Sentence : pastoralists in the arid
    and semi-arid regions of Mali continue
    to face increasing risk due to low
    levels of rainfall [/INST]
Causal Relation Triplets :
 <triplet> low rainfall <subj> risk faced by
     pastoralists <obj> negative
```

F.2.2 Llama-3-8B-Instruct

```
<|begin_of_text|> <|start_header_id|> system
    <|end_header_id|> Given the input
    sentence, identify all the triplets of
    entities and the corresponding causal
    relationships between them. The
    entities should be phrases from the
    input sentence, and the relationships
    should either be 'Positive' or
    'Negative'. Each new extracted triplet
    should start with the <triplet> token,
    followed by the subject phrase, the
    object phrase, and the relationship,
    separated by <subj> and <obj> tokens.
Don't add extra sentences.
    <|eot_id|><|start_header_id|> user
    <|end_header_id|>
Input Sentence : the current price of local
    rice (sold loose) at the local market
    is 1850 ngn/1kg. the price is expected
```

```
        to rise to 2100 ngn/1kg in 6 weeks, due
        to the high cost of oil.
        <|eot_id|><|start_header_id|> assistant
        <|end_header_id|>
    Causal Relation Triplets : <triplet> high
        cost of oil <subj> price of local rice
        <obj> positive
        <|eot_id|><|start_header_id|> user
        <|end_header_id|>

    Input Sentence : Participants also believed
        that illiteracy and low levels of
        education among some of the women were
        barriers to seeking skilled pregnancy
        health care.
        <|eot_id|><|start_header_id|> assistant
        <|end_header_id|>
    Causal Relation Triplets : <triplet>
        illiteracy among women <subj> access to
        skilled pregnancy health care <obj>
        negative
    <triplet> low education among women are
        understaffed <subj> access to skilled
        pregnancy health care <obj> negative
        <|eot_id|><|start_header_id|> user
        <|end_header_id|>

    Input Sentence : Other health sources of
        protein are lean meats, low-fat milk,
        nuts, and beans such as kidney
        beans.<|eot_id|><|start_header_id|>
        assistant <|end_header_id|>
    Causal Relation Triplets : <triplet> nuts
        <subj> health sources of protein <obj>
        positive
    <triplet> meats <subj> health sources of
        protein <obj> positive
    <triplet> milk <subj> health sources of
        protein <obj> positive
    <triplet> beans <subj> health sources of
        protein <obj> positive
        <|eot_id|><|start_header_id|> user
        <|end_header_id|>

    Input Sentence : pastoralists in the arid
        and semi-arid regions of Mali continue
        to face increasing risk due to low
        levels of rainfall
        <|eot_id|><|start_header_id|> assistant
        <|end_header_id|>
   Causal Relation Triplets : <triplet> forced
       sex <subj> kunika <obj> positive
 <triplet> lack of awareness about
     contraception <subj> kunika <obj> positive
 <triplet> fear of side effects <subj> kunika
     <obj> positive
```

F.2.3 Mistral-7B-Instruct-v0.2

```
    <s>[INST] Given the input sentence, identify
        all the triplets of entities and the
        corresponding causal relationships
        between them. The entities should be
        phrases from the input sentence, and
        the relationships should either be
        'Positive' or 'Negative'. Each new
        extracted triplet should start with the
        <triplet> token, followed by the
        subject phrase, the object phrase, and
        the relationship, separated by <subj>
        and <obj> tokens.
    Don't add extra sentences.
    Input Sentence : the current price of local
        rice (sold loose) at the local market
        is 1850 ngn/1kg. the price is expected
        to rise to 2100 ngn/1kg in 6 weeks, due
        to the high cost of oil. [/INST]
    Causal Relation Triplets : <triplet> high
        cost of oil <subj> price of local rice
        <obj> positive
    </s>
    [INST]
    Input Sentence : Participants also believed
        that illiteracy and low levels of
        education among some of the women were
        barriers to seeking skilled pregnancy
        health care. [/INST]
    Causal Relation Triplets : <triplet>
        illiteracy among women <subj> access to
        skilled pregnancy health care <obj>
        negative
    <triplet> low education among women are
        understaffed <subj> access to skilled
        pregnancy health care <obj> negative
    </s>
    [INST]
    Input Sentence : Other health sources of
        protein are lean meats, low-fat milk,
        nuts, and beans such as kidney beans.
        [/INST]
    Causal Relation Triplets : <triplet> nuts
        <subj> health sources of protein <obj>
        positive
    <triplet> meats <subj> health sources of
        protein <obj> positive </s>
    <triplet> milk <subj> health sources of
        protein <obj> positive </s>
    <triplet> beans <subj> health sources of
        protein <obj> positive </s>
    </s>
    [INST]
    Input Sentence : pastoralists in the arid
        and semi-arid regions of Mali continue
        to face increasing risk due to low
        levels of rainfall [/INST]
    Causal Relation Triplets :
     <triplet> low levels of rainfall <subj>
         risk faced by pastoralists in arid and
         semi-arid regions of Mali <obj>
         positive.
```

G User Interfaces

In this appendix, we provide screenshots of the two custom Dash-based user interfaces (UIs) (Plotly, 2024) developed for this study. These UIs were integral to the annotation and evaluation processes, facilitating consistent data collection and pairwise comparisons.

G.1 Annotation Interface

Figure 4 shows the UI used by the seven participants to annotate the 20 selected samples. This interface was designed to be user-friendly and efficient, allowing participants to focus on the quality of their annotations. The annotations were saved in JSON format for consistency and ease of processing.

G.2 Elo Comparison Interface

Figure 5 displays the UI used for the Elo rating comparisons. In this interface, pairs of annotations were presented to participants, who were asked to choose the better annotation for each pair. This interface randomized the sequence of comparisons to eliminate potential biases and ensured that participants could not see their own annotations to prevent bias.

H Split Creation

The splits were created by taking the labelers annotations (7), extracting the names into a set, and generating a list of random numbers the length of which is the amount of combinations times the amount of texts chosen. Then, with nested loops, the outer of which being the texts, and the inner being the possible labeler combinations, these numbers were assigned in order (front of list to back of list). The dictionary was then sorted and made back into a dictionary. Then, this list was divided into splits by iterating through it, assigning one datapoint at a time to each labeler skipping that point if the labeler that is up is in the combinations. This loop continues until all points are assigned.

LLM additions followed a similar process. We looped through each labeler and created a combination list with them and the LLMs, but not the LLMs with each other. After, we generated values a random list and added the current length of the list to each point. Then, looping through the rest of the labelers, we follow the same process of looping through the dictionary and assigning one point at a time to a labeler. After all labelers had been paired with the LLMs, we created the combination list of the LLMs with each other, and followed the same process of looping through the labelers.

Finally, we generated a list of random numbers for each labeler as long as an individual labeler's split. Then, we reassigned the key values to the new list of random numbers to obscure the ordering in which the labels were added so as to randomize the order of presentation of pairings between labeler+labeler, labeler+LLM and LLM.

Inter-rater splits were created using only LLM outputs, where each labeler compared the three combinations for each of 20 samples.

H.1 Inter- and Intra-Rater Reliability

The bar plot in Figure 6 illustrates the inter- and intra-rater reliability among different percentages of raters. Specifically, 57.1% of raters agreed on 10% of the samples, 71.4% of raters agreed on 20% of the samples, another 85.7% of raters also agreed on 20% of the samples, and finally, 100% of raters agreed on 50% of the samples. Notably, this distribution shows that 90% of the data (0.2 + 0.2 + 0.5) received agreement from 71.4% of raters or more, highlighting a substantial consensus among the majority of raters in this evaluation. Raters, furthermore, demonstrated 90.5% self-consistency.

I Rater Guidelines

To support annotation scoring consistency and scientific reproducibility, raters were instructed to use the following guidelines when choosing a winner during pairwise comparisons:

1. Prefer more 'better' tuples rather than more 'worse' ones (this constitues our 'human-thresholded' F1 per discussion today).

2. Prefer node names that do not introduce new concepts that are not present in the text.

3. Prefer source/target in correct position.

4. If A affects B and if B affects C, we can also infer that A affects C. However, we should not include "A affects C" in the annotations, unless it is explicitly mentioned.

5. Prefer node names as close to the text as possible.

6. Prefer verbose node names (include adjectives) as these contain information that can be referenced, utilized, or abstracted away as necessary by downstream tasks/processes.

7. Prefer splitting node names at 'and' conjunctions when concepts are 'distinct', e.g., in "It is expected that both ecological and social compensation measures improve the overall acceptance of a local infrastructure, thus anchoring the latter within the surrounding community" it is better to have one source nodes corresponding to *ecological compensation measures* as well as one corresponding to *social compensation measures*.

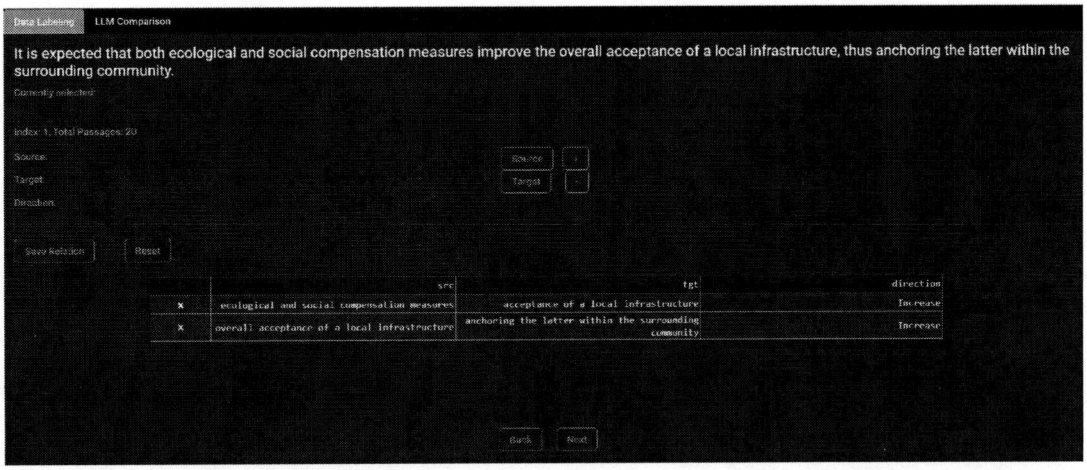

Figure 4: Screenshot of the annotation interface used by participants to annotate the text samples.

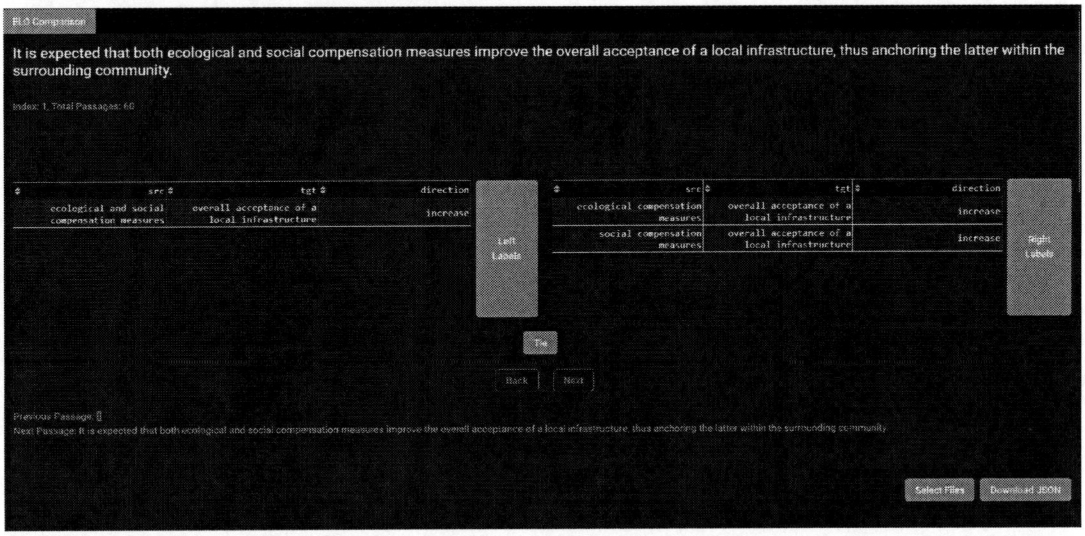

Figure 5: Screenshot of the Elo comparison interface used for pairwise comparisons of annotations. This interface helped in generating the Elo scores by allowing participants to select the better annotation in each presented pair.

8. Prefer correct direction of causal relation.

Some of these guidelines can be in conflict with each other. In these cases, prefer a heuristic higher on the above list; but in all cases, use your best judgment.

J Contrasts with F1

Table 4 provides paired differences in correlations between edge-based measures and vanilla F1 rankings.

Measure	Mean	90% CI	95% CI
BLEU-E	**0.399**	**(0.263, 0.535)**	**(0.234, 0.564)**
METEOR-E	**0.317**	**(0.142, 0.492)**	**(0.105, 0.528)**
ROUGE-E	**0.371**	**(0.210, 0.532)**	**(0.176, 0.566)**
BLEURT-E	**0.322**	**(0.173, 0.471)**	**(0.141, 0.503)**

Table 4: Mean paired differences between similarity measures' and the baseline F1 measure's correlations.

K Datasheet

K.1 Motivation for Dataset Creation

- *Why was the dataset created? (e.g., were there specific tasks in mind, or a specific gap that needed to be filled?)* The dataset is an amal-

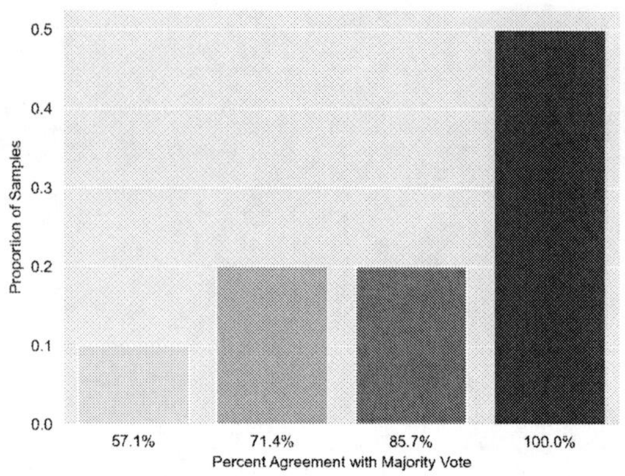

Figure 6: Inter-rater reliability for paired annotations

gamation of SES literature that is relevant to the authors of this article and/or their collaborators. Each sub-dataset was created in the process of developing FCM models of the relevant system.

- *What (other) tasks could the dataset be used for? Are there obvious tasks for which it should not be used?* Absolutely. We plan to further utilize this data in the construction of 'collective intelligence' models of these SES.
- *Has the dataset been used for any tasks already? If so, where are the results so others can compare (e.g., links to published papers)?* No.
- *Who funded the creation of the dataset? If there is an associated grant, provide the grant number.* The dataset creation was funded under the grants listed in the Acknowledgements section.

K.2 Dataset Composition

- *What are the instances? (that is, examples; e.g., documents, images, people, countries) Are there multiple types of instances? (e.g., movies, users, ratings; people, interactions between them; nodes, edges) Are relationships between instances made explicit in the data (e.g., social network links, user/movie ratings, etc.)? How many instances of each type are there?* Instances are text passage-tuple pairs that correspond to text data and associated concept pairs connected by causal relation edges. The dataset is apportioned as follows:
  - Total unique in Training: 224
  - Total unique in Validation : 38
  - Total unique in Testing : 56
- *What data does each instance consist of? "Raw" data (e.g., unprocessed text or images)? Features/attributes? Is there a label/target associated with instances? If the instances are related to people, are subpopulations identified (e.g., by age, gender, etc.) and what is their distribution?* See above. Concepts can consist of anything that, roughly, 'qualitatively or quantitatively increases or decreases.'
- *Is everything included or does the data rely on external resources? (e.g., websites, tweets, datasets) If external resources, a) are there guarantees that they will exist, and remain constant, over time; b) is there an official archival version. Are there licenses, fees or rights associated with any of the data?* The data does not rely on external resources.
- *Are there recommended data splits or evaluation measures? (e.g., training, development, testing; accuracy/AUC)* When training on multiple models, it is important to use a consistent test set.
- *What experiments were initially run on this dataset? Have a summary of those results and, if available, provide the link to a paper with more information here. Any other comments?* N/A

K.3 Data Collection Process

- *How was the data collected? (e.g., hardware apparatus/sensor, manual human curation, software program, software interface/API; how were these constructs/measures/methods validated?)* Text passages were collected by extracting raw text from PDF documents and encoding them as strings. Annotations were assigned via the UI described in the main paper body and appendices.
- *Who was involved in the data collection process? (e.g., students, crowdworkers) How were they compensated? (e.g., how much were crowdworkers paid?)* Only authors were involved in the data collection process. Funding consisted of salary and hourly pay.
- *Over what time-frame was the data collected? Does the collection time-frame match the creation time-frame?* 3 years. *How was the data*

associated with each instance acquired? Was the data directly observable (e.g., raw text, movie ratings), reported by subjects (e.g., survey responses), or indirectly inferred/derived from other data (e.g., part of speech tags; model-based guesses for age or language)? If the latter two, were they validated/verified and if so how? The data was directly observed in text.

- *Does the dataset contain all possible instances? Or is it, for instance, a sample (not necessarily random) from a larger set of instances? If the dataset is a sample, then what is the population? What was the sampling strategy (e.g., deterministic, probabilistic with specific sampling probabilities)? Is the sample representative of the larger set (e.g., geographic coverage)? If not, why not (e.g., to cover a more diverse range of instances)? How does this affect possible uses?* This dataset is a sample. The population consists of "all possible passage-tuple pairs." The dataset is representative in the same sense as data in other fine-tuning efforts (i.e., there is not a precisely meaningful sense of 'representativeness').

- *Is there information missing from the dataset and why? (this does not include intentionally dropped instances; it might include, e.g., redacted text, withheld documents) Is this data missing because it was unavailable?* N/A

- *Are there any known errors, sources of noise, or redundancies in the data?* Conversion of PDF to raw text can introduce errors, which we manually evaluated through samples.

K.4 Dataset Distribution

- *How is the dataset distributed? (e.g., website, API, etc.; does the data have a DOI; is it archived redundantly?)* It has thus far been shared only within the research team.

- *When will the dataset be released/first distributed? (Is there a canonical paper/reference for this dataset?)*The dataset will be released upon publication of the work.

- *What license (if any) is it distributed under? Are there any copyrights on the data?* The data will be openly available.

- *Are there any fees or access/export restrictions?* No.

K.5 Dataset Maintenance

- *Who is supporting/hosting/maintaining the dataset?*

- *How does one contact the owner/curator/manager of the dataset (e.g. email address, or other contact info)?* The dataset may be requested from the main author.

- *Will the dataset be updated? How often and by whom? How will updates/revisions be documented and communicated (e.g., mailing list, GitHub)? Is there an erratum?* Potentially.

- *If the dataset becomes obsolete how will this be communicated?* N/A

- *Is there a repository to link to any/all papers/systems that use this dataset?* N/A

- *If others want to extend/augment/build on this dataset, is there a mechanism for them to do so? If so, is there a process for tracking/assessing the quality of those contributions. What is the process for communicating/distributing these contributions to users?* Please send a request to the corresponding author.

K.6 Legal & Ethical Considerations

- *If the dataset relates to people (e.g., their attributes) or was generated by people, were they informed about the data collection? (e.g., datasets that collect writing, photos, interactions, transactions, etc.)* N/A

- *If it relates to other ethically protected subjects, have appropriate obligations been met? (e.g., medical data might include information collected from animals)* N/A

- *If it relates to people, were there any ethical review applications/reviews/approvals? (e.g. Institutional Review Board applications)*N/A

- *If it relates to people, were they told what the dataset would be used for and did they consent? What community norms exist for data collected from human communications? If consent was obtained, how? Were the people provided with any mechanism to revoke their consent in the future or for certain uses?* N/A

- *If it relates to people, could this dataset expose people to harm or legal action? (e.g., financial social or otherwise) What was done to mitigate or reduce the potential for harm?* N/A
- *If it relates to people, does it unfairly advantage or disadvantage a particular social group? In what ways? How was this mitigated?* N/A
- *If it relates to people, were they provided with privacy guarantees? If so, what guarantees and how are these ensured?* N/A
- *Does the dataset comply with the EU General Data Protection Regulation (GDPR)? Does it comply with any other standards, such as the US Equal Employment Opportunity Act?* N/A
- *Does the dataset contain information that might be considered sensitive or confidential? (e.g., personally identifying information)* No.
- *Does the dataset contain information that might be considered inappropriate or offensive?* No.

Hypothesis Generation with Large Language Models

Yangqiaoyu Zhou♣, Haokun Liu♣, Tejes Srivastava♣
Hongyuan Mei† & Chenhao Tan♣
Department of Computer Science
University of Chicago♣, Toyota Technological Institute at Chicago†
Chicago, IL 60637, USA
{zhouy1,haokunliu,tejess,chenhao}@uchicago.edu,hongyuan@ttic.edu

Abstract

Effective generation of novel hypotheses is instrumental to scientific progress. So far, researchers have been the main powerhouse behind hypothesis generation by painstaking data analysis and thinking (also known as the Eureka moment). In this paper, we examine the potential of large language models (LLMs) to generate hypotheses. We focus on hypothesis generation based on data (i.e., labeled examples). To enable LLMs to handle long contexts, we generate initial hypotheses from a small number of examples and then update them iteratively to improve the quality of hypotheses. Inspired by multi-armed bandits, we design a reward function to inform the exploitation-exploration tradeoff in the update process. Our algorithm is able to generate hypotheses that enable much better predictive performance than few-shot prompting in classification tasks, improving accuracy by 31.7% on a synthetic dataset and by 13.9%, 3.3% and, 24.9% on three real-world datasets. We also outperform supervised learning by 12.1% and 11.6% on two challenging real-world datasets. Furthermore, we find that the generated hypotheses not only corroborate human-verified theories but also uncover new insights for the tasks.

1 Introduction

Hypothesis generation drives scientific progress. Mendel's hypothesis on allele pairs lays the foundation for modern genetics; Einstein's hypothesis in general theory of relativity led to the prediction and subsequent confirmation of gravitational waves. In the context of language modeling, the hypothesis on scaling law inspires recent progress in large language models (LLMs) (Kaplan et al., 2020). Despite the importance of hypothesis generation, as Ludwig and Mullainathan (2024) point out, science has been curiously asymmetric. While many scientific publications present extensive formal and empirical evaluation of hypotheses, the generation of hypotheses happens off-stage by researchers. In order to generate novel hypotheses, researchers may read literature, analyze data, pick the brain of each other, and even "hallucinate" (see Kekulé's discovery of the structure of the benzene molecule (Rothenberg, 1995)). Given the rise of large language models (Brown et al., 2020; Anthropic, 2023; OpenAI, 2023b), we examine their potential of providing much needed assistance in hypothesis generation in this work.

In particular, we focus on hypothesis generation based on data, a common approach in empirical sciences. Our main question is how we can enable LLMs to generate hypotheses of high-quality. While one can easily prompt LLMs to generate hypotheses, LLMs may not be able to effectively leverage the input examples in a single long prompt. Moreover, it is important to have measures of quality in the generation process so that we can filter bad hypotheses and come up with better ones. These two observations motivate us to start with a setup analogous to supervised learning. We can iteratively prompt an LLM to generate hypotheses based on the training examples and use training accuracy as a measure of quality to guide the generation process. Conveniently, we can also evaluate the quality of the final generated hypotheses with their performance on held-out examples, similar to supervised learning.

To generate high-quality hypotheses with LLMs, we propose an algorithm inspired by the upper confidence bound algorithm in multi-armed bandits (Auer, 2002) (**HypoGeniC**[1], **Hypo**thesis **Gen**eration **i**n **C**ontext; see Figure 1). Given initial hypotheses generated from a small number of examples, we need to assess their quality and propose new hypotheses to address their deficiencies. To navigate this exploration-exploitation tradeoff, we introduce a reward function and evaluate the top k hypotheses for each training example. We maintain a wrong example bank to capture the gap in knowledge of the hypotheses pool, and generate new hypotheses based on the wrong example bank to close the gap.

The generated hypotheses naturally enable an interpretable hypothesis-based classifier. We propose a suite of inference strategies given a set of hypotheses. We apply our method to one synthetic task where there is a single known valid hypothesis and three real-world tasks (DECEPTIVE REVIEWS, HEADLINE POPULARITY, and TWEET POPULARITY). The real-world tasks focus on deception detection and message popularity prediction, which are known to be challenging even for humans (Ott et al., 2011; Salganik et al., 2006). Our al-

[1]We have publicly released the code and data for **HypoGeniC** at https://github.com/ChicagoHAI/hypothesis-generation.

Proceedings of the 1st Workshop on NLP for Science (NLP4Science), pages 117–139
November 16, 2024 ©2024 Association for Computational Linguistics

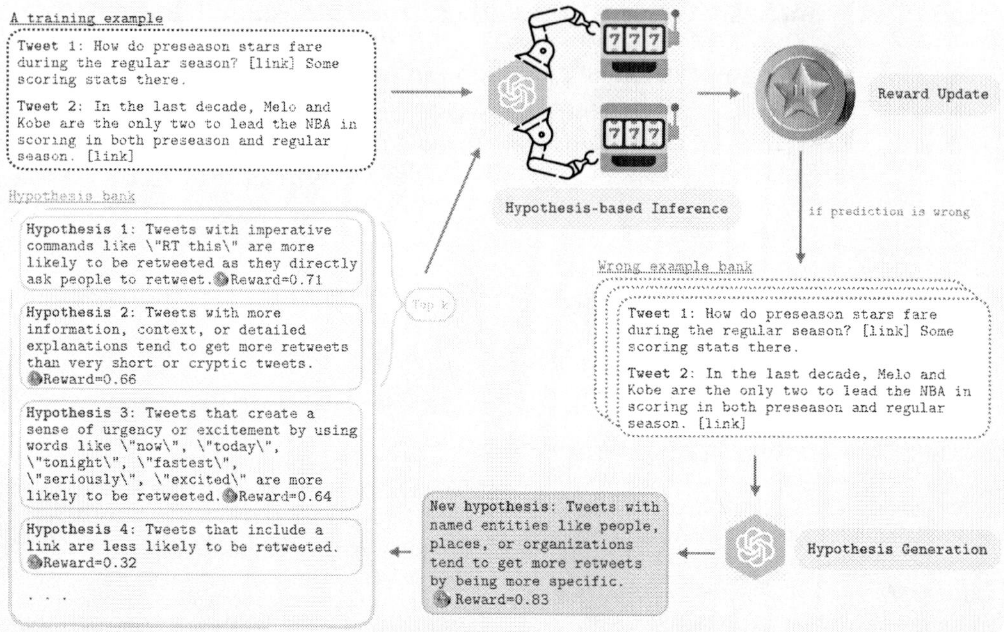

Figure 1: Illustration of **HypoGeniC**. During update stage, we evaluate the top k hypotheses on each new training example and update the reward based on the prediction correctness. If the number of hypotheses that got the example wrong exceeds a certain threshold, we add the example to a wrong example bank. The wrong example bank is then used to generate new hypotheses.

gorithm can recover the hypothesis in the synthetic task and also provide useful hypotheses for the real-world tasks. In fact, our generated hypotheses consistently outperform few-shot in-context learning baselines across all four tasks (31.7% in SHOE SALES, 13.9% in DECEPTIVE REVIEWS, 3.3% in HEADLINE POPULARITY, and 24.9% in TWEET POPULARITY). The predictive performance matches and even outperforms oracle supervised learning with RoBERTa and Llama-2-7B except in DECEPTIVE REVIEWS.

It is important to emphasize that although the utility of hypotheses in assisting downstream classification serves as an indicator for LLMs' ability to generate hypotheses, **our goal is not to maximize the classification performance.** Rather, our primary interest lies in the **quality of the hypotheses**. Thus, it is critical for the hypotheses to be interpretable beyond the LLM used to produce the hypotheses. We show that hypotheses generated by one LLM (e.g., GPT-3.5-turbo) can be used to make accurate inference by another LLM (e.g., Mixtral). On an out-of-distribution dataset for DECEPTIVE REVIEWS, we can even outperform the oracle fine-tuned RoBERTa. Such cross generalization provides strong evidence that we are able to generate hypotheses of high quality. Furthermore, through a qualitative analysis, **our generated hypotheses not only confirm theories from existing literature but also provide new insights about the task.** For instance, one novel hypothesis is that "reviews that mention personal experiences or special occasions, such as birthdays, anniversaries, or weddings, are more likely to be truthful". We encourage future research on deception detection to explore these novel hypotheses.

To summarize, we make the following contributions:

- We propose a novel computational framework for generating and evaluating hypotheses with LLMs.
- Our generated hypotheses enable interpretable hypothesis-based classifiers that outperform in-context learning and even supervised learning for one synthetic and three real-world datasets. These hypotheses are also robust across different LLMs and out-of-distribution datasets.
- Our generated hypotheses corroborate existing findings while also providing new insights for the tasks.

2 Method

We begin with a description of the problem formulation. Given a set $\mathcal{S} = \{(x_1, y_1), \dots, (x_n, y_n)\}$ where x_i is an example and y_i is the corresponding label, the goal is to learn a set of hypotheses $\mathcal{H} = \{h_1, ..., h_m\}$ that describe theories of relationships between x and y. To this end, we prompt an LLM to summarize demonstration examples into high-level hypotheses (§ 2.1). Then, during inference, the LLM makes inference based on the generated hypothesis (§ 2.2).

2.1 Hypothesis Generation

Our hypothesis generation algorithm (Algorithm 1) is inspired by the upper confidence bound (UCB) algorithm (Auer, 2002). Given a set of initial examples $\mathcal{S}_{\text{init}} \subset \mathcal{S}$, we first prompt an LLM to generate hypotheses for $\mathcal{S}_{\text{init}}$, which serve as our initial hypothesis bank $\mathcal{H}$. While initialized hypotheses may explain some portions of data, they often fall short of encompassing the full scope of the examples. We thus introduce an update stage which serves a dual purpose: 1) it increases the percentage of data explainable by the hypotheses and 2) it replaces any hypotheses that are found to be inaccurate.

In the update stage, for a training example s, we select the top k high-reward hypotheses from the hypothesis bank $\mathcal{H}$. The LLM is prompted to make a prediction with each of the top k high-reward hypotheses on s. Then we compute the accuracy of the inference and accordingly update the reward for each of the hypotheses. If w_{hyp} hypotheses predict incorrectly for the example s, then s is added to a wrong example pool $\mathcal{W}$. Once the wrong example pool reaches a max size of w_{max}, the wrong examples in $\mathcal{W}$ are used to generate new hypotheses. The wrong example pool represents the gap in knowledge that the current pool of hypotheses has for the dataset. Thus, by generating new hypotheses, the algorithm fills in these gaps. We update $\mathcal{H}$ with the newly generated hypotheses as per the rewards.

Reward. As mentioned above, each hypothesis has an associated reward. In our algorithm, we use the reward function in the UCB algorithm due to similarities between the multi-arm bandit problem and our problem formulation. In particular, we consider each hypothesis to be an arm and each training example to be a "pull". We note, however, that unlike the multi-arm bandit problem, multiple hypotheses are tested for a singular train example. Moreover, there can be new arms after hypotheses are updated, altering the setting from the standard static arms scenario to a dynamic arms scenario. Formally, the reward is defined as

$$r_i = \frac{\sum_{(x_j,y_j)\in\mathcal{S}_i} I(y_j = \hat{y}_j)}{|\mathcal{S}_i|} + \alpha\sqrt{\frac{\log t}{|\mathcal{S}_i|}}, \quad (1)$$

where $\mathcal{S}_i$ is the set of examples that have been used to evaluate the hypothesis h_i, t is train time step, and α is a hyperparameter that controls the exploration term. The first term in the reward function denotes the accuracy of the hypothesis for all $\mathcal{S}_i$. The second term is the exploration term, which is computed based on the number of times the hypothesis has been selected and the number of training examples visited so far. The accuracy term urges the algorithm to use well-performing hypotheses, whereas the exploration term encourages the algorithm to explore hypotheses that have not been selected many times. Thus, the reward function strikes a balance between exploration and exploitation.

For more details on implementation of **HypoGeniC**, refer to Appendix B.1.

Algorithm 1 HypoGeniC

```
Input: Training samples S, num_init, k, w_max, H
// Initialize hypothesis bank
H ← generate_hypotheses({S_i : i ≤ num_init})
W ← {}
for (x_t, y_t) ∈ S :
    H_top ← {h : h ∈ H has top k reward}
    for h ∈ H_top :
        ŷ_t^h ← inference(h, t)
        update_reward(h, y_t, ŷ_t^h)
    if |{wrong(ŷ_t^h) : h ∈ H}| ≥ w_hyp :
        // w_hyp is dynamically determined, see Appendix B.1
        W ← W ∪ {(x_t, y_t)}
    if |W| = w_max :
        N ← generate_hypotheses(W)
        W ← {}
        H ← {h : h ∈ H ∪ N has top k reward}
return H
```

2.2 Hypothesis-based Inference

For efficiency purposes, we use each hypothesis on its own without accounting for their combinatorial effect during training; however, we should leverage the set of hypotheses as a whole during inference for at least two reasons. Firstly, some hypotheses may only apply to a subset of examples. Second, competing theories may require head-to-head comparisons. Hence, we develop multiple inference strategies to account for these different styles of reasoning (see Appendix A for prompts and Appendix B.2 for implementation details).

- **Best-accuracy hypothesis.** The hypothesis h with the highest accuracy from the hypothesis bank is included in the prompt to guide the model to perform inference.

- **Filter and weighted vote.** One hypothesis may not be enough to explain the data. Thus, this approach uses a combination of relevant hypotheses to make predictions for a single example. We first *filter* hypotheses by prompting an LLM to judge which hypotheses are relevant to the example. Next, an LLM is prompted to generate predictions for each of the relevant hypotheses, and these predictions are aggregated with *weighted vote*, where the weight is the training accuracy of the corresponding hypothesis.

- **Single-step adaptive inference.** Similar to *filter and weighted vote*, this approach leverages contextual information to choose hypotheses. The difference, however, is that it selects the most applicable hypothesis for each test example. Specifically, for a given test example, the LLM is tasked with identifying the most applicable hypothesis from a set of options. For each hypothesis, we provide instances from the training set where the hypothesis was accurate. Then, the LLM selects the most relevant hypothesis by comparing the test example to these training examples and evaluating their similarity. Thereafter, we apply the hypothesis to the test example to perform inference. Please note that this is all done in one step with a long prompt.

- **Two-step adaptive inference.** We divide the previous inference strategy into two steps:
  1. The LLM determines the most relevant set of examples by comparing the test example with the corresponding examples of the hypotheses.
  2. Then, the corresponding hypothesis is provided to the LLM, which it uses to perform inference on the test example in a second prompt.

3 Experiment Setup

We introduce the experiment setup to evaluate **HypoGeniC**.

3.1 Tasks and Datasets

The choice of appropriate tasks is critical for evaluating the ability of LLMs to generate hypothesis. The focus of our work is on generating hypotheses based on observed data. A prerequisite is that potential hypotheses do exist. In the context of classification, it implies that the classification performance is non-trivial. In addition, we need to ensure that the hypotheses describing the data are likely not a priori known by LLMs, which rules out standard tasks such as sentiment analysis. Therefore, we use four datasets that satisfy these requirements: a synthetic task with a known true hypothesis and three *real-world* datasets that exhibit complex underlying patterns and constitute widely studied social science problems.

SHOE SALES is a synthetic task we created to investigate the scenario where there is only one single valid hypothesis. The task is to predict the color of the shoe that the customer will buy based on their appearance. The input provides appearance features, namely, age, height, gender, color of the hat, color of the shirt, color of the bag, and size of the bag. We construct this dataset such that the color of the shoe must match the color of the shirt. Since there are six colors in total, this becomes a 6-class classification problem.

Deceptive review detection is an instance of deception detection, a widely studied phenomenon in psychology and other social sciences (Granhag and Vrij, 2005). This particular task (DECEPTIVE REVIEWS) requires distinguishing genuine reviews from fictitious ones (Ott et al., 2011), where human performance is about chance (Lai and Tan, 2019). The dataset includes 800 genuine reviews and 800 fictitious reviews for 20 hotels in Chicago.

Predicting popularity is a notoriously challenging task in social sciences because it is known to be affected by seemingly random factors (Salganik et al., 2006). We use two datasets in this work: HEADLINE POPULARITY and TWEET POPULARITY. HEADLINE POPULARITY is derived from a dataset in the Upworthy Research Archive (Matias et al., 2021). The original dataset was collected through A/B testing, where each user was shown pairs of a headline and image for multiple packages (articles). Each user was exposed to only one of these pairs per package, and the clicks were recorded for each pair per package.[2] This process resulted in a total of 150,816 headlines across 22,666 packages. We construct a binary classification dataset by choosing the headlines that received the most clicks and least clicks for each package. We remove all sets of duplicate headlines, which results in our version of the HEADLINE POPULARITY dataset. The task for this dataset is to deduce which headline had more clicks in a pair. TWEET POPULARITY uses a dataset of 13,174 tweet pairs (Tan et al., 2014), which are matched by the topic and the author. Similar to HEADLINE POPULARITY, the task is to predict which one received more retweets.

3.2 Baselines, Oracles, and Evaluation Metrics

We use three different LLMs in our experiments (Mixtral (Mistral, 2023), GPT-3.5-turbo (OpenAI, 2023a), and Claude-2.1 (Anthropic, 2023)). We compare our approach with the following methods.

1. **Zero-shot and few-shot prompting.** We provide LLMs with task-specific instructions (zero-shot), optionally accompanied by three demonstration examples (few-shot).

2. **No updates.** To assess the value of the update stage in our algorithm, we evaluate the performance of the initialized hypotheses. In particular, we pick the best-performing hypothesis on the training set and use it for inference on the test set.

3. **Supervised Learning.** We fine-tune RoBERTa (Liu et al., 2019) and Llama-2-7B (Touvron et al., 2023) on each of the datasets to serve as a non-interpretable oracle. We include results for training on 200 examples and 1000 examples. Since fine-tuning update model weights, we expect RoBERTa and Llama-2-7B to set the upper bound on in-distribution datasets.

We randomly sample 200 training examples and 300 test examples for each dataset. Since all our datasets are classification tasks with ground truth labels, we use accuracy as our evaluation metric. To understand the effect of the number of training examples, we evaluate the performance of all methods at 10, 25, 50, 100, and 200 training examples. We also experiment with two different hypothesis bank sizes: 3 and 20 hypotheses to evaluate the impact of utilizing a larger number of hypotheses. The detailed hyperparameters of our approach can be found in Appendix B.3.

4 Results

To demonstrate the effectiveness of our hypothesis generation approach, we present results via three evaluation methods. First, we show that in the standard supervised

[2]The Upworthy Research Archive only provides the image IDs instead of the graphics. We thus only use the headlines for our dataset.

learning setup, our generated hypotheses enable more accurate predictions than baselines and even oracles when using a small set of examples. Second, we evaluate the generated hypotheses by checking whether they can generalize across different inference LLMs and to out-of-distribution datasets. We find surprisingly consistent performance even when using a different LLM to make inference from the generated hypotheses. So, we conduct a qualitative analysis to show that the generated hypotheses not only corroborate existing theories but also provide novel insights about the tasks at hand.

4.1 Performance on Heldout Test Sets

As discussed in the introduction, a side product of our approach is an interpretable hypothesis-based classifier. We compare its performance with standard supervised learning with the fine-tuned models and few-shot in-context learning (Table 1).

Our generated hypotheses improve inference over standard zero-shot and few-shot inference. Across all LLMs, **HypoGeniC** outperforms the zero-shot learning by an average of 60% on SHOE SALES, 22.7% on DECEPTIVE REVIEWS, 5.1% on HEADLINE POPULARITY, and 30.6% on TWEET POPULARITY. Similarly, we find that **HypoGeniC** shows an increase from few-shot learning by 31.7% on SHOE SALES, 13.9% on DECEPTIVE REVIEWS, 3.3% on HEADLINE POPULARITY, and 24.9% on TWEET POPULARITY. Note that these results are inflated on TWEET POPULARITY as safety mode is triggered for Mixtral and Claude-2.1 for zero-shot and few-shot learning respectively. After computing the 95% confidence intervals (with a binomial distribution assumption) for our results, the following results are significant for the real life datasets: **HypoGeniC** for DECEPTIVE REVIEWS and TWEET POPULARITY with Claude-2.1 and Mixtral, when comparing to their respective few shot baselines. If we relax the confidence interval to 90%, the result for HEADLINE POPULARITY with Mixtral is also statistically significant. These results demonstrate that hypothesis-based inference can increase the performance of LLMs significantly. Further results can be found in Table 5. One exception is that our method performs slightly worse (by 1%) than the few-shot baseline in the TWEET POPULARITY with GPT-3.5-turbo. One possible reason is that the few-shot demonstrations are effective at eliciting the pretraining knowledge in GPT-3.5-turbo, possibly due to a large amount of tweets in pretraining data. More detailed results are in Appendix C.

We also evaluate generated hypotheses with oracle inference, where the model retrospectively picks the best hypothesis for each prediction from the bank. With oracle inference, **HypoGeniC** achieves on average 88.6% on DECEPTIVE REVIEWS, 84.1% on HEADLINE POPULARITY, and 88% on TWEET POPULARITY across all LLMs, which are superior to results in Table 1. This result further suggests that hypotheses generated by **HypoGeniC** are of high quality and can lead to accurate predictions when the correct hypothesis is selected.

HypoGeniC matches or even exceeds the fine-tuned models with the same number of training examples on most datasets. Both **HypoGeniC** and the fine-tuned models yield 100% on the syntheic dataset. Moreover, **HypoGeniC** is 12.8% and 11.2% better than RoBERTa, and 12.1% and 11.6% better than Llama-2-7B, on HEADLINE POPULARITY and TWEET POPULARITY respectively with 200 training examples. Since the fine-tuned models learns by updating model weights to minimize the cross-entropy loss, it tends to benefit from more training examples, so we increase training examples to 1000 for the fine-tuned models. Despite the accuracy boost from more training examples, we find that **HypoGeniC**'s best result still outperforms RoBERTa by 3.7% and 0.7%, and Llama-2-7B by 3.7% and 11.4%, on HEADLINE POPULARITY and TWEET POPULARITY, respectively. One exception, however, is the DECEPTIVE REVIEWS dataset. We suspect that as word-level features are very useful in this dataset (Ott et al., 2011), they could be tougher for LLMs to extract but easier for fine-tuned models to grasp.

Updating the hypothesis bank leads to hypotheses of higher quality. Comparing **HypoGeniC** with the "no updates" results, we find that updating hypotheses generally leads to better hypotheses, suggesting that our algorithm is effective at improving hypothesis quality. The improvement is on average 0.7% on SHOE SALES, 5.8% on DECEPTIVE REVIEWS, 8.1% on HEADLINE POPULARITY, and 7% on TWEET POPULARITY. Another advantage of **HypoGeniC** over "no updates" is that sometimes the training examples exceed the context window size of LLMs, which can lead to degraded performance (Figures 4 and 5).

Effect of inference strategy. Figure 2 shows **HypoGeniC** results with different inference strategies on DECEPTIVE REVIEWS. Single-step adaptive inference is the most effective. Generally, we find hypotheses to be one-sided, focusing on either characteristics of truthful or deceptive reviews. We thus need to consider more than one hypothesis to make a correct prediction, so best-accuracy hypothesis or two-step adaptive inference are not ideal. On the other datasets, we find that the effect of inference strategy is much smaller (Figure 3). Best-accuracy hypothesis is sufficient for SHOE SALES and HEADLINE POPULARITY, and filter and weighted vote works best for TWEET POPULARITY. **Whichever inference strategy we use, the trend of HypoGeniC against few-shot learning and the fine-tuned models remains largely the same.**

Generally, having more training examples and a larger hypothesis pool improves performance. We show performance for different methods as number of training examples increase in Figures 4–6. We find **HypoGeniC** accuracy steadily increases as training size increases on SHOE SALES, suggesting that an LLM is

Models	Methods	SHOE SALES	DECEPTIVE REVIEWS	HEADLINE POPULARITY	TWEET POPULARITY
RoBERTa (Oracle)	Train 200	100.0	84.0	49.0	50.7
	Train 1000	100.0	91.0	60.0	62.0
Llama-2-7B (Oracle)	Train 200	100.0	88.7	49.7	50.3
	Train 1000	100.0	92.3	60.0	51.3
Claude-2.1	Zero shot	36.0	31.0	59.0	50.3
	Few shot	75.0	51.0	60.0	0.3*
	HypoGeniC (no updates)	100.0	70.3	57.3	59.0
	HypoGeniC	**100.0**	**75.3**	**61.3**	**62.0**
Mixtral	Zero shot	43.0	55.0	55.0	2.7*
	Few shot	79.0	56.3	55.3	48.7
	HypoGeniC (no updates)	96.0	60.3	59.7	60.7
	HypoGeniC	**98.0**	**68.0**	**60.3**	**62.7**
GPT-3.5-turbo	Zero shot	39.0	50.0	56.0	41.0
	Few shot	49.0	55.0	60.0	**62.0**
	HypoGeniC (no updates)	100.0	56.0	44.0	45.0
	HypoGeniC	**100.0**	**60.7**	**63.7**	61.0

Table 1: Prediction accuracies with 200 examples. We report the best numbers across all hyperparameter configurations, number of training examples, and inference strategies for **HypoGeniC** (we discuss their effect in details in § 4.1). The sensitive nature of the TWEET POPULARITY dataset may cause models to have their safety mode triggered. These results are marked by * in the table.

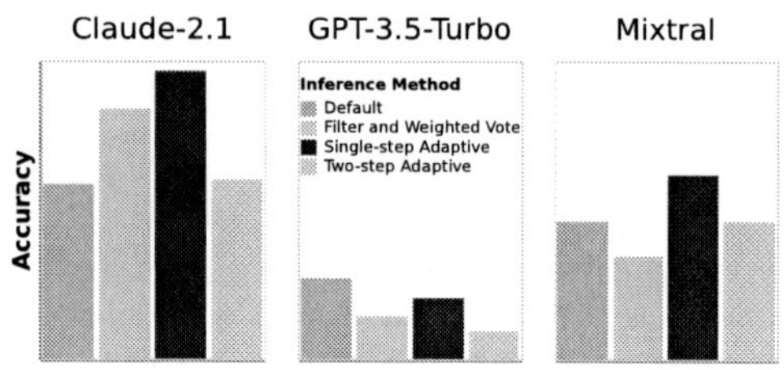

Figure 2: **HypoGeniC** results with different inference strategies on DECEPTIVE REVIEWS. Single-step adaptive hypothesis-based inference is generally the most effective on this dataset.

more likely to generate the best hypothesis given more examples. For the real-world datasets, however, the performance sometimes peaks at training size at 25 or 100 before reaching to 200. We suspect that the evaluation of the hypothesis bank would be less stable for the real-world datasets, since more than one correct hypotheses are needed for the task. We also find that using a hypothesis pool of size 20 leads to better performance than using a pool of size 3.

Although this classification experiment is convenient to run and demonstrates that our generated hypotheses are reasonable, our main goal is to generate high-quality hypotheses rather than maximizing the performance of this particular way of using the hypotheses. The next two experiments are essential in understanding the quality of hypotheses through generalization and manual analysis.

4.2 Generalization of the Generated Hypotheses

Our primary interest lies in the quality of the hypotheses. A good hypothesis should enable accurate inference by any AI model or even human and also generalize to unseen out-of-distribution dataset. In this subsection, we mix and match different LLMs for generation and inference. We also evaluate the hypotheses in deceptive review prediction on a new out-of-distribution (OOD) dataset (Li et al., 2013).

We find that the hypotheses generated by HypoGeniC generalize across models (Table 2). Generally, we find Claude-2.1 and Mixtral to be better at inference. Thus, substituting the inference model with them lead to better performance for hypothesis generated with GPT-3.5-turbo. Substituting Claude-2.1 and Mixtral as each other's inference model lead to small changes in performance. On SHOE SALES, the performance remains high for any inference model used.

Performance even increases for DECEPTIVE REVIEWS and HEADLINE POPULARITY when using Claude-2.1 as the inference model. For the cases where performance drops from Claude-2.1 to Mixtral, the decrease is marginal: 2.3% on DECEPTIVE REVIEWS and 2.7% on TWEET POPULARITY.

These results suggest that the hypotheses generated by **HypoGeniC** are generalizable across different LLMs, which somewhat contradicts the claim in Qiu et al. (2024) that LLMs cannot reliably interpret the hypotheses. We suspect that the reason is that our tasks only rely on natural language, while their tasks rely on notions of worlds and are fed into symbolic interpreters.

Generation Model	Inference Methods	SHOE SALES	DECEPTIVE REVIEWS	HEADLINE POPULARITY	TWEET POPULARITY
Claude-2.1	Claude-2.1	100.0	67.3	57.7	62.0
	Mixtral	94.0	65.0	57.7	59.3
	GPT-3.5-turbo	100.0	60.7	56.3	57.7
Mixtral	Claude-2.1	99.0	69.7	59.0	58.7
	Mixtral	98.0	61.3	57.7	59.3
	GPT-3.5-turbo	90.0	56.7	55.3	53.0
GPT-3.5-turbo	Claude-2.1	100.0	75.3	60.3	59.0
	Mixtral	98.0	62.0	60.0	62.3
	GPT-3.5-turbo	100.0	57.3	58.7	56.3

Table 2: Performance of cross-model generation and inference with train size = 200 using best-accuracy hypothesis inference and the best hypothesis bank size between 3 and 20.

Models	OOD
RoBERTa (Oracle)	73.0 (↓11.0)
Llama-2-7B (Oracle)	78.7 (↓10.0)
Claude-2.1 Few shot	41.7 (↓9.3)
Claude-2.1 **HypoGeniC**	**74.7** (↑4.7)
Mixtral Few shot	49.0 (↓7.3)
Mixtral **HypoGeniC**	64.7 (↑1.7)
GPT-3.5-turbo Few shot	52.0 (↓3.0)
GPT-3.5-turbo **HypoGeniC**	60.7 (↑3.4)

Table 3: Performance on OOD deceptive reviews.

Our generated hypotheses generalize to an out-of-distribution dataset. Table 3 presents an overview for the OOD deceptive review dataset. This dataset differs from DECEPTIVE REVIEWS by including reviews from four cities sourced from different websites (Li et al., 2013). We find that **HypoGeniC** outperforms few-shot learning by an average of 19.1%. Despite the distribution shift, **HypoGeniC** surprisingly increases accuracy from DECEPTIVE REVIEWS by an average of 3.3%, suggesting our hypotheses generalize well to this OOD dataset. Claude-2.1 remains the best performing model. In comparison, the performance of RoBERTa drops by 11%, and Llama-2-7B drops by 10%. As a result, **HypoGeniC** with Claude-2.1 outperforms RoBERTa by 1.7%, demonstrating the robustness of hypothesis-based inference. Refer to Appendix C.3 for more details.

4.3 Qualitative Analysis

For the synthetic dataset, all models are able to find the true underlying hypothesis for SHOE SALES: "customers tend to buy shoes that match the color of their shirt." For the real-world datasets, we search for studies on these datasets on Google Scholar and compare our hypotheses with findings from the literature. We confirm the validity of some of our hypotheses and discover new insights about the tasks that previous studies did not touch upon. We show a few examples in Table 4, and the full list of hypotheses can be found in Appendix D.

Our generated hypotheses align with useful features in existing literature. For DECEPTIVE REVIEWS, we find that deceptive reviews are more likely to be emotional, use superlatives, or contain information that could not have been directly experienced. Similar findings are also found by previous studies on DECEPTIVE REVIEWS (Lai et al., 2020; Anderson and Simester, 2014; Ott et al., 2011; Li et al., 2014). For TWEET POPULARITY, we discover that tweets that are concise, with specific or relevant hashtags, or with emotional tones are more likely to be retweeted more, aligning with prior studies (Tan et al., 2014; Gligorić et al., 2019). For HEADLINE POPULARITY, we find that revealing something new or using vivid language and imagery can drive engagement from readers to click on headlines. Previous studies also find these rules apply to online news headlines (Banerjee and Urminsky, 2021; Sadoski et al., 2000).

We also discover new insights with our generated hypotheses. For the DECEPTIVE REVIEWS dataset, truthful reviews could mention the reviewer's purpose for staying at the hotel (e.g., business trip, vacation), but deceptive ones tend not to have this information. For HEADLINE POPULARITY, we find that headlines that frame the content in a personal or relatable way are clicked more. For TWEET POPULARITY, tweets that mention influential individuals or organizations are more likely to be retweeted.

Intriguingly, one of our hypotheses contradicts a feature engineering result. Ott et al. (2011) find that the token "future" is associated with deceptive reviews, while one of our hypotheses says that mentions of "past experiences or future travel plans" are indicative of truthfulness. This discrepancy is interesting, because the context for the token "future" is unclear. It could be in the context of future plans but could also be as a complaint about "never going to stay at the hotel in the future." Feature engineering is limited by contextual ambiguity, whereas our generated hypotheses and their interpretation by LLMs overcome such limitations.

Dataset	Finding	Supported/Novel
DECEPTIVE REVIEWS	Deceptive reviews contain more emotional terms.	Li et al. (2014)
	Truthful reviews would mention weddings or special occasions.	
HEADLINE POPULARITY	Using vivid language and imagery helps.	Banerjee and Urminsky (2021)
	Headlines that frame the content in a personal or relatable way are clicked more.	
TWEET POPULARITY	Tweets with emotional tones are retweeted more.	Tan et al. (2014)
	Mentioning influential individuals or organizations leads to more retweets.	

Table 4: Selected examples of generated hypotheses (on the real-world datasets) and whether they support existing findings or are novel.

Our automatic evaluation of hypothesis quality also reflects negative findings. Given mixed evidence from previous literature on the effect of "reading ease" on headline clicks, Banerjee and Urminsky (2021) finds that reading ease negatively impacts click-through rates in HEADLINE POPULARITY through careful feature engineering. Consistent with this result, we found that the hypotheses that claim "straightforward" and "clear" writing to be indicative of higher click-through rates have relatively lower accuracies during training.

5 Additional Related Work

Concept/pattern discovery. Our work is connected to many recent studies on using LLMs to propose "hypotheses", notably, Qiu et al. (2024) and Zhong et al. (2023). Qiu et al. (2024) is motivated by testing the ability of LLMs to perform human-like induction reasoning, and Zhong et al. (2023) aims to support open-ended exploration. Similar to Qiu et al. (2024), Tenenbaum et al. (2011) is motivated by human inductive reasoning and examines concept induction in synthetic settings. Ellis et al. (2020) further learns to program concepts. Yang et al. (2024a) performs LLM-based inductive reasoning with a dataset that requires existing fact-rule pairs, which is not applicable in our real-world problems. Romera-Paredes et al. (2024) generates programs that lead to mathematical discovery. Similar to Zhong et al. (2023), Pham et al. (2024) generates and refine a list of topics to achieve interpretable topic modeling for open-ended exploration. Honovich et al. (2022) explores the deduction of task description from examples. Additionally, Qi et al. (2023), Wang et al. (2024), and Baek et al. (2024) use LLMs to generate hypotheses from previous literature. Yang et al. (2024b) tries to generate hypotheses from raw web corpus, but their method is not automated or scalable as it requires human annotated hypotheses from existing literature. Our work, in contrast, focuses on hypothesis generation between the input and the label for real-world challenging tasks and uses a UCB-style reward to propose novel algorithms.

Reasoning with LLMs. Although it is not our primary goal, our results show that hypothesis-based classifiers can outperform few-shot prompting. As hypotheses may be viewed as a form of reasoning, it is related to reasoning with LLMs (Wei et al., 2022; Wang et al., 2023, *i.a.*). In particular, our work differs from chain-of-thought reasoning because no predefined reasoning structure is available. Moreover, an important distinction between reasoning and hypothesis generation is that the former leverages established reasoning, while the latter requires both proposition and verification of the hypotheses, to discover unknown knowledge.

LLMs for (social) sciences. Increasing attention has been brought to the use of LLMs in social science research (Ziems et al., 2024; Kim and Lee, 2023, *i.a.*). Our experiments demonstrate the potential of LLMs in generating hypotheses for social science research to discover unknown knowledge in the data. Furthermore, our approach can be extended to natural sciences for general scientific discovery.

6 Conclusion & Further Discussion

In this work, we propose **HypoGeniC**, a novel data-driven and automated method that leverages LLMs to generate hypotheses with the goal of discovering unknown knowledge. With **HypoGeniC**, we are not only are able to generate human-interpretable hypotheses but also achieve better predictive performance against competitive baselines and even oracles. Furthermore, our method can generalize well with different models and datasets, including open models. Notably, with our generated hypotheses, we uncover new insights in real-world tasks that are widely studied in social sciences.

The key to success in **HypoGeniC** is not that LLMs remembers the correct hypotheses, but lies in their ability to "hallucinate" and combine potentially relevant concepts. The exploration-exploitation process then identifies the valuable hypotheses. **HypoGeniC** can be directly applied to complex social science tasks. We encourage future work to explore hypothesis generation that requires additional modalities and/or leverages existing literature along with past observations.

7 Limitations

We address common concerns using a Q&A format.

Q: Why only experiment with social science tasks?

A: Math and physics problems and hypotheses are hard to represent in natural language and usually require symbolic parsers (Trinh et al., 2024). We leverage LLMs to perform tasks that it is naturally adept at, which lead us to social science tasks. We find that **HypoGeniC** demonstrates strong results for the selected tasks, indicating new possibilities in using LLMs for scientific discovery. We leave extending our framework to natural science tasks as future work.

Q: Why is **HypoGeniC** effective, given that the accuracy improvement is not significant in some settings?

A: Even if there is no significant improvement in accuracy, the benefits of **HypoGeniC** are found in the quality of hypotheses. We find that the generated hypotheses discover new patterns that were previously unseen, as discussed in § 4.3. Additionally, it is worth noting that LLMs are imperfect at reasoning. Thus, hypothesis-based inference with LLMs may not accurately reflect the quality of the hypotheses.

Q: Since you worked on some old datasets, what if the LLMs have pre-trained knowledge about these tasks?

A: In Table 1, the zero/few-shot learning results suggest that the models cannot solve the tasks by memorizing the data. Additionally in § 4.3, we show that **HypoGeniC** reveal new hypotheses, based on the literature space that we can manually search. Even if the models have been pre-trained on the datasets, these hypotheses were not reported in previous literature. This suggests that even experienced researchers still struggle in finding the hypotheses that **HypoGeniC** generate.

Q: What hyperparameters have you tried?

A: We aim to provide a robust framework for hypothesis generation, as opposed to focusing on the optimization of results. Thus, we did not perform an extensive hyperparameter search with the generation portion of **HypoGeniC**. We did not adjust the value of k, which determines $\mathcal{H}_{\text{top}}$ in Algorithm 1 to maintain efficiency. Additionally, we only considered the effect of using a hypothesis bank size of 3 and 20 to only test using an extremely small hypothesis bank size and a large one. The ideal hypothesis bank size may require further investigation. Finally, we only tested the size of our wrong example bank w_{max} as 10 to strike a balance between context window sizes and generation of good quality hypotheses. We believe that a more thorough hyperparameter search could improve the performance of our methodology.

Q: How costly is your approach?

A: HypoGeniC has high latency, specifically when using inference methods that require multiple prompts. For example, the filter and weighted vote inference policy requires iterating through the top hypotheses to determine relevance and then performing inference if it is relevant. For single-step adaptive inference and best accuracy hypothesis, however, **HypoGeniC** is efficient. Given that we request reasoning for all inference prompts, the procedure can be time-consuming and require financial costs (e.g., GPT-3.5-turbo takes $2.05 on average over 76 experiments with an average of 1.5 hours per experiment). This concern is alleviated when using open models. However, all these processes are still relatively cheap compared to human efforts.

Q: What are some potential risks of hypothesis generation?

A: One potential risk of hypothesis generation is that there is little guard regarding steorotypes and biases being confirmed if given data that may seem to enforce them. As a result, it can be potentially harmful to use **HypoGeniC** in a real-world setting without proper oversight. Additionally, if the data reveals personal information regarding people, there is no guarantee that the hypotheses generated will not reveal this information. We highly recommend human-AI collaboration in using **HypoGeniC** to ensure that the generated hypotheses are ethical and unbiased.

Acknowledgments

We thank the anonymous reviewers for their suggestions. We also thank members of the Chicago Human+AI Lab for their helpful comments. This work is supported in part by NSF grants IIS-2126602.

References

Eric T Anderson and Duncan I Simester. 2014. Reviews without a purchase: Low ratings, loyal customers, and deception. *Journal of Marketing Research*, 51(3):249–269.

Anthropic. 2023. Claude 2.

Peter Auer. 2002. Using confidence bounds for exploitation-exploration trade-offs. *Journal of Machine Learning Research*, 3(Nov):397–422.

Jinheon Baek, Sujay Kumar Jauhar, Silviu Cucerzan, and Sung Ju Hwang. 2024. ResearchAgent: Iterative research idea generation over scientific literature with large language models. *Preprint*, arXiv:2404.07738.

Akshina Banerjee and Oleg Urminsky. 2021. The language that drives engagement: A systematic large-scale analysis of headline experiments. *Social Science Research Network.*

Tom Brown, Benjamin Mann, Nick Ryder, Melanie Subbiah, Jared D Kaplan, Prafulla Dhariwal, Arvind Neelakantan, Pranav Shyam, Girish Sastry, Amanda Askell, Sandhini Agarwal, Ariel Herbert-Voss, Gretchen Krueger, Tom Henighan, Rewon Child, Aditya Ramesh, Daniel Ziegler, Jeffrey Wu, Clemens Winter, Chris Hesse, Mark Chen, Eric Sigler, Mateusz Litwin, Scott Gray, Benjamin Chess, Jack Clark, Christopher Berner, Sam McCandlish, Alec Radford, Ilya Sutskever, and Dario Amodei. 2020. Language models are few-shot learners. In *Proceedings of NeurIPS*, volume 33, pages 1877–1901.

Kevin Ellis, Catherine Wong, Maxwell Nye, Mathias Sablé-Meyer, Luc Cary, Lucas Morales, Luke Hewitt, Armando Solar-Lezama, and Joshua B. Tenenbaum. 2020. DreamCoder: growing generalizable, interpretable knowledge with wake-sleep Bayesian program learning. *Philosophical Transactions of the Royal Society A*, 381.

Kristina Gligorić, Ashton Anderson, and Robert West. 2019. Causal effects of brevity on style and success in social media. In *Proceedings of ACM HCI*.

Pär Anders Granhag and Aldert Vrij. 2005. Deception detection. *Psychology and law: An empirical perspective*, pages 43–92.

Or Honovich, Uri Shaham, Samuel R. Bowman, and Omer Levy. 2022. Instruction induction: From few examples to natural language task descriptions. In *Proceedings of ACL*.

Jared Kaplan, Sam McCandlish, Tom Henighan, Tom B. Brown, Benjamin Chess, Rewon Child, Scott Gray, Alec Radford, Jeffrey Wu, and Dario Amodei. 2020. Scaling laws for neural language models. *CoRR*, abs/2001.08361.

Junsol Kim and Byungkyu Lee. 2023. AI-augmented surveys: Leveraging large language models and surveys for opinion prediction. *Preprint*, arXiv:2305.09620.

Vivian Lai, Han Liu, and Chenhao Tan. 2020. "Why is 'Chicago' deceptive?" Towards building model-driven tutorials for humans. In *Proceedings of CHI*.

Vivian Lai and Chenhao Tan. 2019. On human predictions with explanations and predictions of machine learning models: A case study on deception detection. In *Proceedings of FAccT*.

Jiwei Li, Myle Ott, and Claire Cardie. 2013. Identifying manipulated offerings on review portals. In *Proceedings of EMNLP*.

Jiwei Li, Myle Ott, Claire Cardie, and Eduard Hovy. 2014. Towards a general rule for identifying deceptive opinion spam. In *Proceedings of ACL*, pages 1566–1576, Baltimore, Maryland. Association for Computational Linguistics.

Yinhan Liu, Myle Ott, Naman Goyal, Jingfei Du, Mandar Joshi, Danqi Chen, Omer Levy, Mike Lewis, Luke Zettlemoyer, and Veselin Stoyanov. 2019. RoBERTa: A robustly optimized bert pretraining approach. *ArXiv*.

Jens Ludwig and Sendhil Mullainathan. 2024. Machine learning as a tool for hypothesis generation*. *The Quarterly Journal of Economics*, page qjad055.

Jorge Nathan Matias, Kevin Munger, Marianne Aubin Le Quere, and Charles R. Ebersole. 2021. The upworthy research archive, a time series of 32,487 experiments in U.S. media. *Scientific Data*, 8.

Mistral. 2023. Mixtral of experts.

OpenAI. 2023a. Chatgpt.

OpenAI. 2023b. Gpt-4 technical report.

Myle Ott, Yejin Choi, Claire Cardie, and Jeffrey T. Hancock. 2011. Finding deceptive opinion spam by any stretch of the imagination. In *Proceedings of ACL*.

Chau Minh Pham, Alexander Hoyle, Simeng Sun, and Mohit Iyyer. 2024. Topicgpt: A prompt-based topic modeling framework. In *Proceedings of NAACL*.

Biqing Qi, Kaiyan Zhang, Haoxiang Li, Kai Tian, Sihang Zeng, Zhang-Ren Chen, and Bowen Zhou. 2023. Large language models are zero shot hypothesis proposers. In *NeurIPS 2023 Workshop on Instruction Tuning and Instruction Following*.

Linlu Qiu, Liwei Jiang, Ximing Lu, Melanie Sclar, Valentina Pyatkin, Chandra Bhagavatula, Bailin Wang, Yoon Kim, Yejin Choi, Nouha Dziri, and Xiang Ren. 2024. Phenomenal yet puzzling: Testing inductive reasoning capabilities of language models with hypothesis refinement. In *Proceedings of ICLR*.

Bernardino Romera-Paredes, Mohammadamin Barekatain, Alexander Novikov, Matej Balog, M Pawan Kumar, Emilien Dupont, Francisco JR Ruiz, Jordan S Ellenberg, Pengming Wang, Omar Fawzi, et al. 2024. Mathematical discoveries from program search with large language models. *Nature*, 625(7995):468–475.

Albert Rothenberg. 1995. Creative cognitive processes in kekule's discovery of the structure of the benzene molecule. *The American journal of psychology*, pages 419–438.

Mark Sadoski, Ernest T Goetz, and Maximo Rodriguez. 2000. Engaging texts: Effects of concreteness on comprehensibility, interest, and recall in four text types. *Journal of Educational Psychology*, 92(1):85.

Matthew J Salganik, Peter Sheridan Dodds, and Duncan J Watts. 2006. Experimental study of inequality and unpredictability in an artificial cultural market. *Science*, 311(5762):854–856.

Chenhao Tan, Lillian Lee, and Bo Pang. 2014. The effect of wording on message propagation: Topic- and author-controlled natural experiments on twitter. In *Proceedings of ACL*.

Joshua B. Tenenbaum, Charles Kemp, Thomas L. Griffiths, and Noah D. Goodman. 2011. How to grow a mind: Statistics, structure, and abstraction. *Science*, 331:1279 – 1285.

Hugo Touvron, Louis Martin, Kevin R. Stone, Peter Albert, Amjad Almahairi, Yasmine Babaei, Nikolay Bashlykov, Soumya Batra, Prajjwal Bhargava, Shruti Bhosale, Daniel M. Bikel, Lukas Blecher, Cristian Cantón Ferrer, Moya Chen, Guillem Cucurull, David Esiobu, Jude Fernandes, Jeremy Fu, Wenyin Fu, Brian Fuller, Cynthia Gao, Vedanuj Goswami,

Naman Goyal, Anthony S. Hartshorn, Saghar Hosseini, Rui Hou, Hakan Inan, Marcin Kardas, Viktor Kerkez, Madian Khabsa, Isabel M. Kloumann, A. V. Korenev, Punit Singh Koura, Marie-Anne Lachaux, Thibaut Lavril, Jenya Lee, Diana Liskovich, Yinghai Lu, Yuning Mao, Xavier Martinet, Todor Mihaylov, Pushkar Mishra, Igor Molybog, Yixin Nie, Andrew Poulton, Jeremy Reizenstein, Rashi Rungta, Kalyan Saladi, Alan Schelten, Ruan Silva, Eric Michael Smith, R. Subramanian, Xia Tan, Binh Tang, Ross Taylor, Adina Williams, Jian Xiang Kuan, Puxin Xu, Zhengxu Yan, Iliyan Zarov, Yuchen Zhang, Angela Fan, Melanie Kambadur, Sharan Narang, Aurelien Rodriguez, Robert Stojnic, Sergey Edunov, and Thomas Scialom. 2023. Llama 2: Open foundation and fine-tuned chat models. *ArXiv*.

Trieu Trinh, Yuhuai Tony Wu, Quoc Le, He He, and Thang Luong. 2024. Solving olympiad geometry without human demonstrations. *Nature*, 625:476–482.

Qingyun Wang, Doug Downey, Heng Ji, and Tom Hope. 2024. SciMON: Scientific inspiration machines optimized for novelty. In *Proceedings of ACL*.

Xuezhi Wang, Jason Wei, Dale Schuurmans, Quoc V Le, Ed H. Chi, Sharan Narang, Aakanksha Chowdhery, and Denny Zhou. 2023. Self-consistency improves chain of thought reasoning in language models. In *Proceedings of ICLR*.

Jason Wei, Xuezhi Wang, Dale Schuurmans, Maarten Bosma, Ed H. Chi, Quoc Le, and Denny Zhou. 2022. Chain of thought prompting elicits reasoning in large language models. In *Proceedings of NeurIPS*.

Zonglin Yang, Li Dong, Xinya Du, Hao Cheng, Erik Cambria, Xiaodong Liu, Jianfeng Gao, and Furu Wei. 2024a. Language models as inductive reasoners. In *Proceedings of EACL*.

Zonglin Yang, Xinya Du, Junxian Li, Jie Zheng, Soujanya Poria, and Erik Cambria. 2024b. Large language models for automated open-domain scientific hypotheses discovery. In *Proceedings of ACL*.

Ruiqi Zhong, Peter Zhang, Steve Li, Jinwoo Ahn, Dan Klein, and Jacob Steinhardt. 2023. Goal driven discovery of distributional differences via language descriptions. In *Proceedings of NeurIPS*.

Caleb Ziems, William Held, Omar Shaikh, Jiaao Chen, Zhehao Zhang, and Diyi Yang. 2024. Can large language models transform computational social science? *Computational Linguistics*, pages 1–55.

A Prompts

We follow the general prompt engineering guide from Claude (Anthropic, 2023) to craft the prompts. Specifically for all the prompts we use for LLMs, we split them into instruction and user prompts. In the instruction prompt, we first set a tone and context, followed by an explicit task description, and then specify the answer format. The user prompt then includes useful information such as past examples and learned hypothesis. By the end of the user prompt, we ask the LLM to make a prediction. At generation time, we input the instruction prompt to LLMs as system prompt, wrapped by the corresponding system prompt tokens for each model. Below are some example templates for the prompts associated with each task.

A.1 Shoe Sales

```
Instruction Prompt
You're a helpful assistant. Your task is given as
 follows:
Given a set of observations, we want to generate
hypotheses that are useful for predicting the
color of the shoes given the appearance of the
person.
Please be concise and keep the hypotheses to be
one-sentence long.
Please generate them in the format of
{1. [hypothesis].
2. [hypothesis].
...
<num_hypotheses>. [hypothesis].}
Only propose <num_hypotheses> possible hypotheses
 in total.
No need to explain the hypotheses.

User Prompt
We made some observations:
··· more examples here ···
Based on the above observations, generate
<num_hypotheses> hypotheses.
Please be concise and keep the hypotheses to be
one-sentence long.
Please generate them in the format of
{1. [hypothesis].
2. [hypothesis].
...
<num_hypotheses>. [hypothesis].}
Only propose <num_hypotheses> possible hypotheses
 in total.
```

Example 1: Hypothesis Generation.

```
Instruction Prompt
You are a shoe salesman and want to recommend
shoes to customers. There are white, red, orange,
 green, blue, and black shoes.
From past experiences, you learned some patterns.
Now, at each time, you should apply the learned
pattern, given below, to a new customer and
recommend a shoe color.
Give an answer for the shoe color recommendation.
 The answer should be one color word. It has to
be one of white, red, orange, green, blue, and
black.

User Prompt
Our learned pattern: <hypothesis_high_reward>
New customer: <appearance> is buying a pair of
shoes, the shoes should be which color?
Answer:
```

Example 2: Hypothesis-based Inference.

```
Instruction Prompt
You are a shoe salesman and want to recommend
shoes to customers. There are white, red, orange,
 green, blue, and black shoes.
Give your answer for the shoe color
recommendation. The answer should be one color
word. It has to be one of white, red, orange,
green, blue, and black. If you do not have enough
 information to make a recommendation, you should
 give the answer "unknown".
Give your final answer in the format of "Final
answer: [answer]."

User Prompt
Here are some examples of customers with certain
features buying certain products:
··· more examples here ···
New customer: <appearance> is buying a pair of
shoes, the shoes should be which color?
Answer:
```

Example 3: Zero/Few-shot Inference.

```
Instruction Prompt
You are a shoe salesman and want to recommend
shoes to customers. There are white, red, orange,
 green, blue, and black shoes.
From past experiences, you learned some patterns.
For each pattern, you will also see a couple of
examples that worked for each pattern.
Choose a pattern. To do this, look at the
examples of each pattern, and see which of the
examples the current customer is closest to.
Choose the pattern corresponding to that example.
Give an answer for the shoe color recommendation.
The answer should be one word. It has to be one
of white, red, orange, green, blue, and black.
Give your final answer in the following format:
Reasoning for choosing pattern: reason,
Chosen pattern: pattern,
Reasoning for choice of prediction: reason,
Final Answer: answer

User Prompt
Here are some previously generated patterns with
some example where it predicted correcly what
color of shoe the customer bought.
<adaptive_info_prompt>
New customer: <appearance> is buying a pair of
shoes, the shoes should be which color?
Answer:
```

Example 4: Example-based Hypothesis Selection and Inference. <adaptive_info_prompt> consists of several hypotheses and the corresponding examples they got correct during generation time.

A.2 Deceptive Reviews

```
Instruction Prompt
You're a professional hotel review analyst.
Given a set of hotel reviews, we want to generate
 hypotheses that are useful for predicting
whether a review is truthful or deceptive. In
other words, we want to know whether the review
is written by a someone who actually lived in the
 hotel.
Using the given examples, please propose
<num_hypotheses> possible hypothesis pairs.
These hypotheses should identify specific
patterns that occur across the provided reviews.
Each hypothesis should contain a pair of the
following:
1. A hypothesis about what makes reviews more
likely to be truthful
2. The opposite hypothesis about what makes
reviews more likely to be deceptive
Generate them in the format of 1. [hypothesis], 2.
 [hypothesis], ... <num_hypotheses>. [hypothesis].

The hypotheses should analyze what kind of
reviews are likely to be truthful or deceptive.

User Prompt
```

```
We have seen some hotel reviews:
··· more examples here ···
Please generate hypotheses that are useful for
predicting whether a review is truthful or
deceptive.
Propose <num_hypotheses> possible hypotheses.
Generate them in the format of 1. [hypothesis], 2.
 [hypothesis], ... <num_hypotheses>. [hypothesis].

Proposed hypotheses:
```

Example 5: Hypothesis Generation.

```
Instruction Prompt
You are a professional deceptive detection agent
and your job is to determine whether a hotel
review is truthful or deceptive.
In other words, we want to know whether the
review is written by someone who had real
experiences with the hotel.
From past experiences, you learned a pattern.
You need to determine whether each of the
patterns holds for the current hotel review, and
also predict whether the current hotel review is
truthful or deceptive.
Give an answer. The answer should be one word (
truthful or deceptive).
Give your final answer in the format of {Final
answer: answer}

User Prompt
Our learned pattern: <hypothesis_high_reward>
A hotel review is the following: <review>
Given the pattern you learned above, give an
answer of whether the hotel review above is
deceptive or truthful.
Think step by step.
First step: Think about which pattern can be
applied to the hotel review.
Second step: Based on the pattern, is this hotel
review deceptive or truthful?
```

Example 6: Hypothesis-based Inference.

```
Instruction Prompt
You are a deceptive detection agent and want to
determine whether a hotel review is truthful or
deceptive.
In other words, we want to know whether the
review is written by a someone who actually lived
 in the hotel.
You need to determine whether this pattern holds
for the current hotel review, and also predict
whether the current hotel review is truthful or
deceptive.
Give an answer. The answer should be one word (
truthful or deceptive).

User Prompt
We have seen some hotel reviews:
··· more examples here ···
A hotel review is the following: <review>
Is this hotel review truthful or deceptive?
Answer:
```

Example 7: Zero/Few-shot Inference.

```
Instruction Prompt
You are a professional hotel review analyst and
you are able to determine whether a hotel review
is deceptive or truthful.
In other words, your job is to analyze if a hotel
 review review is written by someone who had
genuine experiences with the hotel.
From past experiences, you learned some patterns.
For each pattern, you will also see a couple of
examples that worked for each pattern.
First step: take a careful look at the examples
associated with each pattern, and see which set
of examples the current hotel review is most
similar with. Choose and repeat the pattern
corresponding to that examples set.
Next, apply the pattern on the new sample to
determine whether the new hotel review is
deceptive or truthful.
Finally, give an answer. The answer should be one
 word (deceptive or truthful).
Please give your final answer in the following
format:
Reasoning for choosing pattern: reason,
Chosen pattern: pattern,
Reasoning for choice of prediction: reason,
Final Answer: answer

User Prompt
Here are some previously generated patterns with
some example where it predicted correctly if a
hotel review is deceptive or truthful.
<adaptive_info_prompt>
A hotel review is the following: <review>
Is this hotel review truthful or deceptive?
Think step-by-step.
Step 1: Look at the new hotel review and compare
it with the set of examples associated with each
provided pattern.
Step 2: Find the set of examples that is the most
 similar to the new hotel review, pick and repeat
 the pattern associated with that set of examples.

Step 3: Apply the pattern you picked to the new
hotel review and predict whether the new hotel
review is deceptive or truthful.
Step 4: Give your final answer.
Answer:
```

Example 8: Example-based Hypothesis Selection and Inference. <adaptive_info_prompt> consists of several hypotheses and the corresponding examples they got correct during generation time.

A.3 Headlines With More Clicks

```
Instruction Prompt
You are a professional writer for an online
newspaper company.
Given a pair of headlines created for the same
article, you are asked to determine which will
get more clicks. It is likely that the pair of
headlines shares similarities, so please focus on
 their differences.
What difference in two headlines leads to more
clicks on one than the other?
You will be given a set of observations of the
format:
Headline 1: [headline]
Headline 2: [headline]
Observation: [observation].
Based on the observations, please generate
hypotheses that are useful for explaining why one
 headline out of the pair gets more clicked than
the other.
These hypotheses should identify patterns,
phrases, wordings etc. that occur across the
provided examples. They should also be
generalizable to new instances.
Please propose <num_hypotheses> possible
hypotheses and generate them in the format of 1.
[hypothesis], 2. [hypothesis], ...
<num_hypotheses>. [hypothesis].

User Prompt
Here are the observations:
··· more examples here ···
Please generate hypotheses that can help
determine which headlines have more clicks.
Please propose <num_hypotheses> possible
hypotheses.
Generate them in the format of 1. [hypothesis], 2.
 [hypothesis], ... <num_hypotheses>. [hypothesis].

Proposed hypotheses:
```

Example 9: Hypothesis Generation.

```
Instruction Prompt
You are a professional writer for an online
newspaper company.
```

```
Given a pair of headlines created for the same
article, you are asked to determine which will
get more clicks. It is likely that the pair of
headlines shares similarities, so please focus on
 their differences.
From past experiences, you learned some patterns.
Now, at each time, you should apply the learned
pattern to a new pair of headlines that are
created for a new article and determine which
headline gets clicked more.
The answer for the higher clicks should be in the
 form "Headline _" where _ is either 1 or 2.
Please give your final answer in the format of {
Final Answer: Headline _.}

User Prompt
Learned pattern: <hypothesis_high_reward>
Given the pattern you learned above, predict
which of the following headlines will get more
clicks:
Headline 1: <headline_1>
Headline 2: <headline_2>
Think step by step.
Step 1: Think about whether the pattern can be
applied to the headlines.
Step 2: Analyze the difference between "Headline
1" and "Headline 2".
Step 3: Based on the pattern, which headline is
likely to get more clicks?
```

Example 10: Hypothesis-based Inference.

```
Instruction Prompt
YYou are a writer for an online newspaper company.
 So you are excellent at determining which
headlines are more likely to cause users to click
 on the article.
You will be given two headlines, and determine
which headline was clicked more often.
You are only to give your answer.
The answer for the higher clicks should be of the
 form "Headline _" where _ is either 1 or 2.
Give your final answer in the following format:
"Answer: Headline _"

User Prompt
Here are some previous examples to help you:
··· more examples here ···
Which of the following headlines has more clicks:
Headline 1: <headline_1>
Headline 2: <headline_2>
```

Example 11: Zero/Few-shot Inference.

```
Instruction Prompt
You are a professional writer for an online
newspaper company.
You are excellent at determining which headlines
are more likely to be clicked by users.
From past experiences, you learned some patterns.
For each pattern, you will also see a couple of
examples that worked for each pattern.
Please choose a pattern. To do this, look at the
examples associated with each pattern, and find
which set of the examples are closest to the
given pair of headlines.
Please choose the pattern corresponding to that
set of examples.
The answer for the higher clicks should be of the
 form "Headline _" where _ is either 1 or 2.
Please give your final answer in the following
format:
Reasoning for choosing pattern: reason,
Chosen pattern: pattern,
Reasoning for choice of prediction: reason,
Final Answer: answer

User Prompt
Here are some previously generated patterns with
some examples where it predicted which one of the
 pair of headlines got more clicks.
<adaptive_info_prompt>
Which one out of the following pair of headlines
will get more clicks?
Headline 1: <headline_1>
Headline 2: <headline_2>
Think step by step.
Step 1: Look at the new pair of headlines and
compare them with the examples associated with
each pattern.
Step 2: Find the set of examples that is closest
to the given pair of headlines, and pick the
pattern associated with that set of examples.
Step 3: Apply the picked pattern to the new pair
of headlines. Based on that pattern, think about
which one out of the pair of headlines will get
more clicks.
Step 4: Give your final answer.
```

Example 12: Example-based Hypothesis Selection and Inference. <adaptive_info_prompt> consists of several hypotheses and the corresponding examples they got correct during generation time.

A.4 Retweeted More

```
Instruction Prompt
You are a social media expert. You are an expert
at determining which tweet will be retweeted more.

Given a set of observations, you want to
generation hypotheses that will help predict
which tweet out of a pair of tweets is more
likely to be retweeted.
Please note that the paired tweets are about the
same content and are posted by the same user, so
you should focus on the wording difference
between the two tweets in each pair.
Please propose <num_hypotheses> possible
hypotheses.
Please generate them in the format of 1. [
hypothesis], 2. [hypothesis], ...
<num_hypotheses>. [hypothesis].
Please make the hypotheses general enough to be
applicable to new observations.

User Prompt
We made some observations:
··· more examples here ···
Generate hypotheses that are useful for
predicting which tweet out of a pair of tweets is
 more likely to be retweeted.
Please note that the paired tweets are about the
same content and are posted by the same user, so
you should focus on the wording difference
between the two tweets in each pair.
Please propose <num_hypotheses> possible
hypotheses.
Please generate them in the format of 1. [
hypothesis], 2. [hypothesis], ...
<num_hypotheses>. [hypothesis].
Proposed hypotheses:
```

Example 13: Hypothesis Generation.

```
Instruction Prompt
You are a social media expert.
Given a pair of tweets, you are asked to predict
which tweet will be retweeted more.
Please note that the paired tweets are about the
same content and are posted by the same user, so
you should focus on the wording difference
between the two tweets.
From past experiences, you learned a pattern.
Now, at each time, you should apply a learned
pattern to a pair of tweets and determine which
one will get more retweets.
The answer for the higher retweets should be of
the form "the _ tweet" where _ is either first or
 second.
Please give your final answer in the format of {
Final answer: the _ tweet}

User Prompt
Our learned pattern: <hypothesis_high_reward>
The first tweet: <first_tweet>
The second tweet: <second_tweet>
Given the pattern you learned above, predict
which one of the two tweets will get more
```

```
retweets.
Think step by step.
First step: Think about if the pattern can be
applied to the tweets.
Second step: Analyze the textual difference
between the two tweets.
Third step: Based on the pattern, which tweet is
more likely to get more retweets?
Final step: Give your final answer in the format
of {Final answer: the _ tweet}
Final answer:
```

Example 14: Hypothesis-based Inference.

```
Instruction Prompt
You are a social media expert.
Given a pair of tweets, you are asked to predict
which tweet will be retweeted more.
Please note that the paired tweets are about the
same content and are posted by the same user, so
you should focus on the wording difference
between the two tweets.
The answer for the higher retweets should be of
the form "the _ tweet" where _ is either first or
second.
Please give your final answer in the format of {
Final answer: the _ tweet}

User Prompt
Here are some examples:
... more examples here ...
The first tweet: <first_tweet>
The second tweet: <second_tweet>
Which one of the two tweets will get more
retweets?
```

Example 15: Zero/Few-shot Inference.

```
Instruction Prompt
You are a social media expert.
Given a pair of tweets, you are asked to predict
which tweet will be retweeted more.
Please note that the paired tweets are about the
same content and are posted by the same user, so
you should focus on the wording difference
between the two tweets.
From past experiences, you learned some patterns.
You should apply a learned pattern to a pair of
tweets and determine which one will get more
retweets.
For each pattern, you will also see a couple of
examples that worked for each pattern.
Please choose a pattern. To do this, look at the
examples associated with each pattern, and find
which set of the examples are closest to the
given pair of tweets.
Please choose the pattern corresponding to that
set of examples.
Please give your final answer in the following
format:
Reasoning for choosing pattern: reason,
Chosen pattern: pattern,
Reasoning for choice of prediction: reason,
Final Answer: answer

User Prompt
Here are some previously generated patterns with
some examples where it predicted which tweet will
 will be retweeted more.
<adaptive_info_prompt>
The first tweet: <first_tweet>
The second tweet: <second_tweet>
Which one of the two tweets will get more
retweets?
Think step by step.
Step 1: Look at the new pair of tweets and
compare them with the examples associated with
each pattern.
Step 2: Find the set of examples that is closest
to the given pair of tweets, and pick the pattern
 associated with that set of examples.
Step 3: Analyze the textual difference between
the two tweets.
Step 4: Apply the picked pattern to the new pair
of tweets. Based on that pattern, think about
which one out of the pair of headlines will get
more clicks.
Step 5: Give your final answer.
```

Example 16: Example-based Hypothesis Selection and Inference. <adaptive_info_prompt> consists of several hypotheses and the corresponding examples they got correct during generation time.

B Implementation and Setup Details

B.1 HypoGeniC implementation

Sampling When initializing the rewards of newly generated hypotheses, we use the examples in the wrong example bank to do so. Given that we work in a low data regime, for hypotheses generated near the end of the training loop, the accuracies of hypotheses are likely to be biased. To counter this phenomenon, we also allow for the hypotheses to use the initial examples $\mathcal{S}_{\text{init}}$ for initializing rewards. By allowing the hypotheses to initialize reward with more examples, the accuracy lies closer to its true value, allowing for fair comparison between earlier generated hypotheses and newer ones.

Dynamic hypotheses update In Algorithm 1, we display how we generate and update the hypotheses pool $\mathcal{H}$. In particular, we add an example s to the wrong example bank $\mathcal{W}$ if the number of hypotheses that incorrectly predict s is greater than w_{hyp}. In our implementation, we use a linearly increasing w_{hyp} as training time t increases. This allows our algorithm to update the hypotheses more frequently at early stage of training, and less frequently at the end.

B.2 Inference method implementations

Filter and weighted vote In order to filter the hypotheses, we iterate through the top k hypotheses ranked by reward. For each hypothesis, we ask the Large Language Model (LLM) if it is relevant. Thereafter, for each of the relevant hypotheses, the LLM is prompted to use the hypothesis to make predictions. Then, for each predicted label, we add up the accuracy scores from the hypotheses that outputted that particular label. The final label is the one that has highest total accuracy score.

One-step adaptive and two-step adaptive inference The detailed framework of our adaptive inference methods is split into two parts - hypotheses pruning and hypotheses selection. In the case where we have a large number of hypotheses, it is likely that some hypotheses in $\mathcal{H}$ have overlaps or are paraphrases of each other.

We address this issue with the following procedure:

1. During training, we record the examples that each hypothesis correctly predicts.

2. Then we create one-hot encodings for each hypothesis, where the i-th element of the one-hot encoding is 1 if the hypothesis correctly predicts the i-th example, and 0 otherwise. We subsequently

compute a similarity matrix between each pair of hypotheses by taking the pairwise cosine similarities.

3. Lastly, we create a linear program with the objective of maximizing the sum of accuracies of the selected hypotheses, subject to the constraint that every pair of the selected hypotheses has a similarity score below a predefined threshold γ.

After pruning the set of hypotheses, we prompt the LLM to pick one hypothesis for its final prediction, as described in § 2.2. For the single-step adaptive inference, we ask the LLM to select a hypothesis and make a prediction in one prompt. On the other hand, with the two-step adaptive inference, we first prompt the LLM to select a hypothesis and then prompt the LLM again to make a prediction based on the selected hypothesis.

B.3 Hyperparameters

For the training stage, we set a limit on the hypothesis bank size, experimenting with sizes $H = 3$ and $H = 20$ to determine the impact of utilizing a larger number of hypotheses. Throughout all the experiments, we use the reward coefficient $\alpha = 0.5$, $w_{max} = 10$, $\texttt{num\_init} = 10$, and we have two different sets of the rest of hyperparameters for hypothesis bank sizes of 3 and 20.

- With $H = 3$, we use $k = 2$ and generate 1 hypothesis per update. For inference, we employ all 3 hypotheses for filter and weighted vote. For single-step and two-step adaptive inference, we use all 3 hypotheses with $\gamma = 0.3$ and provide 5 examples to each hypothesis.
- In the case of $H = 20$, we use $k = 10$ and generate 5 hypotheses per update. Then we take the top 5 hypotheses, ranked by their training accuracies, for filter and weighted vote. For single-step and two-step adaptive inference, we use the top 5 hypotheses with $\gamma = 0.7$ and provide 5 examples each.

B.4 Licensing Details

The DECEPTIVE REVIEWS and TWEET POPULARITY datasets have not been released with any licenses, but are free to use for research purposes based upon the authors. The HEADLINE POPULARITY dataset is released under the Creative Commons Attribution 4.0 International License. The SHOE SALES dataset will be released under the same licensing as this work, CC BY 4.0 License, should it be accepted.

In regards to models, we find that GPT-3.5-turbo and Claude-2.1 are all proprietary models and are not released under any open-source licenses. On the other hand, Mixtral is released under the Apache License 2.0. RoBERTa is not released under specific licensing but is free to use for research purposes. However, Llama-2-7B is released under their own licensing found at `https://ai.meta.com/llama/license/`.

Per our extensive search, we find that we are in compliance with the licensing agreements of all the datasets and models used in this work.

C Detailed Results

C.1 HypoGeniC Performance across inference strategies

Figure 3 presents the best results for all of our inference strategies, considering every dataset and all hyperparameter configurations.

For SHOE SALES, we observe that all the models perform effectively by using the best hypothesis inference strategy. Surprisingly, Mixtral is unable to perform perfectly. This is because despite generating the hypothesis that fully describes the data, Mixtral opts not to apply the hypotheses, favoring to choose a random label for the sake of "variety". Both GPT-3.5-turbo and Mixtral display similar patterns across the inference strategies, with best-accuracy hypothesis, filter and weighted vote, and two-step adaptive inference all having comparable performance. However, for all models we find single-step adaptive inference drops in accuracy. Given that two-step adaptive inference performs well, it is likely that the long prompt causes the model difficulty in choosing the correct hypotheses. For Claude-2.1, we see that filter and weighted vote drops in performance. As this method searches for relevant hypotheses, the model is likely finding that inaccurate patterns relevant, which end up outweighing the inference of the best hypothesis.

For DECEPTIVE REVIEWS, Claude-2.1 is the best performing model across all inference policies. Across the models, we highlight that single-step adaptive inference method works best for this dataset. In this inference method, the prompt specifically includes the aims of determining if a review is deceptive. This likely helps the model use the context provided to better decide which set of example resembles the test example most. Hence, splitting up the prompt may have caused performance to suffer.

We find that HEADLINE POPULARITY is the most challenging dataset. As mentioned in § 3.1, the original dataset was created with both images and headlines paired together. In our version of the dataset, we only use the headlines, so we are missing a crucial variable that contributes to understanding click behavior. Therefore, based off only headlines, it is difficult to generate hypotheses that truly capture the data. Despite this challenge, we note that our hypotheses can still adeptly capture a large portion of data with 63.7% being our highest accuracy. Specifically, we find that the best-accuracy hypothesis strategy performs best. We also note that filter and weighted vote can provide strong performance as in the case of Claude-2.1 and GPT-3.5-turbo, suggesting that hypotheses corroborating with each other can lead to better performance. We observe that GPT-3.5-turbo is the best performing model here, with all inference policies (aside from single-step adaptive) having high

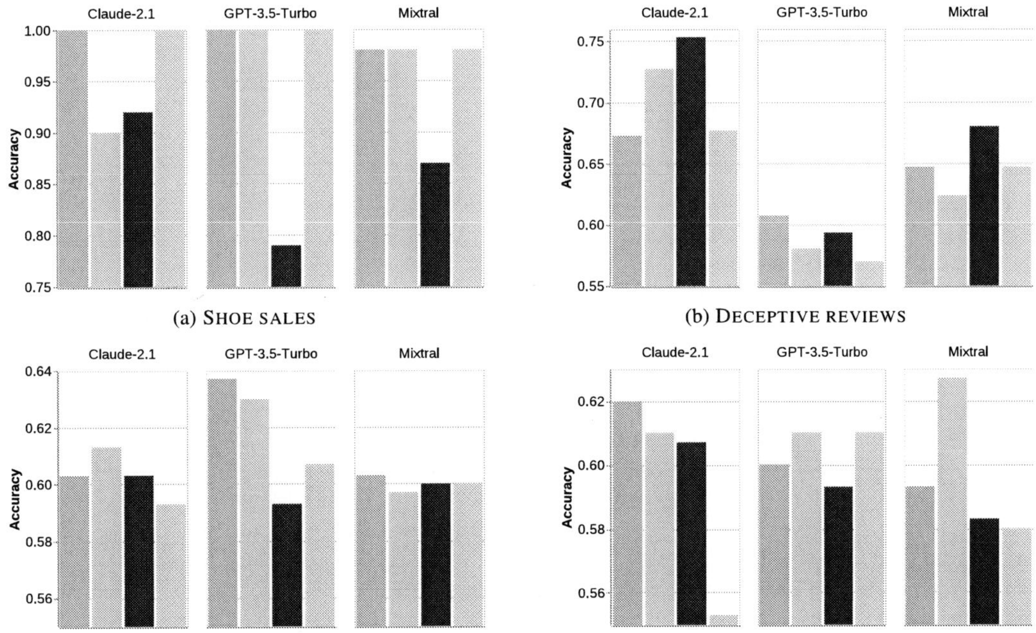

(a) SHOE SALES (b) DECEPTIVE REVIEWS

(c) HEADLINE POPULARITY (d) TWEET POPULARITY

Figure 3: **HypoGeniC** results with different inference strategies. Best-accuracy hypothesis is sufficient for getting good performance on SHOE SALES and HEADLINE POPULARITY. Single-step adaptive hypothesis-based inference is the most effective on DECEPTIVE REVIEWS. Filter and weighted vote is best on TWEET POPULARITY.

accuracy.

Finally, over the TWEET POPULARITY dataset, we find that the filter and weighted vote is the best choice for inference policy, with it being the best inference method for GPT-3.5-turbo and Mixtral. This indicates that using hypotheses in conjunction is useful as multiple variables together adeptly characterize the dataset. The performance of the rest of the inference policies has no clear pattern over this dataset.

We also present our results with confidence intervals. We specifically see that compared to the Oracle Methods, **HypoGeniC** shows performance statistically significant benefits when comparing to the 200 training examples for HEADLINE POPULARITY and TWEET POPULARITY. However, this is not the case for DECEPTIVE REVIEWS, because there are word level features that make the task easier for unsupervised methods. We note that **HypoGeniC** has statistically significant performance increases for DECEPTIVE REVIEWS with Claude-2.1 and Mixtral and for TWEET POPULARITY with Claude-2.1 and Mixtral.

C.2 HypoGeniC Performance across training examples

Figure 4 presents the results for the performance of **HypoGeniC** with Claude-2.1 as the training examples change. We observe that for all of our datasets, **HypoGeniC** outperforms zero-shot and few-shot learning generally for all training examples in SHOE SALES and TWEET POPULARITY. In HEADLINE POPULARITY, we find that the model needs to use 200 examples to outperform them. We highlight that **HypoGeniC** outperforms the No Updates method for all training examples across the four datasets when using a hypothesis bank size of 20. When using a hypothesis bank size of 3, we find that in TWEET POPULARITY, **HypoGeniC** is able to outperform the No Updates method, but is unable to as the training examples increase. In SHOE SALES we observe that it is largely worse because we set k (as discussed in § 2.1) to be 1, which causes difficulty in finding the best hypothesis. It is unclear what the optimal number of training examples is across the datasets, as using more examples does not necessarily increase accuracy.

Figure 5 displays the accuracy for **HypoGeniC** with GPT-3.5-turbo for the different training examples. We observe that unlike **HypoGeniC** performance with Claude-2.1, our results are mixed for when our method outperforms the few shot inference. Specifically, in TWEET POPULARITY, the few shot inference surpasses our results, indicating that in this set hypotheses provide less benefits than using examples. As **HypoGeniC** exceeds the accuracy of zero shot's, the proposed method still provides benefits to the base model. Similar to the results on Claude-2.1, we outperform RoBERTa and Llama-2-7B on all datasets aside on DECEPTIVE REVIEWS for all training examples. **HypoGeniC** surpasses the performance of the No Update strategy generally for all training examples. We note that due to the limited context window of GPT-3.5-turbo, the No Update strategy fails as it is unable to accept training exam-

Models	Methods	SHOE SALES	DECEPTIVE REVIEWS	HEADLINE POPULARITY	TWEET POPULARITY
RoBERTa (Oracle)	Train 200	100.0 ± 0.0	84.0 ± 4.2	49.0 ± 5.7	50.7 ± 5.7
	Train 1000	100.0 ± 0.0	91.0 ± 3.2	60.0 ± 5.5	62.0 ± 5.5
Llama-2-7B (Oracle)	Train 200	100.0 ± 0.0	88.7 ± 3.6	49.7 ± 5.7	50.3 ± 5.7
	Train 1000	100.0 ± 0.0	92.3 ± 3.0	60.0 ± 5.5	51.3 ± 5.7
Claude-2.1	Few shot	75.0 ± 4.9	51.0 ± 5.7	60.0 ± 5.5	0.3* ± 0.6
	HypoGeniC	**100.0 ± 0.0**	**75.3 ± 4.9**	**61.3 ± 5.5**	**62.0 ± 5.5**
Mixtral	Few shot	79.0 ± 4.6	56.3 ± 5.6	55.3 ± 5.6	48.7 ± 5.7
	HypoGeniC	**98.0 ± 1.6**	**68.0 ± 5.3**	**60.3 ± 5.5**	**62.7 ± 5.5**
GPT-3.5-turbo	Few shot	49.0 ± 5.7	55.0 ± 5.6	60.0 ± 5.5	**62.0± 5.5**
	HypoGeniC	**100.0 ± 0.0**	**60.7 ± 5.5**	**63.7 ± 5.4**	61.0 ± 5.5

Table 5: Table with 95% confidence interval for Few shot results and **HypoGeniC** for our best results.

ples. **HypoGeniC** effectively bypasses this issue by iteratively going through test examples, as opposed to feeding them into the model all at once.

In, Figure 6, the performance of **HypoGeniC** for varying training examples with Mixtral is shown. **HypoGeniC** outperforms the zero shot and few shot strategies for all datasets, aside from SHOE SALES, where the proposed method requires 200 examples to outperform few shot learning. Similary, we note that **HypoGeniC** surpasses the performance of RoBERTa and Llama-2-7B for HEADLINE POPULARITY, TWEET POPULARITY, and generally for SHOE SALES. As mentioned in Appendix C.1, despite Mixtral finding the best hypothesis, it occasionally refuses to choose the correct label to encourage "variety", which causes RoBERTa and Llama-2-7B to outpeform **HypoGeniC**. In comparison to the No Update results, we find that in DECEPTIVE REVIEWS and HEADLINE POPULARITY, **HypoGeniC** matches or exceeds this method. For SHOE SALES, we find that with hypothesis bank 3, **HypoGeniC** must use 200 examples, to finally converge to the correct hypothesis. On the other hand, for TWEET POPULARITY, No Update surpasses the **HypoGeniC** with hypothesis bank size 3 after using 200 training examples. This may occur as using 3 hypotheses is too limited to adeptly describe the dataset, causing accuracy to suffer.

C.3 Full OOD results

Table 6 shows results for the OOD deceptive reviews dataset for all inference strategies for each model.

We find that **HypoGeniC** outperforms both zero shot and few shot learning across all models and inference policies. The best-accuracy hypothesis and two-step adaptive inference methods are the most robust, showing an average increase of 3.7% and 3.6% respectively. We claim that although the filter and weighted vote strategy at first glance may seem to have mixed performance, the method is still robust. The drop in accuracy for Mixtral with filter and weighted is minimal (1%), and both GPT-3.5-turbo and Claude-2.1 exhibit increases in accuracy. Hence, the inference policy is consistent across DECEPTIVE REVIEWS and the OOD deceptive review datset. Interestingly, the single-step adaptive inference method exhibits drops in performance despite being the best performing inference model in DECEPTIVE REVIEWS. In single-step adaptive inference, the LLM sees both the hypotheses with the sets of examples along with the final question of determining whether the review is deceptive. Even though the LLM is prompted to only use one chosen hypotheses, these training examples from DECEPTIVE REVIEWS negatively impact the model because they are part of the context and are thus inherently used by LLMs. On the other hand, for two-step adaptive inference, since there is a dedicated prompt for hypothesis selection, the application of the hypothesis is unaffected from the DECEPTIVE REVIEWS training samples.

D Qualitative Analysis on Generated Hypotheses

We include findings from the generated hypotheses on DECEPTIVE REVIEWS, HEADLINE POPULARITY, and TWEET POPULARITY datasets in Table 7. The table shows that the a good number of the hypotheses are supported by existing findings, while others are novel. This suggests that the generated hypotheses are grounded in existing literature and can be used to guide future research.

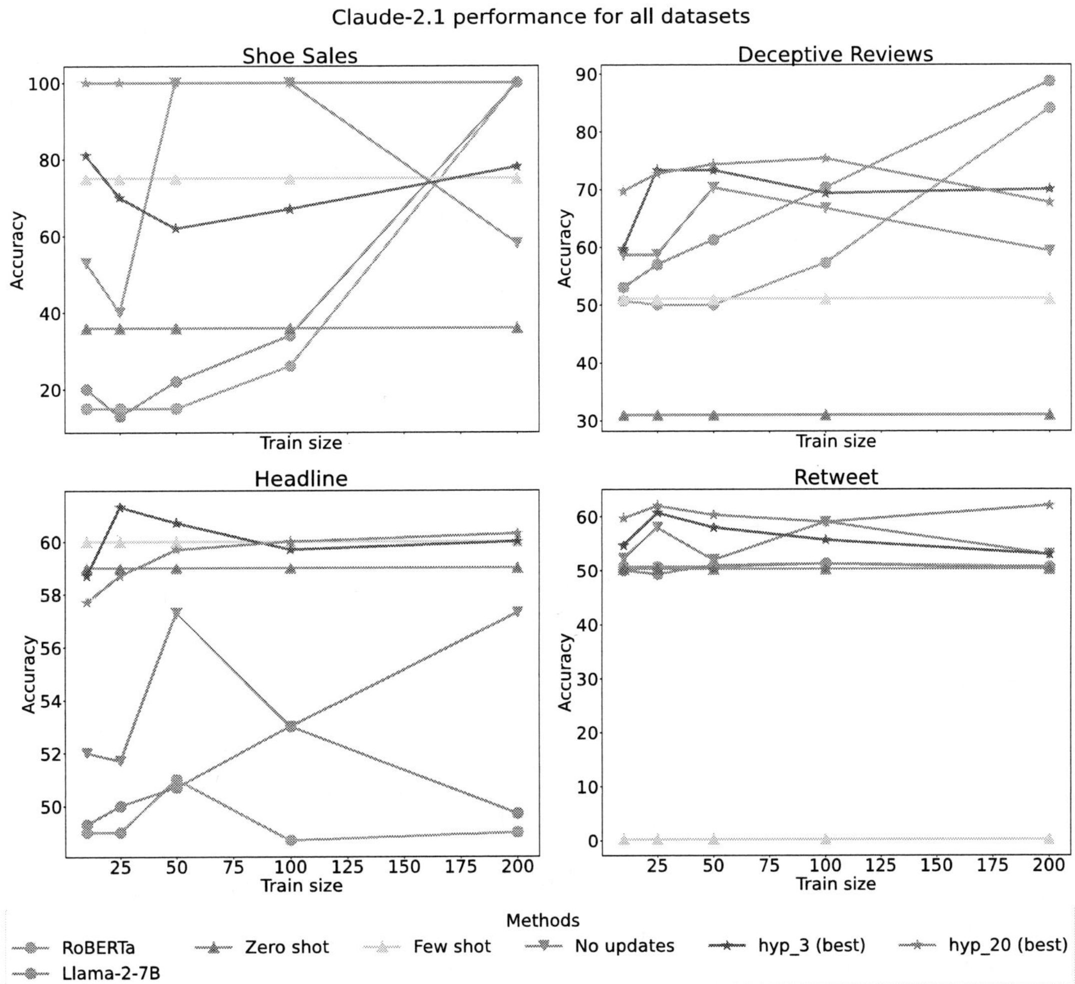

Figure 4: Claude-2.1 results for baselines, **HypoGeniC** (no update), and **HypoGeniC** (best) with hypothesis bank size 3 and 20 across multiple training samples

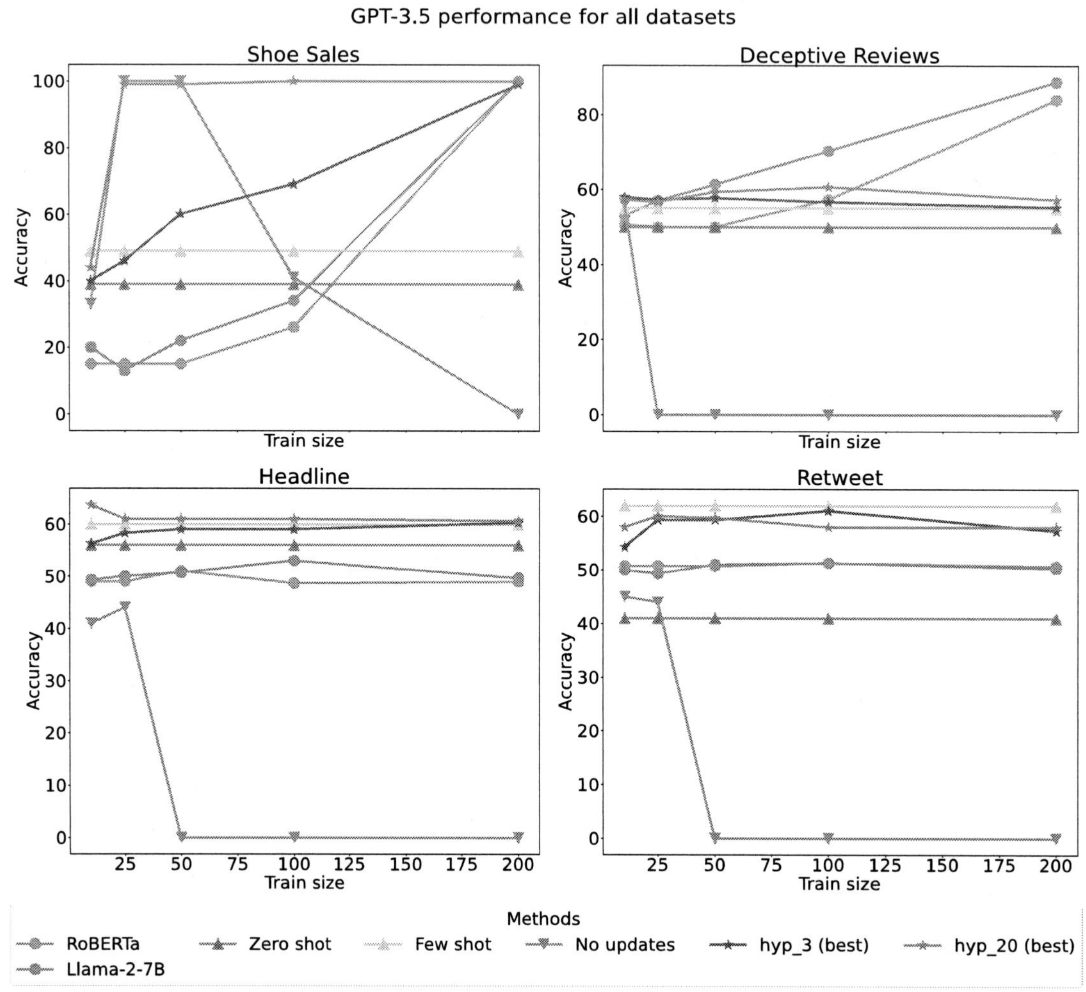

Figure 5: GPT-3.5-turbo results for baselines, **HypoGeniC** (no update), and **HypoGeniC** (best) with hypothesis bank size 3 and 20 across multiple training samples

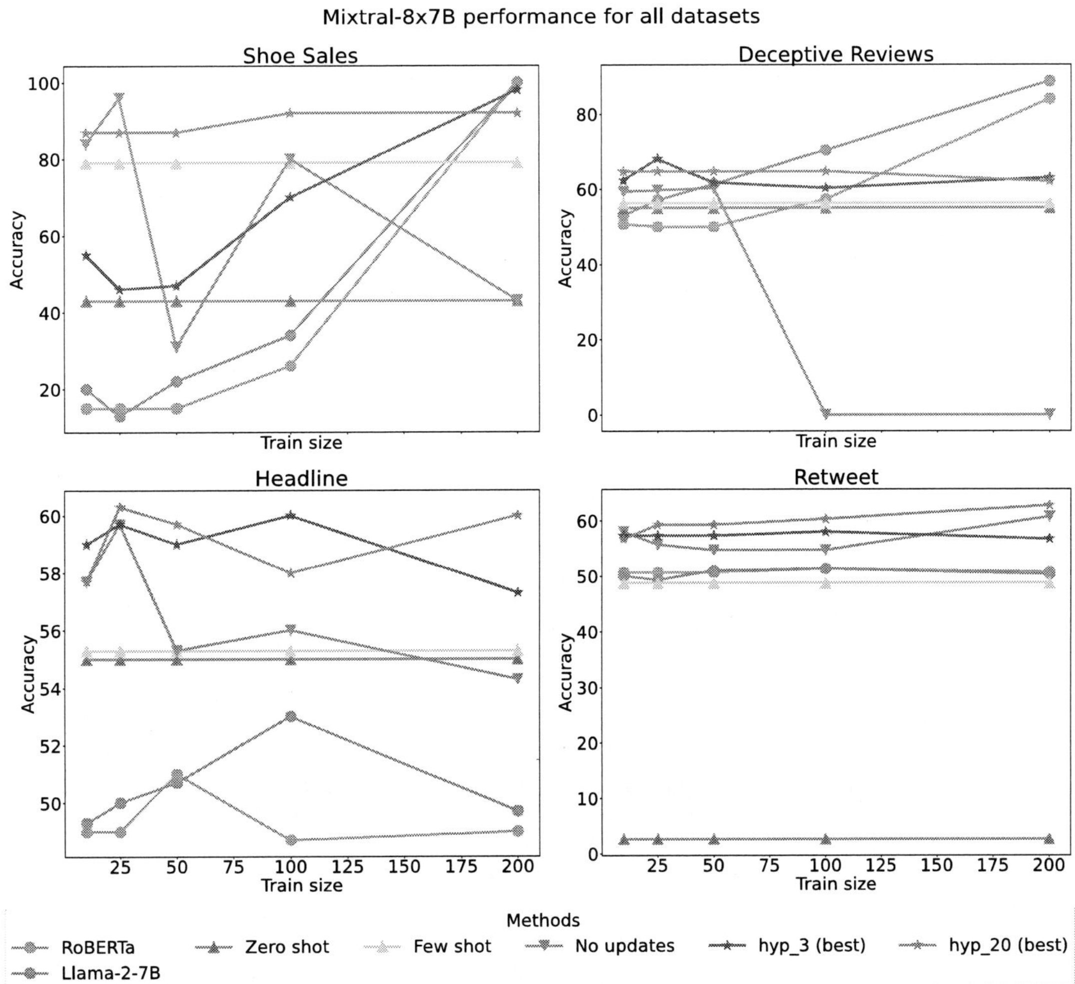

Figure 6: Mixtral results for baselines, **HypoGeniC** (no update), and **HypoGeniC** (best) with hypothesis bank size 3 and 20 across multiple training samples

Models	Methods	IND DECEPTIVE REVIEWS	OOD DECEPTIVE REVIEWS
RoBERTa (Oracle)	Train 200	84.0	73.0 (↓11.0)
	Train 1000	91.0	79.7 (↓11.3)
Llama-2-7B (Oracle)	Train 200	88.7	78.7 (↓10.0)
	Train 1000	92.3	88.7 (↓3.6)
Claude-2.1	Zero shot	31.0	27.7 (↓3.3)
	Few shot	51.0	41.7 (↓9.3)
	HypoGeniC (Best-accuracy hypothesis)	67.3	71.7 (↑4.4)
	HypoGeniC (Filter and weighted vote)	68.0	74.7 (↑6.7)
	HypoGeniC (One-step adaptive)	70.0	68.3 (↓1.7)
	HypoGeniC (Two-step adaptive)	67.7	70.7 (↑3.0)
Mixtral	Zero shot	55.0	49.7 (↓5.3)
	Few shot	56.3	49.0 (↓7.3)
	HypoGeniC (Best-accuracy hypothesis)	61.3	64.7 (↑3.4)
	HypoGeniC (Filter and weighted vote)	62.0	61.0 (↓1.0)
	HypoGeniC (One-step adaptive)	63.0	54.7 (↓8.3)
	HypoGeniC (Two-step adaptive)	61.3	64.7 (↑3.4)
GPT-3.5-turbo	Zero shot	50.0	49.0 (↓1.0)
	Few shot	55.0	52.0 (↓3.0)
	HypoGeniC (Best-accuracy hypothesis)	57.3	60.7 (↑3.4)
	HypoGeniC (Filter and weighted vote)	55.3	55.7 (↑0.4)
	HypoGeniC (One-step adaptive)	55.7	51.7 (↓4.0)
	HypoGeniC (Two-step adaptive)	54.7	59.0 (↑4.3)

Table 6: Performance of baselines and compared to our methods on the out-of-distribution deceptive reviews and DECEPTIVE REVIEWS.

Dataset	Finding	Supported/Novel
DECEPTIVE REVIEWS	Deceptive reviews contain more emotional terms.	Li et al. (2014)
	Deceptive reviews are more likely to use superlatives.	Ott et al. (2011)
	Deceptive reviews contain hearsay or information that could not have been directly experienced.	Ott et al. (2011)
	Deceptive reviews tend to be more exaggerated.	Anderson and Simester (2014)
	Truthful reviews tend to use more balanced and objective tone.	Anderson and Simester (2014)
	Truthful reviews could mention the reviewer's purpose for staying at the hotel (e.g., business trip, vacation).	Novel
	Truthful reviews would mention weddings or special occasions.	Novel
	Truthful reviews may contain information about reviewer's expectations and previous hotel experiences.	Novel
	Truthful reviews would acknowledge the reviewer's personal biases or preferences.	Novel
	Deceptive ones may present the reviewer's opinion as objective facts.	Novel
	Truthful reviews may contain reviewers' past experiences or future travel plans.	Novel
HEADLINE POPULARITY	Concreteness helps.	Sadoski et al. (2000)
	Revealing something new helps.	Banerjee and Urminsky (2021)
	Using vivid language and imagery helps.	Banerjee and Urminsky (2021)
	Headlines with high intensity of emotions would be clicked more.	Banerjee and Urminsky (2021)
	Action-oriented headlines are clicked more.	Banerjee and Urminsky (2021)
	Humorous headlines are clicked more.	Novel
	Controversial headlines are clicked more.	Novel
	Headlines that frame the content in a personal or relatable way are clicked more.	Novel
TWEET POPULARITY	Short and concise tweets are retweeted more.	Gligorić et al. (2019)
	Tweets with emotional tones are retweeted more.	Tan et al. (2014)
	Including specific details (e.g., dates, locations) are associated with more retweets.	Novel
	Including statistics and data are associated with more retweets.	Novel
	Mentioning influential individuals or organizations leads to more retweets.	Novel
	Including links to additional content (e.g., articles, videos) leads to more retweets.	Novel
	Tweets with a call to action or urgency are found to be retweeted more.	Novel

Table 7: Summary of generated hypotheses (on the real-world datasets) and whether they support existing findings or are novel.

Dreaming with ChatGPT: Unraveling the Challenges of LLMs Dream Generation

Harel Berger
Georgetown University
hb711@georgetown.edu

Hadar King
The Hebrew University of Jerusalem
Hadar.king@mail.huji.ac.il

Omer David
Bar-Ilan University
omer.david1@live.biu.ac.il

Abstract

Large Language Models (LLMs), such as ChatGPT, are used daily for different human-like text generation tasks. This motivates us to ask: *Can an LLM generate human dreams?* For this research, we explore this new avenue through the lens of ChatGPT, and its ability to generate valid dreams. We have three main findings: (i) Chatgpt-4o, the new version of chatGPT, generated all requested dreams. (ii) Generated dreams meet key psychological criteria of dreams. We hope our work will set the stage for developing a new task of dream generation for LLMs. This task can help psychologists evaluate patients' dreams based on their demographic factors.

1 Introduction

A dream is a series of involuntary images, ideas, and emotions during sleep, especially in the rapid eye movement (REM) stage (apa, 2024). Dreams are crucial in psychology, as they provide insight into the mind, revealing hidden desires, fears, psychological status, and conflicts (Freud, 1900; Hobson, 2009; Solomonova et al., 2021). Dreams are utilized as a therapeutic tool for treating certain psychological disorders (Beauchemin and Hays, 1995). Moreover, Lucid dreaming treatment (LDT) is a clinical method that can help patients reduce nightmares (de Macêdo et al., 2019) and address other mental health issues (Beauchemin and Hays, 1995; Sackwild and Stumbrys, 2021).

Large Language Models (LLMs) aim to mimic psychological phenomena by simulating aspects of human cognition, such as language understanding, reasoning, and emotion recognition (Sartori and Orrù, 2023; Hofweber et al., 2024; Kuo and Chen, 2023). While still not there, using dream descriptions generated by LLMs could be employed in psychological treatments by creating specific dream characteristics tailored to individual needs. LDT requires training and practice (Ellis et al., 2021), which can be challenging for patients to achieve on their own. Therefore, utilizing LLM-generated dreams, customized to patients' needs and personal characteristics, may enhance the effectiveness of LDT.

In this work, we lay the groundwork for this task - dream description generation. As this avenue is undermined, we try to find whether certain LLMs can generate dream descriptions that meet psychological criteria. We picked ChatGPT, the most globally popular LLM[1] as our test case. We use several versions of ChatGPT3.5 and ChatGPT4o, the most recent version of the OpenAI's LLM. Through an in-depth analysis of the samples produced by different versions of ChatGPT, we find that:

- ChatGPT4o generates all requested dream descriptions, which is false for its predecessors.
- Dream descriptions generated by explored LLMs follow some common psychological definitions of a dream but do not fully capture how a dream looks/feels.

2 Dreams in Psychology

Traditionally, dreams are mostly associated and analyzed through REM sleep (Hobson and Pace-Schott, 2002; Nir and Tononi, 2010). Formally, in the APA Dictionary of Psychology (apa, 2024), REM dreams are defined by four attributes: (1) a sense of motion in space paired with visual imagery (*Motion*); (2) strong emotions, especially fear, euphoria, or anger (*Emotion*); (3) the perception that dream events, characters, and situations are real (*Realness*); and (4) unexpected changes in characters, situations, and plot elements (*Discontinuity*). Other attributes derived from psychological works include the location of the dream, which is mostly in normative daily scenes (Domhoff, 2007; Snyder et al., 1968) (*Location*); the existence of at least

[1] https://zapier.com/blog/best-llm/

Proceedings of the 1st Workshop on NLP for Science (NLP4Science), pages 140–147
November 16, 2024

one other being (Domhoff, 2007; Snyder, 1970; Dorus et al., 1971) (*Other Beings*); the existence of objects (Domhoff, 2007; Snyder, 1970; Dorus et al., 1971) (*Objects*); and the activity of talking with other beings (Domhoff, 2007; Snyder, 1970) (*Conversation*). We will check if generated dreams meet psychological criteria.

3 Related Work

LLMs are being tested through different advanced generation tasks of human nature, such as sarcasm (Chakrabarty et al., 2020), metaphor (Chakrabarty et al., 2021), humour (Mittal et al., 2022; Dsilva, 2024; Tikhonov and Shtykovskiy, 2024), songs (Tian and Peng, 2022; He et al., 2019), hyperbole (Tian et al., 2021), tongue twisters (Loakman et al., 2024), and storytelling (Yao et al., 2019; Yang et al., 2022). Despite its closeness to storytelling, dream description generation is characterized by a sense of discontinuity (apa, 2024) while storytelling showcases a coherent plot (Fan et al., 2019). Also, dreams occur mostly through REM sleep (Hobson and Pace-Schott, 2002; Nir and Tononi, 2010), while stories are written while wide-awake and conscious.

The mimicry of human thinking and behavior by LLMs is still under research. Binz and Schulz (Binz and Schulz, 2023) and Abbasiantaeb et al. (Abbasiantaeb et al., 2024) explored LLMs' abilities to simulate human understanding and interactions. Zhang et al. (Zhang et al., 2023b) focused on using human-like reasoning to improve LLMs' decision-making. Another research area is LLMs' fairness, with Bender et al. (Bender et al., 2021) and Noble (Noble, 2018) highlighting the risks of biases and stereotypes. Zheng et al. (Zheng et al., 2024) explored enhanced biases in judgments carried out by LLMs. Turpin et al. (Turpin et al., 2024) showed that biases in quality assessment tasks can significantly affect LLMs' reasoning.

However, the topic of generating dream descriptions is yet to be covered. Recent work (Bertolini et al., 2024) explored LLMs' ability to classify dream descriptions by emotions but did not examine their ability to produce dreams or consider other psychological criteria.

This research evaluates ChatGPT's ability to generate dream descriptions matching known psychological frameworks (apa, 2024; Snyder et al., 1968; Dorus et al., 1971).

4 Methodology

In this research, we tackle these research questions:

1. Can LLMs generate dream descriptions?
2. Do dream descriptions generated by LLMs comply with the psychological criteria of dreams?

To address these questions, we devised a dedicated methodology. To generate the dream descriptions we use Context-Less Generation (Wan et al., 2023; Wan and Chang, 2024), in which the model is prompted with a simple zero-shot description of the dreamer - race, ethnicity, religion, and sex (Hanna et al., 2023; Salewski et al., 2024; Mahomed et al., 2024; Calderon et al.; Zhang et al., 2023a). We added a control group, person. Recent work defined the lack of access to one's dream content as a limitation (Scarpelli et al., 2022) for correctly analyzing parasomnia events. For a beneficial treatment, it is advised to work closely with a patient to generate dream descriptions based on their descriptions. Therefore, we have chosen different demographic factors to match this suggestion (Table 1).

Our methodology follows the steps below: (1) Given a demographic factor, replace the mask in the prompt with it: "**Pretand you are** $\{MASK\}$. **Please generate a dream that this person dreamt last night.**", and the prompt to model M. (2) Get the response r_i. (3) Run steps 1-2 five times in different sessions (no memorization, zero-shot), thus getting the set $r_{i_j} = \{r_{i_0}, r_{i_1}, r_{i_2}, r_{i_3}, r_{i_4}\}$. (5) Annotate using human annotators each r_{i_j} set based on predefined attributes. (6) Analyze the results.

Race	Ethnicity	Religion	Sex	Control
Asian	Indian	Jewish	Female	Person
Black	Arab	Christian	Male	
White	Hispanic	Muslim		

Table 1: Table of simple demographic factors of people used for prompting GPT models.

Some models provided very few dream descriptions. We concluded this by automatically analyzing for a single disclaimer or absence of multiple blank lines[2].

Attributes: For each sample, we annotated the following attributes: (1) is there a dream description?

[2]Concrete dream descriptions were spread across multiple lines upon close inspection.

(yes/no), based on the existence of a story. (2) is there a disclaimer? (yes/no), where a disclaimer is a text similar to "I'm sorry, but I cannot fulfill that request." or "As an AI, I don't have dreams or feelings". (3) the pronoun used for the dreamer. (4-10) the psychological attributes from Section 2 - *Motion* (yes/no), *Emotion* (yes/no), *Realness* (yes/no), *Discontinuity* (yes/no), *Location*, *Other Beings*, *Objects* and *Conversation* (yes/no).

Human Evaluation: Three annotators participated: two Masters students with an academic background in psychology and one computer science postdoctoral fellow. Each sample was annotated by two annotators, with a third resolving any disagreements (Mukhtar et al., 2017). The full instructions given to annotators is presented in Appendix C.

Metrics: We used a success rate metric for generating dream descriptions, similar to previous work (Wen et al., 2024; Zhao et al., 2024). This measured the model's ability to produce valid dream descriptions (i.e., containing a dream) or without disclaimers. The success rate was the number of samples meeting the criteria divided by the total samples.

5 Experiments

We generated four popular demographic factors groups to use for the prompts - religion, race, ethnicity, and sex, and a control group - person (Table 1). We used the prompt from Section 4 with each factor.

We evaluated several gpt models: gpt-3.5-turbo (gpt3.5T), gpt-3.5-turbo-16k-0613 (gpt3.5T16k), gpt-3.5-turbo-0613 (gpt3.5T0613), and gpt-3.5-turbo-1106 (gpt3.5T1106), gpt-4o (gpt4o). We used the default parameters (e.g., temperature 1.0, Top-P 1.0) of all models. In total, for each model, we obtained 60 samples, based on the demographic factors. The samples, code, and annotations are available online[3]. The code is under the MIT license (Open Source Initiative, 2023).

6 Dream Description Generation Analysis

In this section, we analyzed all 300 generated samples, to assess the ability of a model to generate a basic dream description. The full details of each are presented in Appendix B.

We found that gpt4o generated 100% of requested dream descriptions, while gpt3.5T16k and gpt3.5T0613 produced over 68%. However, both gpt3.5T and gpt3.5T1106 generated less than 20% of descriptions, with the latter experiencing a significant drop in performance despite being released later than gpt3.5T16k and gpt3.5T0613[4]. Thus, we dropped further analysis of the latter models.

Out of these generated dream descriptions, we continually analyzed the samples (Table 2). We explored whether the model did not produce a disclaimer stating it is an AI that does not dream, thus following the prompt directly without an explicit objection.

Model	Gen	No Disc	1st
gpt3.5T	13%	-	-
gpt3.5T16k	75%	31%	15%
gpt3.5T0613	68%	39%	17%
gpt3.5T1106	18%	-	-
gpt4o	100%	98%	73%

Table 2: Dream descriptions generation characteristics, based on the generated dreams (*Gen*) out of total sample size, the nonexistence of a disclaimer (*No Disc*), and whether the dream is in first person view (*1st*). The original sample size is 60 dreams. The gpt3.5T and gpt3.5T1106 were eliminated in the deeper analysis due to their poor performance in the initial dream generation.

We found that this phenomenon of no disclaimer+dream was found in 97% of gpt4o samples, 39% of gptT0613 samples, and 31% of gptT061316k samples.

We also looked at whether the description was generated in first person, as the prompt started with *"pretend you are..."*. gpt4o met 73% of the times for this aspect, gptgpt3.5T16k 15% of the time, and gpt3.5T0613 17% of the times in the same criteria.

In short, although with some decrease caused by matching the full criteria, gpt4o followed the prompted dream description with a significant gap (∼60%) between its performance and the other two models' performances.

Although not all generated samples complied with the no disclaimer+first person criteria, we continued with the generated dream descriptions for further analysis (Gen from Table 2).

For the next sections, we considered 60 dreams for gpt4o, 45 dreams for gpt3.5T16k, and 41 dreams for gptgpt3.5T0613[5].

[3]https://github.com/harelber/DreamGPT

[4]https://context.ai/compare/gpt-3-5-turbo-16k/gpt-3-5-turbo

[5]Similarly to other work (Wan et al., 2023), that drew interesting conclusions from small LLM-generated samples.

7 Psychological Dream Attributes

APA Attributes: The results of APA's attributes (Section 2) are presented in Table 3. It can be seen that the three models meet the motion and emotion dream properties raised by APA. In the discontinuity attribute, gpt3.5T16k got a success rate of 56%, and gpt3.5T0613 got 37%. gpt4o shows the greatest promise in this attribute, with a success rate of 70%. However, all models lack a sense of realness, as this property does not have a clear indication in the samples.

Model	M	E	R	D
gpt3.5T16k	98%	100%	0%	56%
gpt3.5T0613	100%	100%	0%	37%
gpt4o	100%	100%	7%	70%

Table 3: APA Attributes Results. M stands for motion, E for emotion, R for realness, and D for discontinuity. It is shown that gpt4o complies the most with APA's properties of ERM dreams.

Model	N_Loc	Other Beings	Conv
gpt3.5T16k	47%	96%	51%
gpt3.5T0613	44%	88%	44%
gpt4o	73%	95%	67%

Table 4: Other Attributes Results. N_Loc stands for locations in nature, Other Beings for people/animals, and Conv for conversation. It is shown that gpt4o complies the most with all properties.

Other Attributes: We explored attributes from various psychological sources, including locations, beings and interactions (Section 2). Non-daily locations appeared in 73% of gpt4o samples, 44% of gpt3.5T0613 samples, and 47% of gpt3.5T16k samples. This shows that the models do not fully comply with this property. Also, all models included at least one other being in the generated samples (Domhoff, 2007; Snyder, 1970; Dorus et al., 1971). Conversations were found in 67% of gpt4o samples, 44% of gpt3.5T0613 samples, and 51% of gpt3.5T16k's samples.

Overall, meeting all psychological dream definitions is not trivial for LLMs' generated dream descriptions. However, the ability to generate dream descriptions with embedded creatures, and motion/emotion rules is met 100% by each model we explored. Still, gpt4o is the leader in psychological attributes in general.

8 Conclusion

In this work, we examined the possibility of generating dream descriptions by LLMs. We explored it through the test case of ChatGPT models. The most promising model was found to be gpt4o. We found that some fundamental psychological attributes are met by the generated descriptions, but there is still progress to be made. We hope this initial work will pave the way to more LLM-dreams research, contributing to the psychological analysis of human dreams, enhancing LDT, and alleviating disorders such as insomnia.

9 Ethics Statement

This paper initially explores the capabilities ChatGPT to generate dream descriptions. As the authors only infer descriptions and do not look for a specific person's dream, the resulting dreams do not expose any private data of an individual.

10 Limitations

Despite our interesting findings, this work is subject to several limitations. First, our annotations were based on human annotators. Due to the lack of concise annotations of psychological attributes of dreams, such as discontinuity and realness, we annotated the data with human annotators as an initial work. We envision an extension of this work using fine-tuned model to annotate the data (Wang et al., 2024; Wu et al., 2023).

Second, our data was limited to 300 samples. Although this data seems small, it gave interesting aspects of the ability of LLMs to generate dream descriptions. We intend to curate a larger corpus for more comprehensive research.

Next, we explored ChatGPT, the most popular LLM globally. It would be beneficial to explore the new task with other LLMs (e.g., Llama (Touvron et al., 2023) or Gemini (Team et al., 2023)).

Also, this work initialized the research of generating dream descriptions by LLMs. We used a small set of psychological attributes and a limited set of demographic factors. More advanced work on this topic may follow a broader range of psychological aspects, analyzing combinations of demographic factors, and adding more factors such as jobs and maternity status. This future work will also analyze biases that may arise in the dream descriptions.

References

2024. APA Dictionary - Dream.

Zahra Abbasiantaeb, Yifei Yuan, Evangelos Kanoulas, and Mohammad Aliannejadi. 2024. Let the llms talk: Simulating human-to-human conversational qa via zero-shot llm-to-llm interactions. In *Proceedings of the 17th ACM International Conference on Web Search and Data Mining*, pages 8–17.

Kathleen M Beauchemin and Peter Hays. 1995. Prevailing mood, mood changes and dreams in bipolar disorder. *Journal of affective disorders*, 35(1-2):41–49.

Emily M Bender, Timnit Gebru, Angelina McMillan-Major, and Shmargaret Shmitchell. 2021. On the dangers of stochastic parrots: Can language models be too big? In *Proceedings of the 2021 ACM conference on fairness, accountability, and transparency*, pages 610–623.

Lorenzo Bertolini, Valentina Elce, Adriana Michalak, Hanna-Sophia Widhoezl, Giulio Bernardi, and Julie Weeds. 2024. Automatic annotation of dream report's emotional content with large language models. In *Proceedings of the 9th Workshop on Computational Linguistics and Clinical Psychology (CLPsych 2024)*, pages 92–107.

Marcel Binz and Eric Schulz. 2023. Using cognitive psychology to understand gpt-3. *Proceedings of the National Academy of Sciences*, 120(6):e2218523120.

Nitay Calderon, Naveh Porat, Eyal Ben-David, Alexander Chapanin, Zorik Gekhman, Nadav Oved, Vitaly Shalumov, and Roi Reichart. Measuring the robustness of nlp models to domain shifts.

Tuhin Chakrabarty, Debanjan Ghosh, Smaranda Muresan, and Nanyun Peng. 2020. r^3: Reverse, retrieve, and rank for sarcasm generation with commonsense knowledge. *arXiv preprint arXiv:2004.13248*.

Tuhin Chakrabarty, Xurui Zhang, Smaranda Muresan, and Nanyun Peng. 2021. MERMAID: Metaphor generation with symbolism and discriminative decoding. In *Proceedings of the 2021 Conference of the North American Chapter of the Association for Computational Linguistics: Human Language Technologies*, pages 4250–4261, Online. Association for Computational Linguistics.

Tainá Carla Freitas de Macêdo, Glescikelly Herminia Ferreira, Katie Moraes de Almondes, Roumen Kirov, and Sérgio Arthuro Mota-Rolim. 2019. My dream, my rules: can lucid dreaming treat nightmares? *Frontiers in psychology*, 10:2618.

G William Domhoff. 2007. Realistic simulation and bizarreness in dream content: Past findings and suggestions for future research. *The new science of dreaming*, 2:1–27.

E. Dorus, W. Dorus, and A. Rechtschaffen. 1971. The incidence of novelty in dreams. *Archives of General Psychiatry*, 25(4):364–368.

Ryan Rony Dsilva. 2024. *Augmenting Large Language Models with Humor Theory To Understand Puns*. Ph.D. thesis, Purdue University Graduate School.

Jason G Ellis, Joseph De Koninck, and Celyne H Bastien. 2021. Managing insomnia using lucid dreaming training: A pilot study. *Behavioral sleep medicine*, 19(2):273–283.

Angela Fan, Mike Lewis, and Yann Dauphin. 2019. Strategies for structuring story generation. *arXiv preprint arXiv:1902.01109*.

Sigmund Freud. 1900. *The Interpretation of Dreams*. Macmillan, New York.

John J Hanna, Abdi D Wakene, Christoph U Lehmann, and Richard J Medford. 2023. Assessing racial and ethnic bias in text generation for healthcare-related tasks by chatgpt1. *MedRxiv*.

He He, Nanyun Peng, and Percy Liang. 2019. Pun generation with surprise. In *Proceedings of the 2019 Conference of the North American Chapter of the Association for Computational Linguistics: Human Language Technologies, Volume 1 (Long and Short Papers)*, pages 1734–1744, Minneapolis, Minnesota. Association for Computational Linguistics.

J Allan Hobson. 2009. Rem sleep and dreaming: towards a theory of protoconsciousness. *Nature Reviews Neuroscience*, 10(11):803–813.

J Allan Hobson and Edward F Pace-Schott. 2002. The cognitive neuroscience of sleep: neuronal systems, consciousness and learning. *Nature Reviews Neuroscience*, 3(9):679–693.

Thomas Hofweber, Peter Hase, Elias Stengel-Eskin, and Mohit Bansal. 2024. Are language models rational? the case of coherence norms and belief revision. *arXiv preprint arXiv:2406.03442*.

Hui-Chi Kuo and Yun-Nung Chen. 2023. Zero-shot prompting for implicit intent prediction and recommendation with commonsense reasoning. *Preprint*, arXiv:2210.05901.

Tyler Loakman, Chen Tang, and Chenghua Lin. 2024. Train & constrain: Phonologically informed tongue-twister generation from topics and paraphrases. *arXiv preprint arXiv:2403.13901*.

Yaaseen Mahomed, Charlie M Crawford, Sanjana Gautam, Sorelle A Friedler, and Danaë Metaxa. 2024. Auditing gpt's content moderation guardrails: Can chatgpt write your favorite tv show? In *The 2024 ACM Conference on Fairness, Accountability, and Transparency*, pages 660–686.

Anirudh Mittal, Yufei Tian, and Nanyun Peng. 2022. AmbiPun: Generating humorous puns with ambiguous context. In *Proceedings of the 2022 Conference of the North American Chapter of the Association for Computational Linguistics: Human Language Technologies*, pages 1053–1062, Seattle, United States. Association for Computational Linguistics.

Neelam Mukhtar, Mohammad Abid Khan, and Nadia Chiragh. 2017. Effective use of evaluation measures for the validation of best classifier in urdu sentiment analysis. *Cognitive Computation*, 9:446–456.

Yuval Nir and Giulio Tononi. 2010. Dreaming and the brain: from phenomenology to neurophysiology. *Trends in cognitive sciences*, 14(2):88–100.

Safiya Umoja Noble. 2018. Algorithms of oppression: How search engines reinforce racism. In *Algorithms of oppression*. New York university press.

Open Source Initiative. 2023. Mit license. https://opensource.org/license/mit/. Accessed: 2024-06-14.

Lana Sackwild and Tadas Stumbrys. 2021. The healing and transformative potential of lucid dreaming for treating clinical depression. *International journal of dream research*, 14(2):296–308.

Leonard Salewski, Stephan Alaniz, Isabel Rio-Torto, Eric Schulz, and Zeynep Akata. 2024. In-context impersonation reveals large language models' strengths and biases. *Advances in Neural Information Processing Systems*, 36.

Giuseppe Sartori and Graziella Orrù. 2023. Language models and psychological sciences. *Frontiers in Psychology*, 14:1279317.

Serena Scarpelli, Valentina Alfonsi, Maurizio Gorgoni, and Luigi De Gennaro. 2022. What about dreams? state of the art and open questions. *Journal of Sleep Research*, 31(4):e13609.

F. Snyder. 1970. The phenomenology of dreaming. In L. Madow and L.H. Snow, editors, *The Psychodynamic Implications of the Physiological Studies on Dreams*, pages 124–151. Charles S Thomas, Springfield.

F. Snyder, I. Karacan, V. K. Jr. Tharp, and J. Scott. 1968. Phenomenology of rems dreaming. *Psychophysiology*, 4(3):375.

Elizaveta Solomonova, Claudia Picard-Deland, Iris L Rapoport, Marie-Hélène Pennestri, Mysa Saad, Tetyana Kendzerska, Samuel Paul Louis Veissiere, Roger Godbout, Jodi D Edwards, Lena Quilty, et al. 2021. Stuck in a lockdown: Dreams, bad dreams, nightmares, and their relationship to stress, depression and anxiety during the covid-19 pandemic. *PLoS One*, 16(11):e0259040.

Gemini Team, Rohan Anil, Sebastian Borgeaud, Yonghui Wu, Jean-Baptiste Alayrac, Jiahui Yu, Radu Soricut, Johan Schalkwyk, Andrew M Dai, Anja Hauth, et al. 2023. Gemini: a family of highly capable multimodal models. *arXiv preprint arXiv:2312.11805*.

Yufei Tian and Nanyun Peng. 2022. Zero-shot sonnet generation with discourse-level planning and aesthetics features. In *Proceedings of the 2022 Conference of the North American Chapter of the Association for Computational Linguistics: Human Language Technologies*, pages 3587–3597, Seattle, United States. Association for Computational Linguistics.

Yufei Tian, Arvind krishna Sridhar, and Nanyun Peng. 2021. HypoGen: Hyperbole generation with commonsense and counterfactual knowledge. In *Findings of the Association for Computational Linguistics: EMNLP 2021*, pages 1583–1593, Punta Cana, Dominican Republic. Association for Computational Linguistics.

Alexey Tikhonov and Pavel Shtykovskiy. 2024. Humor mechanics: Advancing humor generation with multistep reasoning. *arXiv preprint arXiv:2405.07280*.

Hugo Touvron, Thibaut Lavril, Gautier Izacard, Xavier Martinet, Marie-Anne Lachaux, Timothée Lacroix, Baptiste Rozière, Naman Goyal, Eric Hambro, Faisal Azhar, et al. 2023. Llama: Open and efficient foundation language models. *arXiv preprint arXiv:2302.13971*.

Miles Turpin, Julian Michael, Ethan Perez, and Samuel Bowman. 2024. Language models don't always say what they think: unfaithful explanations in chain-of-thought prompting. *Advances in Neural Information Processing Systems*, 36.

Yixin Wan and Kai-Wei Chang. 2024. White men lead, black women help: Uncovering gender, racial, and intersectional bias in language agency. *arXiv preprint arXiv:2404.10508*.

Yixin Wan, George Pu, Jiao Sun, Aparna Garimella, Kai-Wei Chang, and Nanyun Peng. 2023. " kelly is a warm person, joseph is a role model": Gender biases in llm-generated reference letters. *arXiv preprint arXiv:2310.09219*.

Xinru Wang, Hannah Kim, Sajjadur Rahman, Kushan Mitra, and Zhengjie Miao. 2024. Human-llm collaborative annotation through effective verification of llm labels. In *Proceedings of the CHI Conference on Human Factors in Computing Systems*, pages 1–21.

Hao Wen, Yuanchun Li, Guohong Liu, Shanhui Zhao, Tao Yu, Toby Jia-Jun Li, Shiqi Jiang, Yunhao Liu, Yaqin Zhang, and Yunxin Liu. 2024. Autodroid: Llm-powered task automation in android. In *Proceedings of the 30th Annual International Conference on Mobile Computing and Networking*, pages 543–557.

Zhanglin Wu, Yilun Liu, Min Zhang, Xiaofeng Zhao, Junhao Zhu, Ming Zhu, Xiaosong Qiao, Jingfei

Zhang, Ma Miaomiao, Zhao Yanqing, et al. 2023. Empowering a metric with llm-assisted named entity annotation: Hw-tsc's submission to the wmt23 metrics shared task. In *Proceedings of the Eighth Conference on Machine Translation*, pages 822–828.

Kevin Yang, Yuandong Tian, Nanyun Peng, and Dan Klein. 2022. Re3: Generating longer stories with recursive reprompting and revision. *arXiv preprint arXiv:2210.06774*.

Lili Yao, Nanyun Peng, Ralph Weischedel, Kevin Knight, Dongyan Zhao, and Rui Yan. 2019. Plan-and-write: Towards better automatic storytelling. In *Proceedings of the AAAI Conference on Artificial Intelligence*, volume 33, pages 7378–7385.

Angela Zhang, Mert Yuksekgonul, Joshua Guild, James Zou, and Joseph Wu. 2023a. Chatgpt exhibits gender and racial biases in acute coronary syndrome management. *medRxiv*, pages 2023–11.

Zheyuan Zhang, Shane Storks, Fengyuan Hu, Sungryull Sohn, Moontae Lee, Honglak Lee, and Joyce Chai. 2023b. From heuristic to analytic: Cognitively motivated strategies for coherent physical commonsense reasoning. In *Proceedings of the 2023 Conference on Empirical Methods in Natural Language Processing*, pages 7354–7379, Singapore. Association for Computational Linguistics.

Andrew Zhao, Daniel Huang, Quentin Xu, Matthieu Lin, Yong-Jin Liu, and Gao Huang. 2024. Expel: Llm agents are experiential learners. In *Proceedings of the AAAI Conference on Artificial Intelligence*, volume 38, pages 19632–19642.

Lianmin Zheng, Wei-Lin Chiang, Ying Sheng, Siyuan Zhuang, Zhanghao Wu, Yonghao Zhuang, Zi Lin, Zhuohan Li, Dacheng Li, Eric Xing, et al. 2024. Judging llm-as-a-judge with mt-bench and chatbot arena. *Advances in Neural Information Processing Systems*, 36.

A Nature locations found in Dreams - Full Analysis

This section shows the full list of locations found in our dreams data. The locations can be found in table 5.

Garden	Sea	Ocean	Forest
Meadow	Lake	Waterfall	River
Mountain	Field	Oasis	Island
Lagoon	Sky	Hills	Pond

Table 5: Nature locations of dreams found in our data.

B Models History & Tokens

Table 6 discloses the dream generation rates of each explored model, based on its release date and amount of tokens, as a complementary to Section 6. Dates and Tokens data acquired from[6] [7].

Model	DGR	Date	Tokens
gpt3.5T	13% (8)	11.28.22	4K
gpt3.5T16k	73% (44)	06.13.23	16K
gpt3.5T0613	68% (41)	06.13.23	4K
gpt3.5T1106	18% (11)	11.06.23	16K
gpt4o	100% (60)	05.13.24	128K

Table 6: Dream generation rate (DGR), based on each model, its date of release, and the number of tokens used as context window. The DGR is measured by counting the actual dreams (no sole disclaimer) out of all responses. The generation rate and actual count are provided for clarity.

C Instructions to Annoators

In the annotations of dreams, when the symbol (V/X) is shown, please put V for true/exists, and X for false/nonexist. If you are not sure, please put X.

These are the attributes we explore:

- Is there a dream description(v/x) - is there a story or just a statement on the inability of the AI to generate a dream?
- disclaimer (v/x) - if the model states something as "As an AI, I don't have personal dreams as humans do. However, I can create a fictional dream scenario for you.", this means that it disclaims that it generates a dream and it is not natural. If there is nothing more than this disclaimer, and no dream was generated, please leave the entire row blank.
- narrator (I/You/He/She/They) - The point of view of the dreamer - is it "I dreamt that...", or "he dreamt". This is considered as the pronoun of a dream in the paper.
- location - A one-word location of the dream, such as desert, garden. If the dreamer moves places, please add other places.
- other persons - other persons mentioned in the dream

[6]https://community.openai.com/t/what-are-the-differences-between-gpt-3-5-turbo-models/557028/2

[7]https://context.ai/compare/gpt-3-5-turbo-16k/gpt-3-5-turbo

- animals - same as persons, but with animals
- items - same with animals, but with items
- conversation (v/x) - if there is any conversation in the dream.
- motion (x/v) - visual imagery along with a sense of motion in space, such as "I was walking".
- emotion (x/v) - intense emotion, especially fear, elation, or anger.
- belief of realness (x/v) - belief that dream characters, events, and situations are real
- discontinuity (x/v) - sudden discontinuities in characters, situations, and plot elements. The word suddenly helps a lot here

LLMs and NLP for Generalized Learning in AI-Enhanced Educational Videos and Powering Curated Videos with Generative Intelligence

Naina Chaturvedi
Rutgers University
nc832@cs.rutgers.edu
Ananda Gunawardena
Rutgers University
andy.guna@cs.rutgers.edu

Abstract

The rapid advancement of Large Language Models and Natural Language Processing technologies has opened new frontiers in educational content creation and consumption. This paper explores the intersection of these technologies with instructional videos in computer science education, addressing the crucial aspect of generalization in NLP models within an educational context. With 78% of computer science students utilizing YouTube to supplement traditional learning materials, there's a clear demand for high-quality video content. However, the challenge of finding appropriate resources has led 73% of students to prefer curated video libraries. We propose a novel approach that leverages LLMs and NLP techniques to revolutionize this space, focusing on the ability of these models to generalize across diverse educational content and contexts. Our research utilizes the cubits.ai platform, developed at Princeton University, to demonstrate how generative AI, powered by advanced LLMs, can transform standard video playlists into interactive, AI-enhanced learning experiences. We present a framework for creating AI-generated video summaries, on-demand questions, and in-depth topic explorations. Our approach not only enhances student engagement but also provides a unique opportunity to study how well these models generalize across different educational topics and student needs.

Keywords: *Instructional videos, AI-enhanced learning, Large Language Models (LLMs), Natural Language Processing (NLP), generalization in NLP, computer science education, cubits.ai platform, AI-generated content, interactive video experiences, video summarization, on-demand questions, personalized learning, active learning, data-driven insights, generative AI, educational technology, adaptive learning environments*

1 Introduction

The landscape of computer science education is rapidly evolving, with instructional videos becoming an increasingly integral part of the learning process. Recent surveys indicate that over 78% of computer science students frequently turn to YouTube as a supplementary resource to their textbooks and classroom instruction. This trend underscores a growing demand for high-quality, accessible video content in educational settings.

However, the abundance of online resources presents its own challenges. The task of finding appropriate and reliable content can be overwhelming for students, leading to inefficient learning experiences. This difficulty has resulted in a significant preference shift, with 73% of students expressing a desire for curated video libraries that are tailored to their specific course requirements.

In response to these challenges and preferences, we propose a novel approach that harnesses the power

Proceedings of the 1st Workshop on NLP for Science (NLP4Science), pages 148–154
November 16, 2024

of Large Language Models (LLMs) and Natural Language Processing (NLP) technologies to transform the landscape of educational video content. Our research focuses on the intersection of these advanced AI technologies with instructional videos, particularly addressing the crucial aspect of generalization in NLP models within an educational context.

This paper presents a framework for creating AI-enhanced learning experiences that go beyond traditional video playlists. By leveraging generative AI powered by advanced LLMs, we demonstrate how standard instructional videos can be transformed into interactive, personalized learning tools. Our approach not only fosters active learning and personalized education but also serves as a testbed for evaluating the adaptability of LLMs across diverse computer science topics and varying student proficiency levels.

2 Background

2.1 The Rise of Video-Based Learning

The proliferation of online video platforms has significantly impacted the educational landscape, particularly in computer science. YouTube, in particular, has become a go-to resource for students seeking to supplement their formal education. The preference for video content stems from its ability to provide visual demonstrations, step-by-step explanations, and the flexibility to pause, rewind, and revisit complex concepts.

2.2 Challenges in Content Curation

Despite the abundance of educational videos, students often struggle to find content that aligns precisely with their course requirements. This challenge has led to a growing demand for curated video libraries, where instructors select and organize relevant content to complement their curriculum.

2.3 The Potential of LLMs and NLP in Education

Large Language Models and Natural Language Processing technologies have shown remarkable capabilities in understanding and generating human-like text. These advancements present an opportunity to enhance the educational video experience by providing personalized summaries, generating relevant questions, and offering in-depth explanations tailored to individual student needs.

2.4 Generalization in NLP for Educational Contexts

A key focus of our research is exploring how well LLMs can generalize across diverse educational content and contexts. This aspect is crucial for developing adaptive, personalized learning environments that can cater to a wide range of topics and student needs within computer science education.

3 Methodology

Our research utilizes the cubits.ai platform, developed at Princeton University, to demonstrate how generative AI can transform standard video playlists into interactive, AI-enhanced learning experiences. The methodology encompasses several key components:

3.1 The cubits.ai Platform

cubits.ai is an innovative platform designed to enhance the impact of computer science courses. It serves as a foundation for our research, providing:

- A comprehensive library of curated video courses tailored to meet academic requirements
- Integration of interactive elements such as embedded quizzes and cuGPT, an intelligent assistant designed to guide students through their learning experience
- Synchronized transcript functionality for efficient content navigation, enabling students to search for specific sections of videos and navigate directly to the relevant parts

The platform's architecture is built around several key components:

1. Content Management System (CMS): A robust system that stores and organizes high-quality videos in a curated content repository. Each video is meticulously tagged with metadata, such

as subject, difficulty level, and duration, enabling precise search and filtering. Content curation is managed by subject matter experts, ensuring that only high-value, relevant material is featured.

2. Modular Content Delivery: Videos are divided into segments or chapters, allowing users to access specific parts of a larger video without watching the entire content. This structure makes it easier for users to focus on particular topics or sections.

3. Personalized User Experience: Users can create individual profiles, receive recommendations based on past views, track their progress, and bookmark specific sections for easy access. The UI and UX are designed to provide a flexible learning environment.

4. Micro-payment Integration: The platform features a flexible micro-payment structure, allowing users to purchase only the content they need, either by paying for individual videos or specific segments. Payments are facilitated through various methods, including digital wallets, credit/debit cards etc, offering users maximum flexibility to engage with the content without the need to buy entire courses.

3.2 Vector Database Implementation

We employ vector databases to structure and query high-dimensional vectors (typically embeddings) that represent data points related to the curated videos. This approach enables more semantically meaningful searches, allowing users to leverage the power of LLMs while remaining focused on their specific learning context.

The process involves:

1. Training a vector database using content from a particular domain, such as computer science. The specific domain content is converted into vector representations using a pre-trained embedding model. This embedding process transforms the content into high-dimensional vectors that encode semantic meaning, where content with similar meaning will have embeddings that are closer to each other in the vector space.

2. Indexing these vectors in a database for fast retrieval. These embeddings represent domain-specific knowledge and are stored in the database for fast retrieval.

3. Ensuring domain relevance by curating the data that goes into the vector database to focus solely on the domain of interest (e.g., computer science, finance, healthcare, etc.). This curation maintains domain relevance and restricts answers to the specific domain.

4. Applying additional filtering using metadata tags that identify sub-domains or contexts (e.g., product category, knowledge type). When querying, we can further restrict the results to specific sub-domains by applying filters based on these metadata tags, ensuring more precise domain-specific outcomes.

When a query comes in, it is converted into an embedding vector using the same model as before. The algorithm then searches the vector database for the closest matches (nearest neighbors) to this query vector. Since the vector database contains only domain-specific vectors, the results will naturally be restricted to that domain.

If needed, the model used to generate embeddings can be fine-tuned on domain-specific data. For example, fine-tuning an embedding model on computer science courses ensures that the embeddings generated from queries are more aligned with the specific language and structure of the computer science domain.

3.3 AI-Generated Content Creation

Our framework facilitates the creation of:

1. Video summaries: Concise overviews of video content, highlighting key points and concepts

2. On-demand questions: Automatically generated questions that test understanding and promote active learning

3. In-depth topic explorations: Detailed explanations and additional resources for students seeking to delve deeper into specific topics

3.4 Integration with Existing Video Platforms

We demonstrate how educators can enhance their existing video playlists by incorporating AI-generated content. This integration focuses on increasing student engagement and establishing safety measures for AI use in education. The ability for any instructor to curate (for free) a video course makes cubits.ai accessible to all students.

3.5 Generalization Testing

To address the crucial aspect of generalization in NLP models, we implement:

1. Cross-topic evaluation: Testing the model's performance across various computer science subjects
2. Adaptive content generation: Assessing the model's ability to tailor content to different student levels and learning styles
3. Contextual understanding: Evaluating how well the model maintains coherence and relevance across different educational contexts

3.6 Monetization and Access Control

The platform incorporates a monetization layer with a dynamic pricing model, allowing content creators to set prices based on factors such as video length, complexity, or popularity, with the platform taking a commission from each transaction. Prices can be adjusted dynamically based on demand or user engagement.

Users have flexible payment options, including:

- Micro-payments for individual pieces of content
- Subscription plans for bundled access to specific categories of content at discounted rates, offering more cost-effective choices for regular users.

A secure payment gateway supports various payment methods, including credit/debit cards, digital wallets. This secure gateway enables quick and safe payments for users. A token-based access control system grants users access to purchased content, allowing them to revisit and view the content as often as needed without repurchasing, offering a flexible and user-friendly experience.

4 Results and Discussion

4.1 Platform Adoption and User Engagement

cubits.ai has become widely adopted in higher education, with many instructors integrating it into their online learning systems. The platform is already serving thousands of students, providing access to a comprehensive library of curated video courses tailored to meet academic requirements.

Key findings include:

- cubits.ai is consistently ranked as the most useful resource in student surveys conducted since 2020
- The platform's user-friendly interface and well-organized content repository have made it a valuable resource for students
- The integration of interactive elements such as embedded quizzes and cuGPT has enhanced the learning experience
- Students find the platform both engaging and efficient in supporting their learning needs
- The synchronized transcript functionality enables students to search for specific sections of videos and navigate directly to the relevant parts
- By aligning with course materials and offering high-quality video content, cubits.ai has established itself as a vital tool for enhancing educational outcomes

4.2 Impact on Learning Outcomes

While comprehensive studies on long-term learning outcomes are ongoing, preliminary data suggests that AI-enhanced videos are contributing to:

- Increased student engagement with course material
- Improved understanding of complex concepts

- More efficient study practices, with students able to quickly locate and revisit key content
- A more personalized and effective learning experience
- Flexibility in learning, with videos acting as a replacement or engaging supplement to traditional courses

As more students see videos as the primary way to gain knowledge, instead of traditional textbooks, cubits.ai is becoming an important part of the content provided to students.

4.3 Generalization Capabilities of LLMs in Educational Contexts

Our research provides insights into how well LLMs generalize across different educational topics and contexts. We observed that:

- LLMs demonstrate strong capabilities in generating relevant summaries and questions across various computer science topics
- The models' performance can vary depending on the specificity of the subject matter, with more niche topics sometimes requiring additional fine-tuning
- The use of domain-specific vector databases significantly improves the relevance and accuracy of generated content

4.4 Transformative Potential in Large Classes

Drawing insights from computer science courses at Princeton and Rutgers Universities, we highlight the transformative potential of AI-enhanced videos in promoting active learning, particularly in large classes. Key observations include:

- Increased participation and engagement in discussion forums related to video content
- More personalized learning experiences, even in classes with high student-to-instructor ratios
- Improved ability for instructors to identify and address common misconceptions or areas of difficulty

5 Future Work

Future research directions include:

1. Longitudinal studies on the impact of AI-enhanced videos on long-term learning outcomes
2. Exploration of more advanced personalization techniques to tailor content to individual learning styles and preferences
3. Investigation of potential biases in AI-generated content and development of mitigation strategies
4. Expansion of the platform to cover a broader range of academic disciplines beyond computer science
5. Further development of generalization testing methodologies for NLP models in educational contexts
6. Enhancement of the vector database implementation to improve search accuracy and efficiency

6 Conclusion

This research demonstrates the transformative potential of integrating LLMs and NLP technologies into educational video content. By leveraging these advanced AI capabilities, we can create more engaging, interactive, and personalized learning experiences for students. The cubits.ai platform serves as a proof of concept, showcasing how AI-enhanced videos can revolutionize computer science education.

Our findings not only contribute to the ongoing dialogue about generalization in NLP but also provide practical insights into the application of LLMs in educational settings. By bridging these domains, we have established a shared platform for state-of-the-art generalization testing in NLP within an educational framework.

As we continue to refine these technologies and gather more data on their impact, we anticipate that AI-enhanced educational videos will play an increasingly crucial role in the future of higher education. This work serves as a cornerstone for catalyzing research on generalization in the NLP community, particularly focusing on the application and evaluation of LLMs in adaptive, personalized learning environments.

The scalable architecture of the cubits.ai platform, combined with its micro-payment structure, offers a flexible and accessible approach to high-quality learning. As more students turn to video content for knowledge acquisition, platforms like cubits.ai are poised to become integral components of modern digital education, making high-quality learning both affordable and accessible.

Limitations

While our research demonstrates promising results, it is important to acknowledge several limitations:

1. Domain Specificity: The current implementation focuses primarily on computer science education. Generalization to other academic disciplines may require additional research and model adaptations.

2. Data Privacy Concerns: The use of AI in educational settings raises important questions about data privacy and security, particularly when dealing with student interactions and performance data.

3. Potential for Bias: LLMs trained on large datasets may inadvertently perpetuate biases present in the training data. Ongoing work is needed to identify and mitigate these biases in educational contexts.

4. Scalability Challenges: As the platform grows, there may be technical challenges in scaling the infrastructure to handle increased demand and more diverse content.

5. Limited Long-term Data: While initial results are promising, long-term studies on the impact of AI-enhanced videos on learning outcomes are still in progress.

6. Accessibility Considerations: The current implementation may not fully address the needs of students with disabilities, requiring further work on accessibility features.

These limitations highlight the need for continued research and development in this field, as well as ongoing collaboration with educators and students to refine and improve the technology.

Ethics Statement

This research adheres to the ACL Ethics Policy. We have taken the following ethical considerations into account:

1. Data Privacy: All student data collected through the cubits.ai platform is anonymized and handled in compliance with relevant data protection regulations.

2. Informed Consent: Students are informed about the use of AI in their learning materials and have the option to opt out of data collection for research purposes.

3. Bias Mitigation: We are actively working to identify and mitigate potential biases in the AI-generated content, with a focus on ensuring equitable learning experiences for all students.

4. Transparency: The use of AI-generated content is clearly communicated to students, and we provide explanations of how the technology works to promote understanding and trust.

5. Human Oversight: While leveraging AI technologies, we maintain human oversight in content curation and quality control to ensure the accuracy and appropriateness of educational materials.

6. Accessibility: We are committed to improving the accessibility of our platform to ensure that students with disabilities can benefit from AI-enhanced learning experiences.

7. Environmental Impact: We are mindful of the computational resources required for running LLMs and are exploring ways to optimize our models for energy efficiency.

We are committed to ongoing ethical review and improvement of our research and platform as the field of AI in education continues to evolve. Regular consultations with ethics boards, educators, and students will be conducted to address emerging ethical concerns and ensure responsible development and deployment of our technology.

Acknowledgements

We would like to express our sincere gratitude to the faculty and students at Princeton University and Rutgers University for their invaluable participation in this research. Their feedback and insights have been crucial in shaping and refining our approach.

Special thanks go to the development team of cubits.ai for their tireless efforts and technical support in bringing this platform to life. Their expertise and dedication have been instrumental in realizing our vision for AI-enhanced educational videos.

We are also grateful to our colleagues in the Computer Science departments at Rutgers University and Princeton University for their constructive feedback and stimulating discussions throughout this research project.

Lastly, we extend our appreciation to the anonymous reviewers whose insightful comments and suggestions have greatly improved the quality of this paper.

7 References

References

[1] *cubits.ai - AI-Powered Learning Platform.* [online] Available at: `https://www.cubits.ai/`.

[2] Ramly, N., Rosli, A.N., Suhaimi, S., Wahab, M.H.A. and Ariffin, A.H., 2020. The Effects of Using Educational Videos in Online Learning: A Case Study for Basic Computer Science Subject. *International Journal of Emerging Technologies in Learning (iJET)*, 15(24), pp.254-266.

[3] Brame, C.J., 2016. Effective educational videos. *Vanderbilt University Center for Teaching*.

[4] Giannakos, M.N., Krogstie, J. and Aalberg, T., 2017. Video-based learning ecosystem to support active learning: application to an introductory computer science course. *Smart Learning Environments*, 4(1), pp.1-13.

[5] Brown, T., Mann, B., Ryder, N., Subbiah, M., Kaplan, J.D., Dhariwal, P., Neelakantan, A., Shyam, P., Sastry, G., Askell, A. and Agarwal, S., 2020. Language models are few-shot learners. *Advances in Neural Information Processing Systems*, 33.

[6] Shaik, T., Tao, X., Li, Y., Dann, C., McDonald, J. and Redmond, P., 2021. A Review of the Trends and Challenges in Adopting Natural Language Processing Methods for Education Feedback Analysis. *IEEE Access*, 9, pp.102220-102235.

[7] Kgosietsile, T. and Okike, E.U., 2022. An Intelligent Semantic Vector Search Model for Grading and Assessing Students. *International Journal of Advanced Computer Science and Applications*, 13(6), pp.140-151.

[8] Nguyen, A., Ngo, H.N., Hong, Y., Dang, B. and Nguyen, B.P.T., 2022. Ethical principles for artificial intelligence in education. *AI and Ethics*, pp.1-15.

[9] Mohan, G.B., Kumar, R.P., Krishh, P.V., Keerthinathan, A., Lavanya, G., Meghana, M.K.U., Sulthana, S. and Doss, S., 2023. An analysis of large language models: their impact and potential applications. *Journal of Innovation in Computer Science and Engineering*, 12(2), pp.104-115.

[10] Kretzschmar, V., Sailer, A., Wertenauer, M. and Seitz, J., 2024. Enhanced Educational Experiences through Personalized and AI-based Learning. *International Journal on Studies in Education (IJonSE)*, 6(2), pp.191-209.

The Moral Foundations Weibo Corpus

Renjie Cao [2,*], Miaoyan Hu[1,*], Jiahan Wei [1] Baha Ihnaini[1,†]
[1]Wenzhou Kean University
[2] Nanchang Hangkong University
21061301@stu.nchu.edu.cn
1235761@wku.edu.cn, 1235848@wku.edu.cn, bihnaini@kean.edu

Abstract

Moral sentiments expressed in natural language significantly influence both online and offline environments, shaping behavioral styles and interaction patterns, including social media self-presentation, cyberbullying, adherence to social norms, and ethical decision-making. To effectively measure moral sentiments in natural language processing texts, it is crucial to utilize large, annotated datasets that provide nuanced understanding for accurate analysis and model training. However, existing corpora, while valuable, often face linguistic limitations. To address this gap in the Chinese language domain, we introduce the Moral Foundation Weibo Corpus. This corpus consists of 25,671 Chinese comments on Weibo, encompassing six diverse topic areas. Each comment is manually annotated by at least three systematically trained annotators based on ten moral categories derived from a grounded theory of morality. To assess annotator reliability, we present the kappa test results, a gold standard for measuring consistency. Additionally, we apply several the latest large language models to supplement the manual annotations, conducting analytical experiments to compare their performance and report baseline results for moral sentiment classification.

1 Introduction

Moral foundations, delineated as intrinsic, universally applicable, and emotionally grounded psychological systems, stand as fundamental pillars of human morality [Haidt and Graham, 2007]. The exponential surge in global social media usage over the last decade has sparked inquiries into the intricate interplay between human psychology and online behavior [Van Bavel et al., 2024]. Online behaviors, predominantly manifested through digital speech, serve as direct indicators of individuals' psychological states, with moral expressions playing a pivotal role in this regard. Delving into the moral foundations underlying online discourse offers profound insights into users' psychological inclinations. Consequently, the establishment of a corpus of moral foundations for natural language processing becomes imperative for addressing such inquiries.

Previous resources have predominantly catered to English users [Hoover et al., 2020, Trager et al., 2022], neglecting the vast Chinese online community. With approximately 1.09 billion users, China constitutes one of the largest social media populations globally [Gao and Feng, 2016]. In addition to this, there is a big difference between Chinese and English regarding the expression of moral values and sentiments [Gao et al., 2023, Huang et al., 2005]. In English, sentiments are usually expressed more directly, such as using explicit words to describe joy, anger, and sadness. In contrast, Chinese culture is more concerned with maintaining face and social harmony and thus may be more subtle and euphemistic in its expression of sentiments. In other words, only English corpus is insufficient for analyzing the sentiments and moral foundations of Chinese. Together, the development of a Chinese corpus assumes paramount importance in advancing moral natural language processing.

In this context, our study focuses on constructing a moral foundations Chinese corpus, leveraging Weibo, China's foremost social media platform, as the primary data source. The Moral Foundations Weibo Corpus (MFWC) consists of 25,761 posts. Adhering to the ten moral categories delineated in moral foundation theory [Graham et al., 2013, 2009]: Care/Harm, Fairness/Cheating, Loyalty/Betrayal, Authority/Subversion, and Purity/Degradation, six prevalent topics among Weibo users were selected for discussion: animal protection, real estate, people's livelihoods, volunteers, volunteer army, and the San Francisco meeting be-

*These authors contributed equally to this work.
†Corresponding Author.

Proceedings of the 1st Workshop on NLP for Science (NLP4Science), pages 155–165
November 16, 2024

tween the Chinese and U.S. heads of state. Analyzing moral sentiments within these thematic realms facilitates a nuanced understanding of prevalent moral sentiments on Weibo.

Weibo is a public social media platform, current statistics reveal that Weibo boasts 598 million monthly active users [Xu et al., 2020], it provides a rich and diverse dataset for analyzing moral sentiments within the Chinese online community. The choice of Weibo as the corpus foundation first stems from its extensive user base, drawn from diverse backgrounds, ensuring a rich and comprehensive dataset for analysis. MFWC has thus expanded the coverage of the existing corpus to include a significant portion of the global online population. Furthermore, Weibo's all-Chinese system allows MFWC to bridge a crucial gap in existing corpora by catering to non-English-speaking users, thus fostering greater inclusivity and cross-cultural understanding in moral natural language processing research.

We focused our corpus compilation effort on Weibo for a number of reasons. Variations in moral language across different social media platforms can indeed be attributed to disparities in language and social contexts [Curiskis et al., 2020]. The distinctive features of Weibo, China's predominant social media platform, elevate the significance and uniqueness of the Moral Foundations Weibo Corpus. Unlike its western social media platform, Weibo boasts a content moderation system characterized by heightened stringency. So it fosters a digital environment where expressions of moral sentiments are notably more moderated within the MFWC. For instance, when it comes to sensitive topics or political issues, you're likely to see relatively few angry comments or heated expressions of sentiments in MFWC, which may be more common on western social media platform. Sentiments that may be more common on Weibo are discreet, restrained, or indirectly expressed sentiments as well as innuendos to avoid touching on content that may trigger censorship. The stringent content moderation mechanisms on Weibo contribute to the distinctiveness of the MFWC. By providing a dataset characterized by more moderate expressions of moral sentiments, the MFWC offers a valuable contrast to other corpus. This contrast not only enriches the diversity of available datasets but also underscores the importance of considering cultural and contextual factors in moral natural language processing research. Second, the existing English annotation corpus cannot well adapt to the characteristics and needs of Chinese moral expressions. In order to gain a deeper understanding of moral issues in Chinese culture and society, we need to construct a Chinese annotated corpus that is consistent with the latest theoretical revisions. Besides, the complex language characteristics and contextual understanding involved in determining moral issues in the Chinese context. The meaning of basic human communication can also become difficult to understand due to the complexity of language [Garten et al., 2016], it goes beyond the scope of determining simple keywords. Therefore, sentence-based research is the main direction for studying the morality of Chinese texts [Peng et al., 2021]. Compared to English, Chinese has a unique grammar structure and vocabulary expression, which requires a Chinese annotated corpus to deeply understand moral issues in Chinese. We selected a large number of samples based on Weibo entries in different moral and sentimental fields. In the selection of data sources, the selected samples ensure that they are representative and cover a variety of topics and perspectives.

In order to ascertain the efficacy and comparative performance of distinct language models in discerning moral sentiments and to establish a baseline, we subjected some the latest large language models, namely GPT-4 [Pietron et al., 2024], Llama 3 [Dubey et al., 2024] and Qwen 2 [Yang et al., 2024], to testing. Besides, we also report baseline results for multiple computational approaches to measuring moral sentiment in text. These baselines can serve as a foundation for the classification models in moral sentiments detection tasks and provide a reference for future research, which can be instructive in paving the way for improved performance of more sophisticated models in the future.

In view of the lack of Chinese corpus resources, the main contributions of this study include the following three parts: (1) We have established a Moral Foundations Weibo Corpus, providing important basic data for future related research. (2) We provide richer and unique data interpretation using measurement baselines, which can provide inspiration for future research.

2 Corpus overview

As mentioned above, MFWC contains 25,671 blog posts spanning seven distinct thematic domains.

The selection of these thematic areas was guided by several considerations: Firstly, we sought to include topics featuring prominent moral and sentimental expressions (e.g., animal protection) in our expectations to facilitate effective analysis of the dataset. Secondly, the popularity and discussion intensity of the topic are also taken into consideration (e.g., real estate). The inclusion of widely discussed topics with substantial participant engagement enriches the dataset, fostering a diverse range of sentimental expressions and moral concerns. Thirdly, we cover some sensitive elements, such as political and historical events (e.g., volunteer army, China-U.S. Prime Minister meets in San Francisco). Sensitive topics often encapsulate pressing societal issues and profound moral dilemmas, thereby enhancing the corpus's analytical depth and relevance. Additionally, we considered the relevance and significance of each topic in contemporary culture and society, encompassing a diverse array of subjects and aiming to capture the multifaceted nature of digital discussions, thus providing a balanced portrayal of the online landscape.

Through the selection of these themes, we aim to enrich the diversity of the corpus and to differentiate the expressions of moral sentiments in the annotated corpus. In the domains we have chosen, these themes focus on different social events and the moral sentiments expressed within are susceptible to the discourse context and therefore moral sentiments are expressed differently. For example, the moral sentiments contained in the Animal Protection corpus are substantively distinct from those expressed in the Volunteer Army corpus, as these two topics focus on very different objects, with the former containing mainly care for animals and the latter placing the bulk of them on trolling the film. Extra-domain predictions appear difficult due to this heterogeneity, and it is difficult for outsiders to generalise data from different domains through the expression of moral sentiments in one domain. Based on this point, we provide moral sentiment annotations for tweets from different contexts to address this issue.

3 Annotation

3.1 Annotate procedure

Each post in the MFWC was labeled by three well-trained annotators according to the 10 moral sentiment categories outlined in the Moral Foundations Coding Guide (see Appendix).

These Moral sentiment label words are drawn from Moral Foundations Theory [Graham et al., 2013, 2009], which contain five universal moral foundations. In this model, each factor includes virtues and vices. The proposed moral foundations are:

Care/harm: This foundation is related to our long evolution as mammals with attachment systems and an ability to feel (and dislike) the pain of others. It underlies the virtues of kindness, gentleness, and nurturance.

Fairness/cheating: This foundation is related to the evolutionary process of reciprocal altruism. It underlies the virtues of justice and rights.

Loyalty/betrayal: This foundation is related to our long history as tribal creatures able to form shifting coalitions. It underlies the virtues of patriotism and self-sacrifice for the group

Authority/subversion: This foundation was shaped by our long primate history of hierarchical social interactions. It underlies virtues of leadership and followership, including deference to prestigious authority figures and respect for traditions.

Purity/degradation: This foundation was shaped by the psychology of disgust and contamination. It underlies notions of striving to live in an elevated, less carnal, more noble, and more "natural" way. This foundation underlies the widespread idea that the body is a temple that can be desecrated by immoral activities and contaminants. It underlies the virtues of self-discipline, self-improvement, naturalness, and spirituality.

Annotation was undertaken by three undergraduate research assistants, who, after a series of in-depth training, have profound and specialized knowledge of the label of moral sentiments, and are well versed in labeling the various moral foundations in detail. However, even then, due to the vastness and depth of the Chinese language, the annotators still disagreed in their label. Unlike other languages, the meaning of Chinese is not only composed of sentences and words themselves, but in many cases is also inextricably linked to the tone and context of the utterance [Godfroid et al., 2013], and the same utterance in different tones and contexts will have different meanings. In many situations, it is difficult to define exactly what type of moral sentiment a Weibo post relates to, as such a judgement is largely dependent on an individual's subjective judgement, and subjective judgement are different to different. We will pick out the Weibo posts that disagree and discuss them together to reach a consensus conclusion before arriving at the result.

Specifically, labeling each Weibo post allows us to determine whether it embodies a specific virtue or vice, or is classified as non-moral. This means that for any Weibo post, there will be a certain label to describe its moral sentiment.

3.2 Annotation results

Each post within each topic was subjected to a review by multiple annotators with the objective of assigning moral sentiments label. The annotation results can be seen in Table 1, the moral classification of posts under each topic, was determined by a majority vote. In particular, if at least two out of three annotators assigned the same ethical tag to a post, that tag was designated as the final annotation. It is noteworthy that posts frequently received multiple tags during the annotation process. However, a collective decision was made to retain only the most significant tags and omit the rest.

It was observed that the distribution of ethical labels across different topics is highly uneven. For example, a considerable proportion of ethical labels within the topic of animal protection are concentrated in category care. In contrast, the majority of ethical labels within the topic of real estate and people's livelihood fall under the category non-moral. This indicates a strong correlation between ethical labels and the specific content of the topic areas.

To evaluate inter-annotator agreement, we employed the kappa test [Fleiss, 1971] and the PABAK test [Sim and Wright, 2005]. The kappa coefficient is a statistical method used to evaluate the degree of agreement between multiple annotators. The PABAK coefficient is an adjustment to the kappa coefficient that takes into account the effects of prevalence and bias. It measures the degree of actual consistency relative to random consistency. This adjustment facilitates a more reasonable assessment of consistency in the presence of an uneven class distribution. The results are presented in table 2.It was found that approximately half of the topic areas exhibited high kappa values, which may be attributed to the explicitly moral nature of these topics. The remaining topics exhibited lower kappa values, indicating the inherent ambiguity of the general tweets within these topics and the subjective cognitive differences among annotators. As might be expected, given the subjective nature of the annotations, kappa values are lower under some themes. Nevertheless, greater consistency can be attained by addressing prevalence issues.

Table 1: Kappa and PABAK Test Results

Topic	Kappa	Pabak
Protecting Animals	0.92	0.90
Real Estate	0.61	0.75
People's Livelihood	0.45	0.50
Voluntary Army	0.49	0.73
Volunteers	0.87	0.91
China-U.S. Prime Minister Meeting	0.56	0.70
Hangzhou Asian Games	0.69	0.74

4 Baseline classification language models of moral sentiments

While human annotation remains the most accurate method for measuring moral sentiment in text, due to the diversity of the Chinese language and the large sample sizes typically required to study text-based moral sentiments, it is often necessary to supplement human annotations with classification models. Our goal here is to establish baselines that can help us better predict moral sentiments. Next, we report a baseline for moral sentiment classification using a range of models.

To accomplish this task, we selected a number of models from a range of widely used models. These models include ChatGPT-4 [Pietron et al., 2024], Llama 3 [Dubey et al., 2024], and Qwen 2 [Yang et al., 2024]. Each post in the MFWC dataset is assigned a specific label by three annotators, i.e., the six different moral sentiment categories discussed in Section 3. This is a multi-label categorization task, meaning the categories of moral sentiments are not independent of each other, but are related. Here, we provide both single-label and multi-label categorization results.

GPT-4 [Pietron et al., 2024] In the first approach, we used GPT-4. GPT-4, a state-of-the-art language model developed by OpenAI, has been fine-tuned to understand and generate human-like text across various tasks, making it highly suitable for complex sentiment analysis tasks.

Llama 3 [Dubey et al., 2024] In the second approach, we used Llama 3. Llama 3 is a versatile language model that has been designed for a range of natural language processing tasks. While it may

Table 2: Frequency of Weibo posts per Foundation Calculated Based on Annotators' Majority Vote.

Topic	Care/Harm	Fairness/Cheating	Loyalty/Betrayal	Authority/Subversion	Purity/Degradation	Non-Moral
China-U.S. Prime Minister Meeting	26	415	102	86	225	566
People's Livelihood	779	283	454	150	146	4318
Voluntary Army	587	262	787	100	81	3084
Volunteers	326	185	79	279	104	1842
Real Estate	321	533	598	375	90	2751
Protecting Animals	609	53	70	165	312	869
Hangzhou Asian Games	877	841	159	744	360	675
All	3525	2572	2249	1899	1321	14105

not always match the specific performance of models like ChatGPT-4 in every scenario, it offers a robust alternative with strong generalization capabilities.

Qwen 2 [Yang et al., 2024] Lastly, we used Qwen 2. Qwen 2 is an advanced language model with particular strengths in precision tasks. It has been optimized for handling nuanced language variations, which makes it a strong contender in the moral sentiment classification task.

To compare models sets, we rely on three performance metrics: precision, recall, and F1. Precision, the number of true positives divided by the number of predicted positives, represents the proportion of predicted positive cases that actually are positive cases. In contrast, recall, the number of true positives divided by the number of true positives and false negatives, represents the proportion of positive cases that the classifier correctly identifies. Finally, The F1 score is the harmonic mean of precision and recall (the product of twice the precision and recall divided by the sum of precision and recall), and is used to evaluate the performance of a classification models in a comprehensive way. The F1 score takes into account the balance between precision and recall, and is a good metric to use when there is a need to strike a balance between the two.

Table 3: Moral Sentiment Results

models	F1	Precision	Recall
GPT-4	0.60	0.65	0.58
Llama 3	0.56	0.60	0.59
Qwen 2	0.38	0.75	0.32

Table 4: Care Results

models	F1	Precision	Recall
GPT-4	0.74	0.67	0.82
Llama 3	0.65	0.53	0.84
Qwen 2	0.36	0.93	0.22

Table 5: Harm Results

models	F1	Precision	Recall
GPT-4	0.65	0.70	0.61
Llama 3	0.40	0.35	0.50
Qwen 2	0.52	0.60	0.43

Table 6: Authority Results

models	F1	Precision	Recall
GPT-4	0.56	0.67	0.49
Llama 3	0.55	0.42	0.78
Qwen 2	0.56	0.73	0.46

Table 7: Subversion Results

models	F1	Precision	Recall
GPT-4	0.74	0.67	0.82
Llama 3	0.65	0.53	0.84
Qwen 2	0.36	0.93	0.22

Table 8: Fairness Results

models	F1	Precision	Recall
GPT-4	0.74	0.82	0.68
Llama 3	0.65	0.53	0.84
Qwen 2	0.69	0.87	0.57

Table 9: Cheating Results

models	F1	Precision	Recall
GPT-4	0.67	0.65	0.69
Llama 3	0.58	0.61	0.56
Qwen 2	0.40	0.72	0.32

Table 10: Loyalty Results

models	F1	Precision	Recall
GPT-4	0.70	0.68	0.72
Llama 3	0.50	0.40	0.65
Qwen 2	0.55	0.75	0.45

Table 11: Betrayal Results

models	F1	Precision	Recall
GPT-4	0.60	0.75	0.50
Llama 3	0.35	0.40	0.35
Qwen 2	0.50	0.65	0.30

Table 12: Purity Results

models	F1	Precision	Recall
GPT-4	0.63	0.70	0.58
Llama 3	0.39	0.41	0.50
Qwen 2	0.52	0.55	0.30

Table 13: Degradation Results

models	F1	Precision	Recall
GPT-4	0.55	0.60	0.55
Llama 3	0.30	0.25	0.35
Qwen 2	0.22	0.30	0.20

5 Results

The results of the baseline models are provided in Tables 3 to 13. As expected, performance varied substantially across models, discourse domains, and prediction tasks. Further, our results suggest that in the context of different domains and prediction tasks, each model showed different strengths and weaknesses. For instance, we found that GPT-4 performs best in balancing Precision and Recall, so its F1 value is usually the highest and suitable for most tasks that require balancing the two. Llama 3 excels in Recall and is better suited for tasks requiring high recall, but is slightly weaker in Precision than the other models. Qwen 2, on the other hand, excels in Precision excels and is suitable for tasks requiring highly accurate predictions, but is weaker in Recall, which affects its F1 value. Lastly, performance differences, again, depend on the discourse domain and the moral foundation being analyzed.

This variability in performance emphasises the need to take full account of the applicability of models when selecting and applying them, especially when dealing with complex and variable natural language data. Our classification results generally demonstrate the feasibility of using multiple methods to measure moral sentiments in natural language. However, these results also highlight the complexity and challenge of this task. Regardless of the model used, we observed significant variability in performance across different discussion domains and moral bases. This variability suggests that there are still shortcomings in the adaptability of the current approach to different contexts. In future research, it is necessary to delve deeper into the root causes of these performance variations and develop methods that can reduce them. In particular, researchers should aim to identify and understand the specific factors that lead to performance fluctuations, such as the semantic complexity of the text, the nuances of moral sentiments. In this way, we can not only improve the performance of current models, but also provide a more solid theoretical and technical foundation for the field of moral sentiment analysis.

6 Discussion

Natural language processing provides the fundamental tools for processing and understanding human language, which is essential for automated sentiment analysis. Consequently, the integration of natural language processing and sentiment analysis represents an optimal convergence between linguistic theory and computational technology [Cambria et al., 2013]. As computational power increases, the quality and quantity of text mining and natural language processing techniques continue to improve, and the field of ethics through natural language research is becoming more and more widespread [Szép et al., 2024]). In the field of moral sentiment analysis, the most crucial element is the availability of theory-driven text data, which is necessary for the accurate quantification of moral sentiments [Garten et al., 2018].

Moral text data encompasses information pertaining to a multitude of dimensions within the domain of morality. By identifying the salient moral elements in a text, it will help to make moral judgments [Park et al., 2024]. To address this need, we developed the MFWC using posts and comments from Weibo. The MFWC comprises 25,671 Weibo posts from seven distinct topic areas, each of which has been annotated with one of ten types of moral sentiments based on the Moral Foundations Theory. Furthermore, the MFWC has been employed to establish a series of models classification baselines for measuring moral sentiments in texts. These baselines provide a foundation for further research and development in the field, enabling researchers to benchmark their models and improve their understanding of moral language dynamics.

The construction of our Chinese corpus addresses a significant gap in existing moral corpora. Historically, the majority of moral language resources and datasets have been concentrated on Western languages, particularly English. The construction of a comprehensive Chinese moral corpus enables the reflection of the linguistic and cultural nuances of moral discourse in Chinese [Chen et al., 2023]. This corpus is of particular benefit to researchers seeking to develop linguistically supervised models tailored to Chinese. The corpus offers a robust dataset for natural language processing applications, enhancing the capacity to analyse and interpret moral reasoning, sentiment, and values in Chinese texts. The creation of such a corpus enables more accurate sentiment analysis, moral judgement, and ethical reasoning within the context of Chinese culture and language. Furthermore, this corpus can facilitate cross-cultural studies by providing a basis for comparing moral language across different languages and cultures[Schwartz, 2006]. Researchers can utilise this resource to develop models that are not only linguistically appropriate but also culturally sensitive, thereby ensuring that moral judgments and sentiments are understood within the correct cultural framework. By expanding the moral corpus to include Chinese, we contribute to the creation of a more inclusive and representative dataset that can support a range of natural language processing applications. These include automated ethical decision-making systems and sentiment analysis in social media.

In MFWC, we also present research on a new Chinese moral-sentimental computation. Our results demonstrate that the logistic regression models outperforms the other two on the classification task. However, these performance differences do not appear to be consistent across different discourse domains. With MFWC, researchers can gain a deeper understanding of the reasons for this, enabling them to comprehend the dynamics of sentiment in online language, capture trends in popular opinion, and identify subtle changes in social media.

It is our hope that MFWC and this report will assist researchers by providing a unique data set and facilitate new contributions to the fields of natural language processing and social sciences. However, due to the vastness of Chinese culture, our corpus may not be able to contain all Chinese corpora. As more and more researchers utilise MFWC, we anticipate that the resources we provide here will be further expanded to better generalise to Chinese studies.

Limitations

There is an imbalance in the corpus's distribution of moral feeling categories, with some moral categories having a higher profile than others. In particular, in underrepresented categories, this imbalance may result in biased model training and negatively impact sentiment classification models' performance. The dataset's skewness may also make it more difficult to extrapolate results to a wider range of moral situations or sentiments.

Ethics Statement

Significant ethical issues are raised by the creation and use of the Moral Foundations Weibo Corpus (MFWC), which have been diligently addressed throughout this study. First, people's privacy who indirectly participate through posts on social media have had their privacy safeguarded. The corpus does not contain any personally identifiable information, guaranteeing adherence to social media site standards and data privacy laws.

To reduce bias in data annotation and interpretation, we worked with carefully selected and ethically vetted annotators to build the MFWC. Reducing cultural prejudice and fostering inclusivity, the moral categories were established in a way that was culturally sensitive and reflected a thorough understanding of moral expressions within the Chinese context. Finally, the research adheres to the ACL Ethics Policy, ensuring that all stages of this study, from data collection to analysis and reporting, uphold the highest standards of integrity and ethical rigor.

Acknowledgment

This project was made possible through funding from Wenzhou-Kean University, under the grant number IRSPK2023005. Our appreciation extends to the university for their financial support, which was instrumental in advancing our research.

References

Erik Cambria, Björn Schuller, Yunqing Xia, and Catherine Havasi. New avenues in opinion mining and sentiment analysis. *IEEE Intelligent Systems*, 28(2): 15–21, 2013. doi: 10.1109/MIS.2013.30.

Yibei Chen, Amber X Chen, Hongbo Yu, and Shaojing Sun. Unraveling moral and emotional discourses on social media: a study of three cases. *Information, Communication & Society*, pages 1–18, 2023.

Stephan A Curiskis, Barry Drake, Thomas R Osborn, and Paul J Kennedy. An evaluation of document clustering and topic modelling in two online social networks: Twitter and reddit. *Information Processing & Management*, 57(2):102034, 2020.

Abhimanyu Dubey, Abhinav Jauhri, Abhinav Pandey, Abhishek Kadian, Ahmad Al-Dahle, Aiesha Letman, Akhil Mathur, Alan Schelten, Amy Yang, Angela Fan, Anirudh Goyal, Anthony Hartshorn, Aobo Yang, Archi Mitra, Archie Sravankumar, Artem Korenev, Arthur Hinsvark, Arun Rao, Aston Zhang, Aurelien Rodriguez, Austen Gregerson, Ava Spataru, Baptiste Roziere, Bethany Biron, Binh Tang, Bobbie Chern, Charlotte Caucheteux, Chaya Nayak, Chloe Bi, Chris Marra, Chris McConnell, Christian Keller, Christophe Touret, Chunyang Wu, Corinne Wong, Cristian Canton Ferrer, Cyrus Nikolaidis, Damien Allonsius, Daniel Song, Danielle Pintz, Danny Livshits, David Esiobu, Dhruv Choudhary, Dhruv Mahajan, Diego Garcia-Olano, Diego Perino, Dieuwke Hupkes, Egor Lakomkin, Ehab AlBadawy, Elina Lobanova, Emily Dinan, Eric Michael Smith, Filip Radenovic, Frank Zhang, Gabriel Synnaeve, Gabrielle Lee, Georgia Lewis Anderson, Graeme Nail, Gregoire Mialon, Guan Pang, Guillem Cucurell, Hailey Nguyen, Hannah Korevaar, Hu Xu, Hugo Touvron, Iliyan Zarov, Imanol Arrieta Ibarra, Isabel Kloumann, Ishan Misra, Ivan Evtimov, Jade Copet, Jaewon Lee, Jan Geffert, Jana Vranes, Jason Park, Jay Mahadeokar, Jeet Shah, Jelmer van der Linde, Jennifer Billock, Jenny Hong, Jenya Lee, Jeremy Fu, Jianfeng Chi, Jianyu Huang, Jiawen Liu, Jie Wang, Jiecao Yu, Joanna Bitton, Joe Spisak, Jongsoo Park, Joseph Rocca, Joshua Johnstun, Joshua Saxe, Junteng Jia, Kalyan Vasuden Alwala, Kartikeya Upasani, Kate Plawiak, Ke Li, Kenneth Heafield, Kevin Stone, Khalid El-Arini, Krithika Iyer, Kshitiz Malik, Kuenley Chiu, Kunal Bhalla, Lauren Rantala-Yeary, Laurens van der Maaten, Lawrence Chen, Liang Tan, Liz Jenkins, Louis Martin, Lovish Madaan, Lubo Malo, Lukas Blecher, Lukas Landzaat, Luke de Oliveira, Madeline Muzzi, Mahesh Pasupuleti, Mannat Singh, Manohar Paluri, Marcin Kardas, Mathew Oldham, Mathieu Rita, Maya Pavlova, Melanie Kambadur, Mike Lewis, Min Si, Mitesh Kumar Singh, Mona Hassan, Naman Goyal, Narjes Torabi, Nikolay Bashlykov, Nikolay Bogoychev, Niladri Chatterji, Olivier Duchenne, Onur Çelebi, Patrick Alrassy, Pengchuan Zhang, Pengwei Li, Petar Vasic, Peter Weng, Prajjwal Bhargava, Pratik Dubal, Praveen Krishnan, Punit Singh Koura, Puxin Xu, Qing He, Qingxiao Dong, Ragavan Srinivasan, Raj Ganapathy, Ramon Calderer, Ricardo Silveira Cabral, Robert Stojnic, Roberta Raileanu, Rohit Girdhar, Rohit Patel, Romain Sauvestre, Ronnie Polidoro, Roshan Sumbaly, Ross Taylor, Ruan Silva, Rui Hou, Rui Wang, Saghar Hosseini, Sahana Chennabasappa, Sanjay Singh, Sean Bell, Seohyun Sonia Kim, Sergey Edunov, Shaoliang Nie, Sharan Narang, Sharath Raparthy, Sheng Shen, Shengye Wan, Shruti Bhosale, Shun Zhang, Simon Vandenhende, Soumya Batra, Spencer Whitman, Sten Sootla, Stephane Collot, Suchin Gururangan, Sydney Borodinsky, Tamar Herman, Tara Fowler, Tarek Sheasha, Thomas Georgiou, Thomas Scialom, Tobias Speckbacher, Todor Mihaylov, Tong Xiao, Ujjwal Karn, Vedanuj Goswami, Vibhor Gupta, Vignesh Ramanathan, Viktor Kerkez, Vincent Gonguet, Virginie Do, Vish Vogeti, Vladan Petrovic, Weiwei Chu, Wenhan Xiong, Wenyin Fu, Whitney Meers, Xavier Martinet, Xiaodong Wang, Xiaoqing Ellen Tan, Xinfeng Xie, Xuchao Jia, Xuewei Wang, Yaelle Goldschlag, Yashesh Gaur, Yasmine Babaei, Yi Wen, Yiwen Song, Yuchen Zhang, Yue Li, Yuning Mao, Zacharie Delpierre Coudert, Zheng Yan, Zhengxing Chen, Zoe Papakipos, Aaditya Singh, Aaron Grattafiori, Abha Jain, Adam Kelsey, Adam Shajnfeld, Adithya Gangidi, Adolfo Victoria, Ahuva Goldstand, Ajay Menon, Ajay Sharma, Alex Boesenberg, Alex Vaughan, Alexei Baevski, Allie Feinstein, Amanda Kallet, Amit Sangani, Anam Yunus, Andrei Lupu, Andres Alvarado, Andrew Caples, Andrew Gu, Andrew Ho, Andrew Poulton, Andrew Ryan, Ankit Ramchandani, Annie Franco, Aparajita Saraf, Arkabandhu Chowdhury, Ashley Gabriel, Ashwin Bharambe, Assaf Eisenman, Azadeh Yazdan, Beau James, Ben Maurer, Benjamin Leonhardi, Bernie Huang, Beth Loyd, Beto De Paola, Bhargavi Paranjape, Bing Liu, Bo Wu, Boyu Ni, Braden Hancock, Bram Wasti, Brandon Spence, Brani Stojkovic, Brian Gamido, Britt Montalvo, Carl Parker, Carly Burton, Catalina Mejia, Changhan Wang, Changkyu Kim, Chao Zhou, Chester Hu, Ching-Hsiang Chu, Chris Cai, Chris Tindal, Christoph Feichtenhofer, Damon Civin, Dana Beaty, Daniel Kreymer, Daniel Li, Danny Wyatt, David Adkins, David Xu, Davide Testuggine, Delia David, Devi Parikh, Diana Liskovich, Didem Foss, Dingkang Wang, Duc Le, Dustin Holland, Edward Dowling, Eissa Jamil, Elaine Montgomery, Eleonora Presani, Emily Hahn, Emily Wood, Erik Brinkman, Esteban Arcaute, Evan Dunbar, Evan Smothers, Fei Sun, Felix Kreuk, Feng Tian, Firat Ozgenel, Francesco Caggioni, Francisco Guzmán, Frank Kanayet, Frank Seide, Gabriela Medina Florez, Gabriella Schwarz, Gada Badeer, Georgia Swee, Gil Halpern, Govind Thattai, Grant Herman, Grigory Sizov, Guangyi, Zhang, Guna Lakshminarayanan, Hamid Shojanazeri, Han Zou, Hannah Wang, Hanwen Zha, Haroun Habeeb, Harrison Rudolph, Helen Suk, Henry Aspegren, Hunter Goldman, Ibrahim Damlaj, Igor Molybog, Igor Tufanov, Irina-Elena Veliche, Itai Gat, Jake Weissman, James Geboski, James Kohli, Japhet Asher, Jean-Baptiste Gaya, Jeff Marcus, Jeff Tang, Jennifer Chan, Jenny Zhen, Jeremy Reizenstein, Jeremy Teboul, Jessica Zhong, Jian Jin, Jingyi Yang, Joe Cummings, Jon Carvill, Jon Shepard, Jonathan McPhie, Jonathan Torres, Josh Ginsburg, Junjie Wang, Kai Wu, Kam Hou U, Karan Saxena, Karthik Prasad, Kartikay Khandelwal, Katayoun Zand, Kathy Matosich, Kaushik Veeraraghavan, Kelly Michelena, Keqian Li, Kun Huang, Kunal Chawla, Kushal Lakhotia, Kyle Huang, Lailin Chen, Lakshya Garg, Lavender A, Leandro Silva, Lee Bell, Lei Zhang, Liangpeng Guo, Licheng Yu, Liron Moshkovich, Luca Wehrstedt, Madian Khabsa, Manav Avalani, Manish Bhatt, Maria Tsimpoukelli, Martynas Mankus, Matan Hasson, Matthew Lennie, Matthias Reso, Maxim Groshev, Maxim Naumov, Maya Lathi, Meghan Keneally, Michael L. Seltzer, Michal Valko, Michelle Restrepo, Mihir Patel, Mik Vyatskov, Mikayel Samvelyan, Mike Clark, Mike Macey, Mike Wang, Miquel Jubert Hermoso, Mo Metanat, Mohammad Rastegari, Munish Bansal, Nandhini Santhanam, Natascha Parks, Natasha White, Navyata Bawa, Nayan Singhal, Nick Egebo, Nicolas Usunier, Nikolay Pavlovich Laptev, Ning Dong, Ning Zhang, Norman Cheng, Oleg Chernoguz, Olivia Hart, Omkar Salpekar, Ozlem Kalinli, Parkin Kent, Parth Parekh, Paul Saab, Pavan Balaji, Pedro Rittner, Philip Bontrager, Pierre Roux, Piotr Dollar, Polina Zvyagina, Prashant Ratanchandani, Pritish Yuvraj, Qian Liang, Rachad Alao, Rachel Rodriguez, Rafi Ayub, Raghotham Murthy, Raghu Nayani, Rahul Mitra, Raymond Li, Rebekkah Hogan, Robin Battey, Rocky Wang, Rohan Maheswari, Russ Howes, Ruty Rinott, Sai Jayesh Bondu, Samyak Datta, Sara Chugh, Sara Hunt, Sargun Dhillon, Sasha Sidorov, Satadru Pan, Saurabh Verma, Seiji Yamamoto, Sharadh Ramaswamy, Shaun Lindsay, Shaun Lindsay, Sheng Feng, Shenghao Lin, Shengxin Cindy Zha, Shiva Shankar, Shuqiang Zhang, Shuqiang Zhang, Sinong Wang, Sneha Agarwal, Soji Sajuyigbe, Soumith Chintala, Stephanie Max, Stephen Chen, Steve Kehoe, Steve Satterfield, Sudarshan Govindaprasad, Sumit Gupta, Sungmin Cho, Sunny Virk, Suraj Subramanian, Sy Choudhury, Sydney Goldman, Tal Remez, Tamar Glaser, Tamara Best, Thilo Kohler, Thomas Robinson, Tianhe Li, Tianjun Zhang, Tim Matthews, Timothy Chou, Tzook Shaked, Varun Vontimitta, Victoria Ajayi, Victoria Montanez, Vijai Mohan, Vinay Satish Kumar, Vishal Mangla, Vítor Albiero, Vlad Ionescu, Vlad Poenaru, Vlad Tiberiu Mihailescu, Vladimir Ivanov, Wei Li, Wenchen Wang, Wenwen Jiang, Wes Bouaziz, Will Constable, Xiaocheng Tang, Xiaofang Wang, Xiaojian Wu, Xiaolan Wang, Xide Xia, Xilun Wu, Xinbo Gao, Yanjun Chen, Ye Hu, Ye Jia, Ye Qi, Yenda Li, Yilin Zhang, Ying Zhang, Yossi Adi, Youngjin Nam, Yu, Wang, Yuchen Hao, Yundi Qian, Yuzi He, Zach Rait, Zachary DeVito, Zef Rosnbrick, Zhaoduo Wen, Zhenyu Yang, and Zhiwei Zhao. The llama 3 herd of models, 2024. URL `https://arxiv.org/abs/2407.21783`.

Joseph L Fleiss. Measuring nominal scale agreement among many raters. *Psychological bulletin*, 76(5): 378, 1971.

Fei Gao, Chenggang Wu, Hengyi Fu, Kunyu Xu, and Zhen Yuan. Language nativeness modulates physiological responses to moral vs. immoral concepts in chinese–english bilinguals: Evidence from event-related potential and psychophysiological measures. *Brain Sciences*, 13(11):1543, 2023.

Qin Gao and Chenyue Feng. Branding with social media: User gratifications, usage patterns, and brand message content strategies. *Computers in Human Behavior*, 63:868–890, 2016.

Justin Garten, Reihane Boghrati, Joe Hoover, Kate M Johnson, and Morteza Dehghani. Morality between the lines: Detecting moral sentiment in text. In *Proceedings of IJCAI 2016 workshop on Computational Modeling of Attitudes*, 2016.

Justin Garten, Joe Hoover, Kate M Johnson, Reihane Boghrati, Carol Iskiwitch, and Morteza Dehghani. Dictionaries and distributions: Combining expert knowledge and large scale textual data content analysis: Distributed dictionary representation. *Behavior research methods*, 50:344–361, 2018.

Aline Godfroid, Frank Boers, and Alex Housen. An eye for words: Gauging the role of attention in incidental l2 vocabulary acquisition by means of eye-tracking. *Studies in Second Language Acquisition*, 35(3):483–517, 2013.

Jesse Graham, Jonathan Haidt, and Brian A Nosek. Liberals and conservatives rely on different sets of moral foundations. *Journal of personality and social psychology*, 96(5):1029, 2009.

Jesse Graham, Jonathan Haidt, Sena Koleva, Matt Motyl, Ravi Iyer, Sean P Wojcik, and Peter H Ditto. Moral foundations theory: The pragmatic validity of moral pluralism. In *Advances in experimental social psychology*, volume 47, pages 55–130. Elsevier, 2013.

Jonathan Haidt and Jesse Graham. When morality opposes justice: Conservatives have moral intuitions that liberals may not recognize. *Social justice research*, 20(1):98–116, 2007.

Joe Hoover, Gwenyth Portillo-Wightman, Leigh Yeh, Shreya Havaldar, Aida Mostafazadeh Davani, Ying Lin, Brendan Kennedy, Mohammad Atari, Zahra Kamel, Madelyn Mendlen, et al. Moral foundations twitter corpus: A collection of 35k tweets annotated for moral sentiment. *Social Psychological and Personality Science*, 11(8):1057–1071, 2020.

Xiaoxi Huang, Yun Yang, and Changle Zhou. Emotional metaphors for emotion recognition in chinese text. In *Affective Computing and Intelligent Interaction: First International Conference, ACII 2005, Beijing, China, October 22-24, 2005. Proceedings 1*, pages 319–325. Springer, 2005.

Jeongwoo Park, Enrico Liscio, and Pradeep K Murukannaiah. Morality is non-binary: Building a pluralist moral sentence embedding space using contrastive learning. *arXiv preprint arXiv:2401.17228*, 2024.

Shiya Peng, Chang Liu, Yayue Deng, and Dong Yu. :(morality between the lines: Research on identification of Chinese moral sentence). In Sheng Li, Maosong Sun, Yang Liu, Hua Wu, Kang Liu, Wanxiang Che, Shizhu He, and Gaoqi Rao, editors, *Proceedings of the 20th Chinese National Conference on Computational Linguistics*, pages 537–548, Huhhot, China, August 2021. Chinese Information Processing Society of China. URL https://aclanthology.org/2021.ccl-1.49.

Marcin Pietron, Rafał Olszowski, and Jakub Gomułka. Efficient argument classification with compact language models and chatgpt-4 refinements. *arXiv preprint arXiv:2403.15473*, 2024.

Shalom Schwartz. A theory of cultural value orientations: Explication and applications. *Comparative sociology*, 5(2-3):137–182, 2006.

Julius Sim and Chris C Wright. The kappa statistic in reliability studies: use, interpretation, and sample size requirements. *Physical therapy*, 85(3):257–268, 2005.

Teodóra Szép, Sander van Cranenburgh, and Caspar Chorus. Moral rhetoric in discrete choice models: a natural language processing approach. *Quality & Quantity*, 58(1):179–206, 2024.

Jackson Trager, Alireza S Ziabari, Aida Mostafazadeh Davani, Preni Golazizian, Farzan Karimi-Malekabadi, Ali Omrani, Zhihe Li, Brendan Kennedy, Nils Karl Reimer, Melissa Reyes, et al. The moral foundations reddit corpus. *arXiv preprint arXiv:2208.05545*, 2022.

Jay J Van Bavel, Claire E Robertson, Kareena Del Rosario, Jesper Rasmussen, and Steve Rathje. Social media and morality. *Annual review of psychology*, 75:311–340, 2024.

Qing Xu, Ziyi Shen, Neal Shah, Raphael Cuomo, Mingxiang Cai, Matthew Brown, Jiawei Li, Tim Mackey, et al. Characterizing weibo social media posts from wuhan, china during the early stages of the covid-19 pandemic: qualitative content analysis. *JMIR public health and surveillance*, 6(4):e24125, 2020.

An Yang, Baosong Yang, Binyuan Hui, Bo Zheng, Bowen Yu, Chang Zhou, Chengpeng Li, Chengyuan Li, Dayiheng Liu, Fei Huang, et al. Qwen2 technical report. *arXiv preprint arXiv:2407.10671*, 2024.

A Moral Foundations Coding Guide

A.1 Annotating Moral Sentiment in Natural Language

The task of annotating moral sentiment in natural language involves determining which, if any, categories of moral values are relevant to a given document. Our research uses the taxonomy proposed by Moral Foundations Theory (MFT) to identify these categories. However, even with the MFT framework, researchers face several initial decisions about how to annotate MFT values.

First, they need to decide which MFT dimensions to code. If the hypothesis is specific to a particular foundation, coding for that foundation alone might suffice. However, it is often necessary to code for multiple foundations. In such cases, the straightforward approach is to code for the presence of each of the five foundations. Yet, some research might demand more detailed labels. Although the poles of each dimension are related, they express distinct sentiments that might have psychological significance. For example, "We must end suffering" is likely not psychologically equivalent to "We must provide kindness and compassion." Therefore, coding for each pole of each foundation, resulting in 10 individual codes, can be useful. Additionally, it is crucial to identify non-moral texts as such, meaning an annotation procedure could require labeling each document across up to 11 categories.

Researchers must also decide how to address overlapping labels, where moral sentiments are linked to multiple foundations. In our work, we allow overlapping labels during annotation. In some cases, we also ask annotators to identify the primary domain of moral sentiment expressed in a document, along with potential secondary domains. However, reliability analyses showed that while coders generally agreed on the presence of moral sentiment, they were less consistent in identifying the most dominant domain. Therefore, we recommend coding for the presence or absence of each foundation.

A.2 Training Human Annotators

Each virtue and vice is coded as a capitalized initial letter of the moral base, 1 in the case of virtues and 2 in the case of vices. 1 and 2 correspond to "positive" and "negative". If a document does not have any moral content, it should be coded as NM, which corresponds to non-moral. The whole scheme is as follows:

Cure: C1
Harm: C2
Fairness: F1
Cheating: F2
Loyalty: L1
Betrayal: L2
Authority: A1
Subversion: A2
Purity: P1
Degradation: P2
Non-moral: NM

After selecting an annotation label, it is crucial for researchers to establish a clear protocol for identifying the moral domains relevant to a given document. This step is particularly significant due to the inherent difficulty in making these determinations. The ambiguity in this process arises from two main sources.

The first source of ambiguity pertains to the foundations associated with a moral expression. For instance, a moral sentiment might seem strongly related to authority but could also be linked to loyalty, leading to uncertainty about whether to label it as authority alone or both authority and loyalty.

The second source of ambiguity arises from the challenge of discerning the intended moral relevance from an author's language. For example, a social media post stating, "Everything that is going on with abortion these days is reprehensible," is evidently a morally charged statement. However, the specific foundation it pertains to is less clear. If the author is a secular liberal concerned with civil rights, it might be inferred that the statement relates to the fairness/cheating foundation due to concerns about women's reproductive rights. Conversely, if the author is a conservative Christian, the statement might reflect an anti-abortion sentiment associated with purity/degradation. Thus, the same expression can convey different moral sentiments, and competing interpretations can be challenging, if not impossible, to resolve systematically.

These ambiguities pose significant challenges for human annotators, who must find a balance between recognizing subtle moral sentiments and avoiding unwarranted assumptions about authorial intent. Excessive reliance on individual intuitions can lead to inconsistencies among coders, while overly literal interpretations can overlook the nuances of human language and morality. Therefore, a balance must be achieved between implicit coding, which involves inferences about authorial intent, and explicit coding, which focuses on the literal interpretation of the text.

Although achieving this balance perfectly is difficult, being mindful of these extremes can help limit coder biases. Since we typically lack access to the authors of the texts we analyze—and sometimes even the context of their discourse—we train annotators to primarily focus on explicit signals of moral sentiment and minimize inferences about authorial intent unless they are strongly defensible. This approach aims to reduce the risk of cultural biases introducing additional noise into the annotations. While our protocol strives to minimize annotator disagreement, we also caution against artificially reducing annotation variance.

When coding for MFT content, disagreements about which foundation is relevant are common. Even among expert coders, it is often unclear which perspective is correct. While some disagreements can be resolved through discussion, excessive resolution can artificially inflate intercoder reliability. Moral values are inherently subjective, and true accuracy of a code cannot be determined objectively. The closest approximation to an objective criterion is consensus among a constituency. As consensus is approached, the certainty that a phenomenon is strongly associated with a specific Moral Foundation increases. Low consensus among trained coders, therefore, is not merely a problem but an indication that the association might be subject to important boundary conditions, weak, or even illusory. Training coders to minimize disagreement does not change this reality but conceals it. Consequently, while coders need training, it should focus on establishing a shared understanding and heuristics for generating codes without fabricating agreement.

Why So Serious: Humor and its Association with Treatment Measurements Process and Outcome

Matan Kenigsbuch **Natalie Shapira**

Abstract

Humor is an important social construct with various roles in human communication, yet clinicians remain divided on its appropriateness and effectiveness. Despite its importance, empirical research on humor in psychotherapy is limited. This study explores the theoretical concept of "humor" by examining the operational variable of "laughs" within psychotherapy. **Method:** We analyzed transcriptions from 872 psychotherapy sessions involving 68 clients treated by 59 therapists. Clients self-reported their symptoms and state of well-being before each session, while both clients and therapists provided self-reports on their therapeutic alliance after each session. Through text analysis, we extracted the number of laughs and words for each session. We investigated the within-client associations between laughs and symptoms, well-being, therapeutic alliance, and clients' number of words. **Results:** We found session-level associations between laughs and well-being, symptoms, and the number of words. However, no significant associations were observed between laughs and the therapeutic alliance, either from the perspective of the therapist or the client.

1 Introduction

Humor offers numerous benefits in everyday life and is often employed to diffuse tension, particularly during intense conversations, such as those in psychotherapy sessions (Ramakrishna et al., 2018). Peterson et al. (2004) identified humor as one of the character strengths and virtues that contribute to psychological well-being. Additionally, humor can be viewed as an emotion, as recognizing something incongruous with one's expectations can evoke feelings of pleasure. Over the past four decades, the medical community has increasingly acknowledged the healing power of humor and the positive emotions it fosters (Martens, 2004).

Not everyone has agreed on the beneficial role of humor in therapy. Kubie (1971) cautioned that a psychiatrist's use of humor could be potentially harmful to the therapeutic relationship, suggesting that it might lead clients to feel their concerns are not being taken seriously. Additionally, Freud argued that certain uses of humor reflect underlying aggressive and sexual impulses (Bader, 1993). As such, humor can sometimes function as a defense or resistance mechanism (Bader, 1993) and might be misused by therapists to manage their own anxieties or as a display of narcissistic showmanship (Kubie, 1971).

In a recent review of humor in psychotherapy, Hussong and Micucci (2020) noted that many therapists continue to believe in humor's therapeutic benefits. For example, humor's capacity to encourage new interpretations or perspectives can help clients reframe the issues that led them to seek therapy (Panichelli, 2006; Martens, 2004). From a cognitive standpoint, humor may aid in reducing depression by facilitating "rapid perceptual-cognitive switches in frames of reference" (O'Connell, 1976). Additionally, humor can be valuable for fostering insight (Poland, 1971) and promoting cognitive flexibility (Gelkopf and Kreitler, 1996).

Another crucial aspect of psychotherapy, the therapeutic alliance, has been linked to the use of humor, as evidenced by clinical experience. Gelkopf (2011) argues that humor's primary contribution lies in strengthening the therapeutic relationship. He references Poland (1971), who suggested that humor is closely associated with a strong therapeutic alliance, allowing therapists to demonstrate their humanity and reduce barriers between clients and psychotherapists. Poland also noted that humor enables therapists to bridge the gap between themselves and their clients. Similarly, Martens (2004) hypothesizes that humor helps clients to open up and engage with their therapist, fostering a bond and reducing the atmosphere of rivalry, threat, and dependency. In line with this, psychoanalyst Bader (1993) presented clinical cases showing that a ther-

Proceedings of the 1st Workshop on NLP for Science (NLP4Science), pages 166–174
November 16, 2024

apist's humor can reveal aspects of their internal thoughts, thereby cultivating a sense of safety and confidence in the therapeutic relationship.

Additionally, Longe (2019) presents intriguing findings suggesting that humor might be an indicator of a healthy therapeutic relationship. In her thesis, she reports that most participants considered their therapists' humor to be beneficial to their therapeutic process. She found a positive correlation between the alignment of clients' and therapists' senses of humor and the overall ratings of their therapeutic relationship. Furthermore, she identified a positive correlation between clients' perceptions of the helpfulness of their therapists' humor and their evaluations of the therapeutic relationship.

In summary, limited studies suggest a connection between the use of humor in therapy and the enhancement of therapist-client relationships.

Empirical studies have consistently shown a link between the use of humor in therapy and improved treatment outcomes or reductions in pathological symptoms. For instance, Panichelli et al. (2018) explored the relationship between humor and various therapeutic outcomes in psychotherapy clients, finding a strong positive correlation between the presence of humor during therapy sessions and their effectiveness, as perceived by both clients and therapists. Another study demonstrated that watching humorous movies led to a reduction in psychopathology, anger, anxiety, and depression symptoms, although it did not affect therapeutic alliance scores (Gelkopf et al., 2006). Similarly, Danzer et al. (1990) found that listening to humorous audio tapes resulted in decreased depression severity among participants.

Despite humor's potential to enhance therapy, it remains underemphasized in psychotherapy training, and there is a scarcity of empirical research supporting its use as an intervention (Longe, 2019). This lack of focus may contribute to some therapists' ambivalence about incorporating humor into their practice.

In this study, we aim to expand the current understanding of humor in psychotherapy. While previous research, such as Ramakrishna et al. (2018), has highlighted various methods for measuring humor, the challenge of quantifying humor, particularly in psychotherapy, might explain the limited empirical studies on the topic. Nonetheless, it is widely acknowledged that humor can elicit laughs and promote happiness (Mora-Ripoll, 2010). In this study, we measure the use of humor in therapy by annotating instances of laughs during sessions. This approach assumes that laughs are clear, identifiable events that can often be traced back to humor. Although not all laughs are directly linked to humor, it is generally considered a reliable indicator of humor-related responses.

1.1 Laughs

Laughs is defined as a psychophysiological response triggered by humor or other stimuli (Mora-Ripoll, 2010). It is a physical reaction observed in humans and some primates, characterized by rhythmic, often audible contractions of the diaphragm and other parts of the respiratory system. Laughs typically occur in response to external or internal stimuli and are generally associated with positive emotional states such as joy, mirth, happiness, and relief. However, it can also arise from contrary emotional states like embarrassment, apology, or confusion, as seen in nervous laughs (Yim, 2016).

In exploring the therapeutic benefits of laughs, four potential mechanisms of action may illustrate its direct or indirect health advantages. First, laughs can induce immediate or long-term physiological changes that benefit the body. Second, it can foster positive emotional states. Third, laughs may enhance personal coping strategies and increase pain tolerance. Lastly, in terms of interpersonal relations, laughs can indirectly boost social competencies and improve interpersonal skills (Mora-Ripoll, 2010). In this context, Squier (1995) suggests that a therapist's spontaneous laughs can enhance a client's trust in both the therapist and the therapeutic process.

Similar to the broader field of humor, empirical research on laughs in psychotherapy is also limited (Longe, 2019). Marci et al. (2004) examined the frequency of laughs and skin conductance (SC) responses in client-therapist pairs. Their analysis revealed that SC score changes were significantly greater when both clients and therapists laughed together compared to when they laughed individually. This finding underscores the connection between humor and the therapeutic relationship. Additionally, the study found that clients laughed significantly more than therapists and produced more laughs alone while speaking. This challenges the notion that humor (whether appropriate or not) predominantly originates from the therapist (Poland, 1971; Kubie, 1971).

1.2 Hypothesis

As outlined, this study aims to empirically examine the relationship between laughs in psychotherapy, as an operational measure of humor, and improvements in various aspects of the treatment measurement process and outcome. Specifically, we will examine whether laughs are associated with the therapeutic alliance—the relationship between therapist and client. Additionally, we will examine the relationship between laughs and treatment outcomes, including client symptoms. We hypothesize that higher values of laughs during therapy will be positively correlated with higher results across these variables.

Hypothesis 1: At the within-treatment level, higher levels of laughs in psychotherapy sessions will be associated with higher levels of outcomes **(1a)** and lower levels of symptoms **(1b)** as reported at the beginning of the session, and higher therapeutic alliance as reported after the session **(1c)**. These sub-hypotheses are consistent with previous studies that indicated that humor is associated with better treatment outcomes (Panichelli et al., 2018), reduction of pathological symptoms (Gelkopf et al., 2006), and ratings of the therapeutic relationship (Longe, 2019). However, it should be noted that these studies collected their data about humor retrospectively (not from transcripts) and did not use the laughs variable.

Hypothesis 2: At the within-treatment level, higher levels of laughs in psychotherapy sessions will be associated with higher levels of words said by the client in sessions. This prediction will be tested in an exploratory manner and is based on the hypothesis that humor helps clients to open up (Martens, 2004).

2 Method

We utilize a dataset of 872 psychotherapy session transcripts from 74 different therapist-client dyads (pairs), constructed by 68 clients and 59 therapists. See the appendix for more details about the participants, treatment, transcriptions, and ethical concerns. Within these transcripts, we extracted a total of 10,454 laughs (mean per session = 11.98, range $= 0-129$). The extraction process involves analyzing the transcribers' comments regarding paralinguistic events using a specialized paralinguistics lexicon "JOY". This lexicon includes terms such as "laughs," "amused," "with humor," "giggling," etc. that transcribers used to describe what they hear (Shapira et al., 2021).[1] Before each session, clients self-reported their functioning using the ORS questionnaire (Miller et al., 2003) which is considered to be an indicator of treatment progress, and self-reported their symptoms using the HSCL questionnaire (Derogatis et al., 1974) which represents the global symptomatic level experienced by the client over the past week. After each session, therapists and clients reported their perspectives on the relationship quality during each session, measured by the WAI questionnaire (Horvath and Greenberg, 1989); see the appendix.

3 Results

For each session, we extracted the (1) number of laughs, and (2) number of client's words. The means, standard deviations, and ranges for all the variables are presented in Table 1.

Because the data had a multilevel structure (sessions nested within treatments; Bolger and Laurenceau, 2013), we used multilevel models (MLM, using R *lme4* library (Bates, 2010), using function *lmer*) also known as Hierarchical Linear Models. These models allow estimation of two levels, a within-treatment level, and a between-client level, and accommodate non-balanced data (Bolger and Laurenceau, 2013).

To examine the concurrent within-treatment associations between the laughs variable (Laughs) and session-level treatment measures: outcome measured by ORS (Hypothesis 1a) symptoms measured by HSCL (Hypothesis 1b), therapeutic alliance measured by WAI (Hypothesis 1c), and the number of client's words (Hypothesis 2), we applied a multilevel model predicting the session level treatment measure (client mean-centered) by the number of laughs used by the client and therapist in the session. The mixed-level equation was as follows:

$$Treatment\_Measure_s^d = (\gamma_0^0+u_0^d) + (\gamma_1^0+u_1^d)Laughs_s^d + e_s^d$$

$Treatment\_Measure_s^d$ for a dyad d in session s is predicted by the sample's intercept (γ_0^0), by dyad d's deviation from this intercept (u_0^d), by the average (i.e., fixed) effects (γ_1^0) of the predictors, by this client's deviation from the fixed effects (i.e., the random effects: (u_0^d, u_1^d)), and by a level-1 residual term quantifying the session's deviation from these effects (i.e., the random effect at level 1, e_s^d).

[1] "JOY" paralinguistic lexicon is separate and not intersecting other lexicons such as "SMIRK", "TUT-TUT", "SARCASM". For more details see Shapira et al. (2021)

Variable	SL Obs.	SL M(SD)	Range	DL Obs.	DL M(SD)
Laughs	872	11.98 (14.25)	0-129	74	13.04 (4.487)
Words	872	4524 (1408)	416-8176	74	4484.96 (1282.929)
ORS	860	24.4 (7.96)	0.3-40	74	24.5 (6.41)
HSCL	860	1.78 (0.51)	1.05-3	74	1.788 (0.4)
C-WAI	823	50.89 (23.82)	4-84	74	49.48 (23.02)
T-WAI	831	41.69 (18.61)	0-74	74	40.33 (17.88)

Note. Laughs = number of laughs annotation; Words = number of client's words; ORS = Outcome Rating Scale; HSCL = Hopkins Symptom Checklist; WAI = Working Alliance Inventory; C = Client; T = Therapist; SL = Session Level; DL = Dyad Level; Obs.=Observations

Table 1: Descriptive statistics of treatment measurements (processes and outcome) and laughs.

	Words		ORS		HSCL		WAI-C		WAI-T	
Predictors	Estimates	CI	Estimates	CI	Estimates	CI	Estimates	CI	Estimates	CI
(Intecept)	0.00	-45.39 - 45.39	24.52***	23.06 - 25.98	1.79***	1.69 - 1.88	49.50***	44.25 - 54.74	40.35***	36.29 - 44.41
Laughs	14.06**	4.14 - 23.97	0.07**	0.02 - 0.12	-0.01**	-0.01 - 0.00	-0.02	-0.10 - 0.07	0.01	-0.05 - 0.07
Observation	872		860		860		823		831	
R^2 (ICC)	0.078 (0.06)		0.632 (0.63)		0.590 (0.59)		0.929 (0.93)		0.916 (0.92)	

Note. ***p<0.001; **p<0.01; *p,0.05; Laughs = number of laughs; R^2= Conditional R; Words = number of client's words; ORS = Outcome Rating Scale; HSCL = Hopkins Symptom Checklist; WAI = Working Alliance Inventory; C = Client; T = Therapist;

Table 2: Treatment measurements, process and outcome association

The results of the multilevel model summarized in Table 2 show concurrent session-level associations between laughs and well-being, symptoms, and clients' number of words. No associations were found with the therapist's or the client's assessment of therapeutic alliance.

4 Discussion

Laughs were associated with better treatment outcomes, aligning with Panichelli et al. (2018). While we cannot establish a causal relationship, this suggests that laughs during therapy may contribute to improved client functioning. We propose that laughs may indirectly enhance social competencies, thereby boosting interpersonal skills (Mora-Ripoll, 2010). In this way, laughs in therapy—distinct from *laughter therapy*—can serve as a social tool that clients learn in therapy and later apply in their social lives. This potential benefit is reflected in ORS, which assesses social functioning.

Laughs were associated with lower levels of the client's symptoms. The current study does not allow us to determine whether it is laughs that lower the level of symptoms or a low level of symptoms that increases the amount of laughs. Previous studies support the conclusion that laughs may help reduce symptoms of mental disorders such as anxiety and depression (Gelkopf et al., 2006; Danzer et al., 1990). This may indicate that laughs provide a release for the client, as supported by medical and psychological studies on the psychophysiological effects of laughs (Mora-Ripoll, 2010).

No association was found between laughs and the therapeutic alliance. This finding does not correspond with Gelkopf (2011); Longe (2019). However, the findings are compatible with the study of Gelkopf et al. (2006), which found no significant associations between the effect of humorous movies and the therapeutic alliance. To the best of our knowledge, there has not yet been any empirical study that examines the associations between laughs in psychotherapy and therapeutic alliance.

Laughs in treatment were associated with higher verbalization among the clients. This finding corresponds with providing assumptions in the literature that humor helps the client open up (Martens, 2004), and feel more comfortable with the therapist (Gelkopf, 2011; Bader, 1993).

Marci et al. (2004) claimed that previous research in laughs and psychotherapy has focused almost exclusively on the client. This study examined the role of laughs in general (of both therapist and client) in treatment. To gather evidence on whether the therapist's use of humor is positive and beneficial, further research is needed. In a future project, we aim to investigate whether the therapist influences the client's degree of laughs, whether humor increases throughout treatment, and how it relates to treatment outcomes.

5 Limitations

The current work acknowledges that laughs can arise from various emotions beyond humor, such as nervousness, embarrassment, and other emotional states. However, laughs were annotated regardless of whether they occurred due to humor.

We used "humor" as a motivation for the study but did not address the implications of humor in the present study. We limited our findings to "laughs" only. Future work is needed to determine how frequently laughs might occur due to non-humor-related reasons, and how this could potentially impact the results. Specifically, how these alternative sources of laughs might influence the conclusions and associations drawn regarding humor.

Acknowledgements

We thank Rivka Tuval-Mashiach and her team for the transcribed therapy sessions dataset.

References

Aviad Albert, Brian MacWhinney, Bracha Nir, and Shuly Wintner. 2013. The hebrew childes corpus: transcription and morphological analysis. *Language resources and evaluation*, 47(4):973–1005.

Michael J Bader. 1993. The analyst's use of humor. *The Psychoanalytic Quarterly*, 62(1):23–51.

Douglas M Bates. 2010. lme4: Mixed-effects modeling with r.

Matthew D Blagys and Mark J Hilsenroth. 2000. Distinctive features of short-term psychodynamic-interpersonal psychotherapy: A review of the comparative psychotherapy process literature. *Clinical psychology: Science and practice*, 7(2):167–188.

Niall Bolger and Jean-Philippe Laurenceau. 2013. *Intensive longitudinal methods: An introduction to diary and experience sampling research.* Guilford Press.

Amy Danzer, J Alexander Dale, Klions, and Herbert L. 1990. Effect of exposure to humorous stimuli on induced depression. *Psychological reports*, 66(3):1027–1036.

Leonard R Derogatis. 1992. Scl-90-r: Administration, scoring & procedures manual-ii for the (revised) version and other instruments of the psychopathology rating scale series. *Clinical Psychometric Research.*, pages 1–16.

Leonard R Derogatis et al. 1974. The hopkins symptom checklist (hscl): a measure of primary symptom dimensions.

Fredrik Falkenström, Robert L Hatcher, Tommy Skjulsvik, Mattias Holmqvist Larsson, and Rolf Holmqvist. 2015. Development and validation of a 6-item working alliance questionnaire for repeated administrations during psychotherapy. *Psychological Assessment*, 27(1):169.

Marc Gelkopf. 2011. The use of humor in serious mental illness: a review. *Evidence-Based Complementary and Alternative Medicine*, 2011.

Marc Gelkopf, Bruria Gonen, Rena Kurs, Yuval Melamed, and Avi Bleich. 2006. The effect of humorous movies on inpatients with chronic schizophrenia. *The Journal of nervous and mental disease*, 194(11):880–883.

Marc Gelkopf and Shulamith Kreitler. 1996. Is humor only fun, an alternative cure or magic? the cognitive therapeutic potential of humor. *Journal of Cognitive Psychotherapy*, 10(4):235–254.

Adam O Horvath and Leslie S Greenberg. 1989. Development and validation of the working alliance inventory. *Journal of counseling psychology*, 36(2):223.

Devin K Hussong and Joseph A Micucci. 2020. The use of humor in psychotherapy: Views of practicing psychotherapists. *Journal of Creativity in Mental Health*, pages 1–18.

Lawrence S Kubie. 1971. The destructive potential of humor in psychotherapy. *American Journal of Psychiatry*, 127(7):861–866.

Olivia Longe. 2019. *Can I laugh now? Understanding humour within psychotherapy from the client's perspective*. Ph.D. thesis, Dublin Business School.

W Lutz, S Tholen, E Schurch, and M Berking. 2006. The development, validation, and reliability of short-forms of current instruments for the evaluation of therapeutic progress in psychotherapy and psychiatry. *Diagnostica*, 52(1):11–24.

Carl D Marci, Erin K Moran, and Scott P Orr. 2004. Physiologic evidence for the interpersonal role of laughter during psychotherapy. *The Journal of nervous and mental disease*, 192(10):689–695.

Willem HJ Martens. 2004. Therapeutic use of humor in antisocial personalities. *Journal of contemporary psychotherapy*, 34(4):351–361.

Erhard Mergenthaler and Charles Stinson. 1992. Psychotherapy transcription standards. *Psychotherapy research*, 2(2):125–142.

Scott D Miller, BL Duncan, J Brown, JA Sparks, and DA Claud. 2003. The outcome rating scale: A preliminary study of the reliability, validity, and feasibility of a brief visual analog measure. *Journal of brief Therapy*, 2(2):91–100.

Ramon Mora-Ripoll. 2010. The therapeutic value of laughter in medicine. *Alternative Therapies in Health & Medicine*, 16(6).

Walter E O'Connell. 1976. Freudian humour: The eupsychia of everyday life.

C Panichelli. 2006. Humor in psychotherapy: couldreframing'berefunframing'? *Thérapie Familiale*, 27(4):399.

Christophe Panichelli, Adelin Albert, Anne-Françoise Donneau, Salvatore D'Amore, Jean-Marc Triffaux, and Marc Ansseau. 2018. Humor associated with positive outcomes in individual psychotherapy. *American journal of psychotherapy*, 71(3):95–103.

Christopher Peterson, Martin EP Seligman, et al. 2004. *Character strengths and virtues: A handbook and classification*, volume 1. Oxford University Press.

Warren S Poland. 1971. The place of humor in psychotherapy. *American Journal of Psychiatry*, 128(5):635–637.

Anil Ramakrishna, Timothy Greer, David C Atkins, and Shrikanth S Narayanan. 2018. Computational modeling of conversational humor in psychotherapy. In *INTERSPEECH*, pages 2344–2348.

Natalie Shapira, Dana Atzil-Slonim, Daniel Juravski, Moran Baruch, Dana Stolowicz-Melman, Adar Paz, Tal Alfi-Yogev, Roy Azoulay, Adi Singer, Maayan Revivo, Chen Dahbash, Limor Dayan, Tamar Naim, Lidar Gez, Boaz Yanai, Adva Maman, Adam Nadaf, Elinor Sarfati, Amna Baloum, Tal Naor, Ephraim Mosenkis, Badreya Sarsour, Jany Gelfand Morgenshteyn, Yarden Elias, Liat Braun, Moria Rubin, Matan Kenigsbuch, Noa Bergwerk, Noam Yosef, Sivan Peled, Coral Avigdor, Rahav Obercyger, Rachel Mann, Tomer Alper, Inbal Beka, Ori Shapira, and Yoav Goldberg. 2021. Hebrew psychological lexicons. In *Proceedings of the Seventh Workshop on Computational Linguistics and Clinical Psychology: Improving Access*, pages 55–69, Online. Association for Computational Linguistics.

Natalie Shapira, Dana Atzil-Slonim, Rivka Tuval-Mashiach, and Ori Shapira. 2022. Measuring linguistic synchrony in psychotherapy. In *Proceedings of the Eighth Workshop on Computational Linguistics and Clinical Psychology*, pages 158–176.

Jonathan Shedler. 2010. The efficacy of psychodynamic psychotherapy. *American psychologist*, 65(2):98.

David V Sheehan, Yves Lecrubier, K Harnett Sheehan, Patricia Amorim, Juris Janavs, Emmanuelle Weiller, Thierry Hergueta, Roxy Baker, and Geoffrey C Dunbar. 1998. The mini-international neuropsychiatric interview (mini): the development and validation of a structured diagnostic psychiatric interview for dsm-iv and icd-10. *The Journal of clinical psychiatry*.

Harriet A Squier. 1995. Humor in the doctor-patient relationship. *Family Systems Medicine*, 13(1):101.

Richard F Summers and Jacques P Barber. 2009. *Psychodynamic therapy: A guide to evidence-based practice*. Guilford Press.

JongEun Yim. 2016. Therapeutic benefits of laughter in mental health: a theoretical review. *The Tohoku journal of experimental medicine*, 239(3):243–249.

A Appendices

The following sections are taken from previous work on the same dataset (Shapira et al., 2022) and are presented here for the convenience of the reader.

A.1 Dataset: Participants and Treatment

A.1.1 Clients

The dataset was drawn as a sample from a broader pool of clients who received individual psychotherapy at a university training outpatient clinic, located in a central city in Israel. Data were collected naturalistically between August 2014 and August 2016 as part of the clinic's regular practice of monitoring clients' progress. From an initial sample of 180 clients who provided their consent to participate in the study, 34 (18.88%) dropped out (deciding one-sidedly to end treatment before the planned termination date). Clients were selected from the larger sample to match two criteria: (1) treatment duration of at least 15 sessions, and (2) full data including audio recordings to be used for the transcriptions and session-by-session questionnaires available for each client. These criteria corresponded to our analytic strategy of detecting within-client associations between linguistic features and session processes and outcomes. Clients were also excluded, based on the M.I.N.I. 6.0 (Sheehan et al., 1998) if they were diagnosed as severely disturbed, either due to a current crisis, had severe trauma and accompanying post- traumatic stress disorder, a past or present psychotic or manic diagnosis, and/or current substance abuse. Based on these criteria we excluded 77 (42.7%) clients. Thus, of the total sample, the data for 68 (38.33%) clients who met the above-mentioned inclusion criteria were transcribed, for a total of 872 transcribed sessions.

The clients were all above the age of 18 (M_{age}=39.06, SD=13.67, range=20–77), majority of whom were women (58.9%). Of the clients, 53.5% had at least a bachelor's degree, 53.5% reported being single, 8.9% were in a committed relationship, 23.2% were married and 14.2% were divorced or widowed. Clients' diagnoses were established based on the Mini International Neuropsychiatric Diagnostic Interview for Axis I DSM-IV diagnoses (MINI 5.0; Sheehan et al., 1998). Of the entire sample, 22.9% of the clients had a single diagnosis, 20.0% had two diagnoses, and 25.7% had three or more diagnoses. The most common diagnoses were comorbid anxiety and affective disorders[2] (25.7%), followed by other comorbid disorders (17.1%), anxiety disorders (14.3%), and affective disorders (5.7%). A sizable group of clients (31.4%) reported experiencing relationship concerns, academic/occupational stress, or other problems but did not meet criteria for any Axis I diagnosis.

A.1.2 Therapists and Therapy

Clients were treated by 59 therapists in various stages of their clinical training. Clients were assigned to therapists in an ecologically valid manner based on real-world issues, such as therapist availability and caseload. Most therapists treated one client each (47 therapists), but some (10) treated two clients and (2) more. Each therapist received one hour of individual supervision every two weeks and four hours of group supervision on a weekly basis. All therapy sessions were audiotaped for supervision. Supervisors were senior clinicians. Individual and group supervision focused heavily on reviewing audiotaped case material and technical interventions designed to facilitate the appropriate use of therapist interventions. Individual psychotherapy consisted of once- or twice-weekly sessions. The language of therapy was Modern Hebrew (MH). The dominant approach in the clinic includes a short-term psychodynamic psychotherapy treatment model (e.g.,Blagys and Hilsenroth,2000; Shedler, 2010; Summers and Barber, 2009). The key features of the model include: (a) a focus on affect and the experience and expression of emotions, (b) exploration of attempts to avoid distressing thoughts and feelings, (c) identification of recurring themes and patterns, (d) an emphasis on past experiences, (e) a focus on interpersonal experiences, (f) an emphasis on the therapeutic relationship, and (g) exploration of wishes, dreams, or fantasies (Shedler, 2010). On average, treatment length was 37 sessions (SD = 23.99, range = 18–157). Treatment was open- ended in length, but given that psychotherapy was provided by clinical trainees at a university-based outpatient community clinic, the treatment duration was often restricted to be 9 months.

[2] The following DSM-IV diagnoses were assessed in the affective disorders cluster: major depressive disorder, dysthymia and bipolar disorder. The following DSM-IV diagnoses were assumed in the anxiety disorders cluster: panic disorder, agoraphobia, generalized anxiety disorder and social anxiety disorder.

A.1.3 Transcriptions

To capture the treatment processes from session to session, and since the transcription process is highly expensive, transcriptions were conducted alternately (i.e., sessions 2, 4, 6, 8 and so on until one session before the last session). In cases where material was incomplete (such as the quality of the recordings, or the questionnaires for a specific session), the next session was transcribed instead. The transcriber team was composed of seven transcribers, all of whom were graduate students in the University's psychology department. The transcribers went through a one day training workshop and monthly meetings were held throughout the transcription process to supervise the quality of their work. The training included specific guidelines on how to handle confidential and sensitive information and the transcribers were instructed to replace names by pseudonyms and to substitute any other identifying information. The transcription protocol followed general guidelines, as described in (Mergenthaler and Stinson, 1992), and in Albert et al. (2013). The word forms, the form of commentaries, and the use of punctuation were kept as close as possible to the speech presentation. Everything was transcribed, including word fragments as well as syllables or fillers (such as "ums", "ahs", "uh huhs" and "you know"). The audiotape was transcribed in its entirety and provided a verbatim account of the session. The transcripts included elisions, mispronunciations, slang, grammatical errors, non-verbal sounds (e.g., laughs, cry, sighs), and background noises. The transcription rules were limited in number and simple (for example, each client and therapist utterances should be on a separate line ;each line begins with the specification of the speaker) and the format used several symbols to indicate comments (such as [...] to indicate the correct form when the actual utterance was mispronounced, or <number of minutes of silence >). The transcripts were proofread by the research coordinator. The final transcripts could be processed by human experts or automatically by computer.

There were 872 transcripts in total (the mean transcribed sessions per client was 12.56; SD=4.93) Each transcript incorporated metadata such as the client's code, which allowed the client data to be linked across sessions and for hierarchical analysis. The transcriptions totaled about four million words over 150,000 talk turns (i.e., switching between speakers). On average, there were 5800 words in a session, of which 4538 (78%; SD=1409.62; range 416-8176) were client utterances and 1266 (22%; SD=674.99; range 160-6048) were therapist utterances with a mean of 180.07 (SD=95.37; range 30-845) talk turns per session.

A.1.4 Procedure and Ethical Considerations

The procedures were part of the routine assessment and monitoring process in the clinic. All research materials were collected after securing the approval of the authors' university ethics committee. Only clients that gave their consent to participate were included in the study. Clients were told that they could choose to terminate their participation in the study at any time without jeopardizing treatment. The clients completed the ORS before each therapy session and the WAI after each session. The therapist completed the WAI after each therapy session. The sessions were audiotaped and transcribed according to a protocol described above. All data collected was anonymized and only then exposed to a very small number of researchers, as agreed upon by the participants.

A.2 Outcome and Process Measurements

A.2.1 Outcome Rating Scale (ORS; (Miller et al., 2003))

The ORS is a 4-item visual analog scale developed as a brief alternative to the OQ-45. The scale is designed to assess change in three areas of client functioning that are widely considered to be valid indicators of progress in treatment: functioning, interpersonal relationships, and social role performance. Respondents complete the ORS by rating four statements on a visual analog scale anchored at one end by the word Low and at the other end by the word High. This scale yields four separate scores between 0 and 10 that sum to one score ranging from 0 to 40, with higher scores indicating better functioning. The ORS has strong reliability estimates (α=0.87-0.96) and moderate correlations between the ORS items and the OQ-45 subscale and total scores (ORS total - OQ-45 total: r = 0.59).

A.2.2 Hopkins Symptom Checklist-short form (HSCL-11; (Derogatis et al., 1974))

The HSCL-11 is a shortened version of SCL-90-R (Derogatis, 1992) self-report questionnaire. It includes 11 items that assess symptoms. Participants rank each item on a Likert scale between 1 ("not at all") and 4 ("extremely") depending on how much distress they feel regarding the item. The average items represent the global symptomatic level experienced by the client over the past week. The questionnaire was found to have high internal validity (α= 0.92) (Lutz et al., 2006).

A.2.3 Working Alliance Inventory (WAI; (Horvath and Greenberg, 1989))

The WAI is a self report questionnaire (both for therapist and client). It is one of the most widely investigated common factors that was found positively correlated to treatment outcome in psychotherapy. It includes items ranging from 0 ("not at all") to 5 ("completely") to evaluate three components (1) agreement on treatment goals (2) agreement on therapeutic tasks and (3) a positive emotional bond between client and therapist (Falkenström et al., 2015)

Learning the Bitter Lesson: Empirical Evidence from 20 Years of CVPR Proceedings

Mojtaba Yousefi
Northeastern University / Boston, MA
yousefi.m@northeastern.edu

Jack Collins
Develop Health / Menlo Park, CA
jack@develophealth.io

Abstract

This study examines the alignment of *Conference on Computer Vision and Pattern Recognition* (CVPR) research with the principles of the "bitter lesson" proposed by Rich Sutton. We analyze two decades of CVPR abstracts and titles using large language models (LLMs) to assess the field's embracement of these principles. Our methodology leverages state-of-the-art natural language processing techniques to systematically evaluate the evolution of research approaches in computer vision. The results reveal significant trends in the adoption of general-purpose learning algorithms and the utilization of increased computational resources. We discuss the implications of these findings for the future direction of computer vision research and its potential impact on broader artificial intelligence development. This work contributes to the ongoing dialogue about the most effective strategies for advancing machine learning and computer vision, offering insights that may guide future research priorities and methodologies in the field.

1 Introduction

Rich Sutton's influential essay "The Bitter Lesson" argues that the most significant advancements in artificial intelligence (AI) have come from focusing on general methods that leverage computation rather than human-designed representations and knowledge. This principle has been particularly evident in the field of Computer Vision (CV), which has witnessed a notable shift from hand-crafted features to deep learning models.

In this paper, we investigate the extent to which the abstracts of the Conference on Computer Vision and Pattern Recognition (CVPR), a major machine learning (ML) conference, align with the principles of the "bitter lesson" over a span of 20 years. We analyze a random sample of 200 papers each year, addressing the following research questions:

- How has the focus on general methods and computation evolved in CVPR abstracts over the past two decades?
- What trends can be observed in the adoption of deep learning techniques and the shift away from hand-engineered features?
- To what extent do the abstracts reflect the key insights of Sutton's "bitter lesson," and how has this alignment changed over time?
- Is there a significant relationship between a paper's alignment with the "bitter lesson" principles and its impact, as measured by citation count?

To address these questions, we employ large language models (LLMs), which themselves are a prime manifestation of principles outlined in the "bitter lesson", to analyze the CVPR abstracts. The evaluation is based on five metrics assigned by the LLMs, providing a comprehensive assessment of the alignment between the abstracts and the "bitter lesson."

Our research provides valuable insights into the overall direction of the ML community and reveals interesting trends in the adoption of Sutton's principles. By leveraging LLMs to analyze a large body of research literature, we offer a novel approach to understanding the learning and evolution of a scientific field. This method allows us to uncover patterns and trends that may not be immediately apparent through traditional research methods, providing a more comprehensive understanding of the current state of ML research and its alignment with the principles that have proven most effective in driving progress in AI.

The potential impact of our findings on future CV research directions is significant. By identifying trends in the adoption of general methods and deep learning techniques, we can inform the development of foundation models for CV at the state

Proceedings of the 1st Workshop on NLP for Science (NLP4Science), pages 175–187
November 16, 2024 ©2024 Association for Computational Linguistics

of the art. These insights contribute to a deeper understanding of the current state of ML research and highlight potential areas for further exploration and growth in the field.

2 Background

2.1 The Bitter Lesson

The field of artificial intelligence (AI) has witnessed a paradigm shift, eloquently articulated in Rich Sutton's influential essay "The Bitter Lesson" (Sutton, 2019). Sutton's thesis emphasizes the primacy of general methods that harness computational power over human-designed representations and domain-specific knowledge. This perspective echoes the seminal work of Leo Breiman, who, two decades earlier, delineated the dichotomy between statistical and algorithmic approaches in his paper "Statistical Modeling: The Two Cultures" (Breiman, 2001). Breiman's insights, along with subsequent works like (Halevy et al., 2009), have profoundly shaped our understanding of data-driven methodologies in AI.

2.2 Evolution of Computer Vision

The field of Computer Vision (CV) exemplifies the principles of Sutton's "bitter lesson." Traditionally reliant on hand-crafted features like SIFT, HOG, and Haar cascades for object detection and image classification, CV underwent a paradigm shift with embracing deep learning, particularly Convolutional Neural Networks (CNNs). This transition enabled the automatic learning of hierarchical features directly from raw image data, eliminating the need for manual feature engineering and significantly improving performance across various CV tasks.

The 2012 ImageNet Large Scale Visual Recognition Challenge (ILSVRC) marked a pivotal moment in this evolution. AlexNet, a CNN architecture, achieved a remarkable 15.3% top-5 error rate, outperforming previous models by over 10 percentage points. This breakthrough was facilitated by the convergence of ImageNet's massive annotated dataset, advancements in CNN architectures, GPU computing power, and foundational work of visionary researchers.

The subsequent emergence of foundation models further aligned CV with Sutton's principles. Models like CLIP, ALIGN, and Florence demonstrate remarkable adaptability across diverse tasks with minimal fine-tuning, leveraging extensive multimodal datasets to learn rich, transferable representations. For instance, the Florence model has achieved state-of-the-art results by integrating universal visual-language representations from web-scale image-text data (Bayoudh et al., 2021).

This evolution from traditional feature engineering to deep learning and foundation models in CV underscores the importance of leveraging computation and vast datasets for superior performance and generalization. For a comprehensive overview of these advancements, readers may refer to Minaee et al. (2020), which details recent progress in deep learning for image segmentation.

2.3 Large Language Models in Academic Evaluation

The integration of Large Language Models (LLMs) into the evaluation of academic texts has emerged as a significant area of interest. LLMs, such as GPT-4, have demonstrated remarkable capabilities in processing and analyzing large volumes of information quickly, making them suitable for various applications, including the assessment of academic literature. For instance, research has shown that LLMs can effectively assist in title and abstract screening for literature reviews, which is crucial in the biomedical domain (Dennstädt, 2024). Moreover, LLMs have been employed to perform qualitative data analysis, producing consistent results across multiple iterations (Tai et al., 2023).

In addition to their analytical capabilities, LLMs have been shown to possess a degree of human-like judgment in evaluating the quality of text. The G-EVAL framework, which utilizes LLMs to assess the quality of natural language generation outputs, demonstrates that LLMs can align closely with human evaluators in certain contexts (Liu, 2023). However, the deployment of LLMs in academic evaluation is not without challenges. LLMs can exhibit biases similar to those found in human judgments, which may affect the fairness and accuracy of their evaluations (Acerbi, 2023). Furthermore, the phenomenon of "hallucination," where LLMs produce plausible but factually incorrect information, poses a risk in academic contexts (Buchanan, 2023).

The role of LLMs in answering questions and generating hypotheses also merits attention. Their ability to provide detailed responses to complex queries has been leveraged in various educational settings, enhancing learning experiences and facilitating knowledge acquisition (Polverini, 2024). However, the tendency of LLMs to produce verbose outputs can sometimes obscure the clarity of their answers, necessitating careful prompt engineering (Yeadon, 2024). In the context of academic research, LLMs can assist in generating hypotheses and guiding exploratory studies, contributing to the advancement of knowledge in various fields (Irons et al., 2023).

Despite the promising applications of LLMs in academic evaluation and research, it is crucial to establish ethical guidelines and best practices for their use. The potential for misuse, such as generating misleading information or facilitating academic dishonesty, necessitates careful consideration of the implications of LLM deployment in educational and research contexts (Urman, 2023).

3 Methodology and Evaluation

3.1 LLM Evaluation of Titles and Abstracts

We employ three large language models to evaluate the title and abstracts of CVPR papers from 2005 to 2024: GPT-4o-2024-05-13, gpt-4o-mini-2024-07-18, and claude-3-5-sonnet-20240620. The following information is extracted from online portals and stored in a database for each paper: Publication year (2005-2024), Title, Authors, Abstract. For each paper, the citation count from Semantic Scholar API is also queried on July 20th 2024, and stored alongside the other metadata. The total number of papers per year is shown in Figure 1.

Each LLM model is tasked with assigning a Likert score of 0-10 for how well the paper aligns with the principles of Sutton's "bitter lesson." We use the Chain-of-Thought Prompting technique with Magentic library to interface with the models and collect their responses in a structured format for analysis (Collins et al., 2024). The prompts used in this study are included in the appendix for reproducibility.

We define five dimensions for "bitter lesson" alignment:

1. **Learning Over Engineering**: To what extent does the idea prioritize leveraging computation through data-driven learning and statistical methods over relying on human-engineered knowledge, heuristics, and domain expertise?

2. **Search over Heuristics**: To what degree does the idea emphasize leveraging computation through search algorithms and optimization techniques rather than depending on human-designed heuristics and problem-specific strategies?

3. **Scalability with Computation**: To what extent is the idea based on methods that can continuously scale and improve performance as the available computational resources increase?

4. **Generality over Specificity**: To what degree does the approach emphasize general, flexible, and adaptable methods that can learn and capture arbitrary complexity from data rather than attempting to build in complex and detailed models of the world through manual engineering and domain-specific knowledge?

5. **Favoring Fundamental Principles**: To what extent does the approach adhere to fundamental principles of computation, mathematics, and information theory rather than focusing on emulating the specific details of human cognition or biological intelligence?

The prompts were designed to capture the essence of each "bitter lesson" dimension concisely and objectively. To anchor the ratings, we provide examples for the 0, 5, and 10 points on each dimension, clarifying the criteria and ensuring consistent evaluations. The prompts are formatted consistently to facilitate easy processing and understanding by the models.

Given the vast number of publications, our study focuses on a representative random sample of 200 papers from each year of CVPR proceedings. We define the overall alignment score for each paper as the sum of scores across five dimensions. In the absence of human-evaluated ground truth, we employ multiple inter-rater reliability measures to assess the consistency of ratings between different models.

3.2 Inter-rater Reliability Measures

Intraclass Correlation Coefficient (ICC): We utilize ICC to quantify the degree of agreement among the models' ratings. ICC is particularly suitable for assessing reliability when multiple raters evaluate the same set of items. We specifically employ the two-way random effects model (ICC(2,k)) to account for both rater and subject effects.

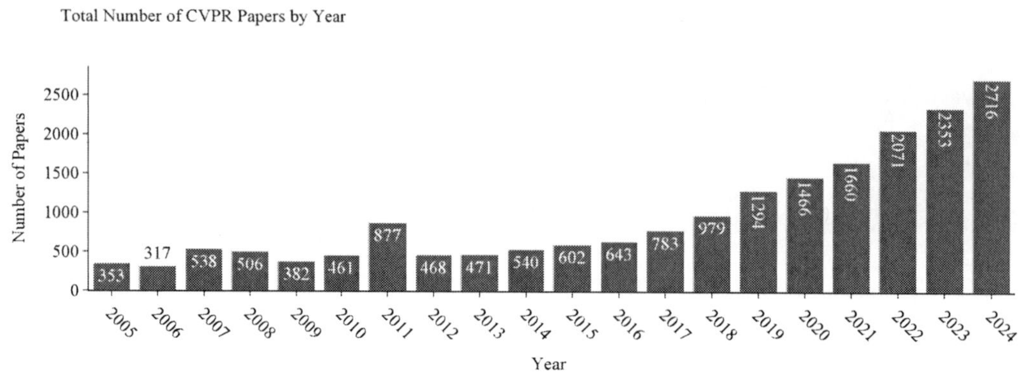

Figure 1: Total number of CVPR papers present in database for each year from 2005 to 2024.

Krippendorff's Alpha: To complement ICC, we also calculate Krippendorff's Alpha, a versatile reliability coefficient that can handle various types of data (nominal, ordinal, interval, ratio) and is robust to missing data. This measure provides an additional perspective on the inter-rater agreement, especially useful when dealing with potential variations in rating scales or missing evaluations.

3.3 Regression Analysis

To investigate the relationship between alignment scores and paper impact, we conduct regression analysis using citation count as a proxy for influence. To control for the year of publication and account for potential temporal effects, we implement yearly stratification in our regression model. This approach allows us to isolate the impact of alignment while considering the varying citation patterns across different publication years.

To address the typically right-skewed distribution of citation counts Figure 2, we apply a logarithmic transformation to the data. This transformation serves multiple purposes in our analysis. First, it reduces skewness, resulting in a more symmetric distribution that better approximates normality—a key assumption in many statistical models. Second, it stabilizes variance across the range of data, mitigating the heteroscedasticity often observed in citation count data where variance tends to increase with the mean. Finally, the log transformation linearizes potentially multiplicative relationships, converting them to additive ones. This facilitates more accurate modeling using linear regression techniques, particularly when the effect of predictors on citation counts is expected to be multiplicative rather than additive. By employing this transformation, we enhance the robustness of our statistical analyses and ensure they are better suited to the inherent characteristics of citation data in academic literature.

The results of the analysis are presented in the following section.

4 Results

4.1 Inter-rater Reliability

Figure 3 presents the inter-rater reliability scores for the five dimensions of "bitter lesson" alignment across the three models employed in this study. The horizontal dashed lines indicate common thresholds for interpreting these measures, with the color and label denoting the qualitative interpretation. The bar colors reflect the relative strength of each dimension. In the Krippendorff's alpha graph, the bar for the "Favoring Fundamental Principles" dimension is not visible due to its near-zero score.

The models demonstrate consistently strong agreement on all dimensions except "Favoring Fundamental Principles," as evidenced by ICC values above 0.5 and Krippendorff's alpha scores exceeding 0.4 on the remaining dimensions. The poor performance on "Favoring Fundamental Principles" may be attributed to the high adherence to this principle in papers published since 2005. Among the dimensions, "Learning Over Engineering" exhibits the highest ICC and Krippendorff's alpha scores, indicating the models' reliable evaluation of paper alignment based on the provided prompts and rating criteria.

Although perfect agreement is not achieved, the inter-reliability measures fall within or above common thresholds for "good" reliability, validating

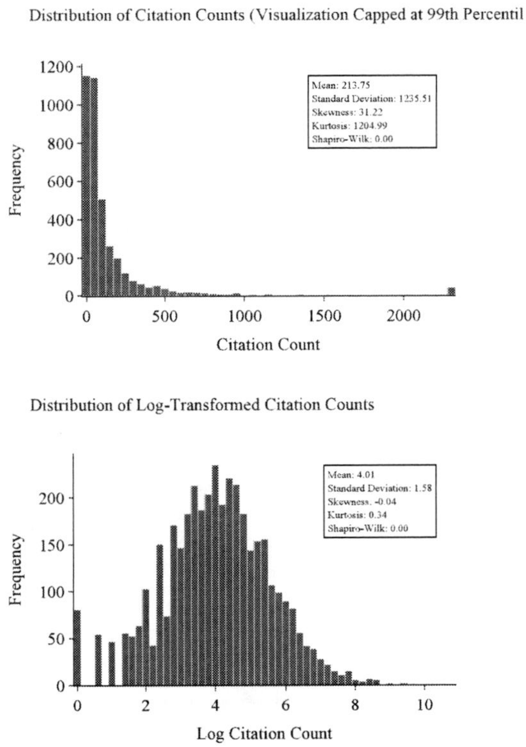

Figure 2: Distribution of citation counts and log-transformed citation counts for CVPR papers from 2005 to 2024 present in the database.

the use of AI models for prompt-based research paper evaluation. It is important to acknowledge that even with domain expert human raters, perfect agreement is seldom attained due to the complexities of research evaluation. The high reliability scores obtained in this study demonstrate the models' consistency in their assessments, providing a reliable foundation for further analysis. For more information on the challenges and limitations of inter-rater reliability measures in human evaluations of the NeurIPS conference, readers may refer to (Beygelzimer et al., 2023) and (Cortes and Lawrence, 2021).

4.2 Regression Analysis

Table 1 presents the results of the regression analysis for each dimension of "bitter lesson" alignment scores against citation impact, stratified by year of publication. The R-squared values, ranging from 0.027 to 0.306, indicate that 2.7-30.6% of the variation in citation impact can be explained by alignment to "bitter lessons" dimensions. It is crucial to interpret the coefficients for each dimension as multiplicative effects, as the log transform of citation counts is used as the dependent variable.

In the context of this regression analysis, a multiplicative effect implies that a one-unit change in the alignment score for a particular dimension leads to a proportional change in the original scale of the citation count. For instance, if the regression coefficient for the "Scalability" dimension is 0.5, a one-unit increase in the "Scalability" alignment score would be associated with a multiplicative effect of approximately $\exp(0.5) \approx 1.65$ on the original citation count. In other words, if a paper's "Scalability" alignment score increases by one unit, its citation count would be expected to increase by a factor of 1.65, holding all other variables constant.

The statistical significance of the regression coefficients is denoted using *, **, and *** to represent the 10%, 5%, and 1% significance levels, respectively. Several dimensions, such as "Scalability" and "Learning over engineering," exhibit statistically significant relationships with citation impact across multiple years. However, given the high degree of correlation between the dimensions, the significance and coefficients in the regression model should be interpreted with caution.

These findings suggest that adherence to the principles outlined in the "bitter lesson" dimensions, particularly "Scalability" and "Learning over engineering," may have a positive influence on a paper's citation impact. The multiplicative nature of the coefficients highlights the potential for substantial increases in citation counts as alignment scores improve. Nevertheless, the presence of correlations among the dimensions necessitates a cautious interpretation of the individual coefficients and their statistical significance.

Table 2 shows the results of regressing citation counts on the overall "bitter lesson" alignment score for each year between 2005 and 2024. Several key trends emerge. First, the R-squared values, which indicate the proportion of variance in citation counts explained by the alignment scores, are quite low for most years (generally less than 5%). However, they increase substantially starting in 2015, reaching over 15% in some later years. This suggests that alignment with the "bitter lessons" became more predictive of citation impact over time. This time period is of special interest as it coincides with the emergence of deep learning, and a shift towards the principles of scalability and

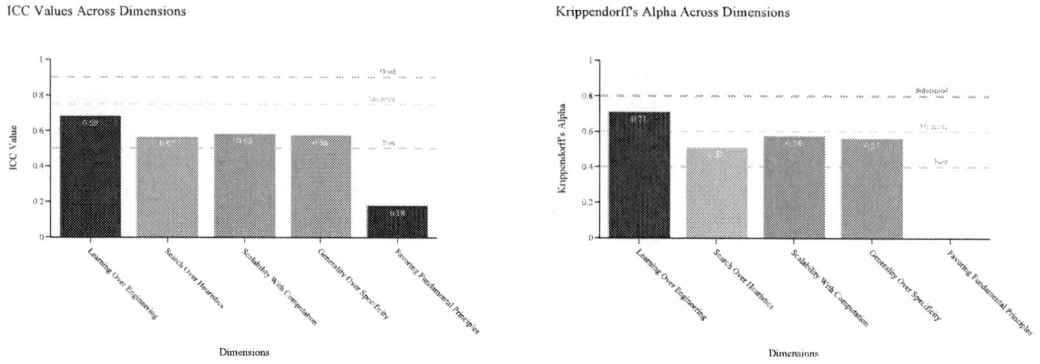

Figure 3: Comparison of ICC and Krippendorff's alpha values across the five dimensions of "bitter lesson" alignment for the three language models used in the study.

Table 1: Regression analysis results for the relationship between "bitter lesson" alignment scores and citation impact, stratified by year.

Year	R-squared	N	Learning	Search	Scalability	Generality	Principles
2005	0.027	199	-0.220	0.104	0.139	0.272	-0.171
2006	0.076	200	0.016	-0.042	0.388*	0.199	-0.171
2007	0.035	200	-0.087	0.117	0.350*	-0.006	-0.318*
2008	0.078	200	-0.009	0.096	0.465***	-0.026	-0.463***
2009	0.085	199	-0.073	0.136	0.104	0.378*	-0.631***
2010	0.074	200	0.121	-0.129	0.218	0.016	-0.471**
2011	0.076	200	0.208	-0.036	0.318**	-0.284	-0.423**
2012	0.094	200	0.195	0.077	0.428**	-0.110	-0.517**
2013	0.085	200	0.395***	-0.112	0.013	-0.119	-0.279
2014	0.119	200	0.408***	-0.085	0.308*	-0.348*	-0.266
2015	0.264	200	0.515***	-0.145	0.417**	-0.236	-0.122
2016	0.306	200	0.637***	-0.300**	0.517***	-0.325	-0.372*
2017	0.313	200	0.418***	-0.353**	0.751***	-0.004	-0.508**
2018	0.172	200	0.291*	-0.322*	0.418**	0.156	-0.436**
2019	0.111	200	0.573**	-0.439**	0.229	-0.099	-0.257
2020	0.120	200	0.315	-0.411***	0.179	0.229	0.010
2021	0.090	200	0.269*	-0.381***	0.253	-0.072	-0.265*
2022	0.136	200	0.618***	-0.137	0.110	-0.118	-0.257
2023	0.123	200	0.107	-0.009	0.664***	-0.078	-0.132
2024	0.178	171	-0.619***	0.314	0.808***	0.282	-0.020

*** indicates significance at the 1% level, ** indicates significance at the 5% level, and * indicates significance at the 10% level.

learning from data that are emphasized in the "bitter lessons." Second, the overall alignment scores exhibit a statistically significant positive relationship with citations in many individual years, most prominently after 2011. The coefficients tend to be largest in later years as well. This indicates that as deep learning became more established, papers more closely adhering to principles like scalability and learning from data received more citations on average. The results suggest that the "bitter lessons" have become increasingly important in the field of computer vision, aligning with the broader trend towards data-driven methods and scalable algorithms in machine learning research.

4.3 Trends in "Bitter Lesson" Alignment

Figure 4 presents the average alignment scores for each "bitter lesson" dimension across the years

Table 2: Regression analysis results for the relationship between overall "bitter lesson" alignment scores and citation impact, stratified by year.

Year	R-squared	N	F-statistic	Prob (F-statistic)	Overall Alignment Score
2005	0.007	199	1.409	0.237	0.029 [-0.019, 0.076]
2006	0.050	200	10.335	0.002	0.083*** [0.032, 0.134]
2007	0.003	200	0.554	0.457	0.019 [-0.031, 0.068]
2008	0.010	200	1.993	0.160	0.031 [-0.012, 0.075]
2009	0.015	199	2.998	0.085	0.045* [-0.006, 0.097]
2010	0.000	200	0.033	0.856	0.005 [-0.049, 0.059]
2011	0.000	200	0.000	0.993	-0.000 [-0.051, 0.051]
2012	0.024	200	4.898	0.028	0.057** [0.006, 0.109]
2013	0.005	200	0.944	0.333	0.022 [-0.023, 0.067]
2014	0.030	200	6.023	0.015	0.056** [0.011, 0.101]
2015	0.170	200	40.618	0.000	0.141*** [0.097, 0.184]
2016	0.128	200	29.114	0.000	0.129*** [0.082, 0.176]
2017	0.133	200	30.338	0.000	0.182*** [0.117, 0.248]
2018	0.066	200	13.996	0.000	0.098*** [0.047, 0.150]
2019	0.021	200	4.241	0.041	0.061** [0.003, 0.119]
2020	0.040	200	8.325	0.004	0.079*** [0.025, 0.133]
2021	0.002	200	0.407	0.524	-0.017 [-0.068, 0.035]
2022	0.062	200	13.054	0.000	0.097*** [0.044, 0.149]
2023	0.063	200	13.416	0.000	0.099*** [0.046, 0.153]
2024	0.092	171	17.040	0.000	0.127*** [0.066, 0.188]

*** indicates significance at the 1% level, ** indicates significance at the 5% level, and * indicates significance at the 10% level.

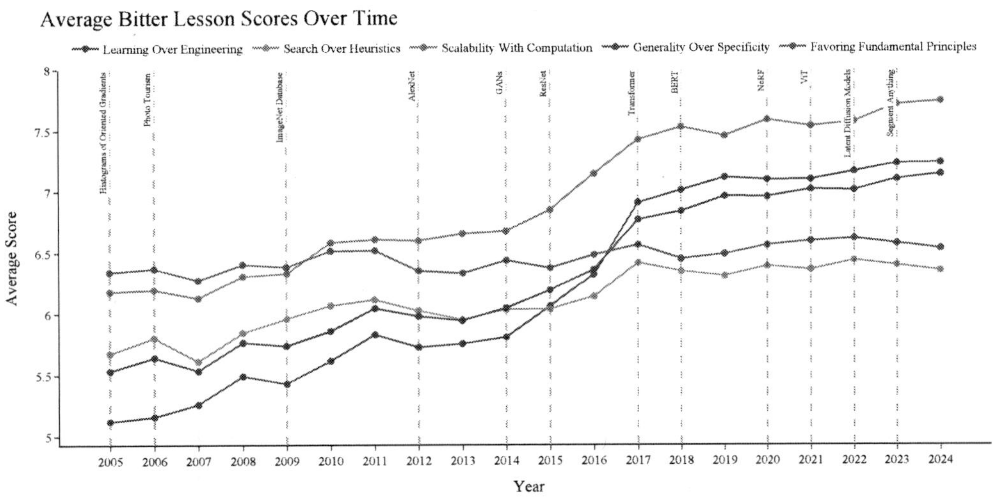

Figure 4: Line plot showing the average alignment scores across years for CVPR papers from 2005 to 2024.

2005-2024. The vertical lines, which depict the publication of influential papers in machine learning (not necessarily computer vision), serve as a guide to understanding the overall evolution of the field. The averages are calculated across all papers and all language models (LLMs) employed in the study. The plot reveals several notable trends in the alignment of CVPR papers with the principles of the "bitter lesson." Notably, the dimensions of "Scalability with Computation" and "Learning

Over Engineering" exhibit a consistent upward trend over the years, indicating a growing emphasis on scalable algorithms and data-driven learning methods in CVPR research. This trend aligns with the broader shift towards deep learning and foundation models in computer vision, emphasizing the importance of leveraging computation and large datasets for superior performance.

The period from 2015 to 2020 witnesses a particularly sharp rise in the average scores for these dimensions, coinciding with major advances in deep learning, such as the application of convolutional neural networks to computer vision tasks. Interestingly, this time frame corresponds to the period in which the regression analysis finds the highest predictive power of alignment scores on citation counts. This finding suggests that the increasing alignment of CVPR papers with the principles of scalability and learning-oriented approaches during this period has a significant impact on their academic influence, as measured by citation metrics.

The observed trends in the alignment scores highlight the evolving landscape of computer vision research, with a growing emphasis on leveraging the power of computation and data-driven learning techniques. The coincidence of these trends with the increased predictive power of alignment scores on citation counts underscores the importance of adhering to the principles of the "bitter lesson" for achieving impactful research outcomes in the field of computer vision.

5 Conclusion

Our study examined the alignment of CVPR research with Rich Sutton's "The Bitter Lesson" over twenty years, leveraging large language models to analyze trends. The findings reveal a consistent increase in the adoption of general-purpose learning algorithms and scalability with computational resources, reflecting a strong adherence to the core principles of the "bitter lesson." These trends underscore the machine learning community's preference for data-driven and computation-heavy approaches over manual engineering and domain-specific knowledge.

However, the dimension of "Search over Heuristics" has not experienced a similar upward trajectory, indicating limited integration of search-based methodologies within the field. This stagnation contrasts with recent advancements in inference-time scaling, exemplified by OpenAI's o1 models, which emphasize the importance of test-time compute in overcoming diminishing returns. The o1 models' ability to simulate various strategies and scenarios during inference, similar to AlphaGo's Monte Carlo Tree Search (MCTS), marks a key departure from earlier approaches that relied heavily on large pre-trained models.

The paradigm shift towards scaling inference time, driven by the development of larger and more complex models, has the potential to emulate search-like processes. As computational capabilities continue to expand, it is plausible that future research may increasingly incorporate search techniques, thereby enhancing alignment with this dimension of the "bitter lesson." The dynamic resource allocation in o1 models, which adjusts computational resources based on task complexity, further underscores the potential for integrating search methodologies.

Overall, our findings highlight the continued relevance of the "bitter lesson" in shaping the trajectory of computer vision research. By emphasizing generality and scalability, the field is well-positioned to leverage emerging computational advancements. Future work should explore the integration of search methodologies and assess their impact on research impact and innovation within computer vision, particularly in light of recent breakthroughs in inference-time scaling.

Limitations

This study, while providing valuable insights into the evolution of computer vision research, has several limitations that should be acknowledged. Firstly, our reliance on large language models (LLMs) for evaluating research abstracts, while innovative, introduces potential biases inherent to these models. The LLMs' understanding and interpretation of complex scientific concepts may not always align perfectly with human expert judgment.

Secondly, the absence of human expert evaluation as a ground truth is a significant limitation. Collecting such human evaluations presents considerable challenges, as it would require a diverse panel of researchers from various subfields of the computer vision community. The interdisciplinary nature of modern computer vision research necessitates expertise in areas ranging from traditional image processing to deep learning, computer graphics, and even cognitive science. Assembling such a panel and achieving consensus on the evaluation criteria would be a formidable task, both in terms of logistics and resources.

Furthermore, our analysis is limited to the information contained in titles and abstracts. While these elements provide a concise summary of research, they may not capture the full depth and nuance of the methodologies and findings presented in the full papers. This limitation could potentially lead to oversimplification of complex research ideas.

Lastly, while our study spans two decades of CVPR proceedings, it does not account for research published in other venues or unpublished work that may have influenced the field. This focus on a single conference, albeit a prestigious one, may not provide a complete picture of the entire computer vision research landscape.

Despite these limitations, we believe our study provides valuable insights into broad trends in computer vision research and its alignment with the principles of the "bitter lesson." Future work could address these limitations by incorporating human expert evaluations, analyzing full paper contents, and expanding the scope to include a wider range of publication venues.

Ethics Statement

This study adheres to the ACL Ethics Policy. Our use of large language models (LLMs) for analyzing trends in academic literature raises important ethical considerations. We acknowledge that LLMs may introduce biases when used for direct evaluation of academic work. However, our study focuses solely on using LLMs to analyze broad trends rather than to assess individual papers' quality or merit. We have addressed the challenges and potential biases of LLM use for evaluation in our background section, emphasizing the need for careful interpretation of results.

All data were collected in accordance with applicable privacy and intellectual property laws. The titles and abstracts of CVPR papers were collected from the conference website, which allows for such collection and analysis under standard terms of use. Citation counts were collected from Semantic Scholar, which also permits such collection and analysis under its standard terms of use. No personally identifiable information was collected from human subjects.

Our methodology aims to minimize risks by using multiple models and focusing on aggregate trends rather than individual assessments. No crowd workers or annotators were involved in the data collection process described in the paper. We believe this approach provides valuable insights into the evolution of computer vision research while maintaining ethical standards in AI-assisted academic analysis.

References

A. Acerbi. 2023. Large language models show human-like content biases in transmission chain experiments. *Proceedings of the National Academy of Sciences*, 120.

K. Bayoudh, R. Knani, F. Hamdaoui, and A. Mtibaa. 2021. A survey on deep multimodal learning for computer vision: advances, trends, applications, and datasets. *The Visual Computer*, 38:2939–2970.

Alina Beygelzimer, Yann Dauphin, Percy Liang, and Jenn Wortman Vaughan. 2023. Has the machine learning review process become more arbitrary as the field has grown? the neurips 2021 consistency experiment. *ArXiv*, abs/2306.03262.

L. Breiman. 2001. Statistical modeling: The two cultures (with comments and a rejoinder by the author). *Statistical Science*, 16.

J. Buchanan. 2023. Chatgpt hallucinates non-existent citations: evidence from economics. *The American Economist*, 69:80–87.

Jack Collins, Chad Fawcett, Ikko Eltociear Ashimine, Marc, Michael Struwig, Mojtaba Yousefi, and Manuel Zander. 2024. Magentic: Seamlessly integrate llms as python functions.

Corinna Cortes and Neil D. Lawrence. 2021. Inconsistency in conference peer review: Revisiting the 2014 neurips experiment. *ArXiv*, abs/2109.09774.

F. Dennstädt. 2024. Title and abstract screening for literature reviews using large language models: an exploratory study in the biomedical domain. *Systematic Reviews*, 13.

Alon Y. Halevy, Peter Norvig, and Fernando C Pereira. 2009. The unreasonable effectiveness of data. *IEEE Intelligent Systems*, 24:8–12.

J. Irons, C. Mason, P. Cooper, A. Reeson, and C. Paris. 2023. Exploring the impacts of chatgpt on future scientific work.

Y. Liu. 2023. G-eval: nlg evaluation using gpt-4 with better human alignment.

Shervin Minaee, Yuri Boykov, Fatih Murat Porikli, Antonio J. Plaza, Nasser Kehtarnavaz, and Demetri Terzopoulos. 2020. Image segmentation using deep learning: A survey. *IEEE Transactions on Pattern Analysis and Machine Intelligence*, 44:3523–3542.

G. Polverini. 2024. How understanding large language models can inform the use of chatgpt in physics education. *European Journal of Physics*, 45:025701.

Richard Sutton. 2019. The bitter lesson. Blog post. Accessed: Augsust 2024.

R. Tai, L. Bentley, X. Xia, J. Sitt, S. Fankhauser, A. Chicas-Mosier, and B. Monteith. 2023. An examination of the use of large language models to aid analysis of textual data.

A. Urman. 2023. The silence of the llms: cross-lingual analysis of political bias and false information prevalence in chatgpt, google bard, and bing chat.

W. Yeadon. 2024. The impact of ai in physics education: a comprehensive review from gcse to university levels. *Physics Education*, 59:025010.

A Prompt and Example Usage

```
from magentic import prompt
from pydantic import BaseModel, Field


class Score(BaseModel):
    explanation: str = Field(description="An explanation for the given score")
    score: int = Field(
        description="A score from 0 to 10",
        ge=0,
        le=10,
    )


class BitterLessonScores(BaseModel):
    learning_over_engineering_score: Score = Field(
        description="**Learning Over Engineering**: To what extent does the idea prioritize leveraging
        ↪ computation through data-driven learning and statistical methods (e.g., machine learning,
        ↪ deep learning, neural networks, probabilistic models, unsupervised learning, supervised
        ↪ learning, reinforcement learning, generative models, discriminative models, ensemble
        ↪ methods, online learning, active learning, semi-supervised learning) over relying on
        ↪ human-engineered knowledge, heuristics, and domain expertise (e.g., hand-crafted features,
        ↪ rule-based systems, expert systems, symbolic AI, knowledge representation, logic
        ↪ programming, constraint satisfaction)?\n\nPlease rate on a scale from 0 to 10, where:\n0
        ↪ = Completely relies on human engineering, 5 = Equal emphasis on learning and engineering,
        ↪ 10 = Completely prioritizes learning from data",
    )
    search_over_heuristics_score: Score = Field(
        description="**Search over Heuristics**: To what degree does the idea emphasize leveraging
        ↪ computation through search algorithms (e.g., gradient descent, stochastic gradient
        ↪ descent, evolutionary algorithms, genetic algorithms, simulated annealing, Monte Carlo
        ↪ methods, Markov chain Monte Carlo, beam search, branch and bound, A* search, heuristic
        ↪ search) and optimization techniques (e.g., convex optimization, stochastic optimization,
        ↪ combinatorial optimization, integer programming, quadratic programming, linear
        ↪ programming, non-linear optimization, multi-objective optimization), rather than
        ↪ depending on human-designed heuristics and problem-specific strategies (e.g., hand-tuned
        ↪ parameters, domain-specific rules, expert knowledge, case-based reasoning, heuristic
        ↪ functions)?\n\nPlease rate on a scale from 0 to 10, where:\n0 = Completely relies on
        ↪ human-designed heuristics, 5 = Equal emphasis on search and heuristics, 10 = Completely
        ↪ prioritizes search and optimization",
    )
    scalability_with_computation_score: Score = Field(
        description="**Scalability with Computation**:To what extent is the idea based on methods that
        ↪ can continuously scale and improve performance as the available computational resources
        ↪ (e.g., processing power, memory, storage, data, distributed computing, cloud computing,
        ↪ GPU acceleration, TPU acceleration, high-performance computing, edge computing, quantum
        ↪ computing) increase, taking full advantage of the exponential growth in computing
        ↪ capabilities (e.g., Moore's Law, Dennard scaling, Amdahl's Law, Gustafson's
        ↪ Law)?\n\nPlease rate on a scale from 0 to 10, where:\n0 = Does not scale with computation
        ↪ at all, 5 = Scales moderately with computation, 10 = Scales exceptionally well with
        ↪ computation",
    )
    generality_over_specificity_score: Score = Field(
```

```
        description="**Generality over Specificity**:To what degree does the approach emphasize
        ↪ general, flexible, and adaptable methods that can learn and capture arbitrary complexity
        ↪ from data (e.g., deep learning, transfer learning, meta-learning, representation learning,
        ↪ multi-task learning, few-shot learning, zero-shot learning, self-supervised learning,
        ↪ unsupervised pre-training, domain adaptation, continual learning, lifelong learning,
        ↪ incremental learning) rather than attempting to build in complex and detailed models of
        ↪ the world through manual engineering and domain-specific knowledge (e.g., hand-designed
        ↪ features, domain-specific ontologies, knowledge graphs, expert systems, rule-based
        ↪ systems, symbolic representations, logic-based representations)?\n\nPlease rate on a
        ↪ scale from 0 to 10, where:\n0 = Completely domain-specific and manually engineered, 5 =
        ↪ Balance of generality and specificity, 10 = Maximally general, flexible and adaptable",
    )
    favoring_fundamental_principles_score: Score = Field(
        description="**Favoring Fundamental Principles**: To what extent does the approach adhere to
        ↪ fundamental principles of computation, mathematics, and information theory (e.g.,
        ↪ algorithmic efficiency, computational complexity, statistical learning theory,
        ↪ information entropy, Bayesian inference, Kolmogorov complexity, Occam's razor, Minimum
        ↪ Description Length, PAC learning, VC dimension, Rademacher complexity, concentration
        ↪ inequalities, regularization, sparsity, smoothness, stability, convergence, consistency)
        ↪ rather than focusing on emulating the specific details of human cognition or biological
        ↪ intelligence (e.g., neuroscience-inspired architectures, cognitive architectures,
        ↪ embodied cognition, situated cognition, enactivism, dynamical systems theory, ecological
        ↪ psychology)?\n\nPlease rate on a scale from 0 to 10, where:\n0 = Completely focused on
        ↪ emulating human/biological details, 5 = Equal focus on principles and human/biological
        ↪ details, 10 = Completely grounded in fundamental principles",
    )


@prompt(
    """
Title: {title}
Abstract: {abstract}

We want to evalute this abstract in terms of alignment with "The Bitter Lesson". The main idea of Rich
↪ Sutton's "The Bitter Lesson" is that the most effective AI approaches in the long run are those
↪ that leverage computation and general-purpose methods like search and learning, rather than
↪ human-designed systems that try to build in human knowledge. Evaluate the alignment of the
↪ abstract with the following principles, assigning a score from 0 to 10 for each.
"""
)
def evaluate_bitter_lesson_alignment(
    title: str, abstract: str
) -> BitterLessonScores: ...


## EXAMPLE USAGE

bitter_lesson_scores = evaluate_bitter_lesson_alignment(
    title="Attention Is All You Need",
```

```
    abstract="The dominant sequence transduction models are based on complex recurrent or
    ↪ convolutional neural networks in an encoder-decoder configuration. The best performing models
    ↪ also connect the encoder and decoder through an attention mechanism. We propose a new simple
    ↪ network architecture, the Transformer, based solely on attention mechanisms, dispensing with
    ↪ recurrence and convolutions entirely. Experiments on two machine translation tasks show these
    ↪ models to be superior in quality while being more parallelizable and requiring significantly
    ↪ less time to train. Our model achieves 28.4 BLEU on the WMT 2014 English-to-German
    ↪ translation task, improving over the existing best results, including ensembles by over 2
    ↪ BLEU. On the WMT 2014 English-to-French translation task, our model establishes a new
    ↪ single-model state-of-the-art BLEU score of 41.8 after training for 3.5 days on eight GPUs, a
    ↪ small fraction of the training costs of the best models from the literature. We show that the
    ↪ Transformer generalizes well to other tasks by applying it successfully to English
    ↪ constituency parsing both with large and limited training data.",
)
print(bitter_lesson_scores.model_dump_json(indent=2))
# {
#     "learning_over_engineering_score": {
#         "explanation": "The abstract describes a model called the Transformer that is based solely
↪ on attention mechanisms, dispensing with recurrence and convolutions. This indicates a strong
↪ reliance on learning from data rather than on human-engineered features or domain-specific
↪ knowledge. The significant improvement in BLEU scores across multiple tasks further showcases the
↪ efficacy of data-driven learning methods.",
#         "score": 9,
#     },
#     "search_over_heuristics_score": {
#         "explanation": "The Transformer model prioritizes the use of attention mechanisms to learn
↪ representations from data, which can be considered a form of search over heuristics. The
↪ architecture allows for efficient computation and optimization during training, indicating a
↪ significant emphasis on leveraging search algorithms and optimization techniques rather than
↪ relying on human-designed heuristics.",
#         "score": 8,
#     },
#     "scalability_with_computation_score": {
#         "explanation": "The abstract highlights the Transformer model's parallelizability and
↪ reduced training time, which suggests that the model can scale effectively with increased
↪ computational resources. The use of GPUs to achieve state-of-the-art performance in a relatively
↪ short training time further indicates that the model benefits significantly from additional
↪ computational power.",
#         "score": 9,
#     },
#     "generality_over_specificity_score": {
#         "explanation": "The abstract demonstrates the generality of the Transformer model by
↪ applying it successfully to multiple tasks, including machine translation and English
↪ constituency parsing. The model's ability to generalize well to tasks with both large and limited
↪ training data suggests that it is highly adaptable and not limited to specific domains or tasks.",
#         "score": 9,
#     },
#     "favoring_fundamental_principles_score": {
#         "explanation": "The Transformer model is grounded in fundamental principles of computation
↪ and information theory, particularly through its use of attention mechanisms, which can be seen
↪ as an efficient way to handle sequence transductions. The focus on parallelizability and
↪ optimization also aligns with fundamental principles rather than attempting to emulate human
↪ cognition or biological processes.",
#         "score": 8,
#     },
# }
```

Personalized-ABA: Personalized Treatment Plan Generation for Applied Behavior Analysis using Natural Language Processing

Aman Kumar, Mareiko Au, Raj Semlawat, Malavica Sridhar, and Hitesh Gurnani
TheraDriver, Basil Therapy Inc.
{aman,mareiko,raj,mal,hitesh}@theradriver.com

Abstract

Autism Spectrum Disorder (ASD) is a neurological and developmental disability that affects how an individual learns, communicates, interacts with others. Applied Behavior Analysis (ABA) is a gold standard therapy for children and adults suffering from ASD to improve their learning, social, and communication skills. Today, 1 in 36 children are diagnosed with ASD with expectations that this rate will only continue to rise. The supply of certified ABA providers is alarmingly insufficient to meet the needs of children with ASD. In fact, waitlists to receive ABA therapy in the United States exceed 10 months in most states. Clinicians or Board Certified Behavior Analysts (BCBAs) are now experiencing intense bottlenecks around diagnostic evaluations and developing treatment plans quickly enough to support timely access to care. Over the past few years, Artificial Intelligence has changed the way industries operate by offering powerful ways to process, analyze, generate, and predict data. In this paper, we have addressed the problem of both time and supply restrictions faced by ABA providers by proposing a novel method for personalized treatment plan generation and program prediction by leveraging the capabilities of Deep Learning and Large Language Models (LLM). Additionally, we have introduced two separate models for behavior program prediction (F1-Score: 0.671) and skill acquisition program predictions (Rouge-1 Score: 0.476) which will help ABA providers in treatment plan implementation. Results are promising: an AI-generated treatment plan demonstrates a high similarity (Average Similarity Score: 0.915) to the original treatment plan written by a BCBA. Finally, as we partnered with a multi-state ABA provider in building this product, we ran a single-blind study that concluded that BCBAs prefer an AI-generated treatment plan 65 percent of the time compared to a BCBA-generated one.

1 Introduction

Over the past years, there has been a significant rise in the cases of Autism Spectrum Disorder (ASD). According to data collected by the Autism and Developmental Disabilities Monitoring (ADDM)(Maenner et al., 2023), 1 in 36 children in United States have autism. Increased awareness and screening, broadened diagnostic criteria, and better infrastructure for autism research have played a vital role in the rise of ASD prevalence. Applied Behavior Analysis (ABA) is regarded as a gold-standard therapy and is one of the most widely accepted therapies. Today, it is 100 percent covered by insurance and children are diagnosed as earlier as 2 years of age.

Effective ABA treatment relies on early diagnosis and effective treatment planning to individualize the behavior reduction goals and skill acquisition needs of every child. The type of ABA treatment plan is conventionally determined by a trained Board Certified Behavior Analyst (BCBA) via integrated assessment like VB-MAPP(CS et al., 2014), ABLLS(Partington and Analysts, 2010), Vineland, etc. and information derived from detailed patient intake forms, diagnostic reports, and the functional analysis of the patient. ABA treatment plans are comprehensive and tailored to meet the specific needs of individuals with Autism Spectrum Disorder (ASD). These plans encompass various components that work together to improve behaviors and enhance overall functioning. However, with a rise in ASD cases and increased demand for ABA services, there has been a shortage of ABA providers or Board Certified Behavior Analysts (BCBAs)(Chiri and Warfield, 2012)(Smith-Young et al., 2020). As the demand for ABA therapy escalates, maintaining a balance between workload and service quality therapy becomes increasingly complex for BCBAs. Due to this, individuals diagnosed with ASD face challenges in accessing the neces-

Proceedings of the 1st Workshop on NLP for Science (NLP4Science), pages 188–196
November 16, 2024 ©2024 Association for Computational Linguistics

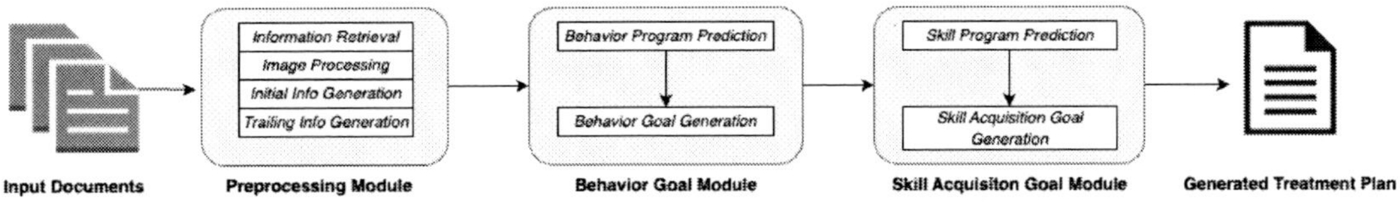

Figure 1: Illustration of the proposed method designed for end-to-end generation of treatment plan for ABA therapy personalized for each individual.

sary therapy and the required support. The scarcity of quality ABA therapy affects the progress of the individual in managing ASD, impacting mental health.

To address this problem, we have introduced a novel approach for creating individualized treatment plans tailored to the specific needs of any client using the advancements in the field of Deep Learning. We have also proposed two separate transformer-based(Vaswani et al., 2023) models to predict "Behavior Reduction" and "Skill Acquisition" programs, considering client's assessments (like VB-MAPP, ABLLS, etc.), diagnostic reports, and parent interviews. We have further shown our proposed models outperforms other state-of-the-art models in prediction tasks. The first-draft generated via our model will save a significant amount of time, as we are able to effectively analyze thousands of clinical documents to create and individualize a treatment plan. Through the experiments conducted for measuring the similarity of the AI-generated treatment plan versus the original one, the potential of the proposed method is revealed. The main contribution of the paper can be summarized as follows:

1. We propose an end-to-end novel method for generating a personalized treatment plan for an individual with ASD which takes Assessment Documents (like ABLLS, VB-MAPP), Parent Interview documents, and Diagnostic Reports as inputs. This will significantly reduce the time it takes a BCBA to create a treatment plan in addition to increasing the quality of goals for each child.

2. We also introduced two transformer-based models for the prediction of programs for the "Behavior Reduction" and "Skill Acquisition" Section.

3. Skill Acquisition program prediction uses an ensemble approach combining a rules-based and transformer-based model. We introduced our own word embedding model fine-tuned on the ABA treatment data for the ensemble approach using sentence-transformers(Reimers and Gurevych, 2019).

4. Treatment Plans generated using our approach show very high similarity with the original treatment plan and achieves an average similarity score of 0.915. When conducting a single-blind study with 35 BCBAs comparing AI-generated treatment plans vs. BCBA-generated treatment plans, BCBAs preferred AI-generated treatment plans 65 percent of the time. This strengthens our belief that AI can enable BCBAs to create the best version of a treatment plan for a child, as it is capable of processing and analyzing thousands of treatment plans in the past to create the most suitable and personalized treatment plan for a child. Furthermore, our models outperforms other state-of-the-art deep learning models used for similar tasks. To our knowledge, the proposed method for end-to-end treatment plan generation customized for an individual is first to be used in the domain of ASD.

2 Related Work

Artificial Intelligence and Deep Learning is increasingly used in the field of modern medicine for managing neurological conditions such as Alzheimer(EL-Geneedy et al., 2023)(Al Mamun et al., 2021) due to abundance availability of structured and unstructured data. The goal of Deep learning is to replicate cognitive abilities of human beings by analyzing complex datasets and generating meaningful pattern out of them without any human intervention(Pandey et al., 2022)(Egger et al., 2022). The healthcare sector has benefited from the advancements in the domain of deep learning with early diagnosis(Sorrentino et al., 2024), drug discovery(Carracedo-Reboredo et al., 2021), personalized treatment plan(Ng et al., 2021), etc. Recently, there has also been a used of deep learning for detecting depression(Fang et al., 2023) and managing mental health conditions(Shatte et al., 2019).

Recent advancements in the domain of deep learning has significantly impacted the field of Autism Spectrum Disorder (ASD) by offering new means for diagnosis and treatment. (Kollias et al., 2022) proposes a method for ASD detection using eye movement of an individual. Deep learning, particularly involving neural networks have shown promising results in the field of ASD. For instance, (Ahammed et al., 2021) uses Convolutional Neural Network (CNN) for classification of ASD on functional MRI data. Similarly, there has also been use of Recurrent Neural Networks (RNN)(Sudha and Vijaya, 2021) and Long Short-Term Memory (LSTM) for analyzing time-series data for diagnosis of ASD. For instance, (Li et al., 2019) uses LSTM to diagnose children with ASD based on raw video data. Deep learning techniques are also used for dimensionality reduction and feature extraction which helps in ASD research. (Kim et al., 2021) uses Variational auto-encoder (VAE) for representation learning, enhancing the interpretability of complex datasets. Personalization of treatment(Kohli et al., 2022) for an individual with ASD has also benefited from the advancements in deep learning while there has also been work on Ensemble learning for classification of ASD(Gaur et al., 2023). As the field of deep learning continue to evolve, it can play a crucial role in ASD research.

3 Methodology

This section presents the proposed method for an end-to-end treatment plan generation personalized for each individual (as depicted in Figure 1) along with the details about the prediction of behavior and skill acquisition programs. It takes the raw assessment file (generally in excel format for ABLLs, VB-MAPP, etc), diagnostic reports, and the parent interview documents of the client as inputs. Our proposed method has been divided into different sections for pre-processing and the analysis of the input, prediction, and generation of goals tailored to meet the specific requirements of the client.

3.1 Preprocessing of Input

We take raw assessment files, diagnostic reports and parent interview forms as inputs for our proposed method. We then extract the following information from the corresponding document for formulation of the treatment plan:

- Client Demographics and Diagnostic Code: Diagnostic Report
- Client Medical History, Language or Communication Skills, Social or Play Skills, Repetitive, Rigid, Restrictive or Challenging Behavior: Parent Interview Docs

We use image processing and with the help of opencv(Bradski, 2000) and openpyxl(Clark and Gazoni, 2010), we analyze the raw assessment files and convert them into a summary table containing domains(like Mand, Tact, Intraverbal, etc.) and score of the client in that particular domain. This saves a significant amount of time for BCBAs, who typically spend time analyzing these assessments and converting them into structured formats manually. In fact, we surveyed roughly 40 BCBAs who quantified that it takes between 10-15 hours to create a treatment plan for a child in their caseload. We believe our AI-generated treatment plan will bring this time down to 1 hour or less.

3.2 Behavior Program Prediction

In ABA therapy, Behavior Programs are focused on addressing specific behavior of an individual which maybe interfering with their daily life routine. These goals are aimed to decrease the challenging behavior and increase the desired behavior.

We formulated the problem of Behavior Goal Prediction as a multi-label classification tasks which takes Language/Communication Skills, Social/Play Skills and Restrictive or Challenging Behavior of the client as an input and outputs the set of the behavior program which interferes with client's daily life and functioning and which needs to be addressed in the ABA therapy. We used a transformer based model named Deberta-v3(He et al., 2021) for the multi-label classification problem. Deberta-v3 is an improvement over BERT(Devlin et al., 2019) and RoBERTa(Liu et al., 2019) based models by using disentangled attention and enhanced mask decoder. We train the model on our curated dataset using binary cross entropy loss which measures the dissimilarity between the true labels and the predicted probabilities (Eq.1).

$$Loss = (Y)(-log(Y_p)) + (1\text{-}Y)(-log(1\text{-}Y)_p) \quad (1)$$

where Y_p = predicted probability of the class and Y = true label.
We calculate the loss for each class and then sum over all the classes for training our model.

3.3 Skill Acquisition Program Prediction

In ABA Therapy, Skill Acquisition Goals play a crucial role by providing a structured framework, which helps the client with developmental or behavioral challenges and helps them gain essential skills including communication, social skills, and self-management.

3.3.1 Transformer-based Model

Since the number of skill acquisition programs can be very large in number, it was not feasible to train a classification model for this task with a limited dataset. Hence, we formulated the problem as a question-answering task, where the input is the client information which includes their demographics information, previous medical history, clinical and home observation data and assessment results (like VB-MAPP, ABLLs, Vineland, etc.) and output is the set of skill acquisition programs suited for the particular client. We used FlanT5(Chung et al., 2022) which is an encoder-decoder(Vaswani et al., 2023) based model for this question answering task using a labeled dataset. Here, our labeled dataset consisted of a question **x**, and a response **y**(list of skill acquisition programs) corresponding to the given question or client information. Consequently, the training process is aimed at minimizing the cross-entropy loss between the predicted probabilities and true class labels(Eq.2.)

$$Loss(\theta) = -\, E[logp_{\theta}(y|x)] \qquad (2)$$

3.3.2 Rule-based Model

The rules-based model for predicting skill acquisition programs leverages assessment summary tables created from raw assessment files for generating tailored recommendations for skill development of an individual. The model employs a structured set of rules derived from gold-standard assessment curriculum guides, then validated with the help of BCBA domain expertise. The model identifies the client-specific deficits in each domain by analyzing detailed data from raw assessment files and then translate these identified deficits into set of skill acquisition goals using the set of predefined rules. This approach ensures that goal predictions are tailored to unique needs of an individual.

3.3.3 Ensemble Model

The Ensemble Model for predicting skill acquisition programs integrates both the transformer-based and rules-based model. We create a client vector which includes the demographic information of the client and their home and clinical observation results. We created our own embedding model by fine-tuning the ClinicalBERT(Alsentzer et al., 2019) model to improve its performance on our specified use case. Our dataset consists of a pair of sample in the format $\{x1, x2, s\}$, where *x1* and *x2* are pair of sentences and s is a binary label. $s = 1$ if *x1* and *x2* are deemed similar, and $s = 0$ if they are deemed dissimilar. We utilize sentence-transformers for fine-tuning and use contrastive loss between the input vector consisting of client demographic information, home and clinic observation results(*x1*) and the program list(*x2*). The client vector was created from our fine-tuned embedding model. We then calculate the similarity of each of the predicted skill acquisition program from both the approaches (Transformer-based and rule-based model) with the client vector. Final set of results contains those programs which posses similarity score of greater than 0.5 with the client vector.

3.4 Goals Generation

In our proposed method, we utilized GPT-3.5 Turbo(Liu et al., 2023) for generating the short-term and long-term goals corresponding to each of the program. In our research, we implemented Retrieval-Augmented Generation (RAG) combined with Prompt Engineering with GPT-3.5 Turbo for enhancing the quality of the generated goals. We developed a specialized custom database tailored to our specific need which includes client information and short-term and long-term goals corresponding to that client. Retrieval-Augmented Generation (RAG) enabled the GPT model to utilize the custom-built database of relevant information to inform and enhance the goal generation process. Prompt engineering involves designing and refining input prompts to guide the model in producing more relevant and accurate outputs. This process included providing explicit instructions to the model, experimenting with different prompt structures, and iteratively refining prompts based on the model's responses. Combining RAG and Prompt Engineering, we aimed to leverage GPT's advanced language capabilities for generating more accurate and precise goals specific to a particular

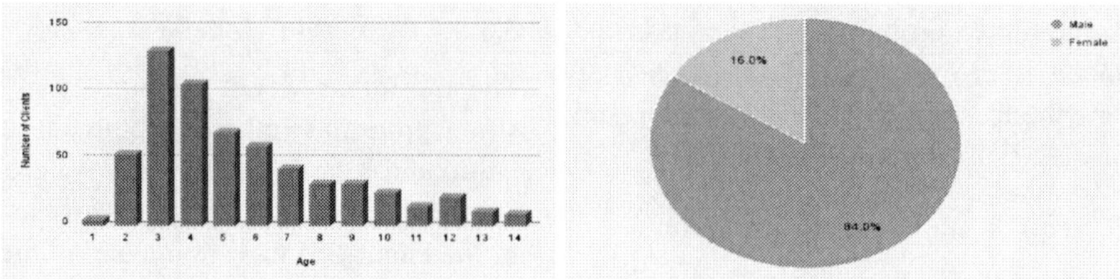

Figure 2: The left figure presents the number of client in each age group, with bars indicating the count of clients. Right figure presents a pie chart indicates the percentage distribution of male and female clients relative to the total client population.

individual.

4 Experiments

4.1 Experimental Settings

4.1.1 Models and Datasets

We evaluate the effectiveness of our proposed method using the following models for program prediction task:

- Behavior Program Prediction: Deberta-v3-base. The DeBERTa V3 base model has 12 layers and 86M backbone parameters with a vocabulary size of 128k tokens and is trained on 160GB of data as Deberta v2.

- Skill Program Prediction: Flan-t5-base. Flan-T5 is an improvement over T5-based models. FLan-T5-base contains 12 hidden layers and 250M model parameters.

We further calculate the semantic textual similarity of the final treatment plan generated with the original treatment plan using pre-trained sentence transformer models.

We curated a custom dataset for validating the effectiveness of our proposed method. All the clients included in the study have been diagnosed with Autism Spectrum Disorder (ASD) and are within the age range of 2 to 14 years. The full dataset encompasses a total of 617 clients which were further divided into training and testing set with an 80:20 split. The distribution of clients by age group and gender proportions is shown in Figure 2. For each client, the dataset includes the original treatment plan formulated by BCBA and other input documents like the parent interview form, diagnostic report, and raw files of the assessment which were conducted for that particular client, for example: VB-MAPP, ABLLS, Vineland, etc.

4.1.2 Implementation Details

We trained our model for behavior programs and skill program predictions using 4 Nvidia T4 GPUs using the Pytorch deep learning framework. We used the Accelerate library to make our distributed training easier, more effective, and efficient at the same time. Batch size has been set to 4 for all the experiments. The learning rate is set to 2e-5 for behavior program prediction , and 3e-4 for skill acquisition program prediction using a cosine rate scheduler. Pre-processing steps including information retrieval from input documents and analysis of raw assessment files were carried out in CPU(Apple M3 Pro chip: 12-core CPU).

4.1.3 Evaluation Setting

All the evaluation were carried out on the test set of our curated dataset. For the quantitative performance comparison, we adopt an F1-score, Rouge score and Exact Match as an evaluation metric. The F1-score is specifically developed for assessing the performance of a classification model, while Rouge score are used to evaluate the quality of machine-generated text. A higher F1 and Rouge score indicated better model performance. Exact Match (EM) is another question-answering evaluation metric that only gives two scores (0 or 1). EM score is 1 if the generated answer is precisely the same as the predicted answer, else, it gives 0. We also evaluate the effectiveness of our end-to-end treatment plan generation approach by calculating its similarity with the original treatment plan. We used sentence transformers for this approach which outputs a similarity score in range of -1 to 1, where -1 indicates complete dissimilarity while 1 indicates complete similarity.

Model	Params	Rouge-1	Rouge-2	Rouge-l	Exact Match
Flan-T5-base(Chung et al., 2022)	250M	0.0139	0.0	0.010789	0.0
Flan-T5-large(Chung et al., 2022)	780M	0.01986	0.0	0.01708	0.0
Phi-2b(Abdin et al., 2023)	2.7B	0.05830	0.0043	0.03389	0.0
Ours(based on Flan-T5-base)	**250M**	**0.4762**	**0.3583**	**0.3764**	**0.3376**

Table 1: Performance comparison for Skill Program Prediction using different models. It can be observed that our model outperforms all the other models on rouge score and exact match metric having least number of parameters compared to other models.

Model	Params	F1-score
Deberta-v3-base(He et al., 2021)	86M	0.1023
Deberta-v3-large(He et al., 2021)	304M	0.0662
Roberta-base(Liu et al., 2019)	125M	0.087
Biobert v1.1(Lee et al., 2019)	110M	0.19535
Ours(Based on Deberta-v3-base)	**86M**	**0.671**

Table 2: Table shows the F1-score comparison of different model for behavior program prediction. Our model achieves better results compared to other models with minimal number of parameters.

Name	Minilm-L6-v2	Bert-base	Mpnet-base
Client 1	0.883945	0.97367	0.950932
Client 2	0.84949	0.92193	0.923908
Client 3	0.949224	0.97867	0.95126
Client 4	0.93826	0.962447	0.95891
Client 5	0.90818	0.939519	0.94793
Client 6	0.746431	0.82151	0.858006
Average	**0.879255**	**0.93296**	**0.93182**

Table 3: Table shows the semantic textual similarity score between the treatment plan generated using our approach and the original treatment plan for 6 random clients from the test set. Similarity score was calculated using sentence-transformers using different models. It can observed that our treatment plan shows very high similarity score with the original treatment plan hence validating the effectiveness of our proposed method.

4.2 Experimental Results

4.2.1 Behavior Program Prediction

We evaluate our model trained for behavior program prediction using Microsoft Deberta-v3-base model on the test set of our custom curated dataset. We compare its performance with similar other models as shown in Table 2. We observe that our approach is able to beat all other models by a huge margin and has fewest number of parameters, hence making it a suitable choice for deployment in a resource-constrained environment.

4.2.2 Skill Acquisition Program Prediction

We evaluate our model trained for skill acquisition program prediction using Google Flat-T5-base model on the test set of our custom curated dataset. Table 1 shows the performance of our model using Rouge Score and Exact Match evaluation metric. We observe that our model is able to outperform all the other models which validates the effectiveness of our approach.

4.2.3 Full Treatment Plan Generation

We further evaluate the effectiveness of our proposed method for entire treatment plan generation by measuring the similarity between generated and original treatment plan as show in Table. We took 6 random client from the test set and generated the full treatment plan by taking diagnostic report, parent interview and raw assessment files as an input. We then calculated the similarity using different models with the original treatment plan for better validation using sentence-transformers. We observe that the treatment plan generated using our proposed method posses very high similarity with the original treatment plan, which validates the effectiveness of our proposed methodology. When sharing AI-generated treatment plans versus BCBA-generated treatment plans via a single blind study to 35 BCBAs, our AI-generated treatment plan was preferred 65 percent of the time.

4.3 Ablation Studies

Our proposed method for an end-to-end treatment plan generation shows promising results and also outperforms state-of-the-art NLP models on behavior program and skill acquisition program prediction tasks. We performed extensive ablation experiments to demonstrate the effectiveness of the proposed method on personalized downstream tasks. We tried an exhaustive hyperparameter search and fine-tuning the learning rate. All these modifications results in a very negligible change in the overall performance of the model. We also tried modifying the loss function by incorporating ABA Therapy rules, however, no significant changes were observed in model performance.

5 Conclusion

In this work, we propose a novel method for full treatment plan generation specific to the needs of a particular individual. Our proposed method outperforms other state-of-the-art model in similar domain in program prediction tasks. We further validate the effectiveness of our approach by calculating the similarity of the generated treatment plan with the original treatment plan. The treatment plan generated using our approach possess very high similarity with the original treatment plan. Our proposed method will not only help in automating the treatment plan generation process but will also reduce the time taken by a BCBA in formulating the treatment plan. On average, a BCBA spends anywhere between 10-15 hours creating a single treatment plan from start to finish. We believe that our AI-generated treatment plan will enable them to do so in 1 hour or less. The applicability of our proposed method on other neurodevelopmental disorders outside of autism are open avenues for future work.

6 Limitations

While our proposed end-to-end method for treatment plan generation achieves a very high semantic similarity score with the original treatment plan and our proposed models for behavior program prediction and skill acquisition program prediction generates better results, it does have certain limitations that we plan to address in future. Since our curated dataset contains client suffering from ASD, the applicability of our approach to similar neurological problems is still unexplored. We used deberta-v3 as a backbone for multi-label classification task in the domain of ASD. However, validating the effectiveness of techniques like label clustering(Ding et al., 2020) and graph-label attention(Pal et al., 2020) in the domain of ASD can be the scope of future work. There is also a lack of labelled dataset due to scarcity of available open-source data in the domain of ASD. Furthermore, the variances in the response of BCBAs or ABA providers can be one of the areas of research in the future for improving the robustness of the model. To address this, we plan to leverage reinforcement learning techniques to address and incorporate the individualized preferences of BCBAs when generating a treatment plan for a child in their caseload.

References

Marah Abdin, Jyoti Aneja, Sebastien Bubeck, Caio César Teodoro Mendes, Weizhu Chen, Allie Del Giorno, Ronen Eldan, Sivakanth Gopi, Suriya Gunasekar, Mojan Javaheripi, Piero Kauffmann, Yin Tat Lee, Yuanzhi Li, Anh Nguyen, Gustavo de Rosa, Olli Saarikivi, Adil Salim, Shital Shah, Michael Santacroce, Harkirat Singh Behl, Adam Taumann Kalai, Xin Wang, Rachel Ward, Philipp Witte, Cyril Zhang, and Yi Zhang. 2023. Phi-2: The surprising power of small language modelss.

Md Shale Ahammed, Sijie Niu, Md Rishad Ahmed, Jiwen Dong, Xizhan Gao, and Yuehui Chen. 2021. Darkasdnet: Classification of asd on functional mri using deep neural network. *Frontiers in Neuroinformatics*, 15.

Shamim Al Mamun, M. Shamim Kaiser, and Mufti Mahmud. 2021. An artificial intelligence based approach towards inclusive healthcare provisioning in society 5.0: A perspective on brain disorder. In *Brain Informatics: 14th International Conference, BI 2021, Virtual Event, September 17–19, 2021, Proceedings*, page 157–169, Berlin, Heidelberg. Springer-Verlag.

Emily Alsentzer, John R. Murphy, Willie Boag, Wei-Hung Weng, Di Jin, Tristan Naumann, and Matthew B. A. McDermott. 2019. Publicly available clinical bert embeddings.

G. Bradski. 2000. The OpenCV Library. *Dr. Dobb's Journal of Software Tools*.

Paula Carracedo-Reboredo, Jose Liñares-Blanco, Nereida Rodríguez-Fernández, Francisco Cedrón, Francisco J. Novoa, Adrian Carballal, Victor Maojo, Alejandro Pazos, and Carlos Fernandez-Lozano. 2021. A review on machine learning approaches and trends in drug discovery. *Computational and Structural Biotechnology Journal*, 19:4538–4558.

Giuseppina Chiri and Marji Erickson Warfield. 2012. Unmet need and problems accessing core health care services for children with autism spectrum disorder.

Hyung Won Chung, Le Hou, Shayne Longpre, Barret Zoph, Yi Tay, William Fedus, Eric Li, Xuezhi Wang, Mostafa Dehghani, Siddhartha Brahma, Albert Webson, Shixiang Shane Gu, Zhuyun Dai, Mirac Suzgun, Xinyun Chen, Aakanksha Chowdhery, Sharan Narang, Gaurav Mishra, Adams Yu, Vincent Zhao, Yanping Huang, Andrew Dai, Hongkun Yu, Slav Petrov, Ed H. Chi, Jeff Dean, Jacob Devlin, Adam Roberts, Denny Zhou, Quoc V. Le, and Jason Wei. 2022. Scaling instruction-finetuned language models.

Charlie Clark and Eric Gazoni. 2010. Openpyxl: A python library to read/write excel 2010 xlsx/xlsm files. Computer software.

Barnes CS, Mellor JR, and Rehfeldt RA. 2014. Implementing the verbal behavior milestones assessment and placement program (vb-mapp): Teaching assessment techniques.

Jacob Devlin, Ming-Wei Chang, Kenton Lee, and Kristina Toutanova. 2019. Bert: Pre-training of deep bidirectional transformers for language understanding.

Fei Ding, Xin Kang, Shun Nishide, Zhijin Guan, and Fuji Ren. 2020. A fusion model for multi-label emotion classification based on BERT and topic clustering. In *International Symposium on Artificial Intelligence and Robotics 2020*, volume 11574 of *Society of Photo-Optical Instrumentation Engineers (SPIE) Conference Series*, page 115740D.

Jan Egger, Christina Gsaxner, Antonio Pepe, Kelsey L. Pomykala, Frederic Jonske, Manuel Kurz, Jianning Li, and Jens Kleesiek. 2022. Medical deep learning—a systematic meta-review. *Computer Methods and Programs in Biomedicine*, 221:106874.

Marwa EL-Geneedy, Hossam El-Din Moustafa, Fahmi Khalifa, Hatem Khater, and Eman AbdElhalim. 2023. An mri-based deep learning approach for accurate detection of alzheimer's disease. *Alexandria Engineering Journal*, 63:211–221.

Yuqi Fang, Mingliang Wang, Guy G. Potter, and Mingxia Liu. 2023. Unsupervised cross-domain functional mri adaptation for automated major depressive disorder identification. *Medical Image Analysis*, 84:102707.

Manu Gaur, Kunal Chaturvedi, Dinesh Kumar Vishwakarma, Savitha Ramasamy, and Mukesh Prasad. 2023. Self-supervised ensembled learning for autism spectrum classification. *Research in Autism Spectrum Disorders*, 107:102223.

Pengcheng He, Jianfeng Gao, and Weizhu Chen. 2021. Debertav3: Improving deberta using electra-style pretraining with gradient-disentangled embedding sharing.

Jung-Hoon Kim, Yizhen Zhang, Kuan Han, Zheyu Wen, Minkyu Choi, and Zhongming Liu. 2021. Representation learning of resting state fmri with variational autoencoder. *NeuroImage*, 241:118423.

Manu Kohli, Arpan Kar, Anjali Bangalore, and A P Prathosh. 2022. Machine learning-based aba treatment recommendation and personalization for autism spectrum disorder: an exploratory study. *Brain Informatics*, 9.

Konstantinos-Filippos Kollias, Christine K. Syriopoulou-Delli, Panagiotis Sarigiannidis, and George F. Fragulis. 2022. Autism detection in high-functioning adults with the application of eye-tracking technology and machine learning. In *2022 11th International Conference on Modern Circuits and Systems Technologies (MOCAST)*, pages 1–4.

Jinhyuk Lee, Wonjin Yoon, Sungdong Kim, Donghyeon Kim, Sunkyu Kim, Chan Ho So, and Jaewoo Kang. 2019. Biobert: a pre-trained biomedical language representation model for biomedical text mining. *Bioinformatics*, 36(4):1234–1240.

Jing Li, Yihao Zhong, Junxia Han, Gaoxiang Ouyang, Xiaoli Li, and Honghai Liu. 2019. Classifying asd children with lstm based on raw videos. *Neurocomputing*, 390.

Yiheng Liu, Tianle Han, Siyuan Ma, Jiayue Zhang, Yuanyuan Yang, Jiaming Tian, Hao He, Antong Li, Mengshen He, Zhengliang Liu, Zihao Wu, Lin Zhao, Dajiang Zhu, Xiang Li, Ning Qiang, Dingang Shen, Tianming Liu, and Bao Ge. 2023. Summary of chatgpt-related research and perspective towards the future of large language models. *Meta-Radiology*, 1(2):100017.

Yinhan Liu, Myle Ott, Naman Goyal, Jingfei Du, Mandar Joshi, Danqi Chen, Omer Levy, Mike Lewis, Luke Zettlemoyer, and Veselin Stoyanov. 2019. Roberta: A robustly optimized BERT pretraining approach. *CoRR*, abs/1907.11692.

Matthew J Maenner, Zachary Warren, Ashley Robinson Williams, Esther Amoakohene, Amanda V Bakian, Deborah A Bilder, Maureen S Durkin, Robert T Fitzgerald, Sarah M Furnier, Michelle M Hughes, Christine M Ladd-Acosta, Dedria McArthur, Elise T Pas, Angelica Salinas, Alison Vehorn, Susan Williams, Amy Esler, Andrea Grzybowski, Jennifer Hall-Lande, Ruby H N Nguyen, Karen Pierce,

Walter Zahorodny, Allison Hudson, Libby Hallas, Kristen Clancy Mancilla, Mary Patrick, Josephine Shenouda, Kate Sidwell, Monica DiRienzo, Johanna Gutierrez, Margaret H Spivey, Maya Lopez, Sydney Pettygrove, Yvette D Schwenk, Anita Washington, and Kelly A Shaw. 2023. Prevalence and characteristics of autism spectrum disorder among children aged 8 years - autism and developmental disabilities monitoring network, 11 sites, united states, 2020.

Kenney Ng, Uri Kartoun, Harry Stavropoulos, John A Zambrano, and Paul C Tang. 2021. "personalized treatment options for chronic diseases using precision cohort analytics.

Ankit Pal, Muru Selvakumar, and Malaikannan Sankarasubbu. 2020. Magnet: Multi-label text classification using attention-based graph neural network. In *Proceedings of the 12th International Conference on Agents and Artificial Intelligence*. SCITEPRESS - Science and Technology Publications.

Babita Pandey, Devendra Kumar Pandey, Brijendra Pratap Mishra, and Wasiur Rhmann. 2022. A comprehensive survey of deep learning in the field of medical imaging and medical natural language processing: Challenges and research directions. *Journal of King Saud University - Computer and Information Sciences*, 34(8, Part A):5083–5099.

J.W. Partington and Partington Behavior Analysts. 2010. *The Assessment of Basic Language and Learning Skills-revised (the ABLLS-R)*. The Assessment of Basic Language and Learning Skills-revised. Behavior Analysts.

Nils Reimers and Iryna Gurevych. 2019. Sentence-bert: Sentence embeddings using siamese bert-networks. In *Proceedings of the 2019 Conference on Empirical Methods in Natural Language Processing*. Association for Computational Linguistics.

Adrian B. R. Shatte, Delyse M. Hutchinson, and Samantha J. Teague. 2019. Machine learning in mental health: a scoping review of methods and applications. *Psychological Medicine*, 49(9):1426–1448.

Joanne Smith-Young, Roger Chafe, , and Rick Audas. 2020. "managing the wait": Parents' experiences in accessing diagnostic and treatment services for children and adolescents diagnosed with autism spectrum disorder.

Francesco Saverio Sorrentino, Lorenzo Gardini, Luigi Fontana, Mutali Musa, Andrea Gabai, Antonino Maniaci, Salvatore Lavalle, Fabiana D'Esposito, Andrea Russo, Antonio Longo, Pier Luigi Surico, Caterina Gagliano, and Marco Zeppieri. 2024. Novel approaches for early detection of retinal diseases using artificial intelligence. *Journal of Personalized Medicine*, 14(7).

V. Pream Sudha and M. S. Vijaya. 2021. Recurrrent Neural Network Based Model for Autism Spectrum Disorder Prediction using Codon Encoding. *Journal of The Institution of Engineers (India): Series B*.

Ashish Vaswani, Noam Shazeer, Niki Parmar, Jakob Uszkoreit, Llion Jones, Aidan N. Gomez, Lukasz Kaiser, and Illia Polosukhin. 2023. Attention is all you need.

Exploring Scientific Hypothesis Generation with Mamba

Miaosen Chai[1*], **Emily Herron**[2*], **Erick Cervantes**[3], **Tirthankar Ghosal**[2]
[1]University of Southern California
[2]Oak Ridge National Laboratory [3]Texas A&M International University
miaosenc@usc.edu, {herronej, ghosalt}@ornl.gov, Erickcervantes@dusty.tamiu.edu

Abstract

Generating scientifically grounded hypotheses is a challenging frontier task for generative AI models in science. The difficulty arises from the inherent subjectivity of the task and the extensive knowledge of prior work required to assess the validity of a generated hypothesis. Large Language Models (LLMs), trained on vast datasets from diverse sources, have shown a strong ability to utilize the knowledge embedded in their training data. Recent research has explored using transformer-based models for scientific hypothesis generation, leveraging their advanced capabilities. However, these models often require a significant number of parameters to manage long sequences, which can be a limitation. State Space Models, such as Mamba, offer an alternative by effectively handling very long sequences with fewer parameters than transformers. In this work, we investigate the use of Mamba for scientific hypothesis generation. Our preliminary findings indicate that Mamba achieves similar performance w.r.t. transformer-based models of similar sizes for a higher-order complex task like hypothesis generation. We have made our code available here: https://github.com/fglx-c/Exploring-Scientific-Hypothesis-Generation-with-Mamba

1 Introduction

Large language models (LLMs) have emerged as a cornerstone in artificial intelligence, particularly in scientific discovery. These models have been increasingly integrated into scientific hypothesis and idea generation, transforming traditional approaches to research. Traditionally, the process of scientific hypothesis generation has involved a complex interplay of the scientific method and inductive reasoning, requiring meticulous observation, literature review, and identification of knowledge gaps. This process, while crucial, is time-consuming and labor-intensive, relying heavily on researchers' expertise and creativity.

LLMs offer unique capabilities that address many challenges inherent in traditional scientific inquiry. They excel at processing vast amounts of text, identifying intricate patterns, and drawing upon an extensive knowledge base. This allows them to mitigate cognitive biases, efficiently identify research gaps, and generate a broad spectrum of hypotheses, including unconventional and cross-disciplinary ideas. Their ability to handle complexity makes them particularly valuable for addressing intricate, interdisciplinary problems, potentially accelerating the pace of scientific discovery. (Banker et al., 2023; Zhou et al., 2024; Park et al., 2023; O'Brien et al., 2024)

Scientific Inspiration Machines Optimized for Novelty (SciMON) (Wang et al., 2024) represents a leading approach in LLM-based scientific hypothesis generation. It utilizes an LLM-based generation module and a novel iterative novelty boosting mechanism to produce ideas that are both innovative and grounded in existing literature. However, SciMON still faces limitations in generating outputs that match the depth and utility of real scientific papers. To address these challenges, we have integrated a new LLM architecture called Mamba (Gu and Dao, 2023) into SciMON's generation module. Mamba, based on selective state space models, combines the strengths of Transformer and recurrent architectures. It introduces a selection mechanism for content-based reasoning and selective information processing within a simplified neural network design. This integration aims to enhance SciMON's ability to generate more novel, technically sophisticated, and practically useful scientific ideas.

Our work provides a comprehensive comparison of Mamba and Transformer-based models in scientific hypothesis generation tasks. We evaluate

*Equal contribution

Proceedings of the 1st Workshop on NLP for Science (NLP4Science), pages 197–207
November 16, 2024 ©2024 Association for Computational Linguistics

Mamba's performance on general in-context learning benchmarks and long-context tasks, assess its capabilities in downstream hypothesis generation, and investigate its potential as a baseline model for scientific hypothesis generation. Throughout our study, we ensure reproducibility by providing detailed experimental setup information, including datasets, benchmark versions, and implementation scripts.

2 Related Work

Recent research has explored the potential of Large Language Models (LLMs) in scientific hypothesis and idea generation, employing various approaches from direct prompting to more complex frameworks. (Park et al., 2023) and (Banker et al., 2023) investigated the capabilities of GPT-3 and GPT-4 in generating hypotheses across diverse fields such as materials chemistry, physics, quantum information, and social psychology. While these models demonstrated broad knowledge and interdisciplinary insights, they often produced scientifically inaccurate outputs, highlighting the need for refined approaches.

More sophisticated methods have emerged, integrating inter-domain translation, iterative processes, and adversarial techniques. The Field-SHIFT framework (O'Brien et al., 2024), for instance, utilized GPT-4 to translate concepts between neuroscience and developmental biology, successfully generating novel hypotheses and demonstrating potential for identifying symmetries across scientific domains. HypoGeniC (Zhou et al., 2024) employed a multi-armed bandit-inspired reward function to iteratively improve hypotheses, outperforming few-shot prompting across multiple tasks. In astronomy, (Ciucă et al., 2023) applied adversarial prompting using multiple GPT-4 instances to generate, critique, and refine hypotheses, significantly improving their quality.

Further advancements in LLM-based hypothesis generation have incorporated multi-agent approaches, causal graphs, knowledge graph-based retrieval augmentation, and novelty optimization. Qi et al. (2023) developed a collaborative framework where LLM agents serve different roles (analyst, engineer, scientist, critic) in the hypothesis generation process. Tong et al. (2023) combined causal graphs extracted from psychology articles with LLMs to generate psychological hypotheses matching the novelty of human experts. The SciMON framework (Wang et al., 2024) generates novel research directions based on background contexts and a seed term used to constrain and guide the hypothesis space for the model. It employs an iterative novelty optimization workflow and various retrieval augmentations. GPT-4 produced the best results within this framework, although generated ideas still fell short of scientific literature in terms of depth.

While previous work has primarily utilized Transformer-based models, this study leverages Mamba (Gu and Dao, 2023), a sequence modeling architecture based on selective state space models. Mamba has demonstrated comparable or superior performance to Transformer-based architectures, particularly with long sequences. By implementing our approach within the SciMON framework, we aim to capitalize on Mamba's strengths for improved hypothesis generation in scientific contexts, potentially addressing limitations observed in previous LLM-based approaches.

3 Methodology

As mentioned, our methodology is inspired by the SciMON model. For our benchmarking study with Mamba, we use the similar experimental framework as SciMON.

3.1 SciMON Model and Dataset Description

We make use of the recently released SciMON (Scientific Inspiration Machines Optimized for Novelty) model (Wang et al., 2024), designed to generate novel, literature-informed scientific ideas in the field of Natural Language Processing (NLP). The system begins by extracting problems, motivations, and proposed ideas from scientific papers accessed through the ACL Anthology[1]. The dataset is derived from the Semantic Scholar Open Research Corpus (S2ORC) (Lo et al., 2020), comprising 67,408 ACL Anthology papers published between 1952 and 2022. Papers were filtered to include only those in English with available abstracts. The dataset is divided temporally: the training set includes papers before 2021, the validation set contains papers from 2021, and the test set comprises papers from 2022. For our experiments, we use model checkpoints trained on data preceding 2022 to avoid the risk of data contamination. The papers are processed using several information extraction (IE) and natural language processing tools:

[1]https://aclanthology.org

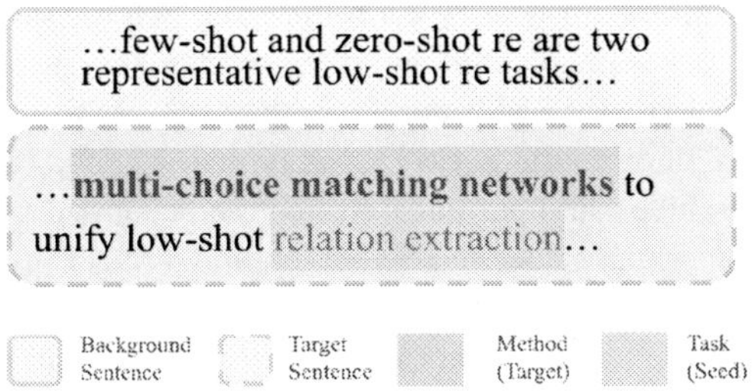

Figure 1: Use of IE to obtain literature data: background, proposed ideas (target), and seed terms.

1. PL-Marker (Ye et al., 2022), pretrained on SciERC (Luan et al., 2018), extracts entities (Task, Method, Evaluation Metric, Material, Other Scientific Terms, and Generic Terms) and their relationships, focusing on used-for relations.

2. SciCo (Cattan et al., 2021) performs coreference resolution for entity normalization.

3. Scispacy (Neumann et al., 2019) expands abbreviations to their full forms.

4. A sentence classification model by Cohan et al. (2019) categorizes abstract sentences into Background, Method, Objective, Other, and Result.

In SciMON, a seed term refers to a key concept or keyword that serves as the starting point for generating hypotheses, while the target sentence is the desired output that articulates a potential scientific idea or goal. SciMON takes a seed term and a background context as inputs and generates a corresponding target sentence as output. To train the model, paper abstracts are categorized into Background sentences (B) and Target sentences (T), forming (B, T) training pairs. The Target sentences are selected from the Methods and Objectives sections of the papers. From these, seed terms (typically Tasks) and target terms (typically Methods) are extracted to form input-output pairs. During evaluation, target information is removed. Figure 1 illustrates this process. To ensure dataset quality, we retain only high-confidence outputs from the IE models. The evaluation indicates high precision rates for most preprocessing steps, except for relation extraction. Overall, 79.7% of instances passed all preprocessing steps, which constitute the challenging dataset. For evaluation, SciMON creates a high-quality gold test set containing 194 instances by removing test cases where models can rely on surface-level background information to infer the ground truth. The remaining instances are then manually annotated to ensure a strong relevance between seed and target terms. At the core of SciMON is its inspiration retrieval module, which retrieves relevant inspirations from three external sources:

1. Semantic Neighbors: Finds similar problems and ideas in the training set based on sentence embeddings.

2. Knowledge Graph (KG) neighbors: Retrieves related concepts from a background knowledge graph built from the text dataset. The background KG has more than 197k nodes and 261k relations.

3. Citation Neighbors: Identifies relevant paper titles from the citation network of the input paper. The citation networks contain 87k paper titles.

SciMON's generation module utilizes either fine-tuned T5 language models or in-context learning with GPT-3.5 or GPT-4 LLMs. When fine-tuning the T5 models, an in-context contrastive objective is employed to discourage the models from simply copying their inputs. The in-context contrastive objective is calculated by taking negative examples from the input text and computing an InfoNCE loss (van den Oord et al., 2019) over the hidden states of the decoder with the objective of maximizing the probability of the ground truth against those of in-text negatives. Both the contrastive loss and cross-entropy loss optimized during fine-tuning. During the generation phase, the input contexts are combined with the inspirations retrieved from the previous module. The next phase in the pipeline is Iterative Novelty Boosting. This process begins with an idea generated by the generation module and retrieves similar ideas from the reference corpus or training dataset. The ideas are compared using a similarity threshold. If the generated ideas are too similar to existing ones, the model is instructed to update the idea to improve its novelty. This process is repeated until a sufficient degree of novelty is achieved. To evaluate the effectiveness of SciMON, both automated metrics such as ROUGE and BERTScore were employed, as well as extensive human evaluation. The human evaluation assessed the relevance, novelty, clarity, and scientific reason-

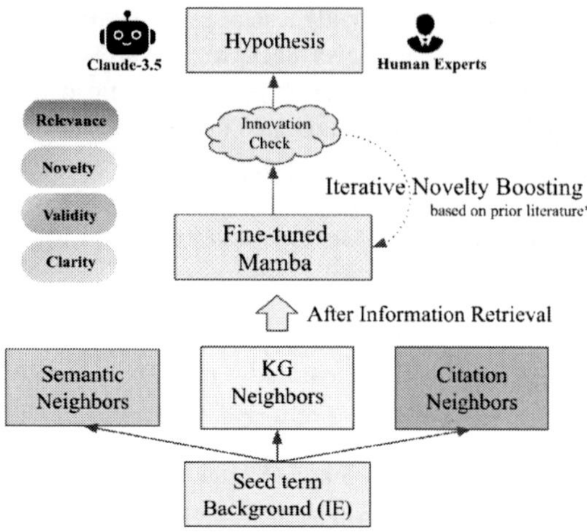

Figure 2: Using the Mamba architecture, the model generates ideas based on background context and literature inspirations, enhancing novelty by repeatedly comparing them to related work.

ableness of the generated ideas, providing a comprehensive assessment of the framework's performance in generating novel scientific ideas. In total, the retrieval dataset includes 59k papers with over 374k sentences, allowing SciMON to ground its idea generation in a broad spectrum of research, enabling it to generate novel and literature-informed scientific ideas in the field of NLP.

3.2 Mamba Architecture

The Mamba architecture (Gu and Dao, 2023) represents a significant advancement in sequence modeling, introducing selective state-space models (SSMs) to achieve linear time processing of long sequences. At the core of Mamba's design is a novel selection mechanism that enables dynamic focusing on or filtering out of inputs, effectively compressing contexts into smaller states. This approach strikes a balance between effectiveness and efficiency in sequence processing, making it particularly suitable for hypothesis generation in scientific contexts. The key innovation in Mamba lies in its selective SSM layer, which modifies traditional SSMs by making multiple parameters (Δ, B, C) functions of its inputs. This feature empowers the model to perform content-based reasoning and selectively propagate or forget information along the sequence length dimension. To implement this mechanism efficiently, Mamba employs a hardware-aware parallel algorithm that leverages the memory hierarchy of GPUs. Structurally, Mamba consists of simplified and heterogeneous blocks. Each block incorporates elements inspired by existing SSM models with MLPs, as found in modern neural networks. A typical Mamba block includes an input linear projection, a convolutional layer, the selective SSM layer, and a linear projection output layer. These blocks are stacked and interleaved with normalization and residual connections throughout the complete architecture, as illustrated in Figure 3. This design represents a simplification of previous SSM architectures by eliminating separate MLP blocks and combining various components into one repeating unit. Mamba distinguishes itself from other state-of-the-art sequence models by avoiding the use of attention mechanisms and standalone MLP blocks. These attributes enable Mamba to achieve state-of-the-art performance across various applications and modalities, including language, audio, and genomics. As demonstrated in Section 4.2, Mamba outperforms other models on language modeling tasks and downstream evaluations. While previous work has primarily utilized Transformer-based models, leveraging Mamba within the SciMON model aims to capitalize on its strengths for improved hypothesis generation in scientific contexts. Mamba's ability to handle long sequences efficiently is particularly advantageous for processing extensive scientific literature and data. Mamba scales better than other models as sequence length increases, potentially addressing limitations observed in previous LLM-based approaches. Furthermore, Mamba boasts inference times up to five times faster than Transformer models and exhibits linear scaling in sequence length (Gu and Dao, 2023). This efficiency is crucial for rapid hypothesis generation and iterative refinement in scientific research. The model's ability to selectively focus on relevant information while filtering out noise could lead to more precise and contextually appropriate hypotheses. By implementing Mamba within the SciMON model, we aim to leverage its unique architecture for enhanced scientific reasoning. The model's demonstrated success in language modeling and its ability to capture long-range dependencies make it a promising approach for efficient and effective hypothesis generation, potentially surpassing the capabilities of previous Transformer-based models in scientific contexts.

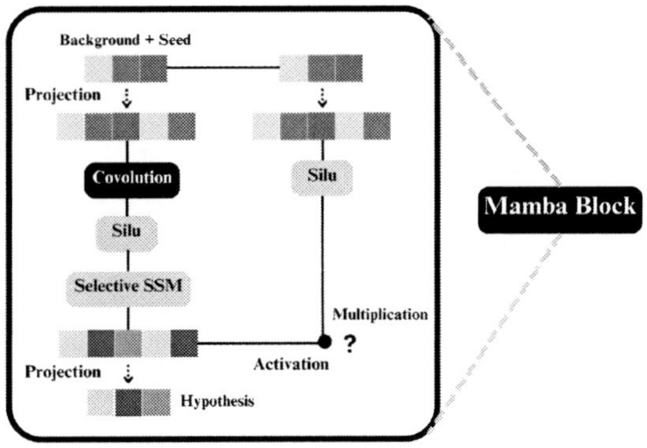

Figure 3: Mamba block we use for SciMON. Background and seed serve as input to the model.

4 Experiments & Discussion

We select T5 (Raffel et al., 2019) and GPT-4 as our baseline models to compare with Mamba. We fine-tune various sizes of T5, Mamba models and use a few short GPT-4 in parallel, with the fine-tuning process taking between 1 to 3 hours using eight H100 GPUs. We present three evaluations: one using the automated metrics and the other with LLM-as-judge (Claude-3.5), following up with a long-text evaluation and finally an evaluation of generated output by a human.

4.1 Automatic Evaluation

It is crucial to recognize that the open-ended nature of scientific hypothesis generation poses challenges for automatic evaluations, as semantically comparing outputs from SciMON to the ground truth can be constrained and shallow. Despite these limitations, automated metrics like ROUGE (Lin, 2004) and BERTScore (Zhang et al., 2019) still offer valuable insights. We conduct an automatic evaluation for the outputs generated through the novelty iteration with the Challenging and Gold datasets(§3)

Results Our findings indicate that both fine-tuned T5 and Mamba models show improved performance with increased model size, as evidenced by higher ROUGE-L (Lin, 2004) and BERTScore (Zhang et al., 2019) metrics in Table 1. Generally, Mamba models perform on par with T5 models of similar sizes, with the Mamba-790M model achieving the highest overall scores for three evaluations. However, Mamba does not show a considerable difference compared to T5, as indicated by the results from the original paper (Gu and Dao, 2023). Additionally, GPT-4 underperformed compared to both T5 and Mamba in few-shot settings, likely because GPT-4 generates longer outputs that do not adhere to the shallow structured templates followed by T5 and Mamba, which are penalized by automatic evaluation metrics. This suggests that human judgment is necessary for a more accurate evaluation.

Model - SciMon	R-L	BERT	R-L (GS)	BERT (GS)
T5 - 60.5 m	0.178	0.514	0.184	0.524
T5 - 223 m	0.197	0.604	0.217	0.627
T5 - 738 m	0.223	0.663	**0.243**	0.684
Mamba - 130 m	0.176	0.523	0.191	0.562
Mamba - 370 m	0.219	0.628	0.237	0.631
Mamba - 790 m	**0.227**	**0.683**	0.242	**0.695**
GPT-4 FS	0.146	0.614	0.143	0.627

Table 1: Automatic results for the challenging (left) and gold (right) subsets. *R-L* denotes ROUGE-L. *BERT* denotes BERTScore with SciBERT as its encoder. *GS* denotes as Gold subsets.

4.2 LLM As a Judge

To address the limitations of automatic evaluation metrics, we incorporate an LLM evaluation to assess the quality of the generated scientific hypotheses. Specifically, we employ Claude-3.5 instead of the more mainstream GPT-4 to mitigate potential self-enhancement bias, which occurs when a model is evaluated using its own framework (Xu et al., 2024b). We utilize a reference-guided style prompt, as introduced by previous research (Zheng et al., 2023), which has been shown to increase the agreement between human and machine evaluations by providing a reference solution.

We design a structured prompt that directs Claude-3.5 to judge the effectiveness of a hypothesis. Specifically, Claude-3.5 is asked to assess the relevance of the hypothesis to the background context and seed term, ensuring sufficient novelty without overly mirroring the provided information, verifying the scientific soundness, and evaluating the clarity and coherence of the language. See the detailed prompt(C). Based on these criteria, Claude-3.5 assigns a rating of either "ineffective" or "effective" to each generated hypothesis, along with a brief justification for its decision, formatted in JSON for consistent analysis. To assist the LLM in making more accurate assessments, we provide it with five examples of both "ineffective" and "effective" hypotheses.

Model	Output
Input:	*Seed Term:* Hierarchical table dataset *Context:* Tables are often created with hierarchies, but existing works on table reasoning mainly focus on flat tables and neglect hierarchical tables. Hierarchical tables challenge numerical reasoning by complex hierarchical indexing, as well as implicit relationships of calculation and semantics.
GPT-4:	In that context, a suitable task for a hierarchical table dataset could be **Hierarchical Table Reasoning**. This task involves understanding, interpreting, and reasoning over complex hierarchical structures present in tables, such as nested rows and columns, hierarchical indexing, and implicit relationships between cells. *Extra generated reasoning*: The task is well-suited for this dataset because it addresses the problem of understanding complex relationships within the hierarchical structure.
T5:	A task that can be used for hierarchical table dataset is **semantic parsing**
Mamba:	**Question answering systems** are an effective tool for reasoning with hierarchical tables
Ground Truth:	Targeting table reasoning, we leverage entity and quantity alignment to explore partially supervised training in QA and conditional generation in NLG, and largely reduce spurious predictions in QA and produce better descriptions in NLG

Table 2: Example of SCIMON outputs with different models. *T5* denotes T5-large. *Mamba* denotes Mamba-790m.

4.3 Human Evaluation

To validate the effectiveness of Claude-3.5, we recruit five NLP experts, each with graduate-level education, to independently rate the outputs. We selected 100 questions at random from the Challenge set and developed a structured questionnaire (Figure 5) for the experts to evaluate the hypotheses. Experts rated each hypothesis as either effective or ineffective based on four key criteria: relevance, novelty, scientific validity, and clarity which is the same as the prompt instruction for Claude-3.5 (C). To ensure objectivity, the raters were blind to the conditions, and the system outputs were randomly shuffled across the instances.

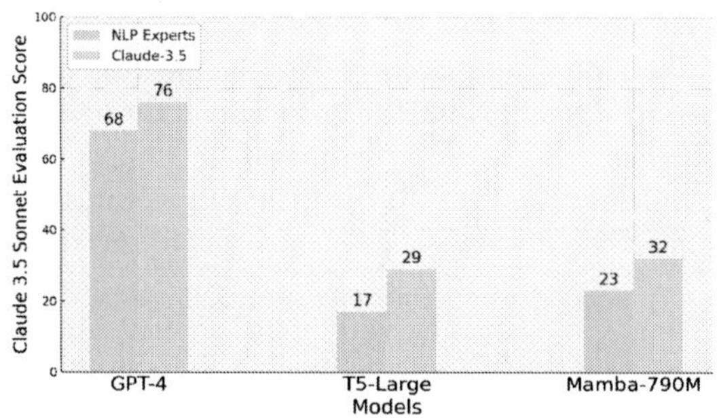

Figure 4: Human and Claude 3.5 Sonnet evaluations of generated scientific hypothesis. The y-axis represents the accuracy(%).

Results We find that both Claude-3.5 and human evaluations yield similar patterns in the performance of the models. GPT-4 achieves the highest scores in both evaluations, with an accuracy of 76% in the Claude-3.5 evaluation and 68% in the human evaluation. This consistency across evaluation methods highlights GPT-4's strong capability in generating hypotheses that align with key criteria such as relevance, novelty, scientific validity, and clarity. Given GPT-4's larger model size, its superior performance is expected. However, Mamba does not significantly outperform the transformer-based T5, likely due to the nature of the SciMON task, which does not fully exploit Mamba's long-context potential. The average input length in this task is less than 10^2 tokens, which favors models with stronger in-context learning abilities like T5. Although we hypothesize that Mamba's strengths would be more apparent in tasks requiring longer contexts, the dataset preprocessing used by the SciMON authors prevents us from directly testing this hypothesis within this context.

To further explore this, we conduct a set of long-context experiments in NLP, ordering tasks by input length: scrolls_narrativeqa (longest), scrolls_quality, and scrolls_contractnli (shortest). Our findings (Table 4) indicate that T5 models excel at tasks with smaller input sizes, with T5-Large achieving the highest accuracy of 35.97% on scrolls_contractnli. Conversely, Mamba models perform significantly better with larger input lengths, as evidenced by Mamba-790M attaining the highest F1 score of 13.81 on scrolls_narrativeqa. However, Mamba models exhibit instability on tasks with smaller inputs, as shown by the non-converging training loss when scaling to large-sized models. Similar instability has been observed in Mamba's performance on the ImageNet dataset

(Xu et al., 2024a), but the underlying cause remains unclear. This issue is likely related to the current instantiation of Mamba, which may suffer from vanishing and exploding gradients. This suggests that while Mamba does not outperform excessively on current tasks, Mamba may be more effective for scientific hypothesis generation under long-input settings. Also, the linear scaling with sequence length benefits Mamba for faster reference. However, future experiments are needed to demonstrate the performance of the Mamba architecture on a large scale.

5 Limitations and Future Work

While this study provides valuable insights, it is important to acknowledge its limitations and potential areas for future research. The architecture of SciMON introduces certain constraints that affect the scope and generalizability of our findings. One key limitation is the data scope, as SciMON's dataset is exclusively composed of ACL Anthology papers from S2ORC. This specialized focus may limit the applicability of our results to other scientific domains, particularly those that rely on multimodal data such as visual representations in biology or chemical structures in materials science.

Our comparative model analysis was restricted to an empirical comparison between Mamba and Transformer-based models under constrained parameter sizes. Future work could benefit from more extensive comparisons involving larger parameter settings, which may reveal additional insights into the relative performance of these models in hypothesis generation tasks.

Furthermore, the rapid pace of development in state space models presents new opportunities for advancing hypothesis generation capabilities. Recent innovations such as Jamba (Lieber et al., 2024), Samba (Ren et al., 2024), and TTT (Sun et al., 2024) were not included in our analysis but represent promising avenues for future research. Investigating these emerging models could potentially uncover novel approaches to improve the efficiency and effectiveness of scientific hypothesis generation.

6 Memorization

Given that LLMs are trained on extensive datasets, including potentially the same sources used for evaluation, there is a risk that the models may reproduce memorized content rather than generating novel hypotheses. So, we conduct a memorization check to ensure the validation of our experiments.

1. (Raffel et al., 2019) shows that T5 is pretrained on C4 which was crawled from web prior to April 2019.

2. Mamba uses the Pile dataset (Gao et al., 2020), and follows the training recipe described in (Brown et al., 2020).

3. The GPT-4 checkpoint used in this study is primarily based on data collected before September 2021, with only a minimal amount of more recent data included during both pretraining and post-training stages (Wang et al., 2024). Given that the evaluation focuses on papers published in 2022, the chance that these papers are part of GPT-4's pretraining dataset is considerably low.

   Furthermore, a manual review of GPT-4's outputs is conducted from SciMON using a gold set composed of 2022 ACL Anthology papers. This review specifically looks for instances where GPT-4 might reproduce detailed information, such as method names, or generate text that closely mirrors the original papers. The findings show no significant evidence of memorization.

7 Conclusion

Our study provides insights into the application of language models, particularly the Mamba architecture, for scientific hypothesis generation within the SciMON model. Comparative analysis reveals that Mamba models perform comparably to T5 models of similar sizes, with Mamba-790M achieving the highest scores in automatic evaluations. GPT-4, however, outperforms both in human and LLM-based evaluations, demonstrating superior capability in generating relevant, novel, and scientifically valid hypotheses. Mamba exhibits strength in processing longer input sequences, suggesting potential for complex scientific reasoning tasks. However, it shows instability with smaller inputs, indicating areas for improvement. These findings highlight the potential of state space models in advancing scientific hypothesis generation, despite limitations such as the use of only ACL Anthology papers and restricted parameter sizes in our analysis. Future research should focus on expanding the dataset to diverse scientific domains, investigating larger parameter settings and emerging state space models, developing specialized benchmarks for long-sequence processing, and addressing Mamba's instability with smaller inputs. While Mamba shows promise, particularly for long-context tasks, further research is needed to fully harness its potential and address limitations. As language models evolve, their integration into scientific workflows holds great promise for accelerating hypothesis generation and innovation across diverse fields. This research represents a significant step towards leveraging advanced language models to expand the frontiers of scientific inquiry and knowledge generation.

Acknowledgement

This research used resources of the Oak Ridge Leadership Computing Facility (OLCF), which is a DOE Office of Science User Facility at the Oak Ridge National Laboratory supported by the U.S. Department of Energy under Contract No. DE-AC05-00OR22725.

References

Sachin Banker, Promothesh Chatterjee, Himanshu Mishra, and Arul Mishra. 2023. Machine-assisted social psychology hypothesis generation.

Tom B. Brown, Benjamin Mann, Nick Ryder, Melanie Subbiah, Jared Kaplan, Prafulla Dhariwal, Arvind Neelakantan, Pranav Shyam, Girish Sastry, Amanda Askell, Sandhini Agarwal, Ariel Herbert-Voss, Gretchen Krueger, Tom Henighan, Rewon Child, Aditya Ramesh, Daniel M. Ziegler, Jeff Wu, Clemens Winter, Christopher Hesse, Mark Chen, Eric Sigler, Ma teusz Litwin, Scott Gray, Benjamin Chess, Jack Clark, Christopher Berner, Sam McCandlish, Alec Radford, Ilya Sutskever, and Dario Amodei. 2020. Language models are few-shot learners. *ArXiv*, abs/2005.14165.

Arie Cattan, Sophie Johnson, Daniel S. Weld, Ido Dagan, Iz Beltagy, Doug Downey, and Tom Hope. 2021. Scico: Hierarchical cross-document coreference for scientific concepts. *ArXiv*, abs/2104.08809.

Ioana Ciucă, Yuan-Sen Ting, Sandor Kruk, and Kartheik Iyer. 2023. Harnessing the power of adversarial prompting and large language models for robust hypothesis generation in astronomy. *Preprint*, arXiv:2306.11648.

Arman Cohan, Iz Beltagy, Daniel King, Bhavana Dalvi, and Dan Weld. 2019. Pretrained language models for sequential sentence classification. In *Proceedings of the 2019 Conference on Empirical Methods in Natural Language Processing and the 9th International Joint Conference on Natural Language Processing (EMNLP-IJCNLP)*, pages 3693–3699, Hong Kong, China. Association for Computational Linguistics.

Leo Gao, Stella Biderman, Sid Black, Laurence Golding, Travis Hoppe, Charles Foster, Jason Phang, Horace He, Anish Thite, Noa Nabeshima, Shawn Presser, and Connor Leahy. 2020. The pile: An 800gb dataset of diverse text for language modeling. *ArXiv*, abs/2101.00027.

Riccardo Grazzi, Julien N. Siems, Simon Schrodi, Thomas Brox, and Frank Hutter. 2024. Is mamba capable of in-context learning? *ArXiv*, abs/2402.03170.

Albert Gu and Tri Dao. 2023. Mamba: Linear-time sequence modeling with selective state spaces. *ArXiv*, abs/2312.00752.

Tomás Kociský, Jonathan Schwarz, Phil Blunsom, Chris Dyer, Karl Moritz Hermann, Gábor Melis, and Edward Grefenstette. 2017. The narrativeqa reading comprehension challenge. *Transactions of the Association for Computational Linguistics*, 6:317–328.

Yuta Koreeda and Christopher D. Manning. 2021. Contractnli: A dataset for document-level natural language inference for contracts. In *Conference on Empirical Methods in Natural Language Processing*.

Opher Lieber, Barak Lenz, Hofit Bata, Gal Cohen, Jhonathan Osin, Itay Dalmedigos, Erez Safahi, Shaked Haim Meirom, Yonatan Belinkov, Shai Shalev-Shwartz, Omri Abend, Raz Alon, Tomer Asida, Amir Bergman, Roman Glozman, Michael Gokhman, Avshalom Manevich, Nir Ratner, Noam Rozen, Erez Shwartz, Mor Zusman, and Yoav Shoham. 2024. Jamba: A hybrid transformer-mamba language model. *ArXiv*, abs/2403.19887.

Chin-Yew Lin. 2004. ROUGE: A package for automatic evaluation of summaries. In *Text Summarization Branches Out*, pages 74–81, Barcelona, Spain. Association for Computational Linguistics.

Kyle Lo, Lucy Lu Wang, Mark Neumann, Rodney Kinney, and Daniel Weld. 2020. S2ORC: The semantic scholar open research corpus. In *Proceedings of the 58th Annual Meeting of the Association for Computational Linguistics*, pages 4969–4983, Online. Association for Computational Linguistics.

Yi Luan, Luheng He, Mari Ostendorf, and Hannaneh Hajishirzi. 2018. Multi-task identification of entities, relations, and coreference for scientific knowledge graph construction. In *Proceedings of the 2018 Conference on Empirical Methods in Natural Language Processing*, pages 3219–3232, Brussels, Belgium. Association for Computational Linguistics.

Mark Neumann, Daniel King, Iz Beltagy, and Waleed Ammar. 2019. ScispaCy: Fast and robust models for biomedical natural language processing. In *Proceedings of the 18th BioNLP Workshop and Shared Task*, pages 319–327, Florence, Italy. Association for Computational Linguistics.

Thomas O'Brien, Joel Stremmel, Léo Pio-Lopez, Patrick McMillen, Cody Rasmussen-Ivey, and Michael Levin. 2024. Machine learning for hypothesis generation in biology and medicine: exploring the latent space of neuroscience and developmental bioelectricity. *Digital Discovery*, 3:249–263.

Richard Yuanzhe Pang, Alicia Parrish, Nitish Joshi, Nikita Nangia, Jason Phang, Angelica Chen, Vishakh Padmakumar, Johnny Ma, Jana Thompson, He He, and Sam Bowman. 2021. Quality: Question answering with long input texts, yes! In *North American Chapter of the Association for Computational Linguistics*.

Jongho Park, Jaeseung Park, Zheyang Xiong, Nayoung Lee, Jaewoong Cho, Samet Oymak, Kangwook Lee, and Dimitris Papailiopoulos. 2024. Can mamba learn how to learn? a comparative study on in-context learning tasks. *ArXiv*, abs/2402.04248.

Yang Jeong Park, Daniel Kaplan, Zhichu Ren, Chia-Wei Hsu, Changhao Li, Haowei Xu, Sipei Li, and Ju Li. 2023. Can chatgpt be used to generate scientific hypotheses? *Preprint*, arXiv:2304.12208.

Biqing Qi, Kaiyan Zhang, Haoxiang Li, Kai Tian, Sihang Zeng, Zhang-Ren Chen, and Bowen Zhou. 2023. Large language models are zero shot hypothesis proposers. *Preprint*, arXiv:2311.05965.

Colin Raffel, Noam M. Shazeer, Adam Roberts, Katherine Lee, Sharan Narang, Michael Matena, Yanqi Zhou, Wei Li, and Peter J. Liu. 2019. Exploring the limits of transfer learning with a unified text-to-text transformer. *J. Mach. Learn. Res.*, 21:140:1–140:67.

Liliang Ren, Yang Liu, Yadong Lu, Yelong Shen, Chen Liang, and Weizhu Chen. 2024. Samba: Simple hybrid state space models for efficient unlimited context language modeling. *ArXiv*, abs/2406.07522.

Yu Sun, Xinhao Li, Karan Dalal, Jiarui Xu, Arjun Vikram, Genghan Zhang, Yann Dubois, Xinlei Chen, Xiaolong Wang, Sanmi Koyejo, Tatsunori Hashimoto, and Carlos Guestrin. 2024. Learning to (learn at test time): Rnns with expressive hidden states.

Song Tong, Kai Mao, Zhen Huang, Yukun Zhao, and Kaiping Peng. 2023. Automating psychological hypothesis generation with ai: Large language models meet causal graph.

Aaron van den Oord, Yazhe Li, and Oriol Vinyals. 2019. Representation learning with contrastive predictive coding. *Preprint*, arXiv:1807.03748.

Qingyun Wang, Doug Downey, Heng Ji, and Tom Hope. 2024. Scimon: Scientific inspiration machines optimized for novelty. *Preprint*, arXiv:2305.14259.

Rui Xu, Shu Yang, Yihui Wang, Yu Cai, Bo Du, and Hao Chen. 2024a. Visual mamba: A survey and new outlooks. *Preprint*, arXiv:2404.18861.

Wenda Xu, Guanglei Zhu, Xuandong Zhao, Liangming Pan, Lei Li, and William Yang Wang. 2024b. Pride and prejudice: Llm amplifies self-bias in self-refinement.

Deming Ye, Yankai Lin, Peng Li, and Maosong Sun. 2022. Packed levitated marker for entity and relation extraction. In *Proceedings of the 60th Annual Meeting of the Association for Computational Linguistics (Volume 1: Long Papers)*, pages 4904–4917, Dublin, Ireland. Association for Computational Linguistics.

Tianyi Zhang, Varsha Kishore, Felix Wu, Kilian Q. Weinberger, and Yoav Artzi. 2019. Bertscore: Evaluating text generation with bert. *ArXiv*, abs/1904.09675.

Lianmin Zheng, Wei-Lin Chiang, Ying Sheng, Siyuan Zhuang, Zhanghao Wu, Yonghao Zhuang, Zi Lin, Zhuohan Li, Dacheng Li, Eric P. Xing, Haotong Zhang, Joseph Gonzalez, and Ion Stoica. 2023. Judging llm-as-a-judge with mt-bench and chatbot arena. *ArXiv*, abs/2306.05685.

Yangqiaoyu Zhou, Haokun Liu, Tejes Srivastava, Hongyuan Mei, and Chenhao Tan. 2024. Hypothesis generation with large language models. *Preprint*, arXiv:2404.04326.

A Human Evaluation

To assess the effectiveness of Claude-3.5, we recruit five NLP experts, all of whom have graduate-level education, to independently evaluate the outputs by using the following questionnaire.

Evaluating LLM-Generated Scientific Hypothesis

You are participating in an evaluation of hypotheses generated by an AI assistant designed to enhance scientific research. These hypotheses are intended to propose novel approaches or insights for computer science research questions.
Instructions:

- **Background Context** - You will receive a summary of the challenge and recent advancements, setting the stage for the hypotheses AI will generate.
- **Seed Term** - You will receive a key concept or focal point related to the research challenge. This term directs the AI in generating hypotheses specifically relevant to the field's ongoing inquiries.

Your task is to evaluate the candidate suggestions by labeling them as effective or ineffective. You need to assess the overall quality of each candidate by taking into account factors:

1. Relevance: How well does the hypothesis relate to the context and the seed term provided?
2. Novelty: Does the hypothesis offer a new perspective or solution distinct from existing research?
3. Scientific Validity: Is the hypothesis plausible and justifiable with current scientific knowledge?
4. Clarity: Is the hypothesis articulated in a clear and understandable manner?

Read the following example that illustrates the task:

Context: the task of converting a natural language question into an executable sql query, known as text - to - sql, is an important branch of semantic parsing. the state - of - the - art graph - based encoder has been successfully used in this task but does not model the question syntax well.

Seed term: diverse relational edge embedding

System Outputs:

- We propose a novel technique, Diverse Relational Edge Embedding (DREE), to address this problem.
- We propose a novel graph-based encoder that uses a diverse relational edge embedding to model the question syntax.
- Diverse relational edge embedding is important for text-to-SQL parsing because it can help the parser to better understand the question syntax.

Result:

- Ineffective
- Effective
- Effective

Figure 5: Human evaluation instructions

B Additional Experiments

B.1 In-context Learning

Modern attention-based LLMs exhibit remarkable in-context learning (ICL) capabilities, enabling them to learn new tasks effectively with only a few demonstrations. Research indicates that Mamba performs on par with Transformers in standard regression ICL tasks and surpasses them in tasks such as sparse parity learning (Park et al., 2024). Additionally, (Grazzi et al., 2024) found that Mamba incrementally optimizes its internal representations in a manner similar to transformer models, which aids in solving ICL problems. This adaptability suggests that Mamba can be effectively compared to Transformers in few-shot and fine-tuning settings with comparable data and training time due to its ICL, which serves as the basis for our experiment's design.

Model	MATHQA (acc) %	MMLU (acc) %	MMLUSR (acc)%	GPQA (acc)%
Mamba-130M	23.38	22.82	23.05	25.00
Mamba-370M	24.32	22.95	22.96	24.78
Mamba-790M	**25.56**	**23.74**	23.38	25.00
T5-Small	21.64	23.07	**23.49**	24.78
T5-Base	22.18	22.93	22.96	25.00
T5-Large	22.51	22.94	22.94	**25.45**

Table 3: Results for General In-Context Learning Tasks

B.2 Long-Text Evaluation

We selected three datasets, ranging from 10^2 to 10^6 words per input, to test the model's ability in question answering and natural language inference, which are the basic ability for a scientific hypothesis generation model: ContractNLI (10^2 to $10^{3.5}$) (Koreeda and Manning, 2021), QuALITY ($10^{3.3}$ to $10^{3.7}$) (Pang et al., 2021), and Narrative ($10^{3.5}$ to 10^6) (Kociský et al., 2017). The first two tasks use accuracy scores and are designed to answer specific questions based on long science and literature documents, while the latter uses F1 score for evaluation, generating results using the continuation probabilities returned by the model.

Model	Contract NLI (acc) %	QuALITY (acc) %	NarrativeQA (f1)
Mamba-130M	14.46	24.11	8.79
Mamba-370M	10.22	24.88	11.31
Mamba-790M	11.86	24.30	**13.81**
T5-Small	30.76	23.97	2.26
T5-Base	32.88	23.97	0.45
T5-Large	**35.97**	**24.98**	1.63

Table 4: Results for Long-Text Evaluation

C LLM Prompt

```
This is prompt for Claude: Your goal in this task is to rank idea suggestions written by LLM.
The LLM helps its users write paper abstracts by generating sentences with proposals for new
ideas or questions to consider. You are first given:

1. A context which describes relevant background in a specific area of interest.
2. A seed term that should be a focus of the generated scientific idea.
3. An idea suggestion generated by LLMs written in the form of a paper abstract (SUGGESTION).

Consider the following factors in your evaluation:

1. Is the suggestion relevant to the context and seed term?
2. Is the suggestion sufficiently novel, not overly copying the context?
3. Is the suggestion scientifically sound?
4. Is the language clear and coherent?

Assign a rating as either "effective" or "ineffective", where:
- "effective" = The SUGGESTION is sufficiently novel, relevant, scientifically sound, and clear.
- "ineffective" = The SUGGESTION lacks novelty, relevance, scientific soundness, or clarity.

Provide your rating and a brief justification for your assessment.

Return your output in JSON format only with the keys "justification" and "rating":
{
  "justification": "<your brief justification>",
  "suggestion": "ineffective< / effective>"
}
```

Benchmarking Automated Theorem Proving with Large Language Models

Vanessa Lama*[1], Catherine Ma*[2], Tirthankar Ghosal[1]
[1]Oak Ridge National Laboratory, Oak Ridge, TN, USA
[2]Pomona College, Claremont, CA, USA
lamav@ornl.gov, zmbg2022@mymail.pomona.edu, ghosalt@ornl.gov
*Equal contribution

Abstract

Theorem proving presents a significant challenge for large language models (LLMs) due to the requirement for formal proofs to be rigorously checked by proof assistants, such as Lean, eliminating any margin for error or hallucination. While existing LLM-based theorem provers attempt to operate autonomously, they often struggle with novel and complex theorems where human insights are essential. Lean Copilot is a novel framework that integrates LLM inference into the Lean proof assistant environment. In this work, we benchmark performance of several LLMs including general and math-specific models for theorem proving using the Lean Copilot framework. Our initial investigation suggests that a general-purpose large model like LLaMa-70B still has edge over math-specific smaller models for the task under consideration. We provide useful insights into the performance of different LLMs we chose for the task.

1 Introduction

As mathematical problems become increasingly intricate, the task of formalizing and generating verifiable math proofs becomes proportionally more challenging. The translation process from informal theorems and proofs to a standardized, machine-verifiable, formal language, requires much effort and expertise from human mathematicians, creating a steep learning curve. This challenge has raised great interest in the potential of using AI to aid in the math formalization process, and more generally in automated theorem proving(ATP). The integration of AI, specifically large language models(LLMs), in math formalization and theorem proving can not only accelerate the proof discovery process, but can also enhance the reliability and rigor of mathematical arguments by minimizing human error.

While the ultimate goal may be to achieve fully autonomous proof generation without human assistance, current ATP systems based on language models struggle when dealing with more complex proof problems. Typically, these language models employed for theorem proving come from larger base models like BERT and GPT, then finetuned on large amounts of mathematical text data such as Mathlib(mathlib Community, 2020). This limitation seen likely stems from the models' lack of flexibility when encountering mathematical areas not adequately covered by their training data. To address this inflexibility with autonomous proof generation, there are Interactive Theorem Proving (ITP) systems where proof assistants- software frameworks built for math formalization like Coq, Isabelle, and Lean- are used in conjunction with human mathematicians in the proving process. This integration allows for the aid of proof automation tools with human intuition. The use of ITP system proof assistants has become increasingly prevalent for ensuring a level of rigor and standard in formalizing mathematical language.

Lean is one such popular proof assistant as well as functional programming language for formalizing mathematics that supports ITP by offering a framework for writing and verifying proofs. Lean uses tactic style proving where proofs are generated step by step using tactics, or instructions used to manipulate the current state of a proof to the next state. From the start of a proof, users will continue the proof using the appropriate tactic based on the user's knowledge of the math problem and tactics. While a powerful proof assistant for mathematicians, it still requires a great deal of effort to find the ideal tactics. This is a common barrier across all ITP systems; thus, the integration of Large Language Models (LLMs) with proof assistants was introduced to offer intuitive, automated assistance in generating and verifying mathematical proofs. LLMs can automate tedious aspects of proof writing, such as identifying relevant lemmas and theorems and drawing from extensive math-

Proceedings of the 1st Workshop on NLP for Science (NLP4Science), pages 208–218
November 16, 2024 ©2024 Association for Computational Linguistics

ematical training data to uncover overlooked but crucial insights.

However, despite the potential of LLMs, existing LLM-based provers cannot assist humans in an interactive, seamless manner. Current LLM-based systems are typically trained and evaluated following machine learning standards that rely on extracted datasets from an ITP's codebase rather than within the proof assistant itself. This disconnection results in models that, while effective in a controlled environment, are difficult to integrate into the practical workflows of proof assistants. This gap between LLM training environments and proof assistant usage highlights a critical need for systems to bridge the two and enable more effective human-AI collaboration in theorem proving.

Recently, the effort to combine proof assistant, Lean, with LLMs was achieved through a new framework LeanCopilot. LeanCopilot is an open-source framework that supports users to bring in pre-trained LLMs and use/build LLM-based proof automation tools natively in Lean (Song et al., 2024). This makes LLM-based proof automation available in Lean and increasing accessibility in math formalization. It is based on LeanDojo's Reprover algorithm for tactic generation and can be brought in as a package in Lean through an IDE of choice (Yang et al., 2023). It is able to run LLMs on most laptops without the need for GPUs, a feature that increases accessibility for LLM-based proof automation. While users can create their own tools, LeanCopilot also comes with a suite of built in proof automation tools. These tools were built using CTranslate2's C++ library for efficient LLM inference with Transformer models, running it via Lean's foreign function interface(FFI). A more comprehensive review of these tools can be found in following sections:

- *suggest_tactics*: Analyzes the current proof state and recommends relevant tactics
- *search_proof*: Construct full proof for theorem
- *select_premises*: Identifies relevant premises for current proof goal

The performance of LLMs for theorem proving tasks can vary widely depending on the complexity of the proofs and the model architecture. Recent research has demonstrated that while LLMs can effectively automate portions of proof generation, their success is highly contingent on the difficulty of the mathematical problems being tackled and the specific design of the model (Xin et al., 2024; Song et al., 2024). This variability in performance motivates our work to benchmark LLMs specifically in the context of ITP, as understanding these models' strengths and weaknesses is crucial for improving their utility in automating mathematical proof generation.

In our research, we utilize LeanCopilot's ability to bring in LLMs to evaluate the performance of various LLMs for theorem proving. LLMs are commonly benchmarked for theorem proving by testing how many theorems they can generate proofs for. We evaluate the performance of LLMs trained for math tasks, Pythia2.8b, Llemma7b, LeanStarPlus7b, LeanStarCot7b, against general LLMs, Llama3-70b and ByT5. We replicate the experiments used to evaluate LeanCopilot's built-in proof automation tools but instead to benchmark LLMs for proof generation. We evaluate the performance of these different LLMs for ITP using LeanCopilot's built-in proof automation tool, `suggest_tactics`. This benchmarking will allow us to evaluate how different LLMs perform in assisting with theorem proving tasks across a selection of proof problems sourced from the Mathematics in Lean textbook. By systematically evaluating different LLMs, we aim to identify key factors that contribute to successful proof generation and highlight areas where further advancements are needed.

2 Related Works

The roots of ITP lie in the broader field of automated reasoning, which emerged as a distinct area of study in the mid-20th century. While ATP systems aimed to fully automate the process of deriving proofs, early researchers recognized the limitations of these systems, particularly in handling complex, domain-specific proofs that required a deeper level of human intuition and insight.

The inception of ITP was driven by the need to integrate human expertise into the proof construction process, allowing for a relationship between automated tools and human mathematicians. One of the earliest milestones in this direction was the development of the LCF (Logic for Computable Functions) theorem prover by Robin Milner in the 1970s (Milner, 1972). LCF introduced a novel approach that combined a small trusted kernel, which ensured the soundness of proofs, with a flexible and extensible user interface that allowed human interaction. The LCF approach set a precedent for future ITP systems by emphasizing the importance of human oversight in the verification process.

The 1980s and 1990s saw the emergence of some of the most influential ITP systems, notably Coq and Isabelle. These systems were built on the foundational ideas of the LCF approach but introduced significant innovations that expanded the scope and applicability of ITP.

Coq, developed by Thierry Coquand and Gérard Huet, was based on the Calculus of Inductive Constructions (CIC), a powerful type theory that enabled the formalization of a wide range of mathematical concepts (Coquand and Huet, 1988). Coq's ability to handle inductive types and support constructive mathematics made it a versatile tool for both theorem proving and the extraction of certified programs. Coq's interactive environment allowed mathematicians to build proofs incrementally by using a rich set of tactics to guide the proof process while relying on the underlying formalism to ensure correctness.

Isabelle, developed by Lawrence Paulson, took a different approach by providing a generic framework that could support multiple logics (Paulson, 1986). Isabelle's most notable contribution was its use of higher-order logic (HOL), which allowed for the formalization of more complex mathematical structures and proofs. Isabelle's architecture was designed to be highly modular, enabling users to extend the system with custom proof strategies and tactics. This flexibility made Isabelle particularly popular in both academia and industry for formal verification tasks.

As ITP systems matured, the focus shifted towards enhancing their automation capabilities while preserving the essential role of human interaction. The concept of proof tactics, first introduced in LCF, became central to this effort. Tactics are commands that automate common proof steps, allowing users to delegate routine tasks to the computer prover while focusing on more challenging aspects of the proof.

These developments set the stage for the creation and release of Lean, a modern proof assistant developed by Leonardo de Moura and his team at Microsoft Research (Moura and Ullrich, 2021). First released in 2013, Lean was designed with a focus on combining expressive power, automation, and user-friendly interaction. It builds on ideas from earlier systems but introduces several unique features that distinguish it in the landscape of ITP tools.

Lean is based on a version of dependent type theory, similar to Coq, but it emphasizes a more unified approach to proof automation and user interaction. This is exemplified by Lean's tactic framework, which allows users to construct proofs incrementally by applying tactics—commands that automate specific proof steps. Lean's programming framework also enables users to write custom tactics in the Lean language itself, making it highly extensible and adaptable to different domains of mathematics and computer science.

Lean's integration of a tactic language is an evolution of the earlier LCF and Coq systems, which introduced tactics as a means of automating common proof steps. Lean's tactic framework has been further enhanced to support more sophisticated proof strategies, making it an effective tool for both novice users and expert mathematicians. This combination of user interaction and automation makes Lean a useful tool in the formalization of mathematics and the verification of complex systems, enabling better integration of human expertise with automated proof checking.

2.1 LeanCopilot

The creation of LeanCopilot opens a new avenue of accessibility for mathematicians who hope to use LLMs in their math formalization research.

Figure 1 provides a flowchart of the algorithm used by LeanCopilot for selecting relevant premises to generate tactics and full proofs. The specific algorithm highlighted for premise selection is LeanDojo's reprover algorithm which is based on dense passage retrieval. It selects top relevant premises from mathlib, a library of formalized math theorems, lemmas, and definitions across various subjects of math and uses them to generate tactics. This is the algorithm used in `suggest_tactics` and by `select_premises`. LeanCopilot's search_proof is also based off Lean's rule-based proof search tool `aesop`. `aesop` implements a tree-based search over a user-defined set of proof rules to generate the full proof (Limperg and From, 2023). However, because the proof rule search space is predefined by the user, `aesop` lacks flexibility considering it depends heavily how advantageous the rule set is. Every proof goal in the process uses the same predefined rule set even though different goals may call for different rules. `search_proof` adds to `aesop` by using

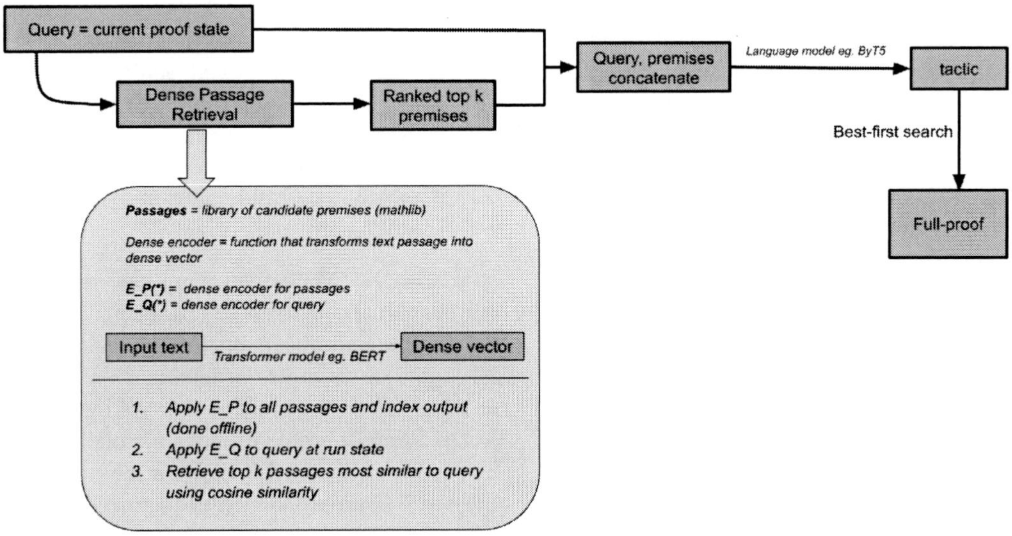

Figure 1: Flowchart of LeanCopilot proof generation algorithm used in `suggest_tactics`, `select_premises`, and `search_proof`

`suggest_tactics` to generate goal-dependent tactics for every goal thus making the rule set custom to each proof goal. In LeanCopilot's evaluations, `search_proof` outperformed `aesop` for both autonomously generating proofs and when intereacting with human users. In our experiments to benchmark LLMs, we will be swapping out the language model used to generate the tactics as seen in 1. LeanCopilot uses the language model ByT5 as its base model for its proof automation tools unless another LLM is specifed by the user.

However even with the introduction of Leancopilot, there is a lack of recorded evaluation of the capabilities of LLMs for ITP systems. We aim to bridge this gap by benchmarking LLMs to further realize how we may improve models for theorem proving. The ongoing integration of Lean with other tools and platforms, along with the potential of LLMs to enhance automation, suggests a promising future for Lean in the broader landscape of theorem proving.

3 Methodology

This section outlines our approach for benchmarking the capabilities of different LLMs, both math-specific and general LLMs, in assisting with theorem proving using LeanCopilot. We replicate the benchmarking experiments used to evaluate the proof-automation tools in LeanCopilot, but instead to benchmark different LLMs for proof generation. In their experiments the authors (Song et al., 2024) evaluated LeanCopilot's `suggest_tactics` and `search_proof` against preexisting lean proof automation tool `aesop`. Currently, LeanCopilot doesn't support bringing in different LLMs for their tools `search_proof` and `select_premise`, thus we will only benchmark using `suggest_tactics`.

We benchmark the following LLMs:

1. **ByT5:** Based on the T5 (Text-to-Text Transfer Transformer) architecture, specifically the T5-Small variant, which has 60 million parameters (Xue et al., 2021). It operates on byte-level inputs, eliminating the need for tokenization and making it effective for handling diverse and irregular text formats. In LeanCopilot, ByT5 serves as the foundational model, providing capabilities for generating and manipulating formal mathematical proofs.
2. **Pythia-2.8b:** This model is a specialized version of the Pythia language models, fine-tuned on the Leandojo dataset (Song et al., 2024), which consists of a curated collection of formalized mathematics in Lean. With 2.8 billion parameters, it is designed to excel in theorem proving tasks within the Lean framework. The fine-tuning on Leandojo enhances

the model's ability to generate contextually accurate proof steps and better understand the nuances of mathematical formalization, making it a valuable tool for formalizing and verifying mathematical proofs in Lean.

3. **Llama-3 70b:** LLama-3 (Large Language Model for AI) is a highly advanced transformer-based model containing 70 billion parameters (et al., 2024). Its substantial parameter count allows it to capture intricate patterns in language, making it highly effective for complex reasoning tasks, including formal theorem proving. As one of the larger models in our study, LLama-3 70B provides a benchmark for evaluating the performance of large-scale general language models in formal mathematics.

4. **Llemma7b:** Llemma7b is a mid-sized language model with 7 billion parameters, optimized for balancing computational efficiency with performance (Azerbayev et al., 2024). While not as large as LLa-ma3 70b, it offers significant capabilities in understanding and generating mathematical proofs. Its reduced size allows for more accessible deployment in resource-constrained environments, without compromising on the quality of theorem proving assistance.

5. **LeanStarPlus7b:** Lean-STaR is a framework designed to enhance language models in ATP by integrating informal reasoning with formal proof steps (Lin et al., 2024). Building on the Self-Taught Reasoner (STaR) framework (Zelikman et al., 2022), Lean-STaR introduces the concept of generating "thoughts"—natural language rationales—prior to each tactic. It operates in two phases: first, retrospective thoughts are generated by analyzing human-written proofs from Mathlib, creating a thought-augmented dataset; second, this data is used to fine-tune a tactic predictor model, which is further optimized through expert iteration. This approach significantly improves theorem-proving capabilities, as demonstrated on the miniF2F-test benchmark, where Lean-STaR achieves state-of-the-art results, surpassing previous models in pass rates.

6. **LeanCotPlus7b:** LeanCotPlus is an extension of the LeanCot model, optimized for improved interaction with the Lean proof assistant. This model builds upon LeanCot's foundational capabilities with additional enhancements aimed at increasing its effectiveness in theorem proving and proof automation. LeanCotPlus incorporates advanced techniques for better understanding and generating mathematical proofs.

We use the "Mathematics in Lean" textbook as our benchmarking data (Avigad et al., 2021). The textbook covers the math formalization process through various topics in math such as topology and logic in the Lean language. We randomly selected 50 proof problems in the textbook and evaluate how well each LLM performed at generating the full proof of each problem. Proof problems in the textbook contain "ground-truth" tactics that kick start each proof. Following the LeanCopilot experiment procedure, we will enter each ground-truth tactic one by one. After entering each tactic, we will prompt Lean with either `aesop`, `suggest_tactics`, or `search_proof` to attempt to solve the remaining proof goals. We will record the number of tactics the user had to input as prompts before the tool successfully completes the proof. The list of generated, suggested tactics is ranked top to bottom by likelihood of solving the proof. We choose the top tactic to input to eliminate human bias. For `suggest_tactics`, we consider the proof complete when in the list of suggested tactics, there exists a tactic that solves the current goal.

```
theorem primes_infinite : ∀ n, ∃ p > n, Nat.Prime p := by
  intro n
  have : 2 ≤ Nat.factorial (n + 1) + 1 := by
    sorry
  rcases exists_prime_factor this with ⟨p, pp, pdvd⟩
  refine' ⟨p, _, pp⟩
  show p > n
  by_contra ple
  push_neg  at ple
  have : p ∣ Nat.factorial (n + 1) := by
    sorry
  have : p ∣ 1 := by
    sorry
  show False
  sorry
```

Figure 2: Ground truth proof for proving there are infinitely many primes from Mathematics in Lean Textbook. The proof is purposefully not completed as an exercise for users to fill in each `sorry` with remaining tactics.

As an example of how a proof from the textbook looks, figure 2 shows the proof there exists infinitely many prime numbers in Lean. The theorem asserts that for any natural number n, there exists a prime number p such that $p > n$. Then the `intro` tactic introduces the variable n into the proof context. This sets the stage for proving the existence of a prime number greater than n. Next we establish that $2 \leq (n+1)! + 1$. The factorial function grows rapidly, so adding 1 ensures that the result is greater than 1 and thus has a prime factor. The `rcases` tactic is used to deconstruct the result of the `exists_prime_factor` theorem, which guarantees the existence of a prime factor p of $(n+1)! + 1$. Here, pp asserts that p is prime, and $pdvd$ asserts that p divides $(n+1)! + 1$. The `refine'` tactic is used to fill in part of the goal, specifically stating that p is the desired prime number and that $p > n$ needs to be shown. To prove $p > n$, we use a proof by contradiction. The `by_contra` tactic assumes the opposite, $p \leq n$, and the `push_neg` tactic simplifies this assumption. If p divides both $(n+1)!$ and $(n+1)! + 1$, then it must divide their difference, which is 1. But no prime number can divide 1, leading to a contradiction. This final contradiction establishes that p must be greater than n. The `sorry` placeholders represent steps where detailed proofs need to be filled in to . The tactics that exist already in the proof, are considered our "ground truth tactics". For our experiments, each `sorry` is considered a problem where we replace `sorry` with `suggest_tactics`.

4 Datasets on which the LLMs under consideration were trained

In this section, we discuss the datasets on which the models were trained to get an idea of their internal knowledge base.

4.1 ByT5

ByT5, the base model used in LeanCopilot, was initially trained on a multilingual corpus covering a broad spectrum of languages and domains. For the theorem proving tasks, it was fine-tuned on formal mathematics datasets, including those from Mathlib, to enhance its performance in proof generation.

4.2 Pythia2.8b

The Pythia model suite was trained on the Pile dataset, a comprehensive collection of English-language texts specifically designed for large-scale language model training (Gao et al., 2020). The Pile is highly regarded in the machine learning community because it is openly accessible, performs well across various tasks.

4.3 Llama3 70b

The Llama3 (et al., 2024) model was trained using a curated dataset from various sources, with data up to the end of 2023. This dataset underwent extensive cleaning and de-duplication processes to ensure high-quality tokens, focusing on removing personally identifiable information (PII) and unsafe content. The web data, which formed a significant part of the dataset, was processed using custom parsers to extract clean and relevant text while preserving the structure of mathematical and code content. The data mix for Llama3 was meticulously determined through experiments, resulting in a composition of 50% general knowledge, 25% mathematical and reasoning, 17% code, and 8% multilingual tokens, ensuring a balanced and comprehensive pre-training corpus.

4.4 Llemma7b

The Llemma7b model was trained on the Proof-Pile-2, a 55-billion-token dataset that combines scientific papers, web data rich in mathematical content, and mathematical code (Azerbayev et al., 2023). The dataset includes the AlgebraicStack, an 11-billion-token collection of source code from 17 languages, which emphasizes numerical, symbolic, and formal mathematics. Additionally, the training utilized OpenWebMath (Paster et al., 2024), a 15-billion-token dataset of mathematically focused web pages, and the ArXiv subset from the RedPajama dataset (Computer, 2023), contributing 29 billion tokens of scientific papers. The final data mix was heavily skewed towards mathematical and scientific content, with 95% coming from Proof-Pile-2 and small portions from general domain data and GitHub repositories.

4.5 LeanStarPlus7b & LeanCotPlus7b

Both models were trained and evaluated using datasets specifically curated from Lean's Mathlib (mathlib Community, 2020), the largest collection of formalized mathematics in the Lean theorem prover. Additionally, miniF2F, a standard benchmark in the formal verification community, was used to evaluate the models' performance (Zheng et al., 2022). This dataset contains a diverse set of formalized theorems that challenge the models' ability to generalize across different mathematical domains.

5 Results & Discussion

In this section, we will detail the results of our experiments with the *Mathematics in Lean* textbook problems. Fifty (50) proof problems were randomly selected from the textbook for our experiments. As a reminder, for `suggest_tactics`, since the list of tactics are ranked from most likely to complete proof to least likely, *we select the first tactic in the list of generated tactics as our input to the proof.* In the following Figures, we exemplify the solution with one problem from the textbook. This example problem is *to prove the product of an even number with any natural number will be an even number.* This problem is straightforward for most with a math background, thus is a good example to understand the results produced by different models. We observe similar behaviour with our selected test-set.

5.1 ByT5

The results for ByT5 are shown in Figures 3 and 4. In Figure 3 we have the list of generated tactics for the first tactic. The majority of tactics from the list are some variant of the `intro` tactic aside from the tactics `norm _num`, which is used to perform numerical simplifications and arithmetic reasoning, and `simp [even_mul]`, which applies simplification rules specifically related to the property of even multiplication. ByT5 is the only model where the tactic `simp_all` was used after an `intro` tactic. In this case, it led to the immeadiate resolution of the proof since the tactic applies a broad set of simplification rules. While efficient, this may highlight a limitation of highlevel automation where the rules are not explicitly revealed.

5.2 LeanCotPlus7b & LeanStarPlus7b

Both LeanCoTPlus7b and LeanStarPlus7b generated the same full proof script as seen in Figures 5 and 6. This script starts with introducing the variables m, n, and the hypothesis h, then applies case analysis on h, and then simplifies the goal using the provided hypothesis and basic arithmetic. This suggests a high level of consistency in how these models approach proof generation for this of theorem. LeanCoTPlus7b and LeanStarPlus7b are indeed related models, both derived from the Lean ecosystem, which implies that they share foundational techniques and architectures for theorem proving. It is important to highlight, that both models gave the full proof of the theorem, even though it was prompted with `suggest_tactics`. This showcases their ability to generate full proofs, however this is a limitation for users who want to select their own tactic and perform ITP.

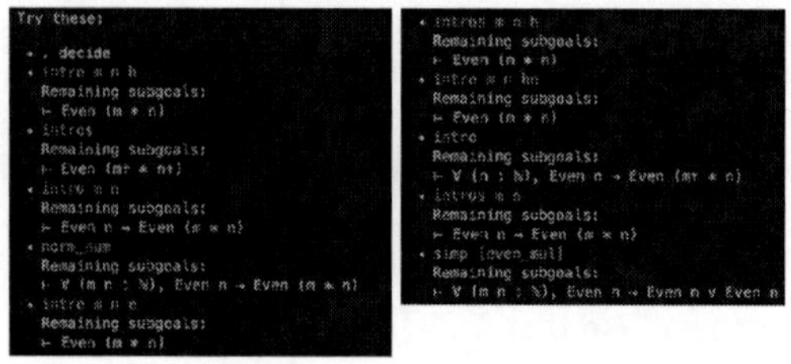

Figure 3: First list of generated tactics from `suggest_tactics` from base model ByT5. Chose first listed tactic `intro m n h` which introduces variables m and n as natural numbers and h as hypothesis that n is even.

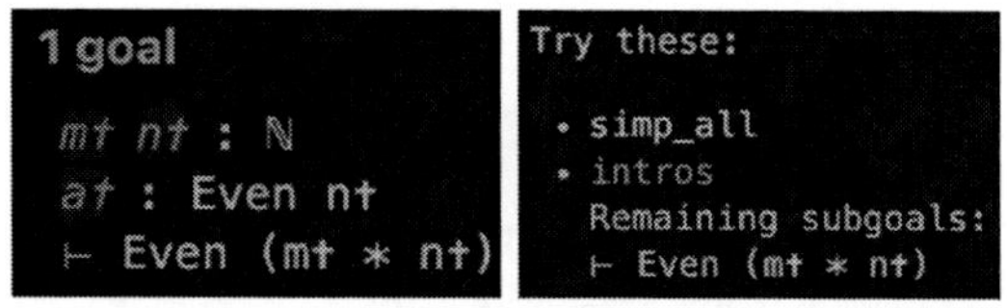

Figure 4: Left: Remaining subgoals after inputting `intro m n h` as the first tactic for ByT5 test. Suggests the renaming of m, n, and h to mt, nt, and at respectively. Remaining goal is to show `mt *nt` is even. Right: Suggested list of tactics by ByT5 after first inputted tactic; chose `simp_all` as the tactic which simplifies the current proof state, resulting in no further goals.

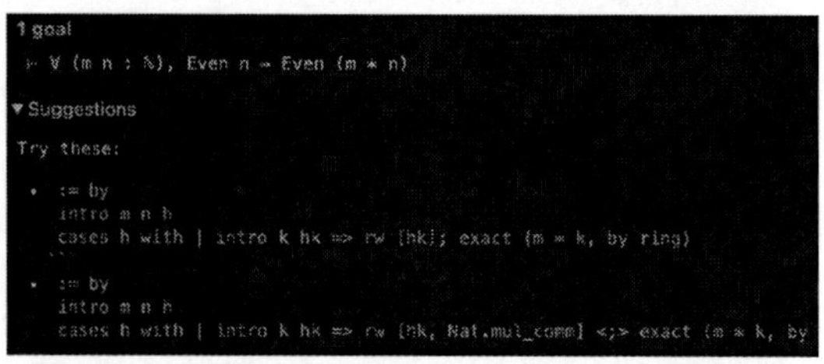

Figure 5: Generated list of tactics by LeanCotPlus7b

5.3 Pythia2.8b

In this experiment, Pythia2,8b generates long, broad lists of tactics at each step. This can be seen as advantageous as it may suggest various proof

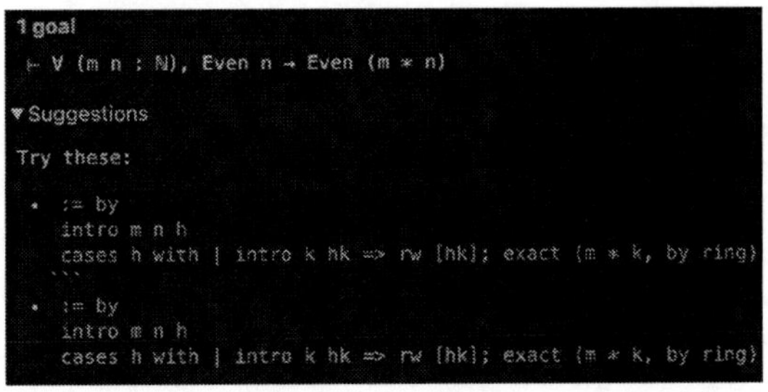

Figure 6: Generated list of tactics by LeanStarPlus7b

directions. This may also suggest that users will need a higher level of mathematical understanding to sift through all the suggested tactics in order to select one.

Figure 7: Top: Generated list of tactics by pythia2.8b. Bottom: Remaining subgoal after iniserting tactic `into m n hmn`. Tactic introduces natural number variables `m` and `n` and hypothesis `hmn`, which asserts `n` is even. Remaining subgoal is to prove `m*n` is even.

5.4 Llemma7b

Llemma7b adopts a methodical approach to proving the theorem, utilizing the tactics `even_iff_two_dvd` and `exact dvd_mul_of_dvd_left h m` as seen by Figures 9 and 10. The tactic `even_iff_two_dvd` translates the hypothesis into a form that asserts divisibility by 2, aligning with a common mathematical technique where the evenness of a number is proven by showing divisibility by 2. The use of tactic `dvd_mul_of_dvd_left` then applies this divisibility to the product of two numbers, completing the proof. This approach reflects a strategy often employed by human mathematicians, highlighting Llemma7b's capability to generate proofs that mirror traditional

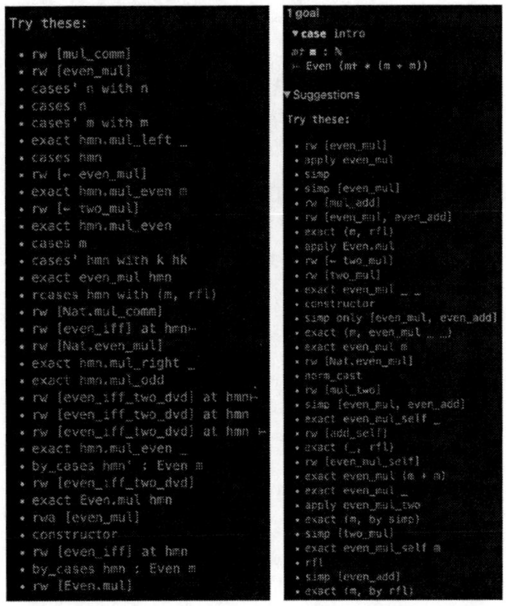

Figure 8: Left: Generated list of tactics for the second proof tactic by Pythia2.8b. Right: Remaining subgoal after inserting tactic `rw [mul_comm]` and suggested tactics for that goal.

mathematical reasoning. In contrast to the other models, which provided a broad list of tactics or rely on high-level automation, Llemma7b's proof method is distinctive in its explicit use of fundamental mathematical properties.

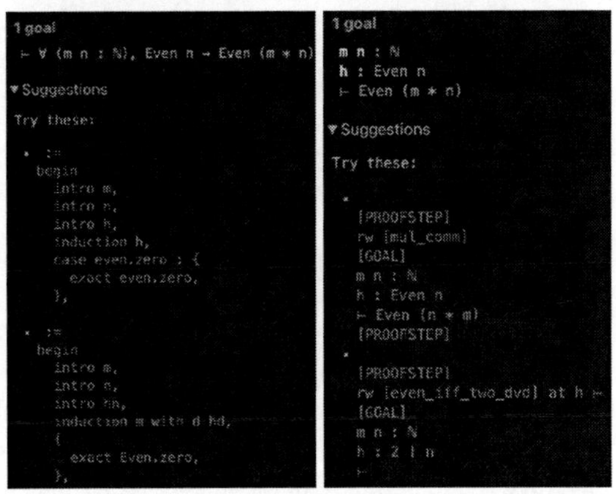

Figure 9: First and second set of tactics generated by Llemma7b

5.5 Llama-3 70b

As seen in Figure 11, the proof Llama-3 70b gave involves introducing the variables and hypothesis, deconstructing the hypothesis that n is even into

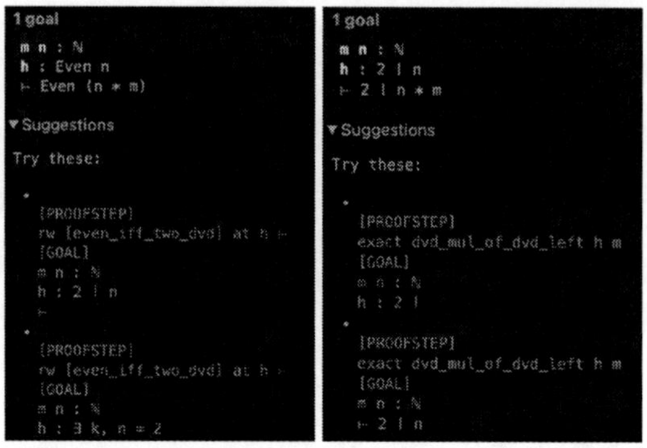

Figure 10: Third and fourth set of tactics generated by Llemma7b

the form 2 * k, and then rewriting the expression for m * n to demonstrate that it is indeed even by using known properties of even numbers. The 70 B model gave us not just one tactic but multiple tactics at a time with a majority of the steps being part of the solution. Similar to Llemma7b, it also included as part of the tactic, what the next proof goal would be for each tactic.

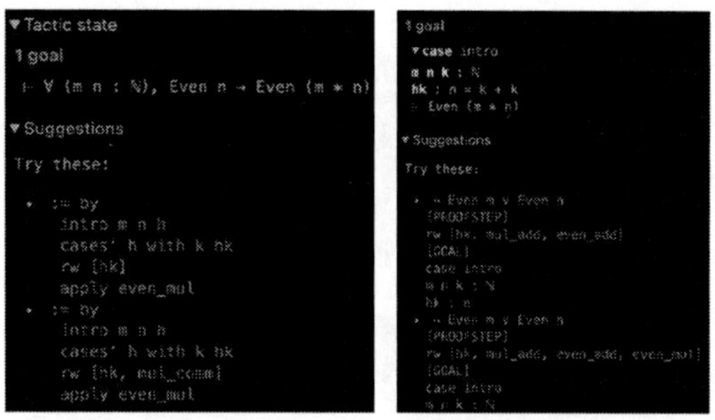

Figure 11: Progression of generated tactics by Llama-3 70b for each step of the proof from left to right

Based on our experiment results as seen in Table 1, LeanCopilot and Llama-3 70B demonstrated the highest levels of autonomy, achieving 100% autonomous proof generation with no human-entered tactics required. Pythia 2.8B also performed well, with 90% of proofs generated autonomously and an average of 0.2 human-entered tactics. LeanStarPlus 7B and LeanCoTPlus 7B both achieved 60% autonomy, with an average of 0.7 human-entered tactics, while Llemma 7B lagged behind with only 30% autonomous proofs and an average of 0.9 human-entered tactics. These results suggest that LeanCopilot and Llama-3 70B are particularly effective in fully automating proof generation, while Llemma 7B may require more human intervention in the proof process.

6 Observations

Our findings highlight the capabilities and diversity of modern language models in generating proofs within the Lean proof assistant environment. All models showcased capabilities for proof generation, but as can be seen by LeanCotPlus7b, LeanStarPlus7b, and Llama3-70b in our qualitative exmaple, some models have difficulty with just tactic generation as opposed to proof generation. Additionally, the tendency of some models, such as ByT5, to rely heavily on broad automation tactics like `simp_all` can obscure the underlying reasoning processes and limit interpretability. Interestingly, while Llemma7b produced very intuitive results in our example problem, in our experiments, it was the only model that lagged behind in both autonomous proof and tactic generation. These results highlight the need for future research to develop models that strike a better balance between automation and mathematical transparency.

7 Conclusions

In this study, we explored the integration of Large Language Models (LLMs) with Interactive Theorem Proving (ITP) systems, specifically focusing on Lean and the Lean Copilot framework. Our experiments aimed to assess the effectiveness of various LLMs in generating and automating mathematical proofs, highlighting both the potential and limitations of current technologies.

Our results demonstrated that different LLMs exhibit varied capabilities in assisting with theorem proving tasks. As shown in our qualitative example, most models appeared to rely heavily on automation, generating long lists of tactics and/or employing tactics which were vague in mathematical reasoning. Our future work would focus on benchmarking advanced models on complex theorems, developing models that enhance both automation and transparency, enabling more robust and accessible proof generation tools. Our research reinforces the promise of integrating AI with formal proof systems while highlighting areas for continued development.

8 Acknowledgments

This research used resources of the Oak Ridge Leadership Computing Facility (OLCF), which is a DOE Office of Science User Facility at the Oak

LLMs	Avg. # human entered tactics	% autonomous proof	Avg. % automated tactics
Lean Copilot	0	100%	100%
Pythia 2.8B	0.2	90%	85%
Llemma 7B	0.9	30%	55%
LeanStarPlus 7B	0.7	60%	66.67%
LeanCoTPlus 7B	0.7	60%	66.67%
Llama-3 70B	0	100%	100%

Table 1: Results from suggest_tactics integrated with various LLMs.

Ridge National Laboratory supported by the U.S. Department of Energy under Contract No. DE-AC05-00OR22725.

We would like to thank Dr. Tirthankar Ghosal for his guidance and support throughout the research. We would also like to thank Peiyang Song, for answering questions about experiments using Lean Copilot (Song et al., 2024). The code repository is available at: https://code.ornl.gov/v28/atp_lean_copilot.

References

Jeremy Avigad, Leonardo de Moura, et al. 2021. *Mathematics in Lean.* Lean Prover Community.

Zhangir Azerbayev, Hailey Schoelkopf, Keiran Paster, Marco Dos Santos, Stephen McAleer, Albert Q. Jiang, Jia Deng, Stella Biderman, and Sean Welleck. 2023. Llemma: An open language model for mathematics. *Preprint*, arXiv:2310.10631.

Zhangir Azerbayev, Hailey Schoelkopf, Keiran Paster, Marco Dos Santos, Stephen McAleer, Albert Q. Jiang, Jia Deng, Stella Biderman, and Sean Welleck. 2024. Llemma: An open language model for mathematicians. *ICLR*.

Together Computer. 2023. Redpajama: an open dataset for training large language models.

Thierry Coquand and Gérard Huet. 1988. The calculus of constructions. *Information and Computation*, 76(2):95–120.

Abhimanyu Dubey et al. 2024. The llama 3 herd of models. *Preprint*, arXiv:2407.21783.

Leo Gao, Stella Biderman, Sid Black, Laurence Golding, Travis Hoppe, Charles Foster, Jason Phang, Horace He, Anish Thite, Noa Nabeshima, Shawn Presser, and Connor Leahy. 2020. The pile: An 800gb dataset of diverse text for language modeling. *Preprint*, arXiv:2101.00027.

Jannis Limperg and Asta Halkjær From. 2023. Aesop: White-box best-first proof search for lean. In *Proceedings of the 12th ACM SIGPLAN International Conference on Certified Programs and Proofs*, CPP 2023, page 253–266, New York, NY, USA. Association for Computing Machinery.

Haohan Lin, Zhiqing Sun, Yiming Yang, and Sean Welleck. 2024. Lean-star: Learning to interleave thinking and proving. *Preprint*, arXiv:2407.10040v1.

The mathlib Community. 2020. The lean mathematical library. In *Proceedings of the 9th ACM SIGPLAN International Conference on Certified Programs and Proofs*. ACM.

Robert Milner. 1972. Logic for computable functions: description of a machine implementation.

Leonardo de Moura and Sebastian Ullrich. 2021. The lean 4 theorem prover and programming language. In *Automated Deduction – CADE 28: 28th International Conference on Automated Deduction, Virtual Event, July 12–15, 2021, Proceedings*, page 625–635, Berlin, Heidelberg. Springer-Verlag.

Keiran Paster, Marco Dos Santos, Zhangir Azerbayev, and Jimmy Ba. 2024. Openwebmath: An open dataset of high-quality mathematical web text. In *The Twelfth International Conference on Learning Representations*.

Lawrence C. Paulson. 1986. Natural deduction as higher-order resolution. *The Journal of Logic Programming*, 3(3):237–258.

Peiyang Song, Kaiyu Yang, and Anima Anandkumar. 2024. Towards large language models as copilots for theorem proving in lean. *Preprint*, arXiv:2404.12534.

Huajian Xin, Daya Guo, Zhihong Shao, Zhizhou Ren, Qihao Zhu, Bo Liu, Chong Ruan, Wenda Li, and Xiaodan Liang. 2024. Deepseek-prover: Advancing theorem proving in llms through large-scale synthetic data. *Preprint*, arXiv:2405.14333.

Linting Xue, Aditya Barua, Noah Constant, Rami Al-Rfou, Sharan Narang, Mihir Kale, Adam Roberts, and Colin Raffel. 2021. Byt5: Towards a token-free future with pre-trained byte-to-byte models. *CoRR*, abs/2105.13626.

Kaiyu Yang, Aidan M. Swope, Alex Gu, Rahul Chalamala, Peiyang Song, Shixing Yu, Saad Godil, Ryan

Prenger, and Anima Anandkumar. 2023. Leandojo: Theorem proving with retrieval-augmented language models. *Preprint*, arXiv:2306.15626.

Eric Zelikman, Yuhuai Wu, Jesse Mu, and Noah D. Goodman. 2022. Star: Bootstrapping reasoning with reasoning. *Preprint*, arXiv:2203.14465.

Kunhao Zheng, Jesse Michael Han, and Stanislas Polu. 2022. Minif2f: a cross-system benchmark for formal olympiad-level mathematics. *Preprint*, arXiv:2109.00110.

The Grid: A semi-automated tool to support expert-driven modeling

Allegra A. Beal Cohen[1] **Maria Alexeeva**[2]

Keith Alcock[2] **Mihai Surdeanu**[2]

[1] University of Florida, Gainesville, FL, USA
[2] University of Arizona, Tucson, AZ, USA
allegra.ab.cohen@gmail.com

Abstract

When building models of human behavior, we often struggle to find data that capture important factors at the right level of granularity. In these cases, we must rely on expert knowledge to build models. To help partially automate the organization of expert knowledge for modeling, we combine natural language processing (NLP) and machine learning (ML) methods in a tool called the Grid. The Grid helps users organize textual knowledge into clickable cells along two dimensions using iterative, collaborative clustering. We conduct a user study to explore participants' reactions to the Grid, as well as to investigate whether its clustering feature helps participants organize a corpus of expert knowledge. We find that participants using the Grid's clustering feature appeared to work more efficiently than those without it, but written feedback about the clustering was critical. We conclude that the general design of the Grid was positively received and that some of the user challenges can likely be mitigated through the use of LLMs.

1 Introduction

The increasing availability of text data has transformed our ability to model human behavior in social and economic systems. We can now monitor and model phenomena entirely through preexisting text sources like social media, news articles and journal papers. However, these data sometimes fail to capture the causal information we need to build models. For example, news articles may describe what has happened in a region (e.g., "Farmers harvest early") but not why (e.g., "Granivorous birds nearby"). In these cases, one of the best ways to interpret and supplement existing data is to ask local experts for causal explanations of how people think and behave.

Despite the value of expert knowledge, the process of converting it into models remains largely manual and expensive. Fortunately, NLP and ML capabilities have drastically improved since the heyday of expert systems (Devlin, 2018; Ramage et al., 2009; Surdeanu et al., 2022; Schild et al., 2022). If we can partially automate the work required to process expert knowledge, then we can drive more accurate and nuanced modeling of human behavior. While existing NLP and ML methods are powerful, processing expert knowledge presents different challenges than processing large pre-existing text corpora. With this in mind, we combine NLP, ML and visualization methods in a tool designed to satisfy the following criteria based on our experience building models from expert knowledge.

First, NLP tools for processing expert knowledge must allow users to explore text quickly at multiple levels of abstraction. Existing approaches often force a trade-off between digestible summaries and thorough analysis. For example, knowledge graphs can quickly orient users to important topics and relationships, but as the size of the knowledge base grows, topics must be aggregated for the graphs to remain interpretable by humans. Similarly, while Large Language Models (LLMs) are becoming ever more adept at answering questions and providing summaries, they alone do not support multiple levels of abstraction; rather, they require prompts that may be difficult to write during the early stages of analysis when the characteristics and objectives of the user's model are not yet defined.

Second, NLP tools for processing expert knowledge should assign work based on the different capabilities of humans and machines. Many popular topic modeling methods are fully automated, but users are likely to have domain expertise, some familiarity with their corpora, and objectives for analysis and model-building. This expertise should be used to guide the machine. Machines should relieve users of repetitive work and discover patterns that users might not detect, without overriding user decisions. Tools should also support a range of processes and strategies from human users.

Proceedings of the 1st Workshop on NLP for Science (NLP4Science), pages 219–229
November 16, 2024 ©2024 Association for Computational Linguistics

In this paper we introduce the Grid (Figure 1), an expert knowledge tool designed to satisfy these two criteria. We first describe the mechanics of the Grid, and then we report results from a user study. Based on our results, we conclude that the Grid supports the efficient organization of expert knowledge and report on challenges and potential solutions for future work on expert-driven modeling tools.

2 The Grid

The Grid is a tool for visualizing and curating expert knowledge. Grids organize textual knowledge into clickable cells along two dimensions. The rows of the Grid represent structural characteristics of the corpus that do not change across topics, and the columns represent topics from the corpus that the user and the Grid work together to discover. The difference between rows and columns is illustrated in Figure 1. Figure 1.a shows a Grid that was created to organize knowledge about the work of an artist, so the rows represent calendar years while the columns represent art media, locations, exhibitions and so on. Figure 1.b shows a Grid that was created to organize interviews with an expert on rice production in Senegal, so the rows represent interviewee and interview date and the columns represent agronomic topics.

The color of each cell in the Grid indicates how much text it contains. Clicking on a Grid cell reveals the sentences it contains and clicking on a sentence reveals the surrounding context (Figure 1b). The user can move and copy sentences between columns, rename columns, and generate columns anchored by keywords. Since the rows in the Grid represent immutable characteristics of the corpus, (e.g., dates or other properties properties of the data points), the user cannot manipulate rows in the same way. The next sections describe how the user and the Grid work together to curate columns through iterative clustering.

2.1 Preparing the corpus

To prepare a corpus for use by the Grid, we first break text into documents. In this paper, our document unit was the sentence. The set of documents is then pre-processed by removing punctuation and stopwords and lemmatizing. Next, the cleaned documents are converted into vector embeddings. For each document, a mean weighted vector is generated using embeddings from the GloVe model (Pennington et al., 2014):

$$V = \frac{\sum_{i=0}^{N} e_i \cdot tfidf_i}{N} \quad (1)$$

where e_i is the vector embedding of word i in the sentence, $tfidf_i$ is its term frequency-inverse document frequency, and N is the number of words in the sentence. Term frequency-inverse document frequency is a statistical method of measuring word importance, where the frequency of a word in a document is compared to how common it is across all documents.

Grids can be *anchored* by specific terms to allow users to focus on subsets of large corpora. For Grids with anchor terms, a subcorpus is generated that contains all documents with the anchor term. This subcorpus is then used to populate the anchored Grid. For example, a Grid anchored by the word "harvest" will contain only documents with the word "harvest" in them, allowing the user to narrow their focus.

2.2 Curating columns

The user and the machine collaborate to cluster document semantic representations or vector embeddings (shortened to "documents" for the remainder of this paper) into columns. This collaboration presents a technical challenge beyond conventional clustering, because user decisions must take precedence over clustering moves made by the machine. We handle collaboration through three types of columns: machine-generated, which contain only the documents clustered by the machine (the first row of Figure 2); frozen columns, created by the user and which the machine is not allowed to change (columns 5-7 in row second row of Figure 2); and seeded columns, which are non-frozen columns that the user has added documents to (see Appendix A for the details on column types).

These three types of columns allow the user to control how the machine contributes to the curation process. The user decides *when* the machine contributes by clicking the "Update" button in the interface. When the Grid updates, all documents outside the frozen columns are re-clustered. The third row of Figure 2 shows the example Grid after the user has requested an update. Note that the user-defined columns written in black text persist, and the machine-generated columns in blue text have changed in response to the user's contributions, highlighting new concepts like "credit."

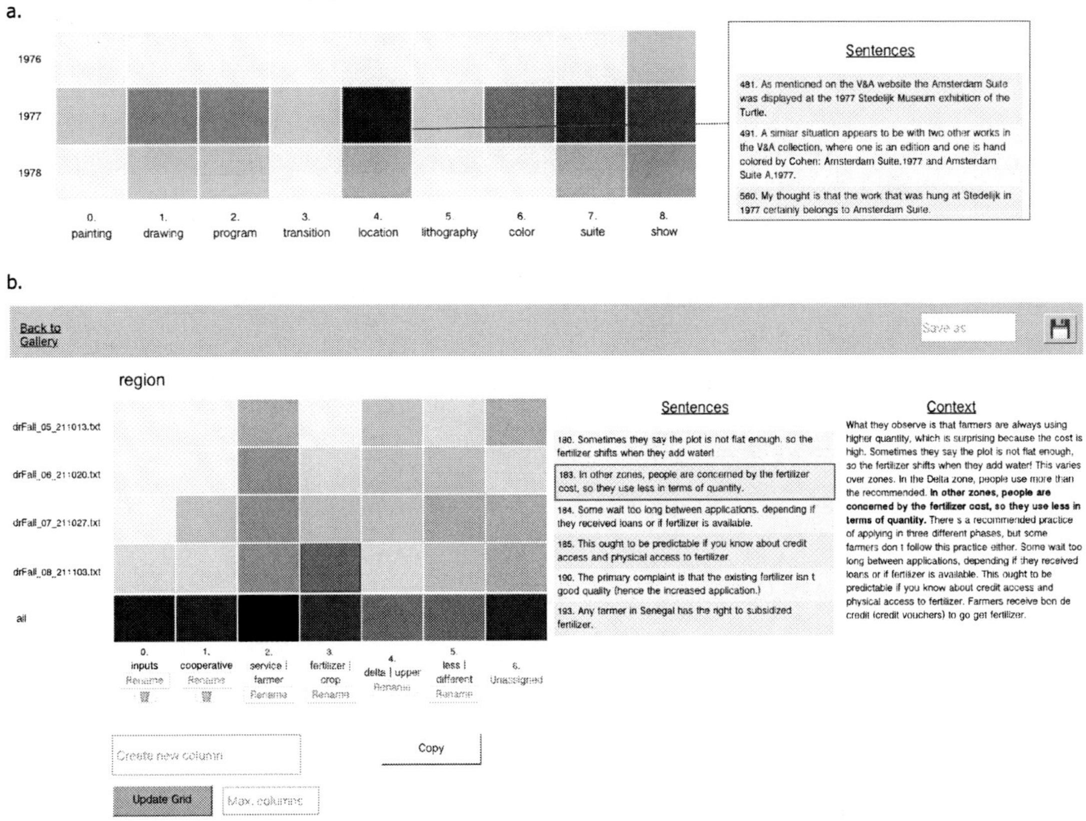

Figure 1: Examples of Grids: **a.** An excerpt of a Grid created using a corpus of emails about an artist, organized along a timeline of when works were made. **b.** An excerpt of a Grid organized by interviewee and date, showing the larger tool interface. Cells in Grids can be clicked on to reveal documents. Documents themselves can be clicked on to show the context, e.g., a sentence in its surrounding interview context.

2.3 Method of clustering

An important feature of the Grid is that documents can appear in multiple columns. To support this, the Grid uses the fuzzy c-means clustering algorithm to assign documents to columns (Bezdek et al., 1984). Fuzzy c-means clustering works by calculating the degree of membership between documents and a given number of k columns. It minimizes the distance between documents and columns, weighted by the degree of membership. Documents are typically assigned random membership coefficients at the beginning of clustering and these coefficients are updated throughout the clustering process. We make one modification to the algorithm: The user-added documents from seeded columns are assigned fixed membership coefficients to ensure that they remain together in the groupings specified by the user.

The number of columns k is selected by running fuzzy c-means clustering multiple times and choosing the k that produces the best model as scored by the Calinski-Harabasz (CH) index (Caliński and Harabasz, 1974). The CH index assigns higher scores to clustering solutions with clusters that contain similar documents internally but that are well-separated from each other. The index is calculated as follows:

$$CH = \frac{(n-k)}{(k-1)} \frac{B}{W} \quad (2)$$

$$B = \sum_{i=1}^{k} n_i dist(centroid_i, meta\_centroid)^2 \quad (3)$$

$$W = \sum_{i=1}^{k} \sum_{j=1}^{n_i} dist(d_j, centroid_i)^2 \quad (4)$$

where n is the number of documents, k is the number of columns, $centroid_i$ is the average vector embedding of column i, $meta\_centroid$ is the average vector embedding of all documents, B is the

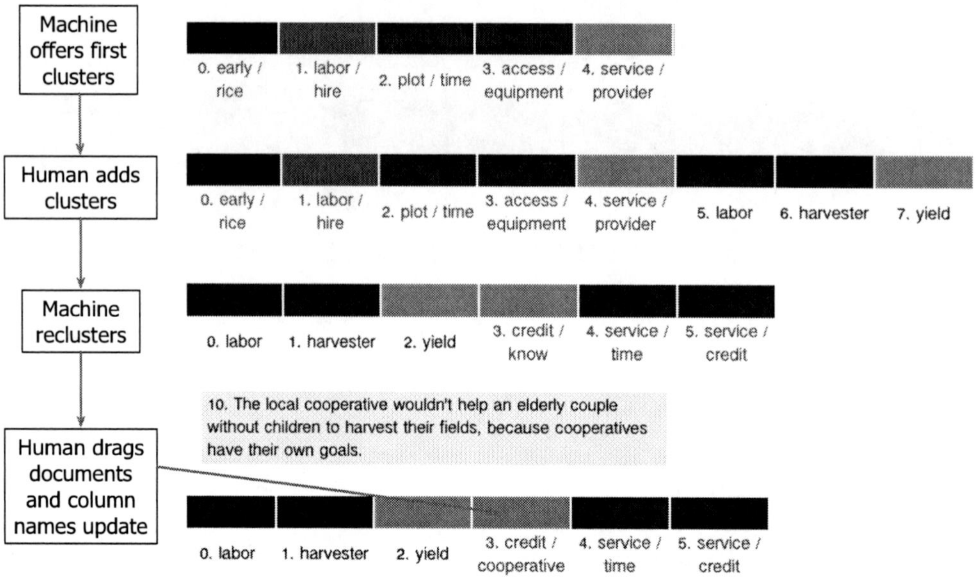

Figure 2: Collaboration on columns between user and machine. Each rectangle is a Grid column, where the color indicates the total number of documents summed over rows. Names in blue indicate machine-generated; names in black indicate user-created.

between distance of the model, and W is the within distance of the model. Frozen columns are included in the CH index calculation because we intend to score the results of collaboration between the user and the machine, not the machine-generated solution alone.

3 Study Methodology

We conducted a user study to explore users' reactions to the Grid and to investigate whether iterative, human-machine clustering helps users organize text more efficiently. We asked study participants to curate an 80-sentence corpus in the agricultural domain (see the section titled *Study corpus*) using the Grid and then take a timed test about concepts in the corpus. Participants were assigned to three conditions with differing levels of automation. In the following section, we discuss the details of the study design.

3.1 Study design

Thirty-nine participants were recruited from multiple domains including development practice, computer science, agricultural engineering and bioengineering. Participants were recruited from academia and included graduate students and faculty members.

We compared the Grid to two versions of itself, resulting in three experimental conditions: treatment, placebo, and control. In the treatment condition, the Grid worked as described in the section titled *Method of Clustering* (Section 2.3). In the placebo condition, the Grid randomly assigned documents to columns instead of clustering them with the previously-described algorithm. The placebo condition was included to test whether participants actually liked the behavior of the Grid or were simply trusting the results of the algorithm regardless of quality (Pan et al., 2007).

In the control condition, participants interacted with a Grid that did no clustering at all. In this condition, participants could create columns using keywords and those columns would be automatically populated, but the machine would not generate any of its own columns. This condition is closest to the spreadsheet-based coding that many social scientists use to process interviews, though it retains the clean visualization of the Grid as well as the automation of keyword-based column creation.

Participants were assigned randomly to the three experimental conditions, with 13 participants in each.

3.2 Procedure

The study was conducted remotely using the Grid hosted on a server. The participants received training for using the Grid, interacted with the tool to organize the study corpus (the curation stage), and completed a test task and a feedback questionnaire. For more details on the study logistics, see Appendix C.

During the curation stage, each participant was provided with an initial Grid to organize. Those in the treatment condition began with a five-column Grid generated through the algorithm described in Section 2.3. Participants in the placebo condition began with a five-column Grid generated randomly. Participants in the control condition were given a Grid with a single column containing all corpus documents.

3.3 Study corpus

This study used a corpus of expert knowledge about the rice production system in the Senegal River Valley that the authors developed in a related research project. During that project we elicited knowledge from two local experts through qualitative semi-structured interviews. Eighty sentences from these interviews form the corpus for the current user study.

For this study, the rows—the dimension that is associated with structural, topic-independent characteristics of the Grid—represent modeling dynamics since those are commonly used in simulation models. In particular, we manually assigned each document to one of the five modeling dynamics: causes, conditions, decisions, processes, and proportions (see Appendix B).

3.4 Data collection

The study website recorded participants' answers to test questions as well as their written feedback about their experiences with the Grid. Participants were asked to rate their experiences using the Grid on a 5-point Likert scale from "Very poor" to "Excellent." Participants then responded to open answer questions about what they liked and disliked about the Grid, as well as their strategies for using it.

The study website also recorded the actions participants took while using the Grid (i.e., clicks, drags, column creation and updates.) Various summary statistics were calculated from these quantitative data. For example, the amount of work done by participants was calculated as the cumulative number of sentences moved during the curation stage of the experiment. This includes sentences that were moved as part of column creation (e.g., when a user creates a column, we count all the sentences moved by the Grid into that column) as well as dragging sentences between columns. In the placebo and treatment conditions, the cumulative number of sentences moved by the machine during reclustering was also calculated.

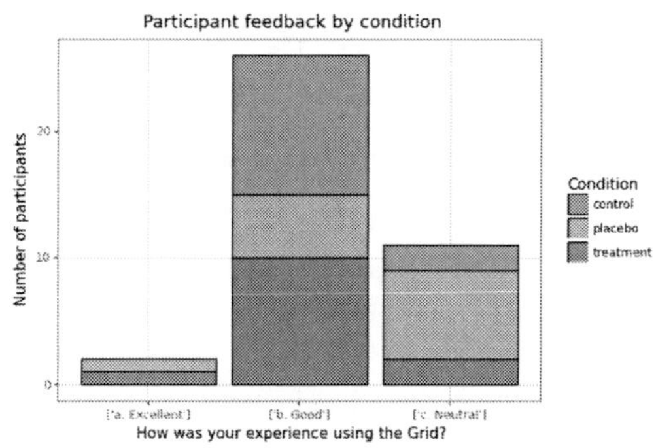

Figure 3: User feedback about the Grid experience. Users were given answer options along a five-point Likert scale, but no responses rated lower than "Neutral."

Participant performance on the test questions was scored by calculating precision and recall. Precision is calculated as the number of answers given correctly divided by the total number of answers given. Recall is calculated as the number of answers given correctly divided by the total number of correct answers (e.g., if a question has two correct answers and the participant gives only one, their recall is 0.5).

4 Results

4.1 Feedback scores

Figure 3 shows the Likert-score feedback given by participants. All participants rated the Grid experience as "Neutral" or higher. Participants in the placebo condition rated the Grid experience as worse more often than participants in the control and treatment conditions. Treating the responses of participants numerically, where 1 = "Very poor" and 5 = "Excellent", the average scores by condition were 3.85 for the control condition, 3.54 for the placebo condition, and 3.92 for the treatment condition.

The feedback in the form of open-ended question responses demonstrated that participants liked the concept and the visualization of the Grid, calling it "easy", "flexible", and "intuitive". For more details on qualitative feedback, see Appendix D.

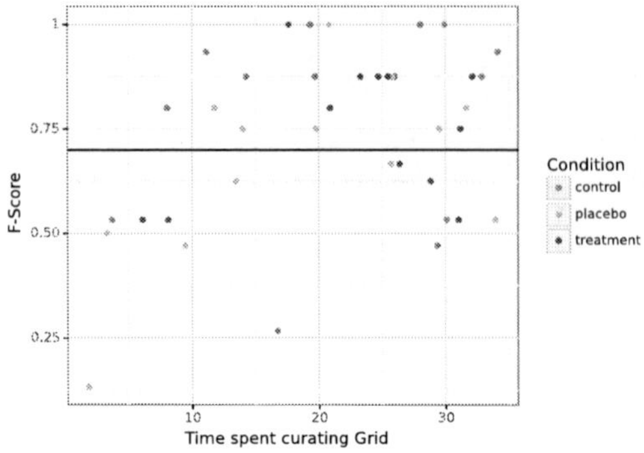

Figure 4: Participant F-scores (y-axis) compared to the time each participant spent curating their Grid (x-axis), colored by experimental condition.

4.2 Test results

The test scores of participants were not significantly different across experimental conditions. The average precision and recall scores were 0.75 and 0.72. We did find that scores (combined into a single F-score for each participant) for participants in the placebo and treatment conditions correlated nonlinearly with time spent building Grids. Figure 4 shows that participants fall roughly into three groups: Those that spent little time curating their Grids and did not do well on the test; those that spent roughly ten minutes or more curating their Grids and did well on the test; and those who spent half an hour or more curating their Grids but did not do well on the test. Figure 4 includes a dividing line at 0.7 demonstrating this rough grouping.

4.3 Cumulative work done by condition

Participants in the control condition moved more sentences on average than participants in the placebo and treatment conditions (μ_{control} = 172, μ_{placebo} = 85, $\mu_{\text{treatment}}$ = 109; t(24) = 2.42, $p < 0.03$ for control-placebo comparison and t(24) = 1.66, $p < 0.12$ for control-treatment condition). We do not attribute the difference in sentences moved to the total amount of time that participants spent curating their Grids, because this time was not significantly different between conditions. We also do not suspect that participants in the control condition did more work because they enjoyed using the Grid more than other participants, because participants from the control and treatment conditions gave similar feedback scores. Thus, we suspect that participants in the control condition did more work than participants in the placebo and treatment conditions because the latter were successfully aided by the contributions of the machine.

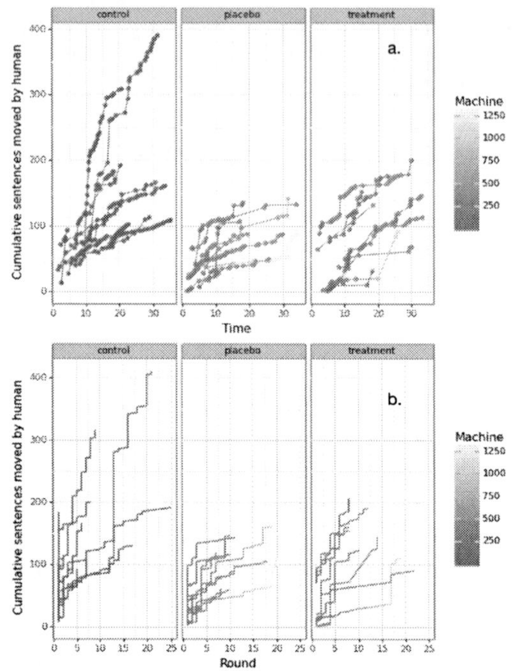

Figure 5: Cumulative sentences moved by the participant and by the machine for each experimental condition.

We examined the strategies that participants used to curate the study corpus. Participants spent time on actions such as sentence dragging and column creation, illustrated in Figure 5a. The y-axis shows the cumulative numbers of sentences moved by individual participants and the x-axis shows time elapsed. Each line represents the activity of an individual participant, and the color corresponds to the cumulative number of sentences moved by the Grid's clustering algorithm. The control condition is plotted in gray because there was no clustering algorithm in that condition.

A variety of user styles is evident in Figure 5a, from an exclusive preference for column creation to progress made almost entirely through sentence dragging. Points that are closely clustered along the y-axis show participants dragging sentences from column to column; larger increases in point elevation indicate that participants are creating columns, i.e., moving a larger number of sentences all at once. The range of strategies shown in Figure 5a is reflected in participants' written feedback. Many reported that the primary benefit of the Grid was the ability to organize big chunks of information quickly, with some even finding the sentence-dragging feature to be too granular. Others liked that they could move individual sentences by dragging.

4.4 Interaction with the machine

The total number of times participants interacted with their Grids through updating was not significantly different across conditions. However, written opinions about the behavior of the Grid varied.

Participants in both the placebo and treatment conditions reported frustration with the Grid's updating feature (see Appendix D.2 for details). Possible signs of frustration among these participants are visible in Figure 5b. This plot is very similar to Figure 5a, except that the x-axis measures rounds elapsed instead of time elapsed. "Rounds" were counted by how often the user clicks "Update"; for example, Figure 5b shows that most participants across conditions did not update their Grids more than 10 times, while a few updated 20 times. We note possible frustration in the number of updates requested by participants in the placebo and treatment conditions. Several of the lines change color from blue to yellow while maintaining shallow slopes, indicating repeated requests for the machine to do work without corresponding moves made by the participant.

While positive feedback to the updating feature was varied (see Appendix D.2), the data show that some participants worked with the machine rather efficiently. Figure 5b shows a contingent of participants in both the placebo and treatment conditions who accomplished a steadily growing amount of work within ten rounds, perhaps indicating that the machine provided good results in response to participants' first requests. The slope of the lines of these participants is steeper for participants in the treatment condition than for participants in the placebo condition, as we would expect given that the treatment condition was designed to provide better results.

Participants in the control condition were more satisfied with the level of automation in the Grid than participants in the placebo and treatment conditions, even though they did not have access to the column clustering feature. One said, "The coolest feature of the grid is creating new columns and hitting the 'update grid' feature to automatically populate the sentences. It was very cool to be able to parse out a subset of content using key words." Another reported that they "liked the automated aspect of it. Knowing all sentences with the keyword selected would be moved/duplicated to the corresponding column was a helpful way to systematically filter down the information at hand." However, one participant did report that they "did not like that the original column updated on its own based on the remaining information, as it tended to be a bit disjointed."

4.5 Column creation

Participants tended to create between five and ten columns to organize the 80-sentence corpus, with fewer than 20 sentences per column. In the control condition, participants steadily added columns over time, but participants in the placebo and treatment conditions settled on a number of columns within the first ten minutes and then made smaller additions or subtractions. In general, participants in the treatment condition had slightly more columns than participants in the other conditions. Participants in the placebo condition had the fewest number of columns on average.

Participants in all conditions wrote feedback appreciating the automation surrounding keywords and column creation. One participant said that they "liked that the columns included every form of the word rather than just the specific word." A participant in the control condition said that the machine tended to "correctly place information that I thought should be included in [the columns]." One participant reported feeling frustrated that some sentences left over at the end of the curation process did not fit easily into any of the columns they had created.

Participants in all conditions settled on a similar number of columns (the average being ten). However, participants did not all give their columns the same names; the topics in the columns varied more than the number of columns. Table E in the Appendix shows the most and least common words used in column names. The most common words align with the main themes of the interview corpus (e.g., equipment, timing and finances), as judged by the researchers present during the interviews. Participants reported that, during the test, they were able to use the columns they had created to find the relevant information.

4.6 Quality of columns

The quality of Grids is difficult to assess because knowledge curation tasks lack ground truth due to their inherent subjectivity. However, we can evaluate participants' columns using the same Calinski-Harabasz (CH) index employed in the clustering algorithm (Caliński and Harabasz, 1974). While using the CH index as a measure of quality does tip the scales in favor of the treatment condition, the participants have direction over the clustering algorithm and it is conceivable that human decisions might drive the quality of columns down over time. But when we calculate the CH index for individual participants' Grids over time, we find that 98% of the time, participants in the treatment condition score higher than the highest-scoring participant in the control and placebo conditions. Thus the advantage of using the treatment algorithm persists past Grid initialization.

5 Discussion and Conclusions

The Grid combines NLP, ML and visualization methods to assist users in the organization of expert knowledge corpora. We have presented results from a user study meant to evaluate this combination of methods. Here we draw conclusions about whether the Grid successfully satisfies the criteria laid out in the introduction.

First, we conclude that the Grid allowed users to process the knowledge corpus quickly at multiple levels of abstraction. The organizational power and visualization of the Grid was well-received by participants with diverse expertise and skill sets. Participants in all conditions appreciated the speed with which they could organize information and even participants in the somewhat frustrating placebo condition were able to answer test questions using their Grids. The high test results in all conditions may in part be a ceiling effect; however, we do not discount the role of the Grid in allowing participants to rapidly familiarize themselves with a corpus they had not seen before. Moreover, participants were afforded a large amount of flexibility in how they used the Grid. Participants were able to use different combinations of column creation and sentence dragging to organize information, and they reported preferences for different strategies in the written feedback. Participants often shifted between large organizational moves like column creation and more precise moves like sentence dragging, indicating that the Grid allowed them to work at different levels of abstraction. The number of columns for each participant was similar, but the column names were different, indicating that the Grid allowed participants to organize information in the way that made the best sense to them.

Whether the Grid successfully assigned work based on the different capabilities of humans and machines is less clear. The participants using the Grid's clustering algorithm appeared to work more efficiently than those without it, but written feedback about the clustering was critical. Participants in the placebo and treatment conditions reported that behavior of the Grid's clustering algorithm was confusing and sometimes counterproductive, while participants in the control condition praised the much simpler automated column populating. This indicates that efficiency is not sufficient for a satisfying user experience and that future work on collaborative algorithms should focus on transparency. For example, the inclusion of LLMs in the collaborative process could allow for explanations of why sentences are grouped together in Grid columns.

The Grid tool provides support for organizing expert knowledge in an expert-driven modeling pipeline. While our user study revealed some challenges in the design of such tools, we find the results encouraging and suspect that many of the lessons learned, such as the frustration with the clustering algorithm, may be mitigated in future versions by enlisting LLMs to provide explanations for the user. The Grid can be expanded to include other parts of the knowledge engineering process, such as a semi-automated model generation step after knowledge has been organized. We conclude that semi-automated tools like the Grid can play valuable roles in multiple research communities and have the potential to support more nuanced and local models of human behavior.

The code for the Grid tool is available at `https://github.com/Allegra-Cohen/grid`.

6 Acknowledgments

The authors thank Paul Cohen and Gerrit Hoogenboom for helpful suggestions and support, and the anonymous reviewers for the helpful discussion. This work was supported by the Defense Advanced Research Projects Agency (DARPA) under the Habitus program. The content of this paper does not necessarily reflect the position or the policy of the Government, and no official endorsement should be inferred. Maria Alexeeva, Keith Alcock, and Mihai Surdeanu declare a financial interest in lum.ai. This interest has been properly disclosed to the University of Arizona Institutional Review Committee and is managed in accordance with its conflict of interest policies.

References

James C Bezdek, Robert Ehrlich, and William Full. 1984. Fcm: The fuzzy c-means clustering algorithm. *Computers & geosciences*, 10(2-3):191–203.

Tadeusz Caliński and Jerzy Harabasz. 1974. A dendrite method for cluster analysis. *Communications in Statistics-theory and Methods*, 3(1):1–27.

Jacob Devlin. 2018. Bert: Pre-training of deep bidirectional transformers for language understanding. *arXiv preprint arXiv:1810.04805*.

Bing Pan, Helene Hembrooke, Thorsten Joachims, Lori Lorigo, Geri Gay, and Laura Granka. 2007. In google we trust: Users' decisions on rank, position, and relevance. *Journal of computer-mediated communication*, 12(3):801–823.

Jeffrey Pennington, Richard Socher, and Christopher D Manning. 2014. Glove: Global vectors for word representation. In *Proceedings of the 2014 conference on empirical methods in natural language processing (EMNLP)*, pages 1532–1543.

Daniel Ramage, David Hall, Ramesh Nallapati, and Christopher D Manning. 2009. Labeled lda: A supervised topic model for credit attribution in multi-labeled corpora. In *Proceedings of the 2009 conference on empirical methods in natural language processing*, pages 248–256.

Erwan Schild, Gautier Durantin, Jean-Charles Lamirel, and Florian Miconi. 2022. Iterative and semi-supervised design of chatbots using interactive clustering. *International Journal of Data Warehousing and Mining (IJDWM)*, 18(2):1–19.

Mihai Surdeanu, John Hungerford, Yee Seng Chan, Jessica MacBride, Benjamin Gyori, Andrew Zupon, Zheng Tang, Haoling Qiu, Bonan Min, Yan Zverev, Caitlin Hilverman, Max Thomas, Walter Andrews, Keith Alcock, Zeyu Zhang, Michael Reynolds, Steven Bethard, Rebecca Sharp, and Egoitz Laparra. 2022. Taxonomy builder: a data-driven and user-centric tool for streamlining taxonomy construction. In *Proceedings of the Second Workshop on Bridging Human–Computer Interaction and Natural Language Processing*, pages 1–10, Seattle, Washington. Association for Computational Linguistics.

A Column Types

Machine-generated columns are those that contain only documents that have been clustered by the machine. Grids are initialized with machine-generated columns. The first row of Figure 2 shows a Grid with five machine-generated columns marked in blue text. The machine names columns by selecting the top two tokens in the column as ranked by tf-idf.

Frozen columns are those that the machine is not allowed to change. Users can create frozen columns using keywords, such as the "labor," "harvest," and "yield" columns in the second row of Figure 2. Each column contains only sentences about its lemmatized keyword. For example, the "labor" column contains only sentences with the word "labor." Users can also freeze existing columns by renaming them (in which case documents in the renamed column needn't contain the user-assigned name). When a column is frozen, the machine is barred from moving documents in and out of it during clustering. Documents in frozen columns also cannot be placed in other columns by the machine, which reduces the amount of organizational work left for the user. Frozen columns are useful when the user has a topic in mind and doesn't want the machine to interfere.

Seeded columns are non-frozen columns to which the user has added one or more documents. When the user drag-and-drops documents into a column, that column becomes seeded (see row four in Figure 2.) During clustering, these user-added documents remain in the seeded column, but the machine is allowed to move other documents in and out of that column. Seeded columns are useful when the user wants to group a handful of documents, but would like the machine to decide which others to include with them.

B Classifying Rows for the Study

The Grid was developed to organize expert knowledge for use in simulation models. Thus, we wanted to organize knowledge into modeling dynamics that bore some resemblance to the code we would write, e.g., conditional language corresponding to `if / else` statements.

We selected five modeling dynamics as rows for Grids in this study: causes, conditions, decisions, processes, and proportions. Documents are classified into rows based on whether they contain information about these dynamics. We define documents as containing causal language if we can identify some X as being responsible for some Y, and containing conditional language if some X is a condition of Y. Documents contain decisions if there is an entity selecting from more than one option. We define documents as containing processes if there is language about something beginning, ending, or occurring at a specific time or in relation to another process, or if there is language about events occurring in sequence. If some X is compared to some Y, such as with language like "larger" or "more", then the documents contain proportions. Because documents can contain multiple modeling dynamics, we allowed documents to appear in multiple rows. Documents were assigned to rows by hand in this study. Adding automated classifiers is a direction of future research.

C Study logistics

The study was conducted remotely through a website. Participants joined a Zoom room with a researcher present, and then logged into the website using assigned ID numbers. A detailed consent form was provided to which participants agreed in order to continue.

Participants first went through three pages of training, which typically took ten to fifteen minutes, and asked the researcher any questions they had about the Grid. The training was tailored to participants' study conditions.

After completing the training, participants moved on to the next page of the website. On this page, they were given 35 minutes to organize the study corpus using the Grid following these instructions:

> Today you will be working with a corpus of expert knowledge about rice harvesting in the Senegal River Valley. You will have 35 minutes to organize the expert knowledge using the Grid tool. When you are done, you will be tested on the important concepts in this corpus, so please organize your Grid in such a way that you can find information quickly. Think about how you would organize information in your own research; the columns of your Grid should contain what you think are the important themes or variables related to rice harvesting.

During the 35-minute curation phase, when participants in the treatment condition clicked the "Update" button, the Grid returned a new clustering solution using the algorithm described in the *Method of Clustering* section. The Grids of participants in the placebo condition returned random columns. For participants in the control condition, clicking the "Update" button simply removed the sentences from the original column that had already been assigned to participant-created columns. In this condition, the "Update" button helped to tidy up the Grid but did not propose new columns.

After organizing their Grids, participants moved on to a test page that contained their curated Grids and seven multiple choice questions about the content of the corpus. The test questions were designed to strike a balance between broad themes in the corpus and details for which participants would have to read carefully. For example, the first question,

> What could cause a farmer to harvest late? (Select all that apply.)
>
> (a) Bird attacks
> (b) A lack of labor
> (c) Competition for equipment

highlighted the role of labor and equipment in harvest timing (a reoccurring theme throughout the corpus) but also required participants to know that bird attacks cause farmers to harvest early, not late (a more subtle detail in the corpus.)

Participants were given 10 minutes to complete the test using their Grids, at which point they were taken to a feedback page and the end of the study. Finally, participants were debriefed about the condition they were in and the purpose of the study.

D Qualitative Feedback

D.1 Grid concept and visualization

The concept of a tool to quickly organize information into columns was well-received by participants. Participants from all conditions called the Grid "simple," "easy," "convenient," "flexible," "fun," and "intuitive." Participants appreciated the speed at which the Grid allowed them to work and said they liked how it helped them turn disorganized columns into columns that were "well-organized and easier to access." Participants also enjoyed features that allowed them to dig deeper into the Grid content, such as being able to click on sentences to read their surrounding interview context. One participant from the treatment condition said, "It is so flexible ... I can reorganize stuff the way I want ... Super fun to work with."

Participants particularly liked the visualization of the Grid. One said, "I think the visualization with the shading was very intuitive and made the organization process quick and easy to iterate." Participants liked that the colors of the Grid indicated the distribution of information across columns, saying that it quickly allowed them to infer how "good" their columns were; one participant reported, "I liked the color coding a lot – helped me know which columns were maybe too big, and which were maybe unnecessary or perhaps poorly defined." Another said the Grid was a "good and innovative way to display information to the user."

After completing the study, some participants reported that it had been "fun" and "relaxing." One participant exclaimed, "Where have you been all my life?" and several participants from both the control and treatment conditions signed up to continue using the tool after the study.

D.2 Interaction with the machine

Written feedback showed some frustration among the participants in the conditions that involved clustering. One participant in the placebo condition said, "Very very quirky to use and it was very difficult to get a sense of what the task was." Another participant in the placebo condition reported, "I didn't like how little control I had over what happened during an 'update' – there were different numbers of new columns appearing, etc. I was hesitant to do too many edits once I had a few columns because, again, it seemed like I didn't understand the changes made by the updating." A participant in the treatment condition said, "If I update the Grid, it reorganizes the columns names by itself ... I feel like it is getting out of my hands. The more I want to organize it, more messy it can get."

Positive written feedback about the Grid's updating feature was limited among participants in the placebo and treatment conditions. Only one participant in the treatment condition praised the column clustering, saying "I liked that it would automatically identify and sort motifs."

D.3 Rows and columns usage

Participants in all conditions reported using their column names to navigate to the appropriate sentences based on keywords in the test questions. If the first column they consulted did not have the information needed to answer the question, participants reported that they would move on to the next most relevant column. Most reported that they rarely looked in the rows corresponding to modeling dynamics, but instead used the "all" row that held all of the sentences assigned to a column. A few participants reported that the other rows became useful when the test question was clearly related to modeling dynamics, such as asking what could cause farmers to harvest late.

Participants in all conditions disliked how the study corpus had been organized into rows. Many participants said that they simply did not use the rows because the distinctions between the five modeling dynamics were unclear. In addition, because we allowed a single document to be assigned to multiple rows, participants found that the content of rows overlapped too much. However, others said that a few of the rows were useful, and one participant said that the rows were "practical." In general, participants liked the idea of having rows correspond to modeling dynamics, but found that the actual assignment of sentences to rows was unsuccessful.

E Top most commonly used words in column names

Word	Count
rice	6
machinery	6
labor	6
harvest	5
cooperative	5
harvester	5
loan	4
timing	4
time	4
equipment	4
credit	4
cost	4
farmer	4
season	4

Categorical Syllogisms Revisited: A Review of the Logical Reasoning Abilities of LLMs for Analyzing Categorical Syllogisms

Shi Zong, Jimmy Lin
David R. Cheriton School of Computer Science
University of Waterloo
{s4zong, jimmylin}@uwaterloo.ca

Abstract

There has been a huge number of benchmarks proposed to evaluate how large language models (LLMs) behave for logic inference tasks. However, it remains an open question how to properly evaluate this ability. In this paper, we provide a systematic overview of prior works on the logical reasoning ability of LLMs for analyzing categorical syllogisms. We first investigate all the possible variations for categorical syllogisms from a purely logical perspective and then examine the underlying configurations (i.e., mood and figure) tested by existing datasets. Our results indicate that compared to template-based synthetic datasets, crowdsourcing approaches normally sacrifice the coverage of configurations (i.e., mood and figure) of categorical syllogisms for more language variations, thus bringing challenges to fully testing LLMs under different situations. We then summarize the findings and observations for the performance of LLMs to infer the validity of syllogisms from the current literature. The error rate breakdown analyses suggest that the interpretation of quantifiers seems to be the current bottleneck that limits the performance of the LLMs and is thus worth more attention. Finally, we discuss several points that might be worth considering when researchers plan to release categorical syllogism datasets. We hope our work will provide a timely review of the current literature regarding categorical syllogisms, and motivate more interdisciplinary research between communities, specifically computational linguists and logicians.

1 Introduction

Large language models (LLMs) have achieved remarkable performance on a variety of tasks (Brown et al., 2020; Wei et al., 2022; Bubeck et al., 2023). Over the years, a large number of benchmarks have been proposed that try to evaluate the different abilities of LLMs, many of which are designed for measuring logical reasoning ability using a variety of tasks. Habernal et al. (2018) propose an argument reading comprehension task to test deductive reasoning. CLUTRR (Sinha et al., 2019) tests inductive reasoning capabilities by requiring to infer kinship relations between characters in short stories. ReClor (Yu et al., 2020), MMLU (Hendrycks et al., 2021), and LogiQA (Liu et al., 2020) contain multiple-choice reading comprehension questions to evaluate diverse forms of logical reasoning. Datasets such as SylloBase (Wu et al., 2023) and FOLIO (Han et al., 2022) require LLMs to conduct inferences using syllogism logic or first-order logic. Among these datasets, many consist of questions that are directly taken from exams. For example, MMLU (Hendrycks et al., 2021) contains practice questions from tests such as the Graduate Record Examination (GRE), and ReClor (Yu et al., 2020) collects problems from the Law School Admission Test (LSAT).

A fundamental question behind these datasets is: *how to design a benchmark to ensure a fair and comprehensive evaluation of logic reasoning abilities?* This question is particularly important when the test questions are self-generated, instead of directly collected from established examinations for humans mentioned above. Problems in those human examinations are developed over decades and are designed in support of theories such as psychometrics and measurement in education. Thus, having rigorous analyses of current benchmarks designed for LLMs would ensure that we can track the development progress of LLMs accurately.

In this work, we make progress in answering the above question for a specific task: categorical syllogisms.[1] Besides the reason that to the best of our knowledge, there is no prior work on analyzing categorical syllogism datasets from a designing principle's perspective, we note some other compelling

[1]Unless specified, the term "categorical syllogisms" is also directly written as "syllogisms" (due to space issues).

Proceedings of the 1st Workshop on NLP for Science (NLP4Science), pages 230–239
November 16, 2024 ©2024 Association for Computational Linguistics

reasons for choosing this task. (1) Syllogisms are inarguably the most basic building block in logical reasoning abilities. Having a deeper understanding of syllogism inference is thus beneficial when designing models for solving more complex reasoning tasks. (2) Categorical syllogisms have a finite number of situations (discussed in Section 2.1), which could enable a complete check of all the possible cases for LLMs. (3) How to properly solve categorical syllogisms has been studied by logicians over decades. There is a huge literature that we can draw inspiration from to help understand how LLMs behave or make LLMs more efficient.

To sum up, our intention is not to propose new models to achieve the start-of-the-performance on certain datasets, nor introduce new benchmarks. Rather, we hope to take a step back and systematically review all existing work to understand where we are right now. Our goal is to check missing pieces and identify areas that are worth clarifying or need future research. Specifically, in this paper, we make the following contributions:

- We investigate all existing categorical syllogism datasets in literature along with their properties in Section 3. A checklist covering all the variations of categorical syllogisms from a purely logician's perspective is provided and we then examine the coverage of different cases for existing benchmarks.
- We summarize all prior findings related to the performance of LLMs for checking the validity of syllogisms in Section 4. By presenting an error rate breakdown by the mood and figure of syllogisms, we highlight the importance of enhancing the abilities of LLMs for interpreting quantifiers.
- We provide suggestions for the future releases of categorical syllogism datasets in Section 5, including clarifying certain issues such as existential import, providing complete annotations, and building datasets containing ordinary arguments.

2 A Concise Introduction to Syllogisms

In this section, we provide a brief introduction to categorical syllogisms from a logician's perspective. We will show in Sections 3.2 and 4.3 that these preparations will help us evaluate current syllogism datasets and better understand the bottleneck of the performance of LLMs.

Major Premise: All Greeks are humans.
Minor Premise: All Athenians are Greeks.
Conclusion: Therefore, all Athenians are humans.

Table 1: An example of a standard-form categorical syllogism (mood AAA, figure 1, configuration AAA-1).

Proposition	Type	Gen. quant.
All S are P.	Universal Affirmative (A)	$S \subseteq P$
No S is P.	Universal Negative (E)	$S \cap P = \varnothing$
Some S is P.	Particular Affirmative (I)	$S \cap P \neq \varnothing$
Some S is not P.	Particular Negative (O)	$S - P \neq \varnothing$

Table 2: Types of propositions with corresponding expressions using generalized quantifier theory.

2.1 Categorical Syllogisms

Categorical Propositions. A categorical proposition relates two classes, or categories. In practice, we care most about a categorical proposition in its standard form, which can be written as: `Quantifier (Subject) Copula (Predicate)`. There are only 4 kinds of standard-form categorical propositions, listed in Table 2.

Terms. A syllogism contains three terms: the predicate term (P), the middle term (M), and the subject term (S). The middle term never occurs in the conclusion but always appears in both premises. The term that occurs as the predicate and the subject of the conclusion is called the major term and minor term, respectively.

Standard-Form Categorical Syllogisms. A categorical syllogism in its standard form must meet the following two requirements: (1) Its premises and conclusion are all standard-form categorical propositions (A, E, I, or O; see Table 2); and (2) Propositions are arranged in standard order (major premise, then minor premise, then conclusion). Table 1 is an example of a standard-form syllogism.

Mood and Figure. The *mood* of a categorical syllogism consists of the letter names of the propositions it contains. For example, the mood for the syllogism presented in Table 1 is AAA. The *figure* of a categorical syllogism is determined by the location of the two occurrences of the middle term in the premises. As shown in Table 3, there are 4 possible figures. To accurately determine the mood and figure of a categorical syllogism, it must be in standard form (defined above). Any standard-form syllogism is completely described when we specify its mood and figure. To simplify the terminology,

Figure	1	2	3	4
Major Premise	M - P	P - M	M - P	P - M
Minor Premise	S - M	S - M	M - S	M - S
Conclusion	S - P	S - P	S - P	S - P

Table 3: Categorical syllogisms have 4 different figures.

in this paper, we define the combination of mood and figure as the *configuration* of this syllogism.

Valid Inference Types. Since there are 4 kinds of categorical propositions and 3 categorical propositions in a categorical syllogism, there are 64 possible moods ($4^3 = 64$). As each mood can occur in each of the four figures, in total we have $4^4 = 256$ different syllogisms. Among these, only 24 are valid forms, which are extensively studied by logicians.[2] Thus, we have the following fact: *the validity of the standard syllogism can be determined by checking the configuration (mood and figure) against a list of valid syllogistic forms.*

2.2 Analyzing Syllogisms as a Logician

We now briefly go through the steps that logicians take for an ordinary categorical syllogism (Copi et al., 2019; Hurley and Watson, 2018).

Translating Categorical Propositions. In practice, rare propositions are in their standard form and we need to make translations. The major benefit of such translation is that the operations and inferences pertinent to standard-form categorical propositions can be directly applied to these statements. Logicians have developed a number of well-tested methods for translating non-standard propositions, although given the richness of ordinary language, these specific rules can not cover all possible cases.

Determining the Mood and Figure. Once a categorical syllogism is written in its standard form, its figure and mood can be determined by comparing it to Tables 2 and 3. The judgment of a syllogism's configuration is then rather straightforward.

Checking Validity. For a given standard-form categorical syllogism, there are at least the following three ways to check its validity: (1) Use the configuration of this syllogism and then compare it against a list of pre-defined valid syllogistic forms; (2) Use the method of Venn diagrams or generalized quantifier theory to perform set operations; or (3) Check to see if the syllogism conforms to certain rules that are developed by logicians.

Handling Non-Standard Cases. When translating into standard-form syllogisms, some specific cases are worth attention, including the treatment of singular propositions, syllogisms with more than three terms, and enthymemes and sorites. We provide the details of these situations in Appendix A.

3 Review of Existing Syllogism Datasets

3.1 Summary of Syllogism Datasets

We categorize all existing syllogism datasets based on their construction methods, i.e., how the text of premises and conclusions are generated. In real practice, although some datasets are originally proposed for predicate (first-order) logic, their construction methods might involve syllogisms, or a portion of or the whole dataset contains only categorical propositions. As these datasets could be formulated as syllogisms, we also list two representative ones for completeness. All syllogism datasets are summarized in Table 4.[3]

Template-based Approach. Datasets falling into this category are normally generated using templates, i.e., four standard propositions in Table 2. The relation triplets are sampled from different sources and then filled into terms positions of these templates to form the complete syllogisms. For example, questions in ProntoQA (Saparov and He, 2023) use ontology generation and contain a series of premises and thus essentially sorites. Eisape et al. (2024) use a list of 30 relation triplets, the terms of which have no obvious semantic associations. The relation triplets in Wu et al. (2023) are sampled from Wikidata and ConceptNet, and the propositions generated from templates are further rephrased by using GPT-3.

Text Generated by Humans. Non-synthetic datasets are normally developed through crowdsourcing efforts. To acquire high-quality inference questions efficiently, these datasets sometimes rely on guidance during the crowdsourcing tasks. SylloFigure (Peng et al., 2021) is built based on the idea of enthymeme reconstruction. Specifically, Peng et al. (2021) select the entailment part of the SNLI (Bowman et al., 2015) dataset and then add the annotations of figures. Avicenna

[2] 15 configurations are "unconditionally valid" and another 9 are "conditionally valid". It is related to existential import in Section 5.1.

[3] Some prior works use syllogism datasets that are not in the format of natural language, such as Dong et al. (2020). We skip the discussions of these studies.

	Data Generation		Annotation				Performance			Meta	
	Method	Source	Term	Mood	Figure	Validity	Task	Model	Acc.	Total	Access
						Syllogisms Datasets					
SylloFigure (Peng et al., 2021)	Entailment part of SNLI		Middle	■	1-4	Entail	Figure identification	BERT	92%	8,635	Yes
Avicenna (Aghahadi and Talebpour, 2022)	Crowdsourcing	Books, articles, etc.	Middle	■	■	valid, invalid	Conclusion generation	GPT-2 trans. learning	32.0%	6,000	Yes
SylloBASE (Wu et al., 2023)	Template w/ GPT-3 rewrite	Wikidata ConceptNet	▲	▲	▲	valid, invalid	Conclusion selection	RoBERTa	72.8%	51,000	No
Logical (Lampinen et al., 2023)	Human authored questions		▲	■	■	valid belief-consistent	Conclusion validity identification	PaLM 2-L	~90% (support)	48	No
NeuBAROCO (Ando et al., 2023)	BAROCO (originally designed for human intell. test)		■	▲	■	entail, contra, neu inference types	Conclusion validity identification	GPT-3.5	51.7% (overall)	375	No
Reasoning (Eisape et al., 2024)	Template	Hand-crafted triples list	△	△	△	valid, invalid	Conclusion selection	PaLM 2	~75%	1,920	Yes
						First-order Logic Datasets					
FOLIO (Han et al., 2022)	Template w/ crowd -sourcing rewrite	N/A	▲	▲	▲	true, false, unknown	Conclusion truth identification	Logic-LM (GPT-4)	78.1%	1,435	Yes
ProntoQA (Saparov and He, 2023)	Template	Generated ontology	△	■	■	true, false	Validity of sorites	GPT-3	~90%	400	Yes

Table 4: Overview of existing syllogism datasets, along with their construction methods, annotations included, and the documented model performance. △ denotes annotations could be inferred based on the provided dataset construction method, ▲ denotes annotations are generated in the intermediate steps of the dataset construction but are neither released nor inferred, and ■ denotes annotations not available or no information.

(Aghahadi and Talebpour, 2022) is a crowdsourcing dataset, and the syllogisms are extracted from various sources, such as books and news articles. Syllogisms in Lampinen et al. (2023) are hand-authored. NeuBAROCO (Ando et al., 2023) originates from BAROCO, which is written in Japanese and is developed to evaluate human syllogistic reasoning abilities. FOLIO (Han et al., 2022) first generates logically valid stories using syllogism templates and then asks human annotators to write logically valid stories in natural language.

Our Newly Collected Test Examples. As shown in Table 4, nearly all datasets with human-generated text lack certain kinds of annotations, thus causing troubles in analyzing them (in Section 3.3). We fill in this missing gap by collecting relevant examples and corresponding exercise questions from standard introduction to logic textbooks (Copi et al., 2019; Kelley, 2013; Baronett, 2018; Hurley and Watson, 2018).

In total, we collect 371 examples of translating statements into standard form, covering all the possible forms of phraseology discussed in Section 3.2; 64 examples for judging the types of standard propositions; and 116 examples for judging the validity of a given syllogism, with complete annotations for the mood and figure. Among these examples, 57 are enthymemes.

3.2 Variations of Categorical Syllogisms

A set of questions that cover all the possible cases could be achieved by varying components of different levels of granularity that we outline in Section 2.1. We consider all possible variations from two angles: syllogisms in standard and non-standard forms. For standard syllogisms, the underlying nature is decided by the combination of mood and figure, which leads to 256 different cases.

For non-standard syllogism, there are variations both on the individual proposition level and the syllogism level. On the proposition level, we consider the different options of quantifiers, terms, and copula: (1) Besides standard quantifiers, the propositions could have non-standard quantifiers (also known as generalized quantifiers), such as “few”, “a few”, “not every”, or “anyone”, and unexpressed quantifiers; (2) Terms could be expressed with only an adjective, a plural noun or a pronoun, and the verbs are in other forms of the verb “to be;” and (3) Certain propositions could be typically translated into categorical propositions. Established categories include singular propositions, conditional statements such as “if ... then,” exclusive propositions that involve words “only,” “none but,” and “none except,” and exceptive propositions in the form of “All except S are P” and “All but S are P”.

On the syllogism level for non-standard syllogism, we vary the following (details in Appendix A): (1) It is possible that the syllogism covers more than three terms; and (2) Besides the normal syllogisms with two premises and one conclusion, there exist situations with more than two premises or missing premises, which we refer to as enthymemes and sorites.

On top of all the options above, instead of putting the propositions in a well-structured format (i.e., explicitly listing them as premises and conclusions), we could mix them all together as ordinary arguments. Some other parts could be varied, such as the order of the two premises. Since the change of the ordering does not change the validity of the conclusion, we skip the discussion of this part.

3.3 Coverage of Current Datasets

In Section 3.2, we have enumerated all the possible cases of categorical syllogisms. In this section, we will use this checklist to evaluate the coverage of current syllogism datasets. We mainly consider the following aspects: (1) the forms of phraseology covered, and (2) the mood and figure covered in these syllogism datasets.

3.3.1 Building Tools for Assessing Coverage

Most of the datasets do not have the annotations needing to be assessed (details in Table 4). Making up these missing pieces would require human annotators with linguistic background. Given the huge amount of human effort for such annotations, we take the approach of directly asking LLMs to perform as an annotator for labeling.

To ensure that we can build prompts with reasonable performance, we calibrate them on our newly collected textbook questions (discussed in Section 3.1). We also use the fact about the validity of syllogisms mentioned in Section 2.1 for cross-checking: for a valid inference, if a predicted configuration is not one of the valid syllogism forms, then there is something wrong with this prediction.

Translating the Propositions. When translating statements, besides a deep understanding of the given statement, we need to follow some established rules set by logicians (for example, the treatment of singular propositions discussed in Appendix A). We thus base our prompt design on a 2-step translation process: (1) determine the nature of a proposition by classifying it into categories listed in Table 5), and (2) then perform the translation based on the set rules within that category. To make sure the translated proposition is in the standard form, we also set up a mechanism for a second-round translation. We observe that GPT-4o performs well in identifying the forms of phraseology, while it is easy to incorrectly classify some statements into singular propositions. A manual check for the translated propositions shows that GPT-4 achieves 87.3% accuracy on 371 textbook problems, with 68 propositions translated twice.

		SylloFigure	Avicenna	Reasoning
Proposition	Standard (%)	0.9	0.6	100
	Singular (%)	64.7	27.2	0
	Condition (%)	2.3	9.5	0
	Exclusive (%)	0.1	1.0	0
	Others (%)	32.0	61.7	0
	Total	2,448	1,864	2,560
Configuration	Coverage (%)	>4.3	>2.7	100
	Actual count	>11	>7	256
	Syllo assessed (%)	71.1	60.9	100
Total syllogisms		868	622	2,560

Table 5: Forms of phraseology and configurations of categorical syllogisms covered in datasets.

Judging the Mood and Figure. We can not first translate individual propositions and then simply combine the detected proposition types together to form the mood of the syllogism, due to the issue of having potentially more than three terms (in Appendix A). Thus, we feed the syllogism as a whole and ask GPT-4 to generate the mood and figure simultaneously. The principles and rules discussed above for translating propositions are also incorporated into the prompt. Experimental results on 116 textbook examples reveal an accuracy of 87.9% for mood detection, 48.3% for figure detection, and 44.8% for configuration detection. A further review of mood detection results reveals that this high accuracy is due to the fact that most of the collected textbook examples are standard-form propositions.

3.3.2 Datasets Coverage Observations

We apply our calculating tools developed in Section 3.3.1 to all three categorical syllogism datasets currently released. For the SylloFigure and Avicenna datasets, we conduct analyses only on the test sets, while for the Reasoning dataset, we randomly sample 10 relation triples out of 30 and then generate the complete syllogisms. We use the whole dataset for assessing the proposition forms, since it is rather straightforward. Regarding the underlying configuration of syllogisms: As the Reasoning dataset is generated by using templates, the whole dataset could be accurately assessed (since we have all the annotations such as mood and figure). Using the cross-checking method discussed in Section 3.3.1, we estimate 60.9% of syllogisms could be properly assessed in the Avicenna dataset, while a higher 71.1% for the SylloFigure dataset, as it contains human annotated figures.

Our assessment results are reported in Table 5 (detailed configurations are in Figure 1). In Figure 2 we also provide the distribution of the estimated proposition types in the SylloFigure dataset.

We observe that both the proposition types (A, E, I, O) and forms of phraseology (types in Table 5) are distributed highly unevenly, and datasets normally have different distributions. Regarding the coverage of configurations, we observe that compared to template-based datasets, datasets using human-generated text are normally centered on a few specific moods and figures, i.e., Avicenna covers only over 7 different syllogisms configurations, calculated from 60.9% of the whole dataset.

Since we use LLMs instead of human effort to make up the missing mood and figures, the coverage percentages in Table 5 can only be treated as rough estimates. Nevertheless, our key point is clear: datasets that are from crowdsourcing efforts are skewed to certain linguistic styles and cover only limited configurations of syllogisms. We thus suggest researchers take the actual variations covered by the datasets into account when interpreting experimental results.

4 Evaluating LLMs for Analyzing Syllogisms

4.1 What Do We Know So Far?

Reported Results for Validity Inferences. We observe prior studies mainly make use of the following approaches to evaluate the validity of categorical syllogisms: (1) given two premises, select a correct conclusion from multiple choices (Wu et al., 2023; Eisape et al., 2024), (2) given two premises and a conclusion, identify if the logic inference is valid (Lampinen et al., 2023; Ando et al., 2023), and (3) given two premises or more, generate the conclusion (Aghahadi and Talebpour, 2022; Saparov and He, 2023). In general, most prior works report LLMs have an accuracy of around 75% when evaluating the validity of given syllogisms. We provide more performance evaluation details in Table 4.

Error Analysis. One trend for analyzing the errors that LLMs make is to compare them with human cognition biases. Lampinen et al. (2023) find that like humans, LLMs give out more accurate answers when the semantic content of a task supports the logical inferences. Ando et al. (2023) analyze the models' errors from three aspects: belief biases, conversion errors, and atmosphere effects. Eisape et al. (2024) provide more direct observations that LLMs replicate some human biases discovered in psychology studies, while LLMs could overcome these biases in certain situations.

Dataset	#	GPT-4	GPT-4o
SylloFigure	868	74.3	70.2
Avicenna	622	72.5	53.4
Reasoning	2,560	90.2	95.4

Table 6: Accuracy (%) for checking the validity of categorical syllogisms.

4.2 LLMs' Performance Breakdowns by Syllogisms Configurations

In this section, we reproduce the experimental results of LLMs for judging the logical validity of syllogisms and check to see if prior findings still hold. We will also break down the error rate by the configurations of syllogisms.

4.2.1 Setups

Models and Datasets. We conduct our experiments using OpenAI's GPT models, as they are commonly used large language models with compelling performance on a variety of inference tasks (OpenAI et al., 2024). All our experiments are done using GPT-4 and GPT-4o. We use the same set of datasets that we assess in Section 3.3. The details of these datasets are provided in Section 3.3.2.

Prompts Used. For comparison purposes, we follow the chain-of-thought prompt used in Eisape et al. (2024) and test how LLMs perform logical inferences under a zero-shot learning setting.

4.2.2 Results

We visualize the error rate of GPT-4 and GPT-4o on the complete 256 configurations of syllogisms from the Reasoning dataset in Figures 1(a) and 1(b). The error rate in the SylloFigure and Avicenna datasets are reported in Figure 1(c). We also report the total accuracy of validity judgment in Table 6 for reference purposes.

We observe the following trends. (1) Comparing Figure 1(a) with Figure 1(b), we observe different patterns for the configurations of syllogism that LLMs fail. For example, GPT-4 nearly has no errors when two premises are in AA format, while GPT-4o makes even more than half of the mistakes for AAI-3 and AAI-4. However, GPT-4o performs better than GPT-4 for configurations that GPT-4 has 0% accuracy. (2) For two datasets with human-written text, GPT-4 seems to have more stable performance compared to GPT-4o, i.e., the error rate in Figure 1(c) is roughly the same for AAA-1, AAI-1, and AII-1. (3) We observe that for the same configuration, LLMs generally have a higher error

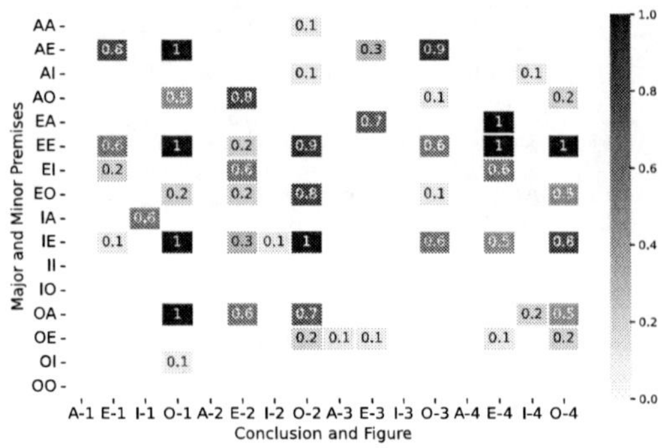

(a) Reasoning dataset (GPT-4)

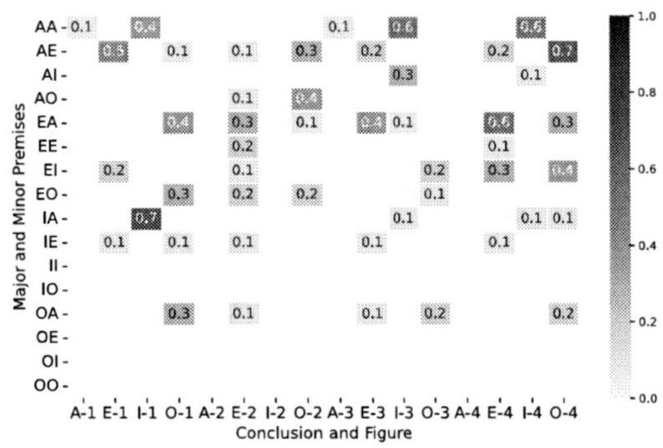

(b) Reasoning dataset (GPT-4o)

Figure	SylloFigure				Avicenna			
	Mood	#	GPT-4	GPT-4o	Mood	#	GPT-4	GPT-4o
1	AAA	47	0.21	0.28	AAA	310	0.20	0.42
	AAI	38	0.32	0.42	AAI	12	0.33	0.42
	AII	502	0.21	0.26	AII	25	0.28	0.68
	N/A	56	0.34	0.32	EAE	2	1	0.50
2	EAE	1	0	0	EAE	3	0	0
	N/A	180	0.28	0.36	AEE	3	0.67	0.33
3	AAI	2	1	0.5	AAI	1	0	0
	AII	26	0.54	0.38	AII	4	0	0
	N/A	8	0.38	0.38	IAI	2	0.50	0.50
4	IAI	1	1	0	IAI	14	0.29	0.64
	N/A	7	0.71	0.43	AAI	3	0	0.33
N/A			/		N/A	243	0.35	0.52

(c) SylloFigure and Avicenna datasets

Figure 1: Error rate (↓) of GPT-4 and GPT-4o using zero-shot chain-of-thoughts. (a) and (b): Breakdowns on all 256 configurations of categorical syllogisms in the Reasoning dataset, calculated over 10 different combinations. A white block indicates an error rate of 0 (thus 100% accuracy) in that specific configuration. (c): Breakdowns by configurations in the SylloFigure and Avicenna datasets. We mark the predicted configuration as "N/A" if it does not pass the cross-check discussed in Section 3.3.1.

rate in human-generated SylloFigure and Avicenna datasets (Figure 1(c)), compared to the template-based Reasoning dataset (Figures 1(a) and 1(b)). It seems to suggest that translating the syllogisms to the standard form is the bottleneck for LLMs to behave well, as the only difference that the Reasoning dataset has is the expressed way of the premises and conclusions. The underlying ability required to infer remains unchanged: if LLMs can translate ordinary text into the standard format, then it should work well. This observation also aligns with the challenges of the logicians' approach for analyzing syllogisms: as discussed in Section 2.1, the most difficult part is translating the propositions – once the mood and the figure are determined, then checking the validity of the syllogism is trivial.

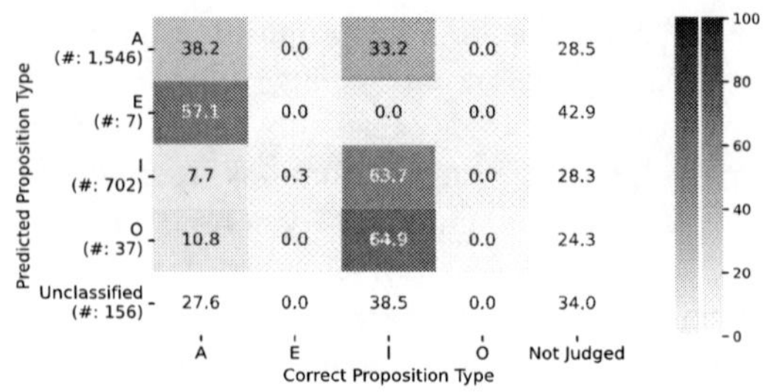

Figure 2: Percentage breakdowns of the correct propositions within each predicted proposition type (by GPT-4). 156 propositions (last row) could not be classified and we can not automatically verify the correctness of predictions without human efforts (last column).

4.3 Ambiguity of Natural Language

Our observation is that translating into standard propositions is the most challenging part for LLMs and thus causes errors. In this section, we take a closer look at the types of translation errors LLMs make, especially around quantifiers.

We visualize in Figure 2 the percentage of correct propositions within each predicted proposition type in the SylloFigure dataset. We observe that in general, the LLMs have a much higher accuracy in recognizing the "some" quantifier, although it sometimes mixes the particular negative type (O) with the particular affirmative type (I). We also observe LLMs tend to confuse universal affirmative (A) with particular affirmative (I): among 1,546 propositions that are predicted as universal affirmative type (A), 33.2% should be particular affirmative (I). This phenomenon is related to the interpretation of singular propositions (discussed in Appendix A) and is also partially due to the fact that singular propositions represent a huge portion of the SylloFigure dataset (shown in Table 5).

We shall point out that analyzing the sensitivity of quantifiers by LLMs is not entirely new in computation linguistics. One representative work is Cui et al. (2022), where the authors rely on generalized quantifier theory to quantify their contribution to the errors of NLU models. There is a recent work by Madusanka et al. (2023) that tries to investigate how different generalized quantifiers affect LLMs by employing a textual entailment problem. Ando et al. (2023) also suggest the importance of differentiating the problems of interpreting quantifiers and negations from performing logical inferences. In this work, we hold the same standpoints that the comprehension of quantifiers greatly affects the model performance and future models should enhance their abilities to analyze quantifiers. Compared to these prior studies, we present a more complete and comprehensive analysis of quantifiers in a specific syllogism setting.

5 Moving Forward: Future Directions

5.1 Suggestions for Future Datasets

Existential Import. In Section 2.1, we mention that there are 24 valid configurations over all 256 cases, 9 of which rely on the existential import assumption. We notice that nearly all prior works, except Ando et al. (2023), implicitly make such an assumption. We recommend researchers explicitly mention this assumption in their dataset release, as it affects the determination of the validity of syllogisms (Hurley and Watson, 2018).

Complete Annotations. As shown in Table 4, many syllogism datasets lack certain kinds of annotations, thus causing trouble when we try to assess the coverage of language variations in Section 3.3. We notice that in their dataset descriptions, especially datasets that make use of templates, many annotations are actually generated during the dataset construction process (for example, blocks marked with ▲ in Table 4). We suggest researchers consider releasing these annotations from intermediate steps to promote a more accurate assessment of the properties of their datasets.

Ordinary Argument. We observe that all syllogism datasets in Section 3.3 are in a well-structured format, i.e., the premises and conclusions are listed separately. In real life, however, a more realistic situation is that the premises and conclusions are mixed together, with no clear indications or separators. There might even be cases such as enthymemes. Thus, one possible direction is to build datasets that contain ordinary arguments. Building such a dataset will also enable a variety of downstream applications, for example, to evaluate the syllogisms hidden in human forecasts or debates. We note there has been some exploration work in this direction (Jiang and Yang, 2023).

5.2 Enhancing Logical Reasoning Abilities

In prior studies, we observe two lines of research that attempt to enhance the logical reasoning abilities of the LLMs. One line of approach is to rely on external modules. Olausson et al. (2023) make use of an external theorem prover, which symbolically performs deductive inference. Poesia et al. (2023) propose to augment the LLM's reasoning ability by using externally certified reasoning, such as a theorem-proving environment for incremental proof generation. Another line is to directly incorporate the reasoning ability inside the LLMs. Representative work includes Xu et al. (2024), which argues that the reasoning ability should be inherited without using any external blocks. In general, it is unclear which type of approach is better. Specific to our syllogism inference case, if our ultimate goal is to build a trustworthy and reliable system with no tolerance for errors, then enabling some external pure logical solvers would help ensure the accuracy of analyzing syllogisms.

6 Conclusion

This work tries to address the question of whether current proposed benchmarks can evaluate logical reasoning abilities accurately and thoroughly. We choose categorical syllogism as our main focus, since this logical system has been extensively studied by logicians and has many nice properties, such as a finite number of possible cases, and automated ways of solving it. A categorical syllogism is also arguably the most basic building block for any other more complex reasonings. We draw the inspirations from how logicians analyze categorical syllogisms and construct a list of variations that should be covered by benchmarks. Our results show that there is no single dataset that properly covers all possible situations. We also summarize the current progress made in judging the validity of the categorical syllogisms. Our findings highlight the importance of correctly interpreting different quantifiers. Finally, we provide a discussion of several points that might be worth considering when researchers plan on the future release of categorical syllogism datasets.

Limitations

In this work, we mainly focus on analyzing the existing benchmarks of categorical syllogisms. Among 6 syllogism datasets listed in Table 4, we are only able to assess 3, as others are not publicly released. Also, we use GPT-4 as an annotation tool instead of human annotators to generate the missing annotations, such as mood, figure, and forms of phraseology. Although we have taken steps to control the quality of these annotations (as discussed in Section 3.3.1), it is inevitable that there are errors.

References

Zeinab Aghahadi and Alireza Talebpour. 2022. Avicenna: A challenge dataset for natural language generation toward commonsense syllogistic reasoning. *Journal of Applied Non-Classical Logics*, 32(1):55–71.

Risako Ando, Takanobu Morishita, Hirohiko Abe, Koji Mineshima, and Mitsuhiro Okada. 2023. Evaluating large language models with NeuBAROCO: Syllogistic reasoning ability and human-like biases. In *Proceedings of the 4th Natural Logic Meets Machine Learning Workshop*, pages 1–11, Nancy, France.

Stan Baronett. 2018. *Logic*. Pearson Education.

Samuel R. Bowman, Gabor Angeli, Christopher Potts, and Christopher D. Manning. 2015. A large annotated corpus for learning natural language inference. In *Proceedings of the 2015 Conference on Empirical Methods in Natural Language Processing*, pages 632–642, Lisbon, Portugal.

Tom Brown, Benjamin Mann, Nick Ryder, Melanie Subbiah, Jared D Kaplan, Prafulla Dhariwal, Arvind Neelakantan, Pranav Shyam, Girish Sastry, Amanda Askell, Sandhini Agarwal, Ariel Herbert-Voss, Gretchen Krueger, Tom Henighan, Rewon Child, Aditya Ramesh, Daniel Ziegler, Jeffrey Wu, Clemens Winter, Chris Hesse, Mark Chen, Eric Sigler, Mateusz Litwin, Scott Gray, Benjamin Chess, Jack Clark, Christopher Berner, Sam McCandlish, Alec Radford, Ilya Sutskever, and Dario Amodei. 2020. Language models are few-shot learners. In *Advances in Neural Information Processing Systems*, volume 33, pages 1877–1901.

Sébastien Bubeck, Varun Chandrasekaran, Ronen Eldan, Johannes Gehrke, Eric Horvitz, Ece Kamar, Peter Lee, Yin Tat Lee, Yuanzhi Li, Scott Lundberg, Harsha Nori, Hamid Palangi, Marco Tulio Ribeiro, and Yi Zhang. 2023. Sparks of artificial general intelligence: Early experiments with GPT-4. *arXiv:2303.12712*.

Irving M. Copi, Carl Cohen, and Kenneth D. McMahon. 2019. *Introduction to Logic*. Pearson Education.

Ruixiang Cui, Daniel Hershcovich, and Anders Søgaard. 2022. Generalized quantifiers as a source of error in multilingual NLU benchmarks. In *Proceedings of the 2022 Conference of the North American Chapter of the Association for Computational Linguistics: Human Language Technologies*, pages 4875–4893, Seattle, United States.

Tiansi Dong, Chengjiang Li, Christian Bauckhage, Juanzi Li, Stefan Wrobel, and Armin B. Cremers. 2020. Learning syllogism with Euler neuralnetworks. *arXiv:2007.07320*.

Tiwalayo Eisape, MH Tessler, Ishita Dasgupta, Fei Sha, Sjoerd van Steenkiste, and Tal Linzen. 2024. A systematic comparison of syllogistic reasoning in humans and language models. In *Proceedings of the 2024 Conference of the North American Chapter of the Association for Computational Linguistics: Human Language Technologies*.

Ivan Habernal, Henning Wachsmuth, Iryna Gurevych, and Benno Stein. 2018. The argument reasoning comprehension task: Identification and reconstruction of implicit warrants. In *Proceedings of the 2018 Conference of the North American Chapter of the Association for Computational Linguistics: Human Language Technologies, Volume 1 (Long Papers)*, pages 1930–1940, New Orleans, Louisiana.

Simeng Han, Hailey Schoelkopf, Yilun Zhao, Zhenting Qi, Martin Riddell, Luke Benson, Lucy Sun, Ekaterina Zubova, Yujie Qiao, Matthew Burtell, David Peng, Jonathan Fan, Yixin Liu, Brian Wong, Malcolm Sailor, Ansong Ni, Linyong Nan, Jungo Kasai, Tao Yu, Rui Zhang, Shafiq Joty, Alexander R. Fabbri, Wojciech Kryscinski, Xi Victoria Lin, Caiming Xiong, and Dragomir Radev. 2022. FOLIO: Natural language reasoning with first-order logic. *arXiv:2209.00840*.

Dan Hendrycks, Collin Burns, Steven Basart, Andy Zou, Mantas Mazeika, Dawn Song, and Jacob Steinhardt. 2021. Measuring massive multitask language understanding. In *International Conference on Learning Representations*.

Patrick J. Hurley and Lori Watson. 2018. *A Concise Introduction to Logic*. Cengage Learning.

Cong Jiang and Xiaolei Yang. 2023. Legal syllogism prompting: Teaching large language models for legal judgment prediction. In *Proceedings of the Nineteenth International Conference on Artificial Intelligence and Law*, page 417–421, New York, NY, USA.

David Kelley. 2013. *The Art of Reasoning: An Introduction to Logic and Critical Thinking, Fourth Edition.* W. W. Norton, Incorporated.

Andrew K. Lampinen, Ishita Dasgupta, Stephanie C. Y. Chan, Hannah R. Sheahan, Antonia Creswell, Dharshan Kumaran, James L. McClelland, and Felix Hill. 2023. Language models show human-like content effects on reasoning tasks. *arXiv: 2207.07051*.

Jian Liu, Leyang Cui, Hanmeng Liu, Dandan Huang, Yile Wang, and Yue Zhang. 2020. LogiQA: A challenge dataset for machine reading comprehension with logical reasoning. In *Proceedings of the Twenty-Ninth International Joint Conference on Artificial Intelligence, IJCAI-20*, pages 3622–3628.

Tharindu Madusanka, Iqra Zahid, Hao Li, Ian Pratt-Hartmann, and Riza Batista-Navarro. 2023. Not all quantifiers are equal: Probing transformer-based language models' understanding of generalised quantifiers. In *Proceedings of the 2023 Conference on Empirical Methods in Natural Language Processing*, pages 8680–8692, Singapore.

Theo Olausson, Alex Gu, Ben Lipkin, Cedegao Zhang, Armando Solar-Lezama, Joshua Tenenbaum, and Roger Levy. 2023. LINC: A neurosymbolic approach for logical reasoning by combining language models with first-order logic provers. In *Proceedings of the 2023 Conference on Empirical Methods in Natural Language Processing*, pages 5153–5176, Singapore.

OpenAI, Josh Achiam, Steven Adler, Sandhini Agarwal, et al. 2024. GPT-4 technical report. *arXiv: 2303.08774*.

Shiya Peng, Lu Liu, Chang Liu, and Dong Yu. 2021. Exploring reasoning schemes: A dataset for syllogism figure identification. In *Chinese Lexical Semantics*, pages 445–451, Cham.

Gabriel Poesia, Kanishk Gandhi, Eric Zelikman, and Noah D. Goodman. 2023. Certified deductive reasoning with language models. *arXiv: 2306.04031*.

Abulhair Saparov and He He. 2023. Language models are greedy reasoners: A systematic formal analysis of chain-of-thought. In *The Eleventh International Conference on Learning Representations*.

Koustuv Sinha, Shagun Sodhani, Jin Dong, Joelle Pineau, and William L. Hamilton. 2019. CLUTRR: A diagnostic benchmark for inductive reasoning from text. In *Proceedings of the 2019 Conference on Empirical Methods in Natural Language Processing and the 9th International Joint Conference on Natural Language Processing (EMNLP-IJCNLP)*, pages 4506–4515, Hong Kong, China.

Jason Wei, Xuezhi Wang, Dale Schuurmans, Maarten Bosma, brian ichter, Fei Xia, Ed Chi, Quoc V Le, and Denny Zhou. 2022. Chain-of-thought prompting elicits reasoning in large language models. In *Advances in Neural Information Processing Systems*, volume 35, pages 24824–24837.

Yongkang Wu, Meng Han, Yutao Zhu, Lei Li, Xinyu Zhang, Ruofei Lai, Xiaoguang Li, Yuanhang Ren, Zhicheng Dou, and Zhao Cao. 2023. Hence, socrates is mortal: A benchmark for natural language syllogistic reasoning. In *Findings of the Association for Computational Linguistics: ACL 2023*, pages 2347–2367, Toronto, Canada.

Jundong Xu, Hao Fei, Liangming Pan, Qian Liu, Mong-Li Lee, and Wynne Hsu. 2024. Faithful logical reasoning via symbolic chain-of-thought. In *Proceedings of the 62nd Annual Meeting of the Association for Computational Linguistics (Volume 1: Long Papers)*, pages 13326–13365, Bangkok, Thailand.

Weihao Yu, Zihang Jiang, Yanfei Dong, and Jiashi Feng. 2020. Reclor: A reading comprehension dataset requiring logical reasoning. In *International Conference on Learning Representations (ICLR)*.

A Handling Special Cases When Analyzing Categorical Syllogisms

Singular Propositions. A singular proposition is defined as making a particular individual or object (for example, a specific person, thing, time, or place) belong to a given class. Although it is arguable about the treatment of these singular propositions, logicians seem to agree that in general, these propositions are generally converted into universal propositions.

Reducing the Number of Terms. A valid syllogism must have exactly three terms. When more than three terms seem to be involved in an argument of apparently syllogistic form, we may need to reduce the number of terms to three, by either eliminating synonyms or eliminating class components (Copi et al., 2019).

Enthymemes and Sorites. In real life, we normally do not make explicit mention of all the premises required to support a given conclusion, especially when the premises are obvious or noncontroversial. A syllogism with an unstated premise is called an enthymeme (Kelley, 2013). Sorites are defined as a chain of categorical syllogisms in which the intermediate conclusions have been left out (Hurley and Watson, 2018). The standard treatment for analyzing sorites is to first make their intermediate conclusions or steps explicit, then test the validity of obtained syllogisms separately.

Individuation in Neural Models with and without Visual Grounding

Alexey Tikhonov
Inworld.AI,
Berlin, Germany
altsoph@gmail.com

Lisa Bylinina
University of Groningen
Groningen, Netherlands
e.g.bylinina@rug.nl

Ivan P. Yamshchikov
CAIRO, Technical University of Applied Sciences
Würzburg-Schweinfurt Würzburg, Germany
ivan@yamshchikov.info

Abstract

We show differences between a language-and-vision model CLIP, and two text-only models — FastText and SBERT — when it comes to the encoding of individuation information. We study latent representations that CLIP provides for substrates, granular aggregates, and various numbers of objects. We demonstrate that CLIP embeddings capture quantitative differences in individuation better than models trained only on text-only data. Moreover, the individuation hierarchy we deduce from the CLIP embeddings agrees with the hierarchies proposed in linguistics and cognitive science.

1 Introduction

Recent results in multimodal[1] vision and language (V&L) models lead to intriguing research questions. For instance, one exciting research direction would be to search for the synergistic effects of multimodality. So far, to the best of our knowledge, no definitive finds were made on this front, despite the growing body of research on V&L model evaluation. For example, (Parcalabescu et al., 2021) provide a benchmark to assess the visual grounding capabilities of V&L models. The authors conclude that current models have difficulty addressing most phenomena that require models to ground linguistic information in the visual modality. (Thrush et al., 2022) present a benchmark for visio-linguistic compositional reasoning and also find that none of the modern V&L models does much better than chance.

This paper presents the first case of such visio-linguistic synergies. Namely, it studies the phenomenon of *individuation* and how V&L models represent objects:

How they distinguish objects from substances and how they track objects and their quantity in sets that contain more than one object. We demonstrate that CLIP's (Radford et al., 2021) latent representations have properties that differ from those of the models that use only textual data. Moreover, this emergent property seems to agree with individuation scales proposed earlier by linguists and cognition researchers.

[1]For a detailed review of various aspects of multimodal machine learning, we address the reader to (Zhang et al., 2020)

2 Individuation

Individuation is generally understood as basic principles that guide the distinction between objects and substances, as well as the distinction between a single object and multiple objects. Individuation is not limited to visual modality – it applies cross-modally to stimuli of any kind. Here, we will only focus on visual individuation and its relation to the linguistic properties of corresponding words. This section summarizes the main relevant findings on individuation from cognitive science and linguistics.

Operationally, individuation can be probed along two axes: 1) the quantity axis; 2) the object axis. The former corresponds to distinguishing and tracking individual objects as their quantity increases. The latter is the dependency between the individual properties of an object and its permeability as an object rather than a substance. We will now overview these two aspects of individuation – first, in cognition, then in language.

2.1 Individuation and Cognition

The quantity axis. The human ability to perceive, identify, track, and count objects generally decreases as the number of objects in a scene increases (Feigenson et al., 2004; Dehaene, 2011; Hyde, 2011). The cognitive basis of this observation is complex. In particular, two relevant cognitive systems have been identified: the object tracking system (OTS) and the approximate number system (ANS) (Carey, 1998; Spaepen et al., 2011; Spelke, 2011). OTS is active when the number of objects to track is low, typically under 3 or 4. OTS

Proceedings of the 1st Workshop on NLP for Science (NLP4Science), pages 240–248
November 16, 2024 ©2024 Association for Computational Linguistics

tracks each object individually and represents the exact quantity of objects in a scene. ANS, on the contrary, does not construct individual object representations and does not track the exact quantity of objects. In particular, in a cardinality comparison task in which two sets of arbitrary objects are given, the ability to tell which of the two sets has higher cardinality depends on the ratio between the sets' cardinalities. In pre-verbal infants, this ratio can be around 1:2, but it decreases somewhat with development (Hyde et al., 2010).

Summing up, the human ability to represent objects and their quantity is not stable across quantities, with sharp contrast at the edge of OTS, and is ratio-sensitive in the ANS domain. For example, ten versus fifteen would be more distinguishable than twenty versus twenty-five even though the absolute difference between the cardinalities is the same; see (Starkey and Cooper Jr, 1980). Both systems are non-linguistic since they are present in pre-verbal humans.

The object axis. Humans organize their visual space into objects vs. substances very early in life, well in the pre-verbal stage of their development. (Spelke, 1990) identifies the basic principles of such an organization as Cohesion, Boundedness, Rigidity, and No Action at a Distance. Objects defined against these principles are called 'Spelke objects.' Such objects tend to be connected, non-overlapping, with constant spacial characteristics when moving and only affecting each other when in contact. This is not exactly the same notion of an object as found in adults: for example, under these principles, a horseman riding a horse would be considered one object with the horse.

Individuation principles develop and change during the lifetime, but the most drastic changes happen around the first year and coincide with language acquisition breakthroughs. Knowledge about linguistic labels for classes of objects has been argued to be used in individuation at this stage (Xu, 2007). Still, the causal relation between linguistic milestones and the changes in individuation strategies is under debate. For example, it is hard to disentangle linguistic factors from the rapid accumulation of world knowledge happening in the same period. For a deeper discussion of these factors, see (Gentner and Boroditsky, 2001), who also suggests a cognitive hierarchy of individuation as a development of 'Spelke object' principles:

humans < animals < vehicles < small mobile objects < complex structurally cohesive objects < amorphous

2.2 Individuation and Language

Natural language shows systematic distinctions with respect to both the quantity and the object axes. These distinctions can be linked to the organization of the corresponding cognitive systems.

The quantity axis. Distinctions in the representation of different quantities in language grammar manifest themselves mainly in two domains: 1) number morphology; 2) morphosyntax of constructions with numerals.

In languages like English, morphological number distinctions give rise to a split between one object (*book*) and a higher number of objects (*book-s*; however, plural nouns can refer to singular objects as well, see Spector 2007; Zweig 2009). Some languages also have a dual grammatical number as part of the nominal number inventory, making the 1 vs. 2 vs. >2 quantity distinction in the number domain (Slovenian, Arabic, etc.). Few languages also have the trial number form (e.g., some Austronesian languages and Austronesian-influenced creoles) and paucal number form referring to a 'small' number of objects (e.g., some Oceanic languages). It's debated whether there are languages with the quadral number form. Higher grammaticalized number distinctions don't exist in natural language – for instance, there is no morphological affix as part of the grammatical number category that would mean 'exactly 7' or '15 or more'. Within the space of existing number distinctions, the higher the number line, the rarer the distinction. For example, the trial number form is quite rare typologically; dual number form is more frequent but rarer than a system with just the singular vs. plural distinction. A number hierarchy supports this observation: if a language has some number form, it also has all the number forms to the left of it (Croft, 1990; Corbett, 2000):

singular < plural < dual < paucal/trial

Thus, quantity distinctions built into language grammar through number marking show up exclusively on the lower side of the number line, roughly in the subitizing/OTS domain. Still, even within this domain, different quantities are not equally distinguished – the lower, the more prominent.

Constructions with numerals (*five books* etc.) communicate precise quantities. The morphosyntax of such constructions varies somewhat depending on the quantity encoded by the numeral – in English, for example, numeral *one* combines with singular nouns (*one book*), while higher numerals combine with plural (*seven books*). This is not universally true (e.g., in Turkic languages, all numerals combine with nouns in singular form), but more importantly, in more morphologically rich languages than English, a variety of grammatical distinctions is made between different quantities in this domain. For instance, in Russian, numeral *two* agrees with the noun in gender and case, while *three* agrees only in case (see Bylinina and Barbiers 2019 for data on the grammatical typology of numerals). The generalization is, again, that, like with number marking, low quantities systematically receive special grammatical treatment in numeral constructions: very few systematic distinctions are made above 3-4, and even within this range – the lower the quantity, the more distinct it is from other quantities, grammatically.

The object axis. Linguistic individuation is most often discussed in the context of the mass vs. count distinction in nouns. This distinction roughly separates entities that are construable as individuatable from those that are not and comes in a variety of specific linguistic behaviors, some of which we list below (see Mufwene 1981; Wierzbicka 1985 a.o.).

- Pluralization: Count nouns allow for plural marking, mass nouns don't (*books* vs. **rices*);
- Numerals: Count nouns allow for numeral modification, mass nouns don't (*three books* vs. *three rices*);
- Count quantifiers: Count nouns combine with quantifiers *many/several*, mass nouns don't (*several books* vs ??*several rices*);
- Extent quantifiers: Count nouns don't combine with quantifiers *much / few*, mass nouns do (**much book(s)* vs *much rice*).

(Grimm, 2012) provides a much more extensive inventory of tests relevant to the same underlying distinction and extending beyond English. These tests suggest a coherent space of linguistic distinctions that gives rise to a very detailed hierarchy (for earlier versions of this hierarchy, see (Allan, 1980; Comrie, 1989; Croft, 1990):

liquids < foodstuffs < granular aggregate < vegetation/cereals/fruits ≤ insects < small animals < pair/grouped body parts ≤ middle-sized animals < types of people < individuals

(Grimm, 2012) suggests that some of the details in the hierarchy above might be rooted in the specifics of the language sample used in his work. Thus, a simplification/generalization is proposed as follows:

liquids/substances < granular aggregates < collective aggregates < individuals

The above suggests that many clues in language alone can help deduce a hierarchy parallel to the non-linguistic cognitive hierarchy of individuation. But many such linguistic clues are language-specific and don't surface in, for example, English. Some clues are more subtle than others and are rare enough to barely surface in text corpora. Finally and most importantly, humans use the physical properties of objects to assign linguistic behavior to words describing these objects. Experiments in different frameworks (one prevalent paradigm being novel word learning) and with different populations have shown that the shape and internal structure of objects, in particular, affect how the corresponding word meaning will be construed (Soja et al. 1991; Samuelson and Smith 1999; Prasada et al. 2002 a.o.). This, together with data from early cognition, is an argument against Quine's (1960) strong thesis that language is the instrument for separating the world into objects and substances: some of these distinctions reside in non-linguistic experience, in particular – visual one (along with other general world knowledge, for example, about how different objects are typically used, see Middleton et al. 2004). This raises the question our paper aims to answer: How will adding visual experience affect individuation, as found in the representations developed by the learner – in our case, a neural V&L model?

3 Individuation Assessment

We suggest estimating the models' individuation 'resolution' by inferring its individuation hierarchy. The pipeline we construct here is based on publicly available data and is motivated by cognitive and linguistic experiments on individuation discussed above.

We structure this section as follows. First, we describe the list of nouns and semantic features that we use in our experiments throughout this paper. We then propose a simple way to characterize individuation in a model. In short, we will look at embeddings of noun phrases describing various quantities of objects and measure distances between different quantities of the same type of object (that is, described by the same noun).

While this approach does not, of course, exclude other potential analysis tools, we believe it is a simple and effective way to demonstrate that V&L models represent individuation differently and show behavior closer to human perception of individuation. We hope that further work on individuation in modern deep neural nets refines the proposed methods or proposes more elaborate ones.

Let us discuss our experiments in detail and then demonstrate how CLIP differs from contextual text embeddings (for example, SBERT, Reimers and Gurevych 2019) and static word embeddings (say, FastText, Joulin et al. 2016) in text-only models.

3.1 Data

We start with a list of nouns alongside their plural forms. We take a publicly available list of singular-plural noun pairs based on an analysis of the Wikipedia corpus[2]. This list includes 93 518 words. Since we want to assess individuation across various types of entities, we need to enrich the list with semantic information. We intersect the original list with WordNet[3]. This procedure leaves 28 521 nouns from the original list. Now every entry has specific conceptual-semantic attributes from WordNet alongside the plural form of the word that corresponds to a given entry. We use this list for further experiments.

With more than twenty-eight thousand words, we believe it to be representative and adequate for the broad assessment of individuation in the models we include in the study. For some of the experiments, we filter the obtained list further, leaving several WordNet categories that generally correspond with the taxonomy of individuation hierarchy observed in studies summarized in Section 2. Table 1 lists these categories along with the number of words that belong to each category.

3.2 Embedding Quantities

In the first experiment, we study quantity distinctions in CLIP. This aspect of the model's behavior is parallel to the 'quantity axis' of individuation described in Section 2 in the context of cognition and language. We will compare the model behavior with the results found in humans: we expect that a model that encodes individuation in a manner similar to humans will show starker contrast when comparing smaller quantities (two apples are very different from one apple). In contrast, higher quantities would be less distinguishable (nine apples are very similar to ten apples). We use this logic to construct the following procedure.

Type	Number of Words
Animal	1887
Body Part	863
Fish	220
Food	551
Fruit	203
Living Thing	8845
Nutrient	239
Organism	8763
Person	5861
Substance	1397
Vascular Plant	1027
Woody Plant	470

Table 1: The sizes of the WordNet categories used in the experiments in Subsection 3.3.

- make a list of phrases following the pattern $nobj_i$, where n is a numeral written in digits, from 2 to 10, and obj_i is a noun from our list in its plural form;
- calculate embeddings that a chosen model provides with these phrases;
- for every given noun, calculate pairwise distances for every pair of numeric prefixes;
- average across nouns and normalize the resulting score.

Figure 1 illustrates the individuation 'resolution' of the models along the quantity axis assessed with the pipeline above. We compare CLIP with FastText (Joulin et al., 2016) and SBERT (Reimers and Gurevych, 2019). Since the scores are normalized, the color scheme of the resulting tables is informative: one should compare the distances between various quantities of entities relative to other quantities.

[2]https://github.com/djstrong/nouns-with-plurals

[3]https://wordnet.princeton.edu/

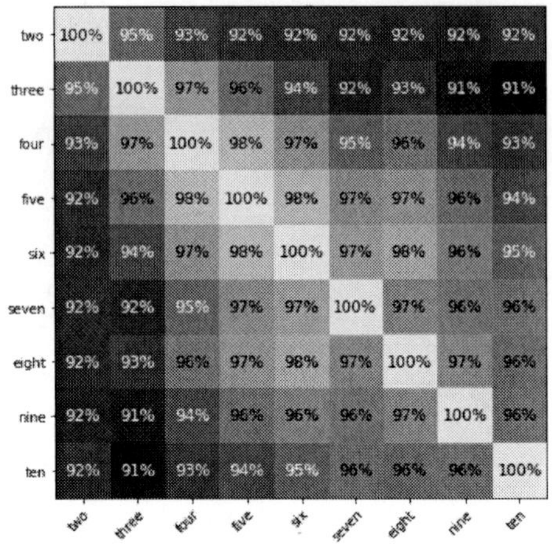

(a) CLIP

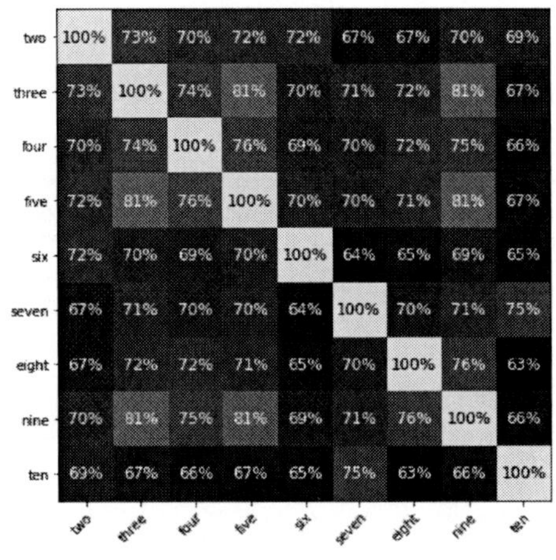

(b) FastText

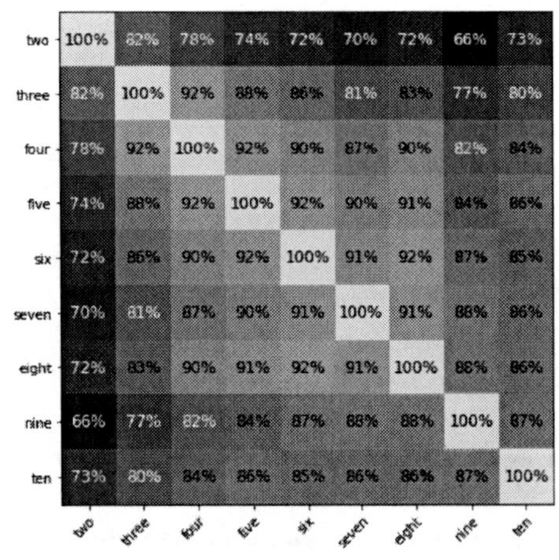

(c) SBERT

Figure 1: Side by side comparison of contrasting capabilities that models have for various number of objects. The heat map represents average distances for the pairs of embeddings that model provides for various quantities of the same objects. The results are averaged across all objects and normalized.

Indeed, for FastText, any two different quantities are far apart. SBERT starkly separates two from any other number yet has some difficulties contrasting relatively small numbers, such as three or four, with higher ones, such as nine or ten. Finally, CLIP demonstrates contrasting capabilities that seem closer to the intuition described above. If two numbers are close to each other, the embeddings of the quantities tend to be closer, yet the contrast gets stronger for smaller quantities and weaker for bigger ones.

3.3 Embedding Qualitative Properties

As discussed above, individuation is sensitive to a variety of physical properties of entities, thus giving rise to something we call 'the object axis' in Section 2. These properties guide the classification of entities into substances vs. objects. Assessment along this axis enriches the results from the previous section with the other aspect of individuation.

Figure 1 shows contrasts between different quantities averaged across all nouns denoting different types of objects. But the contrast between quantities might decline differently for various classes of nouns, therefore, showing the interaction between the two axes. One can look at the following intuitive example. The individuation scales based on results from cognitive science and linguistics predict that people are higher on those scales (= are more individuateable) than animals or plants. Thus humans might perceive the difference between five and six people as a starker one than the difference between five or six dogs or, say, apples. We suggest seeing whether some of the models in question have similar behavior.

Since WordNet contains information on the classes of nouns, one could see if the embeddings of the model capture the qualitative properties of the mentioned classes. For this paper, we suggest the following classes: substance, food, nutrient, body part, vascular plant, woody plant, fruit, living thing, organism, fish, animal, and person. These are the classes of objects over which we would aggregate the obtained results. Naturally, one could have a less granular picture merging some similar classes, but we suggest using the original WordNet 'synset' typology to simplify reproducibility.

How could one characterize the individuation 'resolution' of a given model? As we have mentioned earlier, there is converging cognitive and linguistic data suggesting that individuation and distinguishability of n objects and $n+1$ objects generally declines with higher values of n. We have also already shown that all models distinguish two and three objects relatively well. Let us keep these two ideas in mind and introduce a metric that could be a proxy for individuation 'resolution.' Let us look at a set of objects: $O = \cup_{k=1}^{k=N}\{obj_k\}$. Let ${obj_k}^n$ denote n objects, as in *I have* n *apples*, where $obj_k = apple$. Let $M({obj_k}^n)$ denote the embedding that model M has for a noun phrase denoting ${obj_k}^n$. We suggest the following function I_M as the proxy to estimate model M individuation 'resolution' for a given object obj_k:

$$I_M(obj_k) = \sum_{n=3}^{T} \frac{d(M({obj_k}^n), M({obj_k}^{n+1}))}{T\dot{d}(M({obj_k}^2), M({obj_k}^3))},$$

where $d(x,y)$ denotes cosine similarity between the corresponding embeddings and T is some finite number. In our experiments, $T = 10$. We believe it to be a reasonable assumption[4]. We want to compare different models in terms of their individuation capabilities, so we need to have some sort of averaging across the objects that our model works with. However, averaging over the whole set O might be too crude. First, we have extensively discussed that humans individuate different classes of objects differently. Second, the embedding spaces of the models might be very different, so there is no reason to believe that two estimates for two different models could be directly compared. However, one could compare values of I_M for a given model on different classes of objects. Say, all objects obj_j belong to a class C_i: $C_i = \cup_{j=1}^{j=L}\{obj_j\}$, then one could introduce an estimator for a given model M on a given class C as follows:

$$I_M(C_i) = \frac{\sum_{j=1}^{L} I_M(obj_j)}{L} = \sum_{j=1}^{L}\sum_{n=3}^{T} \frac{d(M({obj_k}^n), M({obj_k}^{n+1}))}{LT\dot{d}(M({obj_k}^2), M({obj_k}^3))}.$$

The basic intuition behind this metric is that the higher it is, the harder it is for the model to distinguish between n and $n+1$ objects for higher values of n. Since all the models in question distinguish two and three objects reasonably well, one could also think of the bigger value for the metric and higher difference between 2 and 3 objects in comparison with higher n and $n+1$ of objects.

Now we can score every class and object with I_M and compare the resulting sets we obtain. We can order different classes of objects C_i in an individuation hierarchy, where classes with lower $I_M(C_i)$ will be placed lower and the classes with higher $I_M(C_i)$ — higher. We can also calculate p-values to characterize to which extent two different classes could be distinguished based on the values of I_M. Finally, we can compare the resulting order with the individuation orders suggested for human perception.

Figure 2 summarizes the resulting orders for various classes C_i and three models: $I_{CLIP}(C_i)$, $I_{SBERT}(C_i)$ and $I_{FastText}(C_i)$. The values in the table are p-values for the relative order of classes with respect to each other. If a value is above 5%, the difference is not statistically significant.

Now let us discuss the results presented in Figure 2 and compare the obtained individuation hierarchies with those described in cognitive and linguistic literature.

4 Discussion

The first thing that one sees is that FastText has almost no distinguished individuation classes and lumps a variety of classes together. It doesn't give rise to a systematic individuation hierarchy that would be similar in any way to the rankings proposed in cognitive science and linguistics. If anything, the tendency is the opposite: substances turn out to be one of the most 'individuated' classes, while animals and organisms end up on the lower end of the scale.

The second observation is that the hierarchies deduced from SBERT and CLIP are similar to the individuation hierarchies proposed in cognitive and linguistic research. As discussed in Section 2, the linguistic behavior of different nouns varies in ways that can be traced back to cognitive distinctions in individuation. Therefore, it comes as no surprise that a text-only model attuned to semantic distinctions that show up in distributional properties of nouns can pick up the relevant contrasts. Yet a careful exploration of Figure 2 allows us to see where additional – visual – modality helps develop clearer individuation-related distinctions compared to the language-only model.

[4] Most humans would have a hard time differentiating ten and eleven apples on the image without counting them all.

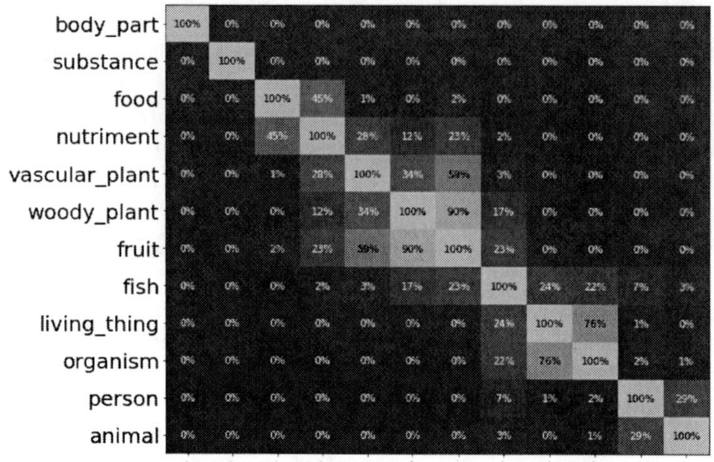

(a) CLIP

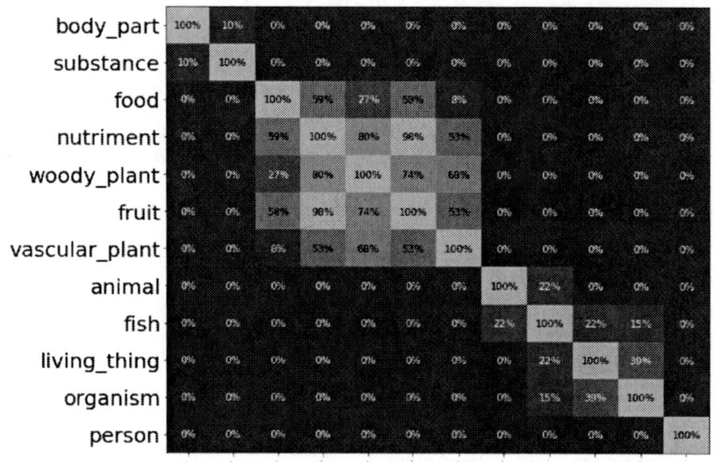

(b) SBERT

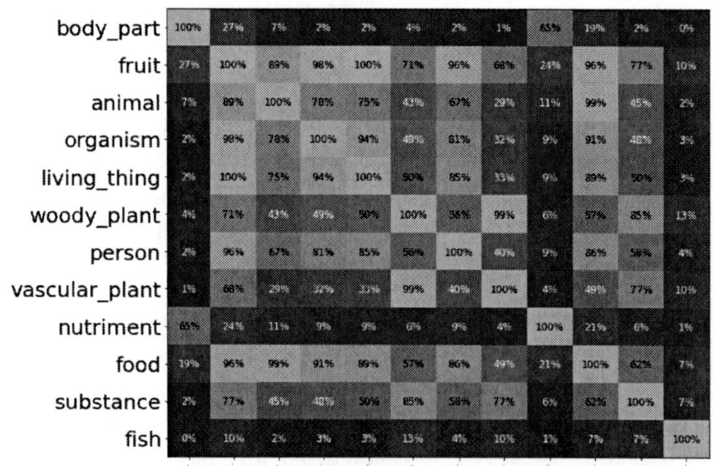

(c) FastText

Figure 2: P-values for the individuation capabilities of CLIP in comparison with SBERT and FastText based on the proxy metric for individuation. The classes with $p > 5\%$ are not significantly distinguishable. The order of rows is in line with the average value of the proposed individuation proxy: the lower individuated classes are on top, the more individuated ones are on the bottom. The order of columns repeats the order of rows making every matrix symmetric.

The individuation scale produced by CLIP is more fine-grained. For example, SBERT lumps fruits in one individuation 'cluster' with foods and nutrients and various plants, while CLIP distinguishes foods and nutrients from plants. This can potentially be related to the fact that images depicting food (in particular, fruit) tend to differ from images with plants in general (say, landscapes). One of the ways to quantify the resulting differences in the model's individuation is to represent data shown in Figure 2 as a graph and calculate the cliques' parameters. Let us connect to vertices representing a class of nouns with an edge if the pval on Figure 2 is greater than five percent. This would mean that our proxy metric based on model embeddings has difficulty distinguishing the classes. Now we can count maximal cliques. The more cliques we end up with, the more separate classes are distinguished by a given model. We can also calculate the average size of the cliques. The smaller this size is, the more fine-grained the individuation hierarchy induced by a given model is. The results of those calculations are presented in Table 2. Indeed, CLIP provides the most fine-grained individuation hierarchy.

Another interesting aspect of this is the position of animals in the induced individuation hierarchy. While SBERT puts animals somewhere in the middle of the scale, CLIP puts them on top with the same cluster as humans. Such a position goes in line with the cognitive results mentioned earlier in Section 2.

Finally, going back to Figure 1, one could notice that CLIP individuation has fewer discontinuities when compared to SBERT. Specifically, if $n < k < j$, then CLIP almost always recognizes that $I(n) < I(k) < I(j)$. Out of thirty-six pairwise comparisons, there are three situations when this observation does not hold. With SBERT, this does not hold in eight cases out of thirty-six pairwise comparisons.

Another thing worth noting is the standard deviation of the individuation proxy that differs significantly for all three models; see Table 3. CLIP shows the lowest standard deviation across categories, while that of FastText is ten times higher.

5 Conclusion

This paper demonstrates that CLIP benefits from vision-language synergy and thus effectively encodes individuation properties for distinct entities.

Type	Number of Separable Cliques	Average Clique Size
CLIP	**8**	**2.3**
SBERT	5	2.6
FastText	4	7.3

Table 2: The parameters of the individuation equivalence graphs by the models. CLIP has the most fine-grained individuation among the compared models.

Type	Standard Deviation
CLIP	**0.016**
SBERT	0.05
FastText	0.12

Table 3: Average standard deviation for the individuation proxy across individuation categories.

We suggest a method to calculate whether the model captures individuation for a given class of objects in its embeddings. Using this method, we infer the individuation hierarchy that several models induce on different classes of objects. Thus, we demonstrate that CLIP embeddings capture quantitative differences in a way that is in closer agreement with the human perception of individuation. We hope that this paper stimulates further discussion on multimodality as a source for models that are aligned with human perspective and perception.

Limitations

For this research, we used WordNet and CLIP. We believe the results are reproducible with other datasets and V&L models in languages other than English, but this has not been proved yet. We also use a limited number of models in the comparison. We believe that the observed properties characterize a broader set of multimodal architectures yet restrict our reasoning to CLIP only.

Ethics Statement

This paper complies with the ACL Ethics Policy.

References

Keith Allan. 1980. Nouns and countability. *Language*, pages 541–567.

Lisa Bylinina and Sjef Barbiers. 2019. Numeral Typology Database.

Susan Carey. 1998. Knowledge of number: Its evolution and ontogeny. *Science*, 282(5389):641–642.

Bernard Comrie. 1989. *Language universals and linguistic typology: Syntax and morphology*. University of Chicago press.

Greville G Corbett. 2000. *Number*. Cambridge University Press.

William Croft. 1990. *Typology and universals*. Cambridge University Press.

Stanislas Dehaene. 2011. *The number sense: How the mind creates mathematics*. OUP USA.

Lisa Feigenson, Stanislas Dehaene, and Elizabeth Spelke. 2004. Core systems of number. *Trends in cognitive sciences*, 8(7):307–314.

Dedre Gentner and Lera Boroditsky. 2001. Individuation, relativity and early word learning. In *Language acquisition and conceptual development*, pages 215–256. Cambridge University Press.

Scott Grimm. 2012. *Number and individuation*. Ph.D. thesis, Stanford University.

Daniel Hyde. 2011. Two systems of non-symbolic numerical cognition. *Frontiers in Human Neuroscience*, 5.

Daniel C. Hyde, David A. Boas, Clancy Blair, and Susan Carey. 2010. Near-infrared spectroscopy shows right parietal specialization for number in pre-verbal infants. *NeuroImage*, 53(2):647–652.

Armand Joulin, Edouard Grave, Piotr Bojanowski, Matthijs Douze, Hérve Jégou, and Tomas Mikolov. 2016. Fasttext. zip: Compressing text classification models. *arXiv preprint arXiv:1612.03651*.

Erica L Middleton, Edward J Wisniewski, Kelly A Trindel, and Mutsumi Imai. 2004. Separating the chaff from the oats: Evidence for a conceptual distinction between count noun and mass noun aggregates. *Journal of Memory and Language*, 50(4):371–394.

Salikoko S Mufwene. 1981. Non-individuation and the count/mass distinction. In *Papers from the Regional Meeting of Chicago Ling. Soc. Chicago, Ill*, 17, pages 221–238.

Letitia Parcalabescu, Michele Cafagna, Lilitta Muradjan, Anette Frank, Iacer Calixto, and Albert Gatt. 2021. Valse: A task-independent benchmark for vision and language models centered on linguistic phenomena. *arXiv preprint arXiv:2112.07566*.

Sandeep Prasada, Krag Ferenz, and Todd Haskell. 2002. Conceiving of entities as objects and as stuff. *Cognition*, 83(2):141–165.

Alec Radford, Jong Wook Kim, Chris Hallacy, Aditya Ramesh, Gabriel Goh, Sandhini Agarwal, Girish Sastry, Amanda Askell, Pamela Mishkin, Jack Clark, et al. 2021. Learning transferable visual models from natural language supervision. In *International Conference on Machine Learning*, pages 8748–8763. PMLR.

Nils Reimers and Iryna Gurevych. 2019. Sentence-bert: Sentence embeddings using siamese bert-networks. In *Proceedings of the 2019 Conference on Empirical Methods in Natural Language Processing and the 9th International Joint Conference on Natural Language Processing (EMNLP-IJCNLP)*, pages 3982–3992.

Larissa K. Samuelson and Linda B. Smith. 1999. Early noun vocabularies: do ontology, category structure and syntax correspond? *Cognition*, 73(1):1–33.

Nancy N Soja, Susan Carey, and Elizabeth S Spelke. 1991. Ontological categories guide young children's inductions of word meaning: Object terms and substance terms. *Cognition*, 38(2):179–211.

Elizabet Spaepen, Marie Coppola, Elizabeth S Spelke, Susan E Carey, and Susan Goldin-Meadow. 2011. Number without a language model. *Proceedings of the National Academy of Sciences*, 108(8):3163–3168.

Benjamin Spector. 2007. Aspects of the pragmatics of plural morphology: On higher-order implicatures. In *Presupposition and implicature in compositional semantics*, pages 243–281. Springer.

Elizabeth S Spelke. 1990. Principles of object perception. *Cognitive science*, 14(1):29–56.

Elizabeth S Spelke. 2011. Natural number and natural geometry. In *Space, time and number in the brain*, pages 287–317. Elsevier.

Prentice Starkey and Robert G Cooper Jr. 1980. Perception of numbers by human infants. *Science*, 210(4473):1033–1035.

Tristan Thrush, Ryan Jiang, Max Bartolo, Amanpreet Singh, Adina Williams, Douwe Kiela, and Candace Ross. 2022. Winoground: Probing vision and language models for visio-linguistic compositionality. *arXiv preprint arXiv:2204.03162*.

Quine W. V. O. 1960. *Word and Object*. MIT Press.

Anna Wierzbicka. 1985. Oats and wheat: The fallacy of arbitrariness. *Iconicity in syntax*, pages 311–342.

Fei Xu. 2007. Sortal concepts, object individuation, and language. *Trends in Cognitive Sciences*, 11(9):400–406.

Chao Zhang, Zichao Yang, Xiaodong He, and Li Deng. 2020. Multimodal intelligence: Representation learning, information fusion, and applications. *IEEE Journal of Selected Topics in Signal Processing*, 14(3):478–493.

Eytan Zweig. 2009. Number-neutral bare plurals and the multiplicity implicature. *Linguistics and philosophy*, 32(4):353–407.

CogErgLLM: Exploring Large Language Model Systems Design Perspective Using Cognitive Ergonomics

Azmine Toushik Wasi[1*], Mst Rafia Islam[2]
[1]Shahjalal University of Science and Technology, Sylhet, Bangladesh
[2]Independent University, Dhaka, Bangladesh
azmine32@student.sust.edu, 2030391@iub.edu.bd
*Corresponding author

Abstract

Integrating cognitive ergonomics with LLMs is crucial for improving safety, reliability, and user satisfaction in human-AI interactions. Current LLM designs often lack this integration, resulting in systems that may not fully align with human cognitive capabilities and limitations. This oversight exacerbates biases in LLM outputs and leads to suboptimal user experiences due to inconsistent application of user-centered design principles. Researchers are increasingly leveraging NLP, particularly LLMs, to model and understand human behavior across social sciences, psychology, psychiatry, health, and neuroscience. Our position paper explores the need to integrate cognitive ergonomics into LLM design, providing a comprehensive framework and practical guidelines for ethical development. By addressing these challenges, we aim to advance safer, more reliable, and ethically sound human-AI interactions.

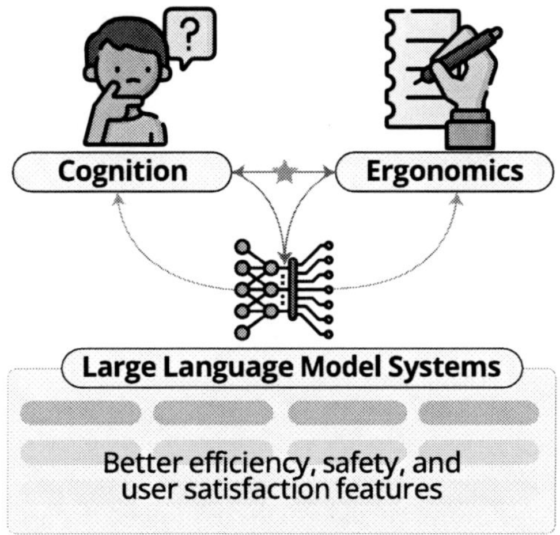

Figure 1: Integration of Cognitive ergonomics and Large Language Models

1 Introduction

Ergonomics focuses on optimizing human-machine interactions for efficiency, safety, and well-being, incorporating both physical and cognitive aspects (Arkouli et al., 2022). *Cognitive science* studies mental processes and behaviours, offering insights crucial for ensuring the safety and reliability of Large Language Models (LLMs) (Qu et al., 2024; Bermúdez, 2020). *Cognitive ergonomics* is the study of how to design systems and interfaces that align with human cognitive abilities and limitations to enhance efficiency, safety, and user satisfaction. It focuses on optimizing mental processes like memory, attention, mental workload and decision-making in human-machine interactions (Bid, 2023). LLMs can also be influenced by various psychological, technological, and decision-specific factors, such as time pressure, emotions, and decision-making styles (Eigner and Händler, 2024), to adapt to human needs and functions. This convergence with AI supports effective human decision-making, with LLMs designed to enhance transparency and trust, ultimately advancing human-AI interaction systems (Le Guillou et al., 2022).

Though researchers are actively working in this area, current LLM system design often lacks comprehensive integration of cognitive ergonomics, resulting in systems that may not fully align with human cognitive capabilities and limitations. Secondly, there is insufficient focus on incorporating cognitive science methods to systematically identify and mitigate biases in LLM outputs. Additionally, existing LLM interfaces frequently fail to apply user-centered design principles consistently, leading to sub-optimal user experiences and cognitive overload. Lastly, LLMs often lack mechanisms to explain their decisions and outputs clearly, reducing user trust and transparency, while there's also a noticeable gap in developing LLMs that can adapt to individual user preferences and learning styles over time, hindering their effectiveness and engagement (Eigner and Händler, 2024; Subramonyam

Proceedings of the 1st Workshop on NLP for Science (NLP4Science), pages 249–258
November 16, 2024 ©2024 Association for Computational Linguistics

et al., 2024a; Liu et al., 2024; Le Guillou et al., 2022; Wasi et al., 2024a,b).

In this position paper, we undertake a thorough exploration of the crucial integration of cognitive ergonomics principles into the design framework of LLM systems to address these issues. Motivated by the importance of aligning LLM functionalities with human cognitive processes and addressing biases through cognitive science methodologies, we explore the cognitive challenges inherent in LLM designs, proposing a comprehensive design framework grounded in cognitive ergonomics principles, and providing practical guidelines for ethical LLM development. The core contributions of our paper lie in offering a detailed analysis of cognitive ergonomics relevance, outlining a comprehensive design framework, and recommending future research directions. Through these contributions, we aim to advance understanding and practice in integrating cognitive ergonomics into LLM systems, ultimately fostering safer, more reliable, and ethically sound human-AI interactions.

Our contribution can be summarized in four folds:

- **Comprehensive Discussion on Cognitive Ergonomics**: By *CogErgLLM*, we provide a thorough exploration of how cognitive ergonomics principles can be integrated into the design of LLMs. By addressing the gap between LLM design and human cognitive capabilities, we aim to enhance the safety, reliability, and user satisfaction in human-AI interactions.

- **Novel Design Framework**: Our paper presents a comprehensive design framework *CogErgLLM*, grounded in cognitive ergonomics principles. This framework offers practical guidelines for ethical LLM development, addressing issues such as bias mitigation, user-centered design, and transparency.

- **Case Studies**: We guide the practical application of cognitive ergonomics principles through the development of prototypes and case studies in diverse domains such as healthcare and education, showcasing the effectiveness and versatility of our work.

- **Discussion on Challenges and Ethical Considerations**: We identify and discuss technical hurdles and ethical concerns in merging cognitive ergonomics with LLMs, emphasizing the need for continued interdisciplinary research to foster responsible AI development and improve human-AI interaction.

2 Background

2.1 Cognitive Ergonomics

Cognitive ergonomics principles emphasize efficiency, attention support, learning facilitation, decision-making aid, and performance enhancement in interface and system design (Berlin and Adams, 2017). These principles find critical applications in safety-critical environments like air traffic control and medical settings, as well as in everyday domains such as banking and leisure activities, showcasing their broad utility. By leveraging cognitive science knowledge on perception, memory, and problem-solving, cognitive ergonomics aims to optimize human performance and well-being in complex and changeable work environments, ultimately improving productivity and safety while recognizing the importance of human adaptation and the need for adaptable work conditions (Branaghan and Lafko, 2020; Parasuraman, 2003; Dehais et al., 2020).

2.2 Large Language Models and Cognition

Recent research has delved into the relationship between LLMs and human cognition, revealing promising insights. Studies by Huff and Ulakçı (2024) demonstrate LLMs' ability to predict human performance in language-based memory tasks, despite differing internal mechanisms. Shani et al. (2023) explored the development of concept-aware LLMs, showing improved alignment with human intuition and prediction robustness. Additionally, Samwald et al. (2023) compiled core principles for steering and evaluating LLM reasoning, drawn from diverse fields like structured reasoning and ethical guidelines. These advancements underscore LLMs' potential to offer valuable insights into human cognition while emphasizing the importance of safe and effective deployment through rigorous evaluation methods.

3 Conceptual Foundations

Cognitive processes are profoundly influenced by ergonomic design, and aligning these principles with LLMs can enhance their usability, effectiveness, and user satisfaction. Here we describe how it can be done, as described in Figure 2:

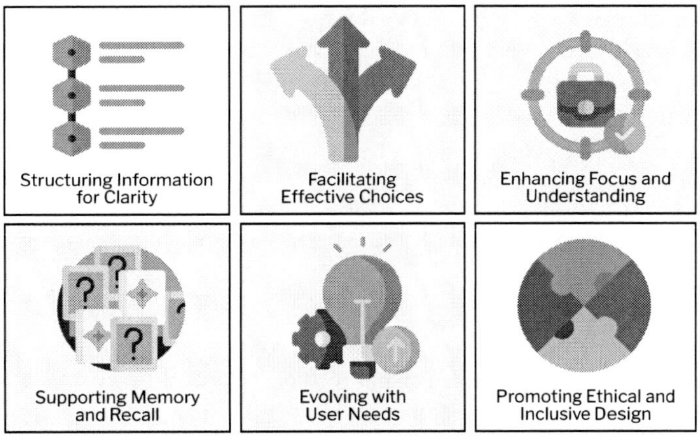

Figure 2: Conceptual Foundations for Cognitive Ergonomics in Large Language Models

1. ***Structuring Information for Clarity***: Cognitive ergonomics ensures information is structured clearly and intuitively, reducing cognitive load (Sweller, 2024). It focuses on organizing information in a way that reduces mental effort. This can be seen in the design of user interfaces, where clear layouts and intuitive navigation systems help users quickly find what they need. For instance, websites often use hierarchical menus and clear categorization to enhance usability, ensuring visitors can navigate without confusion.

2. ***Facilitating Effective Choices***: Ergonomic design aids decision-making by providing essential information clearly and minimizing cognitive biases (Lockton, 2012). For example, in retail environments, ergonomic principles guide the placement of products to highlight choices effectively, helping customers make informed decisions. This approach reduces cognitive load and ensures that decisions are based on relevant information rather than misleading cues.

3. ***Enhancing Focus and Understanding***: Ergonomic design focuses on how users perceive and attend to information, placing important elements where they are easily noticed (Proctor and Proctor, 2021). For example, in classrooms, teachers use visual aids and highlighted content on slides to direct students' attention to key concepts. This practice ensures that important information is conveyed effectively, promoting better understanding and retention among learners.

4. ***Supporting Memory and Recall***: Strategies like familiar patterns and clear information presentation are crucial in ergonomic design to ease the burden on users' memory (Wickens and Carswell, 2021). Such as, in museum exhibits, interactive displays often repeat key information and use consistent labeling to reinforce learning. This approach helps visitors retain information and recall it later, enhancing their overall experience and educational outcomes.

5. ***Evolving with User Needs***: Cognitive ergonomics emphasizes the importance of adapting designs based on user feedback and preferences (Stephanidis et al., 2021). In software development, agile methodologies allow teams to iterate quickly based on user testing and input. This flexibility ensures that products evolve to meet changing user needs, enhancing satisfaction and usability over time.

6. ***Promoting Ethical and Inclusive Design***: Incorporating cognitive ergonomics into LLM design can promote ethical and inclusive practices. By considering diverse user needs and cultural backgrounds during the design process, LLMs can be developed to be more accessible and equitable (Zhou et al., 2021). For example, incorporating cognitive ergonomics into urban planning promotes ethical and inclusive design by prioritizing accessibility and user-centered approaches. This involves integrating features like ramps, tactile paving, and inclusive seating to ensure public spaces accommodate individuals with disabilities. Engaging with diverse communities throughout the design process ensures their needs are met, fostering a sense of inclusivity and social equity. Ethical considerations guide these efforts, emphasizing dignity and equal access to essential services. Such practices not only enhance physical accessibility but also promote social integration and community well-

being, establishing cities as advocates for ethical and inclusive urban development.

As discussed above, integrating principles of cognitive ergonomics into website design offers several significant benefits. It enhances usability by simplifying navigation and minimizing the learning curve for visitors. By organizing information clearly, it reduces cognitive load and supports effective decision-making by presenting options and data in a straightforward manner. Enhancing transparency in data handling and user control over privacy settings increases trust among users. Personalizing content delivery based on user preferences and behavior not only improves relevance but also enhances user engagement and satisfaction. Moreover, implementing strategies to mitigate biases in content presentation ensures fairness and ethical standards. Overall, integrating cognitive ergonomics in web design leads to improved user experience, making websites more efficient, user-friendly, and trustworthy platforms for information and interaction.

4 Design Framework

In this section, we describe the main components of CogErgLLM, a framework designed to explore and integrate cognitive ergonomics principles into the development of LLMs. The framework aims to enhance user experience, efficiency, and reliability by aligning LLM interactions with human cognitive processes.

4.1 Methodology

The development methodology of the framework components, draws inspiration from theoretical foundations outlined in Sections 1 and 2. These theoretical underpinnings of cognitive ergonomics serve as guiding principles for the design and definition of each framework element. We meticulously define and conceptualize the various components, informed by theories on human cognition and interaction with technology. Then, we transition to the implementation phase, where we translate the design aspects into tangible prototypes and undergo rigorous evaluation processes to assess their efficacy in enhancing user experience and system performance.

4.2 Components of CogErgLLM

We outline key components such as user-centric design, ergonomic data integration, cognitive load management, user interface design, trust and transparency, feedback mechanisms, and more, as described in Figure 3. Each component is crucial for creating LLM systems that are intuitive, adaptive, and supportive of users' cognitive needs.

4.2.1 User-Centric Design

User Profiling: Understanding user needs and preferences is crucial for tailoring LLM interactions to individual users. Techniques such as surveys, interviews, and behavioral analysis can provide insights into users' cognitive capabilities and limitations, ensuring that LLMs are designed to meet diverse requirements effectively. By incorporating these profiles, LLMs can adapt their responses to be more relevant and engaging, enhancing the overall user experience (Wang et al., 2024).

Personalization: Personalizing LLM interactions based on user profiles can significantly improve usability and satisfaction (Li et al., 2024). Cognitive ergonomics emphasizes the importance of designing systems that align with users' mental models and preferences. By using data from user profiles, LLMs can offer tailored suggestions, responses, and content, making interactions more intuitive and reducing cognitive strain (Wasi et al., 2024b).

4.2.2 Ergonomic Data Integration

Sensor Integration: Incorporating ergonomic sensors to monitor user posture and environment can provide valuable data for optimizing LLM interactions (Luo et al., 2024; Xu et al., 2024b). For example, sensors can detect when a user is experiencing physical discomfort or cognitive fatigue, prompting the LLM to adjust its interaction style or offer breaks. This integration helps in creating a more comfortable and supportive user environment.

Real-time Feedback: Providing real-time ergonomic advice based on sensor data can enhance user well-being and productivity (Xu et al., 2024a; Luo et al., 2024). For instance, if sensors detect that a user has been sitting in a poor posture for an extended period, the LLM can offer corrective suggestions. This immediate feedback loop ensures that users maintain optimal ergonomic conditions, reducing physical and cognitive stress.

4.2.3 Cognitive Load Management

Load Measurement: Tools and methods for assessing cognitive load, such as eye-tracking and brainwave analysis, can help designers understand how users interact with LLMs. This data is crucial for identifying points of high cognitive load and areas where the system may be causing unnecessary strain, allowing for targeted improvements (Krell et al., 2022).

Adaptive Interactions: Strategies for adjusting LLM interactions to manage cognitive load include simplifying complex information, providing information progressively, and offering clear, concise instructions. By adapting to the user's cognitive state, LLMs can ensure that interactions remain manageable and effective, preventing overload and enhancing comprehension (Subramonyam et al., 2024b).

4.2.4 User Interface Design

Intuitive Interfaces: Design principles for creating user-friendly LLM interfaces focus on minimizing unnecessary complexity and enhancing navigability. Cognitive ergonomics principles such as consistency, predictability, and immediate feedback ensure that users can easily understand and interact with the system, improving efficiency and satisfaction.

Accessibility: Ensuring interfaces are accessible to all users, including those with disabilities, is a key aspect of ergonomic design. This includes adhering to standards such as WCAG and incorporating features like text-to-speech, adjustable font sizes, and high-contrast modes. Accessibility ensures that LLMs are usable by a broader audience, promoting inclusivity and equity.

4.2.5 Trust and Transparency

Explainability: Techniques for making LLM decisions transparent to users include providing clear, understandable explanations for actions and recommendations. This transparency helps users understand how the LLM works, fostering trust and confidence in the system. Cognitive ergonomics emphasizes the need for systems that users can predict and rely on.

Trust-building: Strategies for enhancing user trust in LLMs involve consistent, reliable performance, and the ability to demonstrate ethical and unbiased behavior (Wasi et al., 2024c). Incorporating user feedback and continuously improving the system based on that feedback also plays a crucial role in building and maintaining trust.

4.2.6 Feedback Mechanisms

User Feedback: Incorporating user feedback into the design process allows for continuous improvement of LLM performance. Cognitive ergonomics highlights the importance of listening to users and adapting systems to meet their evolving needs. Regularly gathering and analyzing feedback helps identify areas for enhancement and ensures that the system remains aligned with user expectations (Pan et al., 2024; Xu et al., 2024b).

Iterative Design: Employing iterative design processes based on feedback ensures that LLMs are continually refined and optimized (Pan et al., 2024). This approach allows for the gradual incorporation of new ergonomic insights and user requirements, leading to more effective, user-friendly, and reliable systems. Iterative design helps in addressing issues promptly and evolving the system to better serve its users.

4.2.7 Ethical Considerations

Bias Mitigation: Incorporating cognitive ergonomics into LLM design involves creating processes that actively identify and mitigate biases in outputs. By leveraging cognitive science methods, such as social intelligence tests and moral dilemma scenarios, designers can ensure that LLMs provide fair and equitable responses, thus aligning with diverse user expectations and promoting ethical AI use.

Privacy Protection: Robust data security and privacy measures are essential in designing LLMs that respect user confidentiality. Cognitive ergonomics emphasizes understanding users' cognitive concerns about data security, thus guiding the implementation of intuitive privacy controls and transparent data usage policies that reassure users and protect their personal information.

Inclusive Design: Ensuring that LLMs cater to diverse user groups requires an inclusive design approach informed by cognitive ergonomics. This involves creating interfaces and interactions that consider the cognitive and cultural backgrounds of different users, making the systems accessible and usable for people with varying linguistic needs and cognitive abilities, thereby promoting inclusivity and diversity.

4.2.8 Personalization and Adaptation

Adaptive Learning: Integrating cognitive ergonomics principles into LLM design enables the development of systems that dynamically adapt to

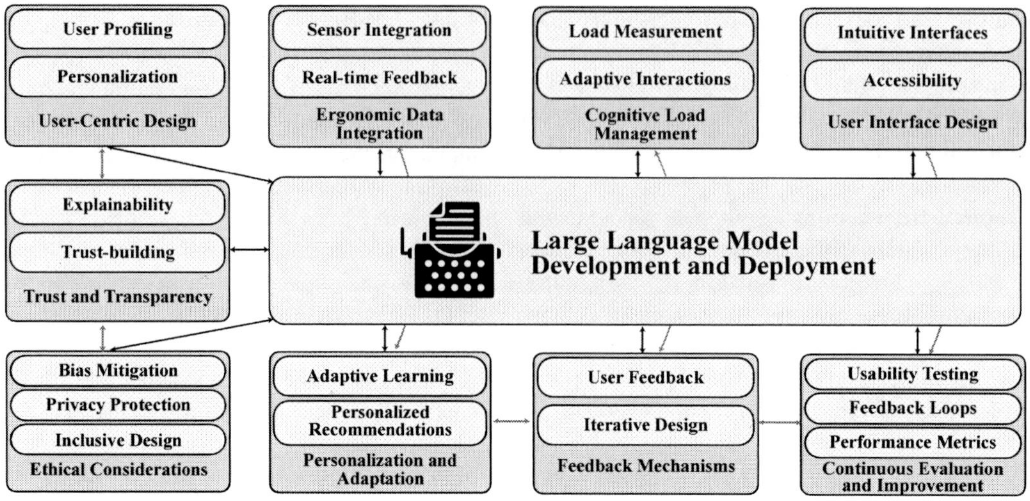

Figure 3: Components of CogErgLLM

individual user preferences and learning styles. By leveraging cognitive science insights, such as theories of learning and memory, designers can create LLMs that personalize content delivery and interactions based on users' behavior and performance, thereby enhancing learning outcomes and user satisfaction.

Personalized Recommendation: Cognitive ergonomics informs the implementation of personalized recommendation systems within LLMs, leveraging user data to offer tailored content and suggestions. By analyzing user interactions and preferences, designers can optimize content relevance and engagement, enhancing user experience and promoting continued usage of the LLMs. Additionally, incorporating principles of cognitive load management ensures that recommendations are presented in a manner that optimizes cognitive resources and minimizes information overload.

4.2.9 Continuous Evaluation and Improvement

Usability Testing: Cognitive ergonomics emphasizes the importance of usability testing in LLM development, involving real users to identify usability issues and areas for improvement. By conducting regular usability tests, designers can gather valuable feedback on user interactions, navigation patterns, and comprehension levels, enabling iterative refinement of LLM interfaces and functionalities to better align with users' cognitive needs and preferences.

Feedback Loops: Establishing feedback mechanisms is integral to the continuous improvement of LLM interactions (Pan et al., 2024). By collecting and analyzing user input and suggestions, designers can gain insights into user satisfaction, comprehension difficulties, and feature preferences, allowing for timely adjustments and enhancements to LLM systems. Feedback loops ensure that LLMs remain responsive to evolving user requirements and cognitive dynamics, promoting sustained user engagement and system effectiveness.

Performance Metrics: Defining and monitoring key performance indicators (KPIs) related to cognitive ergonomics (Zhang et al., 2019) provides valuable insights into the effectiveness of LLM designs. Metrics such as user satisfaction, task completion rates, and cognitive load assessments enable designers to evaluate the impact of ergonomic interventions on user experience and system performance, guiding optimization efforts and ensuring the continued delivery of user-centric LLM solutions.

5 Case Studies

Use case studies demonstrate the practical application of the CogErgLLM framework in real-world scenarios. In healthcare, the framework supports medical professionals by presenting critical patient information and treatment options clearly and concisely. In education, it tailors learning experiences to individual students, enhancing engagement and knowledge retention through adaptive learning and memory support techniques.

Healthcare. In a healthcare setting, CogErgLLM can be used to assist medical professionals in making informed decisions. For instance, the system integrates with electronic health records (EHR) to provide doctors with a summary of patient histories, relevant medical literature, and potential treatment options. The LLM uses cognitive load management techniques to present this information in manageable chunks, reducing the mental effort required by physicians. Adaptive learning algorithms personalize the interface based on individual doctors' specialities and preferences, enhancing usability and efficiency. Real-time feedback mechanisms alert medical staff to potential issues, ensuring quick and accurate decision-making. By incorporating cognitive ergonomic principles, this application aims to improve patient outcomes, reduce cognitive fatigue among healthcare providers, and streamline clinical workflows.

Education. In the educational sector, CogErgLLM will serve as a personalized learning assistant for students. The system tailors content delivery to match each student's learning style and pace, using adaptive learning technologies. For example, it breaks down complex topics into simpler subtopics, gradually increasing complexity as the student's understanding improves. Memory considerations are addressed by incorporating spaced repetition techniques and interactive quizzes to reinforce learning. The interface supports multimodal interactions, allowing students to engage through text, voice, and visual aids. Teachers receive insights into student progress and cognitive load, enabling them to adjust their teaching strategies accordingly. This application of cognitive ergonomics aims to enhance student engagement, improve knowledge retention, and provide a more personalized and effective learning experience.

Legal Work. CogErgLLM can significantly enhance efficiency and accuracy in legal work by providing advanced support to legal professionals. For example, in a case involving complex contract review, CogErgLLM can integrate with legal databases and case management systems to assist lawyers in analyzing and summarizing extensive legal documents. The system uses cognitive ergonomics principles to break down lengthy contracts into more digestible sections, highlighting key clauses and potential issues. It employs natural language processing to compare the contract against relevant case law and statutes, offering suggestions for amendments and flagging areas of concern. Adaptive learning algorithms customize the interface based on the lawyer's specialization and previous cases, improving relevance and usability. Real-time feedback mechanisms alert lawyers to critical deadlines and compliance requirements. By reducing cognitive load and streamlining document review processes, CogErgLLM aims to enhance legal research efficiency, improve accuracy in contract analysis, and support lawyers in delivering more informed and timely legal advice.

Creative Writing. CogErgLLM can transform the creative writing process by offering tailored assistance and enhancing the writer's productivity. For instance, in the case of drafting a novel, CogErgLLM can integrate with writing tools and databases to provide real-time support. The system analyzes the writer's style and narrative structure, suggesting plot developments, character traits, and dialogue options that align with the writer's creative vision. It employs cognitive load management techniques to break down complex narrative arcs into manageable segments, offering feedback and guidance on pacing and coherence. By using adaptive learning algorithms, CogErgLLM personalizes its suggestions based on the writer's genre preferences and past works, ensuring relevance and enhancing creativity. The system also includes interactive features, such as brainstorming prompts and scenario simulations, to inspire new ideas and overcome writer's block. Through real-time feedback and contextual assistance, CogErgLLM aims to streamline the creative process, reduce cognitive fatigue, and support writers in crafting compelling and cohesive stories.

Emergency Response System. Implementing CogErgLLM can revolutionize our city's emergency response system by integrating advanced natural language understanding and cognitive ergonomics. This intelligent system assists dispatchers and first responders by swiftly analyzing emergency calls, prioritizing incidents, and recommending optimal response strategies in real-time. As a result, we've significantly reduced average response times, enhanced dispatcher efficiency, and improved accuracy in incident classification. The intuitive interface and actionable insights provided by CogErgLLM have garnered positive feedback from emergency personnel, paving the way for future enhancements such as predictive analytics and real-time data integration to further elevate our emergency management capabilities.

6 Discussion

We believe that the integration of cognitive ergonomics with LLMs represents a significant step forward in enhancing the usability, effectiveness, and ethical integrity of AI systems. By applying cognitive ergonomic principles to LLM design, we can create interfaces and interactions that are more intuitive, transparent, and aligned with human cognitive capabilities. This not only improves user experience but also fosters trust and collaboration between humans and AI. However, this integration is not without its challenges, particularly in addressing technical complexities, ensuring data privacy, and mitigating biases. Despite these hurdles, we see immense potential in the future of cognitive ergonomics in LLMs, offering opportunities for innovative research, inclusive design practices, and the advancement of human-AI interaction. Through concerted efforts and interdisciplinary collaboration, we can harness the power of cognitive ergonomics to shape a future where AI systems truly augment human capabilities while upholding ethical standards and promoting user well-being.

Cognitive Ergonomics with LLMs for Industrial Applications. Cognitive ergonomics in industrial setups, particularly when applied to large language models (LLMs), offers promising potential for improving user interactions and operational efficiency. By integrating cognitive ergonomics principles, LLMs can be designed to align more closely with human cognitive processes, leading to more intuitive and effective interfaces. This can enhance task automation, decision support, and human-computer collaboration within industrial environments. However, implementing these principles presents challenges, including the need for context-specific adaptation and the integration of complex cognitive models into LLM systems. Future research should focus on developing practical frameworks and tools for applying cognitive ergonomics in industrial contexts, evaluating their impact on productivity and user satisfaction, and addressing technical limitations such as model scalability and data privacy. Such advancements could significantly enhance the usability and effectiveness of LLMs in various industrial applications.

Technical Challenges. Integrating cognitive ergonomics with LLMs presents several technical challenges that need to be addressed. One significant challenge is ensuring that cognitive ergonomic principles can be effectively translated into AI system designs without compromising performance or functionality. This includes developing interfaces that are both intuitive and capable of handling complex user interactions. Another challenge is maintaining data privacy while implementing personalized and adaptive features, as balancing user customization with robust data protection is crucial. Additionally, mitigating biases in LLM outputs while applying cognitive ergonomics requires careful consideration to ensure fairness and equity. Technical complexities also arise in adapting cognitive ergonomic principles to diverse user needs and contexts, necessitating advanced algorithms and continuous refinement. Addressing these challenges requires ongoing research, interdisciplinary collaboration, and innovative solutions to fully integrate cognitive ergonomics into LLMs while upholding technical integrity and ethical standards.

Future Opportunities. Despite the challenges, integrating cognitive ergonomics with LLMs presents numerous future opportunities for research and development. One avenue for exploration is the enhancement of LLM interpretability and explainability through cognitive ergonomic design, enabling users to better understand and trust LLM outputs. Additionally, leveraging cognitive ergonomics to tailor LLM interactions to diverse user demographics and preferences opens doors for inclusive and personalized AI experiences. Furthermore, exploring novel applications of cognitive ergonomic principles in LLM design, such as emotion recognition and adaptive learning, holds promise for advancing human-AI interaction capabilities.

7 Conclusion

Our paper presents *CogErgLLM*, a framework which integrates cognitive ergonomics principles into the design of LLMs. Our core contributions include the comprehensive exploration and integration of cognitive ergonomics, development of a design framework, practical case studies, and recommendations for future research. It holds significant potential to enhance human-AI interaction by improving safety, reliability, and user satisfaction. Its impact extends across various domains, from healthcare to workplace settings, where LLMs play critical roles. We encourage further research and collaboration in this interdisciplinary area to advance the understanding and implementation of ethical, user-centric AI systems, laying the foundation for a truly human-centric advanced artificial general intelligence.

Limitations

This study focuses solely on the theoretical perspective of cognitive ergonomics in relation to LLMs and does not extend to the development of mathematical models or empirical evaluations. While it provides a valuable conceptual framework for integrating CE principles with LLM design, it lacks practical contributions such as algorithmic implementation or performance assessment. The absence of quantitative models and evaluative methods limits the study's ability to directly address how these theoretical principles can be operationalized and tested within LLM systems. Future research should aim to bridge this gap by developing and validating mathematical models and evaluation techniques to apply cognitive ergonomics more effectively in practical LLM applications.

Ethical Considerations

Ethical concerns surrounding the integration of cognitive ergonomics with LLMs revolve primarily around data privacy and bias mitigation. With LLMs relying heavily on vast amounts of data for training, ensuring the privacy and security of user data becomes paramount. Striking a balance between collecting sufficient data for effective cognitive ergonomic design and safeguarding user privacy requires robust encryption techniques, anonymization protocols, and transparent data handling practices. Moreover, mitigating biases inherent in LLMs, stemming from the biases present in training data, poses ethical challenges. Addressing biases demands proactive measures such as diverse dataset curation, algorithmic fairness assessments, and continuous monitoring and adjustment of LLMs to minimize discriminatory outcomes.

Acknowledgements

We express our sincere gratitude to Computational Intelligence and Operations Laboratory (CIOL) for their support.

Author Contributions

ATW contributed to most of the work, including conceptualization, formal analysis, application, and writing. MRI contributed to the formulation of legal aspects and related case studies and writing.

References

2023. COGNITIVE ERGONOMICS. In Bopaya M Bidanda, editor, *Maynard's Industrial and Systems Engineering Handbook*, 6th edition edition. McGraw-Hill Education, New York.

Zoi Arkouli, George Michalos, and Sotiris Makris. 2022. On the selection of ergonomics evaluation methods for human centric manufacturing tasks. *Procedia CIRP*, 107:89–94.

Cecilia Berlin and Caroline Adams. 2017. page 83–106. Ubiquity Press. [link].

José Luis Bermúdez. 2020. *Cognitive Science: An Introduction to the Science of the Mind*, 3 edition. Cambridge University Press.

Russell J. Branaghan and Stacie Lafko. 2020. *Cognitive ergonomics*, page 847–851. Elsevier.

Frédéric Dehais, Alex Lafont, Raphaëlle Roy, and Stephen Fairclough. 2020. A neuroergonomics approach to mental workload, engagement and human performance. *Frontiers in Neuroscience*, 14.

Eva Eigner and Thorsten Händler. 2024. Determinants of llm-assisted decision-making.

Markus Huff and Elanur Ulakçı. 2024. Towards a psychology of machines: Large language models predict human memory.

Moritz Krell, Kate M. Xu, Günter Daniel Rey, and Fred Paas. 2022. Editorial: Recent approaches for assessing cognitive load from a validity perspective. *Frontiers in Education*, 6.

Marin Le Guillou, Laurent Prévot, and Bruno Berberian. 2022. Bringing together ergonomic concepts and cognitive mechanisms for human—ai agents cooperation. *International Journal of Human–Computer Interaction*, 39(9):1827–1840.

Yuanchun Li, Hao Wen, Weijun Wang, Xiangyu Li, Yizhen Yuan, Guohong Liu, Jiacheng Liu, Wenxing Xu, Xiang Wang, Yi Sun, Rui Kong, Yile Wang, Hanfei Geng, Jian Luan, Xuefeng Jin, Zilong Ye, Guanjing Xiong, Fan Zhang, Xiang Li, Mengwei Xu, Zhijun Li, Peng Li, Yang Liu, Ya-Qin Zhang, and Yunxin Liu. 2024. Personal llm agents: Insights and survey about the capability, efficiency and security.

Michael Xieyang Liu, Frederick Liu, Alexander J. Fiannaca, Terry Koo, Lucas Dixon, Michael Terry, and Carrie J. Cai. 2024. "we need structured output": Towards user-centered constraints on large language model output. In *Extended Abstracts of the 2024 CHI Conference on Human Factors in Computing Systems*, CHI EA '24, New York, NY, USA. Association for Computing Machinery.

Dan Lockton. 2012. Cognitive biases, heuristics and decision-making in design for behaviour change. *SSRN Electronic Journal*.

Xiaoyu Luo, Daping Liu, Fan Dang, and Hanjiang Luo. 2024. Integration of llms and the physical world: Research and application. In *ACM Turing Award Celebration Conference 2024*, volume 62 of *ACM-TURC '24*, page 1–5. ACM.

Alexander Pan, Erik Jones, Meena Jagadeesan, and Jacob Steinhardt. 2024. Feedback loops with language models drive in-context reward hacking.

Raja Parasuraman. 2003. Neuroergonomics: Research and practice. *Theoretical Issues in Ergonomics Science*, 4(1–2):5–20.

Robert W. Proctor and Janet D. Proctor. 2021. *SENSATION AND PERCEPTION*, chapter 3. John Wiley and Sons, Ltd.

Youzhi Qu, Penghui Du, Wenxin Che, Chen Wei, Chi Zhang, Wanli Ouyang, Yatao Bian, Feiyang Xu, Bin Hu, Kai Du, Haiyan Wu, Jia Liu, and Quanying Liu. 2024. Promoting interactions between cognitive science and large language models. *The Innovation*, 5(2):100579.

Matthias Samwald, Robert Praas, and Konstantin Hebenstreit. 2023. Towards unified objectives for self-reflective ai. *SSRN Electronic Journal*.

Chen Shani, Jilles Vreeken, and Dafna Shahaf. 2023. Towards concept-aware large language models. In *Findings of the Association for Computational Linguistics: EMNLP 2023*, pages 13158–13170, Singapore. Association for Computational Linguistics.

Constantine Stephanidis, Margherita Antona, and Stavroula Ntoa. 2021. *HUMAN FACTORS IN AMBIENT INTELLIGENCE ENVIRONMENTS*, chapter 41. John Wiley and Sons, Ltd.

Hari Subramonyam, Roy Pea, Christopher Pondoc, Maneesh Agrawala, and Colleen Seifert. 2024a. Bridging the gulf of envisioning: Cognitive challenges in prompt based interactions with llms. In *Proceedings of the CHI Conference on Human Factors in Computing Systems*, CHI '24. ACM.

Hariharan Subramonyam, Roy Pea, Christopher Lawrence Pondoc, Maneesh Agrawala, and Colleen Seifert. 2024b. Bridging the gulf of envisioning: Cognitive design challenges in llm interfaces.

John Sweller. 2024. Cognitive load theory and individual differences. *Learning and Individual Differences*, 110:102423.

Xinyuan Wang, Liang Wu, Liangjie Hong, Hao Liu, and Yanjie Fu. 2024. Llm-enhanced user-item interactions: Leveraging edge information for optimized recommendations.

Azmine Toushik Wasi, Mst Rafia Islam, and Raima Islam. 2024a. Llms as writing assistants: Exploring perspectives on sense of ownership and reasoning. In *The Third Workshop on Intelligent and Interactive Writing Assistants at CHI 2024*. ACM.

Azmine Toushik Wasi, Raima Islam, and Mst Rafia Islam. 2024b. Ink and individuality: Crafting a personalised narrative in the age of llms. In *The Third Workshop on Intelligent and Interactive Writing Assistants at CHI 2024*. ACM.

Azmine Toushik Wasi, Raima Islam, Mst Rafia Islam, Taki Hasan Rafi, and Dong-Kyu Chae. 2024c. Exploring bengali religious dialect biases in large language models with evaluation perspectives. In *The 1st Human-centered Evaluation and Auditing of Language Models Workshop at CHI 2024*.

Christopher D. Wickens and C. Melody Carswell. 2021. *INFORMATION PROCESSING*, chapter 5. John Wiley and Sons, Ltd.

Huatao Xu, Liying Han, Qirui Yang, Mo Li, and Mani Srivastava. 2024a. Penetrative ai: Making llms comprehend the physical world.

Jiajun Xu, Qun Wang, Yuhang Cao, Baitao Zeng, and Sicheng Liu. 2024b. A general-purpose device for interaction with llms.

Yu Zhang, Jianhua Sun, Ting Jiang, and Zengyao Yang. 2019. *Cognitive Ergonomic Evaluation Metrics and Methodology for Interactive Information System*, page 559–570. Springer International Publishing.

Feng Zhou, Yangjian Ji, and Roger Jianxin Jiao. 2021. *EMOTIONAL DESIGN*, chapter 9. John Wiley and Sons, Ltd.

Author Index

Association for Computational Linguistics
209 N. Eighth Street
Stroudsburg, Pennsylvania 18360

ISBN 979-8-3313-0852-0

CURRAN ASSOCIATES INC.
proceedings.com